Modern Economics
Principles and Policy

Modern Economics
Principles and Policy

Second Edition

Kelvin Lancaster
Columbia University

Ronald A. Dulaney
University of Montana

Rand McNally
College Publishing Company/Chicago

Sponsoring Editor Ed Jaffe
Project Editor Stella Jenks
Illustrator James A. Buddenbaum
Designer James A. Buddenbaum

79 80 81 10 9 8 7 6 5 4 3 2 1

Library of Congress Catalog Card Number 78-56521

To Carol Dulaney and Deborah Lancaster

Preface

This book is designed to be a true introduction to economics and economic policy, not a mere preface to it. Its aim is to make you aware of the state of the art of economic policy analysis and prescription, to tell you honestly when economists have not yet found the answer (or disagree among themselves), and to set out the principles upon which economists have based their policy conclusions, all in a manner that is fully within the grasp of the newcomer to economics. The technical analysis is kept at a level appropriate to an elementary text, but the policy discussion is thoroughly sophisticated and timely.

Indeed, the idea of policy permeates the whole book. When there is a chapter devoted to straight economic theory, it is there because that theory is relevant to policy. This does not mean the reader is shortchanged on the basic principles of economics, only that they are not presented as something to be studied just because they are there.

We have used the term *modern* in the title to emphasize that both the economics and the policy coverage are up to date. The analysis uses recent concepts in consumption theory, the role of time, human capital, monetary theory, and econometric model building in an integral way, not as novelties. The policy coverage includes, of course, extensive discussion of such standard problems as unemployment, growth, inflation, and imperfect competition, but also includes equally extensive discussion of poverty and income distribution, the role of the price system in allocation and distribution, the supply of public goods, pollution and other externality problems, manpower policy, urban and agricultural problems, the constraints placed on policy by international relationships, and the pervasiveness of distributional considerations.

The book has thirty-five chapters, divided among nine parts. Part 1 (Chapters 1–3) introduces the reader to economic thinking and the American economy, Part 2 (Chapters 4–8) covers analysis of the market economy as a preliminary to Part 3 (Chapters 9–14) which discusses microeconomic problems and policy. Part 4 (Chapters 15–18) takes up both analysis and policy concerning income distribution. Macroeconomic analysis and policy begins with Part 5 (Chapters 19–22), which lays the foundations of macroeconomics, and continues through Part 6 (Chapters 23–25) which discusses specific problems. Part 7 (Chapters 26–28) covers money and banking, and Part 8 (Chapters 29–32) discusses macroeconomic policy at length. Part 9 (Chapters 33–35) covers international economics.

Although this organization places microeconomic analysis and policy before macroeconomic analysis and policy, the book is written so the reader can begin with Part 5 as easily as with Part 2, and the macroeconomic and microeconomic portions can be taken up separately or in either order.

Organizational Features

In your first glance through the book, you will notice some of the organizational features designed to make it both easy and interesting reading. One of the first things you will notice is the Capsule Supplements, several to each chapter, which are set off in a way to clearly distinguish them from the main text. They provide brief, interesting essays that supplement and illustrate the subject matter of the book. Some, you will find, provide real-world examples of topics discussed in the text, some serve as brief biographies of leading economists of the past, and some discuss methodological or philosophical problems that arise in economics. Others give factual or institutional background materials, present thought-provoking ideas or arguments, or act as extensive footnotes. The separation of these supplements from the main text enables the capsulized material to be presented in a more lively fashion while preserving an uncluttered and clear thread of argument in the text proper. We are sure you will enjoy reading all the supplements, even those in chapters you are not otherwise covering.

At the beginning of each chapter you will find a list of important terms and concepts introduced in that chapter. Another feature is the clearly identifiable lead-in and recap statements for each section of each chapter. Not only do the Recaps act as short summaries of what you should have learned from your reading, but they enable you to find out easily what is contained in the section if, for reasons of time, you are not able to study it. Recaps are provided for each section to give a total picture of the chapter that is more detailed and carries more feeling for the logical development of the chapter than the chapter summaries of other books. For this reason we regard the Recaps as substitutes for a full reading of the chapter if that is not possible.

Although, like all other authors, we believe everything we have labored so hard to put on paper is worth close study, we appreciate that many of you have constraints on your time and will not be able to do more than skim through those parts of the book that are not central to your particular interests. For you, the book contains, in addition to the lead-ins and recaps, a glossary that will provide some guidance when you meet economic terms in your special-interest reading discussed in chapters you have omitted. We hope, of course, that you will read the whole book—if not on first use because of the pressure of other things, then at your later leisure.

At the end of each chapter there are two kinds of materials you should find useful. The first is exercises of the conventional kind, numerical when appropriate, otherwise whatever kind best fits the subject matter of the chapter. The second is questions "For Thought and Discussion," subjects typically open-ended and policy-oriented, often argumentative, designed to inspire discussion but not always amenable to clear-cut answers.

The Second Edition

While the basic organization of the second edition remains much the same as that of the first edition, the book has undergone extensive revision. Virtually every paragraph has been rewritten in an effort to promote easier comprehension and better understanding. Diagrams have also been redrawn and simplified in many instances to better complement the revised text.

Fewer Capsule Supplements appear in the second edition; many have been either deleted or incorporated into the main body of the text. The one major organizational change is the deletion of the final chapter in the first edition and the integration of the material on economic development originally appearing in that chapter into Chapter 24, which is now titled "Economic Growth and Development."

Much of economic significance has occurred since the publication of the first edition and change in the economic order is reflected in the revised treatment of fiscal and monetary policy, international trade and finance, economic growth, and distributional policy. Moreover, in response to the helpful suggestions of numerous instructors and reviewers, the discussions of production possibilities, demand elasticity, index numbers, and interbank financial transactions have been extensively revised and improved. Finally, statistical data have been updated when appropriate to make the book as timely as possible.

Supplementary Materials

As a supplement to this book, a *Student Exercise Book* has been prepared that provides objective questions, essay questions, and numerical problems keyed to each of the chapters in the text. The use of this learning aid in conjunction with your reading of the text is certain to add to your understanding of economic principles and make your study of economics more enjoyable.

An *Instructor's Manual* has also been prepared to provide the instructor with chapter summaries, along with a variety of exercises, questions, and problems for classroom use.

Acknowledgments

We would like to extend our appreciation to Joseph Barr of Framingham State University, R. D. Peterson of Markenomics Associates, Charles Spruill of Hobart and William Smith Colleges, Dennis Sullivan of Miami University (Ohio), and John Walker of Portland State University for their helpful comments on early drafts of this book. Special thanks are also due Jacki Burgad for her tireless travail at the typewriter on behalf of the cause.

Ronald A. Dulaney
Kelvin Lancaster

Contents

Suggested Course Syllabuses

Various combinations of chapters in this book will make it suitable for at least seven separate courses with different emphases. Below is the authors' choice of chapters to be included in the courses described. Please consult the Contents for the chapter titles.

1. A full-scale, one-semester course in macroeconomics

    Chapters 3, 19–32, 35. For a more international orientation, substitute Chapter 34 for 23.

2. A less-intensive version of Course 1

    Chapters 3, 19–22, 25, 29–32. Also include Recaps in Chapters 23, 24, 26, 27, 28, and 35.

3. A full-scale, one-semester course in microeconomics

    Chapters 1–3, 4–12, 15–18, and either 13 or 14. For an international trade emphasis, substitute Chapter 33 for either 13 or 14.

4. A less-intensive version of Course 3

    Chapters 1, 3, 4, 6–9, 11–12, 15, 18. Also include Recaps in Chapters 2, 5, 10, 16, and 17. Consider including Chapter 13 or 14.

5. A full-year course in economics and economic policy

    Combine Courses 1 and 3 in any order, eliminating duplication of Chapter 3.

6. A less-intensive version of Course 5

    Combine Courses 2 and 4 in any order, eliminating duplication of Chapter 3.

7. A one-semester, introductory course covering both microeconomics and macroeconomics

    Chapters 1, 3, 4, 8, 11, 12, 15, 19–21, 29, 32. Also include Recaps in Chapters 6, 7, 9, 22, 30, 31, and 35.

Special note: Students should be encouraged to read the Capsule Supplements in all chapters, no matter which syllabus is used.

Part 1
Introduction

The three chapters in this part are designed to set the stage for the remainder of the book. The chapters should be read whether the reader intends to start a formal study of economics with microeconomics (starting in Chapter 4) or macroeconomics (starting in Chapter 19). Chapter 1 introduces typical economic questions and methods of reasoning by considering prosperity and pollution. Chapter 2 extends the analysis of the economic possibilities open to society. Chapter 3 is designed as an introduction to the major features of the American economy.

Chapter 1
Prosperity and Pollution

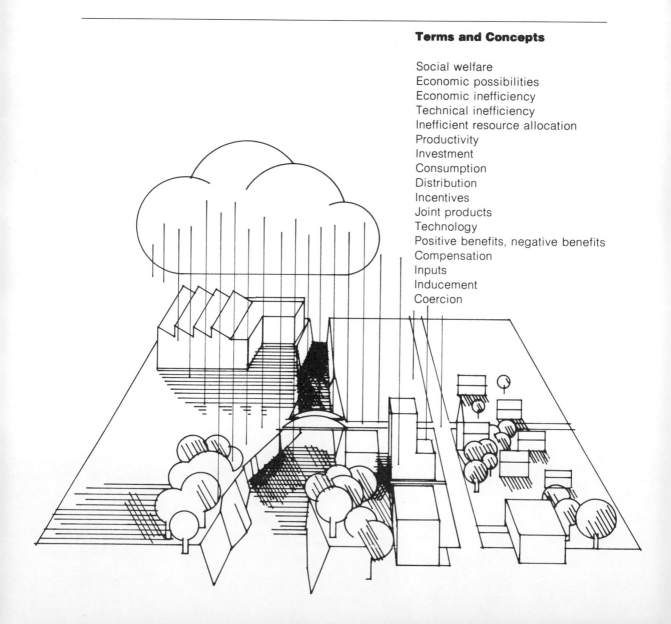

Prosperity and Welfare

The nature of economics

If the debut of modern economics were attributed to a single event, it would no doubt be the publication, some two centuries ago, of a book entitled *An Inquiry into the Nature and Causes of the Wealth of Nations*. But even before that classic was written by Adam Smith, economic thinking had focused on material well-being—how it is attained, sustained, and divided among the members of society. This concern continues to be the focus of economic thinking. The concern does not mean that economists narrowly regard material wealth as an end in itself or lack interest in the nonmaterial aspects of life. It simply reflects the universal observation that material wealth contributes significantly to "happiness," "satisfaction," "welfare," or whatever we choose to call the index that sums up our positive attainments from living.

Economic consideration of the nonmaterial contributions to social welfare, nonetheless, is generally limited to those things that ultimately bear some relationship to the material. Leisure, for example, figures prominently in economic analysis, not only because it provides satisfaction to those who experience it directly, but because a significant increase in leisure will typically reduce society's material output. The economist may thus be observed to cast an occasional cold eye on some aesthetic or spiritual aspect of life by noting that it is attained at the expense of something material. But such an observation merely confirms that the economist is a realist whose professional duty is to inform society that more of one thing usually implies less of something else.

The primary objective of economics is twofold: (1) to describe the behavior of various economic decision-makers in light of the circumstances they face, and (2) to predict how this behavior will be affected by changes in these circumstances.

Recap Economics is primarily concerned with material things, but only insofar as these contribute to the nonmaterial objective of "social welfare."

Capsule Supplement 1.1   **Does Money Make People Happy?**

The old myths that the poor are really happier than the rich were probably invented by the rich to induce the poor to remain that way. Despite the many objections that can be raised to any kind of social survey presuming to ascertain whether people are happy or not, information collected does not support the myth of happy poverty.

In December, 1970, The American Institute of Public Opinion, one of the oldest and most respected institutions of its kind, asked Americans whether they regarded themselves as "very happy," "fairly happy," or "not very happy." The answers were then correlated with various socioeconomic characteristics of the individual respondents. The percentage of individuals claiming to be "very happy" showed a steady decline from 56 percent among those with incomes above $15,000 to only 29 percent among those with incomes under $3,000. The percentage of respondents regarding themselves as "not very happy" rose from 4 percent among the above $15,000 income group to 13 percent among the under $3,000 group. Over a series of polls taken since 1946, the percentage of individuals regarding themselves as "not very happy" (a rather obvious euphemism for "unhappy") was always markedly higher among the lowest socioeconomic groups than among the highest. There would thus appear to be a direct relationship between happiness and income level.

Of course, this shouldn't be taken as evidence that happiness necessarily derives from income *per se*. One alternative explanation of this relationship might be that the psychological characteristics that enable individuals to achieve economic success are themselves the factors most responsible for their personal sense of well-being. Indeed, the old saying that "money isn't everything" is generally borne out by detailed answers in the polls. Most people remarked that such factors as health and family relationships had the greatest influence on their happiness rating. It's noteworthy, however, that financial matters ranked as one of the three main factors among the poor, but were rarely mentioned by the rich—bearing out the maxim that you only think about money when you don't have enough of it.

Several international "happiness" polls have also been conducted in recent years. Needless to say, everything suspect about such polls within individual countries becomes a thousandfold more so when international comparisons are made. Despite such doubts, however, the results are still interesting. They reinforce the notion of a happiness-income correlation; indeed, the proportion of individuals who regarded themselves as "not very happy" was noticeably higher among the poor than among the rich in every country polled. Moreover, the international results, for what they're worth, tend to dispel the myth that the less-developed countries are populated by "happy peasants." The overall ratings on personal happiness for countries like India and Nigeria, for example, are much lower than for the United States, Great Britain, and Japan.

While we shouldn't lean too heavily on this kind of evidence, it does strongly support the economist's premise that material well-being—though perhaps in a relative rather than an absolute sense—contributes to personal happiness.

The Feasibility of Prosperity

An introduction to society's economic possibilities

"Prosperity," like "poverty," is a relative rather than an absolute concept. Evidence of this is the fact that the material standard of living regarded as prosperity has not only changed dramatically over time but also varies markedly from one society to another. Nonetheless, let's assume that we agree on a current standard of prosperity. We define this standard in terms of a list of things required to sustain it—a certain minimum quantity and variety of food, housing, clothing, medical care, entertainment, leisure time, and so forth.

The Basic Questions

For whatever "package" of things we have chosen, we can immediately ask the following questions, fundamental to the study of economics:

1. Is it *feasible* for society to provide everyone with this prosperity package?
2. If it is *not* feasible, why not? Does society lack essential material resources? Would some form of economic reorganization make such provision feasible?
3. If such provision *is* feasible, is it actually achieved? For everyone? If not, why?
4. If feasible for everyone, is the particular prosperity package we've selected identical to the one *everyone* would have chosen? Would some individuals rather have more of certain things, even if it means having less of others?

The question of feasibility suggests a need to investigate society's *economic possibilities*. The most obvious way to determine whether or not society can provide our proposed standard of living is (1) to tabulate an *annual bill of goods*—the minimum annual quantity of every good required to ensure that everyone receives a prosperity package, and (2) to compare this bill of goods with the list of goods actually produced during a typical year.

Note that we have included leisure time as a component of our minimum living standard. By subtracting the required man-hours of leisure from the existing "total stock" of man-hours, we can obtain the maximum number of labor man-hours available for producing material goods. If society successfully produces every good to meet its computed requirements, without taking up more leisure than specified, feasibility is assured.

Suppose, for example, that our required bill of goods consists of 2 million tons of food, 100 thousand bales of clothing, and some specific amount of leisure. Obviously, if society actually produces 2.5 million tons of food and 120 thousand bales of clothing without "cutting into" our specified quantity of leisure, our bill of goods is feasible.

Changing the Product Mix

However, the required bill of goods *may* be feasible even though the actual production of certain goods is less than our list dictates. Suppose that society's actual output is 1.5 million tons of food and 150 thousand bales of clothing. Producing these goods requires *resources*—labor, land, machinery, etc. To a considerable extent, such resources can be shifted between food and clothing production. Therefore, society can increase food production *at the expense of clothing production* by planting corn instead of cotton on some of its land, and by moving workers from textile mills into food-processing plants.

If society currently produces 1.5 million tons of food and 150 thousand bales of clothing, it can almost certainly produce *more* than 1.5 million tons of food if it is willing to settle for *less* than 150 thousand bales of clothing. To produce our required bill of goods, society can reduce clothing output by 50 thousand bales. At the same time, society must be able to produce an additional 0.5 million tons of food. Whether the resources made available by reducing clothing output are sufficient to produce 0.5 million more tons of food is a technological question. If at least 0.5 million extra tons of food can be produced with available resources, our bill of goods is feasible; if not, our collection is obviously infeasible.

If the actual production of *both* goods were less than that required—if food production were 1.5 million tons and clothing production, 80 thousand bales—we would be tempted to conclude that our suggested living standard is clearly infeasible. This conclusion would not necessarily follow, however, because the economy could be *inefficient* in the simple sense of failing to attain its own potential. We shall examine this possibility in the next section.

The feasibility or infeasibility of attaining a minimally acceptable standard of living creates a critical dividing line among societies. If such a standard is not currently feasible, economic policy will typically be directed toward achieving feasibility in the future, that is, toward *economic growth and development*. If the standard is currently feasible, economic policy will typically be directed toward *efficiency*, to ensure its actual attainment, and *distributional equity*, to ensure that all share in the prosperity.

Recap To sustain its population at or above a specified material standard of living, society's economic possibilities must permit a certain minimum amount of all goods to be produced.

Capsule Supplement 1.2   **Adam Smith, 1723–90**

Adam Smith may not have invented economics, but he established it as a field of inquiry and brought it to the attention of the public in a way that had immediate impact. Indeed, his *Wealth of Nations* was one of the most influential books in the latter part of the eighteenth century, a period hardly lacking in ideas or writers.

Smith was a Scot, educated in Glasgow and Oxford, who launched his academic career as a philosopher, being appointed professor of moral philosophy at the University of Glasgow in 1752. His philosophical treatise, *The Theory of Moral Sentiments* (1759), alone would have been sufficient to establish his intellectual credentials, but it would never have brought him the immortality that economics ultimately did. It is interesting to note that his theory of morality was based on the idea of "sympathy"—the ability to identify with others (closer to what we now call "empathy")—while his economic analysis was largely devoted to showing how the economic system would work admirably *in the absence* of this trait with each person behaving in his own best interest without reference to others.

As already suggested, Smith did not invent economics. Rather, he "discovered" it in the works of both contemporary and earlier writers and wove many of the major ideas expressed in those works together in a special way that emerged as a complete system. An important event that initially turned him toward economics was the two-year period (1764–66) he spent as tutor to a young Scottish aristocrat (the Duke of Buccleuch). While being tutor to a young man might now seem beneath the dignity of one holding a chair at a major university, it must be remembered that aristocrats were still VIP's at the time.

Because the essential feature of a young aristocrat's education was the "grand tour" of Europe, Smith obtained the equivalent of a modern professor's foundation-supported foreign-travel fellowship. While in France he met Voltaire and also members of the group known as the Physiocrats. The latter were centered around Francois Quesnay, who was court physician to Louis XV and had devised the *tableau economique,* a table showing the intersectoral flows in the economy. Smith was attracted not by the *tableau* (an idea whose time didn't really come until the 1930s with the development of national income accounting and input-output analysis), but by the Physiocrats' idea that the economic system produces harmony even though each individual acts purely in his own self-interest.

Back in Glasgow, Smith spent ten years concocting his great economic treatise. In it he blended together his own analysis, the thoughts of his contemporaries, numerous real-life examples, and a dash of moralizing. He enlivened the mixture with a gift for turning a phrase, giving his work a quotability that guaranteed both immediate impact and durability. Some of his phrases were too well turned, however, such as his advice to government: "What is prudence in the conduct of every private family can scarcely be folly in that of a great Kingdom"—advice quite contrary to that of modern fiscal policy, but put so neatly as to require an elaborate counter-argument.

The book appeared in 1776, its full title being *An Inquiry into the Nature and Causes of the Wealth of Nations.* The title was designed specifically to address the Mercantilists, a group that had emphasized the importance of accumulating gold and silver to a nation's wealth. Smith established what has remained the foundation of economic thinking ever since, that the true "wealth" of a country is its output of real goods and services, not its stock of gold or silver, the role of money being merely to *facilitate* the production and exchange of goods.

Smith provided the basics of supply and demand analysis, showing how competition would drive out inefficiency in production, as if directed by an "invisible hand." He also outlined how the search for profits would lead competing firms to produce more of those goods valued highly by consumers relative to the costs of production, and fewer of those valued less highly relative to cost. Smith also discussed the technology of production, showing how the *division of labor* into specialized operations could increase productivity. He did not, however, foresee the possibility of large-scale economies, and felt that the more firms in any industry, the better.

Adam Smith advocated that the role of government be confined to ensuring that the private sector be free to get on with business, and thus be concerned with little more than defense, police, and minimal general government operation. He failed to see that the government intervention in the market might one day be essential to bring about the very competitive spirit he believed required no supervision.

Efficiency and Productivity

Some of the underlying determinants of society's economic possibilities

We have seen how it is generally possible to provide more of one good at the expense of some other good. Let us now direct our attention to the question of whether society can produce more of all goods, or at least more of some without reducing the output of others.

Underutilization of Resources

Because goods are produced with resources, the simplest case in which production can potentially be increased is when there are *idle or unemployed resources* that can be used without jeopardizing society's desired quota of leisure time. Because resources already in use will remain unaffected, any production that stems from using previously idle resources will necessarily add to existing output. It has been estimated that during the Great Depression of the 1930s, industrial output in the United States could have increased by as much as 50 percent if it had been possible to tap idle resources.

The existence of idle resources that *could* be used to produce goods generally implies that the economy is operating at less than full potential. This is an example of *economic inefficiency*. However, circumstances may exist under which idle resources cannot be productively used. Most production requires the cooperation of several types of resources—labor and land, or labor and machinery. It may simply be impossible to use more labor without more land or machinery. For example, a peasant society may have spare labor, but may be incapable of growing more food without additional land, farm machinery, or fertilizer.

One of the great economic problems, however, is that workers *and* machinery often are idle within highly industrialized societies. The most notorious occurrence of below capacity operation was, of course, the *Great Depression* of the 1930s. Until World War II, the industrial countries suffered periodic bouts with underutilization of capacity—some severe, some mild. This underutilization led economists to investigate the problem of *business cycles*. Since World War II, however, such occurrences have been much milder, due largely to modern economic policy.

Inefficiency

But alas, even if all of its available resources were fully employed, society may still produce less than is feasible. A particular industry may simply not use resources to its best advantage, or in accordance with the most advanced techniques. We refer to this phenomenon as *technical inefficiency*. It is important not to confuse technical inefficiency with a lack of resources. An underdeveloped country may not use the latest road-building techniques simply because it has no earth-moving equipment. At the same time, it may be technically efficient in the way it uses people and shovels.

A more subtle form of inefficiency may exist in the overall organization of the economy. Specifically, we may have an *inefficient allocation of resources*. This can be likened to the organization of a symphony orchestra in which the string musicians are initially assigned to play wind instruments, and the wind musicians, strings. Simply by appropriately reassigning musicians to instruments, without increasing their total number, we can produce a better orchestra!

To a certain extent, we can judge the working of an *economic system* (capitalism, socialism, and so on) by the way it provides producers with *incentives* or *commands* to be both *technically* and *economically* efficient in the use of available resources.

Productivity

To speak of productivity, as opposed to efficiency, is to place emphasis on the quantity of output produced *per worker*. Because a 10 percent increase in population increases the quantity of goods required to maintain a minimum living standard for all by 10 percent, and also the amount of labor by 10 percent, we cannot actually *increase* living standards unless the output of goods rises by *more* than the increase in population. This involves an increase in *output per worker*, or *productivity*.

Greater efficiency increases productivity but productivity can also be increased *even if the economy is already operating efficiently*.

Specifically, we expect production *per worker* to rise if the existing labor force is provided with increased levels of land, capital equipment, etc., with which to work. Although there may be limits on this, productivity, and thus output per capita, will generally be higher the greater the availability of nonlabor resources in relation to the work force.

To summarize, our chosen living standard may be infeasible simply because society is unable to produce the required bill of goods. This inability may be due to

1. a failure to use all available resources,
2. technically inefficient production,
3. an inefficient allocation of resources, or
4. an insufficient supply of nonlabor resources.

More than half the world's people live in countries that are unable to produce enough goods for their populations to enjoy a higher standard of living than the U.S.'s official "poverty line." For the United States, Canada, Japan, Australia, and the countries of Northwest Europe, however, such a standard is more than feasible.

Recap Goods are produced by using labor and such nonlabor resources as land and machinery. More resources will give more goods, but resources cannot be increased rapidly. Society may fail to produce even what is possible with its existing resources, either because it uses them inappropriately, or because it fails to use some resources altogether.

The Distribution of Output

How poverty may exist even when society can produce enough goods to abolish it

We shall now turn to the case—exemplified especially by the United States—in which a standard of living *above the poverty level* is universally feasible, yet not actually achieved by everyone.

Output Not Consumed

One reason poverty may exist even when its elimination is feasible may be that many of society's resources are devoted to producing goods that do not directly contribute to current material living standards. Such activities as building pyramids, outfitting armadas, and stockpiling nuclear warheads may create a situation in which there are not enough resources with which to produce adequate consumer goods for ordinary households. Society may simply elect to forgo current living standards for other objectives.

If, for example, society were to increase productivity, and thus its *future* living standards, it would need to devote some of its current resources to increasing the stock of resources available for future use. Resources used to build railroads and factories obviously do not contribute to the immediate provision of household commodities. However, the increase in the stock of capital goods that results from such employment of resources ultimately increases society's production possibilities, and thus its *future* ability to provide households with consumer goods.

The production of capital goods is called *investment*. As we have suggested, investment increases future production at the expense of immediate household *consumption*. Just how much current consumption should be sacrificed in order to increase society's capital stock is an important question of economic policy. This question is especially critical to a poor country which, if it is to increase future living standards, must become even poorer in the present.

Distribution

Finally, we come face to face with the problem of *distribution*. Society may produce sufficient consumption goods, even after allowing for investment and its own version of pyramid-building, to provide an acceptable living standard for all. Yet it may actually fail to so provide because it distributes these goods in such a way that some receive more than is called for by this standard while others receive less.

The way in which goods are distributed among the members of society is largely determined by the basic structure of the economic system, subject to whatever special modifications have been imposed on this structure. Although certain small sub-societies (such as monasteries, communes, and Israeli kibbutzim) divide total output equally among their members, all large societies (including all *socialist* societies) rely on some form of *market system* for distribution. While a market system might also result in an equal division of output, this would be a most unlikely outcome.

In a market system, individuals receive *incomes* with which they buy goods. The amount of income required in exchange for a unit of any given good is that good's *price*. Thus, in a market system, the distribution of goods among households is primarily determined by the *distribution of income*, although it may be affected by the "free" distribution of some things (education, for example, or medical treatment in some countries) for which individuals do not directly give up part of their incomes.

The most important source of personal income in every economy is payment for labor services. In most Western-type ("capitalist") economies, however, individuals may also own capital equipment and land, and obtain income from selling their services. The distribution of income is thus determined by the variation in payments to different types of workers and individual differences in the ownership of capital and land.

In all societies, there will be those who neither own property resources nor are capable of working (the old, the sick, and the very young). These individuals may be provided with goods or incomes either through (1) some formal social mechanism—such as government pensions—or (2) the structure of the family—as for the very young everywhere, and the old and the sick in many societies.

Distribution and Efficiency

Distribution is always important in determining the extent of poverty, even though, as in the poorer nations, its significance may be overshadowed by the total unavailability of goods. In the rich industrial nations, however, distribution is *the* critical determinant. If, for example, anyone in the United States is poor, it is *necessarily* because the prevailing distribution of income is unfavorable to them—for there is no question about the feasibility of providing every American with an adequate standard of living.

Just as we can judge the operation of an economic system by the prevailing degree of economic efficiency, which determines the quantity of goods that can be produced with existing resources, so we can also judge a system by how it distributes those goods. Because moral judgments are involved more often in assessing distribution than in assessing efficiency, economists, wishing to keep their discipline as value-free as possible, have tended to understate certain aspects of the distribution problem in their analysis.

Distribution and efficiency, however, are not entirely independent. Differences in income may provide *incentives* for the more efficient use of resources. Those with special talents, for example, may choose not to exercise them if they receive the same income as everyone else. On the other hand, such persons may *enjoy* exercising their talents and do so without special incentives. Unfortunately, the existing evidence of the effect of income differences on incentives is inconclusive.

Recap Even when society can produce enough goods to provide everyone with an adequate material standard of living, it may fail to abolish poverty. One reason may be that it produces significant quantities of defense and/or investment goods that do not contribute to current material living standards. Another is that society's distribution of goods may provide some members with less than an acceptable minimum.

Prosperity with Pollution

An introduction to the economic problems posed by pollution and to the general nature of economic decision-making

Pollution is primarily a problem of rich societies, even though it currently exists in poor societies and existed in currently rich societies even when they were poor.

There are two reasons for this. One is technological—the productive facilities that use capital resources intensively to provide society with a high living standard produce pollution (solid and liquid wastes, smoke, noise) as part of their engineering makeup. The other consists of two separate effects of consumers' affluence. Consumers in rich societies generate waste—especially garbage—expressly because they are rich. An empty can that would be beaten into a steel plate or become a pot in a poor society is simply discarded in a wealthy one. Then again, pollution is a *conscious* problem in a rich society because its members can afford to exercise the choice *not* to have pollution. In an impoverished society, the community water hole may necessarily serve jointly as a cattle bath, a washing facility, and a supply of drinking water. While, in principle, a pollution problem exists, there is nothing to be done; no real choice can be made.

Let's get down to specifics. Suppose a factory spills unpleasant, odorous, and harmful chemical wastes into the river on which it is situated. Presumably no factory would exist for the sole purpose of polluting a river. Whatever its primary product may be (say, paper), the pollution exists expressly *because* it makes this product.

Joint Products

Because making paper involves the simultaneous production of chemical wastes, we say that paper and chemical wastes are *joint products*. Whether or not things are joint products is not a question of economics, but of *technology*—the engineering and chemistry of production. Unlike bicycles, for example, automobiles produce exhaust fumes jointly with transportation—entirely for technical reasons.

The potential existence of pollution is therefore a matter of technology. But whether pollution occurs in fact and, if so, what can be done about it, are questions amenable to economic analysis.

Suppose, in our example, that (1) the only known process for producing paper requires that chemical wastes be discharged into the river; and (2) there is no known technique for disposing of these wastes once discharged. These are both purely technical properties of the situation. How then can we avoid polluting any river that is a potential paper-mill site? Impossible, you may say. But there is one solution—*eliminate paper production altogether*.

The Elements of Choice

Now we can begin to think like economists. We are faced with a *choice between alternatives*—option A, no paper and no pollution, and option B, paper and pollution. Is there any way to decide which is the better alternative?

Obviously, if no one had any use for paper, the choice would be simple.

Because paper would not be desirable to anyone and pollution would be undesirable to everyone, option A would clearly be ''better'' than option B. We can restate this conclusion as follows: While there would be no *positive benefits* from having paper, there would certainly be *negative benefits* (pollution) associated with its production. Hence, even though option A would produce *zero* net benefits to society, this would be preferable to the *negative* net benefits associated with option B.

But paper production clearly does provide positive benefits. In an economy like the United States, people use part of their income in exchange for paper—income that otherwise would be spent on such amenities as razor blades, panty hose, and tuna fish. Paper must therefore provide a benefit of some kind, otherwise why would people voluntarily forgo other things to obtain it?

Our choice is consequently much more difficult. Option B now gives both *positive benefits* (paper) *and negative benefits* (pollution), while option A still brings zero benefits. The question is, do the positive benefits from producing paper outweigh the negative benefits from the associated pollution? It is with just such questions that much modern economic policy is concerned.

Recap It may be technically impossible for a factory to produce paper without discharging chemical wastes into a river. If this is the case, eliminating pollution implies abolishing paper production altogether. The existence of paper provides positive benefits to society and the existence of pollution provides negative benefits to society. The question of whether or not paper (and thus pollution) should be produced can therefore be resolved only by weighing the positive benefits against the negative ones.

Distribution Once More

Even a problem like pollution involves major questions of distribution

To see how the distribution of society's goods (now expanded to include its unwanted things or *bads*) may be affected by the existence of pollution, let us first consider a case in which there is no distribution problem.

Imagine Robinson Crusoe, alone on a south sea island where, among other abundance, there exists an ample supply of *durian fruit*. Now in the opinion of many people (and we'll suppose Crusoe too), this unique fruit has a delicious flavor but a disgusting odor. Therefore, it presents a positive benefit (good taste) associated with a negative benefit (bad smell). If we were to observe Crusoe actually eating the fruit, we would simply conclude that the positive benefit to him outweighs the negative benefit, and we would have no reason to intervene in his decision.

Pollution Involves Distribution

In the case of paper production, however, *the positive and negative benefits do not all accrue to the same people in the same degree.* The main consumers of paper may live miles from any river, while those living on rivers may consume little paper. To make matters even more complicated, benefits, positive or negative, need not accrue only to individuals who are *directly* affected. Even those who do not live near rivers may detest the pollution on general principles. How can we reach any conclusion when the positive and negative benefits associated with alternative courses of action accrue to different people? This is a fundamental problem at the basis of much economic policy and one that cannot be solved without exercising some kind of value judgment.

Assume there were no choice other than between making paper and polluting a river, and ceasing paper production altogether. The policy-maker would somehow then have to judge whether the benefits to society from having paper would outweigh the negative benefits of polluting the river. This decision would have to take into account the fact that the decision itself affects the ultimate distribution of these benefits.

To change from producing paper to banning its production, for example, would increase the benefits of those who use little paper and live near the river *at the expense* of reducing benefits to those who do not live near the river but use much paper.

Compensation

Occasionally, we may be able to simplify such distributional problems by using criteria that reduce the burden of judgment on the policy-maker. If, for example, those living near the river could provide compensation (by giving over part of their income) to the heavy users of paper in such a way that (1) the river dwellers reckoned themselves better off with a clean river than with a polluted river *even after having paid the compensation,* and (2) those receiving compensation also reckoned themselves better off even though they would have no paper, our policy-maker would certainly be on firmer ground in advocating the cessation of paper production.

More on Choice

Let us expand our original problem somewhat and assume that there are now *two* processes for producing paper, one of which produces less pollution per ton of paper than does the other. Which is the "better" process? The low-pollution process, you may well answer. But is it? To investigate this question, we must now take into account certain things we have ignored up to this point.

The paper mill cannot produce something from nothing. It requires *in-*

puts. These inputs will include *raw materials* like wood pulp and chemicals, *labor* (even if required only to watch dials or push buttons), and *capital equipment*.

If the low-pollution process uses the same quantities of all inputs per ton of paper as the high-pollution process, then there would be every reason to regard it as unambiguously better. But suppose low pollution is achieved only by an elaborate filtration process that requires more labor and capital equipment than the high-pollution process to produce a given level of output.

To produce a particular quantity of paper, we now have the following alternatives:

1. The low-pollution process—producing low negative benefits, but using high levels of inputs.
2. The high-pollution process—using fewer inputs, but producing more negative benefits.

The choice between these processes depends on how the inputs fit into our scheme. Other things being equal, it is desirable to use the fewest possible inputs to produce a given level of output. Why? *Because inputs not used here can be used to produce something else.* The extra labor and equipment required for the low-pollution process, for example, might be used to produce better housing for the poor. The low-pollution process would then give us less pollution but also less housing, while the high-pollution process would give us more housing, but also more pollution.

Of course, we cannot actually associate the extra resources used in the low-pollution process with any *specific* loss of output unless we have detailed information about the economy as a whole. All we can say for sure is that, if society's resources are fully employed and paper is produced by the high-pollution process, shifting to the low-pollution process will reduce the availability of resources elsewhere in the economy.

Because productive inputs have *alternative uses,* we must take them into account. By using inputs to produce paper we forgo production somewhere else in the economy. In other words, the benefits we receive from producing paper are obtained at the *cost* of reduced benefits from other things.

We're now faced with the same kind of problem we described earlier. The low-pollution process, as compared to the high-pollution process, produces lower negative benefits but incurs higher costs in terms of things forgone elsewhere in the economy. Once again, deciding which process is "better" involves weighing the desirable against the undesirable.

A Clearer Case

Happily, not all policy decisions require this delicate balancing among alternatives. Sometimes we can make reasonably clear-cut choices.

Consider the case of a paper mill that uses the high-pollution process. Down the river there is a town. The townspeople need relatively unpolluted water for drinking and other purposes. To obtain unpolluted water, the people operate a water-purification plant. Now suppose this water-purification plant uses *more* labor and equipment than would be required to reduce pollution to an acceptable level at the paper mill (whether or not this would be true in reality is, of course, a technological matter).

Regarding the paper mill and the township together as a small economic system, consider the following facts:

1. The paper mill is using the high-pollution process.
2. The townspeople are *demonstrating* their distaste for pollution by devoting inputs (that could be used for other things) to its removal.
3. The paper mill could reduce pollution to an acceptable level by purification at the mill, using *fewer* inputs than required to purify the water at the town.

We can conclude from these facts that there would be an *unambiguous gain* to society if purification were carried out at the mill rather than at the town. Then the economy as a whole would use fewer inputs in the purification process and thus would have surplus labor and equipment with which to produce other things. Purification at the mill would also bring such benefits as relatively clean water over the stretch of river between the mill and the town.

If the economy were actually operating as we have assumed in this example, we would have *economic inefficiency*. A reallocation of resources (specifically, a shift of purification from the town to the mill) would obviously make some people better off without making anyone worse off.

Recap The problem of weighing positive against negative benefits is made more difficult when, as is usually the case, the people on whom the negative benefits impinge are not those who receive the positive benefits. Generally a change to a nonpolluting process uses more resources and thus, while reducing pollution for some, reduces goods available to others.

Capsule Supplement 1.3　**Smoke in the Desert**

Throwing one's trash into a neighbor's yard is a venerable and time-honored method of solving the pollution problem. If something is unwanted in one place, it is simply transported to where it remains no less objectionable but where there are fewer (or politically weaker) people to object. Garbage is collected in the cities and dumped onto the countryside; sewage is piped from population centers and spewed into rivers that smaller towns downstream must rely on for water; junked automobiles are stacked chaotically on the other side of the tracks where, at least for some, they are less visible. One of the most spectacular examples of this approach to pollution has been the construction of electricity-generating plants in the Four Corners region of the Southwest—a region so named because it surrounds the point commonly shared by the states of Arizona, Utah, Colorado, and New Mexico. One of the emptiest parts of the United States and hundreds of miles from the nearest major cities (Salt Lake City, Phoenix, Denver, and Albuquerque), this is an area once noteworthy only for its Indian reservations and pure desert air.

The plan to build six huge generating plants in this region over a twenty-year period originated many miles away, in smog-beshrouded Los Angeles. To solve its own pollution problems, Los Angeles had introduced an antipollution code that could not be met by the standard thermal-generating plants of the period without special costly adaptations. The utilities concerned thus concluded that it would be more profitable to build plants where antipollution devices were not required and transport electric power into the Los Angeles area.

The Four Corners region seemed ideal for this. Out in the crisp desert air no one had ever dreamed of a pollution problem, and hence no restrictive ordinances had been passed. The Angelenos' proposal was initially received with enthusiasm by the four desert states because their major cities were expanding rapidly and worried about future sources of electric power themselves. (Four Corners, it should be remembered, was far away from any of these cities.) Thus, a consortium of twenty-three utilities was formed to build a battery of generating plants in the region to supply electricity to various cities in the Southwest as well as to Los Angeles. The first plant was built in the mid-1960s. With a capacity of more than 2,000 megawatts it constituted one of the largest coal-burning plants in existence, pumping out 250 tons of soot a day—more than the total produced from all sources in New York City. Photographs taken by orbiting astronauts 170 miles up show the plume of smoke from Four Corners competing with the Grand Canyon for attention in that part of the world.

If it were impossible to produce electricity without smoke (which it is not), it might be argued that it would be socially optimal to have the smoke affect the fewest people, as is certainly the case with the plant at Four Corners as opposed to Los Angeles. As with most economic problems, however, the issues involved are much more subtle. For one thing, the population is not homogeneous over the United States. The fact that most of those directly affected by the Four Corners plant are Indians introduces the difficulty of weighing the welfare of a poor minority group against that of a large and prosperous urban center. Even here, there are additional complications. Coal for the plant is strip-mined locally. While, on the one hand, nearby mining operations disfigure the landscape, they also increase the number of jobs available to the Indians and enable some, who would otherwise be forced to seek work in the cities, to continue living in their traditional, if somewhat deteriorated, environment.

There is also the problem of what economists call *externalities.* Most Americans, wherever they may live, feel that they have lost something from the simple fact that the once-pure desert air is now polluted, even though it may not affect them directly. Indeed, it is the existence of just such feelings that has stimulated the growth of the environmental-protection movement in recent years. As evidence of the strength of this movement, public reaction to the environmental effects of the original Four Corners plant has led to the introduction of stringent antipollution measures that affect not only the original but any future generating facilities in the area.

Decision-Making in the Economy

How the structure of the system determines the way in which actual decisions are made

Continuing with our pollution example, let us suppose that, despite society's demonstrably lower total benefits, the upstream paper mill continues to operate the high-pollution process while the downstream townfolk run their own purification plant. How could such an inefficient allocation of resources come about? In the structure of the economic system, what might cause this to happen?

The answer lies in the way in which *economic decisions* are actually made, and what is taken into account in those decisions.

In a market economy, like that of the United States, a paper mill is typically a privately operated firm, concerned primarily (if not entirely) with maximizing its dollar profit, that is, the difference between what it can obtain by selling its output and what it must pay for its inputs. Its salable output is paper; its inputs are labor, capital equipment, and materials. If the decision is left entirely to the firm about which process to use, it will use the *high-pollution* process. The low-pollution process, using more inputs per ton of paper, will clearly involve greater dollar *costs* for those inputs and will thus be less profitable.

Lest we hastily conclude that it is some inherent evil in the capitalist system that causes pollution in a case like this, consider what would happen in a planned economy like the Soviet Union. Typically, the paper mill would be given an allocation of inputs (labor, equipment, materials) and the manager would be instructed to produce as much paper as possible, or to achieve a "target" paper output that would be set as high as feasible. What process would the socialist manager choose? Obviously, the *high-pollution* process with which the most paper can be produced with the resources available.

Influencing Decisions

The issue we face here is thus not one of "profit" versus "target" motives (indeed, the Caspian Sea, like Lake Erie, is polluted), but simply whether decision-makers in general are forced to take into account the pollution they may cause. As we have just shown, there may well be no "automatic" mechanism to ensure that pollution is taken into account, in which case some form of conscious *policy* is required.

Once society (or the government acting on its behalf) becomes aware of the pollution problem, dealing with it becomes much less difficult. In a market economy we could impose a compulsory payment (a *tax*) on every pound of pollutant produced—equal, say, to the township's cost of removing these pollutants—in order to make it *unprofitable* for the paper mill to use the high-pollution process. In a centrally planned economy, planning officials could simply order the manager to avoid pollution, or demand a lower production quota on the condition that no pollution be produced.

Inducement versus Coercion

As indicated in the preceding section, a paper mill can be *coerced* to reduce pollution by charging a sufficiently high tax per unit of pollutant discharged. But the mill could be *induced* to do the same by offering it a large enough tax rebate or outright subsidy, even though this payment would require the government to raise taxes elsewhere in the economy. Which is superior, direct coercion of factory management, or inducement necessitating coercion of the taxpaying public?

Traditional economic thinking about social welfare clearly differentiates between the coercion of firms and the coercion of people. The firm, being an agent or intermediary, does not count in welfare judgments—the economy is presumed to operate exclusively for the *people*. Thus, whether a firm is coerced or induced to behave in a particular way is simply a question of policy technique—the method chosen being whatever is easier, less costly, and/or more effective.

By its very nature, coercion of people implies that they are moved from a situation preferred more to one preferred less. Inducement, on the other hand, implies movement from a situation preferred less to one preferred more. Thus, if everyone can be *induced* to do something, everyone is made better off. On the other hand, if coercion is required, some will necessarily be made worse off. Most economists, anxious to avoid interpersonal welfare comparisons, favor situations in which everything is accomplished by inducement because of the resulting universal betterment. Some might also favor inducement on the grounds that coercion is inherently bad—but this would reflect a strictly moral judgment.

Although in reality many things can be achieved exclusively through inducement, not everything can. While it may be possible to induce the rich to transfer a small fraction of their income to the poor (private charity is evidence of this), major distributional changes cannot be carried out without coercion. Moreover, public goods like national defense and clean air cannot be provided without taxation, and thus coercion. Indeed, it has become apparent in recent years that the major problems plaguing the American economy are those things least easily remedied by inducement alone.

Recap Even when society would choose a low-polluting process using more resources in preference to a high-polluting process, those responsible for determining the process may still choose the latter. This is because the actual decision-makers react to criteria determined by the structure of the economic system, which may not include the effects of pollution. Decision-makers can be coerced or induced to take pollution into account. In general, economists prefer inducement to coercion to achieve policy ends. However, many of the problems that face the American economy today are amenable only to solutions that require coercion.

Capsule Supplement 1.4   **What Should We Do with the "System"?**

The aircraft definitely flies one wing down, forcing the pilot to spend much of his time making corrections. Back in the design department, opinions differ: some believe that the aircraft can never be modified to fly straight, and that it should be scrapped in favor of a completely new design; others note that there has never been a design without faults, and that this one can be modified to fly satisfactorily—perhaps very successfully—in the end.

At the most basic level of economic and social thinking there is a similar difference of opinion. There are those who believe that the faults of the economy are inherent in the prevailing economic system and can be eliminated only by changing the system itself; and those who believe that the present economic system can be modified to bring about any desired standard of performance, subject only to resource availability and the existing technology.

The issue is not whether a particular type of economy does or does not possess faults that call for policy correction, but whether economic policy can correct those faults within the institutional structure that defines the "system." It was Karl Marx who introduced the notion of an inherently flawed system that could never be corrected and hence would necessarily fall apart. His monumental analysis of capitalism was offered as evidence of that system's inherent contradictions and thus its inevitable collapse. Unlike many who talk about changing the system, Marx clearly defined what he regarded as the essential feature of capitalism—private ownership of the "means of production" (nonlabor resources)—and was willing to argue that any economy that preserved this feature would ultimately fail.

Capitalism was, of course, the only economic system that actually operated in the developed economies of Marx's time. Consequently, Marx had only hypothetical alternatives with which to compare it. Today, with alternative systems available for scrutiny, the modern economist can only conclude that economies of different types seem to work, and that all have their own special flaws. If economic policy can do no more than patch up surface wounds of a system whose inherent shortcomings are serious, then China and the Soviet Union, as well as the United States, are all stuck with faulty systems they cannot hope to salvage.

Within every system a majority of economists take the view that, with suitable policy choices, *their* system can be made to do whatever is required of it. An increasing number of economists (call them economic "technicians" if you like) believe that appropriate policy can achieve almost any desired result, regardless of the prevailing institutional structure. In their view, alternative systems differ only in that they provide more or less advantageous starting points for different policy goals. An American economic "technician" and his Soviet counterpart could each devise policies to achieve some specific objective (a given distribution of income, for example). Their policies would differ because of underlying dissimilarities in their respective economies, but each would ultimately achieve the same end.

Radical economists in America strongly criticize this "technical" approach to economic policy. Some are classic Marxists who adhere to the belief that the capitalist system is inherently faulty and that most policy in a capitalist society therefore constitutes either a waste of time or, worse, a postponement of its ultimate collapse, and the advent of a better system. Many are disillusioned liberals or liberal socialists who may accept the technical approach in principle, but believe that the selection process by which the key technicians are chosen and trained will always be biased against those who are likely to develop policies involving major change. The radical critique of economics in recent years has emphasized policy goals that economists have traditionally neglected (such as distributional equity) and attacked certain naive assumptions that have biased economists' results in favor of the status quo (such as their failure to consider the importance of social interactions).

The fundamental premise of this book is that some aircraft tend to fly with the right wing down, some with the left, but that each can be straightened up one way or another without fully discarding the basic structure. It is fully recognized, however, that it may stretch the state of the art to find the exact way to do it.

Exercises

It is estimated that a full-scale antipollution program for the People's Republic of Pluto will require expenditure of $50 billion in the year 2001. The total value of all things produced in the Plutonian economy is predicted to be around $1,000 billion in 2001.

1. If adopting the full program means a loss of goods and services worth the same as the cost of the program, by what percentage will adoption reduce the output of goods and services?

2. Plutonian taxes (of all kinds) are generally equal to about 25 percent of total output. By what percentage will total taxes have to rise if the antipollution program is to be financed entirely from taxes?

For Thought and Discussion

1. Suppose you represent the government of a very poor country that cannot support all of its citizens above the poverty line. What would you choose as your distribution policy?
   a. Equal distribution, with everyone below the poverty level
   b. Some kind of unequal distribution that puts some above the poverty line and leaves others noticeably below, possibly below minimum subsistence

2. The use of chemical fertilizers and pesticides will increase the quantity of food that can be produced with given stocks of land and labor, but almost certainly will cause some deaths through chemical poisoning. Would your attitude toward the use of these chemical agents be different if you represented the government of
   a. a rich country?
   b. a poor country?

3. Economists have been criticized by Marxists for not recognizing that nonmaterial things are ultimately determined by the material. Do you think it possible to separate the material from the nonmaterial?

Chapter 2
Society's Economic Possibilities

Terms and Concepts

Production process
Available technology
Technical inefficiency
Process level
Input substitution
Constant returns to scale
Isoquant
Production possibility curve
Transformation curve
Rate of transformation
Resource scarcity
Efficient allocation of resources
Law of increasing costs

The Underlying Factors

An introduction

The quantities of material, as well as many nonmaterial goods available to society are limited by society's economic possibilities which, in turn, reflect the constraints on society's production alternatives. It is important to stress the *quantitative* nature of these possibilities and constraints because the development of economics as a true social *science* has been largely the result of economists' ability to quantify the concepts with which they deal. The political theorist may have a model in which greater governmental efficiency can be attained only at the expense of less governmental responsiveness to day-to-day community views. But because these two things cannot be quantified easily, the theorist is unable to answer the question, "how much" community responsiveness must be given up for "how much" efficiency? The informed economist, on the other hand, *is* prepared to answer the question, how much of good X must be given up in order to realize an increased quantity of good Y?

Before discussing how society's economic possibilities can be quantitatively determined, let's note those factors that serve to constrain these possibilities. They are as follows:

1. The *resources* available to society. Resources include both things that can be used directly (like stocks of finished consumer goods) and things that can be used to produce other things. Ignoring the former, society's resources can conveniently be divided into
   a. *natural resources*—land, water, timber, sunshine, minerals, etc. In principle, these cannot be increased; but in practice the existence of certain natural resources may be unknown until "discovered."
   b. *human resources*—not only the potential raw labor of society's members, but also their skills and knowledge that can be increased over time by education and training.
   c. *physical capital*—buildings, roads, machines, etc. These resources have been produced in the past and accumulated over time. Some of society's current production will be devoted to increasing its "capital stock."
2. The *technology* available to society. Simply speaking, the technology is the collection of known recipes for doing things, especially using resources to produce goods.

In discussing *possibilities,* we are necessarily talking about the *best* that society can do, given its resources and technology. Specifically, in referring to society's economic possibilities, we mean those circumstances in which

1. output cannot be increased by using idle resources (in which case we have *full employment of resources*), and
2. output cannot be increased by reorganizing production or rearranging

the way in which resources are allocated (in which case we have *technical efficiency* and *efficient resource allocation*).

In the remainder of this chapter we discuss the economist's view of production, the relationship that exists among the various combinations of goods society can produce, and the reasons why society may ultimately fail to achieve its economic possibilities.

Recap Society's economic possibilities are circumscribed by its available resources and its technology and determined by the efficiency with which it operates within these limits.

Capsule Supplement 2.1   **The Gifts of Nature**

The immediate predecessors of Adam Smith in the development of economics—the members of the French school headed by Francois Quesnay and known as the Physiocrats—argued that the "true" source of all wealth was the land, and that other so-called factors of production provided mere barren manipulation of this wealth. Only two generations of economists later, David Ricardo (who directly followed Smith in the lineage) argued and succeeded in convincing his peers, as well as several subsequent generations of economists, that the "true" source of all wealth was labor.

What happened during the short period separating the Physiocrats and Ricardo to inspire this abrupt shift in perspective? It was the spectacular emergence of industry, the output of which was observed to derive from the application of labor to machines (the latter, it was argued, having themselves been built by labor). The role of land (a term traditionally used by economists as a synonym for the "gifts of nature") consequently entered a period of neglect that ended only recently. While the machines that caught the eye of the early economists might have been built *by* labor, they were built *from* the iron ore and derived power *from* the coal that lay in the earth. For a century and a half after the Industrial Revolution, however, those natural resources were assumed to be inexhaustible. It appeared that labor engaged in the process of exploration could simply not fail to locate and tap new resources.

Today, a full two centuries removed from the influence of the Physiocrats, economists are once again emphasizing the role of nature in determining the world's economic possibilities. The now famous "Limits to Growth" report issued by a research group at MIT has predicted that the world's population will begin to decline before the year 2100 because of the depletion of natural resources. This report does not base its conclusions on the old idea that population will outstrip food supplies because of the limits of agricultural land, but on the modern notion that it will outstrip *industrial* supplies of fuels, metals, and other natural materials. Thus industry and the economies built upon it will collapse. In order to survive, the report (based on what have become controversial computer simulations) predicts that the rate of growth in resource use must be cut drastically both by reducing the rate of growth in world output and by recycling wastes to conserve resources.

Does this swing mean that economists will now come up with a "Neo-Physiocratic" theory in which "true" value is, again, attributed solely to natural resources? Some enterprising group of scholars no doubt will. But the general thrust of modern economics is to ascribe the "true" source of value in the economy to *no one* factor of production. Indeed, we note that economic production would fall to zero quite rapidly if either all labor or all natural resources were to disappear.

The case of capital is slightly different. If all the capital in the world were to disappear, it could (in principle) be gradually rebuilt with labor used to fashion simple machines, then labor and simple machines used to produce more complex machines, and so on. But even then, output would initially fall quite drastically, even if not to zero. Thus, it makes little sense to identify any one productive factor as *the* source of all economic value.

The long understatement of the role of natural resources has, however, led to some mistakes that economists must attempt to redress in the coming years. Natural resources have undoubtedly been *undervalued* in making economic policy judgments. Indeed, for the most part, they've been treated as if they were "free" to society in their natural state, any costs associated with their use having been confined to the costs of extracting, processing, or transporting them. To the extent that certain nonrenewable resources are being seriously depleted (and current world concern about limited oil, coal, and natural gas reserves suggests that this possibility constitutes more than idle conjecture), their "true cost" should reflect the reduced output of future generations potentially arising from their current overuse—something which, unfortunately, no private decision-maker is likely to consider.

The Production Process

The economist's view of production

In ordinary usage the term *production* usually refers to the process during which something takes on its own recognizable form. Cotton fiber goes into a textile mill and comes out as cotton fabric. This fabric is then shipped to another location, cut into small pieces, printed with small red hearts, sewn into boxer shorts, distributed through wholesalers, and eventually marketed by retailers. To most people, the various stages of manufacturing *per se* would be regarded as production; but the transport, distribution, and sale would not.

While, as we might suspect, economists also regard manufacturing, along with such kindred enterprises as mining and farming, as *production,* they do not confine this term to these activities alone. Rather, they view production more generally as the transformation of resources or commodities into things that are regarded by consumers as "different." To a resident of Oregon, a Toyota station wagon in a Portland showroom is most assuredly "different" from the same vehicle at the factory in Japan. The transport of an automobile across the Pacific thus constitutes *production* in the broad economic sense. After all, Texas oil "producers" don't actually *make* oil, they merely transport it from its natural state under the ground to the nearest refinery. Similarly, such activities as storage, packaging, and retailing all constitute forms of production.

Nor is production confined to processes that involve tangible things. Production also includes providing services. Accordingly, physicians, mechanics, musicians, lawyers, professors, and prostitutes all are engaged in production.

From the economist's point of view, a critical property of production is that the quantity of whatever is produced is directly related to the quantity of resources used. If the amount of "godliness" in society depends on the number of priests, the time devoted to prayer, and/or the number of maidens sacrificed to the heavens, it comes under the economic theory of production. Then more godliness can be produced only when resources are taken away from other uses.

Production Processes

Were we to ask a French chef how to prepare one of his specialties, say boeuf bourguignon, we would be given an answer in terms of raw materials or ingredients, the proportions and order in which these ingredients must be combined, and appropriate preparation times and temperatures. Because a chef is clearly engaged in processes whose outputs are fundamentally different from their inputs, it might seem that the chef's response to our question would provide the key to the *theory of production* in economics.

But the chef's recipe would be incomplete from the economist's point of view. *Labor* would be needed to bring the ingredients together, as would *capital equipment,* though perhaps only in the form of a mixing bowl. The process would also require *space,* and take *time* to complete.

The economist's analysis of production proceeds from the *complete* recipe, the statement of what specific quantities of inputs—including labor, capital, land, and raw materials—are required to produce a specified level of output. Such a complete recipe constitutes a *production process*.

The Technology

At any given time, some finite number of known processes exists. Taken collectively, these processes are said to constitute society's *available technology*. For a modern industrial society like the United States, the available technology is clearly comprised of a vast array of productive processes. The question arises, however, as to whether all these processes actually constitute relevant production alternatives.

If one process can produce the same level of output as a second process but with less of some inputs and no more of others (or, equivalently, if it can produce more output than the second process with the same level of inputs), the second process is said to be *technically inefficient*. When comparing processes in this fashion, we must take *all* inputs into account. For example, a process that uses more raw materials than others is not technically inefficient if it uses less labor or less capital, or takes less time, than those others.

Because there is no reason why a producer would ever use more inputs than necessary, we can confidently make our first assumption about the nature of production:

A process that is technically inefficient, given the available technology, will never be used except in ignorance of a better process.

We can use the word "never" because a technically inefficient process will remain so forever. To be sure, a process that is technically inefficient today may not have been so a hundred years ago because its inefficiency may be relative only to processes discovered during the intervening century. Nonetheless, it will still be technically inefficient a hundred years from now. The ongoing development of new processes that render old processes technically inefficient, and thereby obsolete, is commonly referred to as *technological progress*.

It is important to recognize that not all new processes necessarily make old processes *technically* inefficient. Driving, for example, is generally quicker, and less tiring, than walking. But driving also requires more inputs (a car, gasoline, etc.). In poor countries, people still walk miles to market despite their acquaintance with the virtues of the automobile. Why? Because they possess resources for walking but not for driving. The choice between these two alternatives is determined by the availability of the resources required for each. It is thus an *economic* choice, not a technical one.

Recap Production is the transformation of resources and/or goods into things that are "different," either because they have been physically changed or because they have been transported to a different time or place. A production process is a complete recipe for producing a given level of output. The collection of all production processes known to society is its available technology. Technological progress occurs when new processes are introduced that, with a given level of inputs, can "outproduce" old processes.

Simple Production

The basic theory of production with two inputs and one output

Most real production processes are complex and require a wide variety of inputs. In order to provide examples that can be illustrated with two-dimensional diagrams, we shall discuss elementary production theory in terms of hypothetical production processes that have a single output and use only two inputs—labor and capital.

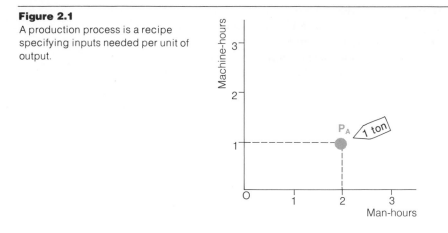

Figure 2.1
A production process is a recipe specifying inputs needed per unit of output.

Consider process A, the unit level of which requires two workers and one machine to produce one ton of output in one hour. For one ton of output, then, the specific inputs required are two man-hours of labor and one machine-hour of capital. We can illustrate this process using a diagram in which the number of man-hours is measured horizontally, and the number of machine-hours is measured vertically. In Figure 2.1, point P_A represents the quantities of both inputs required to produce a unit level of output with process A. Because the diagram shows only *inputs* on two axes, we must *label* the point P_A with the appropriate level of output. Point P_A therefore represents a process in which two man-hours and one machine-hour (as read from the axes) produce one ton of output (as read from the label).

Duplication

Now let's ask the question: If we assemble two more workers and a machine identical to the first one in another corner of the factory so the two groups do not get in each other's way, is there any reason why this second group shouldn't produce exactly the same as the first?

Indeed there is not. In the absence of a specific reason to the contrary, we shall assume that a process can be duplicated. The duplication in our example will use a total of four man-hours and two machine-hours to give an output of two tons.

Figure 2.2 extends the content of Figure 2.1 to illustrate the effect of duplication. Point $2P_A$ depicts the inputs required to duplicate the original level of the process, and is labeled with the duplicated output, two tons.

If the process can be exactly duplicated, obviously it can be reproduced three, four, ten, or any number of times. We shall refer to this number as the *level* at which the process is operated. Operating a process at, say, seven times the unit level will use exactly seven times the amount of each

Figure 2.2

In general, we can expect to double output by doubling all inputs, and obtain any output level by operating the process with more inputs.

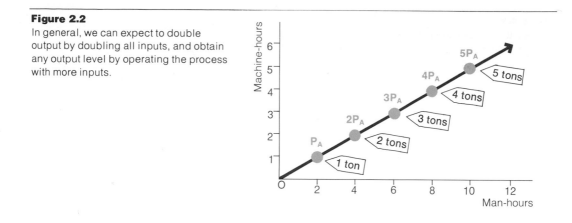

input as at the unit level and produce exactly seven times the amount of output.

Other Processes

Except with the simplest technology, it is likely that there will be more than one process available for producing a particular good. Suppose, in our example, that there is an alternative process, B, that produces one ton of output with *one* man-hour and *two* machine-hours, instead of *two* man-hours and *one* machine-hour as with process A. Figure 2.3 reflects the addition of process B to our technology; the various levels of operation for this process are labeled P_B, $2P_B$ and so on.

With two processes, a *choice* is available. Two tons of output can be produced by process A, using four man-hours and two machine-hours, or by process B, using two man-hours and four machine-hours.

The choice, however, is not confined to using process A or process B exclusively; these two processes may be combined. Assuming that the operation of one process does not affect the operation of the other, we could arrive at two tons of output by producing one ton with process A (using two man-hours and one machine-hour) and one ton with process B (using one man-hour and two machine-hours). Together the two processes would use three man-hours (2 + 1) and three machine-hours (1 + 2). This possibility is represented by point C in Figure 2.4.

Input Substitution

Note that the potential use of different processes or process combinations to produce a given output creates the possibility of producing that output with labor and capital in different proportions. The ratio of man-hours

Figure 2.3
Different processes require inputs in different proportions and thus provide a choice between input proportions for a given output.

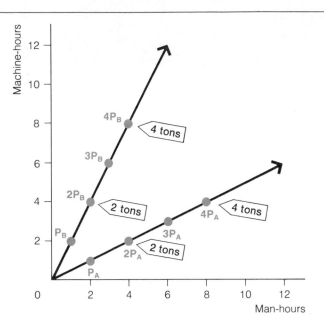

required per *machine-hour* varies from 2 : 1 (using process A) to 1 : 2 (using process B). Process A combined with B at equal levels produces an intermediate ratio of 1 : 1. Thus, we can keep output constant while reducing the number of man-hours and increasing the number of machine-hours, that is, while *substituting* machine-hours for man-hours.

This process of *input substitution* does not involve directly substituting capital for labor—we do not actually *replace* a worker with a machine. Rather, it entails switching to *different* processes or combinations of processes that require more capital and less labor than before.

Isoquants

We now have at least three ways to produce an output of two tons, as illustrated in Figure 2.4 by the points *A*, *B*, and *C*. Those points represent the following:

Point A—operation of process A at level two, using four man-hours and two machine-hours to give an output of two tons;

Point B—operation of process B at level two, using two man-hours and four machine-hours to give an output of two tons;

Point C—operation of processes A and B together, each at unit level, to use three man-hours and three machine-hours and give an output of two tons.

Because we have assumed that any process can be operated at any level, with the level of output varying in proportion to the quantity of inputs (a

Figure 2.4

By combining two processes, input proportions can be varied over a considerable range.

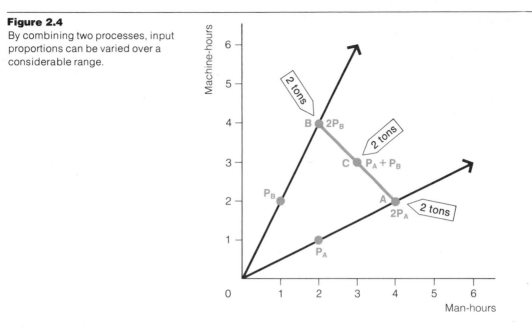

property called *constant returns to scale*), we could produce eight tons of output by operating process A at level eight (using sixteen man-hours and eight machine-hours), process B at level eight (using eight man-hours and sixteen machine-hours), or process A at level four and process B at level four (using twelve man-hours and twelve machine-hours).

But there is no reason why we should confine ourselves to the combined-process case in which processes A and B are operated at the same level. We could, for example, operate process A at level five and process B at level three. By so doing we would obtain eight tons of output (5 + 3) from thirteen man-hours [(5 × 2) + (3 × 1)] and eleven machine-hours [(5 × 1) + (3 × 2)]. Indeed, we can produce eight tons of output with *any* combination of the two processes as long as their respective levels of operation sum to eight.

Given the points that correspond to the input combinations required to produce a specific level of output by using A or B alone (such as points *A* and *B* in Figure 2.4), the various input combinations capable of producing that same output by using these processes together are represented by the line connecting these two points. The line *AB* thus specifically represents *all possible* input combinations capable of producing two tons, and is referred to as the two-ton *isoquant* (meaning an "equal quantity" of output). We could just as easily draw an *isoquant* for eight tons, showing the input combinations that would give that level of output. If drawn on the same diagram as the two-ton isoquant, it would be parallel to it and exactly four times as far from the origin because (assuming constant returns to scale) the

Figure 2.5

A given output can often be produced by a variety of input combinations (*see* Figure 2.4), and the line through the points representing these combinations is known as an isoquant. For combinations derived from two processes only, the isoquant is a straight line.

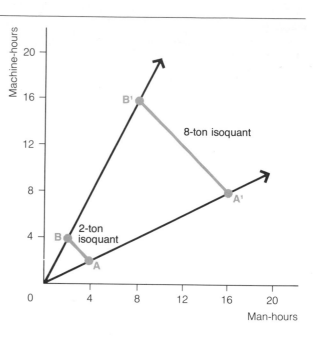

inputs needed to produce eight tons with inputs in some specific proportion would be exactly four times the inputs needed to produce two tons. Figure 2.5 shows the eight-ton isoquant ($A'B'$) compared with the two-ton isoquant (AB).

But, what if there are more than two processes? Consider Figure 2.6(a), which shows unit level input combinations for two processes, P_A and P_B, and two points corresponding to those of a possible third process. If this process were represented by the point P_D, lying farther out than the line joining P_A and P_B, it would never be used. Why not? Because it would be technically *inefficient,* requiring more of both inputs than certain combinations of P_A and P_B. The new process would be used only if it were represented by a point like P_C, lying inside the line $P_A P_B$. If it were, then combinations of P_A with P_C, or of P_B with P_C, would require fewer inputs than combinations of P_A with P_B (which therefore would be rendered inefficient). The resulting isoquant would be the *bent* line $P_A P_C P_B$, described as *convex toward the origin.* A line joining $P_A P_D P_B$ would be *concave toward the origin.*

With more than two processes, an isoquant is thus no longer a straight line, but a bent line like that in Figure 2.6(a) or (b). If the number of technically efficient processes becomes large enough, the bent line becomes indistinguishable from a smooth curve like that in Figure 2.6(c), which is the version of the isoquant generally used by economists.

Figure 2.6
With three or more distinct processes, the isoquant becomes a bent or curved line that is convex toward the origin (never concave toward the origin as $P_B P_D P_A$ would be).

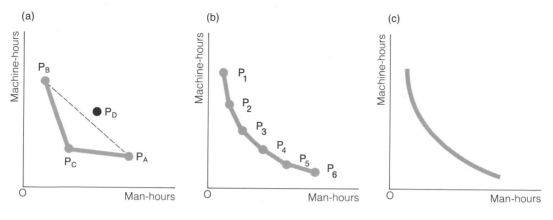

Recap A given process requires specific quantities of each input to yield a particular quantity of output. In the absence of special influences, we assume that doubling the level of inputs doubles the level of output, in which case the process is said to exhibit constant returns to scale. With more than one process available, we can operate processes side by side in various combinations. A given level of output can thus be produced by various process combinations using different input combinations. The various efficient combinations of inputs that yield the same level of output, when portrayed graphically, give a line, bent line, or curve known as an isoquant.

Capsule Supplement 2.2   **The Human Element**

In their conventional models of production, economists treat man-hours of labor as abstract homogeneous inputs whose relationship to output is expressed in terms of fixed technical coefficients. It has long been argued that such failure to consider the human and social aspects of production can lead to serious error in assessing the true state of technology and thus society's production possibilities. Modern corporate management practices, for example, stress the importance of organizing production in such a way that the effects of social and human relationships on productivity are taken into account. Indeed, much technological progress has probably resulted from considering the "human element" in this sense.

But there is a deeper sense in which human and social relationships may affect production. Different *structural* relationships between workers and production processes may give different *technical* relationships between man-hours of labor and levels of output. Karl Marx stressed the alienation of workers from products under industrial methods of organization—the things they produced, or helped to produce, were not "their" products in the direct sense of the preindustrial craftsman. This alienation, it is argued, not only results in workers disliking their work more than they otherwise would, but eventually leads to lower productivity. Like many concepts in Marxian analysis, alienation has taken on a special technical meaning and is applied only to production under capitalism. Workers under socialism are presumed not to feel alienated because their output is not taken away by the capitalists. In reality, however, workers on a Zhuguli assembly line in the Soviet Union probably feel little differently about their jobs than workers on a Ford assembly line in the United States.

There has recently been a revival of interest in the idea of alienation, taken more broadly than in classic Marxism. In the United States, this revival has seen practical expression in attempts to form small-scale production cooperatives, demands by assembly-line workers for greater participation in the production process than the tightening of a single nut, and a rebirth of interest in carrying out production by handicraft methods. While many idealists argue that an entirely different system of production, such as one of cooperatives, would so change production relationships that output per worker would actually increase even in an industrial society like the United States, there is no hard evidence on the subject. The relatively rapid economic development of China in recent years has been suggested as evidence on this point since much Chinese industry is organized on a communal basis. But China did not "switch" from an American, European, or even Soviet form of industrial organization to the commune—it was not industrialized in the first place.

But even if different methods of organizing production do not result in greater productivity, they may lead to greater worker satisfaction and, therefore, deserve to be included among the alternatives considered by the economist. If the aim of economic policy is to increase "social welfare," an increase in worker satisfaction even at the expense of some reduction in material output might well constitute a net social improvement.

Production Possibilities with a Single Scarce Resource

The possibilities open to society when several goods all require the same scarce resource

In the preceding section, we discussed the relationship between inputs and the output of a single good. In reality, of course, an economy will produce many goods. Our interest here is in the various *goods collections* or *output mixes* that can be produced with a given endowment of resources under a given technology. In order to facilitate our analysis of society's production

Figure 2.7
When each of two goods requires the same input and that input is limited in quantity, the combination of goods that can be produced is limited by a production possibility curve.

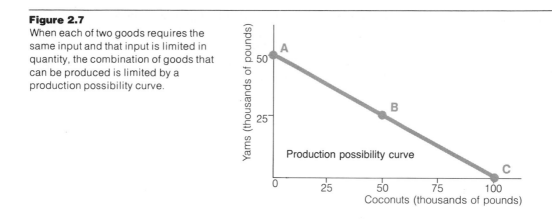

possibilities, let us assume a world that consists of two goods, yams and coconuts.

The simplest case is when unit production of each good requires a fixed amount of a single resource. Let's call that resource *labor,* and suppose that society's available technology dictates the following labor requirements:

yam production: two man-hours per pound at all output levels.
coconut production: one man-hour per pound at all output levels.

Let's assume that there are 100 workers, each of whom contributes a maximum of 1,000 working hours per year. The total of available man-hours is thus 100,000.

If all workers were used to produce yams, total output would be 50,000 pounds of yams. If all were used to produce coconuts, output would be 100,000 pounds of coconuts. If exactly half the labor force were used to produce yams and half to produce coconuts, output would be 25,000 pounds of yams plus 50,000 pounds of coconuts.

A Production Possibility Curve

The various production possibilities open to this society are depicted diagrammatically in Figure 2.7. Point *A* reflects the use of all resources in yam production, point *C* the use of all resources in coconut production, while point *B* reflects the case in which half the available labor is used in each "industry." Note that point *B* lies on the straight line joining *A* and *C*.

In fact, *every* point on the line *AC* represents a production possibility for society. The reader can easily verify that any division of labor between the two industries (say 10 percent to yams, 90 percent to coconuts) will yield an output that is represented by a point on the line *AC*. Our concern here is not with how the choice is made about which combination of yams and coconuts should actually be produced, but simply with which combinations are possible.

A line like *AC* in Figure 2.7, which passes through the points representing society's production possibilities, is known as a *production possibility curve* or a *transformation curve*. The latter name comes from viewing the analysis from a slightly different perspective.

Suppose that, initially, all workers are used to produce yams, yielding 50,000 pounds. Let's investigate what happens when we gradually shift these resources into coconut production.

A shift of one man-hour from yam into coconut production *reduces* yam output by one-half pound (each pound of yams requires two man-hours), but *increases* coconut output by one pound (each pound of coconuts requires one man-hour). By shifting resources from yams to coconuts, we increase coconut output *at the expense* of yams; that is, *we "transform" yams into coconuts, not by magically converting the former into the latter, but by using resources released by reducing yam output to produce more coconuts.* The ratio of coconuts gained to yams lost that results from such a shift in resource use is called the *rate of transformation between yams and coconuts.* In our example, this rate is two pounds of coconuts per pound of yams.

Regardless of what output mix is actually produced in our example, the rate of transformation remains constant. A shift of one man-hour from yam production into coconut production will always result in a sacrifice of one-half pound of yams and a gain of one pound of coconuts. This implies a constant slope for the transformation curve and accounts for its being a straight line.

Such a straight-line transformation curve is a rather special case, however, that arises when there is but a *single efficient process* for producing each good. With a single resource, as in this example, once the output of one good is established (say 20,000 pounds of yams), there will remain a specific amount of labor with which to produce the other good (60,000 man-hours) and thus a *unique quantity* of the other good that can be produced (60,000 pounds of coconuts).

As we shall see, the question of efficient resource allocation arises only when there are several resources—and several processes—from which to choose.

Recap If there are two goods, each requiring the same scarce (and fully employed) resource, we can produce more of one good only by producing less of the other. Given the available technology, the amount of one good that must be given up in order to have an additional unit of the other can be quantitatively defined. It is called the rate of transformation, and will be constant when there is only one scarce resource. Diagrammatically, the set of all points representing possible outputs of the two goods is society's production possibility curve and is a straight line when only one resource is scarce.

Scarcity, Resource Waste, and Technological Change

Some extensions of the case presented in the previous section

If more than one resource is required for production, the analysis of the previous section remains valid *as long as only one resource is scarce*. In reality, the production of both yams and coconuts requires land as well as labor. Suppose that 2 acres of land are required for the annual production of 1,000 pounds of coconuts, and that 1 acre of land is required for the annual production of 1,000 pounds of yams. If all labor were used to produce yams, annual output would be 50,000 pounds and require 50 acres. If all labor were used to produce coconuts, annual output would be 100,000 pounds and require 200 acres. For intermediate output mixes, between 50 and 200 acres will be needed.

If the economy has at least 200 acres of freely available land, the land requirement will not affect its production possibilities. This is true because after allocating the land required to produce any given quantity of coconuts up to 100,000 pounds, sufficient acreage will always remain with which to produce whatever yam output is associated with the quantity of labor unused in coconut production.

A resource is said to be scarce if and only if the output of at least one good can be increased by having more of this resource. In our example, an increase in the availability of land from 200 to 201 or even 250 acres would have absolutely no effect on the output of either yams or coconuts. Consequently, at 200 acres, land would not be scarce.

But scarcity is *relative*. Land, in our example, would always be scarce if less than 50 acres were available. Moreover, it would be scarce, even at 200 acres, if the labor force were increased, say, to 500 members. In that case 250 acres would be required to produce a maximum yam output of 250,000 pounds and 1,000 acres would be required to produce a maximum coconut output of 500,000 pounds. Hence, a given resource, existing in fixed supply, may or may not be scarce depending on what quantities of *other* resources are available to work with it to produce society's output.

The production possibility curve represents an *outer limit* on society's economic options. Therefore, society cannot achieve output mixes lying "beyond" this curve, which is often referred to as the *production possibility frontier*. In Figure 2.8, for example, the combination of yams and coconuts represented by point *X* is simply unattainable.

In fact, society may succeed only in attaining points *inside* the frontier, like *Y* in Figure 2.8. Aside from inefficient resource allocation, the topic of the next section, the most likely reason for being restricted to such a point is society's simple failure to use all available resources.

Figure 2.8

Society cannot attain points, such as X, that lie beyond its production possibility frontier. Indeed, it may even fail to attain points on this frontier because of inefficiency or a failure to use all potential resources. In such cases, it will only be able to achieve points like Y lying within the frontier.

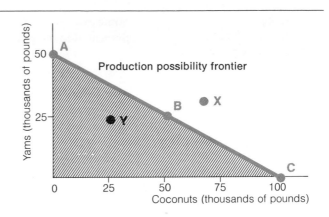

Technological Change

A production possibility frontier is determined by the resources and technology available to society and thus will be affected by changes in these factors. An increase in available labor, for example, will push the frontier outward.

Technological progress—the discovery of new processes yielding more output from given inputs than previously possible—will also expand the frontier. While this general proposition is obvious enough, we should note that technological progress in the production of *either* yams *or* coconuts will lead, in general, to expanded production possibilities for *both*.

Suppose a new yam-growing technique is discovered that permits twice as many yams to be produced per man-hour of labor than before. If we were initially producing the combination of yams and coconuts indicated by point *B* in Figure 2.9, this technological breakthrough would enable us to alter our output in several ways.

Specifically, we could (1) sustain our original allocation of labor between yams and coconuts and thus double our yam production as shown by the move from point *B* to point *D*; (2) maintain our original level of yam output, thus freeing labor exclusively for increased coconut production as shown by the move from point *B* to point *E*; or (3) reduce the allocation of labor to yam production, but by less than half, so as to increase *both* yam *and* coconut production as shown by the move from point *B* to *any* point on the new production possibility frontier between *D* and *E*. Obviously, the only case in which technological progress in yam production would have no effect on output is when yams are *never* produced, as at point *C* in Figure 2.9.

In general, then, we can conclude that technological progress in one industry will normally increase society's production possibilities in terms of all goods.

Figure 2.9
Technological progress, even if only in one industry, will generally enable society to obtain more of all goods.

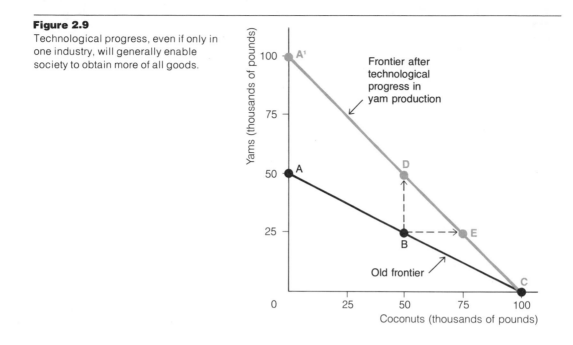

Recap A resource may be required for production, but may not be scarce, as in the case in which more land is available than can be worked by the existing labor force. More of a resource that is not scarce will not affect production possibilities, but more of a scarce resource will expand these possibilities, as will technological progress. Society may, however, fail to achieve its production possibilities by underutilizing its scarce resources.

The Efficient Allocation of Resources

With more than one scarce resource, society can be economically inefficient if it does not allocate its resources appropriately

With a single scarce resource, and thus a single efficient process for each of two goods, the amount of one good that can be produced is fully determined once the amount of the other good is decided. This is not true, however, if there is more than one scarce resource and more than one process for producing each good.

Consider a society whose production possibilities are subject to the constraints set out in Table 2.1. There are two goods, Frisbees and pretzels, each of which can be produced by either, or some combination, of two

Table 2.1
Society's Economic Constraints,
The Availability Technology

Process	Man-hours required	Machine-hours required	To produce
F_1	3	0	1 Frisbee
F_2	0	1	1 Frisbee
P_1	1	0	1 box of pretzels
P_2	0	5	1 box of pretzels

The technology is assumed to exhibit constant returns to scale. Available resources: 120 man-hours, 50 machine-hours.

processes. There are two scarce resources, labor and capital. We've labeled the four processes involved F_1, F_2 and P_1, P_2 to clarify whether the output of a given process is Frisbees or pretzels.

Note that the processes are rather unusual because each uses only *one resource*. We can produce one Frisbee with three man-hours of labor and no capital, or one machine-hour of capital and no labor. Such unrealistic processes have been chosen to simplify the arithmetic. Our conclusions would still hold even if, more realistically, we assumed that every process required some amount of *both* labor and capital.

To find out how many Frisbees the economy can produce if it devotes all of its resources to their production is simple. The 120 man-hours can be used to produce 40 Frisbees using process F_1, and the 50 machine-hours can be used to produce 50 Frisbees using process F_2, for a grand total of 90. Stated a little differently: processes F_1 and F_2 can be operated at levels 40 and 50, respectively, thus using up all available resources to produce 90 Frisbees. Similarly, by using all available resources in pretzel production, we can operate process P_1 at level 120, and P_2 at level 10, giving 130 boxes of pretzels.

Because either labor or capital by itself can be used to produce either commodity, we will never leave any resource unused if we seek to maximize output.

Producing Both Goods

Suppose we decide to produce only 40 Frisbees. How many pretzels can we then produce? Unlike the single-process case, there is no one answer to this question. It depends on which process is chosen for Frisbee production and which for pretzel production.

The 40 Frisbees might be produced by (1) process F_1, (2) process F_2, or (3) some combination of the two.

1. Using process F_1 exclusively, the production of 40 Frisbees will require 120 man-hours of labor. This uses up all the available labor, leaving 50 machine-hours of capital with which we can produce 10 boxes of pretzels using process P_2. Thus, by using process F_1 for Frisbees and P_2 for pretzels, we can produce 40 Frisbees and 10 boxes of pretzels.

2. Using process F_2 exclusively, the production of 40 Frisbees will require 40 machine-hours of capital but no labor. The resources still available for pretzel production will consist of 120 man-hours of labor plus 10 machine-hours of capital. We can produce 120 boxes of pretzels using process P_1, and an additional 2 boxes using the remaining capital in process P_2. Thus, by using process F_2 for Frisbees and a combination of P_1 and P_2 for pretzels, we can produce 40 Frisbees and 122 boxes of pretzels.

3. By using various combinations of F_1 and F_2 to produce Frisbees, then combinations of P_1 and P_2 to produce pretzels with whatever resources remain, we will obtain 40 Frisbees along with from 10 to 122 boxes of pretzels, depending on our exact "mix" of processes.

Efficiency

Thus we can produce 40 Frisbees along with any quantity of pretzels between 10 and 122 boxes without varying the quantities of resources used. In each case, however, there is a different *allocation* of labor and capital between the two industries. Taking the extreme cases of (1) and (2), the first represents an allocation of 120 man-hours to Frisbee production and 50 machine-hours to pretzels, while the second represents an allocation of 40 machine-hours to Frisbee production and 10 machine-hours plus 120 man-hours to pretzels.

Obviously, society will want to produce the *maximum* possible quantity of pretzels along with its 40 Frisbees. This is 122 boxes, obtained by allocating 40 machine-hours to Frisbee production and the remaining resources to pretzels. This allocation represents an *efficient* allocation of resources; any other allocation would be *inefficient*. The data involved in our comparison of production options are summarized in Table 2.2.

To see what our production possibility frontier looks like, let us assume that all resources are initially allocated exclusively to Frisbee production. As already shown, 90 Frisbees can be produced by using process F_1 at level 40 and process F_2 at level 50.

We now wish to produce some pretzels by cutting back on the production of Frisbees. This cutback can be accomplished in several ways. One way would be to reduce process F_1 only or reduce process F_2 only.

Reducing the level of process F_1 by one unit cuts Frisbee production by one and releases three man-hours of labor. With these three man-hours, we

Table 2.2
Efficient and Inefficient
Resource Allocation

	Allocation 1	Allocation 2
Man-hours allocated to Frisbees	120	0
Man-hours allocated to pretzels	0	120
Machine-hours allocated to Frisbees	0	40
Machine-hours allocated to pretzels	50	10
Mode of Frisbee production	F_1 (level 40)	F_2 (level 40)
Mode of pretzel production	P_2 (level 10)	P_1 (level 120) and P_2 (level 2)
Frisbees produced	40	40
Boxes of pretzels produced	10	122
Allocation is	inefficient	efficient

The constraints on the economy are those set out in Table 2.1.

can produce three boxes of pretzels using process P_1. The resulting rate of transformation, doing things this way, is three boxes of pretzels per Frisbee. On the other hand, if we cut Frisbee production by reducing process F_2 by one unit, we release one machine-hour of capital with which we can produce a mere one-fifth box of pretzels using process P_2. In this case, the rate of transformation is one-fifth box of pretzels per Frisbee.

Efficiency dictates that we attain the *maximum* quantity of pretzels for each Frisbee not produced. We will therefore begin by cutting back on Frisbees produced by process F_1, at a transformation rate of three boxes of pretzels per Frisbee. This transformation line is shown as AC in Figure 2.10.

But F_1 uses labor only. We can reduce the output of Frisbees this way only so long as labor is still being used to produce them. Once we've reduced Frisbee output by 40, we will have exhausted this possibility. At this stage, all labor will have been released from Frisbee production, Frisbee output will have fallen from 90 to 50, and pretzel production will have risen from 0 to 120 boxes. This stage is represented by point C in Figure 2.10.

Because Frisbee production now uses only machines and thus only process F_2, further cutbacks will yield only one-fifth box of pretzels per Frisbee until all resources are allocated to pretzels and we reach point B in the diagram. The slope of CB represents a rate of transformation of one-fifth box of pretzels per Frisbee.

In carrying out the reallocation just described, we have made every move in such a way as to maximize the quantity of pretzels produced for

Figure 2.10

An example of the production possibility frontier when there is more than one scarce resource, showing the effect of inefficient resource allocation.

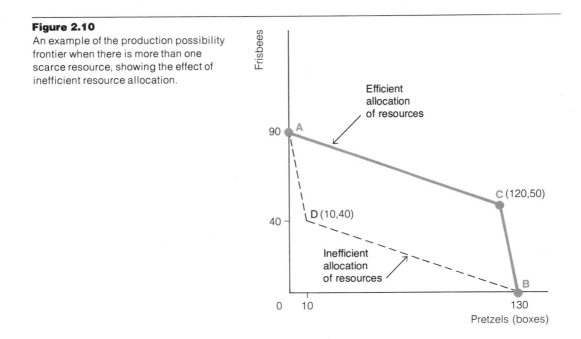

each Frisbee given up. Thus, the various outputs obtained, which all lie on the bent line *ACB* in Figure 2.10, form the *production possibility frontier*.

Inefficiency

Had we reallocated *inefficiently,* by initially cutting back Frisbee production via process F_2, we would have moved from point *A* to point *D* in Figure 2.10 (forty Frisbees, ten boxes of pretzels) rather than to point *B*. The dashed curve *ADB* is thus a kind of "maximum inefficiency curve"—we could do worse, but only by leaving resources idle.

Our point is as follows: by using *all* resources, but allocating them inefficiently, we may well end up at a point far inside our production possibility curve. Indeed, it is not difficult to imagine a situation in which a *less than full* but *efficient* use of resources would result in a larger output of goods than a *full* but *inefficient* use of resources.

With several resources and processes, the production possibility frontier is no longer a straight line as it was with a single scarce resource; it is bent out *beyond* the straight line which, for example, would join the endpoints *A* and *B* in Figure 2.10. Whenever we have two or more technically efficient processes per industry, we will obtain a production possibility frontier of this kind. With more than two processes, the frontier will have more than two kinks and will look like that in Figure 2.11. As the number of processes

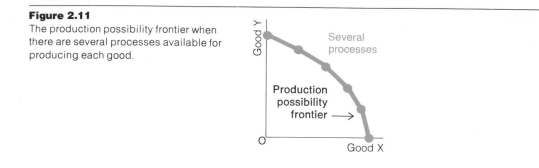

Figure 2.11
The production possibility frontier when there are several processes available for producing each good.

becomes very large, the frontier will become indistinguishable from a continuous curve, as in Figure 2.12.

The Law of Increasing Costs

The broad shape of the production possibility frontier, which is best described as concave toward the origin, is said to reflect the *law of increasing costs*. In general, this law holds that if society's resources are fully and efficiently used in the production of goods X and Y, successive unit increases in X can be achieved only by successively larger and larger sacrifices in the quantity of Y produced, that is, only at an increasing "cost" to society in terms of the quantity of Y forgone.

The logic underlying this law was established in the previous example in which increases in pretzel production were accomplished initially by taking *labor* out of Frisbee production (labor having been relatively better suited for pretzel production than Frisbee production in the first place). When this was no longer possible, *capital* was then taken out of Frisbee production, even though this dramatically increased the "cost" of each additional box of pretzels in terms of Frisbees forgone (from one-third Frisbee per box to five Frisbees per box).

When there are *many* different processes involved, the cost of a good in terms of what could alternatively be produced varies continuously over its entire range of potential output, as is demonstrated by the case of good X in Figure 2.12.

Recap If there are several scarce resources and alternative production processes for each good, society may fail to achieve its production possibilities because of inefficiently allocated resources. Even from simple examples, we can show that society may use all of its resources, yet not achieve its production possibilities because it has misallocated its resources to different industries. The production possibility frontier consists of those output mixes achieved when society's resources are efficiently allocated.

Figure 2.12
In accordance with the law of increasing costs, successive equal increases in the production of good X require increasingly larger reductions in the output of good Y.

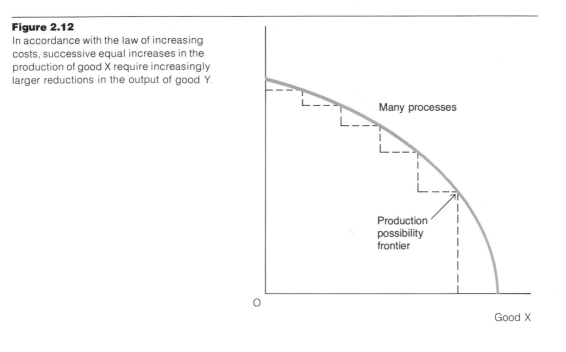

Many processes

Production possibility frontier

O

Good X

Capsule Supplement 2.3   **Can Inefficiency Be Virtuous?**

In our example in the main text, society can fully use its resources to produce 40 Frisbees and 10 boxes of pretzels. In this case, however, these resources are said to be allocated inefficiently. Frisbees are produced by the labor-intensive process and pretzels by the capital-intensive, which is the wrong choice of processes for this output mix. The exact same output mix could be produced "efficiently" in the sense of using no more resources than necessary, by using the capital-intensive Frisbee production process and the labor-intensive pretzel production process. The efficient allocation requires only 10 man-hours and 40 machine-hours, compared with the 120 man-hours and 50 machine-hours needed for the inefficient allocation. For the given output mix, the use of the efficient process combination would release 110 man-hours and 10 machine-hours with which the economy could produce more Frisbees or pretzels or both. When we stress efficiency, are we presuming that the labor or capital released by allocating these resources more efficiently will be used to produce something socially desirable? But suppose, for whatever reason, that there is no use for the resources so released.

It may be that society will simply not buy more than forty Frisbees and ten boxes of pretzels. Where is the virtue in efficiency then, if the resources saved cannot be used for anything else? Indeed, there are strong arguments in this case why *inefficiency* would be preferable to efficiency.

The potential virtue of inefficiency arises from distributional considerations. In most societies, those resources that are used will be paid, and those that are idle will not. Whether our economy is operating efficiently or inefficiently, its output, by assumption, is the same—forty Frisbees and ten boxes of pretzels—and this output will be divided in some way among households. In the inefficient case, the output is divided among everyone in society, because all resources are used. In the efficient case, however, the output will be divided among the relatively small number of individuals actually employed or owning the machines that happen to be in use. These few will receive much more than in the inefficient case, but the rest of society, dependent on the sale of unused resources, will starve. Thus, inefficiency may give a more equitable distribution than efficiency if the latter leads to unemployed resources.

There have been real counterparts to this example. During the Great Depression of the thirties, as much as 30 percent of America's resources (capital as well as labor) stood idle. Would it not have been better to have had an inefficient allocation of resources but no unemployment, had that been a choice? As a matter of ironic coincidence, just as the Great Depression became the fundamental fact of economic life almost everywhere, economics had become heavily influenced by the "Austrian" view, which held that the problem of efficient resource allocation was the chief issue to which economists should address themselves.

In less-developed and preindustrial economies, inefficiency has been and still is widely used as a distributive device. Peasant holdings may support extended families with very inefficient use of labor, simply to give a wider distribution. The rich may support many servants, less because they need them than because it is an implied social obligation to distribute to those who would otherwise be unemployed. The ranks of government bureaucracy may be swollen far beyond the limits of efficient administration by socially accepted nepotism—again, as a device to widen distribution.

Inefficiency is, at most, a second-best solution, even for distribution. The optimal solution to any of the cases cited is obviously to use resources efficiently rather than inefficiently and use those released to produce something that will benefit society. If this simply cannot be done, however, inefficiency may indeed prove itself virtuous.

Exercises

1. Suppose we have two processes, P_1 and P_2, each of which produces twelve tons of hogwash with the following inputs:

| | To produce 12 tons of hogwash | |
	Man-hours	Machine-hours
P_1	1	4
P_2	3	2

Both processes exhibit constant returns to scale and can be operated at any level (including fractional levels).

   a. If both processes are operated at one-half the levels given in the table, what will be their combined output and combined inputs of man-hours and machine-hours?

   b. Using graph paper, draw the twelve-ton isoquant for the technology consisting of these two processes.

   c. Draw the twenty-four-ton isoquant for the same technology.

   d. An additional process, P_3, which uses 2.5 man-hours and 3 machine-hours to produce twelve tons of hogwash, becomes known. Is P_3 a useful addition to the technology?

2. An economy consists of two industries, agriculture and fishing. Each hundred tons of output from agriculture requires, over the course of a year, the services of 3 people and 20 acres of land. Each hundred tons of output from fishing requires, over the year, the services of 5 people, but no land. If the resources of the economy consist of 150 people and 600 acres of land,

   a. what is the maximum possible output of agriculture?

   b. what is the maximum possible output of fish?

   c. Using graph paper, draw the economy's production possibility curve.

For Thought and Discussion

1. Try to think of some production processes that *would* interact if carried on in different corners of the same factory, contrary to the assumption made in the text. Would it be impossible for such processes to be used simultaneously?

2. The development of the Chinese economy since the 1950s has been based on the strategy of "walking on two legs," that is, on using the newest processes that require much capital simultaneously with older processes that use little capital but much labor even in the same industry. Given that China has much labor and little capital, is this a rational policy, or would you expect better results if the high-capital processes were used only in certain industries and high-labor processes in others?

3. The analysis of production has been given for cases in which the only output was something desired, and the inputs were things that could be used elsewhere and thus were not to be used up except for some useful purpose. If the production process were one in which the input were garbage and the output were electric power, how would the analysis be changed? What would now constitute efficiency in production?

Chapter 3
The American
Economy

Terms and Concepts

Corporation
Stocks, stock market
Progressive taxes
Transfer payments
Human capital
Public goods
Fiscal policy

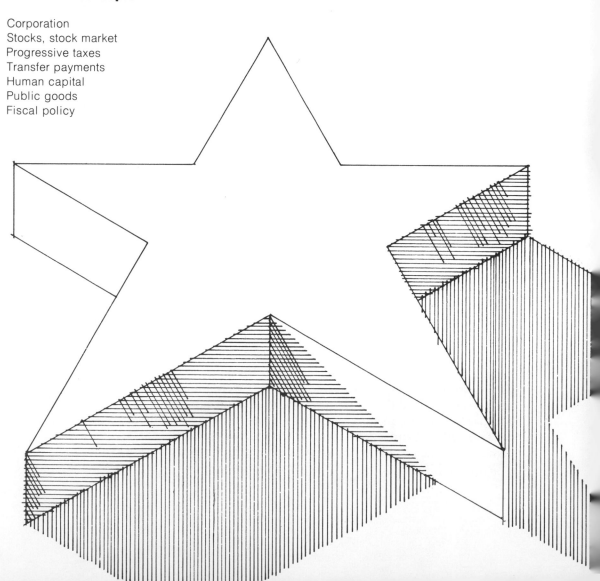

America the Rich

**A brief preview
of America's economy**

A Chamber of Commerce president would consider America to be a rich and successful example of private enterprise. A Marxist would consider it a rich and anachronistic example of capitalism living unexpectedly beyond its time. Others would consider it variously as a rich example of mixed public and private enterprise, a society rich in material things but poor in human values, a rich society enclosing a poor subculture, a rich society in which wealth is justly distributed to those who created it, a rich society in which wealth has been unjustly extracted from those who created it, a rich society that should stop trying to become richer, or simply a society like many others—only richer.

All would agree, including those who might wish it otherwise, that the United States is the richest country in the world in terms of total production, and among the very richest in terms of goods and services produced per head of population. Table 3.1 provides estimates of the total output

Table 3.1
International Comparisons of
Output Per Person, 1975

Country	Output per person (U.S. $)	Life expectancy at birth
1. The Top Ten*		
Switzerland	6,930	73
Sweden	6,876	75
United States	6,597	71
Canada	6,463	73
Luxembourg	6,214	70
West Germany	6,198	71
Denmark	6,020	73
Norway	5,825	74
Belgium	5,451	71
Australia	5,448	71
2. A Selection of Others		
Japan	4,152	73
Israel	4,029	71
Britain	3,375	72
Italy	2,706	72
Mexico	1,119	62
India	110	41
Upper Volta	59	32

* Excludes Kuwait and the United Arab Emirates, the oil revenues and small populations of which place them very high on the list.
Source: United Nations, *Statistical Yearbook*.

produced per person in the United States and various other countries in 1975. This table should be read as showing relative levels of prosperity. We should avoid concluding, for example, that the United States is a "hundred times" more prosperous than Upper Volta, simply because the former's output per person is a hundred times greater than the latter's.

Wealth and Welfare

A high rate of output of material goods cannot be counted on to solve all of a nation's social or even economic problems. The second column of Table 3.1 (life expectancy at birth) has been inserted to show that the United States does not rank particularly high in another important indicator of social welfare. Indeed, Sweden and Switzerland both rank ahead of the United States in per capita income *and* life expectancy. Sweden, however, also ranks well ahead of the United States in one of the standard indexes of social dis-welfare—the suicide rate. The lower end of the column (from Mexico down) illustrates how life expectancy is related to income levels below the "European" standard of living.

America does not lack economic and social problems of major proportions. The important questions to be answered are whether these problems exist *because* America is rich, persist *in spite of* America's prosperity, or arise because the "system" that makes America rich necessarily produces them.

It is certainly true that prosperity may produce its own problems. The most obvious example is environmental pollution, which is produced jointly with high levels of production and consumption. Then there are those issues, such as whether or not to legalize marijuana, which constitute "luxuries" in the sense that starving people worry first about where they will find their next meal and about other things only after they've eaten. However, if problems can be solved at all, higher incomes permit more resources to be diverted to problem-solving without reducing the supply of material goods to poverty levels. It can thus be argued that increased prosperity, *if used in the right way,* can eliminate its own problems. We can think of this as the traditional *liberal* outlook, which would regard America's problems as solvable and thus persisting in spite of, not because of, prosperity.

The so-called *radical* approach would be to ascribe both America's prosperity and its problems to the way the capitalist system works. For example, the freedom of employers to fire workers may lead simultaneously to industrial efficiency *and* social inequity. Hence, there may exist a real choice between prosperity and other social goals. Those whose beliefs run on such lines would regard the liberal approach as naively optimistic because it adheres to the idea that problems can be solved as they arise without fundamentally restructuring the entire system.

There is no convincing evidence that poor countries, as a group, have fewer social problems than rich ones (they simply have *different* problems), or that any poor country has decided it is in its best interests to remain poor. Thus, the approach of this book is that of the liberal tradition, focusing on *what has been done* with prosperity, not prosperity itself, as the source of problems. The book emphasizes solutions that involve changes in the mix of things produced and in the distribution of income.

A Brief History

How did America become so rich? Is its high level of prosperity proof that the "American system" is better than any other? These are questions to which everyone would like an answer, but to which no clear answer can really be given.

We must first note that both the United States and Canada seem to have had high per capita incomes relative to Europe almost from the first. The relative prosperity of America definitely antedates modern technology, mass production, and most of the other factors commonly associated with twentieth-century America.

If we look at the world at about 1860, we can pick out two areas—North America and Oceania (Australia and New Zealand)—with output per capita well above that of the rest of the world, including Northwest Europe, then the industrial center. These two areas were both characterized by large endowments of natural resources (land, minerals) relative to their comparatively small populations.

Over the following century, America did not show a spectacular or unusual rate of growth in output per capita—it remained about the same as that in Western Europe, less than that in the Soviet Union and Japan, and larger than that in Latin America and continental Asia. (America did, however, sustain a high rate of population increase, and its total output grew rapidly.) Australia and New Zealand, on the other hand, grew more slowly than most of the industrial countries and eventually fell well behind the United States and Canada.

Because the United States is a large country, as well as one with a high level of production per person, its total production is much higher than that of any other country. Indeed, it currently produces more than one-fourth of the world's total output even though it has only about one-eighteenth of the world's total population.

Factors in Development

Exactly how America grew richer is not really as clear as is commonly supposed. The most ambitious attempt to analyze the various factors responsible for America's growth was made in 1962 by E. F. Denison (*The Source of Economic Growth in the United States*, Committee for Economic Development). Although his results have been viewed with skepticism by some economists, they are well worth summarizing.

From 1909 to 1929, output per worker grew at an average annual rate of

1.22 percent. Of this growth, Denison attributed only 29 percent (not percentage points, but proportionate contribution to actual growth) to increased capital per worker—the traditional primary explanation. Almost 35 percent was attributed to the improved "quality" of labor (with increased education being a main factor), and 46 percent to pure technological progress—more output from the same inputs. The contribution of these three factors adds to more than 100 percent because the rapid population growth from 1909 to 1927 caused a *decline* in land available per worker, a factor that would have actually reduced output per capita in the absence of the above influences.

From 1929 to 1957, during which the U.S. growth rate averaged 1.6 percent per annum, the contribution of increased capital per worker was even less than for the earlier period (less than 10 percent), the contribution of improved worker quality was about the same, while the contribution of pure technological progress was higher (58 percent).

For this period, Denison estimated the various components of the pure productivity change as having the following levels of importance:

Advances in knowledge and its application (technological progress)	63.5%
Economies of large-scale production	31.0%
More efficient allocation of resources	5.5%

We cannot make a direct comparison with the period prior to 1929 because statistics are not available on the same detailed basis. A recent extension of this analysis covering the period 1950 to 1972 shows a generally similar pattern to that given for 1929 to 1957, except that efficient resource allocation appears to have been a much more important factor in the later period.

If we accept Denison's estimates, we can conclude that the following factors have contributed most to the growth in American per capita output:

1. An increasingly educated and skilled work force.
2. Technological progress through the advancement and application of knowledge.
3. Economies of large-scale production—especially available in America because it has the world's largest "market" (in the sense of total purchasing power).

Recap The United States is the richest country in the world, measured in terms of the value of total goods produced. Being rich brings problems of its own, but also the resources to solve these problems. The relative affluence of North America has not been due to a spectacular increase in output over the past century. Indeed, its long-term growth rate has been similar to that of Europe. This relative affluence existed as early as 1860. The sources of American economic growth are somewhat uncertain, but education and technological progress have clearly been important.

Capsule Supplement 3.1   **Standards of Affluence**

The United States Department of Labor has calculated the costs of maintaining three different standards of living for urban families of four persons. While it is difficult to characterize exactly what these mean, the moderate standard (middle of the three) corresponds closely to what government statisticians used to describe as "modest but adequate." All three standards allow for the ordinary amenities of American life (a car, a TV, a washing machine, and so on), the lower standard being based on the cheapest possible way to attain these goods. The higher standard allows for certain trimmings (a dishwasher, long-distance telephone calls, a color television) not included in the lower standard. We might perhaps characterize the three levels as "adequate," "modest," and "comfortable." Incidentally, the higher (comfortable) level was just about equivalent to the median income of economists in 1975.

In addition, the Social Security Administration calculates two other budget levels, "poverty," the amount necessary to just attain an adequate diet and minimal other things, and "near poverty," which is defined as 125 percent of the poverty level.

For 1975, the five budget levels for an urban family of four were:

	Annual family budget ($)	Average per person ($)
Higher standard of living	22,294	5,573
Moderate standard of living	15,318	3,829
Lower standard of living	9,588	2,397
Near poverty	6,875	1,719
Poverty	5,500	1,375

Let's compare the figures in the last column with American aggregate performance in 1975. The standard measure of total output (gross national product) was $7,102 per person in 1975—somewhat above the "comfortable" standard of living. For reasons that will become apparent later, a more appropriate measure here is disposable income per person, which was $5,052 in 1975—a little below the comfortable standard, but well above the moderate standard and far above the poverty line. Thus, the American economy produced enough goods and services in 1975 to very nearly provide a "comfortable" standard of living for everyone.

In fact, because income was unequally distributed over the population, there were some with incomes well above the "comfortable" standard, and many with incomes well below it. No fewer than 12 percent of total households had incomes at or below the poverty level, with an additional 5 percent at or below the near-poverty level.

A major difference between America and a country like India is that an equal distribution of income in America, if achievable, would leave everyone comfortably off, whereas in India it would put everyone well below the poverty line.

The American Economic System

The main institutional features of the American economy

The American economic system is *capitalistic* in the simple sense that non-labor resources (land and physical capital) can be, and predominantly are, owned by private individuals and corporations rather than by the government on behalf of society as a whole. The American system, in principle, is also one of *free enterprise* insofar as there are no general prohibitions against producing and selling. Of course, certain limitations do exist—one cannot own equipment to print money for example, nor can one legally sell such things as medical services, television broadcasts, and liquor without official approval. But anyone is legally free to produce automobiles, or even (in some states) start a university and call himself or herself a professor. For many industries, of course, freedom of entry may be severely restricted by the lack of access to capital or technology, but these restrictions are not imposed by the government.

Finally, the American economy is a *market* economy in which most goods are sold to those willing and able to pay for them, as opposed to being allocated by some rationing system. Most incomes are also market-determined in the sense that employers pay whatever is necessary to obtain the services of both labor and nonlabor resources.

The Importance of the Corporation

The development of the United States to its present economic structure under a system of predominantly private ownership would have been impossible without the legal institution of the *corporation*. The corporation acts as an intermediary in the private ownership system, being equivalent to a single "person" in terms of its ability to own property, but itself owned by a large number, even millions, of individuals. No one person could assemble the property holdings of a typical large corporation, and no system of loosely organized joint ownership would be stable enough to permit the long-range organizational and production decisions that characterize the modern corporation.

Without the corporation, the size of the average U.S. firm would be many times smaller than it is. The existence of corporations has permitted the emergence of large firms where large-scale operations are more efficient. Unfortunately, however, it has also permitted the growth of large firms where these are *not* conducive to economic efficiency.

More than two-thirds of the contribution to total United States output from private business in 1975 came from corporate enterprises. While not *all* these corporations existed to take advantage of size—many tiny corporations are formed for tax and other reasons—more than 65 percent of all corporate assets in 1975 were held by 1,700 firms, each with assets of at least $250 million. Although the very large corporations are traditionally associated with manufacturing, two of the largest (Sears, Roebuck and A & P) are retailers, and two (Exxon and Mobil) are oil producers and refiners.

Ownership

Ownership of a corporation (as contrasted with what the corporation itself owns) is usually defined in terms of shares or *stocks*. Broadly speaking, the corporation's ownership is divided into a certain number (perhaps millions) of equal shares, and any individual owns as much a proportion of the corporation as his shares bear to the total. It is the essence of the modern corporation that these shares are transferable at the will of their owners and can be sold to others. Thus, the corporation as an institution requires a *stock market* where shares can be traded easily. The world's major stock market, the New York Stock Exchange, trades from 10 to 20 million shares daily, and it is not the only market, even in New York.

Control

The large size of the modern corporation, and the existence of transferable stock in conjunction with a well-organized stock market, has led to a divorce between formal ownership and actual control of the corporation. Those associated with the control of most large corporations are key executives (who are themselves employees of these corporations) and/or leaders of alliances among certain major stockholders.

Stockholders typically buy stock for resale. Their interest in the actual operation of the corporation is usually confined to whether it will serve to increase the value of this stock so that it can be sold, at a profit, to other stockholders whose view of the corporation is similar to theirs. The corporation itself, it should be noted, makes no direct gain from the increase in the market value of its stock. While dividends paid to shareholders totaled $33 billion in 1975, net capital gains for the year totaled another $15 billion.

The modern corporation has thus tended to become a more or less autonomous *institution* run by a large, self-perpetuating management that doles out dividends primarily to prevent stockholders from protesting. This tendency, first noted formally in the thirties, was tabbed the "management revolution." It is no longer a revolution, but an established fact of life. One economic consequence of this is that the goals of management are no longer necessarily simply to maximize profits—even though many corporations reward executives in a way that gives them a personal incentive to increase profits or the market value of the corporation's stock.

Control of Production

Table 3.2 shows how production in the United States is divided among various types of control. As can be seen, well over half of total output was generated from production controlled by corporations, and more than 80

Table 3.2
Contribution to Total Output by
Type of Control, United States, 1975

	Contribution to gross output (billion $)	Proportion of total (%)
Corporations	709	58.8
Noncorporate business	260	21.5
General government	178	14.7
Households	50	4.1
Rest of world	11	0.9
Total	1,208	100.0

percent from production controlled by private business enterprises. Government production represents the output of freely provided government services such as education, defense, and highway maintenance.

Households generate output mainly by employing domestic help and residing in the houses they own rather than renting them to others. (If houses are rented to others, the rents appear as business output.) The rest-of-world sector reflects income to Americans derived from other countries, such as dividends from foreign corporations.

Recap The American economy is a capitalistic and predominantly free-enterprise market economy in which goods are distributed to those who pay for them. The large scale of many productive activities has been possible under this system only because of the legal institution of the corporation, and the major part of U.S. business output is controlled by corporations. The growth of the large corporation has led to a separation of ownership (by stockholders) from control (by management).

Distribution and Incentives

Income distribution under the American system

The distribution of output in the United States is almost entirely carried out through the market. With only a few exceptions, goods are available in exchange for dollars without rationing or other restriction. After paying taxes, consumers are free to spend their incomes as they choose. But first they must have incomes.

Most incomes are obtained from the sale of the services of those economic resources that individuals own. For most persons, the only resources that are "owned" are the knowledge and skills they have acquired. Consequently, their incomes derive from the sale of personal services—labor income in the broadest sense. Almost three-fourths of all personal income in the United States is obtained from the sale of personal services.

Property owners can obtain incomes by selling the services of their property instead of, or in addition to, their personal services. Income from selling property services is variously called rent, interest, dividends, royalties, etc., according to the type of property involved. In addition, there will usually be a surplus or residual profit in most production carried out in a market economy, this being the difference between the value of output produced and whatever payments for labor and property services are required for production.

Diffusion of Property Income

One of the characteristics of America, and one that distinguishes it from the stereotyped conception of a capitalist society, is the absence of a truly separate capitalist class. The rise of the corporation has resulted in broad ownership of property and, whatever the reasons (the "Protestant ethic" probably being one), most property owners also sell their personal services. The existence of certain intermediate institutions has dispersed property income even further, so workers with life-insurance policies and even those drawing pensions negotiated by their trade unions are drawing incomes derived ultimately from corporate profits. Thus, we have propertied millionaires drawing wages and salaries (as lawyers and executives rather than as farm laborers, of course), and ordinary wage earners drawing property incomes, although small ones.

The basic distribution system that arises out of the institutions of property ownership and private enterprise has also come to be modified by redistribution through government policy. Individuals pay income taxes that are designed to be *progressive,* that is, individuals with high incomes pay a higher *proportion* of their incomes in taxes than do individuals with low incomes. At the same time, the government pays individuals falling into certain categories incomes or *transfer payments* even though they may have no resource services to sell. In effect, some of the income individuals receive from the sale of resource services is taxed by the government and transferred through welfare, Social Security, and other programs to other individuals.

Income Differences

Under the basic distribution system, each individual's income depends on the resource services he has available to sell, and the prices of these services. A person who doesn't own property can sell only personal services, which are limited in quantity by the physical constraints of time and human endurance. But the prices of different types of personal services vary enormously—from minimal levels for raw labor power to extremely high levels for certain specialized skills. An unskilled laborer may earn $3,000 to $4,000 annually when fully employed, while a top corporation executive may receive $300,000 to $400,000 annually for special talents—indeed, a rock performer in his or her prime may receive considerably more than that. Thus, the distribution of income, even from personal services, can be very unequal—but the maximum possible income is ultimately limited by the physical powers of the human being.

Property income, on the other hand, is subject to no such ultimate physical constraint. Indeed, property cannot only be accumulated without physical limit but can be retained intact if the owner is physically incapacitated, and ultimately handed on to successors after the owner's death. For these reasons, the most spectacularly high incomes are from property—in 1974 tax returns, 84 percent of the income of those reporting incomes of at least $500,000 in the United States was derived from property.

A part of each individual's income from personal services is derived from a special kind of ''property.'' Although certain high-priced personal skills (particularly those of entertainers, artists, and athletes) largely reflect natural endowment, most skills are developed through *training* and *education*. The distribution of this *human capital* through the population is determined by access to appropriate training that, in turn, often depends on parents' incomes. Thus, there is an indirect generation-to-generation transmission of high incomes derived from personal services. While the United States is probably better than many countries in providing the means by which human capital can be accumulated from scratch, transmitted privilege remains.

Incentives

The distribution system determines the incentive system. Because most goods are distributed through the market, most things can be obtained with sufficient income. This makes the prospect of increased income one of the chief driving forces behind individuals in a market economy. In other societies where certain highly valued things—apartments and dachas in the Soviet Union, knighthoods and peerages in Britain—are distributed other than through the market, money incomes alone may be a less important incentive than in the United States.

Because the owners of small businesses obtain their incomes through profits, the ''income incentive'' becomes the ''profit incentive'' for them. This is generally reinforced by the fact that their success among peers is measured largely by profits. In large corporations, however, those in effective day-to-day control derive their incomes from salaries. While these salaries may depend on the corporation's profits, the direct profit incentive is somewhat weaker. Nevertheless, we can assume that corporations have strong incentives to maximize profits, even though this goal may be weakened by the existence of other management incentives.

In the public sector, individual incentives will still be dominated by income maximization. Insofar as increased income is associated with a more efficient execution of government policy, the ultimate effect will be little different than in a system in which execution of policy is primarily a road to official honors or social prestige. However, institutional factors make it quite probable that those possessing the highest skill levels can make more income outside the public sector, and this will tend to drain top individuals from the public to the private sector.

Recap Most goods are obtained in the United States in exchange for incomes. Consequently, the distribution of incomes is the primary determinant of the distribution of goods. Incomes can be obtained by selling personal services (labor) or property services, with a high proportion of individuals obtaining some of their income from both sources. In addition, governments transfer incomes among persons through taxes and such programs as welfare and Social Security. Incomes vary greatly for persons receiving labor incomes as well as for persons receiving property incomes, although the very highest incomes derive predominantly from property. Prospective incomes constitute an important economic incentive in the United States.

Capsule Supplement 3.2   **The Poor in America**

Poverty is relative. A standard of living that would have been regarded as "modest but adequate" in the 1850s might now be considered as below the "poverty" level. For the United States, the Social Security Administration computes poverty income levels (based on minimal satisfaction of basic needs) for families of various sizes in various environments. In 1975, the poverty level, based on this definition, was $2,724 for a single person and $5,500 for a family of four. The official figure is adjusted annually for price changes; in 1970 it was $3,968 for a family of four. Not unexpectedly, the proportion of households at or below the poverty level (the *incidence of poverty*) has shown a downward trend since 1947, the earliest date for which this analysis is available. The incidence of poverty, in fact, has fallen from 30 percent in 1947 to 12 percent in 1975. But poverty still remains.

Poverty is concentrated—in particular age groups, ethnic groups, and geographic areas. It is high among the old, among nonwhites, among isolated individuals who are not members of larger family units, and among rural Americans. The highest incidence is among American Indians and Eskimos on reservations. Although the *incidence* of poverty is higher among nonwhites than whites (by a factor of three in 1975), most poor persons are white—more than two-thirds of all poor families. Immediately above the poverty line are the near-poor. Whereas families at or below the poverty line are predominantly elderly, or headed by a woman of working age, those just above (the near-poor), if not elderly, are usually headed by a man employed at low wages. The *poverty gap* in 1974, the amount that would need to be added to bring the actual incomes of the poor up to the poverty line, was $14.2 billion, approximately 1 percent of GNP.

America easily produces enough to banish poverty completely (something that is true only of the few richest countries in the world), so poverty is due, not to too little total output, but to the way the output is distributed.

The Economic Role of Government

The role of the government in the American economy, and the constraints imposed by political institutions

There are many different governments or bodies acting on public authority in the United States. These range from the federal, state, and municipal governments themselves to highway authorities and school boards. When we use the term *government* without qualification, we mean any or all of these.

Government in the United States avoids certain types of involvement with the private (that is, the nongovernment) sector. It does not, in general, intervene in ordinary market processes (by setting prices, for example), undertake production in direct competition with private industry, or own stocks in corporations. This avoidance is, in some cases, ideologically motivated (as when the government rigidly controls a public utility but chooses not to actually own it). In others, it reflects a policy judgment that the private sector can do these things at least as efficiently as the government. Even in these areas there are exceptions—the government intervenes in the market for many agricultural products, sets a minimum wage, and heavily regulates activity in markets for transport and communication services. Moreover, the government owns the postal service, operates transport facilities, generates electricity, and even runs hotels. Except for the post office, however, actual government production of goods and services that could be sold through the market is very small relative to the private sector.

The Inevitability of Government Influence

Even if the government did not wish to exert a major influence on the working of the economy, it could not fail to do so under modern conditions. The government purchased more than one-third of all goods and services produced in the United States during 1976, the federal government almost two-thirds of these. Because of the sheer size of government expenditure relative to total output, every change in it has major repercussions throughout the economy.

Because the United States is essentially a private-ownership economy, the government does not actually possess any important source of income—as it would, for example, if it owned large stocks of resources rented to the private sector, or earned large profits from productive enterprises. It pays for its expenditure primarily by diverting part of the private-sector's potential income to itself, through taxes, the proportion being broadly the 34 percent that its expenditure bears to total output. Some of this diversion (sales taxes) comes "off the top" before the income is actually allocated within the private sector; the remainder comes from direct taxes on the incomes actually received by corporations and individuals. With taxes so high relative to incomes, every change in total taxes or the structure of taxes has effects that run through the system.

Over and above the inevitable economic influence stemming from the very size of its operations, government in the United States has come, over the years, to accept responsibility for the operation of the private sector. In particular, the government is concerned with the following:

1. *Maintenance of full employment and price stability,* by adjusting its expenditures, taxes, money, and the public debt.
2. *Maintaining or improving economic efficiency in the private sector,* by regulatory laws (such as the antitrust laws) designed to promote competition, regulation (by the Federal Trade Commission and Securities and Exchange Commission, among others) to ensure that markets operate on the basis of adequate information, and many measures of similar kind.
3. *Modification of the private sector's operation,* by tax concessions designed to increase the rate of accumulation of fixed capital equipment, taxes designed to decrease the production and consumption of certain goods (liquor, tobacco), regulatory controls on businesses that are inherently noncompetitive (such as public utilities), and subsidies to encourage certain types of production (shipbuilding).
4. *Modification of the "natural" income distribution in the private sector,* by progressive income taxes (to make after-tax incomes more equally distributed than gross incomes), transfer payments (to provide incomes to those with no resource services to sell), minimum-wage laws and agricultural price supports (to give unskilled workers and farmers higher prices for their services than the market would provide), the provision of some goods and services free (education, for example) so their availability is partly independent of income, and the provision of certain goods (public housing, medical aid) at below market prices to persons with low incomes.
5. *Provision of things that would not be forthcoming from the private sector,* such as defense, police, and maintenance of the institutional structure of

government. These are examples of *public goods,* things the market will not provide because the benefits cannot be "sold" to individuals. Government must supply these things even under the most extreme *laissez-faire* regime.

The last of these governmental concerns represents the fundamental historical role of government. The remaining areas, over the years, have come under the wing of government as it has become apparent that the private sector simply cannot be expected to automatically operate at full capacity, allocate resources efficiently, produce the most socially desirable output mix, and generate an acceptable distribution of income.

Effects of Political Institutions

In carrying out its economic functions, the American "government" is constrained (like all governments) by its inherent political institutions. Two factors have the most impact on economic policy decisions:

1. *The separation of the executive and legislative branches of government.*
2. *The federal structure and the decentralization of local government.*

The first of these presents major problems for *fiscal policy,* the policy designed to influence the economy's overall level of operation by varying taxes and government expenditures. In countries where no such separation exists, the government can announce a tax change at 4:00 P.M., have the legislation passed that evening, and have the tax effective at the beginning of the following day. In the United States it may take months to put such a policy in operation—by which time it may no longer be appropriate. The inflation of the late 1960s was partly due to tax cuts, proposed by President Kennedy under slack economic conditions, but finally enacted two years (and one president) later in the context of a booming economy. This separation thus prevents quick and flexible use of expenditure and taxing powers.

The second—decentralization—makes it difficult to make a broad and unified attack on many economic problems, especially those involving external effects. Pollution of a river may come from a factory in one city, yet primarily affect the residents of another—who are powerless at the source. Certain local government areas can zone out low-income housing. This could force the poor to concentrate in other nearby jurisdictions. A state can refuse to pay acceptable standards of welfare, pushing the poor into other states. Many of the largest cities are surrounded by autonomous local government areas whose residents freely use urban facilities while avoiding urban taxes.

For institutional reasons of this kind, a policy that seems best in terms of economic theory may be either unworkable or inefficient in practice. The general problem is not specific to America—Australia, for example, has a federal structure so rigid that neither the federal nor state governments can control interstate commerce. Each country has its own institutional peculiarities. Hence, although economic policy principles are universal, practices must be tailored to each country.

Recap Although production in the United States comes predominantly from the private sector, the government plays a large and crucial role in the economy. Not only does the government have direct control over one-third of the economy's total output, but it has also assumed responsibility for ensuring high employment, promoting economic efficiency in the private sector, and modifying the distribution of income. At the same time, the particular political structure of the United States—especially the separation of powers and the decentralization of authority—imposes constraints on the uses of economic policy.

Capsule Supplement 3.3   **The Right Output Mix?**

The American economy is unsurpassed in the volume of goods it produces. But does it produce the best *mixture* of goods?

The high level of American productivity must be credited to the private sector. However, this sector is not equally adapted to produce and sell all categories of goods. Goods that the private sector is especially well-suited to produce in response to ordinary market indicators are *private goods.* They are so called, not because they are *produced* in the private sector, but because they give benefits that are private to those who buy them. A household buys a TV set because it cannot obtain the benefits of that set without doing so. Moreover, it is willing to pay the entire bill because those benefits come under its exclusive control.

A *public good,* on the other hand, like unpolluted air, is something that cannot be purchased by an individual household as its own private property. Furthermore, if *someone else* pays to keep the air clean, each household benefits whether it has paid its share or not. The market economy, with its production of different goods determined by distributing incomes to individuals and allowing them free choice in spending, efficiently determines the mixture of private goods. But public goods will not be produced by such a system because there is no demand from individual households that can be made effective through the normal market mechanism.

The contrast, in America, between the high level of private goods and the low level of public goods has been spotlighted in recent years. Elegant apartments (private) open onto dirty streets, polluted air, and filthy rivers (public). Public goods may be produced in the private sector, but they cannot be *sold* through the regular market system. Because firms will not produce what they cannot sell, the supply of public goods depends on community or government action, either to produce the public goods in the public sector itself or pay the private sector to produce them.

There is, of course, a variety of different public goods. Determining the mix of public goods is as complex a matter as determining the proportion in which output is to be divided between public and private goods. It can be argued that the political structure in America has led to an imbalance in the public-goods mixture itself—that public goods traditionally provided by the federal government (like defense) are possibly oversupplied, while many of those traditionally supplied at the local level (like clean streets) are undersupplied because fiscal institutions have channeled an increasing proportion of total government revenues into the federal treasury.

Exercises

1. List a selection of goods that fall into each of the following categories for the United States.
   a. Private goods produced and consumed in the private sector
   b. Public goods provided by government action, but produced in the private sector
   c. Public goods produced by the public sector
   d. Private goods produced by the public sector and sold to consumers
   Try to find at least one good in each category that falls into a different category for some country other than the United States.

2. Sit down with the latest copy of the *Statistical Abstract of the United States* (issued annually by the Census Bureau and available in the reference section of all libraries). Choose any section that catches your interest, examine the tables, and note anything that surprises you. Why were you surprised? Do you expect to find that at the end of your study of introductory economics you should have had no reason to feel surprised?

For Thought and Discussion

1. If the government were to quietly buy up a large number of corporate shares on the stock market, would America be on its way to socialism?

2. In an average recent year, the number of U.S. citizens arriving in the United States was slightly more than the number departing, and the number of aliens arriving considerably more than the number departing. Can we conclude from this that the high incomes in the United States are sufficient to outweigh any nonmaterial disadvantages it may possess?

3. The corporation enables "ownership" of business enterprises to be divided among very large numbers of people. It also enables business enterprises to grow very large. Would you expect wealth to be more or less evenly distributed if the corporate legal form did not exist?

Part 2
The Market Economy

This part of the book, consisting of Chapters 4 through 8, is primarily concerned with establishing the theoretical foundations necessary for the discussion of economic problems and policy in Part 3. Chapters 4 through 7 lead up to the discussion of the *ideal* market system in Chapter 8. This ideal will then provide a reference point for assessing the performance of a real-world market economy.

Chapter 4
Supply, Demand, and the Market

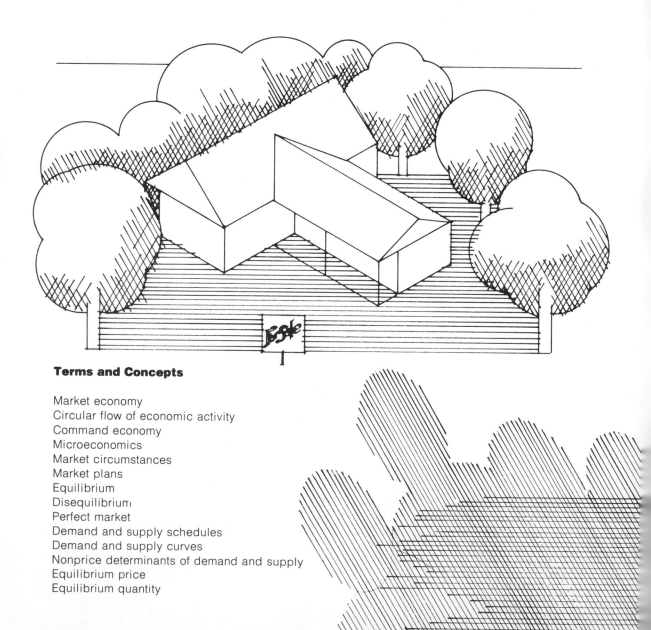

Terms and Concepts

Market economy
Circular flow of economic activity
Command economy
Microeconomics
Market circumstances
Market plans
Equilibrium
Disequilibrium
Perfect market
Demand and supply schedules
Demand and supply curves
Nonprice determinants of demand and supply
Equilibrium price
Equilibrium quantity

Microeconomics and the Market Economy

Why microeconomics is primarily concerned with the market system

Markets are social institutions in which goods and services (including the services of resources) are freely exchanged for other goods and services. In all modern economies this exchange is indirect—one thing is exchanged for money, which is then exchanged for something else. Typically, individuals work for wages (exchanging labor services for money) and then spend those wages (exchanging money for goods). Businesses, on the other hand, sell output (exchanging goods for money) and use their proceeds in part to reimburse employees (exchanging money for labor services).

Perhaps the most important aspect of market exchange is that it is *voluntary*. Thus, it presumably benefits all involved. If a trader has no options—not even the option not to trade—the resulting exchange is not a market transaction. Hence, the government's provision of national defense in "exchange" for taxes fails to qualify as a market transaction because individual citizens have no choice in the matter.

The Role of Markets

Markets function as allocative mechanisms through which society can determine *what, how much, with which means,* and *for whom* to produce.

Consider toothpaste. Most of us take its availability for granted. Yet companies that produce toothpaste are not forced to do so nor to sell it; in the same way, consumers are not forced to buy nor use toothpaste. What guarantees that we'll start the day with that minty fresh feeling? The answer lies in the process of voluntary exchange. Through the market, those of us who want toothpaste communicate our desires to firms that find it in their interest to fulfill this want. These firms then enter the market to purchase the resources needed to produce toothpaste. Eventually, toothpaste is made available, voluntary exchange occurs, and all parties involved benefit.

A society in which the allocation of goods and services is carried out primarily through voluntary exchange is said to have a *market economy*. The basic role of markets in allocating goods and services among both producers and consumers in such an economy is illustrated by the *circular flow diagram* in Figure 4.1.

But the market is obviously not the only way to allocate goods and services. For example, the government may dictate exactly what goes to (or is taken from) particular producers and consumers. In this way, society's productive resources and output are directly allocated. An economic system that allocates resources and output directly is commonly referred to as a *command economy*.

Figure 4.1
The circular flow of economic activity. There are actually two continuous flows: a *real* flow (clockwise) of productive services from households to firms that produce finished goods and services, which, in turn, flow from firms to households; and a *money* flow that exists to facilitate the entire exchange process.

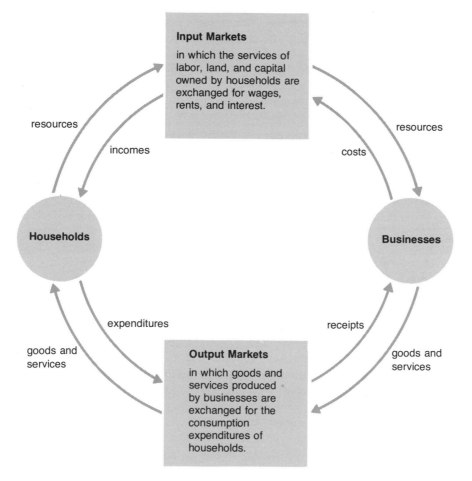

In reality, there is no such thing as a *pure* command economy nor, for that matter, a *pure* market economy. The United States, for example, strongly relies on the market to allocate both productive resources and consumer goods, but operates much of its government sector in command fashion. On the other hand, the Soviet Union essentially has a command economy with respect to the allocation of resources, although goods are allocated to individual households through the market.

Microeconomics is the detailed study of the process by which goods and services are allocated. Our interest here is specifically in the microeconomics of the market economy. Thus, we shall focus on how individual markets work, how prices are established, how producers and consumers make decisions, and what the consequences of these decisions are.

Finally, we shall examine and evaluate the market economy viewed as a whole. Can economic efficiency be achieved through an uncontrolled market system? Should constraints be placed on the operation of the market system to achieve society's desired economic goals? Such questions can be considered only after gaining a thorough understanding of how markets work.

Recap Markets are institutions in which things are voluntarily exchanged, usually using money as an intermediary. To some extent all economies rely on the market as an allocative mechanism. In our analysis of microeconomies—the study of how goods and services are allocated—we shall concentrate on market behavior.

Capsule Supplement 4.1   **The Persistence of Markets and Exchange**

The proposition that exchange occurs because *both* sides gain from it is borne out by the remarkable persistence of exchange even when considerable difficulties are placed in its way. For example, when governments have attempted to prevent free exchange—as during wartime when scarce commodities are rationed to consumers at prices far below what some are willing to pay—black markets have emerged and flourished, despite the risks to the trading parties involved.

This persistence presents a perennial headache to administrators in planned economies who wish to control the terms on which exchanges are made. Countries such as East Germany—relatively prosperous but with consumers officially constrained to buy on controlled markets offering a limited range of goods—generate black markets to an enormous degree. Estimates of the proportion of total goods and services bypassing official markets for the black variety in East Germany have run as high as 20 percent. The Soviet Union discovered many years ago that it was easier to permit a limited free market for products grown on the private plots of collective farm members than to suppress the desire to gain from exchange.

Even within the normal operation of a market economy, the "market" may occasionally fail to do its job (or, more likely, be restricted from doing so) and thus provide opportunities for further gains from exchange. Rarely is there a Broadway smash hit, Super Bowl game, or Rolling Stones concert from which a handsome profit cannot be made by acquiring advance tickets at box-office prices and reselling them at a premium after the event in question is "sold out."

While such "scalping" behavior is generally illegal, and probably regarded by most people as unethical (at least by those who've been "scalped"), there are others who argue that it is no more than a healthy reaction to a maladjusted market.

To be sure, such behavior penalizes those individuals who would otherwise have been able to acquire tickets at the box office by forcing them to either meet the scalper's bounty or do without altogether. However, the very fact that an event is sold out and there are *still people willing to pay more than the box-office price* is evidence that this price may have been too low in the first place. The "appropriate" price, it is argued, would have been sufficiently high as to "just clear the market." To a free-market advocate then, scalping behavior, far from being unethical, is indeed remedial.

Markets and exchange persist even when transactions, market or otherwise, are legally prohibited. This is quite obviously true of drugs and gambling, for example. The addict buys heroin because it is worth more than the money given up *at the time the exchange is made.* The dealer sells because the profit is worth more than the potential risk of arrest. While society, and even the addict, may consider such exchange to be of negative value to the user in the long run, the situation at the actual time of exchange determines behavior.

Thus, we may conclude that any exchange made without coercion implies an immediate gain to those directly involved. This does not mean that the gain is evenly divided, one side may gain much, the other little. Nor does it mean that some patterns of exchange are not superior to others. Indeed, we shall demonstrate later (in Chapter 8) that a pattern of exchange in which everyone trades on the same terms (a pattern called perfect competition) is always preferable to one in which individual exchanges occur on varying terms.

Supply and Demand   An introduction to supply and demand analysis

Conceptually, a market is an institution through which goods or services are exchanged. Practically, a market may be anything from a village square where local truck farmers congregate weekly to sell fresh produce to a huge enterprise like the Chicago Board of Trade where specialized traders meet daily to exchange verbal and paper counterparts of goods that physically are not even present.

When an economist speaks of a market, he means the market for a particular good, like wheat or shoelaces or aluminum foil. In this sense, several different markets may operate under one roof; the Chicago Board of Trade, for example, serves as a medium for markets in a variety of farm products—wheat, corn, soybeans, etc. Indeed, even a term like *wheat* may be too general to define a particular market, given the existence of such distinct varieties as "No. 2 dark winter" and "No. 1 dark northern spring." To have an ideally defined market, a good must be *homogeneous;*

Figure 4.2

Price and quantity variations in the Chicago wholesale egg market covering a typical three-year period.

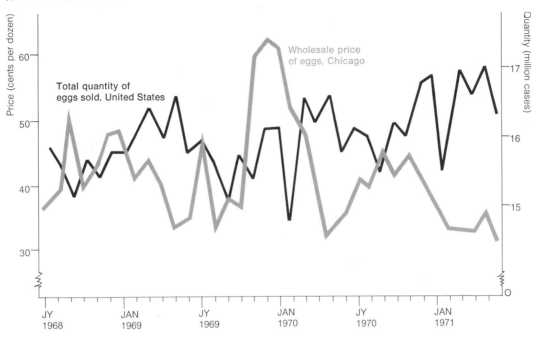

that is, it must be such that any one unit, box, jar, or carload of it is virtually identical to any other. "No. 2 dark winter wheat" denotes a homogeneous good or commodity in this sense while "food" does not.

Let's concentrate on the market for eggs. If we could follow an actual transaction in this market, we would note the following:

1. the transaction involves a sale of eggs by *a given seller* to *a given buyer;*
2. the transaction involves a *price,* the amount of money paid by the buyer to the seller for each dozen eggs sold;
3. the transaction involves a *quantity,* the total number of eggs actually exchanged; and
4. both price and quantity are the result of *mutual agreement* by the buyer and seller—they are necessarily the same for both.

Observable Data

In general, many transactions take place at a given price during a given market period. Observers could add up the number of eggs sold (or, equivalently, purchased) during each period to obtain the total quantity of eggs that changes hands at the prevailing price. Accumulating such data over several years would produce a dated array of prices and quantities, such as those graphically depicted in Figure 4.2.

What causes the price and quantity of eggs sold to rise and fall over time? What determines the exact price and quantity at a particular time? Everybody knows that the answers to such questions have something to do with "supply and demand." But to reply simply that the price of eggs "is whatever it is" at a given time because of "supply and demand" is to give an answer with no content—an explanation that seemingly accounts for everything, yet actually explains nothing.

Look again at Figure 4.2. Obviously something *other* than prices and quantities must have changed between periods. If we were to attempt to explain this market's behavior, we would need to note everything with a potential influence on the market that might have changed from period to period. This would include such variables as the price of chicken feed, farm wages, consumer incomes, and even the weather. In general, we shall refer to those things that comprise the background against which a market operates as *market circumstances*.

Recap To assert that price is determined by "supply and demand" does not tell us why prices are sometimes high and sometimes low. To explain market behavior, we need to identify the circumstances that cause supply and demand to vary. These circumstances may range from consumer income to the weather.

Market Plans and Market Actions

Buyers and sellers each come to the market prepared to trade different quantities at different prices

In general, the only information we can expect to have about the market for a particular good consists of (1) the market circumstances, (2) the price of the good, and (3) the quantity of the good changing hands. Nevertheless, the economist's analysis of supply and demand (and thus of the operation of a market economy) depends on the following basic presumption about buyers and sellers:

Although every actual market transaction takes place under a given set of circumstances and at a specific price, buyers and sellers possess alternative plans about how they would act if the price and/or market circumstances were different from those actually in effect.

By observing market behavior under a sufficient variety of circumstances, we can ascertain just what these alternative plans are, or at least whether or not they conform to any general pattern.

Plans and Behavior

To deduce anything about plans from actual behavior, we must be able to assume that what people actually do under a given set of circumstances is what they had indeed planned to do under these circumstances. This is not a trivial matter because at least one party to a transaction may be unable to fulfill his or her plans.

Suppose that, under a given set of market circumstances, producers plan to sell 1,000 tons of quicksand if the price is $10 per ton, while consumers plan to buy only 900 tons if the price is $10 per ton. Should exchange actually take place at this price, some sellers will obviously be unable to fulfill their plans; there will be 100 tons that buyers are unwilling to purchase at the $10 price, and buyers cannot be made to buy *more* than they choose. An observer would note that 900 tons of quicksand were sold at a price of $10 per ton, but there would be no direct evidence that producers would have been willing to sell another 100 tons at that price.

Equilibrium

Although some transactions undoubtedly do take place under conditions that leave plans unfulfilled, we shall assume that most do not. Specifically, we suggest that the following conditions typify market exchange:

1. *All buyers can buy what they plan to buy at the going price and under existing market circumstances.*
2. *All sellers can sell what they plan to sell at the same price and under the same circumstances.*

If, at the established price and under existing circumstances, all buyers and sellers can indeed fulfill their plans, the market is said to be in *equilibrium*. However, if some buyers cannot buy all that they had planned at the established price, or some sellers cannot sell all that they had planned at that price, the market is said to be in *disequilibrium*.

We shall carry out our analysis of the market by searching for the equilibrium, given the plans of buyers and sellers. Specifically, we shall attempt to determine the *equilibrium price* at which the quantity sellers are willing to sell matches the quantity buyers are willing to buy. We focus on price because it is normally the only factor influencing the quantity traded that is actually determined within the market under consideration.

Recap We presume that although those engaged in the market are observed to behave in a particular way under a given set of circumstances, they have plans about how they would behave under alternative circumstances. By observing behavior under a sufficient variety of market conditions, we can often discover these plans. When all buyers and sellers are able to execute their plans given the relevant circumstances, the market is said to be in equilibrium.

Factors Influencing Market Plans

An empirical example shows how circumstances influence market plans

There are two ways to discover the typical features of market plans. One is to examine the general manner in which buyers and sellers reach market decisions and speculate on how these decisions are affected by changes in various market circumstances. This approach, which characterizes the theoretical analysis of buyer and seller behavior, is the subject of Chapters 6, 7, and 8. Here we shall concentrate on the second approach: the analysis of actual data from a typical market.

These two approaches are complementary and are used together throughout economics. Why? Because we can never be sure that conclusions drawn from a specific market represent markets generally without some theoretical structure. Nor can we rely on theory alone to supply us with the actual data required for most policy formulation.

In this chapter and Chapter 5, the empirical results presented must be accepted as typical of markets in general. These results thus form the basis for a solid theoretical foundation. In any event, using actual rather than hypothetical data will convince the reader that at least one market is factually described.

An Empirical Example

The actual market we have chosen is that for watermelons in the United States. This market has no special or unusual features, and is quite small compared with the total U.S. farm sector (not to mention the entire U.S. economy). We can therefore regard it as "typical."

The statistical analysis of observed prices, quantities, and relevant market circumstances over many years has enabled economists to ascertain how the plans of watermelon buyers and sellers are influenced. The three most important factors found to influence the planned behavior of buyers and sellers in this market are shown in Table 4.1. This table shows how a change in any one of these variables would affect planned behavior.

The first entry in the table shows that a 1 percent *increase* in the farm wage rate would have no effect on the quantity consumers would plan to buy, but would *reduce* the quantity farmers would plan to harvest and sell by 0.3 percent. On the other hand, a 1 percent *increase* in the average consumer income would *increase* the quantity consumers would plan to buy by 1.4 percent, but would have no effect on the quantity farmers would plan to sell. The farm wage rate and average consumer income are *market circumstances,* each affecting either planned purchases or planned sales, but not both.

Table 4.1
Factors Influencing Demand and Supply
in the U.S. Watermelon Market
(Percent change in quantities)

A 1% increase in (1), (2), or (3) gives	(1) Farm wage rate	(2) Average consumer income	(3) Price of water-melons
Planned purchases would change by	0	+1.4	−0.9
Planned sales would change by	−0.3	0	+0.3

Based on data from L'Esperance, "A Case Study in Prediction: The Market for Watermelons," *Econometrica*, 1964.

On the other hand, the price of watermelons *does* affect both sides of the market. A 1 percent *increase* in price would result in a 0.9 percent *reduction* in planned purchases and a 0.3 percent *increase* in planned sales. The relative directions of these movements, planned sales varying directly with price and planned purchases varying inversely with price, typify almost all competitive markets.

Disequilibrium

Suppose that at a given price and under a given set of circumstances, the planned supply of watermelons exceeded the planned demand. This obviously could not result in an equilibrium situation because some sellers would be unable to find buyers for what they had planned to sell. We would describe the market as being in a state of *excess supply*. Equilibrium would occur only if market circumstances or the price were changed in a way that would increase planned demand, reduce planned supply, or both.

From the information in Table 4.1 it is evident that the following changes would result in a movement toward equilibrium:

1. an increase in the farm wage rate, which would decrease the quantity farmers would plan to sell,
2. an increase in average consumer income, which would increase the quantity consumers would plan to buy, and
3. a decrease in the price of watermelons, which would both decrease planned sales and increase planned purchases.

Thus, disequilibrium in the watermelon market could be eliminated by an appropriate change in *any* of the factors that influence planned demand

and/or supply. In a typical market situation, however, economists consider the equilibrating factor to be *price,* because *the values of the variables that comprise market circumstances are determined primarily outside the market in question.*

We certainly would not expect the average level of consumer income in the United States to bear any measurable relationship to what happens in the watermelon market. Nor would we expect farm wages in general to be significantly affected by the watermelon market, as watermelon production represents only 0.0025 percent of the total value of U.S. farm production.

Recap By observing market data under a variety of circumstances, we can determine how the plans of buyers and sellers are influenced by these circumstances as well as by price. The results of such an investigation are presented for the watermelon market. Given an arbitrary set of market circumstances and a price, we can ascertain whether or not the market will be in equilibrium.

Supply and Demand Schedules

The formal construction of supply and demand schedules

We have already stressed that the economic analysis of market behavior is based on the presumption that buyers and sellers possess plans about how they would behave under alternative market circumstances and at various prices.

Given the type of market behavior with which we are presently concerned, we can make one additional assumption:

The plans of each buyer and each seller are totally independent of those of all other buyers or sellers.

This implies that the plans of every buyer and seller depend exclusively on market circumstances and price, and not on guesses about how others might behave. A market for which this assumption holds is called a *perfect market.* A perfect market (or a close approximation to it) exists if there are a large number of buyers and sellers, each of whose transactions are small and thus unimportant in relation to the total volume of transactions in the market.

Complete Schedules

If we knew the complete plans of a typical buyer of some product, we could predict, for each price and under each set of market circumstances, the quantity of the product that would be purchased. This explicit set of plans would be the buyer's *complete individual demand schedule.* Given a specific set of market circumstances and a specific price, such a schedule would indicate the quantity our buyer would plan to purchase. Summing the corresponding quantities for all individuals in the market would yield the total quantity buyers would collectively plan to purchase under the conditions specified. By tabulating similar totals for every possible price under every possible set of circumstances, we could construct a schedule that would show, for *any* set of circumstances and *any* specified price, how much buyers would collectively plan to buy. Such a schedule would be a *complete market demand schedule*.

Similarly, we could compile a *complete individual supply schedule* for each seller, and then, by summing the individual quantities that would be supplied for each possible combination of circumstances and price, derive the *complete market supply schedule*.

Although we may visualize that market schedules are derived from individual schedules in this fashion, available market data are usually confined to aggregates. Indeed, for most markets, nothing short of herculean effort would be required to compile a comprehensive set of individual schedules.

In studying a particular market, we usually take the market circumstances as given and focus on the relationship among price, planned purchases, and planned sales under these circumstances. Thus, we are usually interested in only *part* of a complete demand or supply schedule—*that part corresponding to our given set of circumstances, but covering the entire range of possible prices.*

Extracts from the Complete Schedule

That part of the complete demand (or supply) schedule that shows the planned quantity demanded (or supplied) associated with each price, under a specific set of market circumstances, is usually referred to simply as *the* demand (or *the* supply) schedule. While our attention is normally focused on just such a schedule, *it is extremely important to realize that this is only an extract from a more complete schedule.* Thus, it is crucial that such a demand (or supply) schedule be labeled correctly with respect to the market circumstances for which it is relevant.

Using results from the same study that provided the data in Table 4.1, we can draw up market demand and supply schedules for watermelons that are representative of the economist's general picture of such schedules. These are given in Table 4.2. Because the only market circumstance in this example that affects demand is average consumer income, and because the only market circumstance that affects supply is the farm wage, the relevant labeling is simple. Two extracts are given from the complete demand schedule, one for average income of $2,750, the other for average income of $3,000. Two extracts are also given from the complete supply schedule corresponding to farm wage rates of $8.20 and $7.50.

Table 4.2
Demand and Supply Schedules in the
U.S. Watermelon Market. (Quantities
in millions of tons per year)

(1) Price (cents per pound)	(2) D₁ Quantity demanded at average consumer income of $2,750	(3) D₂ Quantity demanded at average consumer income of $3,000	(4) S₁ Quantity supplied at farm wage of $8.20	(5) S₂ Quantity supplied at farm wage of $7.50
1.5	1.50	1.69	1.26	1.29
1.6	1.42	1.60	1.29	1.32
1.7	1.35	1.51	1.32	1.35
1.8	1.28	1.43	1.34	1.37
1.9	1.22	1.36	1.36	1.39
2.0	1.17	1.31	1.38	1.41

Data modified from same source as Table 4.1.

Recap Complete demand and supply schedules show how much traders plan to buy and sell, respectively, at various prices and under various market circumstances. At any given time, however, we are concerned with the extract from the complete schedule that reflects currently relevant market circumstances.

Supply and Demand Curves

The graphic depiction of
supply and demand schedules

Demand and supply schedules are conventionally depicted in graphic form with *price* represented on the *vertical* axis and *quantity* on the *horizontal* axis.

Figure 4.3 illustrates the graph plotted from the demand schedule of Table 4.2 associated with an income of $2,750. The schedule provides a series of points, which we can join with a smooth curve. The curve so obtained is the *demand curve for watermelons at an income of $2,750.*

Given such a curve, we can read the quantity of watermelons that buyers will plan to buy at any price. At a price of 1.7 cents per pound, for example, the planned quantity demanded (1.35 million tons) is given by the horizontal distance between the point *A* (whose vertical height is 1.7 cents) and the vertical axis. Remember, however, this reading is relevant only if the income level is $2,750.

Figure 4.3

The demand curve for watermelons when per capita income is $2,750 per year. Price is read from the vertical axis; quantity from the horizontal axis.

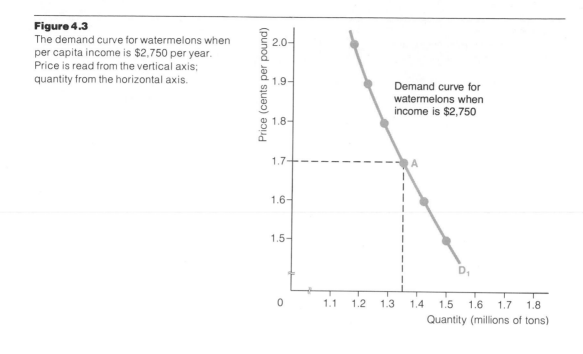

A Curve for Each Set of Circumstances

Associated with each set of market circumstances is a particular extract from the complete demand schedule, and thus a particular demand curve. There is no *single* demand curve, only a curve *relevant to each set of market circumstances*. Figure 4.4 shows, on the same diagram, the demand curves for watermelons at incomes of $2,750 ($D_1$, as in Figure 4.3) and $3,000 ($D_2$).

Despite what we have just said, economists commonly refer simply to *the demand curve* for a particular good. In doing so, however, they are necessarily referring to the demand curve under a specific set of market circumstances that have either been explicitly stated or are implied by the context. The relevant market circumstances are often historically implied. The demand curve for peanut butter in the United States for 1978, for example, is the demand curve for peanut butter under the market circumstances that prevailed in the United States during 1978.

Supply Curves

All that has been said of demand curves applies equally to supply curves. From the complete supply schedule, an extract can be obtained by choosing a specific set of market circumstances. The information in this extract can then be drawn (as was done for the demand schedule), and the points joined to make a supply curve. The convention of measuring price verti-

Figure 4.4
Demand curves for watermelons at two different levels of per capita consumer income.

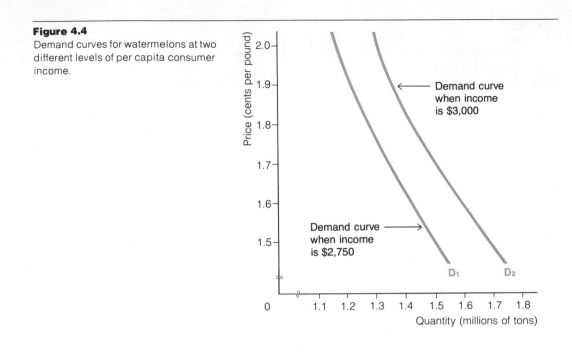

cally and quantity horizontally is observed for supply curves as well as for demand curves.

Figure 4.5 depicts the supply curve for watermelons when the farm wage is $8.20. Figure 4.6 depicts two supply curves, S_1 and S_2, associated with farm wages of $8.20 and $7.50, respectively.

The Appropriate Curves

Because supply and demand curves are both drawn with references to price measured vertically and quantity measured horizontally, they can be combined in a single diagram. For example, Figure 4.7 combines the curves drawn in Figures 4.4 and 4.6.

Although only two demand and two supply curves have been shown in Figure 4.7, theoretically it would be possible to draw an individual demand and supply curve for every conceivable set of market circumstances. A supply curve would correspond to every farm wage and a demand curve would correspond to every consumer income level. Visualize Figure 4.7 expanded by demand curves farther from the origin (O) than D_2, and closer to it than D_1, and supply curves to the left of S_1 and to the right of S_2. There even will be demand curves between D_1 and D_2 (for incomes between $2,750 and $3,000) and supply curves between S_1 and S_2 (for wages between $8.20 and $7.50).

Figure 4.5
The supply curve for watermelons when the farm wage is $8.20.

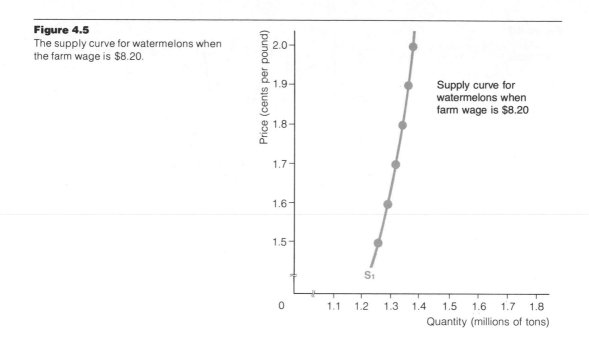

Price (cents per pound)

Supply curve for watermelons when farm wage is $8.20

S₁

Quantity (millions of tons)

Figure 4.6
Supply curves for watermelons at each of two different levels of farm wages.

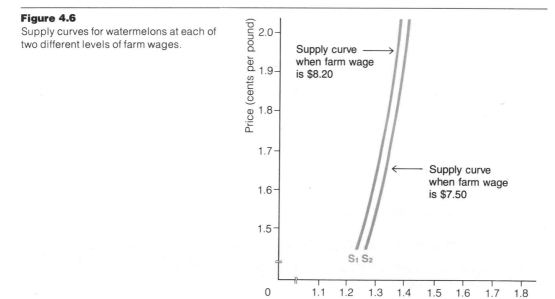

Price (cents per pound)

Supply curve → when farm wage is $8.20

← Supply curve when farm wage is $7.50

S₁ S₂

Quantity (millions of tons)

Figure 4.7
The demand and supply curves for watermelons.

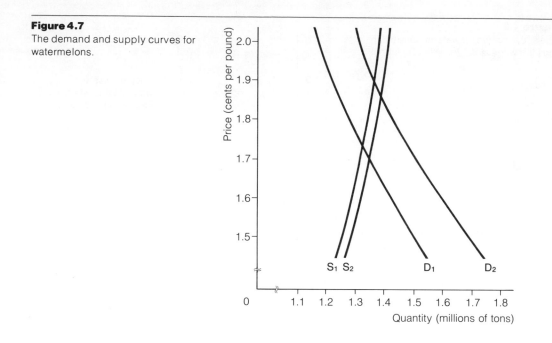

In any event, the *appropriate* demand and supply curves can always be picked out once the relevant income and wage rates are given.

Relevant Market Circumstances

In our watermelon example, income and wage rates are the only relevant market circumstances. In general, a wide variety of circumstances may be relevant to a given market. Economists normally classify such circumstances on the basis of whether they are observed to affect demand or supply.

The market circumstances most commonly observed to affect demand, sometimes called the *nonprice determinants of demand,* are:

1. consumer tastes and preferences,
2. consumer incomes,
3. the number of consumers in the market,
4. prices of consumption-related goods, and
5. consumer expectations about future prices and incomes.

The most commonly observed circumstances that affect supply, the *nonprice determinants of supply,* are:

1. the available technology of production,
2. resource prices,
3. the number of sellers in the market,

4. prices of production-related goods, and
5. producer expectations about future prices and technology.

In any given market situation, the appropriate demand and supply curves must be picked out from the potentially infinite number of such curves once the relevant market circumstances are known.

Visualizing the demand and supply relationships as *curves* has become so embedded in economic thinking that the terms "demand curve" and "supply curve" are commonly used even when their respective *schedules* are actually being discussed.

Recap Extracts from demand and supply schedules are usually depicted graphically as demand and supply curves on a diagram in which price is measured vertically and quantity horizontally. Each curve corresponds to a particular set of market circumstances that must be specified.

Capsule Supplement 4.2   **Supply under Planning**

In a planned economy, such as that of the Soviet Union, consumers spend their incomes on the goods of their choice, just as they do in the United States. The difference between the Soviet and American systems lies not in the nature of demand, therefore, but in the nature of supply.

Under a fully planned system, the appropriate ministry decides how much of a specific consumer good is to be produced and at what price it is to be sold. The resulting quantity supplied may or may not be equal to that which consumers are willing to buy at the specified price. If not, the exact outcome will obviously depend on whether the planned output is more or less than what consumers want. Such outcomes are asymmetrical because consumers can always be forced to do without something but not to buy more of something than they want.

If the Moscow alarm-clock factory produces *less* than the quantity consumers are willing to buy at the going price, the result is excess demand. This becomes apparent in the rapidity with which alarm clocks are sold out after reaching retail stores and in the number of consumers who inquire about when these stores will receive new shipments. This was precisely the situation with respect to alarm clocks and virtually all other consumer goods in the Soviet Union from the early 1920s through the 1950s. In the early 1950s, however, the situation began to change, and the Moscow alarm-clock factory was one of the first to feel the effect. One day, delivery people from this factory noticed that stores still had clocks left over from previous deliveries! The planned supply had become *greater* than what consumers were willing to absorb at the stated price. For the first time, the effects of *demand,* which had remained hidden throughout the chronic shortage of consumer goods, became apparent.

Any ministry of supply is apt to become sensitive to a buildup of unsold stocks of goods because these are not as easily ignored as are consumers struggling for goods in short supply. Consequently, in the early 1950s, consumer preferences began to be taken seriously in the Soviet planning process. The alternatives open to Soviet planners facing excess supply under existing practices of operation are basically the same as those open to a large U.S. corporation—cut back on production, lower prices, and increase demand through style changes and promotional selling. For more than twenty years, Soviet planners, inhibited by ideological constraints on the use of price variations to equate quantities supplied with quantities demanded, have been trying to establish an acceptable policy with respect to the use of these options.

Failure to match planned production and prices with demand conditions is due to the practical and sometimes ideological problems of planned economies; it is not inherent in planning as such. In the *perfect* plan, like the perfect market system, there would be no mismatch between demand and planned production—but perfection is as difficult to achieve in the planning process as it is in the market.

Market Equilibrium

How to determine the equilibrium price, given supply and demand schedules

A market equilibrium exists when the plans of buyers and sellers match. Such an equilibrium requires the existence of an *equilibrium price* at which the quantity sellers plan to sell equals the quantity buyers plan to buy. But, because the plans of both buyers and sellers depend on market circumstances, in setting out to determine the equilibrium price in a market, we must first specify which circumstances are relevant.

Finding the Equilibrium Price

Once we know the relevant market circumstances, it is easy to determine the price at which market equilibrium will occur, using either schedules or curves. In our example, suppose the prevailing market circumstances are a per capita income of $2,750 and a farm wage of $7.50. Then D_1 and S_2 are the relevant schedules in Table 4.3. (This is a restatement of the information presented in Table 4.2.) Schedule D_1 depicts planned purchases at various prices under those circumstances, while S_2 depicts planned sales. Market equilibrium will occur at a price at which planned purchases and planned sales are equal. Glancing down these schedules, we can see that at a price of 1.7 cents per pound consumers plan to purchase 1.35 million tons per year while farmers plan to sell 1.35 million tons per year. Thus, 1.7 cents per pound is the *equilibrium price* at an income level of $2,750 and a farm wage of $7.50.

This equilibrium price can also be arrived at diagrammatically. Figure 4.8

Table 4.3
Equilibrium in the Watermelon Market—I
(Quantities in millions of tons per year)

	Quantity from demand schedules		Quantity from supply schedules	
Price	D_1	D_2	S_1	S_2
1.5	1.50	1.69	1.26	1.29
1.6	1.42	1.60	1.29	1.32
1.7	1.35	1.51	1.32	1.35
1.8	1.28	1.43	1.34	1.37
1.9	1.22	1.36	1.36	1.39
2.0	1.17	1.31	1.38	1.41

The schedules in this table are identical with those of Table 4.2.

Figure 4.8
Equilibrium in the watermelon market, when per capita consumer income is $2,750 and the farm wage rate is $7.50, is represented by the intersection of S_2 and D_1 at point A, which gives P^* and Q^*.

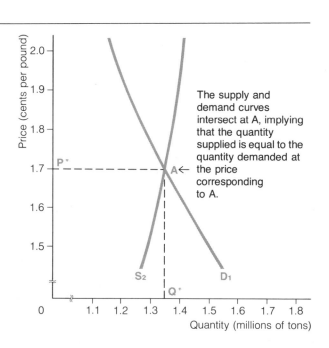

The supply and demand curves intersect at A, implying that the quantity supplied is equal to the quantity demanded at the price corresponding to A.

shows the relevant demand curve (D_1) and supply curve (S_2) drawn on the same diagram. This figure is identical to Figure 4.7 except that the curves D_2 and S_1 have been omitted.

For a point on either D_1 or S_2, the vertical height corresponds to a price and the horizontal distance from the price axis corresponds to the planned quantity associated with that price. Equilibrium will exist only when the vertical height (price) and the horizontal distance (quantity) are the same

Table 4.4

Equilibrium in the Watermelon Market—II
(Quantities in millions of tons per year)

Price	Quantity from demand schedules		Quantity from supply schedules	
	D_1	D_2	S_1	S_2
1.5	1.50	1.69	1.26	1.29
1.6	1.42	1.60	1.29	1.32
1.7	1.35	1.51	1.32	1.35
1.8	1.28	1.43	1.34	1.37
1.9	1.22	<u>1.36</u>	<u>1.36</u>	1.39
2.0	1.17	1.31	1.38	1.41

The schedules in this table are identical with those of Tables 4.2 and 4.3.

for both curves. Such a point necessarily exists *where the two curves intersect*—point A in the figure. The vertical height of A (OP*) is the *equilibrium price* and the horizontal distance from A to the price axis (OQ*) is the *equilibrium quantity*. Because the curves contain precisely the same information as the schedules, these equilibrium values are necessarily identical to those obtained by looking down the latter.

The "cross" in Figure 4.8 is the best-known diagram in economics. It characterizes the typical market equilibrium, with a downward-sloping demand curve intersecting an upward-sloping supply curve. The equilibrium shown in Figure 4.8 is that *for a farm wage of $7.50 and a consumer income of $2,750.*

A Change in Circumstances

If market circumstances were different, we would generally expect a different equilibrium price and quantity. For example, what would happen if S_1 and D_2 were the relevant schedules (a farm wage of $8.20 and a consumer income of $3,000)? Table 4.4 repeats the information in Table 4.3. It is obvious that the equilibrium price cannot be 1.7 cents per pound under these new circumstances because planned purchases would be 1.51 million tons and planned sales would be only 1.32 million tons. Planned purchases at this price would exceed planned sales by 0.19 million tons.

Following schedules S_1 and D_2 down the table, we see that planned purchases equal planned sales at 1.9 cents per pound. Hence, under the new set of circumstances, equilibrium occurs at 1.9 cents per pound at which exactly 1.36 tons of watermelons are traded.

The new situation is illustrated in Figure 4.9, which is essentially the same as Figure 4.7. The equilibrium at a wage of $8.20 and an income level

Figure 4.9
How different market circumstances
determine different equilibrium points in
the watermelon market. There are four
possible equilibrium points.

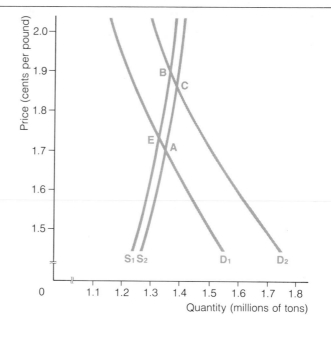

of $3,000 is given by the point B, where S_1 and D_2 intersect, in contrast to
point A, which represents the equilibrium for a farm wage of $7.50 and a
consumer income of $2,750. Points C and E are also possible equilibriums.
Point C represents the equilibrium for a farm wage of $7.50 and consumer
income of $3,000, while point E corresponds to a farm wage of $8.20 and
consumer income of $2,750.

Recap Because an equilibrium occurs when all plans are simultaneously
achieved, and because demand and supply curves represent the respective plans
of buyers and sellers, the equilibrium price and quantity in a given market are determined graphically by the intersection of the appropriate demand and supply
curves. The curves chosen must be those relevant to the actual market circumstances. A change in these circumstances will affect the choice of curves and
produce a new equilibrium point.

Capsule Supplement 4.3   **Dealing with an
Economic "Identity Crisis"**

The design of policy to address the economic problems faced by American agriculture during the Great Depression of the 1930s required a knowledge of the
properties of the demand for farm products. Those economists and statisti-

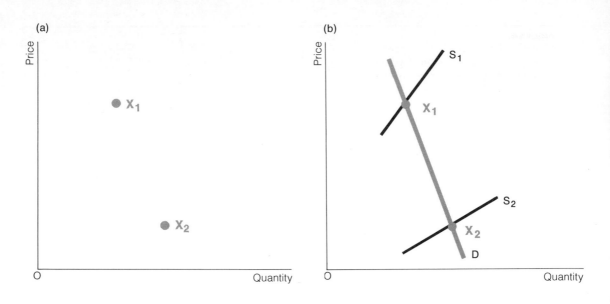

cians who set out to establish these properties found their task to be more challenging than they had expected. They encountered what still remains one of the fundamental stumbling blocks in econometric analysis—the so-called *identification problem*.

Suppose we are given soybean market data for two periods with different equilibriums such as the points X_1 and X_2 in (a) of the diagram. These points happen to be related in such a way that X_1 lies above and to the left of X_2. A line drawn through X_1 and X_2 would thus have the expected slope of a demand curve. But should this line actually be taken as such?

It's certainly *possible* for the line through the two points to be a demand curve, as illustrated in (b). Here D is a true demand curve, S_1 and S_2 are two supply curves, and the change in equilibrium from X_1 to X_2 is unambiguously due to the shift from S_1 to S_2.

But the same two points could also represent equilibriums that differ because *both* demand *and* supply have changed. This possibility is illustrated in (c) of the diagram, in which demand changes from D_1 to D_2, while supply changes from S_1 to S_2. Both D_1 and D_2 have a much flatter slope than D in diagram (b), and to have identified D as a true demand curve would have led to serious error about the nature of demand for soybeans. Note that we can rule out one possibility—that X_1 and X_2, as drawn in (a), represent equilibrium points on the same supply curve resulting from a change in demand only because the line joining them would have the wrong slope for such a curve.

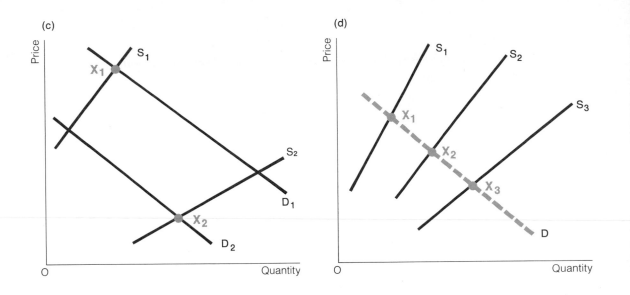

In general, then, equilibrium points derived from market data may well differ because of simultaneous shifts in both supply *and* demand. The problem is to disentangle these two effects. In the physical sciences such a problem could be solved by experimentation. The experiment would be simple: hold all circumstances known to affect demand steady, then shift supply by varying the appropriate circumstances. The resulting equilibrium points would represent the intersections of different supply curves, like S_1, S_2, and S_3 in (d) of the diagram, with a single demand curve. With sufficient variation in supply, such points (like X_1, X_2, and X_3 in the diagram) would eventually "map out" this demand curve for us (like the dashed curve D).

Unfortunately, opportunities for controlled experiments of this kind are extremely rare in economics, and we must usually settle for market data generated from the working economy. Nonetheless, the key to disentangling supply from demand lies in the structure of our hypothetical experiment. For such an experiment to work, we must be able to *hold constant* all the circumstances that affect demand, and *still have* circumstances that can be varied to change supply. In other words, such an experiment will work only if there are circumstances that affect supply but not demand. We can thus solve the identification problem from market data—data that essentially represent a badly organized and uncontrolled experiment by nature—as long as there are circumstances that affect demand exclusively and others that affect supply exclusively. Much econometric research has been devoted to devising techniques that permit selected circumstances to be artificially "held constant" in such a way as to simulate the type of experiment we've described.

Exercises

The jelly bean market has the following supply and demand schedules, both relevant to the prevailing market circumstances:

Price ($/ton)	Quantity (tons/month)	
	Supply schedule	Demand schedule
40	160	340
50	200	320
60	240	300
70	280	280
80	320	260
90	360	240
100	400	220

1. Draw the demand and supply curves. What is special about their shapes?

2. What is the equilibrium price and quantity?

3. What quantity would be sold if the government fixed the *maximum* price at $80 per ton?

4. If the government supported the price at $90 per ton by agreeing to buy any excess supply at that price, how much surplus per month would the government have to buy?

5. Suppose a change in circumstances decreased the quantity supplied by exactly 60 tons per month at every price. If demand is unaffected, what is the new equilibrium price and quantity?

For Thought and Discussion

1. Consider any two goods that you normally buy or think about buying.
   a. Compare the two goods in terms of the market circumstances that would influence your demand for each.
   b. For which of the two goods would your demand have the greatest sensitivity with respect to price?

2. During the Middle Ages there was a religiously sanctioned idea of the "just price" at which something should be sold, whatever the demand and supply conditions. Do you think it immoral for a seller to accept a price much higher than he expects to receive simply because the good is temporarily in short supply?

3. "Scalpers" line up for theater tickets that they resell at much higher prices to those who want to attend the theater in the immediate future

rather than wait for months. This practice is generally illegal. Should it be?

4. Suppose that due to radioactive fallout over part of the United States, the quantity of milk fit for consumption drops by 50 percent. If there is no intervention in the market, the price will obviously rise sharply. If, on the other hand, the price is frozen, rationing will be necessary. If you were president, what would be your policy, and why?

Chapter 5
The Market Mechanism

Terms and Concepts

Comparative statics
Change in demand or supply
Change in quantity demanded or supplied
Elasticity of demand or supply
Unit elasticity
Basic market model
Basic market mechanism
Excess demand or supply
Negative feedback
Arbitrage
Speculation

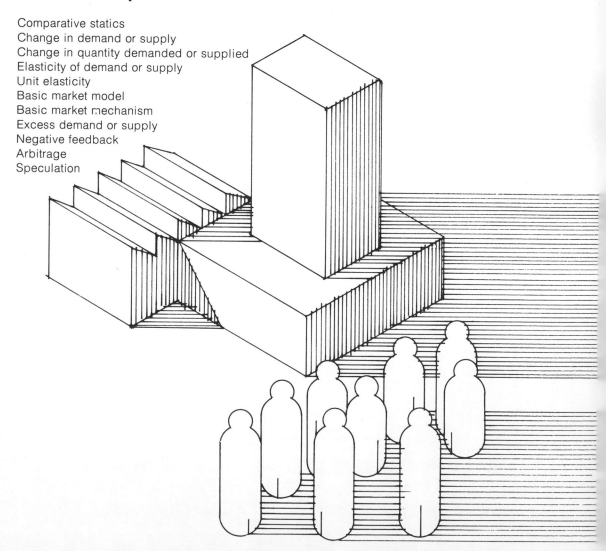

Supply and Demand Analysis

Using supply and demand curves to analyze the effects of changing market circumstances

Consider the supply and demand diagram in Figure 5.1. The curves in this diagram exhibit certain irregularities to emphasize the fact that the only predictable features of the typical market are the *general downward slope of the demand curve* and the *general upward slope of the supply curve.* If the point of market equilibrium under a particular set of circumstances were the only item that interested us, such a diagram would be useless. An equilibrium point, after all, is only a *point,* and the parts of the two curves away from the intersection would have no relevance.

But this is not the case. We *are* interested in the nature of supply and demand curves precisely because we *are* concerned with more than just the equilibrium under a single set of market circumstances. Specifically, we are interested in the following:

1. What happens to a market equilibrium when the relevant market circumstances change?
2. What happens when a market is *not* in equilibrium?

The first question can be restated more precisely. Suppose equilibrium prevails under a given set of market circumstances. Now let these circumstances change. In what way will the new market equilibrium be related to the old? In particular, will the equilibrium price rise or fall? Will the equilib-

Figure 5.1
The traditional market diagram.

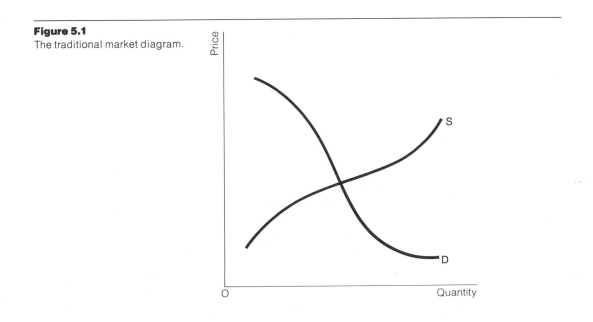

Figure 5.2

The change in equilibrium when demand increases but supply remains constant.

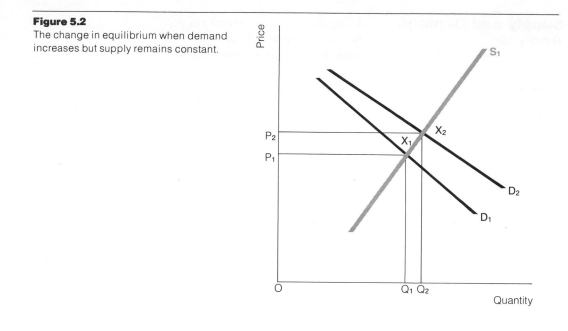

rium quantity rise or fall? This type of analysis involving a comparison of equilibriums under alternative sets of circumstances is called *comparative statics.*

A Change in Demand

An illustration of comparative static supply and demand analysis is given in Figure 5.2. Let's assume that S_1 and D_1 are the appropriate supply and demand curves for some initial set of market circumstances. Now, suppose these circumstances change so D_2 becomes the relevant demand curve while the initial supply curve remains unaffected. As suggested in the previous chapter, such a change could come from several factors (a change in consumer tastes, for example, or an increase in the number of buyers). In any event, the shift from D_1 to D_2 is said to represent an *increase in demand* because the planned quantity demanded is greater on D_2 than on D_1 at every price.

A *change in demand* always refers to a comparison between two different demand curves and should not be confused with a *change in quantity demanded,* which indicates movement along a single demand curve. We can see from the diagram that an increase in demand results in an increase in the equilibrium price from P_1 to P_2 and an increase in the equilibrium quantity from Q_1 to Q_2. A *decrease in demand,* on the other hand, would have reduced both the equilibrium price and quantity.

Capsule Supplement 5.1   **Alfred Marshall, 1842–1924**

While Alfred Marshall may or may not have shrewdly married Mary Paley (a former student of his and one of the first women students at Cambridge) to obtain joint authorship of *Industry and Trade,* he was on all other accounts a sober and respectable figure in economics. Indeed, it would have been difficult for him to have been otherwise because his father held that most respectable of jobs—cashier with the Bank of England.

At Cambridge, Marshall began his career as a mathematician where he was rated "junior wrangler," a term, still used, to designate whoever ranks second in the mathematics tripos examinations—whoever ranks first being, of course, the "senior wrangler." After a short period, however, his puritanical background led him to reject mathematics as "pure pleasure," and he turned to the study of social and economic problems.

He married Mary Paley in 1877, after eleven years as a Fellow at Cambridge. But, Cambridge and Oxford maintained the Medieval institution of celibacy (or at least non-marriage) for their faculty members. Thus, Marshall was forced to resign. He subsequently became a professor of political economy at the University College of Bristol, joined the Oxford faculty in 1883 (the celibacy requirements having been abolished), and then returned to Cambridge where he was awarded the Chair of Political Economy in 1884. He held this chair until retirement in 1908, and it is with Cambridge that his name is most closely associated.

Marshall's influence on economics—which dominated the first quarter of the twentieth century—stemmed primarily from his *Principles of Economics* (1890), a book that was treated by economists as the Bible for many years. The analysis of markets and perfect competition presented in this text are in the direct tradition of Marshall. His contribution was less in the discovery of new aspects of the economic system than in the care with which he conducted his analysis, emphasizing those distinctions between *movements along* supply and demand curves, and *shifts in* these curves due to changing circumstances. These form the fundamental core of market analysis.

A Change in Supply

Now imagine a change in market circumstances (such as an improvement in technology or an increase in the number of sellers) that affects supply but not demand. Figure 5.3 shows the supply curve shifting from S_1 to S_2 as a consequence of such a change. Because planned quantity supplied is greater on S_2 than on S_1 at every price, this shift constitutes an *increase in supply* (with the same caution about the use of this expression as in the case of demand).

   An increase in supply results in a decrease in the equilibrium price from

Figure 5.3

The change in equilibrium when supply increases but demand remains constant.

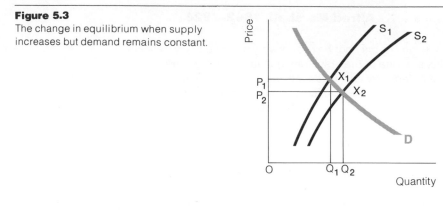

Figure 5.4

The effects of simultaneous increases in both demand and supply.

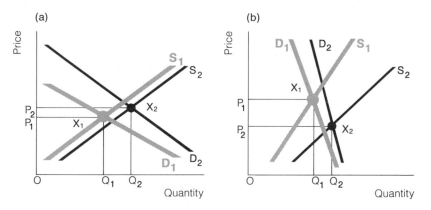

P_1 to P_2 (opposite to the effect of an increase in demand), and an increase in the equilibrium quantity from Q_1 to Q_2 (as in the demand case). Conversely, a *decrease in supply* would have led to an increased equilibrium price and a smaller equilibrium quantity.

Simultaneous Changes in Demand and Supply

What happens if demand and supply increase at the same time? We've established that an increase in either will result in an increase in the equilibrium quantity. Hence, the equilibrium quantity will certainly be expected to rise if both demand *and* supply curves shift to the right. But we've also seen that an increase in demand and an increase in supply will have oppo-

Figure 5.5
How the combination of an increase in demand and a decrease in supply will
cause the price to rise, but may alter the equilibrium quantity in either
direction.

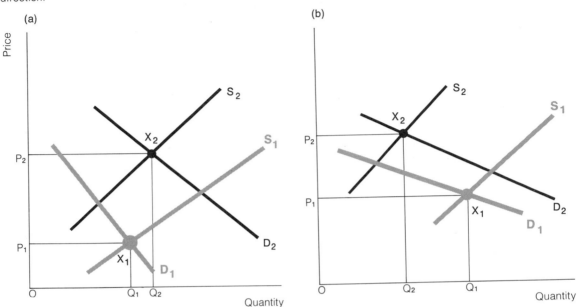

site effects on the equilibrium price. Consequently, the *net* effect of these
increases on price will depend on the relative shifts in the demand and
supply curves. Figure 5.4 shows two cases in which demand and supply
increase simultaneously, one leading to a rise in equilibrium price (Figure
5.4a), and the other to a fall (Figure 5.4b).

Let's consider another possibility. An increase in demand alone will
cause the equilibrium price to rise, as will a decrease in supply. Thus, an
increase in demand accompanied by a simultaneous decrease in supply can
be expected to cause a rise in the equilibrium price. The equilibrium quantity in this case, however, may change in either direction. Specifically, the
increase in demand tends to increase quantity, while the decrease in supply
tends to decrease it. The possible outcomes are illustrated in Figures 5.5 (a)
and (b) in which the old and new equilibrium points are represented by X_1
and X_2, respectively.

From the simple premise that demand curves slope downward and supply curves slope upward, we can predict the following general effects on
equilibrium price and quantity resulting from a simultaneous shift in both
curves:

Shift in		Change in equilibrium	
Demand	Supply	Price	Quantity
increase	increase	either direction	increase
decrease	decrease	either direction	decrease
increase	decrease	increase	either direction
decrease	increase	decrease	either direction

Recap Supply and demand curves can be used to investigate the effect of changes in market circumstances on the equilibrium price and quantity. Knowing only the general directions in which the curves slope, we can predict how both price and quantity will change if the change in circumstances affects either supply or demand exclusively. If supply and demand change simultaneously, however, we need more detailed information about the respective curves (other than general directions of slope) before we can predict the effect on both price and quantity.

Elasticity

How supply and demand curves can be described accurately

The exact manner in which the equilibrium price and quantity in a given market are affected by a given change in market circumstances is determined by the specific character (shape and slope) of the relevant demand and supply curves. Figure 5.6 depicts a market in which demand changes from D_1 to D_2 under two different assumptions about the nature of supply. When the supply curve has the steeper slope (Figure 5.6a), the shift in demand causes a relatively large change in price and a relatively small change in quantity. Alternatively, when the supply curve has the flatter slope (Figure 5.6b), the same shift in demand produces a relatively large change in quantity and a relatively small change in price. Information about the relative steepness or flatness of demand and supply curves would thus appear to be quite useful in predicting just how equilibrium will be affected by shifts in these curves.

Measures of Slope

The slope of a demand or supply curve reflects the change in quantity along the curve associated with a given change in price. Along demand curve D_1 in our earlier watermelon example (see Table 4.2), a change in price from 1.7 to 1.8 cents per pound is associated with a change in quantity demanded from 1.35 to 1.28 million tons. The slope of D_1 over this range can thus be

Figure 5.6
When the demand curve shifts, the price will change more relative to the
quantity when the supply curve has a steeper slope.

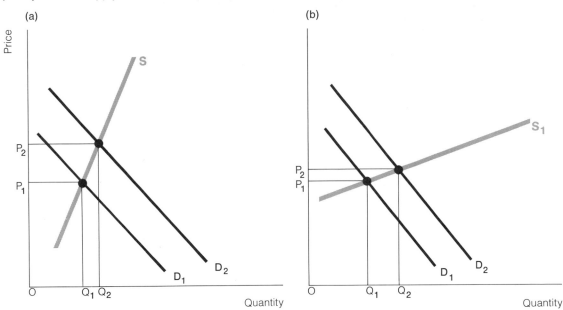

expressed as −70,000 tons per ¹/₁₀ cent, the negative sign indicating that the
slope is downward.

But this slope could just as easily have been expressed as −700,000 tons
per cent, −70 million tons per dollar, or − 140 billion pounds per dollar. The
numerical value of a slope thus depends on the *units* in which both price and
quantity are measured. To express a slope as a simple number (−7, for
example) is meaningless unless we are also given the relevant units of
measurement.

Elasticities Are Independent of Units

Because of the potential difficulties involved in dealing with the numerical
values of slopes, economists make extensive use of descriptive terms called
elasticities, which are independent of units of measurement. Defined generally, an elasticity is *a ratio of the percentage change in one variable to the
percentage change in another.* Just as *percentage changes* in such variables
as quantities, prices, and incomes are independent of the units in which
they are measured, so are *ratios* of percentage changes in these variables.
The numbers given in Table 4.1, for example, are elasticities.

We can see both how an elasticity is calculated and why it is independent of units of measurement by working through a simple numerical example. We shall focus on the *price elasticity of demand,* which is defined as the percentage change in quantity demanded divided by the associated percentage change in price. Suppose that, in the market for pig's feet, the quantity demanded falls from 2,550 tons to 2,450 tons when the price increases from $9.90 per ton to $10.10 per ton. What is the price elasticity of demand over this range? First we calculate the percentage change in price. Because price has risen from $9.90 to $10.10, the absolute change in price is $.20 per ton. Taking this in relation to the average price in the range of variation, $10.00 per ton (midway between $9.90 and $10.10), we arrive at a price change of 2 percent (100 × $.20/$10.00). Likewise, quantity demanded has changed by 100 tons, about an average of 2,500 tons, that is, by 4 percent (100 × 100/2,500). Because quantity has changed 4 percent for a 2 percent change in price, the ratio of the quantity to the price, and hence the absolute numerical value of the elasticity, is 2. We designate the *elasticity coefficient* as −2.0, however, using the negative sign because quantity and price have changed in opposite directions. Had they changed in the same direction, as would be the case for supply, the sign would have been positive.

But what if pig's feet were measured in pounds instead of tons? The relevant quantities would become 5,100,000 pounds and 4,900,000 pounds, and the absolute change in quantity would thus be 200,000 pounds. But because this change is relative to an average quantity of 5,000,000 pounds, the percentage change in quantity would be 100 × 200,000/5,000,000 = 4, as before. Similarly, if price were measured in cents per pound, the two prices would become .495 cent per pound and .505 cent per pound. The absolute change in price would be .010 cent, but around an average price of .50 cent, so the percentage change would again be 100 × .010/.5 = 2, as with the previous units. Thus, the elasticity is still −2.0, even though we've changed units of both quantity and price. Indeed, we could express quantity in kilograms and price in pesos per kilogram, and the elasticity would still be −2.0.

Elasticity is simply a descriptive summary of the relationship between two variables. Because elasticities can be used to describe virtually any relationship, economists use them extensively, although most commonly to describe demand and supply curves. The *price elasticity of supply,* analogous to the price elasticity of demand previously discussed, is defined as the percentage change in quantity supplied divided by the associated percentage change in price.

Because supply and demand elasticities constitute proportional quantity changes divided by proportional price changes, it is often convenient to interpret each as follows:

The price elasticity of demand (or supply) represents the percentage change in quantity demanded (or supplied) resulting from a 1 percent change in price.

Figure 5.7
The flatter the slope of a demand curve at a given point, the greater will be the percentage change in quantity demanded associated with a given percentage change in price, and hence the greater will be the numerical coefficient of elasticity.

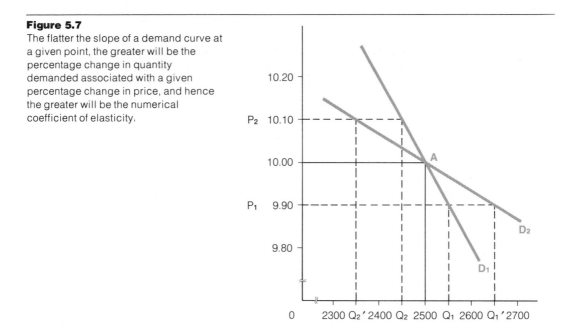

Elasticity: An Index of Responsiveness

Thus, such elasticities indicate the *relative responsiveness* or *sensitivity* of quantity to price changes. High absolute numerical values of the elasticity coefficient indicate that quantity is relatively *responsive* to changes in price; low values, that it is relatively *unresponsive*. The term *elasticity* is used specifically because it suggests the *degree*, though not necessarily the *speed*, of responsiveness.

If we take a supply or demand curve passing through a particular point and rotate it so it has a flatter slope, the numerical value of its elasticity *in the neighborhood of that point* will increase. This is demonstrated in Figure 5.7 in which the demand curve D_1 corresponds to the data given earlier in the calculation of the demand elasticity for pig's feet. An increase in price from \$9.90 to \$10.10 per ton reduces the quantity demanded along this curve from 2,550 to 2,450 tons, thus giving a demand elasticity of -2.0. If the demand curve for pig's feet were *flatter*, like D_2 in Figure 5.7, the absolute numerical value of the demand elasticity over this range would necessarily be *higher* because the same percentage change in price would lead to a larger percentage change in quantity demanded than in the case of D_1. Specifically, a 2 percent increase in price (from \$9.90 to \$10.10 per ton) would reduce the quantity demanded (from 2,650 to 2,350 tons) by 12 percent ($100 \times 300/2,500$), thus giving a demand elasticity of -6.0.

When a curve is horizontal, we say that it is *infinitely* or *perfectly elastic*, because a very small change from a price above the level of the curve to the price on the curve will change quantity from zero to a positive level (an infinite percentage increase). A vertical curve, on the other hand, indicates no change in quantity for any change in price. It therefore has *zero* elasticity and is said to be *perfectly inelastic*.

Elasticity Normally Varies Along a Curve

Elasticity is always calculated with reference to a particular point or segment on a curve. A demand or supply curve can generally be expected to have different elasticities at different points, although this is not necessarily the case. If the curve has the same elasticity at all points, it is called a *constant elasticity curve*. The demand and supply curves for the U.S. watermelon market presented in Chapter 4 are constant elasticity curves.

In examining the watermelon market, the investigators *assumed* constant elasticity at the outset and proceeded to estimate the constant elasticity curves that best reflected the available data. Such empirical investigations are often made under the assumption of constant elasticity in order to simplify the problem enough to allow the investigators to arrive at numerical approximations to actual curves.

Recap An elasticity is a ratio of percentage changes in two variables. Price elasticity of demand is the percentage change in quantity demanded associated with a 1 percent change in price, while price elasticity of supply is the percentage change in quantity supplied associated with a 1 percent change in price. Elasticity values are independent of units of measurement, but are not necessarily the same at different points on a given demand or supply curve. High elasticities indicate a high degree of responsiveness of quantity to price changes; low elasticities indicate a low degree of responsiveness of quantity to price changes.

More on Elasticity

How to compute elasticity values and relate the price elasticity of demand to total expenditure

The method used to calculate the price elasticity of demand in the preceding section can be expressed in the following general terms:

$$\text{elasticity} = \frac{\text{percentage change in quantity}}{\text{percentage change in price}} = \frac{\dfrac{\text{change in quantity}}{\text{average quantity}}}{\dfrac{\text{change in price}}{\text{average price}}}.$$

By assuming D_1 in Figure 5.7 is a typical demand curve, and concentrating on a change in price from P_1 to P_2 and the associated change in quantity demanded from Q_1 to Q_2, we can restate this formula symbolically as:

$$E_D = \frac{\dfrac{Q_2 - Q_1}{(Q_2 + Q_1)/2}}{\dfrac{P_2 - P_1}{(P_2 + P_1)/2}} = \frac{\dfrac{Q_2 - Q_1}{Q_2 + Q_1}}{\dfrac{P_2 - P_1}{P_2 + P_1}}.$$

Note that the expression in the middle differs from the expression on the right only in that the "2" appearing in both the numerator and denominator of the middle expression is cancelled out in the one on the right. The formula for the price elasticity of supply (E_S) would be identical to the one for demand except that the quantities Q_1 and Q_2 would obviously correspond to the quantities *supplied* before and after the price change.

Elasticities calculated this way are often referred to as *arc elasticities* in contrast to *point elasticities,* which are calculated on the basis of infinitesimal changes, and thus require the application of differential calculus.

Demand Elasticity and Expenditure

Each point on a demand curve represents a specific price and the quantity buyers plan to purchase at that price. Each point is therefore associated with a specific level of *planned expenditure* (price times the quantity that will be purchased at that price). If we move from one point on a demand curve to another corresponding to a higher price, will the level of planned expenditure rise or fall?

We cannot answer this question for certain without more information. If, for example, the quantity demanded remained unchanged, expenditure would rise for certain. But we know that the quantity demanded of a good normally falls as a consequence of a price increase. Thus, the net effect on expenditure is the result of two opposing tendencies—that of the increase in price to raise it, and that of the decrease in quantity demanded to reduce it.

Consider a perfectly inelastic (vertical) demand curve. The quantity does not change at all as we move along the curve, so any point higher on the demand curve represents a higher price with no change in quantity, giving an *increase* in expenditure. A perfectly elastic (horizontal) demand curve, on the other hand, has only one price at which any quantity would be bought, so a price increase would cause quantity to fall to zero, giving a *decrease* in expenditure.

These two extremes suggest that the value of the price elasticity of demand provides the key as to whether expenditure on a given commodity will rise or fall as we increase its price.

Suppose we increase a commodity's price by exactly 1 percent. If the quantity demanded did not change, expenditure would rise by 1 percent.

The extent to which quantity demanded actually does change is given by the price elasticity of demand. For an elasticity of −2, our 1 percent price increase will cause quantity demanded to fall by 2 percent. Thus, the effect of the quantity change alone would be to reduce expenditure by 2 percent. The net effect on expenditure is a combination of the price and quantity effects—the price effect is +1 percent (increasing expenditure), the quantity effect is −2 percent (decreasing expenditure), the net effect is the combination: +1 percent − 2 percent = −1 percent. So expenditure will *fall* by 1 percent when price rises by 1 percent.

For a demand elasticity of −0.5, quantity will fall by .5 percent for a 1 percent rise in price and the combined effect of price and quantity changes on expenditure will be: +1 percent − .5 percent = +.5 percent. In this case, expenditure will *rise* by .5 percent when price rises by 1 percent. The boundary case between increasing and decreasing expenditure is when the elasticity is −1. Then the price effect (+1 percent) is exactly balanced by the quantity effect (−1 percent), and expenditure remains unchanged. The general relationships among elasticity, changes in price, and changes in planned expenditure can be summarized as follows:

1. If demand exhibits *unit elasticity* (meaning that the coefficient of elasticity is −1), *planned expenditure is unaffected by a change in price* because the effects of price and quantity on expenditure cancel each other out.
2. If demand is *relatively elastic* (meaning that the coefficient of elasticity has an absolute numerical value greater than unity; for example, −2.0), *expenditure varies inversely with price* because the quantity effect on expenditure outweighs the price effect.
3. If demand is *relatively inelastic* (meaning that the coefficient of elasticity has an absolute numerical value less than unity; for example, −0.5), *expenditure varies directly with price* because the price effect on expenditure outweighs the quantity effect.

The Determinants of Elasticity

Thus far we've cited the virtues of elasticities as descriptive tools, shown how they can be calculated, and indicated how they may be useful analytically. But we need to address these two fundamental questions: (1) What factors actually determine how elastic or inelastic the supply or demand for a given product will be? (2) In which types of markets should we expect supply or demand to be relatively elastic or inelastic? To answer these questions we shall focus first on the *price elasticity of demand* in stating the following three general principles:

1. *The demand for a given product will tend to be more elastic the larger the number of available close substitutes.* We should expect consumers to be fairly responsive to changes in the prices of such products as Crest tooth-

paste, Kent cigarettes, and Right Guard deodorant, each of which has a vast array of close substitutes. Does this seem intuitively reasonable? Given that most brands of toothpaste are quite similar and sell for about the same price, imagine how you would react to a 10 percent increase in the price of your present brand, or to a 10 percent reduction in the price of some competing brand. Of course, billions of advertising dollars are spent each year in attempts to instill brand loyalties among such products. But even the strongest brand loyalties may be broken over time if price differentials persist.

2. *The demand for a given product will tend to be more elastic the larger the fraction of the consumer's total budget represented by expenditures on this product.* It is unlikely that changes in the prices of such inexpensive and infrequently purchased goods as toothpicks and table salt will be even noticed by most consumers, let alone have a significant effect on the quantities demanded of these goods. On the other hand, changes in the prices of stereos and station wagons will not only command the attention of these same consumers but may significantly influence their consumption behavior as well.

3. *The demand for a given product will tend to be more elastic the greater the extent to which it is viewed as a luxury.* If we drive a car, we probably won't be much affected by a general increase in the price of gasoline (even though we may be price-sensitive to different *brands* of gasoline), for this product represents a *necessity* to us. Similarly, if we were suffering from acute appendicitis, it is doubtful that our decision to undergo surgery would be much affected by the fact that the price of appendectomies may have recently doubled. By contrast, such goods as steak dinners and subscriptions to *Playboy* are less likely to be viewed as necessary and thus more apt to be regarded as dispensable. For this reason, our consumption of such goods will tend to exhibit a greater degree of price responsiveness.

While there are a number of factors that may affect the *price elasticity of supply* for a given product, the most important is the *time* a producer has to respond to variations in price. The more time a producer has to adjust to a rise or fall in the price of a given good, the easier it will be to mobilize resources into or out of the production of that good.

Recap The value of the elasticity of demand tells us whether consumers will collectively spend more or less on a commodity when its price changes. If its price rises, expenditure will fall if the elasticity coefficient is greater than unity; expenditure will rise if the elasticity coefficient is less than unity; and it will remain unchanged if the elasticity coefficient is exactly equal to unity. For a given product, demand tends to be relatively more elastic: (1) the more close substitutes it has, (2) the larger is the fraction of the consumer's budget spent on it, and (3) the more expendable it is. Supply tends to be relatively more elastic the more time producers have to adjust to changing prices.

The Market Mechanism

The mechanism that enables a market to reach the equilibrium predicted by the demand and supply schedules

In our basic description of the market, the determination of equilibrium has been made to seem simple; we merely obtained individual supply and demand schedules, aggregated them into market demand and supply schedules, and found the price at which the quantity demanded was equal to the quantity supplied.

Real Markets Are Usually Unorganized

Unfortunately, the determination of equilibrium in real markets is not this straightforward—*there is no one in a position to obtain and assemble market information in the manner described.* Indeed, in the absence of concentrated efforts by statistics-gathering agencies associated with various departments of the U.S. government, the total quantities of goods and services passing through most American markets would remain a perennial mystery.

A commodity's *price* is the only piece of information known in the market because it is common to every transaction. Each market participant, of course, will know the individual amount traded, but not the total amount of the commodity changing hands. This is not due to secrecy, but simply to the fact that no mechanism exists for making such information available automatically.

A Computerized Market

Nevertheless, we can imagine an ideal market in which the process of determining equilibrium resembles the one in our basic description. We'll suppose that such a market operates as follows:

Each trader (buyer or seller) is aware of the market circumstances for the day in question, and possesses a set of plans (a demand or supply schedule) that indicates exactly how much he or she will buy or sell at every conceivable price. An essential presumption of any simple market model is that every such demand or supply schedule represents an absolute commitment to buy or sell the relevant quantities at those prices, whatever may happen in the price-determination process itself. Consequently, each trader can write out an appropriate schedule *in advance.*

Specifically, let's assume that each trader's demand or supply schedule is punched into computer cards. At the opening of the market each trader hands over these cards to the market manager. The identity of individual traders is not required on the cards because the market process is essentially *anonymous* and the identification of the source of each individual schedule would serve no purpose.

The traders now quietly sit back with the morning paper and enjoy a cup of coffee while the market goes to work. The cards are fed into the computer, which simply aggregates the appropriate entries to obtain market demand and supply schedules, then searches these schedules for a price that equates the total quantity demanded with the total quantity supplied. Once the computer has located this price, a bell rings to indicate that the equilibrium price is available for viewing on a closed-circuit television screen.

We would expect no wild scenes to occur because the traders in this idealized model are passive *price-takers* who have already stated exactly what they would do at each price. Sellers may regret that the equilibrium price is so low, and buyers that it is so high, but they would nonetheless proceed to carry out their plans.

Clearing the Market

Once the equilibrium price has been established, the market process is essentially over. To be sure, the commodities involved must still be distributed from the sellers to the buyers. But because at the equilibrium price the total quantity supplied equals the total quantity demanded, the actual method of distribution is academic. Suppliers could simply dump their produce into a pile and be paid (at the equilibrium price, of course) by the market manager, who would then parcel out the produce to the buyers upon receiving payment. Alternatively, buyers and sellers could line up, the first buyer buying from the first seller (or the first several sellers, if purchases are too large to be filled by the first seller alone), and so on down the line.

Whatever scheme is used, the market will be exactly cleared so long as all buyers and sellers adhere strictly to the plans they had originally specified.

Perhaps the most striking feature of this market model is how different the vision of calm passive participants awaiting the outcome of the computation is from the usual portrayal of a market alive with milling, shouting, sweating traders. Yet what we've described is a legitimate model of a market reaching equilibrium in an efficient manner. While no existing market is actually organized this way, developments in technology suggest that some markets may well be so organized in the future.

Traders as a Computer

The work assigned to the computer in our model, in actual markets, must be performed by the traders themselves. This is especially true in large, centralized, stock and commodity markets in which the task of reaching equilibrium is carried out by specialized *floor traders* whose *clients* are equivalent to the passive traders in our example. In any event, the essential fact remains that:

The intense activity in such markets, and for that matter in any centralized marketplace, is the consequence of human beings playing the role of the computer.

A computerized market requires some form of central organization and adherence to strict rules. But most actual markets are decentralized, and thus have no such organization or rules. The logical question follows: How is equilibrium established in most actual markets?

The Basic Market Model

Consider a market that consists of a large number of buyers and sellers, each of whose contribution to total demand or supply is very small. The actions of any one buyer or seller will then have such little effect on the market totals that they can safely be ignored. No buyer or seller will have the power to decide how the market should adjust, and the "market mechanism" will ultimately be nothing more than traders adjusting passively to market circumstances over which they individually have no control. This type of market is called a *perfect market*.

A perfect market is one in which:

1. the commodity being traded is regarded as homogeneous,
2. the only criterion for a particular exchange is that no better bargain is available elsewhere (in other words, that there are no market "loyalties" between specific buyers and sellers), and
3. all traders are aware of all offers available.

While there are probably no markets that satisfy *all* these conditions, there are certainly markets that satisfy *some* of them. We shall regard the model of a market possessing all these characteristics as the *basic market model*. Such a model provides a frame of reference for analyzing all markets that approximate the conditions of a perfect market.

The Basic Market Mechanism

The determination of equilibrium in the basic market model is conventionally viewed as a process of trial and error. A market price is initially set, perhaps by some random event, which both buyers and sellers provisionally accept because:

1. no seller can gain from selling below this price, provided he can sell all he has to offer at the given price (remember, his quantity supplied represents a tiny fraction of the total being traded), and
2. no buyer can gain from offering a higher price, provided he can find a seller at the given price.

Obviously, any seller who asks a higher price or any buyer who offers a lower price will find no one with whom to trade.

Figure 5.8

At any price other than the equilibrium price, there will be either excess demand or excess supply. Because of negative feedback, however, such excess demand or supply will tend to eliminate itself.

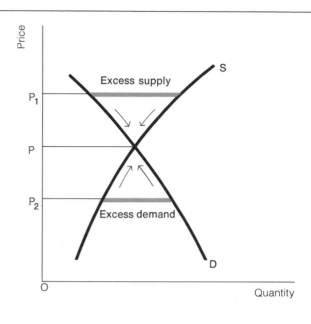

But suppose the price has been set above the equilibrium level. With ordinary demand and supply conditions, such a price, like P_1 in Figure 5.8, will result in an *excess supply* of the market commodity. If trade proceeds at this price, a point must eventually be reached at which buyers will have made all the purchases they wish even though sellers will have positive quantities remaining. However, sellers expecting to be left with unsold goods will probably begin to offer them at lower prices long before this stage is reached. The resulting downward trend in prices will continue as long as excess supply persists, that is, as long as the actual price exceeds the equilibrium price.

Had the price initially been set below the equilibrium level, such as at P_2 in Figure 5.8, frustrated consumers, unable to satisfy their demands, would have bid the price upward until no *excess demand* would have remained. This natural market tendency for divergences from the equilibrium in either direction to generate movement back toward equilibrium is called *negative feedback*.

Once the equilibrium price is established, as at P in Figure 5.8, there is no excess demand and no excess supply, all buyers can find sellers, and all sellers can find buyers. Hence, there is neither incentive for the sellers to cut prices nor for buyers to offer higher prices. These are the very characteristics of the situation that originally led economists to describe it as an *equilibrium*.

Recap Although we can theoretically determine the equilibrium market price and quantity by looking at demand and supply information, real markets have no one to compute and match the appropriate schedules. Nonetheless, such markets are characterized by an inbuilt tendency to eliminate disequilibrium situations, and thus have an automatic mechanism by which the equilibrium price and quantity are established.

Capsule Supplement 5.2   **The Effects of a Specific Sales Tax**

Horseradish is selling for a market price of 15 cents per bottle. The government now imposes a tax of 10 cents per bottle, but does not otherwise intervene in the market. What will happen to the price of horseradish? To the quantity sold? How much revenue will the government receive from its horseradish tax? These questions can be answered using basic supply and demand analysis.

We should first note that wherever the market settles after the tax is imposed, the buyer will be paying 10 cents per bottle more for horseradish than the seller will be receiving. The difference is the tax that is paid by the seller to the government. It may be tempting to simply conclude that the effect of the tax will be to raise the price to 25 cents per bottle. Indeed, the adjustment process may well start this way, with sellers merely lumping the amount of the tax onto the

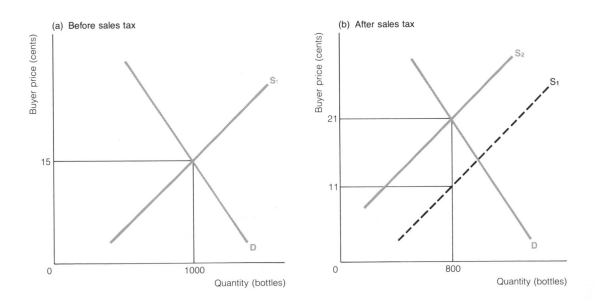

price to which they've become accustomed. But, the increase in the price paid by the customer will reduce the quantity purchased, unless demand is completely inelastic. With falling sales, suppliers will begin to lower the price, offering to sell at less than 25 cents. In effect, sellers would rather accept less than their original 15 cents than have unsold horseradish on their hands. In the end, then, the price paid by buyers will be something less than 25 cents, and that received by sellers (net after tax) will be something less than the original market price of 15 cents.

The exact outcome can be determined directly from the supply and demand schedules, or graphically from the corresponding supply and demand curves. In order to use the curves, we must first deal with the fact that the price paid and the price received will differ by the amount of the tax, instead of being identical as they were in the absence of the tax. This problem can be handled by concentrating on either the price received or the price paid. We choose the latter.

In the diagram, (a) shows the market equilibrium before the tax at a price of 15 cents per bottle (the same for both buyers and sellers) and a quantity of 1,000 bottles. Treating the price measured on the vertical axis as the buyers' price, the effect of the tax is shown in (b) of the diagram. The demand curve is unchanged, but the supply curve is drawn in a new position. Why? Because, in order to supply any given quantity, the sellers must now receive 10 cents more than before. For example, prior to the tax, the sellers were willing to exchange 1,000 bottles of horseradish for 15 cents per bottle. The imposition of the sales tax doesn't change their willingness to do this; it simply changes the amount

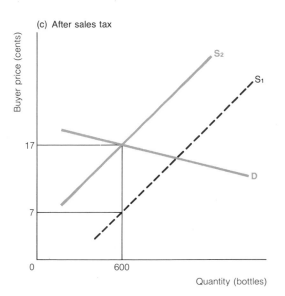

(c) After sales tax

they must *charge* (now 25 cents) in order to *receive* 15 cents. This change, of course, will be true for *all* potential quantities supplied.

The new supply curve, in terms of buyers' prices, therefore, will be shifted vertically upward a distance equal to 10 cents per bottle, so the quantity that corresponds to a price of X cents per bottle on the original curve now corresponds to a *buyers' price* of X + 10 cents per bottle. The new equilibrium, in fact, is at a buyers' price of 21 cents per bottle and a quantity of 800 bottles, with sellers receiving 11 cents per bottle (21 − 10). The buyers' price has gone up, but by less than the amount of the tax, the price received by sellers has gone down, and the equilibrium quantity has fallen. The new equilibrium quantity is lower both because the buyers' price has increased, inducing consumers to buy less, and the sellers' price has gone down, inducing producers to market less.

The more elastic the supply and demand curves are, the more the equilibrium quantity will fall as a result of the tax and, hence, the smaller the government's revenue from the tax will be. In (b) of the diagram, this revenue is equal to the amount of the tax times the after-tax equilibrium quantity, or $80 (= $.10 × 800). By comparison, in (c) of the diagram, where the demand curve is more elastic, the after-tax equilibrium quantity is smaller (600 bottles), and the government's revenue is also smaller ($60 = $.10 × 600). Consequently, a tax assessor who estimates tax receipts by applying the new tax rate to the *before-tax* quantity will inevitably overestimate his revenues, and, if demand is relatively elastic, overestimate them considerably.

Arbitrage and Speculation

How markets may be linked even though separated in time or space

In discussing the basic market model thus far, we've proceeded as though all transactions are made in one place. Let's suppose, however, that the market encompasses a large area and that transactions occur in two distinct places—East and West. Should East and West be treated as two distinct markets, perhaps reaching equilibriums at different prices, or will some market mechanism link the two markets into one?

Arbitrage

In general, spatially separated markets for the same good will be brought into a consistent relationship with one another by a mechanism known as *arbitrage*. This mechanism is actually quite simple. If prices differ between East and West, a profit can be made by buying goods in the low-price market and reselling them in the high-price market. Furthermore, the action of the arbitrageurs in buying in the low-price market increases demand in that market and tends to raise the price, while reselling in the high-price

Figure 5.9

In the absence of arbitrage, equilibrium in West and East markets occurs at points X and X', respectively, with price significantly lower in the West. The promise of economic gain prompts arbitrageurs to buy goods in the West market (thus causing demand to shift to the right, and price to increase) and sell these goods in the East market (thus causing supply to shift to the right, and price to fall). If there are no costs associated with this activity (an unlikely assumption because the goods must be transported somehow from West to East), this process will continue until the price differential between the two markets is eliminated, at P_2.

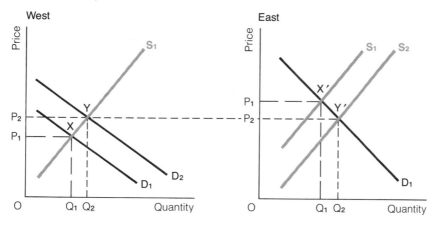

market increases the supply there and tends to lower the price. This effect is illustrated in Figure 5.9.

For ordinary markets with upward-sloping supply curves and downward-sloping demand curves, arbitrage is a simple and satisfactory unifying mechanism. It requires only a profit motive and a knowledge of prices on the part of the traders themselves. Arbitrage may also occur *within* a given market if a uniform equilibrium price has not yet been established. Arbitrageurs will buy from traders selling at low prices and resell in competition with those selling at high prices, hastening the movement toward price uniformity.

Speculation

The term *speculation* tends to conjure up images of sinister market operators who mysteriously amass huge fortunes and precipitate financial disasters. To the economist, however, this term simply means profit-motivated responses to anticipated but uncertain market changes over time. Suppose that market exchange for a certain commodity occurs once a month and that the market circumstances are known *with absolute certainty* for this month and next. Suppose also that ordinary demand and supply conditions for both months would result in a market price higher next month than this. It would thus be profitable to buy on this month's market, hold the commodity, then sell on next month's. Buying this month would tend to raise the price now, just as selling next month would tend to lower the price then, so our action would bring the prices in the two months closer together.

This process is analogous to arbitrage between markets separated in space. Indeed, if there were *certainty* about future events, we would call such a process *arbitrage over time*.

But, because the future status of any market is uncertain, operations involving buying for later resale can only be based on *guesses* about the future that may or may not be well formulated. Such operations, based on an uncertain relationship between present and future markets, constitute *speculation*.

Unlike arbitrage, which always tends to equalize prices in the markets involved, speculation may result in a tendency to either *diminish* or *accentuate* time differences in prices. If speculators guess that prices will be higher in the future, they will buy now to sell later, making present prices higher and future prices lower. If they have guessed incorrectly, they will end up making future prices *even lower*, relative to present prices, than they would have been in the absence of their operations. Speculation based on *incorrect* guesses, therefore, accentuates price fluctuations and is *destabilizing*.

Recap When markets for the same commodity are separated spatially, price variations between them will enable a profit to be made by buying in the market with the lower price and reselling in the market with the higher price. This potential profit will encourage arbitrage transactions that will bring the prices closer together. Markets separated in time will be subject to a similar influence because, if prices are expected to be higher in the future than they are now, speculators will buy now and hold goods for later resale.

Exercises

1. Using the demand and supply schedules given in the exercises for Chapter 4, compute the elasticity of supply about a price of $80 per ton.

2. Using these same market data, show that the numerical value of the elasticity of demand is greater than the elasticity of supply at all prices.

3. Using the watermelon data in Table 4.2, calculate the change in expenditure when price falls from 1.8 to 1.7 cents per pound (use schedule D_1), and demonstrate that this change is consistent with elasticity less than unity.

For Thought and Discussion

1. Would a publicly controlled, computerized market arrangement (like that discussed in the text) represent government interference with the operation of the market system?

2. Using the tools of market analysis, examine the effect of legalization on the price and quantity of a good or service that is generally illegal but nevertheless widespread (prostitution or marijuana, for example).

3. Generally speaking, the demand for farm products has a lower elasticity than that for industrial products. If the output of both farm and industrial goods rises by 10 percent and is all sold, what will have happened to the price of farm products relative to industrial goods (assuming nothing else has changed)?

4. In the text it was suggested that the only market that would truly operate like the economist's simplified model of the market would be one requiring some central organization and equipment (such as a computer). There would obviously be costs associated with operating such a market. Assuming that we wanted every market to operate smoothly and that the only way to achieve this objective was by such organization, who should pay the costs of running it? Both buyers and sellers, by some charge proportional to each trader's volume of transactions? The sellers alone? The buyers alone? The general public through ordinary tax revenues?

5. A can of tomato soup is sold for approximately the same price everywhere in the United States, but the rents of equivalent apartments or houses vary widely among different cities. Why?

6. The extremely rapid rise in the price of Florida real estate during the 1960s was often said to be due to the operations of "land speculators." If there had been no speculators, what do you think would have happened to the price?

Chapter 6
The Consumer in a Market Economy

Terms and Concepts

Consumer
Utility
Product characteristics
Consumer preferences
Budget constraint
Income effect
Real income
Normal good
Inferior good
Income-consumption curve
Engel curve
Income elasticity
Essential goods
Luxury goods
Substitution effect
Complementary goods
The Law of Demand
Product differentiation
Consumer efficiency

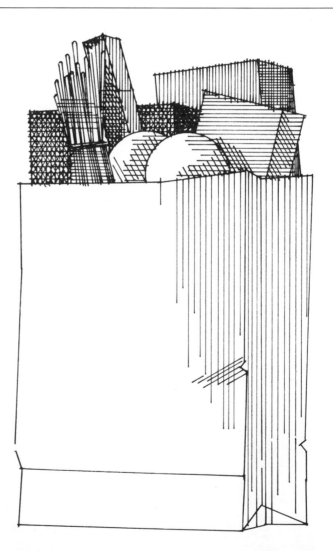

Buyers and Consumers

Why we associate demand with the consumer

Not all buyers who constitute the demand side of the market make purchases for their own immediate benefit. In many markets, such as those for raw materials, buyers are employed to act on behalf of producers who demand these materials. Such materials are demanded not for final consumption, but rather to be used as inputs to production. In other markets, the predominant buyers may be agents of the government. Ultimately, however, all purchases are made either directly by private individuals or for the purpose of producing goods or services that will ultimately benefit such individuals. For this reason, we focus our attention on the *consumer* as the typical buyer.

The Consumer's Role

Consumers act on their own behalf, buying things for themselves or their households rather than for producers or government agencies. Broadly speaking, all decisions made by consumers are made for their own benefit. This includes making decisions such as how much to work at the available wage and how much money to keep in the bank, as well as decisions that relate directly to the purchase of goods and services. Looking at the overall picture, consumers exchange things at hand—labor and/or the services of property—for things not at hand, such as pork chops, theater tickets, and cough syrup. In all but the simplest societies, this exchange requires at least two separate transactions involving some *medium of exchange* or *money*. Consumers must first exchange their resources for money, and then exchange this money for goods. Our concern in this chapter is with the second transaction. We shall assume that consumers have a given amount of money income to spend over a given period of time, and investigate how they allocate this income over the variety of available goods.

Because consumers are assumed to act on their own behalf, presumably they will allocate their income so as to obtain the greatest private benefit possible under the circumstances faced. Economists traditionally use the term *utility* to denote the private benefit of consumers in such a context. By contrast, buyers who act as agents for firms or for the government are concerned with bringing the greatest benefit to their principals. Their own utility is affected only insofar as their income (and hence their ultimate access to consumer goods and services) depends on how well they perform in their capacity as agents.

Individual consumers will generally represent only a minute fraction of total market demand. Consequently, they have no perceptible effect on the market as a whole. No single consumer is going to force up the price of butter by buying another pound or two, nor force it down by switching to margarine. An individual consumer's effect on the market simply won't be noticed. We can thus assume that consumers formulate their market plans on the premise that they can buy as much or as little as they choose of any good at the established price without affecting that price.

Recap Consumers act on their own behalf rather than as decision-makers for someone else. Although considerable buying on the market is accounted for by firms and government agencies, output in the economy flows primarily to consumers. Thus, from consumer behavior, we derive the fundamental properties of demand.

Capsule Supplement 6.1   **Can Consumers Look After Themselves?**

The legal doctrine of *caveat emptor* (let the buyer be wary and judge for himself that he is receiving full value) and the practice of punishing merchants or others who cheat their customers have a long history of coexistence. Indeed, the implied ambiguity about whether the consumer should be his own ultimate judge or whether society should protect him from his own foolishness is as lively an issue today as it has ever been.

There's a touch of ideology in the different views of the consumer as judge of his own fate. Conservatives, especially economic "libertarians," view the consumer as an intelligent, rational, well-informed person who, being fully aware of the potential consequences of his actions, should be given complete freedom to exercise choice as he sees fit. Liberals, on the other hand, express great concern for the "common man" but put little faith in his ability to choose. Thus they tend to favor judicious restrictions on choice. Yet, seeming inconsistency abounds. Many of the same liberals who *support* legislation preventing consumers from buying a new automobile unequipped with antipollution devices are *against* legislation preventing consumers from smoking marijuana.

The problem of choice is not touched upon in Marxian ideology. Marx's observations reflect the early nineteenth century when workers were too poor to have anything but minimal choices. Problems of choice were confined to capitalists whose welfare had little interest to him. The advent of true communism, which Marx and Engel foresaw as the culmination of a long period of socialism (which itself was predicted to follow the collapse of capitalism), would presumably raise some problems of choice, but this "stage of history" was never described in detail. Consequently, as the Soviet Bloc countries have developed and become richer, the problem of what approach to take toward consumer choice has become a major policy issue.

Irrespective of ideology, most would agree that consumers cannot make an optimal choice unless they are properly acquainted with the relevant facts. Because goods are purchased for the characteristics that satisfy the consumers' various objectives, it's important that adequate information be available, both on what characteristics goods possess and on what the implications of these characteristics are. Cancer warnings on cigarette packages provide information of this kind, as do lists of ingredients on boxes of breakfast cereal. Advertising, paid for by sellers, may inform the consumer of those characteristics that are commonly sought in products, but will not likely tell him of those that are not desired. "Consumerism," in drawing attention to either false claims of desired characteristics or failure to note undesired characteristics, clearly plays an important role in this light.

Should consumer policy go beyond providing information and actually prohibit certain choices—ban the sale of cigarettes, for example? We must draw our own conclusions. While alcohol and tobacco may ruin consumers' livers and lungs, rock concerts can impair their hearing; driving without seat belts can be dangerous, but so can skiing and sky-diving. One's judgment as to how far policy should go in actual prohibition, as contrasted with the provision of advice and warning, must be based on one's own view of consumers—their rights and responsibilities, along with their relationship to the rest of society.

The Basis of Choice   The basic determinants of consumer choice

People buy goods for the benefits that can be derived from them. The degree to which a specific good benefits a given consumer depends essentially on two things:

1. the properties or *characteristics* of the good itself, and
2. the consumer's subjective evaluation of these characteristics, that is, tastes and preferences.

Consumers have a wide variety of objectives. Different goods contribute to different objectives as their characteristics permit—a Butterball turkey can be eaten, but it cannot be ridden to the beach as a Suzuki motorcycle can. In turn, a motorcycle cannot easily be made into a sandwich.

Moreover, consumers differ in the benefits they derive from satisfying different objectives, and therefore in the "weight" they give to the importance of these various objectives in the general scheme of things. Some will not buy food in favor of clothing, while others would rather be well fed than well dressed. These differences in weight obviously account for much of the overall variation in preferences among individuals.

And an individual may give differing weights to certain objectives under different circumstances. An individual would probably weight food highly if her budget were near the subsistence level, but weight food lower than, say, designer clothing if her budget were less stringent.

Even if we concentrate on a particular objective, variations in preference will still become apparent. Pork and chicken possess sufficient *similar* characteristics to be potential main courses for Sunday dinner, yet sufficient *different* characteristics for an individual to prefer one over the other on a particular weekend.

Influences on Preferences

Where do consumer preferences come from? Economists have traditionally ignored this question and simply assumed them to be "given." Nevertheless, it is obvious that people are not born with an unchanging set of tastes. To be sure, preferences do reflect physical makeup and hereditary traits. But, they are also affected by general life experience that includes the influence of such factors as social pressure, education, and advertising.

Much of the complexity of developed economies derives from the heterogeneity of consumer preferences. If everyone wanted the same goods in the same proportions, the organization of such economies would obviously be much simpler. Such heterogeneity provides a special headache for planned economies, as has become increasingly apparent in the Soviet Union as consumer incomes have risen.

Constraints on Choice

Given individual preferences, a consumer must choose from among the various collections of available goods, subject to whatever *constraints* may be faced. The most important constraint in a market economy is the consumer's *budget*—individuals obviously cannot choose a collection of goods whose cost, at going prices, exceeds their money income.

While other constraints may also be relevant, they are usually secondary to the budget constraint. A music lover, for example, may find lack of time a greater constraint on concert attendance than lack of money. Or a wealthy family, well able to pay for twenty pounds of prime sirloin a week, may be prevented from doing so during wartime because of constraints imposed by rationing.

In the following discussion we shall concentrate on the more general effects of the budget constraint on consumer choice.

Budget Geometry

To better understand how consumers' choices are constrained by income, consider a simple example in which there are only two goods, *beans* and *jeans*. We can show collections of these two goods by a simple diagram in which we measure pounds of beans along one axis and pairs of jeans along the other. In Figure 6.1, for example, point X represents eight pounds of beans together with three pairs of jeans.

Now suppose that: (1) the price of beans is $.50 per pound, (2) the price of jeans is $2 per pair, and (3) our consumer (we'll call her Wanda) has a money income of $8. Is the collection represented by X in Figure 6.1

Figure 6.1

A collection of goods means specific quantities of each of several goods. Point X represents a goods collection in a world of only two goods.

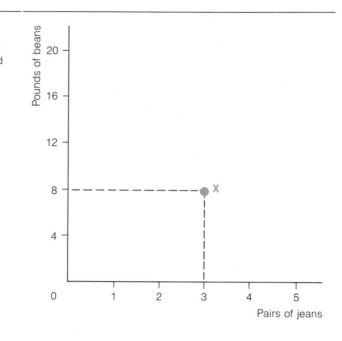

attainable by Wanda? We can easily deduce that it is not, because the cost of this collection is $10 at the prices given [(8 × $.50) + (3 × $2)], while Wanda's income is only $8. To illustrate graphically exactly which collections *can* be attained with this budget, and which *cannot*, we proceed as follows:

1. We calculate the quantity of beans Wanda could buy if she spent her entire income on beans at the prices given. This quantity is sixteen pounds ($8 ÷ $.50), and is represented by the point *A* in Figure 6.2.

2. We calculate how many pairs of jeans Wanda could buy if she spent her entire income on jeans. This is four pairs ($8 ÷ $2) and is represented by point *B* in Figure 6.2.

3. We note that all other collections that cost exactly $8 are represented by points lying on the straight line *AB,* which joins the two points found above. This can be verified by actually "checking out" various points along this line. Its midpoint, *M,* for example, represents the $8 collection of goods consisting of eight pounds of beans and two pairs of jeans.

All collections that lie between line *AB* and the origin, such as *N,* represent less of both goods than some point actually on *AB,* and thus necessarily cost less than $8. On the other hand, all points that lie outside the line *AB* obviously cost more than $8.

The line *AB* is Wanda's *budget line,* and the shaded triangle *OAB* contains all the collections that can actually be attained. Because we assume that

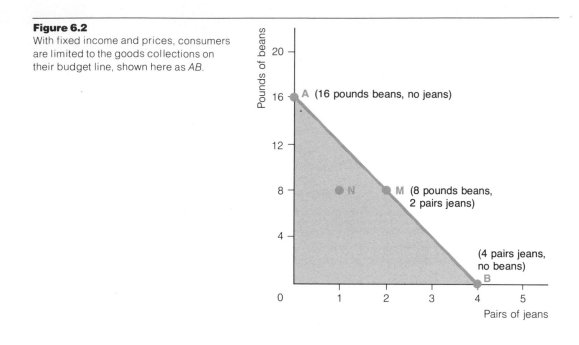

Figure 6.2
With fixed income and prices, consumers are limited to the goods collections on their budget line, shown here as *AB*.

beans and jeans are the only goods in the universe and hence the only sources of utility Wanda can actually buy, we would expect her to spend her entire income on these two goods, that is, to choose some point actually on *AB*.

The Role of Preferences

However, we cannot predict exactly *which* point on *AB* Wanda or any other individual would choose. Figure 6.3 shows two different points, C_1 and C_2, that correspond to the hypothetical choices of Wanda and Charlie who have identical money incomes but different preferences. Wanda, in choosing C_1, exhibits preferences that are "bean-biased" relative to Charlie's because Wanda's collection includes a greater proportion of beans relative to jeans than Charlie's. Conversely, Charlie's preferences at C_2 can be characterized as "jean-biased" relative to Wanda's. The difference in the collections chosen derives entirely from a difference in preferences because both consumers face the same budget constraints.

Marginal Valuations

We can reach a simple conclusion about the nature of consumer choice by noting that the collection of goods a consumer like Wanda will ultimately

Figure 6.3
People with different preferences will choose different collections of goods even when they face the same budget situation.

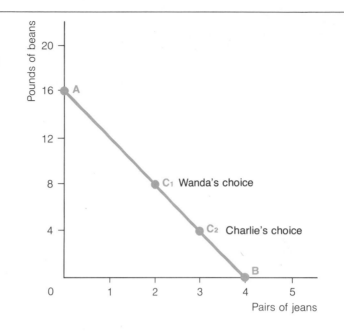

choose must be such that the last dollar spent on jeans as she approaches full expenditure of her budget must bring her the same utility as the last dollar spent on beans. Suppose, to the contrary, that the last dollar spent on jeans brought more benefit than the last dollar spent on beans. She could then gain by spending a dollar less on beans and a dollar more on jeans, her loss in beans being more than compensated for by the gain in jeans. If she could gain in this way, she obviously would not be at the position of highest net benefit and would adjust her purchases accordingly.

Budget Changes

Note that Wanda's budget line depends on both the *prices* of goods and the level of her *money income*. If the price of a good changes, then so does the quantity of that good that can be purchased if the entire income is spent on it. This changes the position of the relevant endpoint of the budget line: point A if the price of beans changes in our example, point B if the price of jeans changes. Similarly, if Wanda's income changes, the quantity of either good that can be purchased with the entire income will change.

Figure 6.4(a) shows what happens to the budget line if the price of beans rises to $1 per pound, the price of jeans and income level remaining constant. The entire income spent on beans will now buy only eight pounds—the top end of the budget line is now lower at point A_1 in the diagram, and

Figure 6.4

The budget line will change when the price of any good or income changes. The diagram shows the effect of (a) a change in the price of beans alone, (b) a change in income with no price change, and (c) changes in the prices of both goods.

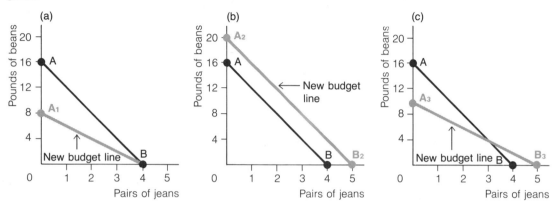

the new budget line is A_1B. Figure 6.4(b) shows what happens if money income increases to $10, with no price changes. Wanda can now buy five pairs of jeans or twenty pounds of beans (at a price of $.50) by spending her income entirely on one or the other. The new budget line is A_2B_2, *parallel* to the old one, but shifted in position. Figure 6.4(c) shows the combined effect of an increase in money income to $10 and a rise in the price of beans to $1 per pound. The new budget line, A_3B_3, has both a different *slope* and a different *position* than the old line AB.

When Wanda's budget line changes, she faces a new set of potential choices. In general, we shall expect her to change the collection of goods she buys, and much of our interest in consumer decision-making is in *how* the new choice is related to the old. The next sections consider the effects of such changes.

Recap Consumers choose from among various collections of goods on the basis of both the characteristics of those goods and the way in which these characteristics contribute to the attainment of their personal objectives. Their normal choice situation involves a budget constraint—consumers can choose only from among those collections their money incomes permit at existing prices. For a simplified world of two goods, the choice situation can be illustrated by a diagram in which a budget line bounds the area of potential choice. The slope of this budget line depends on the relative prices of the two goods: the distance of the budget line from the origin depends on the amount of the consumer's budget.

Figure 6.5

The effect of a change in income on the budget line when the price of goods remains constant.

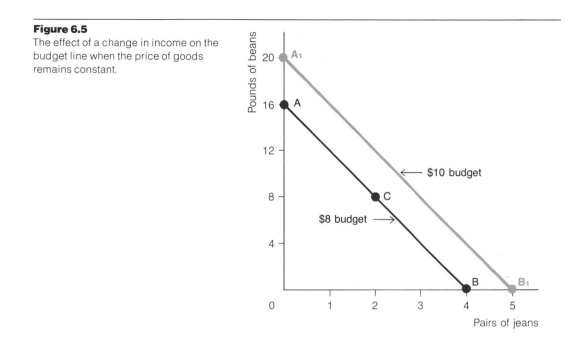

Income Changes

The effect of income changes on consumer choice

A consumer's budget line, and thus the collections of goods from which he is able to choose, changes with both prices and the level of money income. We shall refer to those changes in the actual choice of goods that result exclusively from changes in *real income* (those affecting the position, but not the slope, of the budget line) as *income effects*.

The Effect of Real Income Changes on the Budget Line

Consider the same budget situation faced by Wanda in our earlier example: a money income of $8, beans at $.50 per pound, and jeans at $2 per pair. Let the resulting budget line be AB in Figure 6.5 and suppose that the consumer chooses point C.

Now consider the effect of an increase in money income from $8 to $10, with prices remaining unchanged. This will give a new budget line. Because prices have not changed, the slope of the budget line remains the same, but because Wanda can obviously buy more of all goods than before, the new budget line is farther from the origin than the old. It is depicted as A_1B_1 in the diagram.

Figure 6.6
Wanda's preferences will determine how she changes her purchased goods collections when income changes.

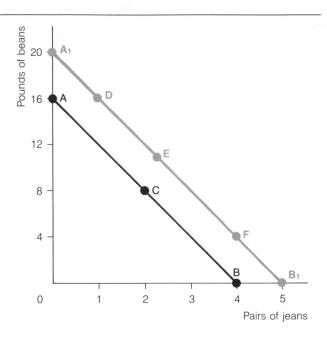

When we state that income effects stem from real income changes, rather than from changes in *relative* prices, we should note that a change in *all prices in the same proportion,* which would not affect relative prices, would have the same effect as a change in money income. Let's suppose that we started with the original budget position, and both prices fell by 20 percent to $.40 for beans and $1.60 for jeans. By spending all income on beans, Wanda could then buy twenty pounds—exactly what she could buy at a money income of $10 and the old prices. Similarly, by spending all her income on jeans, she could buy the same five pairs attainable at an income of $10 and the old prices. The budget line at the reduced prices would thus be A_1B_1, exactly the same as the budget line for the higher money income and the old prices, as in Figure 6.5.

A fall in all prices in the same proportion will have the same effect on the consumer's budget as a rise in money income with prices held constant.

The term *real income* is widely used to characterize the position of the budget line when it is used to measure quantities of goods, as in our budget diagrams. An increase of 25 percent in money income (from $8 to $10) with unchanged prices, a decrease of 20 percent in all prices (to $.40 for beans and $1.60 for jeans) with money income unchanged, or even a decrease of 10 percent in all prices (to $.45 for beans and $1.80 for jeans) together with a 12.5 percent increase in money income (to $9), will all enable Wanda to buy 25 percent more of whatever combination of goods was previously purchased. All these changes will result in the same shift of the budget line, from AB to A_1B_1 in Figure 6.5, and can be considered equivalent to a *25 percent increase in real income*.

The Effect of Changes in Real Income on Choice

How will Wanda's choice change as a result of a change in real income? Figure 6.6 shows her original budget line AB, on which she has chosen point C. As a result of an increase in real income, the new budget line becomes A_1B_1, parallel to the old but lying farther from the origin. If Wanda's real income has increased by, say 25 percent, then she could increase her purchases of both goods by exactly 25 percent with the new budget. But there is no reason why she should necessarily increase her purchases of both goods in the same proportion, or indeed why she should even increase the quantities purchased of *both* goods. She might actually choose to buy less of one of them, and greatly increase her purchases of the other. Any of the points $D, E,$ or F might be chosen on the new budget line. If D or F is chosen, the quantity purchased of one good will obviously be reduced.

Experience suggests that consumers will normally buy more of a good when real income rises. Hence, the term *normal good* is used to indicate a good whose total purchases rise with real income. A good of which less is bought as income rises is called an *inferior good*. In between, with no special name, are goods whose consumption is unaffected by income changes.

The Role of Product Characteristics

A typical inferior good, in the United States, is long-distance bus travel. Air and bus travel share certain characteristics—they both provide basic transportation and offer closely similar seat comfort even though air transport is clearly superior from a ''time-saving'' standpoint. The most essential characteristic of the two, however, is basic transportation. Hence, if bus travel is cheaper, the low-income consumer in need of transportation will choose the bus. But as incomes rise, the relative luxury of spending less time on a journey can be purchased, and consumers will begin to opt for air travel. The demand for bus travel thus tends to decline as incomes rise, even though the demand for travel in general tends to increase.

Other traditional examples of inferior goods are basic filling foods like bread, rice, and pasta. As incomes rise, consumers no longer need to concentrate on maximizing their intake of the most basic characteristic (calories) with their food dollars and will switch to other more flavorful and nutritious foods.

Figure 6.7
A typical income-consumption curve showing how purchased collections change as income changes.

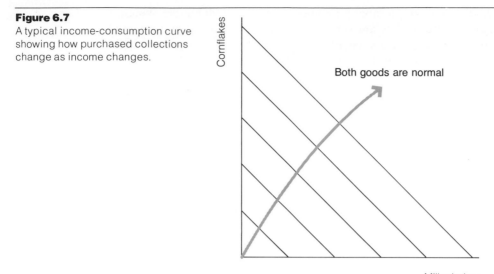

Income-Consumption Curves

By keeping prices constant and increasing income, we could move the consumer's budget line steadily outward and note the point chosen at each income level. Likewise, we could decrease income below the original level, and determine the points chosen between C and the origin. By joining all such points, we would obtain the consumer's *income-consumption curve*. Figure 6.7 illustrates a typical income-consumption curve with both goods normal. Figure 6.8 illustrates a case in which pig's feet become an inferior good at the income level corresponding to point A. We expect goods that are inferior at high-income levels to be normal at low-income levels, and no goods to be inferior at very low incomes.

Engel Curves

The information contained in an income-consumption curve can be treated in another way. Instead of depicting how the consumer's choice between the two goods varies with income, we can select either one of the two goods and show how its quantity purchased varies with income. This is usually done by plotting the expenditure on the good, at fixed prices, against income. The resulting curve is called an *Engel curve*.

Examples of Engel curves are given in Figure 6.9. Diagrams (a), (b), and (c) all show expenditure increasing as income increases (indicating normal goods). Diagram (d) shows expenditure decreasing as income rises beyond income level Y (indicating a good that is inferior beyond this income level).

Figure 6.8
An income-consumption curve when one good is "inferior."

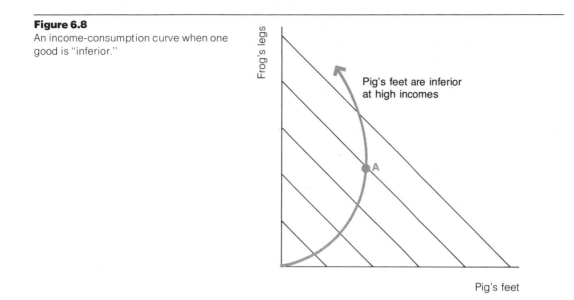

Frog's legs

Pig's feet are inferior at high incomes

A

Pig's feet

Figure 6.9
Engel curves show how the dollar expenditure of any good changes when income changes.

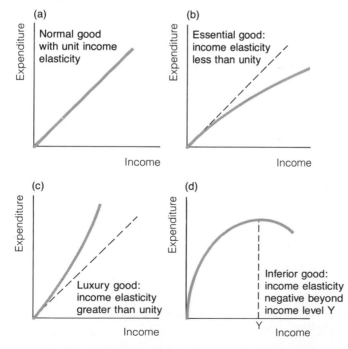

(a)

Expenditure

Normal good with unit income elasticity

Income

(b)

Expenditure

Essential good: income elasticity less than unity

Income

(c)

Expenditure

Luxury good: income elasticity greater than unity

Income

(d)

Expenditure

Inferior good: income elasticity negative beyond income level Y

Y

Income

Income Elasticity

Now compare Figures 6.9(a), (b), and (c). In (a), the Engel curve is a straight line, so the ratio of expenditure on the good to income is constant. In (b), this ratio is falling, while in (c) it is rising.

We define the percentage change in the expenditure on a good associated with a 1 percent change in income as the *income elasticity* for that good, assuming price is constant. If the income elasticity is positive but less than unity, expenditure increases with income, but at less than a proportionate rate. In this case, the ratio of expenditure to income falls as income rises, as in Figure 6.9(b). By the same reasoning, if the income elasticity is greater than unity, the ratio of expenditure to income increases as income rises, as in (c).

Goods for which income elasticity is positive but less than unity are referred to by economists as *essential goods;* those for which income elasticity is greater than unity are called *luxury goods.* We thus have a set of descriptive terms that express the various possible relationships between income and expenditure for a particular good.

If expenditure falls while income rises, income elasticity is negative and the good is inferior. If expenditure rises as income rises, income elasticity is positive, and the good is normal. A normal good may be an "essential" good (income elasticity less than unity) or a "luxury" good (income elasticity greater than unity).

While these terms can be used to describe a given individual's expenditure on a good relative to income, they are most often applied to aggregate expenditure relative to aggregate income. One of the early empirical observations of this aggregate relationship was made by the nineteenth-century economist Ernst Engel who, by comparing the consumption patterns of a large number of families in several income groups, discovered that the income elasticity of food was less than unity. This finding is generally referred to as *Engel's Law.*

Although numerous empirical studies concerning income-expenditure relationships have been conducted, there is nothing in consumer theory to suggest any particular set of such relationships. Our various descriptive terms are invariably used to classify *goods,* although they really refer to patterns of *preferences.* Over a given range of income, a particular good may indeed be regarded as inferior by one consumer, as essential by another, and as a luxury by yet a third.

Recap If prices for goods are held constant and the consumer's money income is changed, or if all prices change in the same proportion while income remains fixed, real income is said to change. With an increase in real income, a consumer can buy more of all goods, but may choose not to do so. If less of a good is purchased when real income rises, this good is called an inferior good; otherwise it is called a normal good. There are several ways to measure how the expenditure on a particular good varies with real income. Among these are income-consumption curves, Engel curves, and income elasticities.

| **Product Substitution** | The effect of a change in relative prices on consumers' choices |

Thus far we've concentrated on changes in consumers' constraints affecting the *position* but not the *slope* of their budget lines. Such changes are straightforward: they either allow consumers to purchase more than they did originally (increasing real income) or constrain them so they must buy less (decreasing real income). The situation is less straightforward if the slope of the budget line changes.

Let's return to our universe of $.50 beans and $2 jeans after having increased money income from $8 to $10, that is, under the assumption that our relevant budget line is A_1B_1, as represented in Figures 6.5 and 6.6. Now suppose the price of beans falls to $.40 per pound, while the price of jeans rises to $2.50 per pair. This will give a new budget line on which the point corresponding to spending the whole budget on beans will be farther from the origin than before and that corresponding to spending the whole budget on jeans will be closer to the origin. The new budget line will have a steeper slope, as shown in Figure 6.10, where A_1B_1 is the old budget line and A_2B_2 is the new one. The two lines intersect at E. With the new budget, the consumer has *gained* the possibility of buying goods collections in the shaded area A_1A_2E, but *lost* the possibility of buying collections in the area B_1B_2E, which could have been purchased with the old budget but cannot with the new.

Note that the collections gained have a high ratio of beans (whose relative price has fallen) to jeans (whose relative price has risen), compared with the collections lost. Any relative price change will necessarily increase the opportunities to purchase more of the good whose price has fallen, relative to the good whose price has risen.

Revealed Preference

Are the collections lost in Figure 6.10 really important to the consumer? This will obviously depend on personal preferences. Nevertheless, we can still reach certain conclusions if we know what point was chosen under the old budget. Three typical points are shown in the diagram, D, E, and F. For the consumer who originally chose collection D, we can deduce that the collections lost are not important. Why? Because, by choosing D when any collection on the original budget line A_1B_1 or in the area A_1OB_1 could have been chosen, the consumer has *revealed a preference* for D over any of those collections that now fall in the area B_1B_2E of Figure 6.10. Because even with the new budget, the consumer can still have D if desired, the loss of those collections that were rated less desirable than D does not matter. We can apply exactly the same argument to the consumer who chose point E on the original budget line (where the two budget lines cross).

Figure 6.10

How a change in relative prices opens new choices to the consumer and closes some former ones, even though money income may not have changed.

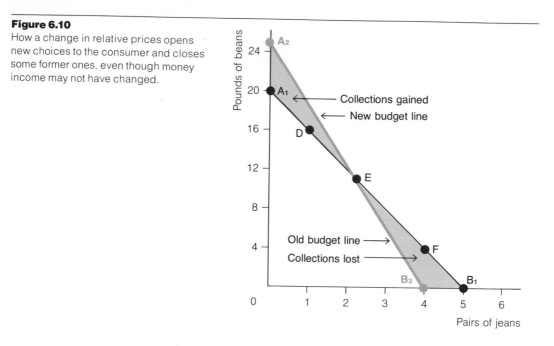

The consumer who originally chose collection F, however, is put in a different situation. He has lost the collection he originally liked best, and without further information, we have no way of knowing whether or not the set of collections gained with the new budget includes one he prefers to his original F.

In summary then, it is evident that the more the consumer's preferences are biased toward the good whose relative price has fallen (beans in our example), the more important are the new opportunities opened up and the less important are the potential collections that may have been lost.

A Pure Substitution Effect

Let's now concentrate on Stanley, the consumer who we'll assume originally chose point E. Because this point lies on both budget lines, the new budget is just such as to enable him to buy his old collection with nothing left over. By way of contrast, the consumer who chose D can still buy his old collection and have money left over, while the consumer who chose F can no longer even afford his original collection. What will Stanley, who chose E under the old budget, do under the new budget? We know, from his revealed preference, that he prefers E to any point on the old budget line. He will therefore not choose any point on the portion EB_2 of the new budget line because he could have had any of those points before had he wanted them. He will either stick with E or choose some collection along the portion A_2E of the new budget line, among the new opportunities opened up. Note that if he chooses any collection other than E, he will end up with *more beans* and *fewer pairs of jeans* than before.

By so choosing, Stanley will therefore *substitute* beans (whose relative price has fallen) for jeans (whose relative price has risen). Because the budget change was such that he can still just buy his old collection, with nothing left over, his real income has remained essentially unchanged. Any resulting change in the collection of goods purchased can thus be referred to as the *pure substitution effect*.

A pure substitution effect will be such that any change in buying patterns will be in the direction of buying more of the good whose relative price has fallen and less of the good whose relative price has risen.

The Importance of Substitution

Simple examples using only two goods tend to overstate substitution effects. With a large number of goods and a change in relative prices, there will certainly be a substitution of *some* goods whose relative prices have fallen for *some* goods whose relative prices have risen. If the price of only one good has fallen, the relative prices of all other goods have necessarily risen, and the substitution effect will result in an increase in the quantity of the good whose price has fallen together with a decrease in the quantity of *at least one* of the other goods.

The more similar the characteristics of two goods are, the more easily they can be substituted for one another without any major rethinking of the consumer's overall objectives. If the price of pork falls relative to the price of chicken, we can expect increased pork consumption at the expense of reduced chicken consumption with only a minor rearrangement of the consumer's eating patterns. Goods so related are called *close substitutes*.

A reduction in the price of pork will not normally be expected to perceptibly affect the demand for stereo tapes and tennis balls because the consumer will presumably confine any adjustment to food consumption. If the price of food in general changes dramatically, however, there may be substitution effects between eating and other consumption activities. Most goods are ultimately substitutes for each other, but this is likely to be revealed only by major changes in relative prices.

By way of contrast, it is possible for goods to be related as *complements* if they are *jointly used* in a consumption activity. A consumer may eat french fries with catsup, in which case catsup consumption will rise with the consumption of french fries. A fall in the price of potatoes, leading to increased purchases of french fries, may thus also increase the consumption of catsup, even if catsup's relative price has risen. Although such complementarity may exist between various pairs of goods, the predominant relationship over the consumer's whole universe will be that of substitution—close for some pairs of goods, more distant for others.

Recap When there is a change in the relative prices of goods, the slope of the budget line changes in such a way as to open up more opportunities for buying increased amounts of the good that has become relatively cheaper than for the good that has become relatively more expensive. If the change in prices, together with any change in money income, is such that the consumer can buy only the originally chosen collection with the new budget with nothing left over, he or she will tend to increase the quantity of the good whose relative price has fallen and reduce the quantity of the good whose relative price has risen. The change in purchasing under these conditions is called a pure substitution effect. In a many-good world, the degree of substitution may range from close to nonexistent between any two goods.

The Demand Curve

The overall effect of a change in the price of one good when money income remains unchanged

A market demand curve shows how consumers collectively react when the price of a good changes. This curve is built up from individual curves, each of which shows how an individual consumer reacts to a change in the price of a single good when money income (along with all other potentially relevant market circumstances) remains unchanged. An important role of the theory of consumer behavior is to show that these individual demand curves will normally have a downward slope, thus giving the downward slope of the market curve we've come to expect. Although we have not yet examined the reactions of a consumer to the type of change implicit in the demand curve, we have now developed the tools necessary to do so.

Income and Substitution Effects Together

Budget line AB in Figure 6.11 depicts the various collections of tuna fish and all other goods available to Dorothy, who we assume initially chooses point C.

Now suppose the price of tuna fish falls, with no other changes. With an unchanged level of money income and cheaper tuna fish, Dorothy could obviously buy more of this good than before if she were to spend her entire budget on it. Thus, the top end of her budget line will move farther from the origin, say from point A to A_1. Alternatively, if Dorothy were to spend her entire budget on goods other than tuna fish, she would obtain the same amount as before because neither her money income nor the price of these goods has been affected. The other end of the budget line therefore remains fixed at B, and the new budget line is A_1B. Dorothy has gained new possibilities (the triangle A_1AB) and lost nothing. Her real income has in-

Figure 6.11
The new choice situation that occurs when the price of one good falls while income and other prices remain constant.

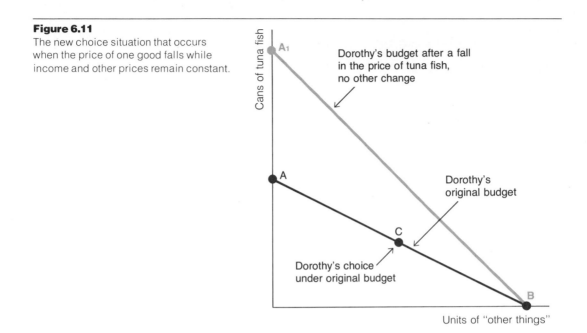

Cans of tuna fish

A_1

Dorothy's budget after a fall in the price of tuna fish, no other change

A

Dorothy's original budget

C

Dorothy's choice under original budget

B

Units of "other things"

creased, but so has the slope of her budget line. Consequently, the total effect of this change can be broken down into two separate effects:

1. *a substitution effect,* because we expect Dorothy to substitute tuna fish, whose relative price has fallen, for other goods that have become relatively more expensive; and
2. *an income effect,* because the fall in the price of tuna fish with money income and other prices left unchanged means Dorothy can buy her previous collection and have money left over to buy more—as if her initial money income *had* increased.

An Imaginary Experiment

We can illustrate this formal division into separate effects by performing a hypothetical experiment in which Dorothy shall serve as our guinea pig. First, once we've permitted the price of tuna fish to fall, let's lower Dorothy's money income so that she can just buy her original collection C. The appropriate budget line then becomes *II* in Figure 6.12 (so labeled to remind us that it is an imaginary construction), intersecting the original budget line at C. Any change in her purchases at this income—say, to point C_1—constitutes a *pure substitution effect* of the kind discussed in the previous section. Now let's restore Dorothy's money income to the original

Figure 6.12
How the total effect of a change in the price of one good is made up of a *substitution effect* and an *income effect*.

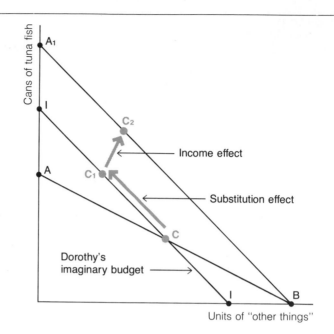

level, giving the final budget line A_1B. Given that A_1B is parallel to II but farther from the origin, the resulting change in Dorothy's purchases from C_1 on the imaginary budget line to C_2 on A_1B constitutes a *pure income effect*.

Given that Dorothy would have obviously chosen point C_2 had she gone directly from a choice on AB to one on A_1B (which, of course, is actually what would have happened), it is clear that the *total price effect* (the change from C to C_2) can legitimately be regarded as a combination of pure substitution and income effects.

The Downward Slope of the Demand Curve

The substitution effect is always such as to increase the quantity demanded of a good whose price has fallen. If the good whose price has fallen is a normal good, the income effect will also tend to cause an increase in the quantity purchased.

Therefore, a fall in the price of a normal good will result in an increase in the quantity purchased by each consumer, both the substitution and income effects working in this direction. Thus, each individual demand curve will slope downward, and the quantity demanded will vary inversely with price.

But what about an inferior good, purchases of which decline as incomes rise? While the substitution effect of a price reduction will tend to increase the quantity demanded of such a good (as it would with any good), the income effect will work in the opposite direction, thus raising the possibility of an upward-sloping demand curve. Such a "perverse" demand relationship requires the existence of a *special type* of inferior good, however, one for which the income effect of a price change actually outweighs the substitution effect.

The *theoretical possibility* of such a demand relationship is illustrated by consumers who subsist entirely on bread and cheese. If the price of bread goes up and they continue to buy the same quantity of bread as before, less income remains with which to purchase cheese. The original amount of bread together with the reduced amount of cheese may be insufficient to satisfy their minimum caloric needs. Consequently, they may cut down even more on cheese and buy more bread because bread, though more expensive than before, remains the cheaper source of calories.

Despite the theoretical appeal of this example, there is no hard evidence to suggest that this sort of behavior actually exists. Consequently, regardless of whether a good is generally viewed by buyers as "normal" or "inferior," it will be expected to have a downward-sloping demand curve. Indeed, the notion of a "downward-sloping demand curve" is so ingrained in economics that the inverse relationship between quantity demanded and price implied by such a curve has come to be known as the *Law of Demand.*

Recap A demand curve shows the relationship between quantity demanded and price when other prices and income are held constant. If the price of one good falls, consumers can buy more of both goods, provided they were originally buying some of the good whose price fell. A fall in price, with constant money income, is thus equivalent to an increase in real income. At the same time, if the price of only one of the two goods falls, their relative prices change. The total effect of such a price change is thus a combination of a pure income effect and a pure substitution effect. If the good whose price has fallen is normal, both the income and substitution effects work in the same direction—to increase quantity demanded. Thus, it is the general expectation that consumers will buy more of a good as its price falls, giving the conventional downward slope of the demand curve. Exceptions are theoretically possible, however.

Capsule Supplement 6.2 **Cardinal Utility Theory**

Although the idea that goods possess value because they render "utility" to consumers is at least as old as Aristotle, the way in which this term came to be used in economics grew out of eighteenth-century thought. Jeremy Bentham (1748–1832), the British moral philosopher, conceived the idea that human conduct is guided by a *felicific calculus,* meaning that an action is taken only if the pleasure it brings outweighs the pain it causes. From this idea it was an obvious next step to associate some actual *amount* of pleasure (or pain) with each action, and it is this quantity that came to be known as *utility*.

A brief description of the role played by this concept in consumer theory from the mid-1800s through the early part of the twentieth century follows.

First, it was assumed that the utility obtained from consuming goods and services could be measured *cardinally,* like weight in pounds or length in meters (specifically in units we shall call *utils*), and that the incremental amount of utility obtained from consuming successive units of a good becomes smaller and smaller. This latter property, known as the *Law of Diminishing Marginal Utility,* is illustrated in the chart where successive dollar bags of both artichokes and pomegranates are observed to give Lulu increasingly less utility. Indeed, it can be seen that the fifth dollar spent by Lulu on pomegranates gives her no utility at all, even though the first four dollars worth give her a total of eighteen (8 + 6 + 3 + 1) utils.

Number of Utils Derived by Lulu from
Consuming Successive $1.00 Bags of
Artichokes and Pomegranates

	Artichokes	Pomegranates
1st dollar bag	9	8
2nd dollar bag	7	6
3rd dollar bag	6	3
4th dollar bag	4	1
5th dollar bag	2	0

Now the question arises: How can Lulu maximize her utility when constrained by a money income of, say, $5.00? The answer lies in the following foolproof procedure: *Spend one dollar at a time—each one so as to maximize the utility derived from it.*

Lulu's first dollar, therefore, should be spent on artichokes, to obtain nine utils (as opposed to the eight utils that would be obtained from pomegranates). Her second dollar should then be spent on pomegranates (for eight utils), her third on artichokes (for seven utils), and her fourth and fifth on a dollar's worth of each (for 6 + 6 = 12 utils). This allocation, where *the last dollar spent on each good yields the same amount of utility,* guarantees that Lulu will maximize her utility at thirty-six (9 + 8 + 7 + 6 + 6) utils. Indeed, any deviation from this allocation will necessarily result in Lulu amassing less utility. For example, had she originally purchased $4.00 worth of artichokes and only $1.00 worth of pomegranates (obtaining thirty-four utils), she could have improved her condition by giving up her fourth bag of artichokes (sacrificing four utils) and using that dollar to buy a second bag of pomegranates (obtaining six utils, or a net increase of two). However, once the utility provided by the last dollar's worth of each good is equated, no further reallocation should be attempted. If Lulu, once having found the above "trade" to be advantageous, had continued to "exchange" artichokes for pomegranates, she would have reduced her total utility (specifically by three utils if she gives up her third bag of artichokes for a third bag of pomegranates).

In general, this process of utility maximization requires the consumer to equate the marginal utility associated with the last dollar spent on *every* good purchased, that is:

$$\frac{MU_x}{P_x} = \frac{MU_y}{P_y} = \cdots = \frac{MU_z}{P_z},$$

where MU_x is the marginal utility per unit of good x, P_x is the price per unit of good x, and y, . . . , z represent all other goods purchased by the consumer.

The problem with this approach was that utility eventually came to be considered, without regard for reality, as something almost tangible that could be measured and compared among persons. This led to oversimplified views of what could or could not be said about the social desirability of specific economic policies. We can never know whether Lulu gets more pleasure or utility from spending a dollar than does Wanda or Charlie. We might sometimes want to make the *social judgment* that Lulu's pleasure from spending an extra dollar is, or is not, of more value to society than someone else's, but that is quite a different thing. Economists have thus come to avoid using the concept of utility any more than necessary.

The Consumer in a Complex Economy

Factors we must consider in order to understand consumer behavior in a complex modern economy

Although the general principles of consumer behavior in a market economy can be illustrated in terms of two goods, real consumer choices are carried out in a far more complicated context. This is especially true in a market economy such as that of the United States where the number of different goods can be measured in the tens of thousands.

Product Differentiation

The most apparent feature of an advanced consumption society is the existence of many makes and models within each product category. There exists a seemingly endless variety of automobiles, laundry detergents, breakfast cereals, headache remedies, and so on. Goods that can be considered "the same product" yet are distinguishable from one another are commonly called *product differentiates* within a given *product class*.

Choice and Characteristics

Because consumer choice in advanced economies so frequently involves choices among product differentiates, the analysis presented in this chapter tends to oversimplify the process of consumer decision-making in such economies. In the standard analytical framework we must choose either to regard all automobile models as the same good and thus ignore the hours of agonizing comparison often spent in picking a particular model, or to regard each model as a separate good and thus ignore the fact that all automobiles perform essentially the same function.

The most useful way to view choice among product differentiates is in terms of the characteristics they possess. What a consumer really seeks from an automobile, for example, is a bundle of characteristics—comfort, size, maneuverability, fuel economy, etc. Indeed, each model derives its uniqueness from its distinct characteristic mix. Even with similar budgets, consumers will buy different automobiles in accordance with their respective preferences concerning characteristics. Cadillac buyers will exhibit their preference for comfort over fuel economy, Porsche buyers their preference for maneuverability over size.

Consequently, consumer decision-making can be regarded as a three-stage process based on:

1. the collections of goods that can be purchased with the consumer's budget;
2. the collections of characteristics that these various collections of goods possess; and
3. the consumer's preferences about characteristics.

The Need for Information

Because choice depends on product characteristics, consumers need *information* about these characteristics. The set of relationships among varieties of goods and the characteristics they possess can be thought of as society's *consumption technology*.

If the consumption technology is *static*, consumers learn from their own experience (and from the experiences of their parents and friends) what the characteristics of various goods are. Once this knowledge has been absorbed into the process of choice, it is simply taken for granted.

With a *changing* consumption technology, however, information about the characteristics possessed by certain goods becomes necessary. If bananas have always been available, consumers will have already incorporated them into their patterns of choice. But if bananas were suddenly invented from scratch, consumers would want to learn about their characteristics in order to determine the place of bananas in their respective consumption schemes.

Advanced consumption technologies are characterized by constant change—new product differentiates are introduced every day. Consumers consequently need information and are prepared to pay for it, as the success of such periodicals as *Consumer Reports* demonstrates.

Advertising

Producers are obviously anxious to inform consumers of the particular collections of characteristics their new product differentiates have to offer. The provision of such information is one role of advertising.

Of course, there is another side to advertising. Producers frequently advertise in an attempt to convince consumers that their products are high in those characteristics of particular interest to those consumers. Such advertising, of course, may be exaggerated or even completely misleading.

Efficient Choice

A related aspect of choice in a complex society is that of *consumer efficiency*. A consumer of a given collection of characteristics may not be aware that it can be obtained *from a different collection of goods* that costs less. If so, this consumer is consuming inefficiently. By moving from an inefficient choice of goods to an efficient one, a consumer with a given budget can obtain more of all desired characteristics. This implies that social welfare can be improved through any type of activity that increases consumer information (including the limitation of false advertising).

The Agonies of Choice

The diversity of consumer preferences, on the one hand, and the personal costs of making decisions (in terms of time and mental anguish), on the other, lead to two divergent tendencies in complex modern societies. Goods become differentiated into a broad variety of models so as to better fit individual preferences and, at the same time, become standardized so consumers can be assured of continued and widespread access to those goods that suit their needs. Having purchased a new Chevrolet or Volkswagen, the modern consumer can drive from coast to coast with complete assurance that there will be not only a McDonald's and a Holiday Inn, but also a factory-authorized Chevy or VW service center around every corner.

Some would argue that the variety of products available to the American consumer has reached the point at which the waste of time and energy in making choices outweighs the hypothetical advantage of having goods closely related to individual preferences. Whether we accept this argument or not, it is clear that the greater the variety of goods, the more difficult it is to make choices, and thus the less certain it is that the choices individuals actually make result in outcomes that are truly most preferred. We can presume that most consumers will eventually settle on a pattern of expenditure once they decide that the costs of further "shopping around" outweigh the potential benefits from making more refined choices.

Recap In an advanced modern economy, consumers face complex choice situations. This complexity derives in large part from the proliferation of closely related but objectively differentiated goods. The most revealing way to analyze choice among product differentiates is to concentrate on the characteristics of these goods rather than on the goods themselves. Consumer information assumes great importance in a complex economy. Indeed, the real costs involved in assimilating and processing consumer information may ultimately outweigh the benefits derived from the virtually limitless choice available to the consumer.

Capsule Supplement 6.3   **The Bad among the Goods**

Economists have long viewed goods like automobiles and cigarettes as the relevant objects of consumer choice. The modern approach, however, is to regard such "goods" as having many characteristics, with consumers reacting to different characteristics in different ways. This enables us to consider the possibility that some things have both good *and* bad characteristics.

It is almost impossible to analyze a complex modern society without noting that many goods have bad characteristics. Despite the many virtues of automobiles, they cause pollution and jam the streets. Likewise, people who derive satisfaction from smoking cigarettes increase the probability that they will die from lung cancer. Those who buy and use goods in such mixed cases can be presumed to conclude that the positive aspects outweigh the negative.

Social welfare can be increased if the "bad" content of things can be diminished without reducing the "good." This is ultimately a technical problem. The bad is there because standard production methods produce it in conjunction with the good. Sometimes the price system can be used to induce consumers to buy goods with a lower ratio of bad to good if they are not already doing so out of free choice. One example is the use of differential sales taxes, such as the New York cigarette tax which is higher for cigarettes having a high-tar content than for those having a lower content. This differentiation is based on the presumption that more tar is associated with a higher probability of cancer (the "bad"), and consumers are induced by the price differential to switch to low-tar cigarettes. The tax on lead in gasoline is the same kind, inducing automobile owners to buy low-lead (and thus minimal-pollution) fuel.

If "bad" and "good" characteristics simultaneously affect the consumer of some product, and him alone, we can presume that the consumer's own opinion as to whether the good outweighs the bad, or vice versa, should be allowed to determine his behavior. The case for intervention exists when these effects do not occur simultaneously or affect others. In the cigarette case, the bad effects are long-run ones that do not appear simultaneously with the immediate enjoyment of smoking. The case for intervention is similar to that for compulsory schooling and Social Security—consumers may take too shortsighted a view of their own ultimate welfare. In the automobile case, the good characteristics (flexible transport on immediate call) accrue to the owner while many of the bad characteristics (particularly pollution) are distributed to persons other than the owner, so the owner's decisions do not take into account enough of the effects on society.

Policy should be formulated relative to specific characteristics rather than in terms of goods *per se*. The solution to the automobile problem is to reduce the bad characteristics, not to throw out the good along with the bad. The same approach is appropriate to a variety of problems, from artificial sweeteners to supersonic aircraft.

Exercises

1. Abner has a money income of $240 to spend on corn whiskey and "other things." The price of corn whiskey is $1 per bottle and the price of other things is $10 per unit. Draw the following points on Abner's budget diagram:
   a. that corresponding to spending his entire income on corn whiskey;
   b. that corresponding to spending his entire income on other things;
   c. that corresponding to buying 48 bottles of corn whiskey and spending the rest of his income on other things;
   d. that corresponding to buying 100 bottles of corn whiskey and spending the rest of his income on other things;
   e. that corresponding to buying 10 units of other things and spending the rest of his income on corn whiskey.
   Show that all five points lie on a straight budget line.

2. Suppose Abner's income remains unchanged at $240, but the price of corn whiskey rises to $1.20 a bottle, and the price of other things falls to $8 per unit. Show that Abner can just buy his originally chosen collection with the new budget, where this collection consisted of 120 bottles of corn whiskey and 12 units of other things.

3. Show that the "new" budget constraint of question 2 is exactly the same as one in which the price of corn whiskey is $1.50, the price of other things is $10 per unit, and money income is $300.

4. If Abner originally purchased 120 bottles of corn whiskey and 12 units of other things with the budget constraint of question 1, then the price of corn whiskey rose to $1.50 a bottle with no other changes in the budget situation, show that the overall change is equivalent to a two-step change of the following kind:

Step 1: The price of corn whiskey rises to $1.50 a bottle and Abner's income is increased to $300.

Step 2: The price of corn whiskey remains at the new level, and Abner's income is cut by 20 percent ($60).

5. Suppose the pure substitution effect in step 1 of the previous question is such that Abner changes from his original 120 bottles of corn whiskey and 12 units of other things to 80 bottles of corn whiskey and 18 units of other things. Abner's income elasticity of demand for spirits is 0.10. How much corn whiskey does he buy when its price is $1.50 a bottle and his budget is $240?

6. Is Abner's demand for corn whiskey relatively elastic or relatively inelastic with respect to price?

7. By how much does Abner change the quantity of other things he buys when the price of corn whiskey changes as above? Why does he change his purchases of these other things even though neither their price nor his money income has changed?

For Thought and Discussion

1. Can you think of any case in which *you* might buy more of a good whose price has risen, when other prices, your income, and your general circumstances have remained unchanged?

2. Is the variety of products and product differentiates in a modern economy so large that consumers can never really ascertain their preferences among different collections? What would this imply, if true, for our study of consumer behavior?

3. Think about the collection of goods you currently buy. Which of these, if any, are inferior goods? For which is your income elasticity especially low, or especially high?

4. Why do we assert the following to be true?
   a. Not all goods consumed by an individual will have income elasticities of less than unity.
   b. At least one good consumed by an individual must have a downward-sloping demand curve.

Chapter 7
Production for the Market

Terms and Concepts

Firm
Perfect competition
Monopoly
Oligopoly
Imperfect competition
Average and marginal revenue
Opportunity cost
Long-run and short-run cost
Fixed and variable cost
Average and marginal cost
Constant returns to scale
Marginal profit
Profit-maximizing rule
Equilibrium level of output
Marginal product
Marginal revenue product
Law of diminishing returns

Sellers and Producers

The role of the firm in a market economy

Just as the *properties of demand* ultimately depend on the *typical behavior of consumers,* a subject explored in the preceding chapter, the *properties of supply* depend on the *typical behavior of producers.* Specifically, supply is determined by the conditions under which producers are willing to engage in production, even though they may not be the ultimate sellers of what they produce.

In a market economy, control over production is exercised by the *firm.* A firm may be anything from a street-corner newsstand to a giant corporation employing hundreds of thousands of workers. A firm may produce a single product or a wide variety of products. Its operations may be carried out at a single location or, as is common in manufacturing, at several different plants. *The essential feature of the firm is that it is a single decision-making unit.* While, in reality, it may be difficult to ascertain whether a large, complex, business corporation constitutes a single firm or several firms in this sense, we shall assume in our basic analysis that the firm can always be identified.

From the broad perspective of the economist, the firm is an *intermediary,* using inputs owned by consumers or the government to produce outputs that are ultimately purchased by consumers or the government. The firm is assumed to have no personality of its own, and criteria for judging its overall effect on the economic system are based solely on the benefits and costs accruing ultimately to consumers (or the government acting on their behalf). "What's good for General Motors," therefore, is not a relevant index of social welfare, even though we're interested in the employees, stockholders, and customers of General Motors as *people.* Despite all this, the firm does not *act* as though it is merely an intermediary. Rather, it behaves in accordance with what it believes to be its own self-interest.

All policy problems relating to the role of firms in a market economy ultimately concern the relationship between the actions taken by a firm in its own interest and the actions desired from it as society's trustee in control of production.

Recap Control over production in a market economy is exercised by the firm. An important task of economics is to analyze how firms behave and how this behavior is related to such broad issues as efficiency and social welfare.

Types of Competition

A guide to the main types of competitive structure among firms

In discussing consumers as buyers, we assumed that the typical consumer represented such a small part of the market that his individual actions had no effect on it. Thus, the typical consumer can be viewed as operating in an environment where as much or as little as desired can be purchased without a noticeable effect on market demand and on the equilibrium quantity and price. The consumer simply reacts *passively* to the state of the market, accepting the price as given and adjusting his own behavior to that price.

In discussing firms, however, we cannot automatically assume that the "typical" firm represents so small a part of the total market for the good it produces that its variations in output have a negligible effect on total supply. Up until the latter part of the nineteenth century, the typical firm could perhaps be regarded in this way legitimately. Indeed, the economic theory of the firm originated as a theory of small, individual firms of this kind. Today, however, firms vary so much in size and in their relationships with one another that we can no longer characterize the "typical" firm as either large *or* small.

Of course, certain markets still exist in which the average firm contributes a negligible share of total supply. This is true for most farm products. Schultz, a Minnesota wheat farmer, doesn't expect the price of wheat to be influenced by whether or not he, as an individual farmer, plants a few more acres—and he is correct in viewing the market this way. When each firm producing a particular product contributes only a minute fraction of total supply, like Schultz's farm, we say that the market for that product exhibits *perfect competition in supply*. Because we can assume that consumers in such a market are typically the ultimate buyers, and that no one consumer can affect the market by his own individual actions, we can characterize the market situation as a whole as being *perfectly competitive*.

Now consider Consolidated Edison, which supplies electricity to New York City. Its relevant market is for electricity within a specific geographical area because buyers cannot buy electricity in New York and transport it elsewhere. Within this market, Con Edison is the only seller, even though there are millions of buyers. If the price elasticity of demand for electricity in New York were, say, -2.0, then a 10 percent increase in the price of electricity would result in a 20 percent reduction in the quantity consumed. This change in quantity would fall entirely on Con Edison, which clearly could not act as if its own sales were completely independent of price. When a single firm is the only supplier of a product, the demand for the output of the firm is identical to the entire market demand for the product. Such a market (and firm) is commonly referred to as a *monopoly*.

A firm like General Motors differs from both Schultz's farm and Con Edison. In the market for automobiles, General Motors is the major supplier. Despite its predominance, however, it is not the *only* supplier of automobiles in the American market, even if we ignore imports. Obviously, General Motors cannot act as if its decisions about the quantity produced will not affect the market. But, unlike Con Edison, General Motors must know more than how the market demand for automobiles relates to price. The firm must also know, or guess, how its major competitors—Ford and Chrysler—will react to its decisions. If General Motors were to raise the price of its cars by 10 percent, the effect on its sales would depend greatly on whether or not Ford and Chrysler also raise their prices. Such a market, in which there is a small number of large firms whose respective actions reflect the possible reactions of rival firms, is known as an *oligopoly*.

There are many other possible market structures, each having some mixture of the characteristics of monopoly and oligopoly. We commonly distinguish between *perfect competition* and *imperfect competition*, the latter being a catch-all term for monopoly, oligopoly, and any other market structure that cannot be considered perfectly competitive. Table 7.1 provides a general guide to the relationship between perfect and imperfect competition. The various subtypes of imperfect competition are discussed more extensively in Chapters 9 and 10.

Recap Firms vary greatly in the relationship between output and total market supply. At one extreme, a firm may have no perceptible impact on market equilibrium when it varies its own output; at the other extreme, a firm's output may constitute the total supply. If there are many small firms, none with more than a minute share of the market, we say there is perfect competition. If, on the other hand, any one firm has so large a share of the market that its individual actions have a noticeable effect on market equilibrium, we say there is imperfect competition.

Capsule Supplement 7.1   **Are There Any Small Firms Left?**

Perfect competition, the primary topic of Chapters 7 and 8, is a market structure characterized by numerous small firms. Bombarded day in and day out with the acronyms of corporate giants such as GM, GE, IBM, and ITT, we may well ask whether a study of competition among small firms can have anything more than purely historical relevance.

One important answer to this question is that perfect competition provides a standard against which we can compare the divergences that result from *imperfect competition*. Moreover, as is brought out in Chapter 8, an economy that is perfectly competitive possesses certain socially desirable properties that form the basis of much economic policy. Thus, there would be a case for the study of perfect competition even if there were no small-firm competition left.

But small firms do still exist, and in large numbers. The United States has almost 11 million proprietorships (businesses owned by single individuals) and partnerships, most of them "small" by any standard, and many of them extremely so. Although this number has not changed much over the past decade, it has grown from less than 2 million in 1939. Not all corporations are giants either—a full one-third of all corporations in the United States had sales of less than $50,000 in 1975, and one-fourth of them had sales of less than $25,000.

The classic small business, however, is the proprietorship: the farm, corner store, newsstand, travel agency, gas station, or beauty shop. There were almost 11 million proprietorships in 1975, of which more than 9 million had sales of less

Table 7.1

A Guide to Competitive Structures

Type	Determining structure	Effect on firm's actions
Perfect competition	No firm large enough for its actions to have a perceptible effect on total supply. Requires many firms supplying the product and lack of any one firm large enough to have an important market share. Examples: wheat or cotton farming, nineteenth-century textiles.	Individual firm adjusts passively to market price, which it cannot influence by its actions.
Imperfect competition	Any structure that diverges from perfect competition, usually due to the existence of only a small number of firms, or of very large firms even if there are also many very small ones. Size is relative to market—a single taxi can have a monopoly of the taxi market in a small town. Imperfect competition can come from the demand side if there is a single or dominant buyer. Examples: automobiles, soap products, and most other manufacturing; public utilities.	Firm does not adjust passively, but considers the effect of its actions on price, which it can influence.

(A guide to the subtypes of imperfect competition is given in Table 10.1.)

than $50,000 and 8 million had sales of less than $25,000. The average net profit (sales less materials, wages, and other costs) of the proprietorships with sales under $50,000 was less than $2,500 per firm. Most proprietorships, as the previous examples suggest, are in agriculture, trade, and services. More than one-third are farms and about one-fourth are in services (barbershops, dry cleaners, and the like). Most of the remainder are small stores, with a scattering in construction (small building firms) and transport (taxi drivers and wildcat truckers). Less than 2 percent are in manufacturing.

In terms of market share, proprietorships still predominate in agriculture, and account for more than 67 percent of total industry sales. They also remain an important part of service industries (32 percent of total sales) and retail trade (22 percent).

Small size alone is insufficient to ensure perfect competition because the relevant market may also be small. A one-chair barbershop in a small village, for example, may be a monopoly relative to the market it serves. Because the typical small business in retail trade or services caters to a small local market, its appropriate market structure is likely to be some form of imperfect competition. Agriculture remains the industry that most closely approximates perfect competition, with almost 3 million small farms in the United States selling produce on huge national and international markets.

Profit Maximization

Why we assume the maximization of profit to be the usual decision rule for a firm

The basic role of the firm in a market economy is to make decisions about production. Like other decision-makers, the firm must consider the potential benefits and costs of alternative actions. Specifically, we'll assume that, from the firm's point of view:

1. *the benefits associated with any production decision are measured entirely by the revenues obtained from selling the resulting output;* and
2. *the costs associated with any production decision are measured entirely by the costs attributable to that production.*

We can suppose that the firm's objective is *to maximize the net benefit to itself.* Because this net benefit is simply the difference between revenues and production costs—or profit—we can thus assume that the firm acts *to maximize its profit.*

Motives Other than Profit

Even in the United States where the "profit motive" supposedly governs business behavior, this decision rule may represent a simplification. Firms do not necessarily measure benefits by revenue alone, nor net benefits by the excess of revenue over cost. A firm may be motivated by the desire to be large, and thus may wish to expand beyond the most profitable level. Or it may seek approval of its technical sophistication or its social actions, achieved at the expense of simple profit. Some would go so far as to argue that simple profit maximization is the exception rather than the rule in the contemporary United States, especially among large corporations.

These points will be taken up later. For now, we'll assume simple profit maximization to be the criterion by which the firm makes its decisions.

Constraints on the Firm

The firm must operate within the *constraints* of the situation it faces. One major constraint is the existing *production technology* for the product in question. Other constraints are:

1. *Input prices and input availability.* These determine the firm's choice of technique, its production costs, and whether these costs are *long run* (no constraints on input availability) or *short run* (existing input limitations or similar constraints) in nature.

2. *The structure of its output market.* As shown in the preceding section, its output market determines the options open to the firm in earning revenue. Under conditions of perfect competition, the firm cannot affect the price it receives. It needs only to decide what output to sell at that price. If competition is imperfect, the firm's actions will affect the price, and it will need to consider (and thus secure information about) demand conditions and possibly the actions of rival firms.

Types of Decisions

Subject to the relevant constraints, the profit-maximizing firm faces four basic decisions:

1. *Entry and exit.* This is the fundamental decision of whether or not to produce the product at all or, if presently doing so, whether or not to continue production.
2. *Size.* Inputs may not be freely available when needed, or, like plants and buildings, require time to install or modify. Therefore, the firm must decide on what size plant and with what level of resource stockpiles it should operate.
3. *Production process.* The firm must decide which input combination to use to produce each level of output within its probable range of operations.
4. *Level of output.* The firm must decide on the amount of output to produce and sell under the market conditions facing it.

The first two decisions really hang on the last two. Given input prices, the firm will maximize its profits at a specific level of output only by choosing the production process producing that level of output at least cost. By comparing the differences between the revenues and least costs associated with each level of output, the firm can then determine which output level is the most profitable.

Only after determining the most profitable level of output, and ascertaining exactly how much profit will be forthcoming, can the firm decide whether or not it is actually worthwhile to enter the market. If the firm decides to enter the market, there are several factors that will determine the size of its operations. These include the choice of production process and the desired level of output, which must be considered in conjunction with any preexisting constraints on, say, the availability of inputs.

The basic theory of the firm thus focuses on the choice of production process and output level, leaving conclusions about size and entry to be determined from these.

Recap The firm acts to maximize its own net benefit in light of whatever constraints it may face. Moreover, we generally assume that this net benefit consists of sales revenue less production costs—or profit. In reality, however, a firm's behavior may reflect objectives other than pure profit maximization.

Revenue

How a firm's revenue varies with the quantity it sells

A firm's revenue consists of its receipts from the sale of its output. Like using the unqualified term *cost* to mean the *least cost* of producing a specific level of output under a given set of constraints, we use *revenue* to mean the *maximum revenue* that can be obtained from selling a specific level of output under a given set of market conditions. While a firm's revenue clearly depends on the *quantity* of output sold, it may be impossible to predict exactly how much revenue will be obtained from selling a given quantity of output. Uncertainty about revenue may arise for essentially two different reasons, and the analysis of the firm depends crucially on which, if either, type of uncertainty is involved.

On the one hand, uncertainty may simply stem from the firm's inability to obtain sufficient information about the market. On the other hand, uncertainty may arise from the very structure of the market itself, in which case it cannot be totally eliminated simply by acquiring ordinary market information. This is likely to occur when the market is characterized by a small number of firms whose respective actions affect each other. An initial action by one firm will affect its competitors who, in turn, may react in various ways. The effect of the initial firm's action on its revenue will therefore ultimately depend on the potentially unpredictable reactions of others. This situation, which is much like a game in which the results of a move by one player depend on the subsequent moves of other players, typically characterizes oligopoly.

We shall discuss oligopoly and the complex decisions faced by certain types of firms in Chapter 10. Here we shall deal with a much simpler case, making the assumption that:

The revenue of the firm is a function of the quantity it sells, which, in principle, can be predicted. We shall furthermore assume that all relevant information is known to the firm.

Average Revenue

We shall define *total revenue* as the revenue obtained from selling a specific level of output, and *average revenue* as the total revenue from selling a specific level of output divided by the number of units sold. That is:

$$\text{average revenue} = \text{total revenue/quantity sold.}$$

Whereas total revenue is measured in simple dollars, average revenue is measured in dollars per unit of output—dollars per ton, for example.

Our concern is generally confined to the case in which the firm sells on an open market to all buyers at the same price. In this event, total revenue is equal to price multiplied by the quantity sold. But total revenue is also equal to average revenue times quantity sold. Hence, we have the following basic relationship:

$$\text{average revenue} = \text{price.}$$

This equality obviously does not hold for a firm selling to different buyers at different prices. Electricity, for example, is commonly sold to domestic and commercial users at different prices. Indeed, the price per kilowatt hour may even vary on the basis of quantity purchased by a particular user. Selling at different prices to different buyers is called *price discrimination*. This can occur only under imperfect competition, and even then only in markets in which buyers paying the lower price cannot resell to buyers paying the higher price. It should be obvious that if a product is sold at, say, two different prices, average revenue lies somewhere between the two. While isolated instances of price discrimination can obviously be found in the real world, our analysis of the firm will focus on the more typical market situation in which there is a uniform price.

Marginal Revenue

The stage is now set to introduce an extremely important concept in economic analysis—*marginal revenue*—defined as the change in total revenue resulting from the sale of an additional unit of output. At first glance, it might seem that marginal revenue is simply equal to price, provided the price charged by the firm is uniform. But this need not be the case. Suppose, for example, that a monopolist can sell 100 units of his product at a price of $10, in which case his total revenue from 100 units is $1,000. Because when we speak of revenue, we mean *maximum revenue,* it's implied that $10 is the highest price at which 100 units can be sold. The marginal revenue obtained from selling the 101st unit cannot then be $10 because the monopolist cannot sell 101 units at that price. To sell 101 units, the monopolist must offer *all* of them (because there is a uniform price) at a price less than $10. New revenue must then be *less than* $101 \times $10 = $1,010$, so the addition to revenue (which was formerly $1,000) must be *less than* $10. If, for example, 101 units can only be sold by lowering the price to $9.99, the resulting total revenue is $1,008.99 ($9.99 \times 101$) giving a marginal revenue of the 101st unit of $8.99 ($1,008.99 − $1,000$). While this example is for a monopoly, a similar argument holds for any form of imperfect competition.

Marginal Revenue under Perfect Competition

In a perfectly competitive market, the actions of any one firm are assumed to be sufficiently unimportant relative to the total market that it can sell as much or as little as it chooses without causing a change in price. Thus, if the market price is $10 per unit, the perfectly competitive firm obtains $10 for every additional unit sold, regardless of how much it was selling to start with, and the marginal revenue remains constant at $10. The marginal revenue for the perfectly competitive firm changes only when the market price changes, that is, when there is a change in market circumstances outside the direct control of the firm. Its own marginal revenue is always equal to the market price, and thus to average revenue.

Although we won't take up the analysis of imperfectly competitive firms until later chapters, it is important to characterize the relationship between marginal revenue, average revenue, and price in a context that portrays the equality of price and marginal revenue under perfect competition as a special case. We may summarize the general relationships:

Type of Competition	Relationship of Marginal Revenue to Price	Relationship of Average Revenue to Price
Perfect	$MR = P$	$AR = P$
Imperfect	$MR < P$	$AR = P$, unless there is price discrimination

Revenue Curves

The relationship between revenue and the level of output is commonly depicted graphically. Under perfect competition, price is independent of the firm's level of output and equal to both average and marginal revenue. Thus, if we measure output along the horizontal axis, and dollars per unit of output on the vertical axis, price, average revenue, and marginal revenue can be represented by a single horizontal line, as shown in Figure 7.1.

The corresponding curves for imperfect competition are given in Figure 7.2. Because average revenue is equal to price, the firm's average revenue (= demand) curve slopes downward to the right, showing that more can be sold only if the price is lowered. Because marginal revenue is less than price, and thus less than average revenue, the marginal revenue curve necessarily lies *below* the average revenue curve.

Recap The total revenue from selling a given output divided by the quantity sold is the average revenue, or price. The addition to total revenue from selling an additional unit of output is marginal revenue. Marginal revenue cannot exceed price, and is less than price if the demand curve for the firm's product is downward slop-

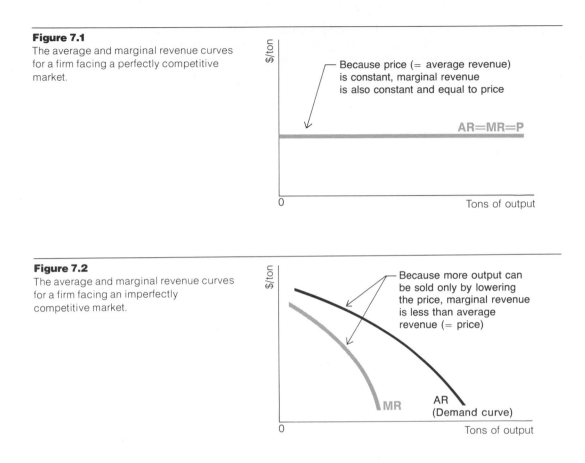

Figure 7.1
The average and marginal revenue curves for a firm facing a perfectly competitive market.

Because price (= average revenue) is constant, marginal revenue is also constant and equal to price

AR=MR=P

$/ton

0   Tons of output

Figure 7.2
The average and marginal revenue curves for a firm facing an imperfectly competitive market.

Because more output can be sold only by lowering the price, marginal revenue is less than average revenue (= price)

$/ton

MR   AR
(Demand curve)

0   Tons of output

ing. Average and marginal revenue (which are measured in the same units) are commonly plotted graphically against output, giving average and marginal revenue curves. The average revenue curve is identical to the demand curve for the firm's product. Under perfect competition, this curve is horizontal because price, average revenue, and marginal revenue are equal for all levels of output. Under imperfect competition, the firm's average revenue (= demand) curve will be downward sloping, and the marginal revenue curve will lie below it.

Costs of Production

Some basic considerations about a firm's costs

To the economist, costs represent alternatives that must be forgone in order to achieve some specific objective. Accordingly, production costs consist of whatever must be given up to produce a given quantity of output.

The outlay or expenditure on inputs purchased in the market obviously constitutes a cost to the firm. But there may be other costs as well. If, for example, the owner of the firm spends forty hours per week supervising production, that time has a cost because it is something that could be avoided if there were no production. We normally value such time in terms of how much the owner could earn by supervising another firm's production instead of his own. This cost is referred to as an *opportunity cost* because working for one's own firm requires that one *forgo the opportunity* of working elsewhere.

We shall assume that all opportunity costs of this kind—which occur when the firm possesses certain inputs that have alternative uses in the economy—are added to the firm's actual outlays, and thereby are implicitly incorporated into the firm's total costs.

A Simple Example

Let's hypothetically engage in the production of a good, say almond fudge, which requires only two inputs, labor and capital. They can be purchased on the market exactly where and when required at fixed prices of $2 per man-hour and $3 per machine-hour.

If the only production process requires six machine-hours of capital and one man-hour of labor to produce ten pounds of fudge, then the total cost of producing ten pounds is uniquely given at $20 [(6 × $3) + (1 × $2)]. It follows that the *average cost* of producing ten pounds of fudge is $2 per pound.

Cost Means Least Cost

If there were alternative ways to produce ten pounds of almond fudge with differing combinations of inputs, then we would have to consider the cost of each process. Because our profit from producing ten pounds, regardless of market conditions, will be maximized only if we produce that quantity at least total cost, we can make the following assumption:

At whatever level of output the firm chooses to produce, it will choose the process that yields that output at least cost, subject to the information available to it and any constraints on its choice.

Now suppose that there are actually two ways to produce ten pounds of almond fudge: the process we've already described (P_1) requiring six machine-hours and one man-hour, and another (P_2) requiring only five machine-hours but three man-hours. If the input prices are those already given ($3 per machine-hour and $2 per man-hour), then the cost of producing ten pounds by P_1 is $20 (as already shown), and the cost by P_2 is $21 [(5 × $3) + (3 × $2)]. So long as input prices remain constant (or, strictly speaking, remain in the same *ratio*), process P_1 will be the least-cost process. In general, then, so long as relative input prices remain constant, and *so long as inputs can be obtained in the least-cost proportion,* the firm will use a single process.

But, if relative input prices change, the optimal process may change as well. Suppose the price of machine-hours goes up to $5 while wages remain constant. The cost of producing ten pounds of fudge by P_1 is now $32 [(6 \times \$5) + (1 \times \$2)], while by P_2, it is only $31 [(5 \times \$5) + (3 \times \$2)]. P_2 has become the least-cost process. To be sure, the total cost of production has gone up as a result of the increase in the price of machine-hours, but by less than would have been the case had P_1 been the only process available. *The choice of process will depend on relative input prices, and the least-cost process can be expected to change if these prices change markedly.*

For a given set of input prices and a given technology, the least possible cost for producing any level of output can be clearly established. A particular firm may be unable to produce at this least possible cost, however, because of constraints on its operations. It might, for example, be restricted in its access to some input (as when its plant, equipment, or land cannot easily be expanded), and be forced to use a lower proportion of this input to other inputs than would give the least possible cost. In our initial example, P_1 (six machine-hours and one man-hour) is the least-cost process. But suppose the firm can obtain only five machines. It may have no alternative but to use process P_2—using two additional man-hours instead of the additional machine-hour.

Long-Run versus Short-Run Cost

The *least possible cost* of producing a specific level of output (input prices and technology being given) is usually referred to as the *long-run cost.* This term reflects the presumption that, given sufficient time to make whatever adjustments are necessary, a firm can remove all obstacles to achieving the least possible cost. Suppose, for example, a firm annually produces 1,000 tons of shampoo with its existing plant, and has no intention of changing this rate of production in the foreseeable future. If the present plant size permits a lower-cost way to produce that annual level of output than would any alternative plant size, it will obviously be retained. The firm will alter its plant size if, and only if, doing so serves to lower the cost of production. Thus, long-run cost (with the choice of any plant) cannot be higher than short-run cost (production confined to the existing plant), and will often be lower. The term *short-run cost* means exactly what the above context implies—the least cost that the firm can achieve for a given output *with whatever facilities are already at hand.*

The distinction between the short run and the long run is not necessarily related to any specific length of time. In some industries, like pretzel vending, a firm may be able to adjust completely within a matter of hours, while in others, like aerospace manufacturing, the comparable adjustment may take years.

Whereas long-run costs are unique, short-run costs are not. Indeed, a different set of short-run costs will prevail for every conceivable size of physical plant. Consequently, we cannot refer to *the* short-run costs of a firm without specifying the exact circumstances currently constraining the firm's operation.

Recap Production costs are what the firm gives up in order to produce. These include the value of forgone opportunities of resources owned and used by the firm (opportunity costs) as well as direct outlays. The firm will choose, for any potential level of output, the least-cost method of producing that output, subject to whatever input limitations it faces. Choosing the least-cost method will involve a cost comparison of different processes. The least-cost process will be expected to change if there is a marked change in the relative prices of inputs required.

Cost Variations

**How a firm's costs vary with
the level of output produced**

Assuming that the firm is aware of the least-cost method of producing *each output level,* given input prices and constraints on input use, we can now describe how its costs vary with the level of output. As we'll demonstrate later, by comparing the respective variations of revenue and cost with output, the firm can ultimately determine the most profitable level of production.

It is possible to look at cost data from three different points of view:

1. *Total cost (TC)* is the overall cost associated with producing a specific level of output. We can thus imagine a statement like "the total cost of producing 1,000 harmonicas is $3,500." Total cost is measured in simple dollars.

Total cost can be broken down into two components. One of these is *fixed cost,* the sum of all outlays and opportunity costs that do *not* vary with the level of output. The rent paid for a factory building, for example, may be a fixed contractual obligation, quite independent of the output produced by the factory. (Strictly speaking, because such an obligation must be met regardless of the conditions of production, it is debatable whether or not it constitutes a true production cost.) *Variable costs* are those components of total cost that depend directly on the level of output. Typically these consist of the costs of inputs that are purchased *only as needed* to permit increased output.

2. *Average cost (AC)* is the total cost of producing a given level of output divided by the number of units produced. If the total cost of producing 1,000 harmonicas is $3,500, the *average cost* of producing 1,000 harmonicas is $3.50 per harmonica. Average cost is not measured in simple dollars but

in *dollars per unit*. As with total cost, we must specify the output level to which it applies.

Because average cost is simply total cost divided by the level of output, and because total cost is the sum of fixed cost and variable cost, we can theoretically distinguish between *average fixed cost* and *average variable cost*. The sum of these two is obviously equal to *average cost* (sometimes called *average total cost* when both fixed and variable components are being discussed).

3. *Marginal cost* (*MC*) is the cost of producing *one additional unit* of output. If the total cost of producing 1,000 harmonicas is $3,500 and the total cost of producing 1,001 harmonicas is $3,504, then the *marginal cost* of producing the 1,001th harmonica is $4. Like average cost, marginal cost is expressed in dollars per unit, and we can compare the two directly.

Because marginal and average cost are both obtained directly from total cost, the information they convey is already implicit in total cost. Marginal cost constitutes the *change* in total cost associated with a one-unit variation in output. Because the fixed component of total cost does not change with output, marginal cost depends only on *variable cost,* and is thus independent of *fixed cost.* Because more output always requires more inputs, it is obvious that total cost increases with output.

However, it is not immediately obvious how marginal and average cost vary with output. Given input prices, the precise manner in which total, average, and marginal costs vary with output depends on the technology and on the constraints impeding the firm's ability to choose the least-cost process.

Constant Returns to Scale

If the production technology is such that increasing all inputs by, say, 10 percent will increase output by 10 percent, it is said to exhibit the property of *constant returns to scale*. Under this property, if input prices are fixed and the firm is free to vary all inputs, a 10 percent increase in output will result in a 10 percent increase in total cost. Because total cost changes in the same proportion as output, average cost remains unchanged. If average cost is constant, marginal cost must also be constant and equal to average cost. For example, a firm produces 231 tons of bubble gum at an average cost of $11 per ton, so the total cost of producing this output is $2,541 ($231 × 11). If output is now increased to 232 tons and average cost remains unchanged at $11 per ton, the cost of producing the new output is $2,552 ($232 × 11). The marginal cost is the increase in total cost of increasing output from 231 tons to 232 tons and is equal to $2,552 − $2,541 or $11, the average cost. Thus, the relationship *MC = AC* is true for all levels of output *so long as average cost is constant*. The arithmetical relationships that underlie this equality are basically the same as those from which we derived the equality of marginal and average revenue when the latter is constant, as under perfect competition. Thus, we can assert that *long-run average and marginal costs are equal and constant if the technology exhibits constant returns to scale.*

Constant returns to scale simply implies that if we can produce one widget in a particular way, we can duplicate the process and produce *two* widgets with *double* the inputs. This result is both theoretically plausible and empirically evident in a wide variety of cases. We shall therefore assume that constant average and marginal costs are a standard property of the *long run.*

Input Limitations

If the available quantity of one input is limited, however, we may not be able to increase all inputs in proportion. Suppose capital equipment is limited in the short run, so increases in output beyond some limit can be achieved only by increasing labor.

If there are constant returns to scale and fixed input prices, the least-cost process for one level of output will also be the least-cost process for every other level. In other words, the firm will prefer to expand output by increasing all inputs in proportion. If it cannot do so, as when its access to capital equipment is limited and output can be expanded only by increasing labor, the firm must change to a process using more labor per unit of capital than was used at the output at which there were no limits on capital equipment. Because these processes are *not* those that would be chosen in the absence of limitations, it follows that they are more costly.

Thus, the effect of input limitations is to force the firm, in expanding output, to use processes that are successively less and less similar to the least-cost process, so total cost will rise more than in proportion to the level of output. Marginal cost will thus increase with output, once the point at which input limitations becomes effective is exceeded. Because we regard input limitations as typical of all firms under short-run conditions, we can expect that *short-run marginal cost increases with output, at least beyond some point.*

Typical examples of short-run cost relationships are shown in Figure 7.3. Note that we can draw both marginal and average cost curves on the same diagram because they are both expressed in the same units. The J-shaped marginal cost curve, shown in both (a) and (b), is suggested by empirical evidence, and is commonly used in the economic analysis of the firm.

The U-shaped average cost curve, shown in (a), is also commonly used in economic analysis. The reason behind the presumption of this shape, *which depends on the existence of fixed costs,* is as follows:

1. Average fixed cost, being a fixed quantity divided by different outputs, is large and tends to dominate average cost at small outputs. For large outputs, however, it is relatively small. A fixed cost of $100 will give an average fixed cost of $100 per ton when output is 1 ton, $1 per ton at 100

Figure 7.3
Possible shapes for the average and marginal cost curves of a firm.

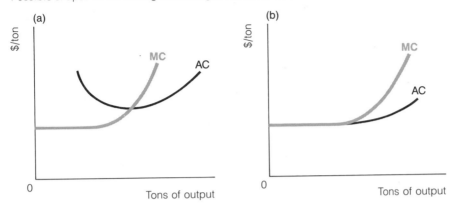

tons, and $.10 per ton at 1,000 tons. Thus, the early part of the average cost curve is dominated by the large, but declining, average fixed cost element, and slopes downward.

2. At large outputs, with input limitations, the necessity of using more and more costly processes causes marginal cost, and thus average variable cost, to increase. The right-hand portion of the average cost curve will thus be dominated by the rising average variable cost element and will slope upward. (As a matter of arithmetic, the marginal cost curve must intersect the U-shaped average cost curve at its lowest point.)

Now look at diagram (b). While the average cost curve in this figure does not reflect the potential effect of fixed cost as does its U-shaped counterpart in (a), it depicts more clearly the essential short-run feature of input limitations (which become effective at the point where both curves turn upward). For this reason, and also because short-run curves so portrayed best permit illustration of the relationship between short- and long-run costs, we shall use short-run cost curves similar to those in (b) in our analysis of the firm.

Our use of such curves for analytical purposes is not meant to suggest that fixed costs are absent in the real world or that U-shaped average cost curves are not potentially relevant for some firms. We have simply chosen to portray short-run costs in a fashion that permits us to simplify the analysis of the firm to the greatest extent possible without sacrificing those elements of cost essential to that analysis.

Recap Assuming the firm has already determined the least-cost method of producing each level of output, we can ascertain how this cost varies with the output level. Associated with each level of output is a total cost (which has both fixed and variable components), an average cost, and a marginal cost. We usually concentrate on how marginal and average costs vary with output, and commonly depict these cost relationships in the form of curves. If the firm faces limitations on the use of its inputs, both marginal and average cost curves can be expected to rise beyond the particular level of output at which this input limitation becomes effective.

The Most Profitable Level of Output	The properties of that output level at which the firm's profits are maximized

Because profit is defined as the difference between revenue and cost, it might seem that the most profitable level of output is that associated with minimum average cost, especially when price is constant, as in perfect competition. Indeed, if price is constant, the *profit per unit* is greatest at that output level at which average cost is least.

But, *total profit* is not necessarily maximized when profit per unit is at a maximum. Suppose the price of organic fertilizer is constant at $4 per ton, and that average cost is a minimum $3 per ton at an output of 1,000 tons. Profit per unit (at its maximum) is $1 per ton for an output of 1,000 tons, and total profit for this output is $1,000. If we produced another ton, even at less profit per ton than $1 (say at $.90 per ton), *we would add further to total profit*. Specifically, total profit for 1,001 tons would be $1,000.90. Consequently, 1,000 tons is clearly not the most profitable output level.

Marginal Analysis

The most profitable level of output is found, not by looking at *average cost*, but by observing how total profit is affected by incremental changes in output. If total profit rises when output is expanded incrementally beyond some particular level, then that level is obviously *less* than the most profitable level. On the other hand, if profit rises when output is contracted slightly from some particular level, then that level is obviously *greater* than the most profitable level. Finally, if total profit cannot be increased by either expanding or contracting output, the existing level is obviously the most profitable.

The kind of approach in which we note the effect of small changes in the value of a variable such as output is known as *marginal analysis*—a simplified version of the mathematical technique of differential calculus.

By considering the effect of a small increase in output, we see that there will be an increase in total profit if total revenue increases by more than total cost. The change in total profit that results from a one-unit increase in output can be called *marginal profit*. If this is positive, the extra unit adds to total profit—if it is negative, the extra unit reduces total profit. Indeed, if marginal profit is negative, total profit will be increased by *reducing* output.

The increase in total revenue associated with a one-unit increase in output is, of course, *marginal revenue,* while the analogous increase in total cost is *marginal cost.* Marginal profit is thus equal to marginal revenue less marginal cost.

From these arguments, we obtain the following basic rules:

1. *If marginal revenue is greater than marginal cost, it will be profitable to expand output, if this is feasible.*
2. *If marginal revenue is less than marginal cost, it will be profitable to contract output, if this is feasible.*

The Profit-Maximizing Rule

The profit-maximizing level of output is thus that level at which marginal revenue is neither greater than, nor less than, marginal cost; that is, where marginal cost and marginal revenue are equal. Abbreviating marginal cost to MC and marginal revenue to MR gives us this profit-maximizing rule in the simple form:

$$MR = MC.$$

A Numerical Example

Data for a hypothetical firm under perfect competition are given in Tables 7.2 and 7.3. Because the market price for this firm's product is $200 per ton, both average and marginal revenue are also $200 per ton. Hypothetical cost data that conform to the generally expected properties of such data are given. Table 7.2 sets out the basic data for total revenue, cost, and profit at each of various levels of output, together with the average revenue, cost, and profit derived from these. This table illustrates the point, already made, that we cannot deduce the profit-maximizing level of output from average data. Average cost is a minimum and profit per ton a maximum at each level of output up to four tons, but total profit is not maximized at any of these output levels. Indeed, total profit is higher at all output levels other than these.

Table 7.3 sets out the basic data for totals once again, but shows marginal cost, marginal revenue, and marginal profit. Here we see that marginal revenue exceeds marginal cost (yielding a positive marginal profit) for all output levels up to seven tons. Above eight tons, however, marginal cost exceeds marginal revenue (yielding a negative marginal profit). The firm's profits will increase if it expands output from any level less than seven tons, and will decline if it expands output beyond eight tons. At an output of seven tons, marginal cost equals marginal revenue, marginal profit is zero, and total profit is maximized.

Table 7.2
Cost and Revenue Data for
a Hypothetical Firm

(1) Output (tons)	(2) Total revenue ($)	(3) Total cost ($)	(4) Total profit ($)	(5) Average revenue ($/ton)	(6) Average cost ($/ton)	(7) Average profit ($/ton)
1	200	100	100	200	100	100
2	400	200	200	200	100	100
3	600	300	300	200	100	100
4	800	400	400	200	100	100
5	1,000	510	490	200	102	98
6	1,200	640	560	200	107	93
7	1,400	800	600	200	114	86
8	1,600	1,000	600	200	125	75
9	1,800	1,250	550	200	139	61
10	2,000	1,560	440	200	156	44

Table 7.3
Determining the Profit-Maximizing
Level of Output

(1) Output (tons)	(2) Total revenue ($)	(3) Total cost ($)	(4) Total profit ($)	(5) Marginal revenue ($/ton)	(6) Marginal cost ($/ton)	(7) Marginal profit ($/ton)
1	200	100	100			
2	400	200	200	200	100	100
3	600	300	300	200	100	100
4	800	400	400	200	100	100
5	1,000	510	490	200	110	90
6	1,200	640	560	200	130	70
7	1,400	800	600	200	160	40
8	1,600	1,000	600	200	200	0
9	1,800	1,250	550	200	250	−50
10	2,000	1,560	440	200	310	−110

But closer inspection reveals that the firm faces a dilemma. Specifically, *the maximum profit level is the same at both seven and eight tons.* Because the marginal revenue and marginal cost associated with increasing output from seven to eight tons are equal, the production and sale of the eighth ton has no effect on total profit. Which output, then, should the firm choose?

The honest answer is that, if profit were the only consideration, a real firm represented by the data in Tables 7.2 and 7.3 would simply be *indiffer-*

Figure 7.4

Cost and revenue curves for the hypothetical firm whose cost and revenue data are given in Tables 7.2 and 7.3.

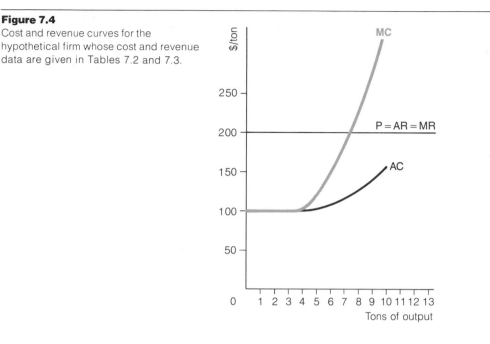

ent about producing seven or eight tons. For convenience, however, we'll assume that a firm would rather produce more than less, and adopt the following working rule: *If there is more than one level of output giving the maximum profit, the firm will choose the largest.* Consequently, in our example, we shall consider eight tons to be the level of output chosen by the firm.

If such an analysis were drawn graphically, we generally would portray all quantities changing continuously along curves instead of in distinct steps, as in tables. Marginal revenue and marginal cost curves will thus normally intersect at a point, indicating a unique profit-maximizing level of output. Figure 7.4 shows marginal cost and revenue curves drawn to fit the data presented in Tables 7.2 and 7.3. Note that as an indication of the continuous nature of these curves, the "unique" profit-maximizing level of output lies *midway* between seven and eight tons.

The Equilibrium Level of Output

Unless input prices, product demand, and/or technology change, a firm has no reason to vary its output from the existing profit-maximizing level. For this reason, the profit-maximizing level of output is often referred to as the *equilibrium level of output*.

The firm's equilibrium level of output obviously depends on both marginal cost and marginal revenue. The firm's marginal revenue in turn depends on the demand curve for *its* output, which in turn depends on both the overall market demand for the product and the amount potentially supplied by other firms. Thus, the output of the individual firm, given costs and the overall demand for the product, is determined by the prevailing *market structure*, that is, the number of and relationship among firms producing this product. We shall take up the effect of market structure on output decisions in the next two chapters.

Recap The most profitable level of output is normally not that at which average cost is least or profit per unit is highest. Rather, it is the output at which profit cannot be increased by either an increase or a decrease in output. A unit increase in output adds to total revenue an amount equal to marginal revenue, and adds to total cost an amount equal to marginal cost. If marginal revenue exceeds marginal cost, an increase in output will increase profit. Consequently, the most profitable level of output will be that at which marginal revenue and marginal cost are equal.

The Firm's Demand for Inputs

How the quantity of an input demanded by a firm varies with its price

Because inputs are used only to produce output, and because the proportion in which a firm employs inputs at each level of output is determined by the appropriate least-cost process, a particular level of output for a firm is associated with a particular collection of inputs. The existence of a most profitable level of output for the firm thus implies the existence of a most profitable collection of inputs, subject to the firm's constraints.

Consider a simple firm using only two inputs, capital and labor, in the typical short-run situation in which the quantity of capital is limited. To expand output beyond the point at which the capital limitation becomes effective, the firm must rely exclusively on additional labor and thus change to processes using a lower ratio of capital to labor than would be optimal if additional capital were freely available.

Marginal Product

We shall assume that our firm is initially at or beyond the level of output at which the capital limitation is effective. If the firm uses one more man-hour of labor with the same capital, output will rise provided input proportions are variable (that is, provided there are several processes). The amount by which the firm's level of output rises when an additional man-hour is used is called the *marginal product of labor*. This quantity is expressed in units of output per unit of input—tons per man-hour, for example.

The addition of labor will, of course, increase the firm's total cost. Because labor is the *only* factor being varied, the increase in total cost can be measured entirely in terms of the additional cost of labor. Because the increase in labor is one man-hour, the increase in total cost is necessarily the price of one man-hour (in dollars per man-hour), or the wage rate.

The increase in total cost occurs because more labor is used, which yields more output. The increase in total cost from producing *one* more unit of output is the *marginal cost*. Because the addition to output from an additional man-hour (marginal product) is not necessarily equal to one unit of output—it could be more than, or less than, or coincidentally equal to one—the resulting addition to total cost is not the marginal cost but is directly related to it.

To take a numerical example, suppose the marginal product of labor at the prevailing level of output is three tons per man-hour and the wage rate is $6 per man-hour. If we use an additional man-hour of labor, we add $6 to total cost and three tons to total output. To add one ton to total output, it follows that we would need to add only one-third of a man-hour, costing $6 $\times$ ⅓. *This* then is the marginal cost—$2.00 per ton.

Thus, we have the following important relationship between the wage rate, the marginal product of labor, and marginal cost:

$$MC = \frac{W}{MPL}, \quad \text{or} \quad MC \times MPL = W.$$

Because at the profit-maximizing level of output, we have $MC = MR$, we will also have

$$MR \times MPL = W.$$

The product, $MR \times MPL$, is often referred to as the *marginal revenue product of labor.*

Suppose the firm is initially in equilibrium (marginal cost and marginal revenue are equal), and the wage rate rises. What will happen? If, as in perfect competition, marginal revenue remains unchanged, the firm must adjust marginal cost to this level.

Because we are specifically assuming that labor is the only input that can be varied, the marginal cost is entirely labor cost. A rise in the wage rate means that every man-hour of labor costs more, including the marginal man-hour. Marginal cost can only be kept constant if the marginal man-hour produces enough extra output to make up for its additional cost. Consequently, the firm must make some adjustment to increase the output of the marginal man-hour, this output being the marginal product of labor. Of course, the only thing the firm *can* vary is the total quantity of labor employed, so the result of the wage change depends on how the marginal product of labor (that is, the output of the marginal man-hour) changes when the total quantity of labor changes.

The Law of Diminishing Returns

We expect the marginal product of labor to *fall* as the quantity of labor is increased with the quantity of other inputs remaining fixed. Why? Our general line of reasoning is as follows:

With capital fixed, additional labor will first be used in those processes that provide the maximum possible addition to output from each unit of labor. As we add more and more labor, however, we become increasingly constrained by the lack of additional machines. We must use the additional labor in processes that yield less and less additional output per additional man-hour.

Thus, if plant and equipment remain unchanged, the marginal product of labor will decline as additional labor is added. This property of production in the short run is commonly called the *law of diminishing returns.*

To revert back to the effect of our original wage change, increasing the marginal product of labor when the wage rises can only be achieved by cutting back on the quantity of labor—taking workers off those processes giving the least return per additional man-hour. Thus, an *increase* in the wage rate will *reduce* the quantity of labor demanded by the firm. Conversely, a decrease in the wage rate will increase the firm's quantity of labor demanded. *Demand curves for inputs thus slope downward just as demand curves for outputs do.*

Although our analysis has focused on labor, it applies to any other input that can be varied while other inputs remain fixed. It does not apply, however, if there are fixed input proportions (that is, a single production process), and hence no possibility of varying a single input.

Recap A firm for which labor is the only input that can be varied will have its variable cost determined exclusively by its labor cost. Each additional man-hour of labor will increase total output by an amount called the marginal product of labor, and will increase costs by the amount of the wage. By dividing the wage by the marginal product of labor, we arrive at the addition to cost per unit of output, or marginal cost. From this we can compute the firm's demand curve for labor. This curve will be downward sloping because the marginal revenue product of labor, which the profit-maximizing firm attempts to equate with the wage rate, declines as more labor is employed.

Capsule Supplement 7.2   **The Role of Finance in Production**

The simple analysis of the firm proceeds as though production and sale occur simultaneously—an approximation that is adequate for most purposes but one that fails to reflect the importance of finance in the productive sector of the economy. Because production normally precedes sale, inputs must be purchased before revenues are obtained from the sale of output. Hence, the firm must be able to pay wages in the *present* for labor used to produce something that will be sold in the *future* (next week, next month, or even next year).

Suppose we form a company and hire labor valued at $800 to produce goods this week that will be sold for $1,000 at the end of next week. (We'll assume that the $200 difference between revenue and wages, representing other miscellaneous payments, does not have to be paid out until the product is sold.) At the end of the first week, our firm must be in a position to meet its initial payroll even though it will not have received a penny in revenue. We must begin with at least $800 for this purpose, in cash or in our bank account.

The financial resources needed by a firm to pay for those inputs that must be acquired before its output can be sold are called *working capital* (or *circulating capital*). Working capital is not confined to payroll requirements, but typically includes payments for raw materials and other physical resources without which a firm simply cannot operate. The amount of working capital required depends not only on the scale of a firm's operations but also on the *period of production*. A haircut, for example, has a very short period of production because it can be sold within minutes of the initial application of labor. A New York skyscraper, on the other hand, will normally be characterized by a long period of production, and the builder may have to finance wage and other payments for months or even years before the product is ready to be sold.

Without adequate working capital, an entrepreneur's hands are tied. If he is sufficiently wealthy, he may be able to supply it himself. Typically, however, he'll need to *borrow* it from a bank or other financial institution. For a product with a lengthy production period, like an apartment house or an aircraft carrier, he may borrow part from the ultimate buyer by requiring partial payments as construction progresses. In any case, when the product is finished, the firm can repay its borrowed working capital out of the proceeds of the sale. But it will need to borrow again for the next production cycle. Working capital thus remains a continuous requirement so long as the firm remains in business.

The shortage of working capital is a major factor that hinders economic growth in many of the poorer countries, and is often caused by inadequate financial institutions. While fertilizer may increase the output of peasant farms by 50 percent, few peasants have the working capital with which to buy fertilizer even though they would easily be able to make repayments from the increase in output. Banks can exert considerable influence on the industrial structure of a region or country by their willingness or reluctance to lend working capital to various types of enterprises. It should be noted that the need for working capital is not confined to capitalist economies—Soviet enterprises must also pay wages in advance of receipts from production, and the state-operated *Gosbank* provides loans for this purpose.

Exercises

1. A firm has two processes available for producing hybrid rutabagas. At levels that each give twenty tons of rutabagas per year, the required inputs of labor and land are:

	To produce 20 tons	
Process	Man-years	Acre-years
P_1	2	120
P_2	3	80

The fixed price for the use of an acre of land for a year is $100. Which of the processes will be used at each of the following levels of annual wage?
   a. $2,500
   b. $3,500
   c. $4,500

2. Compare the change in least total cost of producing twenty tons with the change in the labor cost when the wage changes from $2,500 to $3,500, and then from $3,500 to $4,500.

3. The following table shows total variable cost for a hypothetical firm.

Output	Total variable cost
0	0
1	5
2	10
3	15
4	20
5	25
6	36
7	56
8	96
9	180
10	400

Compute the firm's
   a. marginal cost.
   b. average variable cost.

4. Draw the average and marginal cost curves for this hypothetical firm, assuming zero fixed cost.

5. Draw the average variable cost, average fixed cost, and average total cost curves, as well as the marginal cost curve, for this hypothetical firm if it has a fixed cost of $42.

For Thought and Discussion

1. If you were in charge of a firm, would you operate it to maximize profits? If not, what would you use as the criterion for determining how much you would produce?

2. Under what circumstances might a firm continue to increase output even though each additional unit sold brings in less than the direct cost of producing it?

3. In what ways, if any, do you think higher education would be changed if all colleges were organized as profit-maximizing firms?

Chapter 8

The Perfectly Competitive Economy

Terms and Concepts

Industry
Industry supply curve
Long-run competitive price
Interconnected markets
General equilibrium
Efficient allocation of resources
Optimum output mix
Shadow price

A Frame of Reference

Why perfect competition provides a frame of reference for both analysis and policy

There has probably never been an economy characterized by universally perfect competition, that is, an economy in which the market for every product and every input is such that no one buyer or seller is so important that his actions can perceptibly affect the equilibrium market price. There have, of course, always been individual markets—such as those for certain agricultural commodities—whose structures are essentially perfectly competitive. But such markets have always coexisted with imperfect competition elsewhere in the economy.

Why then do we study the perfectly competitive economy? The answer is not so much to learn about specific markets that may be perfectly competitive, but to establish a frame of reference for analyzing the effects of *imperfect competition* and to lay the groundwork for examining microeconomic policy. Why do we choose perfect competition as our frame of reference? There are three basic reasons:

1. A perfectly competitive economy is the only economy simple enough to analyze in its overall operation. While there are well-defined models of various types of imperfectly competitive *markets,* there exists no clear analysis (even at the most advanced levels) of an *entire economy* that is imperfectly competitive.

2. Whereas perfect competition is a uniquely defined market structure, *imperfect* competition means literally any structure that is not perfectly competitive. Given the diversity of such structures, there is no such thing as *the* model of imperfect competition, only a large number of different models.

3. A perfectly competitive economy possesses certain "ideal" properties with respect to resource use and the allocation of goods among consumers. Because these properties are often sought as ends in themselves, much economic policy involves inducing the economy to perform *as if* it were perfectly competitive.

In this chapter we shall describe the operation of a perfectly competitive economy—albeit a hypothetical one—and outline its optimal properties.

Recap We study perfect competition, which admittedly characterizes no known economy, because it provides a useful frame of reference. This usefulness derives from the fact that a perfectly competitive economy exhibits (1) relative simplicity of analysis, (2) uniqueness of specification compared with the varieties of imperfect competition, and (3) certain optimal properties that form the basis of much microeconomic policy.

| **Production and Supply** | How supply curves in a perfectly competitive economy are derived from the cost curves of firms |

The analysis of the individual firm under perfect competition conforms to the general analysis of the firm presented in Chapter 7, subject to the fact that such a firm is, by definition, one whose share of the market is so small that its variations in output have no perceptible effect on market price. Farmer Schultz, representing a firm of this kind, thus takes the price of wheat (as well as the prices of his inputs) as given, and adjusts his level of output so as to maximize profits at those prices.

Analytically then, the existence of perfect competition implies that the firm can sell as much or as little as it chooses at the going price. Hence, if the product price is $10, the firm will obtain $10 from selling an additional unit whatever its level of output, provided it remains small relative to the market. In other words, the firm's marginal revenue (the increase in total revenue that results from the sale of an additional unit of output) is constant and equal to $10. The general profit-maximizing rule—equality of marginal cost and marginal revenue—therefore takes on a special simplified form under perfect competition:

For the perfectly competitive firm, the profit-maximizing level of output will be that at which marginal cost is equal to price (MC = P), *because price is equal to marginal revenue.*

Figure 8.1 illustrates the equilibrium of a perfectly competitive firm facing a given set of cost curves and a market price of $10. The profit-maximizing level of output is Q, at which the marginal cost curve intersects the line representing price (and thus both marginal and average revenue). The total *profit* of such a firm is equal to the profit per unit (price less *average cost*) multiplied by the quantity sold, and is thus equal to the area of the shaded rectangle.

The Firm's Supply Curve

By studying Figure 8.2, it is easy to see what level of output the firm will sell at different prices. At price P_1, the firm will sell quantity Q_1, at which marginal cost is equal to P_1. At price P_2, lower than P_1, the firm will sell quantity Q_2, at which marginal cost is equal to P_2. Similarly, the output at price P_3 is Q_3. At price P_4, equal to the firm's minimum average cost, the firm will rest on the verge of going out of business, and indeed will do so if the price falls below P_4—say, to P_5—since it will then incur a *loss* on every bushel sold that can be avoided by producing nothing.

Thus, we can ascertain the firm's planned output for any given price from its marginal cost curve. Each point on this curve, corresponding to a price read from the vertical axis, indicates the quantity that will be supplied at

Figure 8.1
The equilibrium output for a firm under perfect competition. The shaded area represents the firm's equilibrium profit.

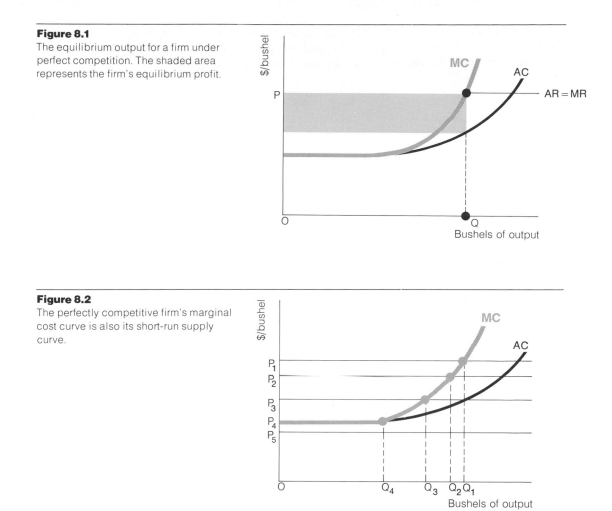

that price, read from the horizontal axis. *The firm's marginal cost curve is thus its short-run supply curve.* Because the marginal cost curve rises for outputs beyond the level past which minimum average cost can no longer be achieved, the supply curve also rises and thus has the positive slope we've come to expect.

Relevant Market Circumstances

Because the firm's supply curve coincides with its marginal cost curve, the supply curve will be affected by any change in the firm's marginal cost structure. The market circumstances that influence the firm's supply— those things that, if changed, would give a different supply curve—are consequently those things that affect marginal cost. These obviously include wages and other input prices, the technology of production, and, in the case of Farmer Schultz's wheat, seasonal weather conditions.

The Industry

Market supply is determined by the collective behavior of all firms that produce the same product. We refer to this collection of firms as the *industry*. If we assume that the number of firms comprising the industry is fixed, we can determine the total quantity supplied by the industry at a given price by summing the planned sales of all firms at that price. By doing this for every price, we can derive the *short-run industry supply curve* that will have the same general shape as each individual firm's supply curve, except that the quantities will be much greater. The supply curve S_1 in Figure 8.3 is such a curve, similar to the curve for the individual firm in Figure 8.2, but with the quantity axis in thousands of bushels rather than in bushels.

An Analysis of the Market

We can now begin our analysis of a perfectly competitive industry, using the short-run industry supply curve in conjunction with the market demand curve. Look again at Figure 8.3. The demand curve may intersect the short-run supply curve, S_1, either on the rising portion, as D_1 does at X_1, or on the horizontal portion, as D_2 does at X_2. If the curves intersect on the horizontal portion, the market price will be equal to each firm's minimum average cost, and profits will be zero. While no firm will have any particular incentive to expand beyond its present size, no firm will have an incentive to shut down either. The status quo will be maintained because the value of alternative employment of each firm's capital and managerial talent will have already been included in its costs. Given the absence of any incentive for firms to expand or shut down, or for new firms to enter the market, market equilibrium under these conditions constitutes a *long-run equilibrium*. This conclusion could also have been reached by noting that the horizontal portion of the short-run cost curve coincides with the long-run cost curve.

Expansion and Entry

If, on the other hand, equilibrium occurs at a point like X_1 on the rising portion of the short-run supply curve, marginal cost, and hence price, will exceed average cost, and firms will receive profits greater than zero. This will have two basic consequences. First, firms already in the industry will attempt to expand their productive capacity by obtaining more of their limited input. Such expansion will move the point at which these firms' marginal cost curves begin to rise to the right. Thus the point at which the industry supply curve begins to rise will also move to the right. Second,

Figure 8.3
Long-run market equilibrium for the industry under perfect competition.

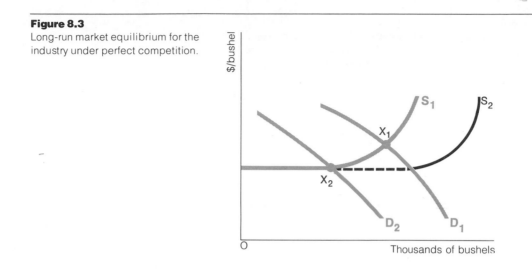

new firms will be attracted into the industry, which will move the rising part of the industry supply curve even farther to the right. Incidentally, entry into a market does not necessarily mean a major change for a firm. By deciding to plant corn instead of wheat, for example, a farmer leaves the "wheat industry" and enters the "corn industry."

These tendencies will persist as long as there are positive profits, that is, as long as the market demand curve intersects the rising part of the industry supply curve. A long-run equilibrium will eventually be reached when the rising part of the industry supply curve has moved sufficiently far to the right (like the curve S_2 in Figure 8.3) that its intersection with the market demand curve occurs on the industry supply curve's horizontal portion.

The Long-Run Competitive Price

The level of the horizontal portion of the industry supply curve is determined by the horizontal portion of the marginal cost curves of the individual firms within the industry. This level represents the minimum average cost at which the product can be manufactured, given the existing technology and input prices. We can thus conclude:

In the long run, if full adjustment has been made to a given technology and constant input prices, the price in a perfectly competitive market will be equal to the minimum average cost of production.

Industry Dynamics

Under perfect competition, adjustments to changing industry conditions will generally occur through the entry and exit of firms.

Suppose the development of a new production technique results in a

Figure 8.4

The effect of introducing a net low-cost technique on (a) the marginal cost curve (and hence the supply curve) of a firm adopting this new technique, and (b) the industry supply curve and long-run equilibrium after all adjustments to the introduction of this technique have been made.

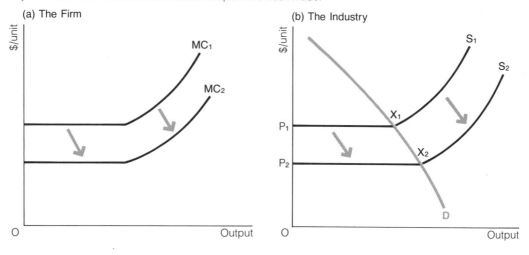

marked downward shift in the cost curves of those firms adopting it. The applicability of this technique to the industry may first become apparent to an outside firm—perhaps because the new process is based on production methods used elsewhere in the economy. What will happen if this firm enters the industry with lower costs than the firms already there?

Under perfectly competitive conditions, the entry of a single firm will have no perceptible effect on the market equilibrium price. Hence, the new firm, subject to the same price as all other firms in the industry, can be expected to reap large profits. The success and profitability of this firm will eventually become apparent to other firms in the industry, and possibly to other potential entrants. These firms will respond by adopting the new technique. This response will normally lead to a reduction in the level of marginal cost associated with each level of output, and thus to a shift to the right in each firm's supply curve, as illustrated in Figure 8.4(a).

The shift in the supply curves of the first few firms that adopt the new technique will not be expected to have more than a negligible effect on industry supply. As the number of such firms increases, however, the effect will eventually become noticeable, and the industry supply curve will begin to shift downward and to the right as S_1 does in Figure 8.4(b). The equilibrium price will then begin to fall, and firms using the old technique will find their profits squeezed—quite severely if a long-run equilibrium initially existed with price equal to (the old) minimum average cost. These firms will be forced either to adopt the new technique or to leave the industry. This latter option may take the form of filing for bankruptcy, selling out to a new entrepreneur, or merely switching to an industry that promises a greater chance of success.

The larger the number of firms adopting the new technique, the more rapid will be the increase in industry supply, the decline in market price, and hence the exit or adaptation of the remaining firms. The only firms surviving this adjustment process will be those employing the new technique. As demonstrated in Figure 8.4(b), the resulting long-run equilibrium price, P_2, will be equal to the new minimum average cost associated with this technique.

Like most long-run economic processes, adjustments like this are rarely completed. It may take years for the full process of entry, exit, and technological adaptation to be achieved. In the meantime, while the "new" technology is still being absorbed, even "newer" technological advances occur. These may require additional adjustments before the original adaptation is at all close to being complete. At any point in time, an industry will contain a broad spectrum of firms in various stages of adjustment to past influences—some employing the latest techniques, some the next-to-latest, and others the oldest.

Recap A perfectly competitive firm accepts the market price as given, and adjusts its output to make the greatest profit at the going price. Because the most profitable level of output is that at which price is equal to marginal cost, we can ascertain the firm's planned output at each price directly from the marginal cost curve, which is thus the firm's supply curve. The market supply curve is constructed by aggregating the supply curves of the individual firms. High profits will cause new firms to enter the industry; losses will cause firms to leave. Thus, market supply is affected by a change in the number of firms as well as in the productive capacity of individual firms. Such adjustments in the number and size of firms result in a long-run equilibrium price equal to the minimum average cost of production.

The Interconnection of Markets

How events in one market affect, and are affected by, events in others

In discussing the operation of a *single* perfectly competitive market in Chapters 4 and 5, we treated everything other than price and quantity in that market as "circumstances" determined elsewhere in the economy. We shall now consider the operation of the economy as a whole, recognizing that all markets operate simultaneously, and hence that the "circumstances'' of one market are heavily influenced by equilibrium conditions in others.

In Chapter 6, we demonstrated that consumers' choices among collections of beans and jeans depend on their income and the relative prices of these two goods. If income remains constant while the price of beans rises, consumers are expected to reduce their beans purchases. But, in adjusting their purchases of beans to the new price, they will generally change the quantity of jeans they buy as well. In other words, *the quantity of jeans demanded depends on the price of beans as well as on the price of jeans themselves.*

Suppose the price of beans changes. Consumers will then buy a different quantity of jeans, even though the price of jeans has remained fixed. This indicates that the demand curve for jeans has shifted. Why? Because the price of beans is one of the circumstances of the jeans market, and that market has changed. But that's not the end of it. The shift in the demand curve for jeans will affect the equilibrium price of jeans and may potentially cause a change in the demand for *beans*. Thus, events in the beans and jeans markets are not independent—equilibrium in one market can be established only when equilibrium is established in the other.

Interconnections occur on the supply side as well. Consider the markets for wheat and corn. Many farmers have the option of growing either, and will grow whichever is the more profitable. A fall in the price of wheat may cause some farmers to "exit" the wheat industry and "enter" the corn industry. This adjustment will increase the supply and thus reduce the price of corn. This will, in turn, have repercussions in the wheat market, and so forth.

Markets for resources are interconnected with output markets in a similar way. A fall in wages will change marginal cost curves and thus affect supply in many product markets. But wages also represent income to those who receive them, and a decline in wages will trigger a change in the demand for many of the goods wage earners buy.

In the real world, there is a diversity of markets. Consequently interconnections between any two markets may be quite small. On the demand side, markets for *close substitutes*, such as beef and pork, will tend to be quite sensitive to one another, whereas markets for unrelated goods, such as brass candlesticks and denture adhesive, will normally bear little, if any, relationship. On the supply side, interconnections will be closest when more than one good can be produced by the same firm with little technical reorganization, as in growing wheat or corn.

Recap Both the demand and supply of a good depend on the prices of other goods. Thus a good's demand and supply curves will shift as prices in other markets vary, and consequent changes in its own price will affect demand and supply in those other markets. Final equilibrium cannot be established in one market until it is also established in all those related to it.

General Equilibrium

The network of compatibility requirements that must be met for all markets to be in equilibrium

We've now outlined the characteristic behavior of the principal decision-makers in the economy—consumers and firms—and shown that, under perfectly competitive conditions, each has specific plans about what and how much to buy or sell under various market circumstances and at various prices. We've also defined market equilibrium as a state in which market prices and circumstances are such that all buyers and sellers can fulfill their plans. Finally, we've shown that markets are interconnected, because the equilibrium price in each market constitutes a "circumstance" that is potentially relevant to every other market.

In advanced industrial societies like the United States, millions of individual decision-makers in households and firms reach billions of independent decisions every day concerning thousands of different goods. Yet these decisions must somehow be *related*—the aggregate quantity demanded of each good does, after all, equal the aggregate quantity supplied. *All decisions in a market economy, though made independently by a large number of individuals, must therefore ultimately be compatible with each other.*

An important question is whether or not compatibility is automatically guaranteed by the structure of the system as a whole. Stated otherwise, is the behavior of each individual consumer in a perfectly competitive economy necessarily compatible with the behavior of every other consumer, with that of every producer, and with equilibrium in every market?

Compatibility Requirements

More specifically, we need to know whether or not equilibrium prices can be found for all goods and factors such that:

1. all consumers can freely choose their most preferred collection of goods and services subject to their budget constraints, which, in turn, are determined by their initial endowment of resources, resource prices, and the prices of goods.
2. all producers can freely maximize their profits subject to the existing technology, any input limitations they may face, and market conditions for their inputs and outputs.

If such prices can be found, these prices, the quantities of all goods produced and consumed, and the quantities of all factors used constitute the conditions of a *general equilibrium* of the economy.

Such a set of conditions need not be unique. There may be other prices and quantities that also constitute a general equilibrium. If, for example, there are constant returns to scale in production and no input limitations on individual firms, we may well have unique relative prices, a unique list of quantities consumed and services provided by individuals, and a unique aggregate output of each good. But we may also have an infinite number of ways in which production can be divided among individual firms. This is because the size of each individual firm is indeterminant, even though the "size" of the industry is not. All policy implications about general equilibrium and social welfare are quite independent of how production is divided among firms, as long as each industry is perfectly competitive.

More on Interconnections

Because everything is interconnected, the determination of whether or not all the pieces fit together is not a simple matter. Consumer incomes, for example, depend on the wage rate that, in turn, is determined by supply and demand conditions in the labor market. But the demand for labor is affected by the prices producers receive for goods and services. These, of course, are determined by supply and demand conditions in output markets. Finally, because demand in such markets is influenced by consumer incomes, we've come full circle—consumer incomes depend on consumer incomes.

Interconnections go not only from consumers to factor markets, to producers, to goods markets, back to consumers, but exist among different output markets and among different factor markets. The demand for labor depends not only on production levels, but also on available quantities of capital and other factors, just as the demand for one good depends on the prices of other goods.

In order for a general equilibrium to exist, therefore, the wage rate must be exactly that at which:

1. consumers will choose to supply the number of man-hours actually used;
2. the amount of labor income generated, when combined with earnings from other sources, will give consumers incomes such that they will just buy the quantities of goods produced at the equilibrium prices;
3. producers, given equilibrium levels of output and prices, will choose to employ the number of man-hours consumers choose to supply; and
4. producers, taking alternative production processes into account, will choose to combine the actual quantities of capital (and other inputs) with the equilibrium quantity of labor.

Conditions analogous to these four must be satisfied by the price of every other factor and every good in the economy. It follows that:

1. *all general equilibrium prices and quantities depend on each other;* and
2. *no one price can be determined without reference to the rest of the economy.*

Could It Work?

Complex though the system is, it can work—at least under perfectly competitive conditions. That is, given specific consumer preferences and an initial endowment of resources, a potential set of product and factor prices that will yield an equilibrium in all markets and make all individual decisions compatible will exist.

Recap An actual society contains millions of individual decision-makers making billions of economic decisions. Our analysis of how individuals make decisions holds only if these decisions are demonstrably compatible with each other. The state of the economy in which these decisions are indeed compatible is called a general equilibrium.

Capsule Supplement 8.1   **Leon Walras, 1834–1910**

Leon Walras (pronounced "Vahl-rah"), more than any other individual, is responsible for modern general equilibrium analysis. While the idea that everything is somehow connected, and that independent decision-makers must behave compatibly if the economic system is to work, had surfaced long before Walras, no one had described the nature of the interconnections or shown that universal perfect competition would guarantee compatibility. Walras painstakingly did both. Because his analysis was mathematically complex, the full impact of his work is not apparent in the elementary treatment of general equilibrium analysis presented in this text.

Ironically, Walras, a patron saint of modern mathematical economics, possessed a weaker mathematical background than did Alfred Marshall, who used little mathematics in his work, and whose followers disavowed mathematical economics right through the 1940s. As a matter of fact, Walras flunked the entrance exam to the Ecole Polytechnique in Paris because of his poor math, and had to settle for the less prestigious Ecole des Mines.

Moreover, Walras had no academic training in economics. What he knew at the outset of his career he had picked up from his father—an unorthodox minor economist who was never given a post in the profession. After studying in the Ecole des Mines, Walras tried his hand at writing. He succeeded in publishing a novel in 1858 before deciding to follow his father's footsteps into economics. Because he had neither formal training in the subject nor access to the "in-group" of economists in Paris, he was unable to obtain a post in the French economics profession. Consequently, he took a succession of different jobs in Paris, including writing and lecturing on social reform.

The most important event in Walras's career occurred in 1870. Though favored by only four of seven members of the appointment committee, he was offered a post to teach economics in the law faculty at the Academy of Lausanne in Switzerland. At Lausanne he all but abandoned the socially oriented economics on which he had previously concentrated and turned to pure theory. Within several years he published a book entitled *Elements d'Economie Pure* that contained his general equilibrium theory, and was to become a classic. Despite the absence of colleagues in his field and the general attitude of his law students, who regarded economics as a tiresome necessity of the curriculum, Walras remained at Lausanne until his death. Because of his isolated position, he carried on an extensive correspondence with economists all over the world.

Walras was a cantankerous and rather paranoid eccentric with little formal training in either mathematics or economics. In spite of—or perhaps because of—these traits, he was able to introduce something important and original to economic theory. Recognition commenced only in his old age, and was truly achieved only after his death.

The "Ideal" Properties of Perfect Competition

How a perfectly competitive equilibrium results in the optimal use of society's resources

We mentioned earlier that a perfectly competitive equilibrium exhibits certain ideal properties. The time has come to spell them out, one at a time.

1. *The existence of a perfectly competitive equilibrium guarantees the absence of any involuntary unemployment of resources.*

Equilibrium in a given factor market implies that, at the prevailing price, resource owners do not want to supply more of the factor than they currently supply. It also implies that producers do not want to employ more of this factor than they currently employ. Equilibrium in the labor market does not necessarily mean that every able-bodied person is employed a full work week, therefore, but simply that everyone who wants to work *at the going wage* has the opportunity to do so—and for as many hours a week as desired.

Suppose the wage is $120 per forty-hour week and Ms. Jones does not work, although she would do so at a wage of $140. Is there a social loss from Ms. Jones's failure to work? The answer is no. By being willing to work for a wage of $140 but not $120, Ms. Jones reveals that she prefers forty hours of leisure per week to $120 worth of goods, but that she values this leisure time at less than $140 worth of goods. If forced to work, she would be exchanging leisure time (worth more to her than $120) for $120, and be worse off in terms of her *own* preferences. The rest of society remains unaffected by her choice. By working she would increase market production by goods worth $120 but increase her own consumption by $120, leaving the same amount for the rest of society whether she works or not.

Thus, *society can achieve an optimum mix of goods and leisure or other nonwork activities only if everyone who wants work at the going wage can find it, and anyone who does not can choose not to work, even though more goods could be produced if everyone worked.*

The existence of *involuntary unemployment*—persons wanting to work at the going wage but unable to do so—would be evidence that the labor market is not in equilibrium.

2. *The existence of a perfectly competitive equilibrium guarantees an efficient allocation of resources.*

Let us consider the consequences of reallocating resources among industries, assuming a perfectly competitive equilibrium. Specifically, let's examine the effect of moving labor from agriculture to textile production.

We'll assume that the type of labor required by the two industries is identical, in which case the wage will be the same in each. Moreover, because both industries are characterized by a perfectly competitive equilibrium, price will equal marginal cost in each. Using the subscripts A for agriculture and T for textiles, and drawing on results presented in Chapter 7, we have:

$$P_A = MC_A = W/MPL_A \text{ in agriculture,}$$
$$P_T = MC_T = W/MPL_T \text{ in textiles,}$$

where P is the price, MC is the marginal cost, W is the wage, and MPL is the marginal product of labor.

By cross-multiplying, we obtain

$$P_A \times MPL_A = W = P_T \times MPL_T.$$

That is, the value of goods produced from the marginal man-hour of labor will be the same in each industry and equal to the wage (say $3). A shift of one man-hour of labor from agriculture into textiles will simply reduce agricultural output by $3 and increase textile output by $3. The value of output will remain unchanged. Thus, *we cannot increase the total value of output* by diverging from the allocation reached by perfect competition. By drawing on the property of diminishing marginal productivity, we could show that any substantial reallocation would actually reduce the total value of output.

Such efficient resource allocation will not generally prevail under imperfect competition. For example, suppose a strong union pushes textile wages up to $4 per hour while farm wages remain at $3 per hour. Even with perfect competition in the textile market, textile firms would only employ labor to the point at which the value of goods produced by the marginal man-hour is $4. Thus, a reallocation of one man-hour from agriculture to textiles would reduce farm output by $3 but would increase textile output by $4—a net gain of $1 in the total value of goods produced. It's obvious that the union, in order to maintain the textile wage at $4, would have to restrict entry into the textile labor force. Consequently, a reallocation of labor to increase output would require policy measures to provide an "open shop" in textiles.

3. *The existence of a perfectly competitive equilibrium guarantees an optimum output mix, in the sense that no improvement can be made by increasing the output of one good at the expense of others.*

In equilibrium, consumers allocate their budgets so the last dollar's worth of every good purchased is worth the same as the last dollar's worth of every other. Otherwise, consumers could improve their status by spending a dollar less on the good that brings the least utility per dollar, and a dollar more on the good that brings the most utility. This implies that in equilibrium no consumer can be made better off by being given an additional dollar's worth of one good and being relieved of a dollar's worth of another. Hence, no one can gain if an additional dollar's worth of one good is produced at the expense of reducing the output of some other good by the equivalent dollar's worth.

For these reasons, an *optimal output mix* cannot be reached under imperfect competition. Suppose manufacturing is imperfectly competitive, while agriculture is not. Firms in both industries will equate marginal cost with marginal revenue. But, as shown in Chapter 7, marginal revenue is necessarily less than price under imperfect competition. Consequently, marginal cost will be less than price in manufacturing. Specifically, let's assume that marginal cost is equal to half the price, so the marginal cost of goods selling for $2 is only $1. Now let's shift resources valued at $1 into manufacturing from agriculture. Because agriculture is perfectly competitive, the market value of goods forgone with the marginal dollar's worth of resources is $1 (since marginal cost equals price). The market value of goods produced with the marginal dollar's worth of resources in manufacturing, however, is $2. Hence, there is a $1 ($2 − $1) net increase in the value of output that results from the reallocation. This proves that the original allocation was non-optimal. This example illustrates that perfect competition represents a social optimum only when *all* markets are perfectly competitive. As we shall demonstrate in Chapter 12, *some* perfect competition in an economy characterized by *some* imperfect competition may be worse than none at all.

Recap The general equilibrium of a perfectly competitive economy is characterized by the absence of involuntarily unemployed resources, an efficient allocation of those resources that are employed, and an optimum output mix. Such an equilibrium is thus "ideal" in the sense that no rearrangement can make anyone better off without simultaneously making someone worse off.

The Market System in a Command Economy

A demonstration of the role of prices in an economic system

Let's consider a hypothetical economy whose structure is essentially perfectly competitive, and examine the possibility of it being operated as a command economy by a government whose only goal is to achieve the best interests of its citizens. We'll assume that the government knows the preferences of all consumers, the production technology, and the distribution of resources among households. In principle, it could then compute the prices and quantities that correspond to a general equilibrium. Such a computation would show:

1. the price of every good and factor.
2. the amount of every good produced by every producer and the quantity of every factor employed by every producer.
3. the amount of every good consumed and of every factor supplied by every consumer.

Centralized Control

The computation would also show the equilibrium quantities produced and consumed, and the required deliveries of each good from each producer to each consumer and of each factor from each consumer to each producer.

The quantities determined by our command economy would correspond precisely to those characterizing a perfectly competitive general equilibrium. Hence, the government could simply order producers to make deliveries of goods and consumers deliveries of factors that were dictated by the computation. In this way, a fully centralized system could be organized to achieve the exact configuration of the economy represented by the competitive equilibrium without the need for prices or market transactions. For the United States this would annually involve about 500 billion orders to individual producers and consumers concerning the delivery of specific quantities of particular goods and factors.

Decentralization

Now consider an alternative to achieve the same end. Our government could issue a general instruction to all producers to buy inputs and sell outputs at certain announced prices and produce whatever level of output that would maximize the value of total revenue less total cost. (Because consumers can be presumed to act in accordance with their preferences, they would need no special instructions.) Having laid down the general rule of producer behavior, the government would then need simply to publish the computed equilibrium prices in the newspapers.

Again, the configuration of the economy would correspond to the competitive equilibrium, but be achieved this time simply by issuing a general rule and announcing a few thousand prices. It would make no difference whether the producers were government agencies or private firms, as long as they obeyed the rule.

Given these two schemes, it is evident that a general equilibrium can be attained under central direction either by

1. exact scheduling of all quantities of all goods and factors to be transferred between all producers and consumers, or
2. issuing a general rule accompanied by a list of prices.

Prices as Information

In other words, all the information required to achieve a general equilibrium can be conveyed by prices alone, once the rules of behavior are established. Thus, prices are highly efficient conveyors of information. This will be true as long as prices are accepted without question, and no attempt is made to influence them by behavior comparable to that of imperfect competition.

Prices that are devised centrally with the object of inducing individual decision-makers to behave in a certain way are called *shadow prices*. Large corporations with numerous internal divisions that use each other's products as intermediate goods are moving toward the use of shadow prices to ensure the proper allocation of these goods. Socialist economies have also begun using methods involving shadow prices in lieu of detailed allocation plans.

Competitive Markets

While shadow prices theoretically enable a central authority to achieve a particular equilibrium point while leaving detailed decisions to decentralized units, *these prices must be computed* nonetheless. Here the special virtues of the market economy become apparent. Under perfect competition, the equilibrium prices determined by the market will be identical to the shadow prices that would otherwise have to be computed. In other words, *a competitive market economy computes its own shadow prices.*

The market mechanism thus automatically generates price information that assures that the actions of individual decision-makers are mutually compatible. Prices serve as *signals* that appropriately guide individual decision-makers when there is universal perfect competition (although they may well *misdirect* decision-makers if imperfect competition exists).

While profit-maximizing firms will obviously obey the rule of producing the level of output at which total revenue less total cost is maximized, they'll accept prices as fixed items of information only if they're perfectly competitive. A centralized economy can order the National Automobile Works to treat the shadow price of automobiles as fixed (and thus act as if it were perfectly competitive), but firms in a private-enterprise economy can be expected to use whatever economic power they can muster to influence price.

A *competitive* equilibrium with all its optimal properties can theoretically be achieved by a command economy using centrally computed shadow prices, or by a market economy in which shadow prices are computed automatically. In practice, the determination of a general equilibrium under a centralized system would be an enormous computational task, especially in light of the need to ascertain individual consumer preferences. The market economy, on the other hand, has many problems of its own that prevent such an equilibrium from being achieved. These are the subjects of discussion in Part 3 of this book.

Recap The prices and output levels associated with a perfectly competitive equilibrium could theoretically be attained by a central authority in either of two ways. Output levels could be computed and plants ordered to produce at these levels, or a list of shadow prices" could be calculated and producers ordered to produce at a level that maximizes total revenue less total cost. Thus, prices are seen to convey information to individual decision-makers. A market economy "computes" its own shadow prices and reaches an optimum state if the behavior of producers and consumers reacting to those prices is perfectly competitive.

Capsule Supplement 8.2   **The Soviet Economy**

In the text, we showed that an economy can potentially attain an optimal state either under perfect competition or under an ideal central plan. No real economy, capitalist or socialist, even remotely approaches this state. The American economy, as a leading example of capitalism, is far from perfectly competitive, while the Soviet economy, as a leading example of socialism (The Peoples' Republic of China would disagree no doubt), certainly does not possess the ideal central plan. Moreover, there are important structural and institutional reasons in both cases why divergences from the ideal are likely to persist.

The Soviet economy is operated not as a fully centralized command economy, but as a mixture of central planning and the use of the market. Generally speaking, consumers freely purchase goods and services out of their incomes, and workers freely choose their occupation and employer. In other words, the *demand side* of the consumer-goods market and the *supply side* of the labor market are much like those in a "free-enterprise" economy. The supply of goods and the demand for labor, on the other hand, are determined (or, at least, heavily influenced) by planning decisions. Finally, the production and distribution of capital goods are directly influenced by the plans on both the supply and demand sides.

The centralized component of the Soviet economy's operation is manifested in two related but not fully coordinated sets of decisions: the *physical plan* and the *financial plan*. The physical plan involves setting desired targets for the production of goods and the employment of resources. This plan must be balanced to ensure that the planned output of, say, electricity is consistent with the amount required to produce other target outputs. The financial plan is an attempt to achieve a broad balance in the flow of money. Such a balance is required to ensure that the total value of consumer-goods output at planned prices is equal to total consumer incomes generated at planned wage rates, and that the payments various productive sectors will be called on to make will be in balance with their financial receipts.

Both the financial plan and the operation of those economic sectors in which output quantities are not actually specified depend on resource and product prices. Such prices are determined, not by the operation of the market, but by state planners. The method for setting these prices has long been the subject of debate within the Soviet economics profession. While mathematical techniques do exist for determining truly optimal shadow prices (one of which, called linear programming, was actually pioneered by the Soviet mathematician Kantorovitch), such shadow prices have generally not been used in the Soviet planning process.

In comparison with the kind of shadow prices that would lead to an optimal allocation of resources and output, Soviet prices are considerably distorted. Prices of consumer goods, for example, are much higher relative to cost than are capital goods and raw materials. In effect, consumers are unable to afford consumer goods whose retail prices are significantly higher than their true social costs, and producers are tempted to use production methods that overemploy capital goods whose accounting costs are lower than their true social costs. Moreover, within the consumer-goods sector, there remains an ideological reluctance (which has been declining over the years) to use prices to match actual production levels with consumer demand. Consequently, some goods accumulate in stores and factories while others cause long lines and waiting lists.

In recent years, there has been a general movement toward economic reform in the Soviet Union, aimed at developing a system in which appropriate shadow prices are set uniformly in relation to social costs throughout the entire economy. Each individual reform has generated a counter-reform, but the net effect seems to be the development of a more efficient allocative mechanism.

Exercises

1. The widget industry contains 1,000 identical firms. Each firm's marginal cost is a constant 10 cents per widget up to an output of 100 widgets. Marginal cost increases by .1 cent per widget for every additional widget above 100—being 10.1 cents for 101 widgets, 10.2 cents for 102 widgets, and so on. Compute and draw the marginal cost schedule for each firm up to an output of 240 widgets. Compute and draw the *industry* supply schedule for prices up to 20 cents per widget.

2. The demand schedule for widgets is as follows:

Price (cents per widget)	Quantity demanded (thousands of widgets)
5	190
10	170
15	150
20	130

What will be the equilibrium price in the widget market if supply comes wholly from the industry described in question 1?

3. Suppose anyone can make widgets with the same costs as the firms in question 1. If the demand schedule for widgets is that given in question 2, what is the maximum number of firms that the widget industry will contain?

For Thought and Discussion

1. In principle, a planned economy can be made to produce exactly the same goods, distributed in the same way, as a perfectly competitive economy. Does this mean that the differences between those who favor planning and those who favor competition are trivial?

2. That a perfectly competitive equilibrium is optimal is based on the assumption that individual consumers are the best judges of their own welfare. Do you view this as a good working assumption for making policy judgments?

3. Adam Smith, universally regarded as the father of modern economics, thought that the government should perform almost no function other than provide defense and a legal system. Would Smith's prescription result in a perfectly competitive economy?

Part 3
Problems and Policy in the Market Economy

Chapters 9 through 14 are concerned with the practical operation of the market economy, with the problems it generates, and with the design of policy to alleviate those problems. Chapters 9 and 10 deal with the causes and effects of imperfect competition in the modern industrial economy and with associated policy matters. Chapter 11 considers situations in which the market cannot provide a solution, and Chapter 12 is concerned with the criteria for policy decisions involving microeconomic problems. Chapters 13 (the cities) and 14 (agriculture) discuss policy applications in specific problem areas that illustrate problem-solving.

Chapter 9
Imperfect Competition

Terms and Concepts

Laissez-faire
Economies of scale
Monopoly
Price-setter
Monopoly price
Barriers to entry
Indivisibilities in production
Monopoly markup
Monopoly profit
Social cost, social benefit
Natural monopoly
Antitrust legislation

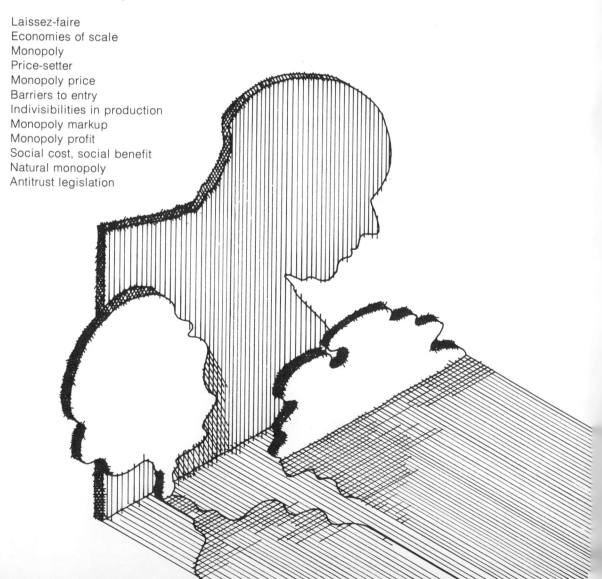

Why Competition Is Imperfect

Firms have incentives, and in some industries obvious means, to avoid perfect competition

In Chapter 8 we showed that, under the simple assumptions of our analysis, a perfectly competitive economy would be ideal from society's point of view. The passive reactions of individual firms to market-determined prices would result in the efficient use of resources and the production of an optimum output mix—all without the need for government intervention. Indeed, a picture of such an anarchistic but efficient economy, in which the role of government is restricted to such matters as law enforcement and national defense, was sketched by Adam Smith at the end of the eighteenth century, and has been the ideal of those who advocate the principle of *laissez-faire* (no government control of the economy) ever since.

But if perfect competition is so ideal, why doesn't it actually exist, especially in countries like the United States and Japan that have no ideological bias against it? The answer is simple: while it is certainly *in society's interest* for individual firms to behave as they would under perfect competition, *it is not necessarily in their own self-interest to do so.* As long as a firm has no control over price, its efforts to maximize profit will also serve to best allocate society's resources provided all other firms face the same conditions. But, as we shall demonstrate in this chapter, if a firm has some control over price, it can increase its profits beyond those attainable under perfect competition.

The typical firm thus has reason to acquire a market share large enough to permit an influence over price. Stated otherwise, *the typical firm has an incentive in the form of increased profits to become imperfectly competitive.*

But despite whatever incentive a firm might have to increase its market share, finding the way to do so is quite another thing. If 10 thousand small firms constitute a single industry, they obviously can't all attain a substantial share of the market. Indeed, an increase in the market share of any one such firm implies a decrease in the share retained by others. In agriculture, the opportunity for a single firm to dominate a national market simply does not exist, and most farms operate within a market structure approximating perfect competition.

In manufacturing, however, there are two important technical factors that tend to facilitate the growth of imperfect competition. One is the existence of *economies of scale* in production. This is the potential to produce large outputs at lower average cost than small outputs. A large firm may enjoy certain cost advantages that enable it to reduce prices, put small firms out of business, and expand its market share. The other special feature of manufacturing is the potential for *product differentiation*. This refers to the ability of firms to produce products that are just different enough from those of other firms that an individualized product market can be established for each—something rarely possible in agriculture. We shall discuss economies of scale later in this chapter; product differentiation will be discussed in the next chapter.

In addition to whatever incentives and means firms might have to avoid perfect competition, society requires certain goods that simply cannot be produced under this market structure. These include public goods, like national defense, which cannot be subdivided and sold to individual consumers, and other goods, like public utilities, for which there are enormous economies of scale. Even without imperfect competition, government policy may be required to ensure that these things are produced. In Chapter 11 we shall discuss cases in which the market completely fails to provide such things.

We should further note that the desirable properties of perfect competition derive from the existence of a *general equilibrium*. As we've demonstrated, no market equilibrium can be regarded as permanent, and disequilibrium may persist indefinitely in industries experiencing the entry or exit of many firms.

Consequently, despite its desirable features, a perfectly competitive economy is neither self-sustaining nor capable of solving all economic problems as economists once believed. The development of *microeconomic policy*—guidelines as to how, when, and where the government should intervene in the operation of the market—was inevitable. From now through Chapter 14, we shall focus our concern on problems requiring definite policy action, criteria for designing policy, and examples of specific policy applications.

Recap While perfect competition may result in the optimal allocation of resources for society as a whole, each individual firm can expect to make higher profits under a monopolistic or other imperfectly competitive structure. If there are economies associated with large-scale operation, it is almost inevitable that some firms will attain an important share of the market. Thus, perfect competition is not self-sustaining, and economic efficiency cannot be attained without some conscious form of microeconomic policy.

Monopolistic Behavior

Price and output determination under monopoly

A firm has a *monopoly* in a market if it is the only supplier of a given product, and if that product is sufficiently different from other products that its demand curve is relatively insensitive to changes in other markets. Regional companies in the Bell Telephone System, for example, have true monopolies in the supply of most telephone services within their respective areas. The Ford Motor Company, on the other hand, while admittedly having a "monopoly" of sorts in the supply of Pintos, Broncos, and Mustangs, operates in markets that are intimately related to those in which vehicles produced by Chrysler and General Motors are sold. Consequently, our basic analysis of monopoly does not apply to it.

Except for certain so-called *natural monopolies,* like public utilities, true monopoly is a rare phenomenon in a large industrial economy. We shall nevertheless begin our discussion of imperfect competition with monopoly both because its analysis is simple and because its social effects are representative of those characterizing other forms of imperfect competition.

The Basic Analysis

A monopolistic firm will adhere to the general behavior of a profit-maximizing firm as described in Chapter 7, producing that level of output at which its marginal cost is equal to its marginal revenue. But while its costs are determined the same way as those of a perfectly competitive firm, its revenues will differ significantly.

Because a monopolistic firm is the sole supplier of a given product, the demand curve for its output will be identical to the market demand curve for that product, and thus will slope downward. Unlike the perfectly competitive firm whose market share is so small that it can sell whatever it chooses at the going price, the monopolistic firm can sell more only by inducing consumers as a group to buy more, that is, by offering its product at a lower price. Another way to look at the difference is to note that the monopolist can raise price, losing some sales but obtaining more per unit for those remaining, while the perfectly competitive firm will sell absolutely nothing if it raises its price above the existing market level.

Diagrammatic Analysis

A diagram of the simple monopoly model is presented in Figure 9.1, which shows the firm's average and marginal cost curves (*AC* and *MC,* respectively) and its average and marginal revenue curves (*AR* and *MR*). The monopolist's average revenue curve is identical to the market demand curve for the product. The marginal revenue curve necessarily lies below the average revenue curve because the marginal revenue associated with any quantity sold is necessarily less than the price at which that quantity can be absorbed by the market. The reader who doubts this fact should refer back to the discussion in Chapter 7.

The most profitable level of output for the monopolistic firm is that at which marginal cost and marginal revenue are equal—at the output level Q_1, the point on the horizontal axis that corresponds to the point at which the *MC* and *MR* curves intersect. Note that the intersection of the *MR* and

Figure 9.1
Determination of price and output by a
monopolist in the short run. The shaded
area depicts total profit.

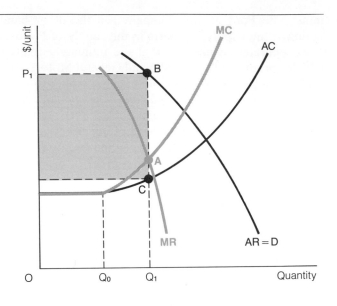

MC curves (at point A) merely gives the profit-maximizing level of output.
The height of point A above the horizontal axis is *not* the price; price must
be read from the demand curve vertically above A at point B.

Normally, a monopolistic firm will be expected to set the price of its
product, and then offer for sale the quantity demanded by the market at that
price. More specifically, its sequence of actions is:

1. Determine the most profitable level of output, Q_1.
2. Set the price, P_1, at a level sufficiently high that buyers will just buy
   quantity Q_1, and offer to sell at this price.

If its information on market demand is correct, the firm will sell exactly
Q_1 at price P_1, and maximize its profit. The average cost of each unit sold is
obtained from point C on the average cost curve. Given that average revenue is price, profit per unit is the vertical distance BC. The firm's total profit
is thus represented by the shaded area, and is equal to profit per unit
multiplied by the quantity sold.

No Supply Curve Under Monopoly

Once a monopolist's demand and cost conditions are established, a unique
optimal price and output can be determined. Consequently, it is meaningless
to ask the monopolist what level of output would be supplied at each of
several prices. The monopolistic firm determines the price at which it

wishes to sell—it is a *price-setter*—in contrast to the perfectly competitive firm that accepts the market price as beyond its own control.

A market supplied by a monopolistic firm therefore has no supply curve of the ordinary kind, because it plans to supply not different quantities at different prices, but only one quantity at one price.

The Long Run

A monopolist has the same opportunity to make long-run adjustments as does a perfectly competitive firm. The firm depicted in Figure 9.1, for example, would not be in long-run equilibrium if it were possible to expand its plant size so outputs larger than Q_0 (corresponding to the point at which average cost commences to rise) could be produced at the same average cost as smaller outputs. It is obvious that the firm's profit would increase if it could produce output Q_1 at the same average cost as it could produce output Q_0, since average cost would then be lowered and nothing else would be changed. Then, however, the firm would not choose output Q_1 because it could increase profits even more by expanding output. If the firm, by increasing its plant size, could extend the horizontal portion of the average cost curve to the right, it would arrive at long-run equilibrium at the point at which average cost and marginal revenue become equal. Marginal and average cost, of course, are equal as long as the average cost curve is horizontal. Thus, when marginal cost equals marginal revenue, it is implied that average cost equals marginal revenue. The firm of Figure 9.1 would expand capacity until the minimum average cost range of output extended just to the profit-maximizing output, as shown in Figure 9.2 where P_2 and Q_2 are the long-run monopoly price and output.

Note that, with constant returns to scale, both the monopolist and the perfectly competitive firm will produce at minimum average cost in the long run. The monopolistic firm, however, will set its price *above* minimum average cost (since it is equating minimum average cost with marginal revenue), whereas the perfect competitor will sell at a price *equal* to minimum average cost.

Barriers to Entry

If a monopoly is profitable, other firms will have an incentive to enter the industry. The preservation of a monopoly, therefore, depends on the existence of one or more barriers to entry by other firms. Among such barriers are the following:

1. *Legal barriers*. These include copyrights and franchises (which directly prohibit entry), patents (which prevent other firms from using essential production techniques), and trademarks (which make it difficult for other firms to convince potential buyers that their products are identical to

Figure 9.2

Long-run adjustment by a monopolist.

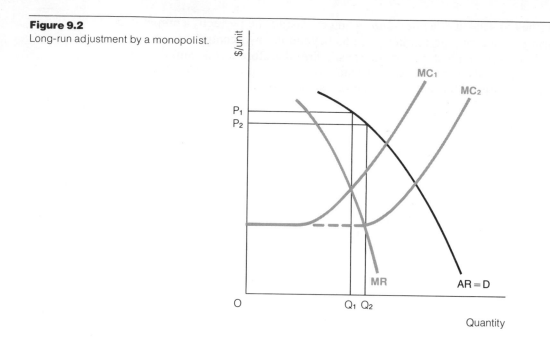

the monopolist's). Legal barriers provide the oldest and most secure foundation for monopoly—in times past, kings frequently granted monopoly rights in reward for services rendered to them. For reasons we shall examine later in this chapter, government franchises in the United States are granted mainly to so-called natural monopolies in transportation, communications, and public utilities. Extensive monopolies have also been built on patents and copyrights, although these generally offer protection for a limited number of years.

2. *Economic barriers.* These derive primarily from the existence of *indivisibilities* in the production technology. Such indivisibilities prevent potential competitors from entering the industry on a small scale and expanding—they must enter as very large-scale operations. Entering on a large scale is riskier for the potential competitor because the market may not be large enough to absorb the production of two large operations at a profitable level. Even if competitors do successfully enter the market under these circumstances, the industry will become oligopolistic (since firms will be few and large) rather than perfectly competitive.

3. *Informal and frequently illegal barriers.* These include physical, financial, and political intimidation of potential competitors. For example, a monopolist may reach an informal agreement with the supplier of some essential raw material that he will not supply potential competitors. Bar-

riers of this kind may involve a cost to the monopolist such as a kickback, bribe, or threat of legal action.

Changes in Demand

Monopoly power is also affected by long-run shifts in demand. A change in the demand curve affects the monopolist's position in a complex way because the nature of the monopolist's equilibrium depends on both the size of the market and the elasticity of demand.

The highest possible (infinite) price elasticity of demand corresponds to a horizontal demand curve such as that faced by a perfectly competitive firm. Thus, the more elastic is the demand for its product, the less monopolistic a firm will be. Shifts in demand that increase elasticity thereby reduce a firm's effective monopoly power.

General economic forces usually operate to increase the demand elasticity of products typically sold under monopolistic conditions. This is due largely to the fact that most of the barriers protecting a monopoly can be bypassed by producing a similar if not identical product. The monopolies sustained by railroad franchises, for example, have been weakened, not by competing railroads, but by truck and airline competition that has served to increase the elasticity of demand for railroad transportation. Likewise, monopolies sustained by patents (like Xerox, Polaroid, and IBM) have met competition from firms producing similar products that do not use the patented process.

Recap A simple monopoly is the sole supplier of a product, so its average revenue curve is the market demand curve for that product. The monopolist is free to vary both price and quantity, but can sell only the quantity given by the demand curve at each price. The most profitable level of output will be that for which marginal revenue and marginal cost are equal. Because the monopolist's marginal revenue is always less than average revenue (price), price will exceed marginal cost. The preservation of a monopoly requires the existence of some economic or noneconomic barrier preventing the entry of other firms into the industry.

Economies of Scale Cost advantages that large firms may enjoy

The terms *economies of scale* and *increasing returns to scale* refer to the phenomenon, especially common in manufacturing and transportation, where large output levels are associated with lower average costs than small output levels. While most firms exhibit some minor economies of scale in moving from near-zero outputs to modest output levels, our inter-

Table 9.1

Economies of Scale
(Costs for a hypothetical automobile
body plant requiring an initial outlay
of $10 million for dies, and a variable
cost of $100 per car body)

Output (no. of car bodies)	Average fixed cost ($ per body)	Average variable cost ($ per body)	Average cost ($ per body)
100	100,000	100	100,100
1,000	10,000	100	10,100
10,000	1,000	100	1,100
20,000	500	100	600
50,000	200	100	300
100,000	100	100	200

est here is in those major economies of scale that create the marked cost advantages large firms have over small firms.

While economies of scale may derive from a variety of sources, most stem from *indivisibilities in the technology of production*. Automobiles can be handcrafted by workers using relatively simple machines, each car being fabricated by making parts one by one and fastening them together. Early automobiles, in fact, were made this way. Then along came Henry Ford who introduced the assembly-line technique in which specialized machines (and workers) were adapted to specific aspects of the total production process. Such technology possesses the property of indivisibility in the simple sense that, while a small assembly line may be capable of producing, say, 100 cars per week, there can be no mini assembly line, using one hundredth the equipment and labor, installed in a small workshop to efficiently produce one car per week.

Fixed Costs

In cost terms, modern mass-production technology involves very large *fixed* outlays—the dies and presses for making automobile bodies, for example, may cost many millions of dollars. Specifically, let's assume that a set of body dies, capable of producing 100,000 auto bodies, costs $10 million, while the cost of labor and materials associated with the assembly of each body is $100. If we assume no other costs, the average cost schedule will be as given in Table 9.1.

In this case, marginal cost is constant at $100 per car body (since it depends only on the cost of labor and materials), but average cost falls from $100,100 at 100 bodies to only $200 at 100,000 bodies. Even if average

Figure 9.3
The economies of large scale. (This figure is based on the data in Table 9.1.)

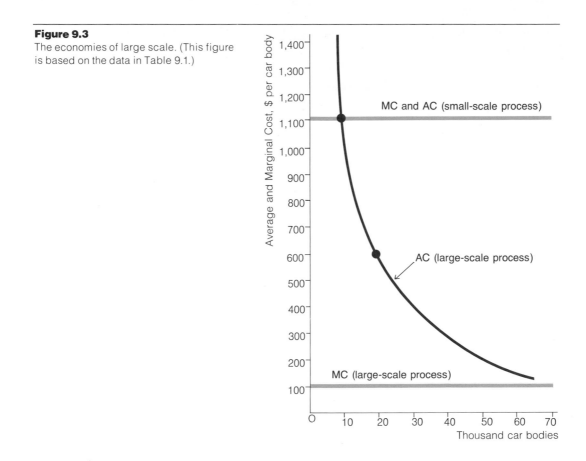

variable cost were to rise somewhat with output, average cost would still very likely fall.

In this example, it is clear that the firm would never plan to mass-produce only 100 car bodies, for handcrafting could surely produce a body for less than $100,100. The choice between whether to use the small- or large-scale process will depend on the planned level of output. At some output level, average costs will be identical for small- and large-scale methods, and mass production will be used only beyond this level.

Suppose handcrafted bodies cost a constant $1,100 per unit. Then, average and marginal cost for the small-scale process would be constant and equal at $1,100 per body. From Table 9.1, we see that average cost for the large-scale process will be less than $1,100 for all levels of output above 10,000. For outputs above 10,000, the firm would therefore choose mass production; for outputs less than 10,000, it would choose the small-scale method.

The cost curves for the large- and small-scale processes are shown in Figure 9.3. Note that the average cost curve for the large-scale process falls continuously, but converges toward the (constant) marginal cost at very large outputs.

The Significance of Scale Economies

Economies of scale are commonly observed in manufacturing, transportation, and public utilities. Due to indivisibilities in such things as management, advertising, and marketing, there can also be significant scale economies in banking and retail trade. In manufacturing, they are usually more pronounced in some phases of production than others. Specialty car manufacturers, for example, may use small-scale methods for final assembly, but purchase engine blocks and transmissions from one of the ''big three'' since the cost savings associated with scale economies on these items are so pronounced.

The existence of major economies of scale has a profound effect on the feasibility and desirability of perfect competition. If average costs decrease continuously with output, for example, an expanding firm gains an increasing cost advantage over its stationary and contracting rivals. Thus, if one firm in an industry of many small firms starts growing, it can lower prices below the average costs of other firms, put them out of business, and expand its market share, perhaps even to the point of monopoly. On the other hand, preventing a firm from growing in this manner will deny society the advantage (fewer resources used per unit of output) to be gained from scale economies.

Recap Economies of scale exist if large outputs can be produced at lower average costs than small outputs. A common source of economies of scale is the existence of technological indivisibilities where certain types of equipment or organizational structure are not feasible at less than a certain minimum size. Major economies of scale are commonly observed in public-utility operations, manufacturing, and transportation.

The Economic Effects of Monopoly

The economic inefficiencies resulting from monopoly

Because we know that a perfectly competitive economy is economically efficient and produces an optimal mixture of goods—at least under certain circumstances—we can judge the effect of a monopoly in a given industry by comparing the price and output under monopoly with that which would prevail if the industry were perfectly competitive with the same cost conditions. Specifically, any divergence of the monopolistic equilibrium from that of perfect competition will provide an indicator of possible economic inefficiency.

Figure 9.4

A comparison of market equilibrium under perfect competition and under monopoly when there are no economies of scale. The shaded area shows monopoly profit.

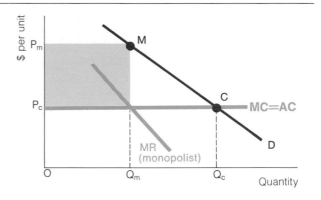

If there are no economies of scale, the comparison is direct and simple. Long-run average cost will be the same for the competitive industry and the monopoly, and marginal cost will coincide with average cost. Demand conditions are assumed to be unchanged by the structure of the industry.

The comparison is given in Figure 9.4. For perfect competition, the market equilibrium will be at point C, the intersection of the industry supply curve and the market demand curve, giving perfectly competitive industry output Q_c and competitive price P_c. For monopoly, however, the supply of the firm will be at point M, giving monopoly output Q_m and monopoly price P_m. The results of this comparison can be stated simply:

A monopoly will produce a smaller output and sell it at a higher price than would an "equivalent" perfectly competitive industry, provided there are no economies of scale.

The difference between the monopoly price, P_m, and the competitive price, P_c, is the *monopoly markup*. This is the most profitable excess the monopolist can charge over the competitive price. The monopolist, of course, could set the price even higher relative to the competitive price, but the additional loss in sales would lower profits. The shaded area in Figure 9.4 is the maximum profit that can be made by using monopoly power, and is usually referred to as the *monopoly profit*.

The economic inefficiency that monopoly produces is the result of the monopolist's ability to restrict output and therefore raise price to the most profitable level. From a broad social point of view, a product's marginal cost represents the value to society of the resources needed to produce one more unit of output. The price of a product, on the other hand, represents the value to consumers (and thus to society) of having one more unit of output. Because the monopolist produces an output level at which price exceeds marginal cost, society could gain from increased output of the monopolized product, because the *social cost* of additional resources shifted to this industry (marginal cost) would be less than the *social benefit* derived from the additional output produced (measured by price).

Figure 9.5

Market equilibrium under perfect competition and under monopoly when there is a low-cost, large-scale process as well as a small-scale process, and the monopoly markup is less than the cost savings.

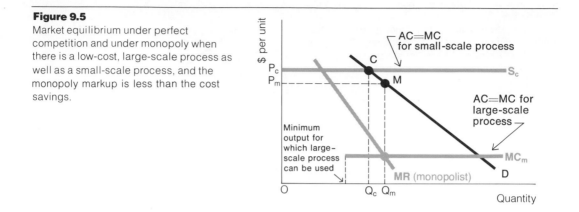

Thus, the primary effect of monopoly is to reduce the proportion of the monopolistically produced goods in the overall output mix below the optimum level.

If manufacturing is largely monopolized while agriculture is not, the economy will be provided with fewer manufactured goods and more farm products than is optimal, while the price of manufactured goods will be higher relative to the price of farm products than would be the case under perfect competition.

The general conclusion that monopoly leads to higher prices and lower levels of output than perfect competition applies to other forms of imperfect competition as well.

The Effect of Scale Economies

We must modify our conclusions about the relationship between perfect competition and monopoly if there are major economies of scale. Then the simple argument just given does not necessarily hold. Consider the case in which there are both small-scale and large-scale processes, the large-scale process having the lower average cost, but usable only at large output levels.

Now, suppose the industry is perfectly competitive and composed of firms that all produce outputs below the level at which the large-scale process is economical. The industry supply curve will be horizontal at the small-scale average cost even though the output of the industry as a whole may be in the range where large-scale production is economical. This case is illustrated in Figure 9.5, where S_c is the supply curve (=average cost curve, since we assume long-run equilibrium) for the perfectly competitive industry producing under small-scale conditions, while MC_m is the marginal cost curve (assumed horizontal and thus coincidental with the average cost

Figure 9.6
Market equilibrium under perfect
competition and monopoly when there is
a low-cost, large-scale process as well as
a small-scale process, and the monopoly
markup is greater than the cost savings.

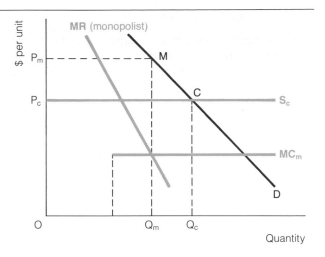

curve) associated with the large-scale process. The perfectly competitive
equilibrium will be at point C giving output Q_c at price P_c. The monopolist,
using the large-scale process, will produce a larger quantity, Q_m, and sell it
at a lower price, P_m.

*A monopolist may thus sell a larger output at a lower price than a perfectly
competitive industry even though he still enjoys a monopoly markup, because
the monopoly markup is less than the cost saving resulting from large-scale
production.*

If, as in Figure 9.6, the monopoly markup (which depends on the elasticity of demand) is *greater* than the cost saving, the monopolist may sell less
output at a higher price than the perfectly competitive industry, despite the
existence of scale economies.

Even when scale economies are sufficiently pronounced that a monopolist
produces a greater output than would a perfectly competitive industry,
there is still a social loss from monopoly because the marginal cost of additional resources shifted into the industry is still less than the marginal value
of additional output. *In this case, neither monopoly nor perfect competition
gives optimal results.* Optimality requires the simultaneous satisfaction of
two conditions:

1. that output is such that marginal cost and marginal price are equal; and
2. that the most efficient (large-scale) process is used.

Perfect competition would satisfy the first condition but not the second;
monopoly, the second, but not the first. An optimum solution would require
a firm large enough to take advantage of scale economies but one producing
to the point at which marginal cost equals price, behavior no monopolist
would undertake voluntarily.

Intermediate Cases

Size sufficient to use the large-scale economies in the above case need not necessarily require a monopoly. If demand is sufficiently large relative to the minimum level of large-scale operation, there may be room for several firms, yielding oligopoly, or even for a sufficiently large number to give perfect competition.

For example, an agricultural sector of 1 million farms could possibly gain some scale economies by moving to farms one-hundred times as large. This would still leave 10 thousand farms, presumably enough for a perfectly competitive structure. Social, political, or legal institutions may result in an agricultural sector that is locked in with too many holdings. Consolidation would permit scale economies, yet not jeopardize agriculture's competitive structure, a change that would be especially desirable in certain less-developed countries having large peasant sectors.

Recap Under constant returns to scale, a monopoly will sell less at a higher price than the equivalent industry under perfect competition. A monopoly makes profits over and above profits that could be made under competition. If there are economies of scale, however, a profit-maximizing monopoly may actually sell more at a lower price than would a competitive industry in which the individual firms are too small to take advantage of large-scale techniques.

Capsule Supplement 9.1   **Scale Economies and Competition**

While many industries possess important economies of scale, detailed information about actual cost differences between large- and small-scale operations within specific industries is rare. In 1963, Marc Nerlove examined electrical utilities in depth. He found that there were considerable scale economies, specifically, a 20 percent decline in average cost for a 10 percent increase in output among smaller suppliers, and a 6 to 7 percent decline in average cost for a 10 percent expansion among the largest firms. Other studies have indicated that supertankers are more economical than conventional tankers, and that cost per passenger mile is lower on jumbo jets than on regular jets.

What little information does exist on economies of scale is confined primarily to industries that are either *natural monopolies,* like public utilities, or heavily regulated, like transportation. Of much greater interest, if less accessible, is information pertaining to scale economies in ordinary industries that are not regulated.

Do major economies of scale exist in conventional manufacturing, for example? If so, is the optimal firm size so large that monopoly is inevitable? The classic attempt to answer these questions was a study conducted by Joe S.

Industry	Optimal firm size as percent of industry capacity	Average percent of market share of 4 largest firms
Fruit and vegetable canning	0.5	6.6
Oil refining	1.75	9.3
Meat packing	0.2 ⎫	⎧ 10.3
Meat products	2.5 ⎭	⎩
Fountain pens	10.0	14.4
Copper	10.0	23.1
Typewriters	30.0	19.9
Flour milling	0.5	7.3
Liquor distilling	1.75	18.7
Metal containers	3.0	19.5
Tires	3.0	19.2
Rayon	6.0	19.6
Farm machinery	6.0	9.0
Automobiles	10.0	22.5
Tractors	15.0	16.8
Shoes	2.5	7.0
Cement	10.0	7.4
Steel	20.0	11.2
Gypsum products	33.0	21.2
Soap	15.0	19.8
Cigarettes	20.0	22.6

Based on Joe S. Bain, "Economies of Scale, Concentration, and the Condition of Entry in Twenty Manufacturing Industries," *American Economic Review*, 1954. Where optimal size was originally given as a range, the top of the range is given here.

Bain in the 1950s. Although his findings are based on data now more than twenty years old, there is no real reason to suppose that they are not still valid.

Bain obtained information for the size of firm considered optimal by engineers in each of twenty important manufacturing industries. The results, *with optimal size expressed as a percentage of total industry capacity at the time,* are shown in the middle column of the accompanying table. Note that optimal size as a proportion of industry capacity is quite small in fruit and vegetable canning (less than 1 percent), but rather large (20 percent or more) in typewriters, steel, gypsum products, and cigarettes.

We can immediately conclude that none of the twenty industries sampled requires a monopolistic structure to gain full advantage of scale economies. However, few if any of these industries could sustain a sufficient number of optimally sized firms to give perfect competition. Even fruit and vegetable canning could sustain no more than 200 such firms. Indeed, half the industries listed could sustain no more than 10 firms of optimal size, implying oligopoly at best. If we were to draw any general conclusion about manufacturing from Professor Bain's sample, it would be that, while monopoly is never implied by the optimal use of resources in manufacturing, some form of oligopoly normally is.

It should be noted that the total productive capacity of most industries listed is considerably larger in the United States than in most other countries. For example, while the United States could very likely sustain ten automobile manufacturers of optimal size, a smaller country seeking to take full advantage of scale economies might be forced to live with one.

The right column of the table shows the average share of industry output for each of the four largest firms in each industry. Note that this figure is larger than the corresponding figure in the middle column for all but four industries. In other words, the largest firms in most industries have a greater share of the market than is required to maintain the optimally sized plant. There is, however, a general correspondence in magnitude between both columns, enough to suggest that the degree of concentration in those industries whose dominant firms have larger market shares is at least partially justified by scale economies.

Monopoly Policy

The principles of government policy toward monopoly

The economic inefficiencies of monopoly have plagued the operation of the market economy and thus have been the object of governmental policy for a long time. The direction taken by monopoly policy in combating these inefficiencies depends critically on the presence or absence of scale economies. In the absence of such economies, monopoly is generally viewed as indefensible, and policy will be directed toward establishing competition. In their presence, however, it is broadly conceded that a policy based on tolerance will ultimately prove wiser than one of promoting an industry of small, inefficient firms.

Do We Need a Policy?

It has been argued that the only necessary anti-monopoly policy is one ensuring that monopoly is not promoted by government action. The logic of this argument can be summarized:

1. Monopolies are inherently self-destructive because their high profits are bound to eventually inspire competition unless there are barriers to entry.
2. It is only with some form of government sanction that most barriers to entry can persist.

While it is true that competitive forces do indeed work against the persistence of monopoly, most evidence suggests that they work very slowly. Furthermore, all known cases of ''monopoly breakdown'' have resulted in the emergence of a small group of large firms (oligopoly), leaving the basic inefficiencies of imperfect competition reduced somewhat, but still there.

Therefore, we cannot escape the necessity for a public policy toward monopoly. Such a policy should generally have the following objectives:

1. To prevent or eliminate monopoly when no scale economies can be shown to exist.
2. To permit a single supplier when scale economies can be shown to exist, but to prevent or inhibit this supplier from adopting a monopolistic pricing policy.

Sound Policy Requires Facts

The first requirement of an effective monopoly policy is *information*, because the basic attitude toward a specific monopoly depends on whether or not scale economies exist, and, if so, to what extent.

There are certain cases in which the existence of scale economies is accepted on a "rule-of-thumb" basis. These are the so-called *natural monopolies*, the provision of telephone and postal services, public utilities, and certain modes of transportation. In these cases, supply characteristically involves the construction of a massive network of telephone lines, transmission lines, pipelines, etc., which, once established, enable additional customers to be supplied at little extra cost.

Living with Monopoly

Given an industry in which a single supplier is unambiguously more efficient than a large number of firms, there are three main policy options:

1. Do nothing, permitting the single firm to operate as an ordinary profit-maximizing monopoly.
2. Permit the firm to operate privately as a monopoly, but *regulate* it by fixing its price or devising some special tax scheme so its pricing and output behavior are brought into line with those of a perfectly competitive firm.
3. Place the firm under public ownership, so its pricing and output behavior are determined directly by the government.

All three types of policy are evident in the United States. Many cities have only one newspaper. Yet, because of the obvious scale economies in this industry, no attempt is made to regulate it or put it under public ownership. Most public utilities, telephone companies, and railroads are privately owned but regulated at both state and federal levels. The postal system, many transportation facilities (primarily urban transit systems), and some public utilities (especially water supply facilities) are publicly owned.

Those industries that are either regulated or publicly owned in the United

States are treated similarly in most other countries. The incidence of public ownership, however, is generally greater outside the United States. Evidence of this is provided by the worldwide prevalence of nationally owned telephone systems and railroads.

Regulation versus Public Ownership

In terms of the simple analytical model of the firm, there are no criteria by which to choose between regulation and public ownership. In principle, a private firm can be regulated to act in exactly the same way a public firm would be instructed to behave. If, for example, operating at a loss were part of the desired behavior, the cost to the government of compensating a regulated private firm for this loss would be equivalent to the loss it would otherwise bear directly.

By focusing on the detailed operation of a firm under realistic conditions, however, certain differences between ownership and regulation become apparent. If the regulated price is set independently of the profit level, the private firm will have a strong incentive toward technical efficiency and cost reduction—something government managers may lack. But if, as is often the case, the firm's *profit rate* is regulated, the private firm may lose this incentive because cost reductions will simply lead to mandatory price reductions with no change in profits.

The most common form of public utility regulation in the United States is one in which some agency sets the maximum price the utility can charge for specific types of service, using as a criterion some *standard rate of profit on capital* that the utility company should not be allowed to exceed. In practice, this standard rate becomes both a maximum and a minimum. The firm cannot set prices so high that its profits exceed this rate, but it is virtually guaranteed that it can always charge prices that will bring this rate of profit. If costs rise, the firm applies for—and usually obtains—a price increase. This system thus provides no guarantee that the least-cost technology is used. Indeed, it tends to encourage heavy capital investment which, while possibly uneconomical, increases the base on which the fixed profit rate is calculated, and thereby enables total profits to rise.

Public ownership has problems of its own, many of them political rather than economic. Publicly owned firms, for example, may face pressures to give concessions having no economic justification to politically powerful groups. Moreover, they may be forced to subsidize other government activities while being criticized if they operate at a loss. For example, an urban transit system may be obligated to provide free rides to police and other municipal employees. Finally, publicly owned firms may be administered by managers whose qualifications are primarily political. Those public enterprises that have proved most successful are those whose structures are much like those of private corporations.

Taking a sufficiently large worldwide sample, there is no compelling evidence that publicly owned monopolies are either more or less successful than regulated private monopolies. There are efficient and dynamic examples, and inefficient and decaying examples of both.

Promoting Competition

Let's turn now to the situation in which scale economies are generally absent, and thus in which there is a clear case for promoting competition. While many countries have virtually no policies in this field, the United States, in its *antitrust legislation*, has what is widely regarded as the most highly developed body of such policies in existence. The primary concern of these policies is to make illegal the most obvious methods by which a firm can obtain and/or maintain a monopoly in an industry without scale economies. Such methods include buying out or merging with competitors, arranging with input producers to stop supplying competitors, enlisting labor unions to boycott competitors, and buying control in a crucial source of supply to the industry or a crucial outlet for its product. While these measures are probably sufficient to prevent the monopolization of an industry, they are acknowledged as being virtually powerless in preventing oligopoly.

If a monopoly already exists, prohibitions against the techniques of monopolization are obviously irrelevant. Either the firm must be broken up into smaller firms, or potential competition must be actively promoted.

While provision for breaking up a monopolistic firm exists under United States law, the practical problems of doing so are enormous. Into how many parts should such a firm be broken? On what basis? Who should be granted ownership of the parts? The classic breakup was that of Standard Oil, which began in 1911 and took many years to achieve. It was eventually broken up into thirty-four parts, most of them very large—Standard Oil of New Jersey, Standard Oil of New York, Atlantic, Continental, and other firms of comparable size. The resulting structure was an oligopoly—actually a network of regional monopolies—within which competition was still quite imperfect.

The policy of promoting competing firms has also been used in the United States. For example, after World War II, surplus equipment was sold to Kaiser Aluminum rather than ALCOA. This was done to break the near-monopoly position of the latter. Other government attempts along this line have included varying its sources of supply in purchases of aerospace equipment and military hardware so as to keep several firms in operation. As in the breakup cases, however, the inevitable if unintended result has been the promotion of oligopoly.

Recap If there are no economies of scale, there is a case for policy designed to ensure the conditions of perfect competition in a monopolized industry. When there are substantial economies of scale, however, the small firms characterizing a competitive structure may be inefficient relative to a large monopoly. Policy in this case is directed toward retaining scale economies, but reducing the monopolist's market power. It is common under these circumstances to place the industry under public ownership, or to regulate the existing private firm.

Capsule Supplement 9.2 **Antitrust Policy in the United States**

The foundation of antitrust policy in the United States is the *Sherman Act* of 1890, a simple law that grew out of campaign promises made by Benjamin Harrison in the 1888 presidential race in response to farmers' concerns about railroad monopolies. When the bill came up, Congress passed it perfunctorily, without a hearing, on a unanimous voice vote in the House and with only one dissenting voice in the Senate. Its content was simple, making illegal "every contract, combination in the form of a trust or otherwise, or conspiracy, in restraint of trade . . . ," and declaring "every person who shall monopolize, or attempt to monopolize, or combine or conspire with any other person or persons, to monopolize any part of the trade or commerce . . ." to be guilty of a misdemeanor.

The *Clayton Act* of 1914 put more teeth into antitrust policy by outlawing specific practices deemed to be in restraint of trade. In that same year, the Federal Trade Commission was established to regulate business practices. Further acts augmenting or amending this basic legislation have since been passed to deal with matters not originally covered. The most important have been the *Robinson-Patman Act* of 1936, which dealt with the practice of selling to different customers at different prices, and the *Celler-Kefauver Amendment* of 1950, which gave courts the power to order a firm to divest itself of the assets of another firm it has acquired or merged with if the acquisition or merger is found to be in restraint of trade.

How effective have these laws been? Thurman Arnold, who was assistant attorney general of the United States in charge of antitrust enforcement for the period 1938–43, and regarded as one of the most diligent enforcers of the law, stated flatly in 1949 that "the antitrust laws have not been effective in the real world." International comparisons with countries having no antitrust enforcement do usually show "concentration ratios" (the percentage of a market held by the four largest firms) to be slightly lower in the United States. But this can be attributed to the simple fact that the United States has larger industry markets than the comparison countries.

The complexities of the judicial process make it poorly adapted to facilitate what are essentially economic judgments. Antitrust suits may involve hundreds of thousands of pages of evidence and arguments. Indeed, the standard strategy corporations involved use is to drown the Justice Department in paper and cause it to withdraw its suit or at least reach a settlement more favorable to the firm than the probable court decision.

Even if a court decision were reached in principle, putting the verdict into practice would be extraordinarily difficult. This is well illustrated by Cellar-Kefauver cases in which the court can order a firm to divest itself of an acquisition that is in restraint of trade. On average, such cases go to court *nineteen months* after the actual acquisition and final court orders are issued *five-and-a-half years* after acquisition! During this period, the finances, plant, and personnel of the acquired firm are thoroughly integrated with those of the parent firm. Even if these can be unscrambled, what is to be done with them? The parent firm will usually have already bought out the stockholders of the acquired firm, leaving no "original" owners to buy the firm back. The "firm" being taken away from the parent can only be sold to another large firm. When the Hazel-Atlas Glass Company was divested from its acquirer, Continental Can, in 1965, it ended up being sold to Brockway Glass, turning the latter from the fourth largest U.S. producer of glass products into the second largest! In some cases, the entire court action proves fruitless because the divested firm cannot be sold, in which case it simply stays acquired.

Antitrust policy has probably prevented the emergence of complete monopoly in some industries, restricting these to oligopolistic structures. But this is at best a minor victory.

It may be that what is essentially an economic policy can simply be better carried out by economic instruments, such as taxes, that are discriminatory against large firms or firms possessing large market shares. But it can be argued that even this approach will ultimately result in complex litigation as firms refuse to pay their taxes.

Exercises

Below is a demand schedule for plastic trochoids. Production of these items is subject to constant returns to scale and a constant long-run average cost of $10 per ton.

Quantity (tons)	Price ($/ton)
4	12.5
5	12.0
6	11.5
7	11.0
8	10.5
9	10.0
10	9.5
11	9.0

Given this information, answer the following questions:

1. What will be the long-run price and output of the plastic trochoid industry if it is perfectly competitive?

2. What will be the long-run price and output if the industry is monopolized?

3. What will be the monopoly markup?

4. What will be the monopoly profit?

5. If the government levies a tax exactly equal to the monopoly profit, what will be the price and output?

6. Suppose someone discovers a large-scale production process that has an average cost of $5 per ton but that can be used only under monopoly conditions. Will price be lower or higher under monopoly than under perfect competition?

For Thought and Discussion

1. How many firms do *you* think would be the minimum necessary to ensure perfect competition in an industry?

2. Suppose the stock of a monopolistic firm were distributed among its workers. To what extent would you expect the price and output policies of the firm to be different under worker control than under capitalist ownership?

3. Devise a tax system that would discourage the growth of very large firms.

4. List the pros and cons of placing an industry, in which economies of scale require a single large firm, under public ownership rather than under regulated private ownership.

5. The right to operate a television station on a specific frequency confers some degree of monopoly power on the conferee. Should the government sell this right to the highest bidder, or should it grant the license only to someone whose moral standards have been thoroughly examined?

Chapter 10
Modern Market Structures

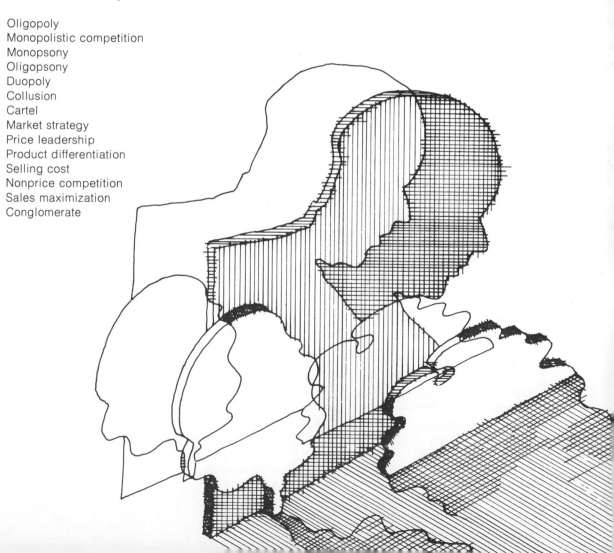

Terms and Concepts

Oligopoly
Monopolistic competition
Monopsony
Oligopsony
Duopoly
Collusion
Cartel
Market strategy
Price leadership
Product differentiation
Selling cost
Nonprice competition
Sales maximization
Conglomerate

| **Defining the Market** | **The nature of a firm's market and the determination of its closest competitors are not always simple and straightforward matters** |

A perfectly competitive market is clearly defined as one in which the goods produced by all firms in the market are regarded by buyers as identical. Such a market is thus the *total* market for a clearly distinguishable product.

A monopolistic firm might also appear to have a clearly defined market—a market for the good over which it has a monopoly. But this clarity may be illusory. What the monopolist is selling may not be *identical* to other products, but it may be *closely related* to them. Amtrak (the government-controlled rail-passenger corporation) is the sole supplier of rail-passenger transport between New York and Washington, and thus has a monopoly if we regard the relevant market as that for rail-passenger transportation between those two cities. But if we view the relevant market as that for passenger transportation *in general* between New York and Washington, Amtrak certainly has no monopoly. Buslines, airlines, and private automobiles all supply such transportation even though these alternatives are clearly not identical. The demand curve for each mode of transport will thus slope downward, but will shift noticeably when the prices of related modes of transport change.

Market Structure Determines Behavior

The designation of the relevant market for a given product does not simply represent an exercise in theoretical "pigeonholing," but bears directly on the *expected behavior* of the firms involved. The specific questions at issue in our example are: (1) To what extent does the behavior of the railroad depend on what happens in road and air transport? (2) To what extent is road and air transport influenced by decisions of the railroad? The railroad can operate as a true monopoly only if it faces a demand curve that is unaffected by its own policies. In practice, it cannot do this—it must take into consideration potential changes in air and bus fares that occur in response to its own pricing decisions, and that will very likely affect the demand for train travel.

In all cases except perfect competition, we must identify what each firm is *really* selling from the consumers' viewpoint. A railroad is selling a mixture of *characteristics*—transportation between two points, a certain degree of comfort during the journey, a given length of travel time, etc. These same characteristics, in different proportions, are also sold by bus and airline operators, and can be provided by consumers themselves if they own an automobile.

Effectively, therefore, Amtrak does not possess a *monopoly,* even though it is the only supplier of rail-passenger transportation. Rather, it constitutes part of an *oligopoly* (direct rivalry among a few large firms) along with bus services and airlines.

Viewing the market this way broadens it from specific rail transportation between two points to general transportation between two points. On the other hand, a critical look from another perspective will show the market to be narrower than it might first appear. People enter the market to buy transportation *between two particular points*—a train ride to Boston is clearly of little value to a New Yorker desiring transportation to Washington. Thus, we must regard New York–Boston transportation and New York–Washington transportation as *essentially two different products*.

Because Amtrak supplies transportation between many pairs of cities, it is really supplying *different products in distinctly different markets*. Given that airline and/or bus competition may be absent on some routes, Amtrak will therefore be subject to a variety of market structures.

Typical Market Structures

The rail-transportation situation differs only in degree from that of the automobile industry. General Motors may have a monopoly on Chevrolet station wagons, but Ford, Chrysler, and American Motors each sell a very similar product. These corporations thus collectively constitute an oligopoly. But their products are more ''similar'' to each other than those of airlines, buslines, and railroads. Thus, firms in the automobile industry will be more sensitive to each other's actions than firms providing alternative modes of passenger transportation. The oligopolistic structures that dominate large-scale industry in modern economies vary greatly in the extent to which individual firms are sensitive to the actions of their rivals.

Despite the pervasiveness of oligopoly, markets that can legitimately be considered monopolistic do remain. Most local telephone companies have a monopoly despite the existence of such seemingly obvious competitors as the U.S. Postal Service and Western Union. Why? Because telephone communication has certain characteristics (immediacy of contact and response) that make it truly unique. Likewise, postal communication has certain characteristics (such as the ability to transmit documents) that cannot be achieved by telephone, at least at present. We can thus consider the markets for both ''telephone'' and ''postal'' communication to be relatively independent, and thus essentially monopolistic.

Recap Defining the relevant market for firms producing differentiated products is no simple matter. Amtrak clearly has a monopoly in the supply of rail-passenger transportation. But it just as clearly competes imperfectly with airlines and buslines in providing passenger transportation in general. Because consumers normally define markets in the broader sense, oligopoly is a common market structure.

The Variety of Market Structures

Market structures cover a wide spectrum

Perfect competition and monopoly represent two obvious extremes in the vast array of possible market structures under which a real firm may operate. Indeed, some economists consider these to be *the* extremes, with all other structures visualized at various positions along a continuum with perfect competition at one end and monopoly at the other.

It seems inappropriate, however, to regard oligopoly as "in between" perfect competition and monopoly. Oligopoly possesses an aspect of market behavior—direct responsiveness to the behavior of rival firms—that these other two structures do not share. Thus, if we wish to visualize a "pattern" of market structures, it would appear to be more appropriately portrayed as *triangular*, with perfect competition, monopoly, and oligopoly at the three corners, as in Figure 10.1.

Mixed Structures

A variety of intermediate cases is possible. For example, we could have a market in which 1 large firm supplies 90 percent of the output and 1,000 small firms supply the remaining 10 percent among them. Because the demand curve for the large firm would be identical to the market demand curve for the product, less the small amount supplied by the remaining firms, the large firm, for all practical purposes, could behave like a monopolist. The small firms, on the other hand, would find themselves in a position equivalent to perfect competition, having no choice but to simply adjust output in accordance with the price set by the "monopolist." From the viewpoint of the economy as a whole, however, the monopolistic element of such a market would be the dominant feature.

Monopolistic Competition

One important intermediate market structure is characterized by a large number of firms producing similar (but not identical) products, whose individual actions have consequences that are widely dispersed through the market. Because the behavior of any one firm has little effect on any other, there is no direct interfirm rivalry. If there were 100 such firms, for example, an expansion of sales by 1 would be partly at the expense of the other 99 (not entirely, since the goods are not identical). But each of the other firms would suffer only $1/99$ of the total loss in sales, which is too small to cause direct reactions. Thus, while there would be no effects of an oligopolistic nature, each firm would behave as a monopolist with a highly elastic demand curve. Such a market structure is called *monopolistic competition*. The "competition" in its name derives from the assumption that

Figure 10.1

Market structures cannot be described in terms of perfect competition and monopoly only.

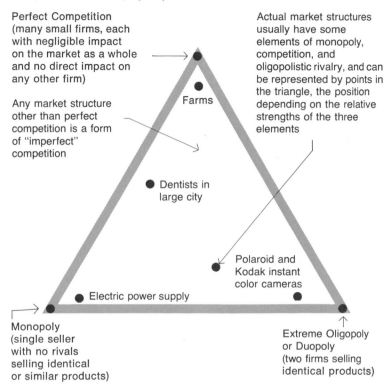

Perfect Competition (many small firms, each with negligible impact on the market as a whole and no direct impact on any other firm)

Any market structure other than perfect competition is a form of "imperfect" competition

Farms

Actual market structures usually have some elements of monopoly, competition, and oligopolistic rivalry, and can be represented by points in the triangle, the position depending on the relative strengths of the three elements

Dentists in large city

Polaroid and Kodak instant color cameras

Electric power supply

Monopoly (single seller with no rivals selling identical or similar products)

Extreme Oligopoly or Duopoly (two firms selling identical products)

profits among existing firms will lead to the entry of new firms. Their market is gained partly at the expense of the old firms, but with the effect dispersed over all existing firms.

Some industries have monopolistically competitive structures. These include retailing and firms that provide services (such as those of dry cleaners, tailors, and hairdressers). Each of these industry types has something, like proximity or familiarity, that leads consumers to prefer one firm to another that offers essentially the same product. This preference is not absolute, however, because the higher the price charged by a given firm relative to its competitors, the more willing customers will be to "shop elsewhere."

In reality, there is normally an element of oligopoly in such a market. For example, to the extent that proximity is a relevant market characteristic, the store next door provides more direct competition than stores farther away. Thus, if one store raises its prices, it is more likely to lose customers to the store next door than to have them evenly dispersed over the entire galaxy of rival stores. Thus, *pure* monopolistic competition in which there are no direct interactions between any firms in the industry is relatively rare.

Multiproduct Firms

Additional complexity is added to our discussion if we consider the existence of multiproduct firms. Virtually all producing units in a modern economy are engaged in the production of more than one good. Large firms may produce hundreds of identifiably different goods, each sold in a different market. Hence, a major corporation may be a monopolist in one market, an oligopolist in a second, and a perfect competitor in yet a third.

Two firms may be intense rivals in one market, as are Xerox and IBM in the market for dry copiers, yet have no rivalry in other markets—IBM makes sophisticated computer hardware, for example, while Xerox does not. On the other hand, firms whose prime markets are not competitive may compete in auxiliary markets. While Loew's Theatres' primary business is showing movies, and ITT's is providing international telecommunications, these firms both own a chain of hotels.

Imperfect competition is not necessarily confined to the seller's side of the market. For example, a market may have only one buyer (*monopsony*), or only a few buyers (*oligopsony*). Markets for certain farm products may have a monopsonistic or oligopsonistic structure—there are relatively few processors, for example, to whom oranges can be sold for juice extraction.

Indeed, it's not uncommon for imperfect competition to appear on *both* sides of the market. When Boeing negotiates with General Electric to buy jet engines, we have a buyer whose purchases and a seller whose sales each represent a large share of the market. There is no simple way to determine the outcome in such a situation. (It may be noted that this situation closely resembles the relationship between a large firm and the labor union that represents its workers, discussed in Chapter 16.)

Most market structures possess a mixture of monopolistic, competitive, and oligopolistic elements. We have already discussed perfect competition (in Chapter 8) and monopoly (in Chapter 9). We shall now discuss the special characteristics of oligopoly. A guide summarizing the basic types of imperfect competition is presented in Table 10.1.

Recap Oligopoly, uniquely characterized by the behavioral interdependence of rival firms, is not just a "cross" between perfect competition and monopoly, but a fundamentally distinct market structure. Because virtually all real market structures contain a mixture of competitive, monopolistic, and oligopolistic elements, it is convenient to view them as lying at various positions within a triangle whose corners represent these three "pure" elements. It is common to refer to all structures other than perfect competition as imperfect competition.

Table 10.1
A Guide to
Imperfectly Competitive Markets

Formal Term	Determining Structure	Example
Monopoly	Single firm, product has no close substitutes.	Your local telephone company.
Oligopoly	Small number of firms, products identical or very similar.	Automobiles (General Motors, Ford, Chrysler, American Motors). Aluminum (ALCOA, Kaiser, Reynolds).
Monopolistic competition	Large number of firms selling different but similar products.	Retail stores (but these often have close rivalries with adjacent stores, and oligopolistic aspects then exist), barbers, laundries.
Mixed structures	Single very large firm, some small rivals, or few large firms and very small firms.	The large firms dominate, small firms follow. The result is effectively monopoly or oligopoly. Most oligopolies (the steel industry for example) have many small firms on their fringes.
Monopsony	Single buyer.	The government in the market for defense equipment.
Oligopsony	Few buyers.	Sale of vegetables or fruit for freezing or canning.
Bilateral bargaining	Both buyer and seller are important in market.	General Motors buying steel from U.S. Steel. Penn-Central buying locomotives from General Electric. Large firms negotiating with a major labor union.

Oligopoly

A market structure with few firms and intense rivalry

The term *oligopoly* literally means "few sellers." As we have stressed, however, the actual number of sellers is not nearly as important as the existence of behavioral interdependence among them. Specifically, a market can be considered oligopolistic if the actions of one firm have effects of such importance on rival firms that these rivals are forced to contemplate reactions that, in turn, may affect the original firm. In short, oligopoly exists if each firm must contemplate the possible reactions of rivals in deciding its own behavior.

Two service stations at the same intersection will typically have this kind of relationship. If either station owner cuts the price of gas, the resulting change in his sales will depend critically on the response of his rival. Thus, each must try to predict his rival's reaction before making a move.

No General Theory

A vast number of markets in the United States are oligopolistic. These vary from the rivalry of a few giant corporations each producing a wide variety of differentiated products—as in the automobile industry—to that of competing liquor stores situated along a given stretch of suburban black top. Each oligopolistic market has its own special features, depending on the exact relationships among firms on a variety of levels. Unlike the cases of perfect competition and monopoly, *there is no general theory of oligopoly, only models of specific oligopolistic situations.* As will become apparent from the analysis that follows, oligopolistic firms face complex decisions that do not always lead to a unique outcome or simple "equilibrium" as with perfect competition and monopoly.

Duopoly as the Simplest Case

Much of the analysis of oligopolistic behavior uses a two-firm model, both because of its relative simplicity and because it best accentuates the effects of interaction. A market consisting of two firms is normally referred to as a *duopoly.*

Imagine two gas stations located across from each other on the north and south sides of a relatively deserted section of highway in the Texas panhandle. We'll suppose that the number of motorists stopping for gas is fixed, unless the price of gas is too high—more than $1.00 per gallon—in which case they'll all risk an empty tank and proceed down the road. Because gas at both stations is the same quality, motorists will cross to the opposite side of the road if, and only if, gas is cheaper there. Finally, we'll assume that each station's cost for a gallon of gas is $.50, and that the number of cars is equal from both directions.

What will be the price of gas at the two stations? Obviously the *highest* possible price is $1.00 and the *lowest* that can be sustained over the long run is $.50. Let's assume that, for some reason, both stations are selling gas at a price of $.75, each servicing all the cars on its side of the road so sales are split evenly. North would clearly make more profit if he raised his price to $.80, *provided he could keep his customers.* North could keep his customers, however, only if South were also to raise his price to $.80. Otherwise the cars would all cross over to South, and North's sales would fall to zero. Would South be likely to follow North's increase in price? One way to find out is to actually list the various ways South could react if North were to increase his price to $.80, and their consequences:

1. If South left his price unchanged, South would capture the entire market and double his sales at the original price, thus doubling his profits.
2. If South matched the increase, leaving his share of the market unchanged, his profits would rise by 20 percent because profit per gallon would have risen from $.25 to $.30 and quantity would have remained unchanged.
3. If South increased his price, but only to $.79, he would capture the entire market and his profits would rise by 132 percent because he would sell twice as much as before, at a profit of $.29 per gallon instead of $.25.
4. If South cut his price, he would capture the entire market, but his profits would rise by less than 100 percent because of the lower profit per gallon than that earned initially.

Safety versus Quick Profits

The reaction most profitable to South is obviously 3, following North's price increase part, but not all, of the way. North must therefore consider this the most likely reaction by South. Because the consequences of this reaction are disastrous to North, he will consider his contemplated $.05 increase in price to be *unsafe*.

From this example, we can generalize that it's unsafe for North to attempt to increase his profits by *any* increase in price. What about a reduction in price? If North reduces his price, and South does not match the cut, North gains all the customers and increases his profits. If we were to set up a tabulation like that for the previous example, we'd discover that South's best reaction would be to cut price *by slightly more* than North, thereby capturing all the sales. Consequently, any price cut by North also turns out to be unsafe.

But North might still cut price if he believes South cannot match the cut. For example, he may believe that South pays more for gas at wholesale than he does. Having lower costs than one's rivals is of enormous competitive advantage for an oligopolistic firm, simply because it cannot then be undercut for any prolonged period. For this reason, oligopolistic firms tend to be quite conscious of and even secretive about their costs whenever there is a threat of price-cutting competition.

If we now return to the original question regarding the eventual price of gas at our two stations, it's evident that there is no clear answer. The only certainty is that the price will be the same at both stations if one station is to avoid being forced out of business.

Collusion

The firms could obviously maximize their joint profits by agreeing to fix the price at $1.00. Such an agreement, a form of *collusion,* would obviously be difficult to maintain because either firm could gain by undercutting its rival and obtaining a monopoly. To prevent this undercutting, the colluding firms could draw up a legally binding agreement called a *cartel* (although this is not permissible in the United States). Alternatively, they could *merge*— taking equal shares, for example, in a corporation operating both stations at a price of $1.00.

Oligopoly as a Game

The gas-station example illustrates oligopolistic rivalry at its most acute. If the situation were less straightforward—the stations sold different types of gas, for example, or if motorists were reluctant to cross a busy highway— reactions would be less predictable.

Competition under oligopoly possesses all the basic elements of a game of chess. Every potential move must be regarded as part of a total *strategy;* potential countermoves must be considered carefully before action is taken. In every move, the oligopolist must weigh potential profitability against safety.

Recap The types of decisions faced by oligopolistic firms can be illustrated by the simple case of two firms (duopoly). The economist's interest in studying such a case is to obtain evidence about the likely outcome, in terms of price and output, of an oligopolistic situation. If we have only two firms, any action by one will affect the other deeply, and may provoke reaction. The behavior of either firm will be influenced by the owner's view of what his rival's goals are. A potential action by either firm that could be expected to evoke retaliation or that makes the original firm worse off than it was to start with is an unsafe strategy. If the firm expects to gain, even after retaliation by a rival, the move represents a safe strategy and will presumably be made. Oligopolistic firms can usually gain by collusion—acting together as a single monopolistic firm and dividing the profits.

Capsule Supplement 10.1   **The Great Air War of 1971**

A good example of how a collusive arrangement in an oligopolistic industry can be upset by a major change in cost structure is provided by the experience of the trans-Atlantic air travel industry during 1971. For many years, fares and flight conditions (down to the size of airline steaks) on trans-Atlantic routes had been set by a formal collusive arrangement among the airlines flying these routes, embodied in the regulations issued by IATA (the International Air Transport Association). The two American carriers involved, Pan Am and TWA, were granted exemption from U.S. antitrust laws to enable them to join in this consortium of airlines, most of which were national airlines of foreign countries. IATA agreements possessed considerable strength because countries whose national airlines were members could deny landing rights to carriers that failed to conform. Icelandic Airlines, which was not a member and which had consistently charged fares below IATA rates, could land on the European mainland only in Luxembourg. It had obtained landing rights in the United States only as part of a package deal involving the U.S. Air Force's use of a base in Iceland.

By the late 1960s, the regular airlines had already begun to suffer from the actions of the "nonskeds," which organized "charter flights" for various organizations. Because these airlines flew planes only if and when they were full, their costs per passenger were much lower than those of the scheduled carriers that flew planes at regular times with whatever passengers happened to buy tickets (average occupancy of such carriers in 1971 was 60 percent). Thus, "nonsked" fares were significantly lower. Indeed, at about half the regular fare, charters were heavily patronized by students during this period.

Then came the final blow—the introduction of the Boeing 747. While no faster than the planes of the previous generation, this first in a succession of "jumbo jets" carried more than twice as many passengers. The 747s were huge and expensive, but due to their immense seating capacity their costs per passenger mile were *potentially* lower than those of conventional jets.

Suddenly, the various airlines found their shiny new planes arriving, but no passengers to fill them. Why did they buy the planes under these conditions? One reason was that the production time for the 747s required the airlines to place their orders two years ahead of delivery (when projections of passenger demand had looked much better). More importantly, no oligopolist can afford to fall behind competitors in technology, especially if bound by regulations to charge the same price for the same product.

The IATA accords finally began to crack in the classic manner of a collusive agreement in the face of impending losses among its members. The first break came when the Belgian government ordered its national airline, Sabena, to offer a student fare of roughly half the regular economy fare in an attempt to catch the charter traffic. Within days, this had been matched by other carriers offering similarly low "youth fares."

Late in the summer of 1971, IATA met in an attempt to bring the impending downward spiral in prices under control. A special low fare was proposed for passengers who would book, and pay, ninety days before a flight—roughly the terms required (officially at least) for a chartered plane. But the competitive pressures were too great, and Lufthansa of Germany refused to ratify the agreement. Under IATA rules, a fare agreement requires unanimous consent of the members. Thus, by September, the airline cartel came "unstuck," leaving fares to be independently determined by each airline. By the end of the year, however, IATA had glued itself together again—but only by permanently incorporating many of the price reductions that had occurred during the price war.

Further Aspects of Interfirm Rivalry

Some additional consequences of oligopoly

The uncertainties and risks, as well as the probable lower profits, associated with oligopoly as compared with monopoly will induce firms to move as close to a monopolistic position as possible.

Driving Rivals Out of Business

If all firms in an oligopolistic market sell identical products, the only way a firm can achieve a monopoly is to collude with its rivals or drive them out of business. The most common way to accomplish the latter is to lower price below average cost. If a firm has a lower average cost of production than its competitors, the firm can take this course without loss, drive the competitors out of business, and then raise the price to the monopolistic level without risking retaliation. Indeed, the very *fear* of this happening serves as a constant incentive for oligopolistic firms to minimize their costs.

Even if a firm does not have a cost advantage, it may still push the price down below the level of average cost if it believes that it can survive a longer period "in the red" than its competitors. Large financial resources may enable a firm to do this. The loss incurred is regarded as a necessary "outlay" for the monopolistic profits that will ultimately result from the bankruptcy of its competitors. The fear of such occurrences is so widespread that a subtle form of implicit collusion—the condemnation of such behavior in the business community as "unfair" or "unethical"—has developed in many market economies.

Price "Stickiness"

To an oligopolist, there is a certain safety in the status quo and considerable risk involved in any unilateral price change. If the oligopolist raises price, rivals may not follow. In this case, the oligopolist's sales may suffer severely. On the other hand, if the oligopolist lowers price, he may precipitate a "price war"—a sequence of price undercutting by rival firms—that may continue until profits disappear altogether.

Thus, even when price would normally be expected to change in a perfectly competitive or monopolistic market (in response to a reduction in costs due to technological progress, for example), no one firm in an oligopolistic market may be willing to take the risk of initiating such a change. Prices under oligopoly are thus likely to be less *volatile* than under other market structures, and may remain steady for relatively long periods even under changing cost conditions.

Price Leadership

One form of implicit collusion that reduces the reluctance of firms to adjust prices in response to changing costs is *price leadership*. An oligopolistic industry may have one firm that, because of its size, age, or simply tradition, acts as the "price leader." When, and only when, this price leader initiates a price change do the others follow. If costs for all firms in the domestic steel industry rise, for example, everyone may wait to see what U.S. Steel does. If U.S. Steel raises prices by 10 percent, this is a signal for other steel firms to adjust their prices as well—not necessarily by exactly 10 percent, but certainly relative to the change instituted by the price leader.

It's clearly advantageous to be the industry price leader. Indeed, a primary objective of many oligopolistic firms is to increase their market share to a level which, while short of the level required for a monopoly, permits the assumption of price leadership.

Product Differentiation

An oligopolistic firm, if its product does not need to be identical to that of its rivals, may follow an alternative road that is closer to the one a monopolist follows. Each firm can differentiate its product by ascribing to it a mix of characteristics that somehow is different from those of other firms. Although most product differentiates do exhibit real differences in the mix of characteristics they possess, it's common for sellers to exaggerate these differences or even "create" differences that have little objective basis. Thus, virtually identical products may be sold under different *brand names* or with different *trademarks*.

Because such products are closely related, the demand for each is sensitive to the prices of others. In this case, the general structure of oligopoly is preserved, even though the pricing and output strategies open to individual firms are relatively "safer" than those facing oligopolistic firms whose products are homogeneous.

Selling Costs

Each producer of a differentiated product (or a product consumers can be induced to believe is somehow different from those of its rivals) will try to increase the demand for the particular good it produces. The most common technique for doing this is advertising. Advertising uses the communications media to put a carefully devised statement before the public that stresses those aspects of the product the seller believes to be desirable. Other techniques may involve salespeople and promotional gimmicks such as free gifts and contests. These techniques all involve *selling costs* that the firm must weigh against potential gains in sales.

The extent of business advertising in the United States varies from market to market. In pharmaceuticals, for example, advertising expenditures are particularly high, and run at about 5 percent of total industry sales, reaching as high as 40 percent for some products. Advertising by oligopolistic firms (the most prevalent form) represents a component of total market strategy, and is thus subject to the same considerations as tactics such as price changes. The effectiveness of advertising by a given oligopolistic firm will strongly depend on the amount of advertising done by its rivals. A firm that doubles its advertising to get ahead of its rivals may well remain where it started if its rivals all double their advertising in response.

Collusion to prevent competitive advertising is largely confined to individuals who provide professional services (such as physicians and dentists) against whom legal or quasi-legal sanctions against "unprofessional" conduct can be upheld.

Oligopolistic tactics like advertising, which do not involve the direct manipulation of price, are said to be forms of *nonprice competition*. Another important form of nonprice competition is the improvement in a product's quality, that is, an increase in the quantity of desirable characteristics per unit of the product. While in some ways this is equivalent to lowering price, it does not (or is believed not to) lead to the same kind of market retaliation as would a straightforward price reduction.

Recap There are strong incentives for oligopolists to increase their independence from the reactions of their rivals. If they cannot drive rivals out of business, they can try to insulate themselves by (1) product differentiation and advertising, (2) making as few price changes as possible, and/or (3) assuming industry price leadership so that rivals will not react adversely to their behavior.

Capsule Supplement 10.2   **Advertising in America**

It has been estimated that by the time the average American is old enough to vote, he or she will have been exposed to 350 thousand television commercials. It's no wonder that the advertising jingle has come to replace the nursery rhyme. No longer can we casually stroll down Main Street or take a drive in the country, much less read a magazine or watch the evening news, without being accosted by Charlie the Tuna, Geraldine the Plumber, or Mr. Cholesterol. Coke, Seven-Up, and Dr. Pepper aren't just three chemical variations on a carbonated soft-drink theme, but charismatic entities with distinct personalities (akin, the cynic might add, to so many TV-generation politicians). Indeed, advertising has become a minor art form with some (unfortunately too few) television commercials having more socially redeeming values than the programs their sponsors help to support. While there are many fascinating dimensions of modern advertising to which we might allude, however, our concern here shall be confined to the economic aspects of this phenomenon.

One function of advertising is to provide information. The classified ads in the daily newspaper represent advertising in this most basic form, and without them the markets in housing, used cars, and jobs would no doubt be more chaotic. Much local retail advertising is also purely informational, giving potential consumers an idea of what goods are available and at what prices. This kind of advertising improves the efficiency with which markets operate, and can thus be regarded as fulfilling a useful role in a world where information is not easily and costlessly available.

But there are major questions about the role of *promotional advertising*—the kind that entreats us to "own a piece of the rock" and "fly the friendly skies."

Such advertising characteristically lacks information (consider the foregoing slogans) and may, either explicity or implicitly, contain misinformation. It is this kind of advertising that generally comes to mind first when the subject is mentioned, illustrating the extent of its impact.

Before examining the economics of promotional advertising, we should note that general views toward it are conditioned by general attitudes about consumers. On the one extreme, consumers are pictured as innocent and relatively ignorant pawns in the hands of advertisers who can sell them anything regardless of whether or not they really want it. There have been enough notable failures of major sales campaigns to suggest that this can only be partly true. At the other extreme, consumers are portrayed as decisive individuals who know exactly what they want and on whom advertising has little, if any, effect. With all due respect to this latter view, advertisers must believe that their campaigns have some effect, for what else would account for the billions of dollars they spend each year?

The most common setting for promotional advertising is an oligopolistic market in which a few suppliers of closely similar products vie to maintain or increase their share of the market. The economist's classic argument against such advertising is that it is an avoidable waste, that each firm advertises only to keep up with its competitors, and that the market would change little if *all* firms ceased advertising. The relative uniformity of advertising expenditures in specific markets tends to support this competitive hypothesis, as advertising tends to be consistently high, or low, from one industry to the next.

The judgment about whether such advertising is socially undesirable and wasteful depends to a certain degree on who pays for it. Do consumers pay through higher prices? Or do firms pay out of potential profits? If the advertising is purely competitive, undertaken to preserve market shares without affecting the total market, it can be argued that prices would be just as high without advertising. In this case, costs are paid from profits and constitute a penalty that firms must pay for being in an oligopolistic market.

Regardless of whether advertising comes largely out of potential profits or out of consumers' pocketbooks, we should look at what happens to advertising expenditures. Although such expenditures exceed $30 billion annually (thereby rivaling total U.S. expenditure on higher education), most of this does not go to the advertising *industry,* employment in which is only about one-sixth as large as total university faculties. The major share goes to subsidize the communications media, whose dependence on this revenue is utterly vital. Indeed, this is virtually the sole source of revenue for commercial radio and television and represents about two-thirds of the total revenue of newspapers and periodicals.

Thus, to the extent that advertising costs are paid from a firm's potential profits, we can treat them as a tax levied on firms in certain oligopolistic industries, the proceeds of which are used to provide free radio and television and relatively inexpensive newspapers and magazines. This might not be the *ideal* way to finance these industries—perhaps "pay TV" and "dollar newspapers" can be shown to be better—but it provides an interesting example of how the market economy sometimes works in mysterious ways.

Policy Toward Oligopoly

The policy implications of oligopoly

In the United States and increasingly in other larger industrial countries, oligopoly is the predominant form of imperfect competition. Even though the typical oligopolistic industry may contain many firms, it is dominated by a small minority of them. While the United States automobile industry (including parts) contains more than 1,600 firms, almost 80 percent of total sales is generated by only four of them.

Appropriate policy toward oligopoly is similar to that toward monopoly. If there are no scale economies, oligopoly cannot be better, and is very likely worse, than perfect competition. If, as is generally the case, there *are* scale economies large enough to be advantageous to oligopolistic firms, the same question arises as with monopoly—should the industry be left alone or regulated?

If an industry is to be fully regulated, a case exists for enforcing the merger of all rival firms (or for giving an exclusive franchise to the most efficient of them), so regulation is confined to a single firm. If the optimum plant size is such as to justify more than one firm, the resulting monopolist could produce in several plants of optimal size but under single control.

There are few fully regulated oligopolies. Virtually all fully regulated firms are public-utility monopolies. There are, however, instances of *partially* regulated oligopolies, such as the petroleum industry. But regulation in such cases usually consists of a variety of *ad hoc* restrictions and is not designed to achieve full control over the industry.

The tradition in the United States has been to leave oligopoly alone. Enforcers of antitrust laws have generally considered the breakdown of monopolies into oligopolies as unqualified victories that require no further interference. This has been due, in part, to a mistaken belief that the "competition" economists have shown to be desirable can be achieved by the existence of only a few firms.

There are valid arguments to suggest that oligopoly is usually better than monopoly and may represent the best structure attainable under realistic conditions. It can be shown that prices and output levels under oligopoly are normally closer to the perfectly competitive ideal than they would be under monopoly, provided there is no explicit or implicit collusion. In addition, the uncertainty and potential ferocity that characterize oligopolistic rivalry provide strong incentives for firms to keep costs low and their technology up to date.

Special Problems of Oligopoly

Oligopoly, however, presents certain difficulties of is own. Rivalry can lead to intense price competition that is "false" in the sense that the ensuing price reductions cannot be sustained in the long run—they are simply designed to force rivals out of business. Of course, economists often argue that inefficient firms *should* go out of business. In saying this, however, they normally visualize the exit of small competitive firms with a tiny share of the market. The collapse of a giant firm employing tens of thousands of workers in a given location is a major event with considerable economic, social, and political repercussions.

Oligopolistic rivalry can also result in wasted resources. Firms may employ numerous salespeople and engage in extensive advertising, merely to maintain their respective shares of the market. Even if the costs of these selling efforts come primarily out of profits (rather than from higher prices), they represent a *pure resource waste* in the sense that sales and advertising personnel are resources that could be productively used otherwise in the economy. They contribute nothing to output as long as their task is to merely maintain *relative* shares in a constant overall market because *total* output would remain the same if there were no selling effort at all.

There is probably no alternative to living with oligopoly if a private-enterprise sector is to be maintained in an advanced industrial economy. Given substantial economies of scale, freedom of entry into an industry will generally serve at best to modify a monopoly into an oligopoly, and antitrust action cannot realistically be expected to do any better.

One possible compromise is the *semiregulated* oligopoly, as exemplified by the United States domestic air-transport industry. This industry is characterized by broad regulations (not necessarily well devised) guaranteeing that price and cost competition do not reduce safety, together with a degree of "keep on your toes" rivalry to promote efficiency. Certain cooperative arrangements (such as ticket transferability) provide the advantages of a single operation. It is possible that other oligopolistic industries—automobile production for example—could be handled within a similar framework.

Recap Oligopoly is a fact of life in modern industrialized economies. From a policy point of view, the arguments against oligopoly are similar to those against monopoly (although usually weaker); but there are additional problems presented by oligopoly. These include resource waste through selling costs, and potentially unstable market behavior. The regulation of oligopoly is inherently more difficult than the regulation of monopoly.

The Giant Corporation

The large multiproduct firm

One of the most spectacular developments over the last half-century in the United States (and to a lesser extent in Japan and Western Europe) has been the growth and emergence of the giant multipurpose corporation. Such corporations are not merely simple firms grown large to take advantage of indivisibilities, but multiproduct enterprises that interact with the rest of the economy on a variety of social and political fronts.

Because of their size, these giants are generally imperfectly competitive in all fields. Not only do they sell their products under imperfectly competitive conditions, they buy their primary and intermediate inputs, and even obtain financing, under these conditions as well. They become institutions in the economy, and their names are elevated to the status of household words—General Motors, IBM, DuPont, General Electric, and Exxon. No one buys from them, sells to them, or negotiates with them without being aware of their enormous size and economic power. Indeed, they are more than large enough to use direct political pressure to attain their economic objectives.

In effect, these corporations aren't just large firms, but outright *subeconomies*. A corporation such as General Motors is a larger economic unit than many of the countries represented in the United Nations. Many of these corporations operate on a broad international scope and play a crucial—even dominant—role in the less-developed countries. Some, like Shell Oil, are truly international, being owned by shareholders in several countries and operating in many more.

Giant Firms as Subeconomies

As subeconomies, these giants possess complex internal structures and face many of the same problems as the economy itself—how to best allocate their available resources, whether to produce inputs internally or "import" them, and how to coordinate the individual decision-makers in charge of their various component units. Indeed, modern general equilibrium theory can be directly applied to their overall operation. In light of this unique character, we might well ask if and how the behavior of such corporations differs from that predicted by the economist's standard model of the firm.

Corporate Objectives

The evolution and growth of the modern corporation has been accompanied by the separation of ownership from management. Corporate ownership consists of shareholders who buy stock primarily for resale and know or care little about the firm's actual operation. Corporate management, on the other hand, is represented by professional executives who may have goals other than the simple maximization of corporate profits that they may consider "wasted" when paid out to shareholders.

There is, however, no widely accepted idea of what such alternative goals might be. For that matter, there's no reason why these goals should be the same from one management group to another. Executives with scientific backgrounds may be unduly interested in technically advanced, though not necessarily economical, products or production processes. Other executives may be preoccupied with their "corporate image" and channel funds into unprofitable but socially beneficial activities.

Of course, profits cannot be altogether neglected. If a corporation fails to make some "reasonable" level of profit, the price of its stock may eventually fall, and borrowing funds (or selling new stock) on favorable terms may become increasingly difficult. There's even the remote possibility that a voting majority of stockholders will exercise its ultimate legal right and dismiss the existing management. Thus, in order to preserve its own existence and ensure that the corporation has access to funds for expansion, management must pay *dividends* sufficient to keep stockholders happy. In addition, it will require sufficient profit, over and above that paid out in dividends, to provide an internal source of funds for investment purposes.

If market or business conditions are such that the corporation is hard put to reach even a "reasonable" level of profit, it will then presumably act as a profit maximizer. It is only when satisfactory profits can be achieved easily along with other goals that a corporation can afford the luxury of putting profits second. During boom periods, then, a firm may regard profits as secondary, while during a recession it will generally cut back first on those activities that do not directly contribute to profits. During the 1973–75 recession, the first executive to get the proverbial axe was quite likely the vice-president for community relations.

Sales Maximization

The simplest alternative goal model is that of a firm maximizing its *sales* (more precisely, its *revenue*), subject to some minimum level of total profit. Sales maximization is an attractive goal for management because a firm's relative importance in an industry is generally measured by its share of sales rather than by its share of profits. Increasing the firm's share of the market enhances the prestige of management and improves the competitive position of the firm under oligopolistic circumstances.

A profit-maximizing firm, of course, will sell the output for which marginal cost and marginal revenue are equal. Provided the profits earned by a sales-maximizing firm at this output are greater than the required minimum, it can then further increase its revenue by lowering price and increasing volume. Each unit sold beyond the maximum profit level will reduce profits below the maximum because marginal revenue will be less than marginal cost. But as long as marginal revenue is positive, total revenue will continue to increase. The sales-maximizing firm will thus lower price until profits reach the minimally acceptable level.

A sales-maximizing firm, it should be noted, will sell more at a lower price than a profit-maximizing firm. From the viewpoint of social welfare, sales maximization will thus bring a firm closer to the perfectly competitive output and price than profit maximization under imperfect competition.

Conglomerates and Mergers

Giant corporations may grow from small firms by accumulating profits withheld from stockholders, by selling new stock, by merging with other corporations, or by a mixture of these. Recent years have brought the merging of corporations from *different industries* to form *conglomerates*. Conglomerates may be giant corporations in terms of their central financial structure without being dominant in any single industry. Although giants operating primarily in a single industry or in related industries gain their strength from such things as large-scale economies in production, conglomerates gain strength from *economies in management* and from *competitive power in finance*.

Recap The giant corporations of modern industry are typically involved in a variety of different markets. While they may not possess a dominant position in any one market, they derive market power from exercising central control over production in many areas. There are doubts about whether the behavior and growth of the corporate giants can be explained in terms of simple profit maximization, and alternative motives, such as sales or growth maximization, have been suggested.

Capsule Supplement 10.3   **Is Bigness Bad?**

Let's consider the implications of a firm's sheer size independently of whether or not it dominates a particular market. Most of the corporations that came under government scrutiny prior to the 1960s were giants *because* they dominated particular markets—corporations like General Motors, U.S. Steel, and IBM. Evolving more recently are the *conglomerates,* firms that are gigantic because the total sum of their operations is huge, even though these operations take place in many markets, none of which may be dominated by them.

The most direct argument against size *per se* is that the growth of giant corporations creates economic units that have excessive social and political power, regardless of whatever economic power they may have in a particular market. It is argued that the balance of power, both between business and consumers and between business and government, has simply shifted too much in favor of big business. At issue, therefore, is the *political clout* that accompanies enormous size rather than power over specific market prices.

It would be foolish to take a conglomerate's share in any one market as representative of its *real* power in that market. However small this share, the enterprise is backed by financial reserves derived from its other operations. Obviously, a huge conglomerate with only a tenth of the market in one of its many activities is a far stronger animal than a firm with the same share of this market and nothing else.

The proponents of the conglomerate movement argue that it is just this "backup" protection in each market that provides the strongest case in their favor. They argue that good management, for example, is one of society's scarcest resources, and that a conglomerate with first-class management at its center can deploy this resource to particular areas at particular times, guaranteeing its efficient use. Moreover, they argue that the lack of total commitment to any one field provides the flexibility the economy needs—the conglomerate being more willing to start new things and to close down unsuccessful operations than traditional one-industry firms.

Prior to 1971, antitrust policy in the United States had been concerned almost exclusively with market dominance, and no real decision had been made about where such policy stood on pure size. The settlement of a suit brought by the Justice Department that year against ITT (International Telephone and Telegraph) is thus generally considered to have established an important precedent.

ITT is an enormous corporation basically rooted in international cable and radio communications. In the 1960s it began to diversify, buying up firms in many fields totally unrelated to its original lines of business. It gradually became the owner of "Wonder" bread and "Hostess" cakes, Avis car rentals, Levitt Construction, Sheraton hotels, and Aetna Insurance. It then acquired Hartford Insurance—an act that finally brought about the end of its conglomeration. The Justice Department agreed to a settlement by which ITT could either drop the Hartford acquisition or divest itself of an equivalent value in other acquisitions. The Justice Department let it be known that this was to be a representative settlement—that giant conglomerates could acquire *new* firms only if they dropped *old* acquisitions in such a way as to leave their overall size unaffected. ITT decided to keep Hartford and Sheraton, but drop Avis, Aetna, and some other minor acquisitions.

The policy established with the ITT decision would seem to be "enough is enough," that giants can remain as large as they are, but grow no larger. This may end up pleasing no one; the opponents of bigness argue that the giants are *already* far too big, while the proponents contend that most U.S. conglomerates aren't big enough for international competitive strength in the face of massive merger movements in Europe and Japan.

Exercises

The following questions are based on the hypothetical data given in the table for two profit-maximizing automobile firms, Alphamobile, Inc., and Betamobile, Inc., producing similar but not identical cars.

If Alphamobiles sell for	And Betamobiles sell for	Alphamobile's profits are (millions of dollars)	Betamobile's profits are
$1,500	$1,500	8	8
	$2,000	12	6
	$2,500	14	2
$2,000	$1,500	6	12
	$2,000	10	10
	$2,500	12	6
$2,500	$1,500	2	14
	$2,000	6	12
	$2,500	7	7

1. Suppose both cars sell initially for $2,000. Alphamobile considers lowering its price to $1,500. What would Betamobile be expected to do?

2. What would happen to Alphamobile's profits if it lowered its price to $1,500 and Betamobile took the expected counteraction?

3. Suppose Alphamobiles were selling initially for $2,000 and Betamobiles for $2,500. Would you expect both prices to remain at those levels? If not, what would you expect final prices to be?

4. If the firms entered into a collusive agreement to sell at the same price, splitting profits fifty-fifty, what price would they set? (Ignore the fact that such behavior might violate antitrust laws.)

For Thought and Discussion

1. General Motors, generally speaking, can raise funds for capital more easily than a new firm because of its size (and thus investor belief in its "safety") and reputation. Does this indicate the desirability of large corporations, or an imperfect stock market?

2. Reducing price to less than average cost is often regarded as "unfair" competition. Should it be made illegal?

3. If you were instructed by the court to prepare plans for the dismemberment of a giant corporation, what would you take into account in determining the parts into which it should be broken?

4. The intense rivalry of an oligopolistic situation is often said to keep firms "on their toes." If you had the job of allocating air routes, and there were travel demands for, say, ten full planes a day between two cities, would you give the route to a single airline? Two airlines? Ten different airlines?

Chapter 11
Failure of
the Market

Terms and Concepts

Bilateral bargaining
Public good
Excludability, non-excludability
Diminishability, non-diminishability
Externality
Club good
Joint product
Undesired product
Public bad
Externalities
Consumer surplus
Price discrimination

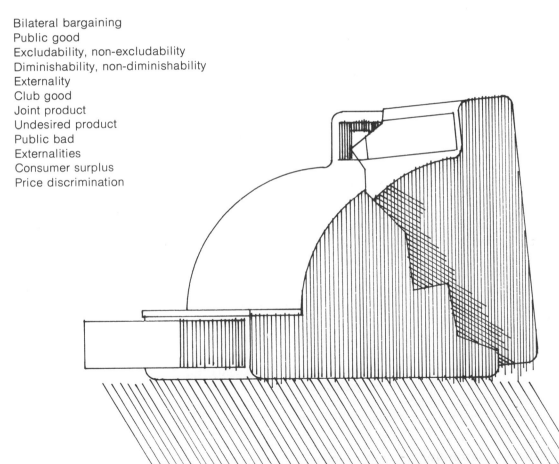

Types of Failure

The market mechanism may fail in several ways and may fail to operate altogether with certain classes of goods

In our discussion of perfectly and imperfectly competitive markets, we assumed that all conditions required for the successful operation of such markets were satisfied. In practice, there is no guarantee that these conditions will be met. Consequently, the market mechanism may fail to operate properly.

Market failure may result from an inability of the market to facilitate the essential exchange of goods and information, to reach equilibrium in a reasonable period of time, or to achieve equilibrium at all. More serious cases of market failure are those in which the market system cannot produce certain goods or produces goods society would prefer not to have.

A Failure of the Market Mechanism

As we saw in Chapter 5, a market must be minimally organized to function smoothly. At the very least, a working market requires not only that each buyer and seller be aware of what other buyers and sellers are offering, but also that isolated segments of the market are kept closely in step by well-developed arbitrage. In the absence of a functioning market, exchange may take the simple form of *bilateral bargaining*. In this situation individual buyers and sellers simply work out deals on the basis of their own respective needs. Thus, an eager seller and a reluctant buyer may exchange at a low price in one place, while an eager buyer and a reluctant seller exchange at a high price somewhere else. In such a situation, there is obviously no true market, and hence no real market price.

In uncomplicated cases, the absence of a market can be rectified without great difficulty. A small coastal village, for example, may organize a municipal marketplace just for the purpose of facilitating exchange between its residents and local fishermen—or these buyers and sellers may organize such a market cooperatively. But some types of markets are more difficult to initiate than others. Well-developed *capital markets,* for example, in which loans for purchasing capital equipment are made available, are noticeably absent in the developing nations. Without such markets, funds are more freely available in some parts of the country (or for some uses) than in others, and the allocation of funds is distorted.

Market Instability

Even when markets do exist, they may be *unstable*. In certain agricultural markets, a high price one season (established after planting has been done) will not affect current supply but may lead to larger plantings next season. When next season comes, the resulting larger supply will precipitate a fall in price that, in turn, will lead to reduced plantings and a high price again the following season. Such cases, in which the price fluctuates around some average long-run equilibrium level, constitute a classic form of instability.

Alternatively, the market may be stable, but be characterized by an adjustment process that is *too slow*, so equilibrium is achieved only rarely. One of the problems of advanced industrial societies, to which part of macroeconomics is devoted, is that the aggregate labor market can remain out of equilibrium indefinitely (resulting in unemployment, or an excess supply of labor at prevailing wages).

Complete Market Failure

This chapter is primarily concerned with cases in which the market either (1) fails to produce goods society wants and values at least as highly as the resources required for their production, or (2) persists in producing un- wanted things (''bads'') society would be willing to pay to eliminate. These basic types of market failure are derived from the properties of either the goods (or bads) themselves or the techniques of their production that lead to undesirable situations. In the case of goods, the *social benefit* from hav- ing them cannot be converted into a large enough *private benefit* to induce a private firm to produce them. In the case of bads, the *social cost* of having them cannot be turned into a large enough *private cost* to prevent their being produced.

Basic market analysis requires the existence of well-defined supply and demand conditions. On the supply side, it is conventionally assumed that producers control the output level of each individual product and that they can establish this level quite independently of the output level of any other goods they may produce. On the demand side, it is assumed that individual consumers can obtain benefits from a good only if they buy it. Furthermore, it is normally assumed that whatever is being produced and consumed is a *good*—something that consumers will give up money to obtain—as opposed to a *bad* that consumers would pay to avoid.

It is when one or more of these conditions are not met that a complete market failure may result. The remainder of this chapter is devoted to cases in which this may occur.

Recap There are various ways in which a market may fail to operate properly. It may fail to reach a uniform price because of structural or informational defects, its adjustment toward equilibrium may be too slow, or it may be unstable and fail to move toward equilibrium at all. A more basic problem arises when the market fails to operate altogether for certain goods whose social benefits (or costs) cannot be converted into private benefits (or costs), and hence for whose production (or elimination) no market incentives exist.

Capsule Supplement 11.1　**The Political Economy
of Regulation**

Regulation always sounds better in theory than it seems to turn out in practice. The frequent failures of regulatory agencies to achieve their presumed objective of improving social welfare can doubtless be attributed to a variety of causes. One such cause may be that the powers given by the government to an agency are inappropriate for achieving its stated goals. Indeed, the idea behind the very formation of an agency may have been poorly conceived. We shall not concern ourselves here with the problem of an agency's deformity at birth, however, but shall explore the causes of failure when the agency can be regarded, in principle, as well founded.

A major problem of regulation is the nature of the regulators. Not that they are necessarily evil, corrupt, or incompetent (although these traits may be evident from time to time), but rather that the context in which they find themselves makes their task difficult from the outset. The typical regulatory agency is headed by an executive and some kind of commission or board. Where can suitable executives and board members be found? The obvious answer might seem to be that they should simply be good citizens concerned with the public interest. But regulation is a technical matter that involves such questions as what the price of electricity should be, whether two airlines should be permitted to merge, whether a domestic industry is really threatened with extinction by import competition, and whether the freight rate on a ton of tomatoes should be greater or less than that on a ton of potatoes.

No one knows the technicalities of an industry better than those who have been associated with it in some way. Consequently, there is a strong tendency for regulators to be chosen from the regulated industry itself—either directly, from among its former executives, or indirectly, from the pool of lawyers, accountants, and economists who have worked for it. Although the individuals concerned may honestly regard themselves as public officials once they've joined the regulatory agency, their background necessarily makes them sympathetic to the "problems" regulation creates for the industry. Thus, the regulatory agency may end up as an institution by which *the industry regulates its own members,* rather than as an institution by which *the public regulates the industry.* The effect, therefore, may be that of a cartel and, hence, worse than if there were no regulation at all. The Civil Aeronautics Board (CAB), for example, has perennially been accused of acting this way, having successfully prevented the entry of a single major airline into the industry for the past thirty-five years.

But an industry is in a strong position to dominate its regulators even when these individuals have no previous ties to it. The industry normally has exclusive possession of detailed information about its affairs and technical expertise about its operation. Such an industry, or even a single firm within it, may find it profitable to spend hundreds of thousands of dollars to support its case on a major issue, employing every favorable expert it can find. Who documents the public's case? Usually a few public bureaucrats who are overworked are bombarded day after day with the industry's case, and spend much of every working day with industry representatives.

Last, even if the problem of industry domination were overcome, there are the dangers of pure bureaucracy. Regulatory agencies have been accused of being in the *regulation business* instead of the *public-interest business;* that is, of typically countering one bad regulation with another rather than simply eliminating the original bad regulation. The Interstate Commerce Commission (ICC) was originally established to regulate the railroads. It has carried out this job with enthusiasm, setting freight rates for each commodity over each route to the point where there are currently some 75 thousand separate rate schedules that differentiate, among other things, between sand to be used in making glass and sand to be used in making cement, and that sometimes specify a different freight rate when a certain commodity is moved from A to B than when it is moved from B to A. In the 1930s, highway freight became competitive with the railroads, especially on certain types of freight for which the rates had been set well above cost. Instead of permitting the railroads to meet the competition by lowering their own rates, the ICC simply started regulating the rates the highway carriers could charge. Interstate freight has become a complex mass of regulations, and the ICC may well be primarily responsible for the decline of the railroads.

All this does not mean that regulation is an impossible way of increasing social welfare. It merely demonstrates that the existence of a regulatory agency does not necessarily guarantee the achievement of this objective.

Public Goods

A major class of goods that
is not supplied through
the ordinary market mechanism

Can a consumer benefit from something without being required to pay for it? For the class of goods known as *public goods,* the answer is yes. A simple example of a public good is the service provided by a lighthouse.

The signal from a lighthouse is visible to *all* ships that pass near it. Because this light cannot be confined to any particular group of ships, we cannot exclude anyone from using it. Furthermore, the services of the lighthouse cannot be diminished because the benefits derived by one ship do not decrease the services available to others in any way.

Consider first the effects of *non-excludability*. Suppose someone built a lighthouse and proposed to sell its services to passing ships. Why should any given ship be willing to pay for these services? A ship will obviously benefit from the services of the lighthouse regardless of whether or not it pays for them. These services are thus unmarketable, because it is to no one's individual benefit to offer something in exchange for them, assuming they are already being provided to someone else.

The property of *non-diminishability* implies that there is no problem *allocating* the lighthouse services. Because no user of these services diminishes the potential use by others, it's obvious that society will be better off when *anyone* needing these services can obtain them. Consequently, the services of the lighthouse require no allocation, and thus require no market. Of course, the ordinary market could not be used anyway because of the non-excludability.

Supplying a Public Good

This example looks very neat, and might even suggest that lighthouses present no economic problem. But, in fact, they present a most difficult one. Building and maintaining a lighthouse requires *resources* that must be diverted from other uses. While *allocating the services* of the lighthouse presents no problem, *allocating resources to it* does. In general, when resources are used to produce output that can be sold in the market, they can be obtained in exchange for part of the proceeds realized from selling the output. This is what happens in the case of normal production. A potential lighthouse producer, by contrast, will receive nothing he can exchange for resources.

To the buyer of an ordinary *private good,* such as a tennis racket, the benefit (in simple money terms) is presumably at least as great as the price of the good. Moreover, the cost of producing such a good must be less than the price. Thus, we can expect the market to provide private goods when benefits to buyers cover the costs of the resources used.

While the services of a lighthouse clearly provide social benefits, the ordinary operation of the market will nonetheless fail to produce these services, regardless of how much these benefits may exceed the cost. To be specific, let's suppose there are 1,000 potential lighthouse users, all of whom are willing to pay at least $100 per year to have the lighthouse rather than do without it. Furthermore, let's assume the lighthouse can be built and maintained for $50,000 per year. The market would *still* not provide the lighthouse even though, if the government built it and taxed all shipowners $50 per year, everyone would consider himself better off.

In this case the difference between having a government supplier and having a private supplier is that the $50 per shipowner could not be collected by the private supplier, but could be by the government. Although each potential user is willing to pay $50 *if he must* (in taxes), he is not willing to do so when he can avoid it and still obtain the benefits.

The Possibility of Exclusion

Non-diminishability does not necessarily imply non-excludability. Consider a beach so large that everyone who wants to use it can find ample space on the sand and uncluttered room in the surf. It's obviously possible to exclude people from such a beach by simply fencing it off. If the benefits are truly non-diminishable, such exclusion will reduce social benefits if anyone wishing to use the beach is actually kept away. But, what if resources are required to maintain the beach? These could potentially be financed from a charge so small that everyone wishing to use the beach is willing to pay it. In this case, it might be possible to give beach benefits to all desiring them through the ordinary market mechanism. Without excludability this would not be possible.

Typical Public Goods

There are many things that have the properties of, and therefore can be classified as, public goods. While such things need not be absolutely non-diminishable and non-excludable to be considered public goods, they must possess these properties to a considerable degree. Excludability, for example, may sometimes be possible, but quite complicated, expensive, or politically difficult.

National defense, in the basic sense of protection from real and immediate dangers, is a typical public good. The government cannot realistically exclude from the benefits of defense those individuals unwilling to pay for it, even though it could theoretically exclude certain sections of the country. The economic analysis of defense is extremely complex, not so much because of the public-good aspect, but because of difficulties in judging the relationship between the quantity of resources devoted to defense and the measurement of ''output'' in terms of protection against events whose occurrence is uncertain.

Basic police and fire services are usually considered public goods. Because exclusion is possible, however, these services are frequently supplemented by market-provided services (bank guards, for example) in circumstances in which the benefits are more private. Indeed, fire services were originally provided by insurance companies. Since they directly benefited from such services, they actually practiced exclusion by refusing to put out fires in uninsured buildings! However, two factors make it desirable to treat fire protection as a public good: *economies of scale* (a fire station, once established, is capable of serving an entire area) and *externalities* (a fire in one building may spread to others). Such facilities as parks and recreation areas can also appropriately be considered public goods, although exclusion from them is possible.

Government Goods and Public Goods

Because public goods cannot usually be supplied through the normal operation of the market, they will normally be supplied, if at all, by the ''government.'' However, not all goods supplied by the government are public goods.

There are certain things which could be supplied through the market but which the government may choose not to have supplied in this fashion. A straightforward example is education. In the absence of public schools, education undoubtedly would be supplied privately through the market. If it were, however, access to it by individual households would depend on income. Because of the government's objective that education be available to everyone regardless of income, it is supplied publicly rather than through the market. In actuality, because school fees are only *part* of the true cost of education (in later years, there is also the potential loss of income during school), education is still more available to the rich than to the poor. However, the difference is obviously much smaller than if its provision were made exclusively through the market.

There are many reasons why the government may choose to supply goods directly to consumers rather than through the market. That a good is a *public good* in the technical sense is only one of the reasons.

Club Goods

There is an intermediate variety of cases between true public goods and ordinary private goods. A golf course, for example, is too costly for any one person to build. But once it exists, there is little loss of benefit to one person if others (though not too many) are also allowed to use it. Such a *club good* typically results when a group of consumers finds it necessary to "club" together in order to have some consumption activity that would not be available to each of them individually. Because actual clubs may (and frequently do) practice social exclusion, and because large clubs are difficult to organize, the government supplies many club goods, such as public golf courses and sports grounds. In a community with a socially homogeneous population (a wealthy suburb, for example), the local government may effectively serve as a "club committee."

Market Ingenuity

Sometimes things that appear to have the general properties of a public good are, in fact, supplied through the market. One example is commercial television.

Television broadcasts most certainly possess the property of non-diminishability. Moreover, at least to owners of television sets, they are generally non-excludable. Of course, exclusion can be, and is, exercised with regard to television broadcasts. In Britain, for example, such exclusion applies to the set itself—to operate one, a license fee must be paid to the British Broadcasting Corporation. In the United States, exclusion takes the form of "pay television" in which the transmission is coded, and can only be decoded by a special apparatus supplied, for payment, by the broadcaster.

Standard commercial television, however, is both non-diminishable and non-excludable, and would seem to fit the mold of a true public good. Yet it is supplied through the market. How?

The answer is that commercial television produces not pure programming, but a joint mixture of programming and advertising. Viewers cannot exclude the advertising from their screen (at least without going to some trouble), while commercial sponsors who derive value from televising their advertisements can, in a sense, be excluded from presenting their material. The public good is provided in this case because consumers will not watch advertising alone (even if free), but will accept an advertising-entertainment mixture. This is evidence that, with some entrepreneurial ingenuity, the market can, under certain circumstances, be induced to offer public goods.

The commercial television solution is due to the existence of joint products—program material together with advertising. Advertising can be sold (to the advertiser); the program material cannot.

Recap Public goods are those from whose benefits individuals cannot be excluded, and whose benefits to one individual are not diminished by their use by others. A classic example is the service provided by a lighthouse. If a public good is produced, individuals are not willing to pay for the benefits because they cannot be excluded if they refuse to do so. Public goods will thus not generally be produced by private firms because revenue cannot be obtained from their sale. They will normally be produced by the government, or in cases in which some exclusion is feasible, by a club or other cooperating group. Some exceptions are possible, however, as shown by commercial television.

Capsule Supplement 11.2   **Men on the Moon**

Outside the fictional world of James Bond, major space programs are initiated and financed by national governments. Can the "output" of a program like Viking, Soyez, or Apollo be regarded as a true public good? If this output represents a generalized national objective—say, putting a Russian or an American (or, for that matter, a Norwegian) on Mars, the resulting achievement is then non-excludable and non-diminishable to the citizens of the successful country. But a space program obviously accomplishes more than this, and many of its benefits (such as scientific information obtained) can indeed be restricted to a select group.

To analyze something as complex as a space program, we must regard its overall output as a bundle of diverse "goods" produced jointly. The particular output we call "national prestige" certainly has all the general properties of a public good (although many may place little value on it). Other joint outputs, such as scientific data acquired, are not true public goods because exclusion is not only possible, but practiced. Some of the data may have limited applicability, such as for "national defense," itself a complex public good. Other data may have direct commercial value. It has been suggested, for example, that truly spherical ball bearings might be more easily manufactured under weightless conditions, giving the possibility of renting out commercial factory space on future Skylabs!

A space project confined to producing a commercially salable output, such as launching an orbiting ball-bearing factory or a communications satellite, must necessarily be regarded as a public utility if not a public good, because of the enormous indivisibilities and scale economies precluding competition.

If the only objective of a major space project, such as sending an exploratory device to another planet, were to gather pure scientific data to be made freely available, the resulting output could be treated as a world public good. The desirability of such a project would rest on whether or not the potential benefit to the world as a whole was sufficient to justify the cost. There exists, of course, no organized mechanism for assessing the effects of a world public good (except, possibly, the United Nations, which in any event lacks the taxing powers of a true government). Currently, the world must rely on such a project being undertaken by a specific country, either as a voluntary donation to the world community or, more realistically, in an attempt to turn the project into as much of a national public good as possible by emphasizing prestige and restricting data to give priority to its own scientists.

Joint Products

Many problems arise because the output of one product cannot always be separated from the output of another

Important cases of market failure, especially those associated with environmental pollution, stem from the existence of production processes having two or more distinct outputs. Petroleum refining, for example, produces several hydrocarbons, from tar and furnace oil to high-grade gasoline— each of which constitutes a joint product having commercial value. In some processes, however, one or more of the joint products may have no commercial value—slag as a joint product with refined metals, for example—and in certain processes, such joint products may actually have a *negative* social value, as is true of certain wastes and pollutants.

If all the joint products of a process are marketable, the analysis of producer behavior is essentially the same as in the simple case. The only difference is that, in computing the firm's total revenue, we must consider the revenue derived from the sale of the *entire package of products* rather than just that derived from the sale of a single good.

Undesired Products

Our interest here is not with cases in which every joint product is marketable, however, but with cases in which certain joint products are not. Of great importance in microeconomic policy, and common in modern industrial society, is the case in which one of the joint products is a *bad,* rather than a good. The best known examples of bads are those outputs that contribute to *environmental pollution*. Take smoke, for example. Firms do not set out to produce smoke, but do so as a joint product along with marketable commodities. The very fact that it is sometimes referred to as a by-product implies that it is produced by an accident of technology.

Smoke, of course, is not a marketable commodity; the producer receives a *zero price* for it. Problems arise because society would rather not have the smoke, and presumably would be willing to pay to get rid of it. Accordingly, smoke should actually have a *negative price,* that is, the producer should have to pay, rather than be paid, to produce it. But the market, under voluntary exchange, cannot handle negative prices. Individuals can be induced to give up money in exchange for something, but they cannot be forced to give up money without receiving anything in return.

Private Choice

If smoke is produced in a *fixed proportion* to the primary output, we have a simple choice between (1) no smoke and no output, and (2) smoke and output.

The analysis becomes more interesting when undesired products are produced in *variable proportions*. Let's suppose there are two processes, both of which use two machine-hours of capital and two man-hours of labor at the unit level. But one (P, the polluting process) produces 2 tons of output and 100 pounds of smoke, while the other (N, the nonpolluting process) produces 1 ton of output but no smoke. The smaller output of process N is obviously due to the partial use of both labor and capital to remove smoke.

If smoke were simply neglected, the producer taking no account of it one way or another, N would appear to be an *inefficient* process because it produces less output than P with the same inputs. Thus, process N would not be used at all, process P would be adopted, and the air would be polluted. This represents the past situation with regard to virtually all industrial production. Only if smoke were regarded by the producer as undesirable, a *bad* as contrasted to a *good,* would process N be considered part of the available efficient technology. From society's point of view, of course, *less* smoke is superior to *more* smoke, and process N, which produces less output with less smoke, is not necessarily inefficient relative to P. Preferable to P, of course, would be a process yielding even more output than P with less smoke, for then, even if smoke were neglected, this process would still be more efficient than P. Diesel locomotives replaced steam locomotives, not because the diesel engines produced relatively less smoke pollution, which they did, but because diesel traction was superior to that produced by steam.

As already pointed out, the private benefits accruing to the producer of joint products consist of the combined revenues from selling the marketable products. If one of the joint products is a bad, *but one the buyer must accept along with the good,* then each buyer must decide whether the price *plus* the bad aspect of the product is more than outweighed by the good. In such a case, the good and bad aspects appear as positive and negative benefits to the same person, and the market can operate as usual.

In the smoke case, however, the bad (smoke) does not necessarily affect the buyer of the good. Although the smoke represents a negative benefit or cost to society, producers do not receive a negative price (that is, they are not obligated to make a payment) for the smoke, but rather count their private benefit solely in terms of the revenue received from the sale of their output. No automatic market mechanism exists to induce producers to deduct some negative smoke "price" from the revenue they receive from their primary output.

Recap If two or more outputs result simultaneously from a production process, we have joint products. Major economic problems arise when one of the joint products is undesired, such as pollution. Because the market will place a zero price on the undesired product, producers will not consider it in their choice of technique for producing a given output of the desired product, and will use a nonpolluting process only if it is less costly than the polluting process.

Public Bads

A class of unwanted outputs that may be supplied through the market mechanism

Certain undesired things, like air pollution, possess the same properties of non-diminishability and non-excludability as do public goods. It thus seems appropriate to refer to these things as *public bads*. Apart from air pollution, typical examples of public bads include jackhammer noise, sonic booms, and tannery odors.

Surely no one would produce a public bad for its own sake. Public bads are essentially joint products. Just as commercial television produces a public good (entertainment) jointly with a marketable product (advertising), so a public bad may be produced jointly with a marketable product. In the case of television, advertising and entertainment are supplied jointly as a matter of *producer choice* because consumers will not accept the advertising without the entertainment. Public bads, like the stench associated with an oil refinery, are produced jointly with marketable goods because of the *technological conditions of production.*

"Unsupplying" a Public Bad

Just as there is no market mechanism to *promote* the production of a public good, there is no market mechanism to *prevent* the production of a true public bad that is produced jointly with a marketable commodity.

Although public bads have always existed, the problems they present have become more apparent in recent years. The reason is simple enough. Because public bads are produced jointly with many marketable goods, the production of public bads rises with private-sector production in general. Automobiles are readily produced and sold through the market despite the fact that they produce air pollution. The higher the output and use of automobiles, the greater the output of the attendant public bad.

An increase in the output of private goods that are valued in themselves despite the fact that they may be associated with public bads results in an overstatement of the corresponding increase in social welfare. It's even possible for increased automobile use to *reduce* overall social welfare. This would not be apparent in standard measures of economic performance, however, in which the *positive* output of automobile services is counted, while the *negative* output of associated bads is not.

Rarely is a bad produced jointly with a good in absolutely fixed proportions. The problem with the market system is that a public bad has no way of influencing market behavior. In particular, if it is more costly to produce a private good with a process yielding less of the associated public bad, the market system will not produce the good in this manner. Some form of intervention is required. Just as the government must step in to provide public goods, so must it intervene if the economy is to *un*produce public bads.

Recap Public bads—like noise, odors, and physical pollutants—are analogous to public goods, except they are undesired. As in the case of public goods, individuals cannot easily be excluded from public bads nor are such bads diminished by their effect on individuals. Just as the market fails to produce public goods, it will fail to remove public bads. The elimination or reduction of public bads will thus normally require government intervention.

Externalities
Economic actions that affect individuals not directly involved

When a choice or action by one person in society directly affects the welfare of individuals who are not involved in that choice or action, we say that there are *consumption externalities*. Such externalities may be "good" (if the affected people consider their welfare increased) or "bad" (if the affected people consider their welfare reduced). A gentleman who chooses to consume a garlic sandwich on a crowded bus certainly creates bad or negative externalities for those in his general vicinity. If, however, that gentleman turns out to be, say, Burt Reynolds, some good or positive externalities will undoubtedly be created simultaneously to at least partially offset the collective nausea produced by his peculiar choice of public snack.

In a perfectly competitive market system, consumers maximize their own private net benefit. The previously stated argument that this leads to a social optimum depends heavily on the presumption that the behavior of each individual consumer has no effect (especially no adverse effect) on the welfare of others. So long as there are no consumption externalities, each consumer's maximization effort makes him better off, and no one worse off, and thus his effort can be presumed to make society better off as a whole.

Let's suppose that Ralph, a resident of a peaceful suburb, buys a motorcycle. We'd normally argue that Ralph prefers this to any other good or collection of goods society could have produced with the same resources, and that his purchase implies an optimal use of these resources. But if the noise from this motorcycle seriously disturbs his neighbors, the private benefit to Ralph overstates the net social benefit derived from the motorcycle—there being a loss to some. Society might be better off if Ralph were constrained to accept other goods produced with the same resources, which he values less than the motorcycle, but to which his neighbors do not object.

Externalities can cause a failure of the market in the sense that, given their existence, a *socially* optimal collection of goods cannot be produced by the market. The market responds to private benefits only—to the potential buyer of the motorcycle but not to those who suffer its negative externalities. There is a basic similarity between the problem of externalities and that of public goods. Indeed, a public good can be regarded as something that consists exclusively of positive externalities with no private impact on any one consumer.

Although commonly neglected by economists in the past (because they made the analysis untidy), externalities have a long history in common law. For centuries it has been recognized that an action by one individual that adversely affects the enjoyment of life by others may be grounds for legal compensation or for a ban on that behavior.

Most externalities have a spatial property—trombone practice in the Mojave Desert will have far fewer external effects than the same activity in a Brooklyn apartment house. The closer consumers are spatially, the more important the externalities will be.

Thus externalities are of great importance relative to urban problems. In fact, the economic analysis of such problems is dominated by two pervasive influences—externalities and joint products—both of which have a long history of neglect. This is why economists have only recently begun to contribute to the study of cities.

Recap An act that affects the welfare of individuals who are not direct parties to the act creates externalities. These externalities can be positive (if the effects are desirable to others) or negative (if the effects are undesirable). Externalities, if they are negative, result in a loss of social benefits that are not reflected in market prices, and the market can be considered as failing by not giving the socially optimal output. Externalities are especially important in urban economic problems.

Capsule Supplement 11.3   **Who Gets the Goods—
and the Bads?**

Although it's useful to consider certain "pure" examples of public goods, such as lighthouses, non-excludability and non-diminishability are rarely absolute. Consequently, the provision of things normally regarded as public goods and bads may have important market and distribution effects.

An obvious example is airport noise. While commonly treated as a public bad, such noise is partially excludable at the cost of installing special sound insulation. Moreover, its impact, far from being uniform over society, diminishes with distance from the airport and its approach paths. Consider the resulting market effects. Other things being equal, householders will prefer not to live near the airport, and rents will consequently tend to be lower in its vicinity. Those who live near the airport will thus be "compensated" by the market for doing so. This implies a market-distribution effect for public bads of this kind. Specifically, the poor, whose access to market goods is constrained by limited money incomes, become the main recipients of public bads.

This effect is less apparent with respect to airports than, say, railroad yards because airport noise at the jet level is a relatively recent phenomenon and adjustments in the real-estate market often take many years. But it's the poor who live near oil refineries, heavy-machine shops, and railroad yards, and it will eventually be the poor who live near airports. In effect, the poor increase their consumption of private goods, like housing, by accepting a lion's share of the public bads.

A similar linkage of locational market and distribution effects occurs with certain goods that narrowly fail to qualify as "pure" public goods. Take public parks, for example. Rent effects will result in those with higher incomes being able to live near such parks and thus benefit most from them. Even when the market is not the main allocative mechanism, as in the case of campus parking spaces, Moscow apartments, or air pollution, those highest in some hierarchy are likely to obtain the greatest access to public goods, and those lowest in the hierarchy are likely to obtain the greatest share of public bads.

Consumer Surplus and Economies of Scale

A market problem that can arise under economies of scale

We have seen that the market often fails to provide public goods even when the beneficiaries of such goods are willing to pay taxes that will cover the cost of their production. A similar case arises with respect to certain private goods that exhibit significant economies of scale and for which *some* consumers are willing to pay more than *others*.

Consider telephone services, which are more valuable to some users than to others. Suppose, in particular, that 1,000 potential consumers are willing to pay $100 per month (but not more) for such services, that another 1,000 are willing to pay a maximum of $50 per month, and another 1,000 are willing to pay a maximum of $10 per month.

For simplicity, let's assume that the system costs $120,000 per month to operate, regardless of the number of subscribers. Because the only cost is fixed, we have economies of scale and decreasing average cost.

While the 1,000 subscribers most anxious to have telephones are willing to pay $100 per month, the average cost for 1,000 subscribers is $120—more than the average revenue of $100. Thus, the telephone company will incur a loss on this level of service at a charge of $100 per month.

If the price is lowered to $50 per month, 1,000 additional subscribers will be added, and average cost will fall to $60 ($120,000 ÷ 2,000)—still above the average revenue of $50. Lowering the price to $10 per month will increase the number of subscribers to 3,000, bringing average cost down to $40 but still above the average revenue. Thus, ordinarily, no telephone services would be provided by the market.

Consumer Surplus

The crucial question, of course, is: Will society actually benefit from the provision of telephone services? Despite the failure of the market to produce them, the answer is yes. Why? Because the most eager subscribers value these services at $100,000 per month ($100 × 1,000), the middle group considers them worth $50,000, and the least eager group $10,000. These figures add to $160,000—more than the total cost ($120,000) of having the system.

If everyone pays the same price, the market does not reflect the full benefits accruing to consumers. If the price is $50 for example, those who would have been willing to pay $100 actually obtain the service for $50 less. This difference between the maximum individuals are *willing* to pay and what they *must* pay is often referred to as *consumer surplus*. Obviously one way (not the only, nor necessarily the optimal, way) of bringing the telephone service into being is for the supplier to charge a *different* price for different consumers—$100 for the most eager, down to $10 for the least.

Such *price discrimination* can only be carried out in certain situations. Those willing to pay $100 will not admit it if they know charges will be based on their admission—while they're *willing* to pay $100, they'd obviously *prefer* to pay less. When feasible, discrimination must therefore be based on *categories* for which voluntary confession of the degree of desire for a telephone is not required. Commercial users, for example, will typically be charged higher rates than households, and private lines will typically be provided at higher rates than party lines.

We shall defer until Chapter 12 the policy question as to what pricing system should be used by a telephone supplier or other public utility. At this stage, we simply note the possibility that the market may fail to produce certain private goods even though the money value of total benefits may be sufficient to cover costs.

Recap A special market problem arises when there are increasing returns to scale over the entire range of industry output. Because marginal cost is below average cost, it may be impossible to produce without a loss (even under a monopoly) if all consumers pay the same price. However, if some consumers place a higher value on the goods than others, it may be that the total social benefits outweigh the total social costs, in which case the good should be produced even though the market may fail to produce it under ordinary market conditions.

Exercises

A city has 1 million inhabitants and no public transit system. Of the total population, 250 thousand would be willing to pay at least $10 per week to ride a transit system, another 250 thousand would be willing to pay $8, another 250 thousand would be willing to pay $4. The remaining 250 thousand would not be willing to pay, but would use the system if it were free. A transit system, if set up, would cost $2.5 million per week in fixed expenses and $4 weekly for every member of the population who used it.

1. Assuming that any fare charged must be the same for all users, would the market provide a transit system?
2. Would society gain from the existence of such a system, assuming the costs represented the true costs to society of the resources used?
3. Would your answers to the above questions be changed and, if so, in what way, if the fixed expenses were $1.5 million weekly?
4. What if the fixed expenses came to $3.5 million per week?

For Thought and Discussion

1. Is commercial television an example of a public good produced jointly with a public bad?
2. Many public goods (including lighthouses) satisfy the non-excludability test, even though only a certain group in the economy is interested in the good. Should taxes to pay for the good be confined to this group?
3. We can regard defense as a public good. But an increase in expenditure on defense can bring more "defense" only in the sense of decreasing the probability that the country can be outmaneuvered on some matter of international politics. The government must surely provide defense, but how can it decide on an optimum amount?

4. Some of the goods provided without direct charge by governments (or local governments) in otherwise market economies are listed. Which are public or club goods in the true sense? Why are the others provided through the government?

education	highways
police protection	garbage disposal
fire protection	parks

Chapter 12
Microeconomic Policy

Terms and Concepts

Social cost, private cost
Social benefit, private benefit
Consumer surplus
Marginal social benefit
Marginal social cost
Subsidy
User charge
Congestion
Marginal cost pricing
Rationing device
Theory of second best

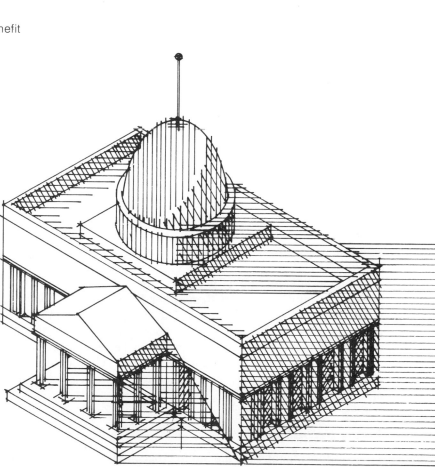

| The Government and the Market | How the activities of the government can be related to the market |

There are two main groups of microeconomic policy objectives, those concerned with economic efficiency and those concerned with society's output mix. In Chapters 9 and 10 we considered policies directed toward increasing the degree of competition and, hence, the degree of efficiency in the economy. In this chapter, we shall focus on the problems of attaining an optimal output mix that arise from the existence of scale economies, externalities, public goods, and public bads. In addressing these problems, we shall consider the various ways in which the government may choose to intervene in the market system to improve its overall operation.

Relation to the Market

In an economy with a substantial market sector, the government may relate its own activities to those of the market in a variety of ways. While it always has the power to *coerce*, it may also work *through the market mechanism* or operate *parallel to the market*. Most governments exercise all three of these options to some degree.

Consider the problem of abating the environmental pollution associated with refining oil. The government could use its coercive powers by simply *forbidding* oil refineries to operate in localities where pollution is especially undesirable. Alternatively, it could use a mixture of coercion and market force by levying *taxes* on refineries that operate in undesired areas. The government could also offer *subsidies* to refineries that move to isolated locations. This is inducement through the market. Finally, the government could simply *refuse to buy* from oil companies that operate in undesired locations.

Taking a different kind of problem, suppose it were socially desirable to have more public transport than either firms would supply or consumers would buy at going market prices. The government could use its regulatory powers to force transport firms to reduce prices. If this meant losses, coercion alone would obviously be insufficient because firms cannot easily be coerced to stay in business against their will. Of course, the government could still offer subsidies to private firms or work parallel to the regular market by operating its own system at a loss.

Policy Instruments

The instruments for carrying out microeconomic policy are limited only by ingenuity. The government can control, prohibit, selectively license, assume ownership, and offer subsidies based on countless different formulas;

it can levy taxes related to output, profits, the use of inputs, or any other measurable aspect of operation; it can supply inputs below market cost, use its own bargaining power as a customer, or produce in competition with private industry—to mention only a few.

The government always has the option, which itself constitutes a policy choice, not to intervene in the private market at all. It cannot, however, avoid the responsibility for public goods (nor, ultimately, for public bads). Hence, the decision about the optimal public-private goods mix is always an explicit or implicit act of government policy.

Some, like John Kenneth Galbraith in *The Affluent Society*, have argued that the greatest failure of the American economic system is that its output mix consists of too many private goods and too few public goods. As one might suspect, critics of the Soviet economy, including many Soviet economists, have argued that the output mix in the U.S.S.R. is too much the other way.

The proportion of total output (including defense) allocated by the government, as opposed to the market, is not actually much lower in the United States than elsewhere. To be sure, it's lower than in Sweden, but higher than in France and the United Kingdom, nations both commonly regarded as placing less emphasis on private goods than the United States and having considerable defense activity.

Recap If the market fails to provide the socially optimal output mix, say, because of the existence of public goods or public bads, the government can modify the mix in many ways. Its choice of a specific policy technique depends on whether it decides to use coercion, thus bypassing the market altogether, to operate through the market by using devices such as subsidies, or to supplement the market by producing certain goods itself.

Social and Private Costs and Benefits

How problems arise from
the divergence between
social and private benefits

The ultimate aim of microeconomic policy is to produce the greatest possible output of the right mixture of goods. Once this output mix is determined, the specific objectives of producing particular amounts of particular goods can be achieved in several ways. It is the determination of the appropriate output mix itself that presents the major problem.

The market system under perfect competition produces the appropriate output mix without any direct information about individual preferences. By acting freely in accordance with their preferences, all individuals are assumed to do as well as they can with their initial resources. Those features that prevent the perfectly competitive system from operating ideally—

public goods, public bads, and externalities—cause a divergence between social and private benefits and social and private costs. These features can thus cause a divergence between the output mix that is actually produced and the mix that is socially optimal.

Divergence Between Private and Social Costs

Consider an electricity-generating plant that emits heavy smoke when it uses the least-cost process, as measured in terms of conventional inputs purchased in the market. The costs the electricity producer must meet, the *private costs,* are simply the payments for these inputs. These payments also represent *social costs* in the sense that they reflect the use of resources that society cannot otherwise employ once they are used in the generating plant. But there is an *additional* ''cost'' to society in the form of the undesired smoke. Assuming we can put a dollar estimate on this, the *full social cost* is the cost of the inputs *plus* the cost of smoke pollution; the private cost to the producer is simply the cost of the inputs.

An alternative process that produces no smoke, but uses more expensive inputs (natural gas instead of oil, for example), would represent *higher private costs.* But, because the social cost associated with smoke would be absent, it might well represent *lower social costs.* The return from the sale of electricity is a *private benefit* to producers, and, in the absence of complications, a measure of *social benefit* because consumers are willing to pay this much for electricity rather than do without.

In the regular market context, producers will simply consider the relationship between their private benefits and private costs and choose the smoke-emitting process because it yields the greatest private net benefit (profit). Social welfare, however, will be maximized with the smokeless process if this production method yields a higher ratio of *social benefit* to *social cost.* If this is the case, government policy can bring about smokeless production in one of the three ways discussed in the previous section.

Other Examples

The lighthouse, cited in Chapter 11 as a classic example of a public good, can also be analyzed in this way. Here the private benefit is zero because there is no way the lighthouse owner can charge for his services, while the social benefit is positive. The costs of building and operating the lighthouse are identical, of course, regardless of whether or not they are borne privately. Consequently, social and private costs are equal, but the social benefit exceeds the private benefit.

We can also apply the technique to externalities. Ms. Smith loves red and hates green, while Ms. Jones loves green and hates red. Both like white well enough. Now let's suppose that these two women buy adjacent white houses on the same street, and each immediately repaints the house her favorite color. Each increases her private benefit by changing white to her favorite color. However, each imposes a negative benefit on her neighbor. The total social benefit associated with repainting is obviously less than the sum of the two private benefits. Indeed, social welfare might have been higher if both houses had been left white.

Note that a *divergence* between social and private costs or benefits merely indicates that a *problem exists,* namely, that the market solution (all consumers maximizing their private benefit) may not be socially optimal. It does not tell us how to *solve* the problem. To do this we need more information.

In the lighthouse example, the social benefit exceeds the private benefit, but the private benefit is less than the private cost. Hence, the market will not produce a lighthouse. But should a lighthouse be provided at all? Suppose the social benefits were assessed at $10,000 per year, while the costs of operating a lighthouse came to $20,000 annually. If there were any alternative way in which those resources could be used to yield a social benefit exceeding $10,000, they would surely be better put to that use.

Policy Requires Information

The procedure for comparing private and social costs and private and social benefits is quite straightforward. Just determine the social benefit and the social cost. If the benefit exceeds the cost, the thing should be done. Then compare the private benefit and the private cost. Again, if the benefit exceeds the cost, the market will provide the good or service. If not, the government must provide the good or service, say by subsidizing production, or society must do without.

But how can social costs and social benefits be measured for purposes of comparison? The fact is, we can't really *measure* them, but we can use various types of evidence to *estimate* them within limits. Indeed, with nothing but the sketchiest of evidence, we can frequently spot potential divergences between private and social costs or benefits, and thus identify situations in which the market may not yield an optimal solution.

We must be careful, however. Let's say a new eighty-story office building has been constructed in the shape of an elongated artichoke. We ask the first passerby for her opinion. She pronounces it ugly—evidence of a negative externality making social benefit less than private benefit. The next passerby, however, proclaims it beautiful—evidence of a positive externality. Situations like this, in which externalities affect different people in different ways, are obviously difficult, if not impossible, to resolve.

Recap A failure of the market system to produce an optimal output mix is primarily caused by divergences between social and private costs and benefits. Public goods, for example, are not produced by the market because no firm can obtain private benefits from their production no matter how large the social benefits may be. In principle, activities should be undertaken if their social benefits exceed their social costs. In practice, however, there are major difficulties assessing social benefits and costs when these differ from private benefits and costs.

Capsule Supplement 12.1   **The Economics of Theft**

We can learn much about the various economic factors that affect social welfare by examining activities not usually regarded from an economic perspective. Consider the case of theft. Ignoring the moral and legal aspects of this phenomenon, its most obvious characteristic is that it constitutes a *transfer* activity—the effective ownership of the stolen object is transferred from its original owner to the thief. In this sense, theft simply constitutes a redistribution of wealth, and as such there is no clear presumption about its effect on social welfare. If the original owner was rich and the thief poor, it might even be argued that the redistribution involved actually yields a net improvement in social welfare.

There is, however, one type of unambiguous welfare loss associated with theft—that associated with an inefficient use of resources. The time and energy expended by a thief *creates nothing new*. In other words, were a thief to work at a "legitimate" occupation for the same amount of time, he would increase the total supply of goods and services available to society, in which case he would theoretically make everyone a little better off. We can, however, presume that a thief's gain from stealing exceeds the value of his equivalent services in a conventional job. Consequently, although *society* would be clearly better off if he had a regular job, *he* would be worse off. Theft thus represents a case in which the *private* benefits accruing to an individual (the thief) exceed the *social* benefits from his actions.

If a thief is caught and convicted, the *direct* economic loss to society will quite probably be greater than if he hadn't been. He will spend time in prison, where his services will not be socially useful (except for the few license plates he may help to produce). He will be paid an income in kind by the government (food, lodging—not of the highest quality, but better than many poor families receive), and require expensive custodial services.

Should the theft victim be fully insured, he does not lose by the transfer, unless, of course, the stolen article has emotional value not covered by the insurance. Who then does lose? Insofar as insurance claims are ultimately covered by insurance premiums, it is the entire group of individuals who insure property of this kind. Hence, the actual redistribution associated with theft is tantamount to a tax on those who insure property, the proceeds of which accrue as transfer income to the thief.

There is, however, yet another type of loss associated with theft. Stolen property is usually "fenced" at less than its "legal market value." The actual gain (in dollars) to the thief and his associates (including his market intermediaries) is thus *less* than the dollar loss to the group of insurers. From the economic point of view, this constitutes a *depreciation* of one of society's assets—the stolen article is converted into something of lower value simply because it has lost its legal title of ownership. This is an institutional loss, rather than a real one because it could be restored by giving those who currently possess the article full legal ownership. But the loss is real relative to existing legal arrangements because the article, no longer freely transferable, has lost some of its usefulness.

Estimating Costs and Benefits

How market data may be useful even when there are divergences between private and social costs and benefits

When the problem of potential divergence between private and social costs or benefits faces the government, it requires estimates of the social valuations relative to the private valuations before it can begin to formulate policy objectives. When the problem involves only a small fraction of total output and there is a substantial market sector in the economy, the government can do much by maximizing its use of *market information*.

Using Market Data

Consider the case of a smoke-emitting factory. If the government's objective is to estimate the extent to which total social costs exceed the cost of resources used, it can carefully observe any costs evident in the market that can be directly attributable to the smoke emitted. Among these may be:

1. costs to residents of painting their houses more frequently than required in nonpolluted areas.
2. costs to residents of household cleaning and laundry above those required in nonpolluted areas.
3. medical costs to residents that can be attributed specifically to illnesses arising from the pollution.

All such costs are directly observable in market terms, and thus measurable in dollars. The total gives one possible estimate of the additional social costs arising from pollution.

Estimates as Limits

Estimates of this kind, however, will surely *understate* the true additional social costs. All are costs associated with restoring adversely affected people or things more or less back to normal. There will inevitably be households that are unable or unwilling to engage in the extra maintenance, and thus, will allow things to deteriorate. Suppose the additional maintenance comes to $1,000 per year per household. A household affected by the pollution suffers a definite loss. The owners may nevertheless consider the loss to be less than $1,000 and not pay for the maintenance. Similarly, there will be many people whose health is adversely affected but not enough to seek medical treatment. Moreover, there is no guarantee that those who do incur medical costs will be restored to the state of health they enjoyed prior to the pollution.

In much the same fashion, we could estimate the social benefits of a lighthouse by assessing the market value of shipping that would be wrecked off the relevant part of the coast if there were no lighthouse. Again, we would tend to underestimate the true social benefit by failing to consider such things as the nervous strain on captains and crew from negotiating the unlighted coastline, even without mishap.

Market Data May Not Be Appropriate

In using market prices to estimate costs and benefits, we must be sure that the data used are reasonable measures of true social valuations. In a perfectly competitive economy with no direct government intervention in the *private* sector, market data will generally tend to be quite reliable. As we concluded in our analysis of general equilibrium, a dollar's worth of any input, under these conditions, would produce the same additional value of any output.

But consider a more realistic example. An irrigation project is currently under way that, among other things, will increase cotton production in Arizona. Included in the assessment of the social benefits to be derived from this project is the market value of the anticipated increase in cotton output. The inclusion of this valuation may seem appropriate, but *it is wrong*. Why? Because cotton prices are artificially supported by the government. Price supports are themselves presumptive evidence that the social value of an extra pound of cotton is *less* than the market price. Because cotton is an ordinary private good, there is no reason why its social value should differ from its private value (what consumers are actually willing to pay). Consequently, it is the price consumers would pay *in the absence of government support* that should be used to measure social benefits. The reader may well ask: Why, then, is cotton subsidized? One answer is that it should not be. An alternative answer is that *farming*, as such, is considered to have a social value higher than the market value of its output.

A comparable effect may result from imperfect competition in the private sector. In the absence of scale economies, a monopolist will charge a higher price for a given output than would prevail under perfect competition. The monopolist's price, which necessarily exceeds marginal cost, thus *overstates* the social value of resources required to produce the output.

When Market Data Fail

Obviously, we cannot use existing market data to estimate the costs and benefits of actions that will substantially change the structure of, and prices in, the market sector, nor can we always readily assemble the precise market data we need. Many space and defense programs, for example, require techniques not previously used. In such cases, we can only *approximate* probable resource requirements (social costs) by looking at comparable operations in the market sector.

The social costs of, say, a defensive weapons system for which no market exists can be estimated from its actual money cost if each component of this cost is determined in some market. If labor and materials required for the system are valued at market prices, then the cost so computed is a reasonable representation of the value of other things that might have been produced with the same resources (subject to the "second-best" considerations discussed later in this chapter).

Estimating the benefits derived from such a weapons system is, of course, another matter. Well-informed authorities may differ about such essential questions as whether the system reduces the probability of disaster (thereby providing a positive benefit), or increases it (providing a negative benefit). Even if all agree that the system reduces the probability of a nuclear holocaust, how does one measure the social benefit derived from reducing this probability from, say, one in a thousand to one in a million?

Problems also arise in choosing the *right* market from which to take prices. For some public-works projects (dams, for example), the chief cost is the interest paid on the funds used for construction. If the federal government builds the dam, it can borrow funds at a relatively low interest rate. A municipal government, whose bonds are rated less safe, must pay a higher interest rate, while a private corporation must pay a higher rate still. Which rate then represents the true social cost of resources incorporated into the dam? Surely the true social cost of the dam cannot depend on which authority happens to build it? Many economists are inclined to use the rate of return on private investment, arguing that such investment consistently represents the most fruitful alternative.

Recap Some external effects are such that market data may be used to estimate social costs. In estimating the social costs of pollution, for example, the costs of cleaning and medical bills for resulting illnesses provide data of this kind. Generally, such data will underestimate true social costs and benefits. The actual data used must also be carefully assessed because market prices may not represent appropriate social valuations if there is imperfect competition or government intervention in the market.

Assessment and Compensation

Techniques for going beyond market data

In the absence of negative externalities, market data will usually understate the private benefits obtained from the availability and use of goods. A case of this kind was studied in Chapter 11, where it was pointed out that a good selling for, say, $10 yields a private benefit of *at least* that much to everyone who chooses to buy it at that price. Specifically, an individual who would have been willing to pay $20 for the good is said to extract a *consumer surplus* equivalent to the $10 difference.

Consumer Surplus

The general notion of consumer surplus can be summarized:

1. Market prices will understate the *money value equivalent* of benefits obtained by some consumers.
2. The extent of the understatement depends on *how many consumers* would be willing to pay *how much more* than the going market price, rather than do without the good.

The second point implies that the *amount of understatement* depends on the *shape of the demand curve* for the product. Figure 12.1 shows two different demand curves, intersecting the same constant cost supply curve at the same market price and market output. The relatively flat (highly elastic) demand curve of Figure 12.1(a) shows that few consumers are willing to pay much more than the actual price, while that of Figure 12.1(b) (exhibiting low elasticity) shows that many consumers are willing to pay considerably more than the going price. The understatement of total benefits that results from using market price as a measure (represented by the shaded areas) may thus be quite small, as in case (a), or quite large, as in case (b).

In the ordinary allocation of private goods through the market, the extent of this surplus is not relevant because ultimately it is the choice *at the margin* that counts. There would thus be no argument in favor of, say, increasing the output of goods with large consumer surpluses relative to those with small ones. The reason for this is: all consumers, in allocating their budgets, buy only enough of each good to make them indifferent between switching one cent from the purchase of one good to the purchase of another. Consumers who would have paid up to $20 for something they can actually obtain for $10 will thus allocate the $10 "saved" among other goods so as to obtain their optimum goods collection.

Assessment

Nevertheless, the notion of consumer surplus is of great usefulness in analyzing cases such as those involving the provision of public goods when there is no possibility of simple adjustment in a working market. If a public good is worth, say, $100 to an individual, this implies that the person would feel better paying $99 for the good than not having it at all.

One technique for determining whether or not a public good should be

Figure 12.1

The extent of "consumer surplus," the shaded areas in the diagrams, depends on the shape of the demand curve.

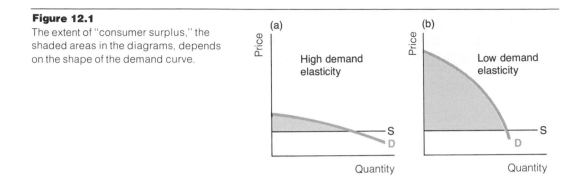

supplied is to convert the consumer surplus associated with the good into an assessment of its benefits. We need simply ask each individual how much he or she would be willing to pay to ensure the provision of the good, rather than do without it. One individual might be willing to pay $100, another $25, another nothing. By adding up all such individual assessments, we could then obtain some idea of the value to be placed on total benefits. If this total exceeds the cost of providing the good, then we could argue in favor of providing the good. If the total is less than the cost, obviously, there would be a case against providing the good.

Problems

For this system to work, it is essential that the assessments be *honest*. In practice, this is difficult to guarantee. If an individual believes he will actually have to *pay* the assessed amount, he has a motive for understatement. If he does not expect to be called on to pay, but expects to gain from having the good, he has a motive for overstatement in the hope of ensuring that the good will be provided. The poor, therefore, will generally be motivated to overstate the value of public goods, the rich to understate them. With some ingenuity, voting and other procedures can be devised to minimize dishonest responses.

Assessment methods have often been advocated and are sometimes used for highly localized public goods, like access roads to residential properties, with the implication that such assessments will actually have to be paid.

In principle, the assessment method could be used to determine the *amount* of a public good to be provided. Let's suppose that we assess the benefits from an increase in police protection—perhaps by simply asking people how much they would be willing to pay for the guarantee of an additional police officer on the block, or more indirectly by estimating the social value of potential reduction in losses from theft, injury, and the like that would result from increased protection. The increase in social benefit from a small increase in police protection—the *marginal social benefit*—can be compared with the increase in cost, measured adequately enough in this case by the additional officer's wages—the *marginal social cost*. If the marginal social benefit exceeds the marginal social cost, police protection should be expanded. If marginal social cost exceeds the marginal social benefit, it should not.

Recap A consumer's willingness to pay $10 for a unit of a good implies that he or she values having that good at least as much as $10. However, the consumer may be willing to pay more than $10, rather than do without the good. The amount of the excess, or consumer surplus, may be useful in reaching decisions about public goods, if it can be determined. One method is to attempt to obtain honest answers to the question: How much would you be willing to give up in order to have a certain public good rather than do without it?

Capsule Supplement 12.2   **On the Uses of Voting**

In a democracy, it might seem that the simplest and most appropriate way to decide whether to produce some public good, or ban some activity yielding a public bad, is to put it to a vote. While this may be desirable on ideological grounds, it's important to realize that a mandate of the majority does not necessarily guarantee an improvement in social welfare.

If each person casts one ballot, someone who is affected significantly by a given proposal has no more weight in the system than someone who is completely unaffected by it. If the distribution of effects is such that many benefit slightly from a proposal while a few lose heavily, it may be easy to obtain a majority in favor of it, even though the overall effect on social welfare is negative.

Bargaining for votes, as among congressmen voting on bills, may help to introduce some weighting into the system. A congressman whose constituency is deeply affected, one way or the other, by a specific proposal can demonstrate concern by being "difficult" about other bills of marginal importance to his constituency until an acceptable compromise is reached.

Simple voting can also produce inconsistent results when there are more than two choices. This is due to the so-called *voting paradox*. Imagine a family consisting of three individuals—Mom, Pop, and Junior—with three alternatives as to how to spend a Sunday afternoon: at an all-Beethoven concert, at the beach, or at a baseball game. The three family members' relative preferences for these three alternatives are as follows:

Order of Preference	Mom	Pop	Junior
1	Beethoven	ball game	beach
2	beach	Beethoven	ball game
3	ball game	beach	Beethoven

None of these activities is the first preference of a majority of the family members. If we compare the activities two at a time, we have majorities for the following rankings:

Beethoven preferred to beach   (Mom and Pop)
beach preferred to ball game   (Mom and Junior)
ball game preferred to Beethoven   (Pop and Junior)

Because each of the three activities is either more or less preferred by a majority than the remaining two, the outcome is indeterminant. Consequently, some other criterion (say, deference to a particular family member out of respect, fear, or obligation) must ultimately be used if a decision is to be made.

Allocating Costs and Benefits

The distributional effects of converting social costs into private costs

One general solution to problems arising from divergences between social and private valuations is policy designed to convert social costs and benefits into private costs and benefits. Such policy, when successful, forces private decision-makers to *internalize* all social costs and benefits in such a way that their actions are consistent with the socially desirable result.

An electricity-generating plant that emits smoke could be charged with all the additional home maintenance and medical costs attributable to its operations. To some extent, the legal system already does this as damage suits can, in general, be brought against polluters. But legal remedies are slow and costly. They also require conclusive proof of responsibility for damage whose value is assessed *after the fact*. The aim of social policy should be to induce the generating plant to use a smokeless process in the first place, rather than simply repair the damage caused by a smoke-emitting process.

Reallocation by Taxes

The government, for example, could simply levy a tax on smoke equivalent to the estimated social costs associated with the pollution. If this tax exceeds the additional costs of using the smokeless process, the manager of the plant will obviously be moved to change the process used. Even if this tax is *less* than the additional costs of employing the smokeless process, however, it might still be desirable to levy the tax (although it would not be sufficient to induce smokeless operation) and use the proceeds to subsidize pollution-associated maintenance in the local community.

Such a tax reallocates costs and benefits. Let's suppose that the generating plant is located in a small town on the outskirts of a large city that it supplies with electricity. To use the smoke-emitting process will provide the city with cheap electricity at the expense of polluting the small town. To compensate the town by a non-prohibitive tax will increase electricity prices in the city. Such a tax thus results in a reallocation of benefits.

Public Bads

Consider a true public bad, such as air pollution from automobiles. Such pollution can be attributed both to automobile producers (who are ultimately responsible for engine design, etc.) and to automobile users. What if a nonpolluting car could be produced for $500 more than a conventional model? Would anyone buy it? The additional expense would obviously constitute a *private cost* to each buyer. But air pollution is a *public bad* yielding *social costs* that cannot be eliminated by the actions of a single individual.

In this case, a *subsidy* to auto manufacturers of at least $500 per car would be called for, provided the estimated social benefit of removing pollution exceeds the resulting total subsidy. (In the United States, this would represent an annual subsidy of more than $5 billion on new motor vehicles.) On the other hand, the government could simply *prohibit* the registration of new cars without antipollution equipment. Consumers would then have to pay $500 more per car because it would no longer be permissible for manufacturers to market conventional models.

In the United States, the general population of taxpayers and that of car owners are virtually identical. Therefore, there would be little difference between forcing car owners to pay $500 more for their cars or increasing taxes by an amount sufficient to finance a general subsidy to the auto industry. *Politically* it might prove more feasible to prohibit sales because the relationship between increased car costs and reduced pollution would be more directly apparent to the population than with the subsidy approach.

Club Goods

Major policy problems arise in allocating the costs of *club goods*. Should the city art museum's operating costs be paid for by charging admission, or should these costs be financed out of general tax revenue to permit free admission?

If every resident of the city considers himself to benefit from the museum, even though he may rarely visit it, there is a case for treating it as a conventional public good. However, if the benefits accrue only to those who visit the museum, there is a case for treating it as a club good and charging admission. Whichever choice is made, there will be distributional effects.

Suppose admission is free, and the museum is financed by a tax that falls more heavily on the rich than on the poor. Then social benefits are redistributed from the rich to the poor. Alternatively, if the tax falls more heavily on the poor than the rich, as is commonly the case with property and other local taxes, the redistribution of social benefits is from the poor to the rich—especially if the rich are more likely to frequent the museum than the poor. Free admission also represents a redistribution from city residents to out-of-towners (including suburbanites) because the latter would have access to the museum but not be required to contribute to its costs.

The art museum case brings up an interesting phenomenon: public goods or things with certain public-good characteristics are sometimes provided independently of both the market and the government by private gift. Society, in giving costless "brownie points" for philanthropic private donations to the public, has devised yet another ingenious mechanism. This has worked especially well in the case of art museums, many of which have been founded with just such gifts. But because the mechanism requires great income inequalities to provide the requisite millionaires, it is not without its own social disadvantages.

When things possess something of a public-goods character, but provide benefits that are limited to a specific *sector* of society, there is a case for allocating costs to the benefiting sector only. Consider the operation of a public airport. This could be supported either from *general tax revenues* or from *user charges* levied on the operators of the aircraft. User charges on commercial aircraft will ultimately be reflected in fares, and thus paid by air travelers. If air travel is distributed over the population in much the same way as the general tax burden, then there is little difference in the impact of the two systems. If aircraft users are a relatively small and specialized group, however, there is obviously a stronger case for financing through user charges rather than out of general tax revenues.

Recap A divergence between social and private costs may be reduced by government intervention. Firms may be taxed on their emission of pollution, in which case the social costs of pollution are converted into private costs. Such a tax will generally result in an increase in the prices of the firm's primary products. Consequently, those who use these products the least and suffer from pollution the most will ultimately gain from such a tax, while those out of contact with the pollution but who consume the products will lose. All tax-subsidy arrangements will be expected to have certain distributional effects of this kind.

Public-Facility Pricing

Whether tolls should be charged for crossing a bridge, and similar pricing problems

Let's turn now to the problem of analyzing the effect of user charges for a public facility. This analysis, focusing on the allocation of *goods and resources* rather than on the allocation of costs and benefits, applies as well to public utilities and the regulation of imperfectly competitive industries.

Let's take the oldest and simplest example. A bridge is to be built across a river joining two towns. Should a toll be charged for crossing the bridge and, if so, how should the size of the toll be determined?

The No-Congestion Case

We'll initially assume that there is no *congestion* problem, in which case even the cheapest bridge can handle all actual and potential traffic. Suppose the bridge has, in fact, already been built. We can reason in the following way. An additional person (or automobile) crossing the bridge has absolutely no negative effect on anything—the *marginal social cost* of using the existing bridge is zero. Clearly, anyone who crosses the bridge does so for some reason (there is a positive *private benefit*). Because there is no congestion, the crossing does not affect anyone else, and also represents a positive *social benefit*. We can thus conclude that allowing free use of the bridge will add social benefits without adding social costs, and no toll should be charged.

If a toll were charged, there would undoubtedly be some whose private benefits would be less than the toll, and who would not pay to cross. Because excluding these people would represent a loss of social benefits without any reduction in social cost, there would be a net loss to society.

In general, there will be a net social loss whenever we exclude from a facility someone whose private gain from it would be at least as great as the marginal social cost of his use of it. If a price is charged, therefore, it should be equal to the marginal cost of providing the facility. Because in the bridge case the marginal cost is zero, the price should also be zero. Note that the equality of price and marginal cost is the result we would achieve under perfect competition, except that most public facilities possess extreme economies of scale and hence would never be provided by the market under perfect competition. The policy of pricing public facilities at marginal cost is generally referred to as *marginal cost pricing*. As we shall observe later in this section, this pricing formula does not necessarily hold if there are externalities like congestion.

Cost Allocation

We have not considered the problem of who should pay to build the bridge in the first place. In the absence of a toll, it could be paid for out of general tax revenue. Is this the best solution?

If the bridge were between two towns and the whole population of both towns used the bridge in approximately equal amounts, there would be a good case for financing it out of tax revenues. But suppose that all the traffic was from North Town going to market in South Town and returning home. Then, it might seem that the bridge should be paid for only by North Town residents. But, because South Town businesses would obviously obtain benefits from North Town customers, there is a case for having South Town pay as well.

If the benefits of the bridge accrue only to certain identifiable groups in both towns, there would be a case for charging these groups. Such costs should *not* be assigned through tolls, however, because this would result in an underutilization of resources. The appropriate solution would be to assign costs by taxing those groups gaining from the bridge, rather than by levying a toll on each person crossing.

Congestion and Other Externalities

The analysis of the bridge problem is radically changed if there is a *congestion problem*. Congestion constitutes a negative externality—each additional person trying to cross increases the delay in crossing for all other persons—and results in the social benefits from, say, 100 people all trying to cross being less than one-hundred times the private benefit from each person crossing unhindered.

In other words, in the congestion case, the total social benefit is less than the sum of private benefits. To take the extreme case, a traffic jam may prevent everyone from crossing, reducing the total social benefit to zero. Because the *marginal* social benefit may be negative in the congestion case (as when marginal attempts to cross jam traffic completely, thus reducing total social benefit from a positive amount to zero), there is now a case for a toll because we want to *restrict* the number of persons using the bridge.

By charging a toll, the bridge is restricted to those whose *private benefit* is at least as great as the toll. The toll, in this case, serves as a *rationing device*. Although toll proceeds may be used to finance the cost of the bridge, this is not its primary purpose. The toll should be related to the *costs of congestion,* rather than to the *costs of building the bridge.* Specifically, it should be sufficiently high that the marginal social benefit equals zero, and is therefore equal to marginal social cost. Toll receipts might ultimately be smaller or larger than necessary to pay for the bridge.

Congestion, however, suggests the alternative of widening the bridge or building a new one. To make the appropriate decision, we would need to compare the total potential social benefits lost by rationing the use of the existing bridge with the social costs involved in expansion. If building another bridge would increase social benefits by more than social costs, it would be appropriate to do so and abolish the toll on the existing bridge.

It should be obvious that rationing the use of a bridge by a toll will generally be optimal only in the short run during which the marginal costs of any potential expansion loom large. In the long run, the optimal solution will generally be to increase bridge capacity.

Increasing bridge capacity, however, may not be optimal if there are other external effects. Let's suppose that the sole purpose of the bridge is to permit access to a lookout commanding a spectacular view. The topography is such that a maximum of 100 cars can be fitted into the lookout's parking lot. Moreover, each car stays at the lookout for approximately one hour. If we assume that there is an even distribution of traffic over time, and that there are *more* than 100 cars per hour whose occupants yearn to see the view, then building a bridge whose capacity exceeds 200 cars per hour (each car must cross twice), even if there were congestion at this capacity, would be an obvious waste of resources. To "decongest" the bridge would simply send more cars into an already full parking lot.

Recap If there is an addition to social benefit from the additional use of a facility, such as a bridge, but no addition to social cost, social welfare will be increased by permitting free usage. Costs of the facility should be financed from general tax revenues or from taxes on those gaining from the facility, but not by tolls related to the actual use of the facility. Externalities, of which congestion is one example, may result in restrictions on the use of a facility. Tolls would then be appropriate, but should be set to ration use appropriately rather than in relation to the costs of supplying the facility.

Capsule Supplement 12.3   **Some Notes on Transportation Policy**

The backbone of transport regulation in the United States is the common-carrier principle. Under this principle, transportation firms are granted franchises with restricted competition on condition that they carry goods or passengers at published fares on fixed schedules. A second basic principle of transport regulation is that of cross-subsidization; carriers are required to accept a mix of routes and/or merchandise so they have both high-profit operations and low-profit or even loss operations, the former offsetting the latter. These principles are broadly applied to air, rail, and, to a lesser extent, commercial road transport.

Cross-subsidization means that air travelers between Chicago and Podunk City pay less than cost for their service which is subsidized by air travelers between New York and Chicago, who pay more than cost. This raises two quite separate policy questions: (1) Is it socially desirable for travelers between Chicago and Podunk City to receive air transport below cost? (2) If so, who should pay the subsidy? Why should it be travelers between other cities? Why not society as a whole? Or residents of Podunk City, whose land values may be increased because of better access to Chicago?

Many might accept the principle that rural routes should be subsidized because they believe society as a whole gains by reducing the isolation of its smaller communities. But few would be prepared to argue that the associated costs should be borne exclusively by other travelers. Nevertheless, cross-subsidization is an administratively easy, and politically acceptable, way to carry out the policy. Similar instances of cross-subsidization characterize urban-transit franchising. For example, operators may receive a franchise for highly profitable routes only if they accept certain less-desirable routes.

Naturally, carriers will try to get rid of unprofitable routes. In contrast to most industries, transport firms cannot exit easily—they must obtain special permission to withdraw from a route, and this is not lightly given. To this end, railroads have gone so far as to deliberately provide poor service and dirty cars on so-called milk runs to chase customers away, then seek permission to terminate service because of a lack of customers. Such tactics have had important external effects on major routes, both from reduced feed-in from branch lines and from the lowered service reputation of the railroad generally.

Railroad passenger services have thus come to be operated under a centralized government subsidy, through the Amtrak Corporation. In making decisions about which routes Amtrak should maintain, the Interstate Commerce Commission has considered certain things other than the simple demand for passenger transportation. Among these are the need to reduce both highway congestion and the effects of automobile pollution, the scenic beauty of some routes, and even international relations—the latter in the decision to preserve a rail link to Mexico City. Such "other factors" provide good examples of the kinds of externalities governments *should* take into account when making policy decisions.

The Theory of Second Best

The problem of doing as well as possible when the very best is out of reach

In Chapter 8, we demonstrated that, in a well-defined general sense, *universal* perfect competition is optimal. Then, in Chapter 9, we showed that in a two-sector economy in which one sector is perfectly competitive and the other is imperfectly competitive, the output mix is non-optimal. There is too much output at too low a price from the perfectly competitive sector, and too little output at too high a price from the imperfectly competitive sector. Under these circumstances, the perfectly competitive sector will not behave optimally, because of the *economic distortions* introduced by the existence of imperfect competition elsewhere in the economy.

Let's consider the nature of these distortions. In the imperfectly competitive sector, price exceeds marginal cost, while in the perfectly competitive sector, price and marginal cost are equal. Because consumers are free to choose goods from both sectors, however, the *marginal private benefits* per dollar spent are the same in each.

A Simple Example

Suppose the market structure in the imperfectly competitive sector is such that marginal revenue is half the price. In this case, price is necessarily twice marginal cost ($P = 2MC$).

Let's assess the true social value of resources used. If we withdraw $1 worth of resources from the perfectly competitive sector, output will decline by $1 because price equals marginal cost. Thus, we might conclude that $1 worth of resources produces $1 worth of output, and that this is the value to be placed on the resources. But if we withdraw $1 worth of resources from the imperfectly competitive sector, output will fall by $2 (since price equals twice marginal cost), suggesting that the social value of $1 worth of resources is really $2.

In general, if we direct resources into some third use, some of them will be drawn out of the perfectly competitive sector, others from the imperfectly competitive sector. Generally speaking, the resources drawn from the two sectors will be in proportion to the respective size of each sector. Suppose that 75 percent of resources are initially employed in the perfectly competitive sector, 25 percent in the imperfectly competitive sector. If we withdraw $4 in resources for other uses, resources in the perfectly competitive sector will fall by $3 (75 percent of withdrawals), while in the imperfectly competitive sector they will fall by $1.

Because $P = MC$ in the perfectly competitive sector, a marginal loss of $3 in resources will result in a loss of $3 worth of output, so output in the competitive sector will fall by $3. In the imperfectly competitive sector, on the other hand, $P = 2MC$. Each dollar of resource reduction causes a loss of $2 in output, the extra dollar being monopoly profit lost that does not represent a social cost. Thus, the withdrawal of $4 worth of resources, $3 from the competitive sector and $1 from the imperfectly competitive sector, leads to a loss of $5 in output. This output loss is $3 in the perfectly competitive sector and $2 in the imperfectly competitive sector. Thus, $4 worth of resources produces $5 worth of output, representing an average social value (in terms of what they can produce) of $1.25 (= $5 ÷ 4) for resources with a market price of $1. The true social value of resources is thus 25 percent higher than their market value.

Now let's consider the position of a third sector in the economy, one whose price-output policy is determined by the government. This might be a public-goods sector or a regulated sector. Upon what basic principle should price-output policy in this sector be determined?

Clearly the economy will not be at an *optimum* so long as any one sector is imperfectly competitive. The "first-best" policy would be to ensure perfect competition throughout the entire private sector, then set price in the public or regulated sector accordingly. Under universal perfect competition, price and marginal cost would always be equal. Thus, the market cost of resources would represent the value of their marginal use in all sectors, and the appropriate third-sector policy would be to equate price and marginal cost also.

Second Best

But what if it is *impossible* to ensure universal competition? In this case, the economy cannot achieve a true optimum, so the most that the government can do with this public sector is achieve a *second-best* situation, that is, the best that can be done given that one sector remains imperfectly competitive.

For a second-best solution, public-sector pricing that equates prices with ordinary marginal cost will not generally be optimal. As previously pointed out, the market prices of resources drawn from the private into the public sector do not necessarily represent their true social value. If $1 worth of resources withdrawn from the private sector causes a decline of $1.25 in the value of private-sector output, there will be a gain from their use in the public sector only if they produce output valued at $1.25 or more. Public-sector prices should thus be set at 1.25 times marginal cost. Using the traditional rule of equating price and marginal cost would give not a second-best solution, but something even farther from the optimum because it would undervalue the resources withdrawn from the private sector.

In other words, a pricing-output policy for a given sector that would be optimal *if there were perfect competition everywhere else* may not be so in the presence of imperfect competition. Ensuring perfectly competitive behavior in one industry may not be the best policy if imperfect competition is permitted elsewhere—although ensuring perfect competition in one industry as part of a sequence in which it will ultimately prevail everywhere would certainly be justified.

The general theory of second best, which really amounts to noting that optimality is a general equilibrium property of the economy as a whole and that the appropriate rules for one sector thus depend on the actual behavior in all others, has wide applicability. The example given illustrates the need for policy-makers to view the economy as a complete system.

Recap If the private sector is perfectly competitive, a public sector selling output in the market should follow perfectly competitive pricing and output rules, equating price and marginal cost. If the private sector is divided between imperfect and perfect competition, however, such rules may be inappropriate. Unless the imperfect competition can be abolished, society will be faced with a second-best problem, in which case it is generally appropriate for the public sector to charge a price exceeding marginal cost.

Exercises

Use the same basic data as given for the exercises in Chapter 11, with fixed expenses for the transit system at $2.5 million.

The city decides to set up the public transit system with the weekly fare to be set at $10, $8, $4, or $0 (free transit), and with a subsidy from general tax revenue at whatever level is required. The policy decision to be made is the level of the fare, with all users paying the same fare.

1. For each of the four possible weekly fares, compute:
   a. revenue from fares,
   b. number of users,
   c. total cost of operation,
   d. subsidy required, if any.
2. What level of fare would require the least subsidy?
3. What subsidy would be required for marginal cost pricing?
4. Suppose abolition of all fares would save $1 million weekly from reduction of staff otherwise required to police fare payment and collect fares. Would marginal cost pricing now be optimal?

For Thought and Discussion

1. Should automobile manufacturers be charged with the costs of air pollution arising from internal-combustion engines?
2. It has been argued that houses near a smoke-emitting factory will be lower in price and rent for less than comparable houses elsewhere, so those living near the factory are already being compensated for its external effects. Consider carefully the merits of this argument, and decide whether or not you agree with it.
3. Supersonic airliners have an associated sonic boom that has unwanted external effects along the route of flight. Assuming that such airliners are permitted to fly, analyze the situation in terms of social costs and social benefits. Will the costs and benefits accrue to broadly similar groups of people, or to quite distinct groups?
4. It has been proposed that tolls be charged on all automobile access routes into Manhattan and that the proceeds be used to subsidize the fare on public transportation. Consider this proposal in terms of (a) the effect on resource allocation, and (b) the implicit redistribution of income.

Chapter 13
The Cities

Terms and Concepts

Consumption externalities
Production externalities
Labor specialization
Benefit differential
Irreversible decision
Handing-down model
Urban renewal
Rent supplements
Redistributive taxes
Property tax
Sales tax
Revenue sharing
Functional specialization

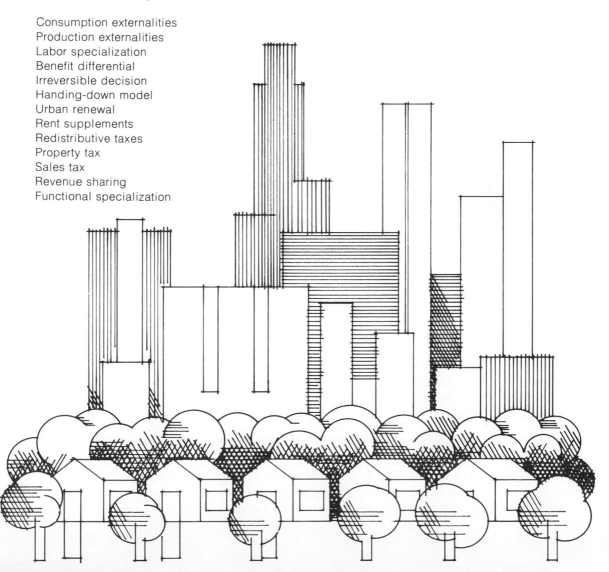

| A Study in Externalities | The crucial role of production and consumption externalities in the study of cities |

Cities develop, thrive, grow, and ultimately strangle themselves on *externalities* taken in the most general sense. Without these externalities, cities and, for that matter, small villages, would have no basis for existence, and their populations would presumably disperse more or less evenly over the countryside.

Positive Externalities

It is the *good* externalities that initially bring people together. These include simple *consumption externalities,* such as those derived from contact with relatives, friends, and neighbors. The private benefit derived by individuals from certain festive, religious, and social activities is greater the more people are engaged in these activities. An additional participant in a gathering thus not only gains personally, but increases the benefits of those already there. In many countries, peasants with small landholdings live in central villages, rather than on isolated plots of land in order to take advantage of such positive externalities.

There are important *production externalities* and *scale economies* as well. A hundred households in a small town may be able to defend themselves more effectively than can a hundred isolated households—a factor historically important to urban growth in certain times and places. Clustering of industry permits *labor specialization* (a form of scale economy) whereby individuals can devote their entire skill and training to some specific craft or trade.

Most externalities, both of consumption and production, have a *spatial* property. They exist only if there is physical proximity. Market towns with a variety of shops and services developed because it is more efficient to buy many things in a single shopping excursion. *Location* with respect to activities whose benefits are sought is also an important source of externalities. The nineteenth-century industrial towns of Europe and America grew up because workers needed to live near the new large factories. The towns continued to grow as other factories located near the existing labor supply. Financial and commercial centers developed because market transactions were mutually advantageous to all traders when they were close to each other.

Negative Externalities

But there are *bad* externalities as well. While an isolated household can dispose of sewage and garbage behind the bushes, such disposal into a city street (common enough in Medieval times) has rather obvious external effects on passersby. Contagious disease spreads rapidly by close contact, as evidenced by the plague that wiped out a large proportion of the population of Medieval European cities. Locational proximity to factories results in widespread exposure to air and noise pollution. Moreover, people themselves have dimension, leading to congestion and crowding.

A Balance Between Good and Bad

Most serious urban problems arise because the bad externalities have a joint relationship to the good. Desirable proximity to friends goes with potentially undesirable proximity to strangers. Indeed, most good externalities require proximity, and it is this proximity that brings on most of the bad externalities. While some separation of the two may be feasible, this can usually only be done at a cost. One certainly need not live within the smoke pall of one's place of work, but the alternative, commuting, is expensive and time consuming.

Technological change affects the relationship among externalities. The development of public transportation has given workers access to the factory without living in its shadow. The telephone has permitted instant communication without physical proximity. The replacement of steam by electric trains has reduced air pollution, but the replacement of horse-drawn carriages by automobiles has increased it. The invention of the elevator has permitted location to be developed in three dimensions, and so on.

A city always remains in an uneasy balance between its good and bad externalities. As technological, economic, and social conditions change, this balance changes. Economic policy toward the cities strives to maximize social benefits (in which good externalities play a major part) relative to social costs (in which we include bad externalities). As might be expected, the strong relationship between good and bad externalities greatly complicates the formulation of effective urban policy.

Recap Cities are built on a complex of external effects associated with spatial proximity. Some of these, such as accessibility to shops and entertainment are "good" externalities in the sense that people gain from them. There are also "bad" externalities, such as noise and congestion, associated with the same proximity. Cities stand in a delicate balance between these good and bad externalities.

Economies and Diseconomies of Size

Their balance in the economic structure of cities

Closely linked with the balance between a city's good and bad externalities, which primarily affect the consumption side, is a balance on the production side between economies and diseconomies of scale.

Many urban facilities—such as communications and mass transit—exhibit economies of scale. Even housing can exhibit such economies, as when the heating and maintenance of individual apartments are centrally provided for an entire apartment building. Retailing also possesses economies of this kind, as found in large department stores.

But there are diseconomies of scale as well. As cities grow, land at the center becomes a limiting resource and population density increases. Buildings must have multiple stories to increase the capacity of the land. As a consequence, building costs rise disproportionately. As more and more automobiles come into the city center, parking becomes more difficult, traffic flow is impeded, and air and noise pollution increase.

Linkages

Diseconomies in one context may have external effects that increase the diseconomies in others. If street space is fixed, an increase in the number of automobiles leads to a shortage of parking space. Motorists are thus forced to double-park, reducing the rate of traffic flow and increasing pollution. Double-parking also impedes and thus increases the cost of garbage collection, street cleaning, and commercial delivery. Even the costs of police services rise as the enforcement of regulations against double-parking increases.

The evidence that the largest cities have outgrown scale economies and are now facing major diseconomies of size is considerable. Although electrical power supply is generally taken as a classic example of an industry with large-scale economies, the costs of supplying electricity to the customer are noticeably higher in New York City than elsewhere in the United States. Because there is no compelling evidence that Con Edison (New York City's supplier) is especially inefficient compared with other large power suppliers, the high costs can be ascribed to diseconomies associated with high urban concentration. Costs of many things involving a large transportation and distribution component are high in cities, because of the diseconomies that arise from congestion.

As size increases, the total effect of many negative externalities increases in an even greater proportion. If the population doubles, for example, apartment-house incinerators burn twice as much garbage and thus produce twice as much smoke. Because smoke is a non-diminishable public bad, we have twice as much smoke affecting twice as many people, a fourfold increase in total effect. For technological reasons, the increase may be even more than this because climatic patterns of certain areas of the city may result in a slower dispersion of the increased quantity of smoke than before, so we may ultimately have twice as much smoke lingering over the city for longer than before, and affecting twice as many people.

Good externalities, if non-diminishable, can also increase with size—the variety of foods offered in the restaurants of a city, for example, will tend to increase with population. Most good externalities, however, exhibit a slowdown in their rate of increase with size beyond some point, while most bad externalities increase at an increasing rate with size. Further growth in the population of Manhattan, for example, would probably not affect the already large selection of restaurants and theaters, but would certainly put increasing pressure on the ability of the atmosphere to clear pollutants and of the transit system to move people effectively.

Recap Some of the things a city must produce in order to sustain itself are subject to economies of scale, while others are associated with diseconomies. Just as the city is balanced between good and bad externalities, so it is balanced between being sufficiently large to obtain economies of scale and being sufficiently small to avoid diseconomies.

Urban Poverty

How poverty, while not created by cities, becomes concentrated and visible in them

Cities have contained large populations of the poor for as long as evidence has been available. Cities are highly visible and have always seemed an obvious place to seek opportunities. Even if such opportunities are available in nonurban areas, information about these opportunities is relatively poor. Moreover, there are economies of job search in cities; instead of having to travel from one isolated employer to another in search of work, many such searches can be carried out in a single day. Given the random element involved in finding a job, it's simply rational to be in a place where there are many employers.

The cities have historically represented *some* hope of personal advancement, however forlorn, for those who see *no* hope where they are. This is especially true of a city like Calcutta, India, where, in the world's largest concentration of urban poverty, an estimated 250,000 people live—and die—on the sidewalks. Rural Bengalis, having no prospects in their villages, migrate to Calcutta where they see some hope, however faint, of a job. Even though they know they may die for their efforts, they view the gamble as worthwhile.

Thus the poor migrate to cities where they often remain poor. There is little evidence that those not already poor become so when they reach the city, although many may find that a given money income produces a lower standard of living in the city than in the rural areas from which they've migrated. It is important, therefore, to place the problem of urban poverty in proper perspective:

The urban poor are not people who have been made poor by living in cities, but people who have been left poor by the working of the economy as a whole, and happen to live in cities.

There is, of course, the question of why the poor who come to the cities generally *remain* poor. In America, the traditional belief was that poor immigrants arrived in cities, worked hard, and ceased to be poor. Even if this partly mythical belief were previously accepted, certain changes have taken place in the larger cities that prevent it from being so readily accepted today.

Manufacturing, the traditional employer of unskilled immigrant labor, has been moving out of the cities—especially out of the central city. For this and other reasons associated with the business structure of cities, employment opportunities for the unskilled and uneducated are greatly restricted in the central-city area. Typists, with high-school diplomas, commute into the city center from the suburbs, passing through poverty areas where education levels are low and unemployment rates high.

Urban Poverty Is Visible

Contrary to popular belief, poverty is *not* especially prevalent in cities. For the United States, the only country in which accurate statistics on poverty exist, the incidence of poverty is lower in metropolitan areas than in rural areas. This is, after all, what we should expect, given that the poor migrate *to* the cities—they presumably would not do so unless there was poverty elsewhere.

An important feature of urban poverty, as with most characteristics of the urban economy, is its externalities. The most obvious externality is simply that urban poverty is *visible*. Rural poverty is scattered and, even if seen by the passing motorist, may be regarded simply as part of the local scene. Evidence of urban poverty, on the other hand, is highly visible to all.

Because the affluent are disturbed by the sight of poverty, they avoid it if possible by moving to locations where poverty is less visible. But the visibility of urban poverty *does* lead to greater attempts (however inadequate) to assist the poor. Local government transfer payments are considerably higher in urban areas than in rural areas. This is another incentive for the movement of the poor into cities.

Slums

The externalities of poverty are multiplied in the urban environment. The poor cannot afford good housing, so the slums remain. If everyone were affluent, no one (except, perhaps, a few eccentrics) would be willing to live in slum housing, *however low the rent*. The demand would all but disappear, and the slums would be demolished and probably replaced quite rapidly by adequate housing through the ordinary working of the market. Like urban poverty itself, slums, a manifestation of that poverty, are highly visible (even though the proportion of substandard housing in the central cities is only one-third that in rural areas).

It is externalities again that cause poverty to be concentrated in special neighborhoods. One deteriorated building on a block creates negative externalities for residents of the area, rents fall, and landlords allow the remaining buildings to deteriorate. Because the poor are crowded into such neighborhoods, their associations are primarily with other poor people. This has its own good and bad externalities. Surviving poverty is an art in which information and help from others in the same position is relevant, but information about how to *escape* poverty is not so easily accessible in this environment.

In the final analysis, poverty stems from the operation of the economy *as a whole*, even though its external effects are felt most acutely in an urban environment. Thus, we may conclude that there is more potential social benefit to be gained from the elimination of poverty in the cities than from its elimination elsewhere.

Recap Cities do not create poverty, even though the poor are both more concentrated and more visible in cities than elsewhere. Externalities cause the poor to be concentrated in specific urban areas. These areas are more visible than equivalent concentrations of rural poverty simply because they are adjacent to the rest of the city.

Capsule Supplement 13.1   **Urban Poverty in America**

In a special survey conducted in 1975, 12.3 percent of the population of the United States was found to be below the officially defined poverty level. Poverty was actually greater in rural areas than in large metropolitan areas, and in the metropolitan areas it was much more prevalent in the central core of large cities than elsewhere. The incidence of poverty was 15 percent in the central cities of the largest metropolitan areas, and only 7.6 percent in the suburban rings surrounding these cities. For the metropolitan areas as a whole it was 10.8 percent, 1.5 percentage points *below* the national average. Of all the nation's poor, about one-third lived in the central cities in 1975, another fourth lived in the suburban rings, with the remainder (about two-fifths) residing outside metropolitan areas.

While these statistics provide the overall picture, it should be noted that urban poverty has a special *social* concentration. In 1975, 29.1 percent of all central-city, black residents were poor, along with 22.5 percent of suburban blacks, compared with 6.7 percent of suburban whites. Again, however, the incidence of poverty among blacks was greater outside the metropolitan areas (specifically, 42.4 percent).

The highly localized concentration of poverty becomes clear by looking at statistics for *poverty areas,* that is, neighborhoods with high concentrations of the poor. About one-half of all the poor families in New York City live in poverty areas, although these areas contain only one-fourth of *all* families. Again there is evidence of social and ethnic concentration. Indeed, more than half of the nonwhites who are *not* poor live in poverty areas, while less than one-sixth of nonpoor whites live in poverty areas.

Contrary to much popular belief, while poverty is less widespread in urban areas than elsewhere in the economy, it is concentrated in the central cities rather than in the suburbs, and in particular neighborhoods within the central cities. Racial and ethnic factors tend to increase this concentration because many nonpoor blacks and Puerto Ricans live in these poor neighborhoods.

Land Use

How the market succeeds and fails to allocate land within the city

A city exists because of externalities derived from proximity. Thus, the *locational* properties of land are critical. Land is the ultimate limiting resource in the economics of cities.

In the ordinary working of the market system, prime locations are limited in supply. Indeed, for simplicity's sake, we can assume that the supply of prime locations is absolutely fixed. Rent for prime land will thus be determined by demand conditions. Each potential user will be willing to pay rent no greater than the value to him of being in that location. In particular, a potential user will be willing to pay a *rent differential* above the rent in alternative locations, equal to, at most, the *benefit differential* from being in the prime location rather than in alternative locations. Thus, market rents will *ration* prime land to those for whom it yields the greatest benefit.

Social and Private Benefits

But such benefits are necessarily *private* benefits. The market system will not allocate prime land to uses in which the *social* benefits exceed the private benefits. No market system would generate a Central Park in Manhattan or a Bois de Boulogne in Paris because the associated social benefits could not be converted into private benefits to the landowners of the areas on which these parks stand. Such parks do generate private benefits, but primarily to those *near* the park rather than to those owning the park land itself. The value of land on the perimeter of a park will generally rise because people will pay higher rents for a view of, or immediate access to, the park.

Although most parks are public goods, this need not be the case. Some parks are club (or group-consumption) goods. "Club" parks have long existed in urban centers. Many of the gardens in the squares of London were once fenced and accessible only to those living on the square. Gramercy Park in New York remains a club park of this kind. Yet even a club park may still provide external benefits to those who pass by. Some suburbs have club parks, closed to all but those with permits issued to residents or taxpayers of the area.

Certain types of park facilities, whose benefits can be confined entirely to those who enter the park, may even be developed on a direct market basis. Typical cases are amusement parks, swimming pools, tennis courts, and other special facilities.

The great city parks, located on land with lucrative alternative uses and bringing external benefits even to those who do not use them, cannot be produced through the market or as a club good. Their creation necessarily requires government intervention.

Irreversibility

One of the characteristics of land use of enormous practical consequence is the near *irreversibility* of land-use decisions. Tearing down a building involves cost. It would be almost inconceivable that a Central Park could be created from an area covered with buildings. The socially optimal use of land thus depends on the estimation of *future* benefits as well as present benefits. Private decisions are generally based on private benefits versus private costs now and in the medium-range future, but socially optimal decisions must be based on a comparison of social benefits and social costs over a long period, lest a potential social gain be lost irretrievably.

The difficulty of reversing previous land-use patterns presents problems even with private development. Technological progress in construction engineering has made it more efficient to build larger buildings on larger lots than was the case with the mortar-and-brick technology of the past. It is not uncommon, however, for subdivision into lots and patterns of ownership to reflect decisions made 50 to 100 years ago. In large city centers, the process of acquiring and assembling small lots into one large enough to erect a modern building is a lengthy process. But the gains are large to those who manage such transactions.

Property Taxes

Local governments, including cities, have traditionally obtained much revenue from property taxes. These taxes constitute market intervention because they affect relative prices.

Most property taxes, from the economist's point of view, are poorly designed. These taxes often make the market less efficient in performing that part of the allocation task to which it is well adapted in the absence of taxes. The ultimate scarce factor in the cities is *land*, in the sense of simple space, and the allocative function of the market should be to encourage the optimal use of this factor. Typical property taxes, however, are levied on the value of buildings as well as on the value of land. Thus, someone who uses scarce land efficiently, say, to construct a high-rise office building, is "penalized" relative to someone who uses the land inefficiently to build, say, a parking lot. Deteriorated buildings tend to remain on scarce land because repairs or improvements to these buildings would result in an increased assessed value of the property and, thus, higher taxes.

The optimal tax structure for allocating resources would appear to be one that taxed *land* at a high rate, and *buildings* little, if at all, encouraging building and improvements on the land. In determining the tax base, the land would have to be appropriately valued, so that an acre of prime land would generate a high tax, and an acre of swamp on the outskirts of the city, a low tax. Of course, society may not always want a particular piece of land to be used intensively (to preserve open space, for example). This should be dealt with as a separate matter of policy, however, and not by a badly devised property tax.

Virtually all urban (and many nonurban) areas place restrictions on the allocation of land use through the market. The most common form of such restriction is *zoning*, where land in certain parts of a city is restricted to certain types of use—residential, commercial, industrial, etc. This practice reflects a long-standing recognition of the existence of externalities. A factory has negative external effects on the use of the immediate locality for residential or commercial purposes, but it may generate positive externalities to other factories. More detailed zoning restrictions (only single-family houses on one-acre lots, for example) are commonly used, especially in suburbs, to preserve an area's socioeconomic homogeneity.

Recap The ordinary working of the market will ration scarce land in the city to those who obtain the greatest private benefit from its use. However, it will not necessarily allocate land according to its greatest potential social contribution—for public parks, to give one example. The irreversibility of land-use decisions suggests that future as well as present social benefits should be considered in allocating the use of land. There are two main policy instruments for intervening in the market allocation of land—the property tax, which is rarely well devised for the purpose, and zoning regulations, which specify the use to which land must be put.

Capsule Supplement 13.2 **Fifth Avenue**

Fifth Avenue in New York City, one of the world's greatest shopping areas, illustrates well the locational externalities on which cities have grown and been sustained. Along this street, a great number of stores simultaneously compete with, and complement, each other. While stores competing for the same customer, such as Bonwit Teller and Bergdorf Goodman, may be rivals in one sense, each also gains from the presence of the other. It is precisely because there are *many* stores, enabling shoppers to stroll down the avenue comparing window displays and interior contents, that so many potential patrons can be reached. Thus we have the following, rather peculiar situation: when one of the stores closes down, its "rivals," far from being overjoyed, become worried because they know that as the number of stores declines, so will the number of potential customers. If Saks Fifth Avenue became the only store for blocks, its sales might well fall rather than rise, even though it would have fewer rivals.

The positive externalities, which depend on the existence of many blocks of successive stores, exhibit a high degree of sensitivity to breaks in the continuity. Replacement of a storefront along one block by an office building will result in such a break, and thus cause great concern to nearby store owners. Indeed, the very success of an area such as Fifth Avenue can set in motion forces that could ultimately destroy it in its present form. This success naturally tends to cause shop rents, and thus land values, to rise. If shops represented the only use to which the land could be put, rents would reach an equilibrium level at which the demand for storefront space would be equal to the supply. But in large cities, and especially in New York, the most profitable use of high-priced land is for high-rise office buildings. Stores, after all, require a relatively high ratio of street frontage to total area while office buildings do not. The rise in land values would thus make the use of land for stores relatively less profitable than for office buildings. Once there were noticeable breaks in store-window displays, the external effects would quite likely lead to fewer customers, lowered sales, and thus an increase in the relative probability of using the land for office buildings rather than for stores. This could eventually change the character of the entire area.

The most appropriate policy for preserving the special character of such areas as Fifth Avenue, theater districts, and so on, is zoning. Once an area is zoned for some special use, market effects will allocate the available space *for that use,* but not allocate it away for some other purpose.

Housing and Housing Policy

Why housing problems, especially for the poor, are almost universal in large cities

In the large cities, housing represents one of the greatest problems facing everyone from the poor to the rich. Near the city center, land used for housing has the alternative of being used for commercial and business purposes. Since it is quite scarce, its market value is high. To minimize this land cost per household, housing will typically be in high-rise apartment buildings. But building costs are then quite high, partly because costs rise sharply with height, and partly because construction carried out where there is restricted access to materials (which characterizes city centers) is costly. The high cost of new housing in the cities thus generally means that, at market prices, it is affordable only to the rich.

New housing, of course, is only part of the stock of total housing available in a large city, and all housing was relatively expensive when new. Thus, it is unlikely that the urban poor ever lived in new private housing in any city at any time.

The Handing-Down Model

The traditional analysis of the urban housing market goes like this. New housing is built, but is so expensive that only the relatively rich can afford it. Thus, the rich move to this new housing, leaving their previous dwellings, which are beginning to show the first signs of age. The owners of these older dwellings, unable to compete with new housing in attracting wealthy tenants, are forced to lower rents. As a consequence, these buildings become the homes of middle-income residents, who, in turn, leave even older and probably deteriorating buildings. Owners of the latter, in turn, reduce their rents and come to house the relatively poor. Finally, the dilapidated housing, which the relatively poor have left for better accomodations, cannot be rented. It is torn down and replaced by new housing, and the process repeats itself.

In the last generation or two, this "handing-down" model has ceased to represent reality—if it ever did. There are several reasons for this. One is that the relative size of different income groups is subject to change—the number of households that can only afford housing in its last *acceptable* phase may exceed the supply. This keeps the prices from falling as far as they might, and, more importantly, leaves much of the dilapidated housing still inhabited. Social factors, giving neighborhood externalities, also intervene—the deteriorating former housing of the rich may be torn down, rather than handed down to the poor, because the owners fear property values in the area will decline if it loses its upper-class-address label. This effect will certainly be more marked if there is racial, in addition to social, discrimination.

In some of the great cities, New York, London, and Paris being notable examples, the flow of rental housing from household to household has been severely impeded by municipal rent controls. Under such controls, as the general price level rises, rents remain relatively fixed in money terms so long as there is no change in occupancy. Rent controls thus keep rents low for rich and poor families alike, and induce elderly widows to remain alone in fourteen-room apartments.

Finally, there may simply not be enough new buildings to satisfy the top- and middle-income housing markets. Thus, the amount of handed-down housing is insufficient to meet the demand for low-rent housing. The failure of the "handing-down" system has important consequences for both low- and middle-income groups, especially in American cities.

Housing the Poor

The persistence of slum neighborhoods, as we've already pointed out, is due to the persistence of poverty. The market for slum housing is a separate market in which the demand comes exclusively from the poor. The abolition of poverty would thus presumably abolish this market and serve to eliminate slum conditions.

The poor are largely trapped in the central cities because the old and thus low-rent housing is there. In the suburbs, not only is housing less capable of being modified to low-income housing (by increasing the number of dwelling units per building, for example), but much potential adaptation is deliberately prevented by zoning and other local regulations.

Because low-income households are simply incapable of paying market rents for new housing, a realistic urban housing policy for low-income families can really do only one of three things:

1. maintain the status quo, allowing the poor to live in dilapidated slum conditions at rents they can afford;
2. build new housing in the cities and charge less than the market, either by renting public housing at less than true cost, or by subsidizing private landlords or tenants directly; or
3. relocate low-income families, building new low-income housing away from the urban center.

Relocation and Renewal

The arguments in favor of the third policy are compelling. First, land at the center is expensive and has many alternative uses capable of yielding a high social return. Second, job opportunities for the poor are not necessarily located at the center, and good public transportation, in any event, could improve access to the center. It is difficult to argue that scarce inner-city land is best allocated from the standpoint of total social welfare to low-income housing that must be heavily subsidized.

In the United States, this potential solution faces many political problems that do not exist to the same extent elsewhere. Both London and Stockholm have built new suburbs (or satellite towns) with extensive low-income housing. Families have moved from crowded slums (at least in London) to an environment characterized by many of the amenities possessed by American suburbanites. Such solutions have been almost impossible in the political context of the United States with its closely guarded local autonomy. For the Michigan or Illinois state legislatures to give Detroit or Chicago the same power over housing developments *outside their own boundaries* as have been given to London and Stockholm would be a radical departure from American tradition. However, initial indications that these traditions may indeed be breakable are beginning to appear in the form of *state* housing authorities with power to override local zoning regulations.

Urban renewal programs in the United States, now attacked so much, have accomplished the first part of the relocation process described without the essential second part. Dilapidated housing has been pulled down and replaced by new housing (generally not low-income housing, however) but an acceptable alternative residence has rarely been provided to those displaced.

In the absence of a bold approach along the lines described, the only socially acceptable alternative is subsidized housing. To maximize the ratio of social benefit to cost, the appropriate policy would appear to be some form of *rent-supplement* program, in which a family receives a subsidy (either directly or indirectly) that bridges the gap between the market value of new housing, whether public or private, and some appropriate percentage of household income.

Such a policy is the only one capable of obtaining rapid results that combine the goal of enabling low-income families to live in respectable housing with the goal of encouraging new building of all kinds. Its chief disadvantage is that its administration would undoubtedly lead to much bureaucratic red tape. In the long run, much reorganization of the structure of local governments is necessary before urban Americans can be well housed.

Recap Housing is provided from the existing stock of buildings and the quantity and type cannot be rapidly changed. Historically, new housing has gone primarily to higher-income households, being "handed down" to lower-income groups as it becomes older and its value declines. Because of high land values, new housing at low prices will not be supplied by the market in urban centers. Such housing must either be subsidized, or built in areas of lower land value. Given the institutional structure of local governments in the United States, it is very difficult for central cities to induce the building of low-income housing outside their boundaries, despite the apparent desirability of this policy.

Capsule Supplement 13.3　**The Black Ghettos**

The black ghettos differ significantly from other ethnic neighborhoods in at least two important respects: one is that certain negative forces—especially racial prejudice in housing—have played a greater part in their creation than the positive forces of religion, culture, and language that served to mold the traditional ethnic ghettos of the past. The other is that the pressures which have created the black ghettos continue to dominate the lives of their inhabitants, thus weakening the desire of these inhabitants to move out, and strengthening the tendencies for such ghettos to be perpetuated. It is hardly necessary to stress that the black ghettos, as neighborhoods, possess virtually every urban problem to a heightened extent. They are areas of high poverty with poor public facilities, their residents suffer from high unemployment and low levels of education, and the available housing is dilapidated or deteriorating.

There are two major approaches to assessing the future of the black ghettos. One is founded on the old liberal dream that prejudices in housing will eventually break down and ghetto blacks will become dispersed throughout urban areas. This happened to the inhabitants of the old ethnic ghettos, so they simply dissolved. The other approach, much more recent, and a product of the ghettos' own thinkers, is to *revive* the ghettos and make them viable and attractive black neighborhoods under black control.

An important feature of the black ghettos, when viewed as subeconomies, has been the relative lack of resources (other than simple labor, much of it unskilled) owned within the community. The immigrant ghettos, although made up predominantly of the poor and relatively unskilled, all contained their own sources of capital because many immigrants arrived with financial resources. Thus, the houses and the businesses within these ghettos were not entirely the property of other groups, and members of the ethnic group had at least some access to capital. For the black ghettos, there is generally no group of black capitalists from which to draw members.

An analogy has often been drawn between black ghettos and colonies. In both cases, business enterprises are predominantly owned by "foreigners." The extent of "foreign" ownership, however, is greater in the black ghettos than in most colonies—even the "rackets" have traditionally been run by outsiders. The interest in reviving the black ghettos as semiautonomous subeconomies is derived largely by analogy with the independence of former colonies. Indeed, the motives involved are quite similar to those of nationalism rather than just simple economic gain.

Most colonies, however, have more resources than simple labor. The typical colony (or small independent country with a colonial relationship in economic matters) has some natural resource, such as bauxite deposits, a tropical climate, or oil, which gives it bargaining power with a foreign government or business interest. Contrary to much Marxist theorizing, the value to international business of colonies as a pure labor pool is quite small. There lies the real problem for black nationalism in the ghetto—not just the lack of capital, but the lack of a basic resource with which to *bargain for* capital. The strongest bargaining powers of the black communities are political, not economic, and these just might be sufficient to kindle a process of development based, initially, on resources imported from outside the black ghetto. On the other hand, some have argued that the more rapidly racial prejudice breaks down in society as a whole, the smaller is the chance for independent ghetto development. This breakdown may well accelerate the movement of those who "make it" outside the ghetto into the regular suburbs, these "escapees" taking with them their newly acquired skills—and their capital.

Urban Transport

**The special problems
of urban transportation**

The externalities of a city depend largely on proximity, which is measured by the true *costs* of moving from one location within (or near) the city to another. The costs involved are not represented merely by cash outlays, but include time, general travel conditions (such as the degree of comfort), and freedom of choice as to time of travel.

Transportation involves externalities of various kinds, although these differ among the different modes. Beyond a certain point, additional travelers will diminish the comfort of other travelers. In a crowded bus or subway car, everyone is made more uncomfortable by the crush of fellow riders. Such crowding may also affect travel time by prolonging loading and unloading, but the major effect is on comfort. Highway congestion from a large number of automobiles also involves discomfort. But its chief effect is to increase travel time and to cause frayed nerves from difficult driving conditions and worry that destinations will be reached late. Automobiles generate another important production externality in the form of air pollution, a public bad, and have adverse external effects on pedestrians and bicyclists.

Automobiles versus Mass Transit

The fundamental problems concerning urban transportation arise from the radical difference between the cost-benefit structure of automobile transport as compared with alternatives.

Consider the comparison between the automobile and a rapid-transit system. *In the absence of externalities,* the *private benefits* of the automobile are very high. It conveys from door to door, provides complete freedom of choice as to time of journey, and generally has a short journey time (at least on uncrowded highways). The *private costs* of the automobile are relatively low, primarily because the road system is provided largely from general revenue, even when automobile gasoline taxes contribute to road costs. Hence, ignoring external effects, the *private* benefit to cost ratio for the automobile is high.

But the total *social benefits* arising from automobile ownership are much lower than the sum of potential private benefits to individual automobile owners. Congestion occurs with a large number of cars, and air pollution is increased. *Social costs* are higher than private costs because the subsidization of roads and curb-side parking results in their being priced at levels below the rental value of land in prime locations. The greater the number of automobiles, the lower the social benefits compared with apparent private benefits. Beyond a certain point, the marginal social benefit may even be negative, even though the marginal private benefit remains positive.

Rapid transit exhibits a benefit-cost pattern that is largely the reverse of the automobile case. Once a large transit system is constructed and operating, the *marginal social cost* of an additional passenger is quite low and may be below the *private cost* if fares are charged. If a subway train is not crowded, it clearly costs little to carry additional passengers, even though all such passengers may still be required to pay fares.

Cost-Benefit Relationships

Thus, if public-transit fares are designed to cover costs (being set at the *average cost* per journey), as is usually the case, marginal social cost is less than private cost (the fare), while social benefits and aggregate private benefits are nearly equal. *Social benefits would be increased at almost no additional social cost by having more passengers, assuming adequate capacity of the transit system.*

In the case of automobile transport, encouragement of more automobile use produces the opposite effect. *Because of external effects on other automobiles, on pedestrians, and on the environment, the marginal social benefit from additional automobile use is not only lower than marginal private benefit, but much lower than the marginal private benefit that would exist if each automobile had sole use of the road system.*

We can sum up the analysis by noting that the ratio of social benefits to social costs *increases* with increased use of the transit system, and *decreases* with increased automobile use. The ratio of private benefits to private costs does not reflect this, however, and thus neither encourages the use of public transit nor discourages the use of the automobile.

A variety of policy measures has been suggested to bring the social and private benefit-cost ratios associated with urban transport into a closer relationship. High charges for parking and for special licenses to drive within the city limits have been suggested to bring the private and social costs of the automobile closer together. Indeed, it has been suggested that the revenue derived from such special charges on automobile use be devoted to the subsidization of public transport. This is obviously the appropriate type of policy to allocate the use of transport facilities, *provided adequate public transport capacity already exists or is developed.*

Recap The major problems in devising policies for urban transportation are the large differences in the cost-benefit structures of different transport modes. Automobile transportation is characterized by high private benefits accompanied by many bad externalities, pollution and congestion in particular, which tend to reduce the social benefits relative to the private. Public transport tends to have a structure of the opposite kind with fewer bad externalities and low marginal social costs. The operation of the traditional pricing systems tends to produce widely different social and private cost-benefit ratios, which lead to suboptimal transport arrangements.

The Suburban Rings

The relationships between the central city and the areas adjacent to it

Most urban areas consist of a central city surrounded by a ring of suburban areas. The relationship between the central city and the suburbs that surround it depends, in part, on local government institutions. In the United States (though not necessarily in other countries), suburbs are typically self-governing, local entities not linked to the government of the central city. In the case of certain cities (New York, Philadelphia, Chicago, and Washington, D.C., for example), some suburbs may even be in a different state.

Externalities and Suburbs

The growth of suburban areas has paralleled the ability of urban dwellers to separate the good and bad externalities of the city by means of transport. The suburbanite can travel into the city to take advantage of the good things it has to offer (entertainment, commercial diversity, etc.) then retire to the suburbs to obtain those things (space, fresh air, etc.) that are scarce in the city.

Suburbs have also permitted the development of other externalities, especially those of the "club" kind. The high degree of autonomy of local governments in the United States has resulted in the development of such club externalities to their highest degree. Zoning laws continue to effectively restrict the residents of many suburban communities to people of certain economic classes. Until made illegal, formal and informal agreements and other arrangements also served to restrict residents to certain religious, ethnic, or racial groups—a practice that still manages to persist. Suburbs developed as clubs with relatively homogeneous memberships so most external effects within the suburb were positive. Because of governmental autonomy, education systems were developed as *de facto* private schools that "just happened" to be supported by general community revenue instead of school fees. Indeed, education, because of its direct "club" impact, continues to be an area in which suburban expenditure is noticeably higher than that in the city.

Redistribution of Costs and Benefits

But suburbs merely permit their residents to escape undesired urban externalities. They do not remove these effects, but serve only to ensure that they are concentrated in the central cities.

Thus, while suburban residents increase their *own* social welfare by maximizing the good externalities for themselves as a group, they create or increase bad externalities elsewhere. The social welfare of a metropolitan area, *taken as a whole,* may actually be decreased by suburban development beyond a certain point. By denying entrance to the poor, suburbs concentrate poverty more heavily in the central city, and increase the bad externalities associated with this concentration.

If local governments continue to exercise a great deal of fiscal autonomy, as has historically been the case in the United States, suburban residents may continue to receive important *private benefits* from the central city, while avoiding many of the *costs* associated with these benefits. While it is true that those in the suburbs often pay higher local taxes than those living in the central city, these taxes are typically for local amenities from which suburban dwellers benefit directly—high-quality schools, clean streets, and a high level of police protection. For these same taxes, middle-income residents of the central city typically receive less in direct benefits than their suburban counterparts, because a higher proportion of their taxes must be used to balance the lower taxability of the poor. Suburban residents thus not only avoid having to live with the poor but also avoid "subsidizing" the poor to remain in the central cities. Moreover, suburbanites can typically use all of the public facilities of the central city, but can close their own parks and beaches to central-city residents.

To maximize social welfare over an entire metropolitan area is a problem that involves a fairly delicate balance. On the one hand, suburbs enhance the social welfare of their residents through "club" arrangements. On the other hand, the social welfare of those excluded from these "clubs" is lowered by their very existence. Thus, part of the increased social welfare of the suburbs is due to a genuine *increase in total welfare* (stemming from an increase in positive externalities), and part to a *transfer of benefits* from central-city residents in the form of *cost avoidance.*

Recap The relationship between the central city and the surrounding suburban areas is heavily influenced by the institutional structure of local government. Residence in the suburbs permits escape from some of the bad externalities of the city while still allowing access to many of its benefits. Suburban autonomy in local government tends to exclude the poor from suburban areas. As a consequence, urban costs bear heavily on central-city dwellers while many benefits accrue to suburbanites. The case for redistributing these costs and benefits is thus quite compelling.

Financing the Cities

The financial problems of local government with special reference to central cities

Local governments in the United States are responsible for approximately 40 percent of nondefense public expenditures. Some of this expenditure is on essentially local things (sanitation, water supply, police and fire protection, local road maintenance), and some is on nonlocal things (education, welfare, and health).

The division of responsibilities between local, state, and federal governments is partly a matter of administrative convenience and partly a matter of history. Whatever the reasons, local governments generally and urban governments in particular are responsible for providing an important slice of total public services. On the average, urban governments annually require resources worth around $500 per person to maintain services at present levels.

In principle, it may seem that there is no separate problem of local government finance, that it is simply part of the overall fiscal picture. But a problem exists nonetheless. Cities have certain traditional areas of responsibility and certain traditional sources of revenue—and the two have not kept in step.

The picture of a local community providing whatever services it chooses, and paying for them from its own resources, may seem attractive, but this idyllic vision does not bear close examination in a highly mobile society. The realistic picture is that of a closed community of the rich, amply provided with all possible public services, and another community of the poor, unable to provide even the most basic social requirements.

Communities Are Not Autonomous

There are two main reasons why local communities cannot operate on a self-contained basis. One is that costs and benefits cannot be confined to specific localities; the other is that the socioeconomic composition of the population varies enormously from one community to another.

Poverty is generated by society as a whole, not by the cities. Associated problems, such as the lack of education, are due in large part to the failures of the communities (or countries) from which the urban immigrants have come. At the same time, educational benefits peculiar to the cities may spill over into other communities. Doctors trained in Baltimore and Philadelphia may practice elsewhere upon graduation. In fact, cities with medical-training facilities may actually wind up short of physicians.

More important is the simple fact that people can move. The federal government can impose income taxes with marginal rates of 70 percent on high incomes. A city that imposed such taxes would quickly lose its rich citizens, and hence the taxes they pay. Likewise, a 40 percent tax on corporate profits would soon result in corporations migrating elsewhere. Thus, personal and corporate income taxes—the most fruitful sources of government revenue—can be levied only at very low levels by local governments.

We can presume that people are willing to pay taxes that are directly related to their private benefits. Hence, if cities needed taxes only to provide services benefiting taxpayers, major problems would not arise. It is *redistributive taxes* that local governments cannot levy. If the rich are taxed to support the poor, they will leave for suburbia where the poor are kept out and all taxes provide services that yield benefits to the rich.

Yet most policy prescriptions for urban ills—public assistance to the poor, subsidized public transport, and subsidized housing—involve redistribution.

Local governments, generally lacking the ability to tax incomes directly, have two major sources of tax revenue—*property taxes* and *sales taxes*. Both of these tend to be regressive, that is, to bear proportionately more on the poor than on the rich. Assuming that the same piece of property yields the same tax whether occupied by the rich or the poor, we would normally expect that the rent paid by the rich will include more services (security personnel, janitors, better heating, and so on) than that paid by the poor. Consequently, a higher proportion of the poor person's rent (and thus income) will be taken by property taxes. Because rent is a higher proportion of low than of high incomes, the effect is enhanced. General sales taxes also bear more on the poor (even when food is exempt) because the rich spend a smaller fraction of their incomes on consumer goods. Thus, increasing property and sales taxes to pay for subsidies to low-income families may bring about little actual redistribution.

Revenue Sharing

Demands for public expenditures are growing at all levels of government. Only the more central levels (federal and state) can use income taxes to a major extent—and it is the revenue from income taxes that is growing fastest. Thus, there is a case for *revenue sharing* or *revenue pooling* in which the states and even smaller governmental units receive revenues that are related to *total* government receipts rather than simply to the receipts from certain types of taxes.

Australia, which has a federal structure (though divided into only six states) has a formula that gives the "least-developed" states proportionately more per person than the others. The United States has had a limited federal revenue-sharing program since 1972. Each year approximately $5 to $7 billion in federal funds is divided up among the fifty states.

The main argument against simple revenue sharing, especially in the context of the United States, is the variation in political and social viewpoints and in the simple quality of administration between the various states and localities. Of two cities receiving $1 million in revenue from the federal government, one may build a new ghetto school, while the other may erect a memorial to its mayor. While such a memorial may be of high priority to the inhabitants of the city, it is difficult to argue that funds raised *from society as a whole* are being appropriately used when devoted to this purpose.

A good case can thus be made that *functional specialization* would be better than simple revenue sharing. Under this method, the federal government would assume all costs for functions either involving income redistribution (the costs associated with poverty policy, for example) or having major externalities extending beyond local areas (pollution control, and higher education). Local governments would be responsible only for matters whose causes and effects are confined to specific localities. Given the growth of major externalities and increasing concern with income redistribution, this would certainly imply a greater role for the federal government in addressing urban problems than it now plays.

Recap The division of responsibility between local and central governments with respect to financing and producing public and other government goods is complex. The crucial problem, whatever the division, is that the requirements for services and the sources of finance do not necessarily keep in step. Local governments are severely limited in their ability to impose redistributive taxes since, if their burden is higher on the rich than on the poor, the rich may move elsewhere. Only the central government, whose taxing authority cannot be escaped, can affect redistribution on a large scale. As the problems of urban areas become increasingly concerned with redistribution—financial assistance to the poor, public education, and housing—the fiscal problems of the cities become more acute. Some suggested solutions involve revenue sharing and functional specialization.

Exercises

1. Consider the community where you live, either at home or at college. Carefully list:
   a. all the good externalities associated with the community.
   b. all the bad externalities.

2. For the list you've drawn up for question 1, estimate which of the externalities, good and bad, would increase if the size of your community were to increase.

3. The population of the United States has more than doubled since World War I, and the urban population has increased by a greater proportion than the population as a whole. Why do you think there have been so few entirely new towns in spite of this large population growth?

4. Suppose, in a typical large city, everyone's income were to double overnight. What would you expect to happen to rents and the supply of different types of housing:
   a. in the short run?
   b. in the long run?

For Thought and Discussion

1. Early urban-renewal schemes abolished slum neighborhoods by simply pulling them down and replacing them with better-quality housing. This method is no longer popular. What was wrong with the original cost-benefit analysis on which urban renewal was based?

2. It has been suggested that urban transport should be provided free, at least within the central city. What are the merits of this idea, and on whom should the costs of operating the system fall?

3. Slum landlords claim they perform a public service because they are the only providers of housing that the poor can afford. Does this mean that the growth of slums should be encouraged as long as poverty persists?

4. Educational and religious institutions (in the United States and most countries) are exempt from paying taxes on their property. Does this lead to a socially undesirable allocation of scarce land?

5. Choose any large city you prefer and imagine it as an independent country. What could it sell to its neighbors to pay for the food and other goods it would import?

Chapter 14
Agriculture

Terms and Concepts

Fallacy of composition
Price stabilization
Buffer stocks
Price controls
Price supports
Price fluctuations
Parity
Redistributive policy

The Universal Problems of Agriculture

Why most countries have an agricultural policy

While the European Common Market is comprised of the greatest industrial powers in Western Europe, most of its internal crises have centered around *agriculture*. Thus, the United States is not the only industrial giant whose agricultural policy is of major significance. Agricultural problems arise in almost every country, but they are often more acute in industrialized countries because the economic properties of agricultural markets in such countries are unique. These properties are:

1. *The relatively low elasticity of demand for farm products, and the relatively small expansion of this demand over time.* These properties reflect the fact that agricultural production is predominantly for food. In the richer countries, most people spend a relatively small fraction of their income on food. Consequently, when incomes and food prices change, people alter their food consumption only slightly.

2. *The relatively low elasticity of supply for farm products in the short run.* Once a farmer has planted his crop, he will harvest and market it at any price high enough to cover his costs. Price changes during a given year will thus have little effect on the size of most farm crops during that year. But unpredictable weather conditions may cause considerable season-to-season fluctuations in farm output.

3. *Rapid technological progress in agriculture.* This has pronounced effects in rich countries where new techniques are more likely to be adopted. Technological progress has only *potential* effects in most poor countries.

4. *The relative immobility of resources devoted to agriculture.* Farming represents a form of social as well as economic specialization. Shifting resources from agriculture to industry requires far greater social adaptation than shifting them from one industry to another.

The Classic Agricultural Problem in a Nutshell

The low elasticities of both demand and short-run supply, coupled with unpredictable output variations due to weather, contribute to the most fundamental and universal problem of agriculture—*pronounced year-to-year fluctuations in prices.*

Technological progress causes other important problems. New techniques enable farmers to produce more with the same land and the same (or even less) labor. Because the demand for farm products does not rise in step, the expansion in output puts downward pressure on prices. The low elasticity of demand implies, in turn, that absorption of even small increases in output will require relatively large reductions in price over time.

Recap Markets for agricultural products are characterized by low price elasticities of both demand and short-run supply. Moreover, farming represents social specialization, so shifts of labor between agriculture and industry have more social consequences than shifts between one industry and another. The universal problems of agriculture derive from these characteristics, coupled with fluctuations in crop yields due to unpredictable weather conditions, and, in the more-developed countries, rapid technological progress.

Farm Price and Income Fluctuations	**Why farm prices and incomes fluctuate greatly in the absence of market intervention**

Fluctuations in farm and industrial prices for a five-year period in the 1960s are compared in Figure 14.1. Obviously, there was a much greater variation in farm prices than in others, despite the government's attempt to stabilize farm prices during this period and no attempt to influence the prices of industrial goods. As already suggested, the variability of farm prices is due to a combination of low, short-run elasticity of supply and low elasticity of demand, with random fluctuations in crop yields.

These circumstances are shown graphically in Figure 14.2. It is assumed that the crop, once harvested, will be sold by all farmers in the market for whatever it will bring them, giving completely inelastic (vertical) supply curves. Two such curves are shown, S_1 for a season with unfavorable weather conditions, and S_2 for a more productive season. Because the demand curve is steeply sloping due to the low elasticity of demand, the fluctuation in harvest between Q_1 (corresponding to S_1) and Q_2 (corresponding to S_2) will result in the relatively large fluctuation in price between P_1 and P_2. The relationship between the fluctuation in price and that in quantity is given directly by the elasticity of demand. As shown in Chapter 5, the coefficient of elasticity, E, is the percentage change in quantity associated with a 1 percent change in price. It follows that a 1 percent change in quantity is associated with a $1/E$ percent change in price, and this change in price will obviously be large if E is small.

Fluctuating Incomes

But a low elasticity of demand results not only in large *price* fluctuations, but in large *income* fluctuations as well. If demand is relatively inelastic, total revenue from farm sales, which constitutes farm income, will vary directly with price. This means that incomes will be *low* when output is high (Q_2) and high when output is low (Q_1). If, by contrast, the demand for farm

Figure 14.1

Historical comparison of fluctuations in farm and industrial prices. During this period, farm-price-stabilization policies were in full swing (unlike later periods).

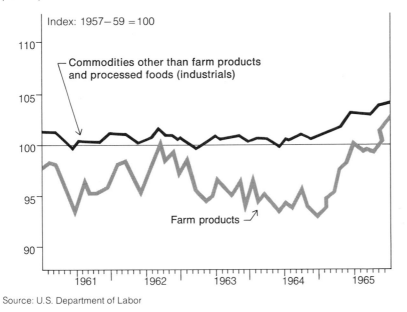

Source: U.S. Department of Labor

products exhibited unit elasticity, incomes would be unaffected by price fluctuations because decreased quantity and increased price would exactly balance each other.

Because low demand elasticity is the general rule, income will tend to fall in years of good harvest and rise in years of bad harvest. Nevertheless, there is no incentive for *individual* farmers to hold back production in a good year because they cannot affect the market price by their own actions. However low this price, each individual farmer will make more income by selling more, although farmers as a group will make less by collectively behaving this way.

Farm incomes, because of the low demand elasticity, are thus subject to the *fallacy of composition*—what is good for each farmer individually is not necessarily good for all farmers taken together. It is this special property of farm incomes that has, ironically, necessitated government intervention in an industry that, more than any other, approximates the classic view of perfect competition.

Figure 14.2

The fluctuations in farm prices are due to the combined effect of seasonal variations in supply and low elasticity of demand.

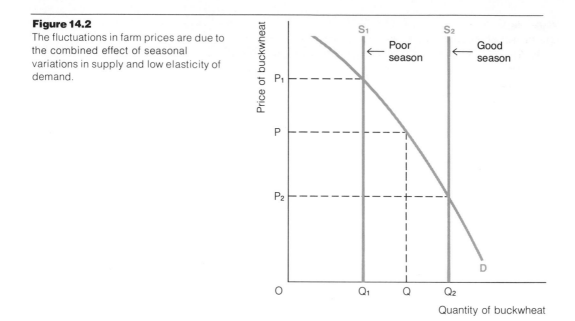

Price Stabilization

If the only source of fluctuations were the seasonal factor, which we can assume causes supply to vary between S_1 and S_2 with equal probability, then the obvious policy is *price stabilization*. The free market price, which fluctuates between P_1 and P_2 with equal probability, on the *average* over a period of years, will be equal to P (midway between P_1 and P_2).

Now suppose the government decides to maintain the price at P, at which level quantity Q will be purchased. In a good crop year, with supply at S_2, P will be *above* the market price, P_2. But buyers will only purchase amount Q at this price, and there will be *excess supply* equal to $Q_2 - Q$. In this event, the government will normally have to do one of two things:

1. *Ration supply*, by allowing farmers to sell only a portion of their crop and making them *destroy* the rest. Proportionate rationing would require each farmer to destroy a fraction of his crop equal to $(Q_2 - Q)/Q_2$. Note that, because of low demand elasticity, each farmer would consequently enjoy a higher income compared with the free market situation, even though part of his crop would have been destroyed.

2. *Add to demand* the amount $Q_2 - Q$. Most typically this is done by *buying up* the surplus, or by some equivalent measure like paying the farmers to store the excess.

Now consider a bad crop year when supply drops to S_1. In the absence of intervention, the free market price would rise to P_1. If the *price ceiling* were fixed at P, however, there would be *excess demand* equal to $Q - Q_1$. The government could handle this by doing one of the following:

1. *Ration demand.* This is difficult to do because farm policy usually gives the government control over farmers but not over consumers.

2. *Add to supply* the amount $Q - Q_1$. This can only be done if the government holds large quantities of farm products, or *buffer stocks,* for just this purpose.

Buffer Stocks

In the idealized simple model, the government could hold the price at P by *accumulating* buffer stocks in good crop years and *selling them off* in bad crop years. Over time, the stabilized price, P, would lead to purchases of Q, and the buffer stocks would rise and fall from season to season but maintain a constant average level. With an ideal buffer-stock scheme, the government would not need to use *direct price controls.* If it simply offered to buy or sell at a constant price, P, the market price would be stabilized at that level, and the buffer stocks would simply fluctuate from season to season.

Note that such a scheme would impose no financial burden on the government (other than administrative costs and the interest forgone on the value of the buffer stocks) because purchases into, and sales from, the buffer stocks would be made at the same price and cancel out over the years.

The Trend Problem

This idealized policy suffers from one near-fatal flaw. Farm outputs and prices do not fluctuate around a constant average level, but around a moving *trend*. Moreover, fluctuations do not always occur in successive years. There may be relatively long periods of potentially high free market prices, the stabilization of which may require aggregate sales larger than existing buffer stocks.

The main problem, however, is the trend. Suppose that if seasonal factors did not vary randomly, the equilibrium free market price would fall steadily by 2 percent each year. Seasonal influences, in fact, would cause fluctuations about this trend, however, so market prices would move up and down from year to year. If the government were to stabilize prices at a *fixed* level, it would find, as time went on, that it would be required to buy increasingly more in larger-crop years and sell increasingly less in smaller-crop years. Its buffer stock would grow steadily on the average rather than fluctuate around a relatively fixed level. Hence, the program would not be financially self-liquidating, like the ideal model, but would become more expensive over the years due to the continuous buildup of stocks.

If there is strong political pressure from the agricultural sector (as is common in all political systems whose representation is based on geographical divisions), it will not be for true price stabilization, but for *price support*. Farmers would prefer to obtain the *free market price* when it is high, but a *support price* when the free market price is low. This leads to programs in which the government buys when the price is depressed, but cannot sell overtly when the price is high. Under these conditions, we do not have *price stabilization,* but outright *subsidization* of agriculture.

Recap Basic market analysis shows that the low demand and short-term supply elasticities in agriculture result in relatively large price fluctuations because crop yields vary randomly with weather. The low demand elasticity also implies large fluctuations in the revenues that constitute farm incomes. If fluctuations occurred around predictable average levels, it would be relatively easy to devise stabilization policies, but the existence of long-term trends makes such stabilization difficult. Thus, stabilization often becomes subsidization.

The Effects of Technological Change

How technological progress can be a problem

It may seem paradoxical that rapid technological advance in agriculture has been a major source of problems in the farm sector. This paradox is further stressed by the fact that *agriculture is the most successful sector of the American economy.*

In the period from 1950 to 1975, output per man-hour in agriculture rose by no less than 300 percent, whereas in manufacturing it rose by only 90 percent, and in the service sector, by even less. This high rate of increase in agricultural labor productivity, which averaged more than 6 percent per year over the period given, was due largely to increases in other inputs such as machine services and chemical fertilizers. Still, even if we adjust for the increase in such inputs, the "pure" productivity increase in agriculture—defined as the excess of the rate of increase in output over the rate of increase of all inputs—was about 2 percent per year, twice the rate for the economy as a whole. Technological progress is clearly beneficial to society as a whole because it pushes out the production possibility frontier. But it can, nonetheless, present major problems to the sector in which it actually occurs.

The Problem of Low Elasticity

In the case of technological progress in agriculture, low demand elasticity is once more the villain. Suppose technological progress is such that every year (with seasonal variations evened out) output increases by 2 percent with the same inputs. Suppose also that demand is stationary and exhibits a price elasticity of $-.5$. Because output rises by 2 percent from one year to the next, selling the increased output *will require the price to decline annually by 4 percent* (since an elasticity of −.5 means that the proportionate change in quantity is only half the proportionate change in price). Farm revenues will thus *decline* by 2 percent (reflecting a 2 percent increase in output less a 4 percent decline in price) and farmers will find their incomes falling by 2 percent a year in spite of (actually because of) rapid technological progress.

The Need for Resource Migration

Must farmer's incomes fall as a result of technological progress? In the example given, *total* farm income can be expected to fall, but average farm income need not, *providing resources leave agriculture for other opportunities.*

It is easy to see that, if 2 percent of all resources leave agriculture each year, output will remain constant because it would have increased by 2 percent with the original resources. Output is unchanged; therefore, prices will remain steady, and total farm income will remain the same, but be divided among 2 percent fewer resources. Thus, average farm incomes will rise by 2 percent per year.

With 1 percent of resources leaving agriculture each year, output will rise by 1 percent (2 percent from technological progress less 1 percent from the fall in inputs). This will cause prices to fall by 2 percent, with total farm income falling by 1 percent (1 percent more output less 2 percent from the fall in price). Under these circumstances, average farm incomes will remain steady.

Consequently, if demand conditions for farm products are relatively stationary with low price elasticity, maintaining or increasing average farm incomes with technological progress would require the migration of resources out of agriculture.

If demand is *increasing*, as will be the case when the population and income per person are growing (the income factor being less important in rich countries), this conclusion must be suitably modified. We can state the following as a reasonable presumption:

In a growing economy that is well above subsistence level, technological progress in agriculture will require either migration of resources out of agriculture, or growth in these resources at a rate lower than that of the economy as a whole if average farm incomes are not to decline relative to other incomes.

The American Experience

Because technological progress in American agriculture has been such as to raise output *per worker* very rapidly, we would expect resource effects to be especially pronounced with respect to labor. This is precisely what we find.

The United States' farm population declined from 32.2 million in 1935 to 24.4 million in 1945. Since the end of World War II, farm population has declined in every year except 1955. In the single year 1953, no less than 2.2 million people left the farm. By 1975, the farm population was down to 8.9 million and still falling.

Other inputs in U.S. agriculture have increased, however. During the period 1945 to 1968, for example, total inputs increased by 13 percent. Moreover, output increased by 48 percent over this period because of technological progress alone. Farm prices rose by 25 percent, but then all prices rose over this period. Indeed, relative to the prices of *things bought by farmers,* farm prices *fell* by 32 percent.

The general picture of U.S. agriculture thus conforms quite well with the simple model we introduced at the beginning of this section. Rapid technological progress has taken place, some resources (especially labor) have moved from agriculture, and total resources have increased at a much lower rate than elsewhere in the economy.

Although demand has increased over the years, supply has increased even more, and output has been sold only because farm prices have fallen relative to other prices. Total real farm income has also fallen. Overall, the decline in farm population has more or less balanced the fall in total farm income (after price adjustment), leaving average real farm income virtually unchanged in an economy where other real incomes have been rising steadily. This has all taken place *in spite of* an intensive series of farm programs. These may have helped, but clearly have not altered, the basic results of the market's operation.

If the United States were a closed economy with no international relationships, our analysis would lead to the simple conclusion that American farm policy should be devoted to moving resources out of agriculture more rapidly than at present so that per-capita farm income could keep in step with the rest of the economy. But, because the United States is not a closed economy, we need to examine agriculture in an international context.

Recap Agriculture has shown steady technological progress. But a steady increase in output for commodities with low demand elasticities implies that prices will fall more than in proportion to increases in output. Thus, technological progress in agriculture may result in steadily declining farm incomes, unless the number of farmers falls as productivity rises. Though these effects are diminished if the demand for farm products is growing, due to increasing population or rising incomes, they pose a major long-run problem in a country like the United States.

Capsule Supplement 14.1   **Agriculture and the Environment**

Because the impact of prehistoric hunting and fishing was small, agriculture represents humanity's earliest and perhaps most extensive modification of the environment. In the United States, one of the more recent areas of the world to come under the plow, the proportion of the total land area in farms rose from less than 16 percent to more than 60 percent in the hundred years from the mid-nineteenth century to the mid-twentieth. While only about one-third of this is cropland, the environmental change has been very large.

In recent years, there has been growing concern about the relationship between agriculture and the environment. This concern is not about the area of land that is plowed, however, but about the environmental effects of modern chemical fertilizers and pesticides. Rachel Carson's *Silent Spring,* published in 1962, which can be used to mark the beginning of modern concern about ecology, specifically dealt with the secondary effects of the pesticide DDT on animal and food chromosome chains.

Economic considerations arise because the growth in farm productivity over the last thirty years has been due primarily to the combined effects of increased mechanization and increased use of chemical products. In the two decades following 1950, agricultural output rose by 11 percent while farm labor fell by 53 percent. During this same period, however, there was a 34 percent increase in the use of mechanical equipment, an increase of no less than 219 percent in the use of fertilizers, and 60 percent in the use of miscellaneous substances including pesticides.

Discontinuing the use of chemical products in agriculture—returning to "organic" farming—would certainly result in a large decline in agricultural productivity. For the reasons outlined in the text, this could presumably cause farm prices, incomes, and employment to increase, though at the cost of higher food prices. Because the poor spend a higher proportion of their incomes on food than the rich, this would effectively lower the real incomes of the poor. Thus, as is often the case in matters of economic policy, two objectives that are both generally considered desirable—protecting the environment and reducing the incidence of poverty—are in direct conflict. In the absence of other policies, one can come close to achieving one objective only at the expense of moving further away from the other. No doubt this dilemma will eventually be solved by the development of techniques that increase agricultural productivity without damaging the environment. But for the time being, the policy-maker must face it.

World Agriculture

Why agricultural policy must be formulated in an international context

Perhaps the greatest economic tragedy of modern times, full of irony as true tragedy should be, is that technological progress in agriculture has taken place at such a rapid rate in the United States and so slowly in many less-developed countries. From 1950 through the mid-1960s, rice yields per acre in Asia grew at less than two-fifths the rate in the United States, while corn (maize) yields in Africa grew at only a slightly higher fraction of the American rate. Yet rice is the staple food of Asia, and corn is one of the staple foods of Africa.

If the situation were reversed, with technological progress more rapid in the poor countries and less rapid in the United States, the American "farm problem" and the food-supply problem in poor countries would obviously *both* be reduced.

Of course, it is not a random or ironic act of fate that has produced the present situation. The rapid technological progress of American agriculture is related to the wealth and industrial technology of the American economy as a whole, just as the slower progress of poorer countries is related to their less-developed economic and social structure.

Trade Effects

However, agriculture is not simply an internal problem of individual countries. Trade in agricultural products is one of the most important components of world trade. One-fifth of total U.S. trade is in agricultural products, and about one-sixth of U.S. farm output is exported. The United States is the dominant world exporter of some agricultural products, and one of a small group of dominant exporters of many others. It is also a major importer of certain agricultural products.

However, the United States is less dependent on its agricultural trade than most other major traders. Although farm exports are about one-fifth of all exports in the United States, total exports represent less than 10 percent of gross national product (GNP). By contrast, Canada's exports run at about 25 percent of its GNP, and Australia's at 17 percent, and these countries' exports are *dominated* by farm products.

Because the United States is one of the largest agricultural producers and traders, its farm policies have major repercussions on international markets in farm products. The behavior of these markets critically affects the economies of many countries, so the United States cannot pursue its farm policy in isolation. U.S. farm policy must take international effects into account.

Many Problems Are International

Some of the basic problems of agriculture are shared by all countries with important trade (either export or import) in agricultural products. One of these is *price fluctuations*. Both importers and exporters have an interest in smoothing prices. There have been, in fact, several international programs designed to stabilize prices of such products as wheat, rice, sugar, and coffee.

Typically, such programs attempt to stabilize prices at specific levels or between certain limits. One of the most ambitious, the International Wheat Agreement, sets upper and lower limits and attempts to solve excess demand and excess supply problems by imposing buyer and seller quotas. Exporting countries promise to sell importing countries a certain maximum amount if the price reaches the upper limit, and importing countries promise to buy a certain minimum quota if the price reaches the lower limit. On the whole, international stabilization schemes have been only moderately successful. Failures have usually occurred because the agreed-upon prices have turned out to be inappropriate to the conditions that developed, or because either buyers or sellers abandoned (or refused to renew) the agreements when free market prices were especially favorable to them. International stabilization schemes therefore tend to suffer from the same problem as national schemes (that of prediction). There is also the additional problem that the buyers and sellers reside in different countries, and a solution satisfactory to one side cannot be imposed on the other— something a government can always do within a country.

Attempts at Isolation

On the other hand, internal stabilization cannot be carried out in isolation from world markets without heavy agricultural *protection* by tariffs and quotas. If, for example, the United States has an internal buffer-stock stabilization scheme for wheat, foreign producers will send their wheat to the American market when the world price is below the support price, and foreign consumers will buy on the American market when the world price is high. The *American* stabilization scheme, in effect, will become a *world* stabilization scheme, but with all costs borne by the United States. Stabilization schemes thus lead to reductions in trade because the stabilizing countries are forced to restrict imports when world prices are low, and to restrict exports when world prices are high. While it's easy for economists to show that the ideal situation is free trade in farm products with foolproof *international* stabilization schemes, organizing such schemes has not yet been proved politically feasible.

Finally, it should be noted that extensive trade in farm products, of itself, can contribute to stability. If good and bad harvests vary over the world, then the flow from areas with good seasons to those with bad will tend to smooth out domestic fluctuations.

Recap The existence of both an American and a world agricultural problem is due largely to the fact that technological progress in agriculture has been most marked in the richer countries, whose demand for agricultural products has risen little. Thus, the United States can be embarrassed by an excess output of food, while starvation occurs in poorer countries. At the same time, because there is extensive international trade in farm products, it is very difficult for one country to stabilize its own farm prices without severely restricting this trade. The inevitable conclusion is that stabilization policies should be international. But first, steps must be taken to eliminate the imperfections of international agreements.

Capsule Supplement 14.2   **David Ricardo, 1772–1823**

It was one of the greatest agricultural crises of history—the tremendous scarcity of wheat (then called corn) in England from the end of the eighteenth century through the Napoleonic wars—that turned David Ricardo's attention to the study of economics. Ricardo was no farmer, however, but an astute stockbroker of Dutch-Jewish ancestry who had become a Quaker. He retired as a rich man at the ripe old age of 25 to devote himself to writing, being a gentleman, and making an occasional "killing" in the stock market.

Ricardo, along with Reverend Malthus of population fame, spearheaded the second generation of economists following Adam Smith. We can regard Ricardo as the first real practitioner of *economic analysis*. His models of the economy, unlike the loose mixture of insight and description that comprised the work of Smith, were fully thought out. Indeed, Ricardo played a special role in the development of economic doctrine. He was the last major economist whose contributions were in the mainstream of both Marxian and non-Marxian economics. Marx depended heavily on many of Ricardo's ideas—especially the labor theory of value (the idea that the relative values of commodities reflect the relative amounts of labor that have gone into their production).

The Ricardian vision of society was dominated by England's agricultural situation and its relationship to the Industrial Revolution. Ricardo noted that, as industrialization grew in England, the population increased to provide the labor supply, and the stock of capital increased as the new industrialists plowed their savings into industry. But the quantity of land from which the food to supply the increasing population had to come remained fixed. The result was that wheat prices rose rapidly, and the real gainers from the Industrial Revolution were the landlords. It is important to realize that farming in England was typically carried out by tenants, so, unlike the situation now common in the United States, the farmer and the landowner were two different people. Ricardo showed that, as the price of wheat rose, the increased gains from farming accrued neither to the workers (whose wages were held down by the ever-growing supply of labor) nor to the tenants, as the scramble for access to the fixed stock of land simply led landlords to raise rents. Rather, economic growth led to increased demand for food, higher agricultural prices, higher rents, and thus higher incomes for landlords.

The injustice of the shift in income distribution away from workers and capitalists and toward landlords was, to Ricardo, that the landlords had performed no productive function in the process. Workers had worked, capitalists had managed factories and explored new economic opportunities, but the landlords had just sat there with pieces of paper stating that they were entitled to all the proceeds from the use of land which they had not created and which would have been there whatever they had done. Thus, Ricardo introduced into economics the concept of *pure rent,* a payment that is not necessary to ensure the existence of a resource and, thus, is not a payment for any productive function even though it is received by the owner of that resource. Ricardo presented this analysis of a simple economic system in which the emphasis was on the *distribution of income* among workers, capitalists, and landlords in his *Principles of Political Economy and Taxation* (1817).

Ricardo later devoted his attention to the support of free trade and developed the idea of "comparative advantage," which showed how all countries gained from trade if their production possibilities differed. His devotion to free trade was closely associated with his attacks on landlords because the main barriers to free trade in England were the Corn Laws, devised to prevent domestic wheat prices from being reduced by competition from imports.

Ricardo eventually became a member of Parliament, and one of the greatest in his day. Members flocked to hear his speeches, not because they were particularly witty or entertaining, but because Ricardo's incisiveness and analytical mind made them important and memorable. It was not until more than a century later with John Maynard Keynes that the economics profession produced an individual who achieved such a combination of intellectual, financial, social, and political success as David Ricardo.

Farm Policy in the United States

A brief history of American farm policy

Major government intervention in the United States' farm sector began in 1933 during the Great Depression. Farm prices had fallen disastrously (by more than 50 percent from 1929) and, even though other prices had also fallen, real income per farm had dropped by almost two-thirds. The Depression decline had come on top of a long-run downward trend that had begun about 1920.

While prices had continuously fallen during the 1920s, farmers had attempted to maintain prices by voluntary crop-withholding movements. These were based on the then-popular belief that the price decline was due to "speculators" who could be defeated by such a move. These attempts had no effect on prices, so farmers turned to more formal measures. The *Agricultural Marketing Act* of 1929 set up a system of cooperative marketing arrangements through the Federal Farm Board, which included some provision for stabilization by purchase operations. By mid-1932, however, the Federal Farm Board had declared its inability to prevent a disastrous fall in farm prices.

President Franklin D. Roosevelt came to office in 1933. His winning campaign had included promises to use the full powers of the federal government to solve the farm crisis. By May, 1933, Congress had passed the *Agricultural Adjustment Act*. This act's main provision was to impose production quotas on farm products that would reduce supply and cause market prices to rise. As a temporary measure, farmers were extended federal loans against some of the crops yet to be harvested. In addition, the idea of a *parity price* emerged—a price for farm products that would enable farmers to buy the same nonfarm goods per unit of farm goods as in some base period. The basic provisions of this legislation—restrictions on production—were ultimately ruled invalid by the Supreme Court in 1936, although farm incomes rose by 50 percent after 1932 due considerably to this legislation.

In the *Agricultural Adjustment Act* of 1938, a new technique of acreage restriction was devised. Farmers were paid to assist in "conservation" by retiring farmland from active cultivation. A buffer-stock program for grains (the "Ever-Normal Granary") was started, and price supports for certain crops were given in the form of loans, related to parity prices. These loans were made on the security of crops, and thus could be "redeemed" by forfeiting the crops to the government.

World War II

Buffer stocks accumulated over the period up to 1941, when wartime conditions dominated the economy. These stocks suddenly became an important national resource, and farm policy made a full turnaround toward encouraging production instead of restricting it. Both output and prices rose during the War, and support prices were raised closer and closer to parity.

Basic postwar policy was set by the *Agricultural Acts* of 1948 and 1949. They provided price supports at 90 percent of parity for many farm products, and price supports at lower levels for certain others. These price-support programs—they were not price-*stabilization* programs as farmers were not limited as to the *upper* level of market prices—were associated with continued acreage restrictions, payments to take land out of crop use, and accumulation of buffer stocks by loans and default.

Korea and After

The Korean conflict (1950–53) led to another policy reversal. Again the emphasis was on increasing output rather than reducing it. At the end of this conflict, however, agricultural policy returned to previous aims.

In 1956, the *Soil Bank* was added to the other instruments of agricultural policy. This program to take land out of farm production was on a much larger scale than any previously devised. Many other adjustments to the farm program have taken place since then, the *Food and Agriculture Act* of 1965 being the most important. But the broad aims and instruments of farm policy remain very much as set in the "New Deal" period of the 1930s.

Because American farm policy has been one of price support rather than one of price stabilization, the government has primarily acted as a buyer in the market. It cannot sell surplus stocks at lower than market prices, so it must devise other methods of disposal. Immediately after World War II, Europe's need for food permitted the export of surpluses to Europe without depressing the market. In recent years, it has become increasingly difficult to dispose of surpluses overseas unless they are sold on terms favorable to poor countries as part of foreign aid. Even then, political problems arise because such exports compete with potential commercial exports by third countries, some of whom are themselves relatively poor. Consequently, there has been a steady increase in internal disposal designed to avoid competition with regular market sales. For example, surpluses are given or sold at below market prices to schools and poor families.

Recap Major intervention in the market for agricultural products began during the Great Depression of the 1930s. The basic agricultural policy was a combination of crop and acreage restriction and guaranteed price minimums. Although modified many times and in many ways, the basic policy has remained that of supporting prices in bad years, restricting acreage to be planted, and allowing farmers to receive market prices when these prices are high.

Farm Incomes Policy

Why it may be better to direct policy toward farmers' incomes rather than farm prices

All agricultural policy, at its roots, has a concern for farm incomes. As has already been pointed out, farm incomes—in the absence of some kind of stabilization—tend to fluctuate more than nonfarm incomes, and for many years have risen more slowly than other incomes in the advanced economies. Having noted this, we need to consider what the justification may be for policies designed to raise farm incomes as such, as opposed to those that merely lessen fluctuations.

Redistribution

Any assistance to agriculture represents a redistribution of income to the farm sector from the rest of society. Direct payments to farmers from general tax revenues can be regarded as representing either taxes that need not have been levied or alternative public projects that had to be scrapped. But even these do not represent the full cost to consumers, if the effect of the policies is to keep agricultural prices higher than they would otherwise be.

One argument in favor of such assistance is simply that many farmers are poor (or at least have lower incomes than people in other occupations).

However, many farmers are rich, and many are not individuals but corporations. If we assist poor farmers by increasing *all* farm incomes, then we help rich farmers too. Indeed, if a given program increases all farm incomes in much the same proportion (as price subsidies and similar policies tend to do), a rich farmer will receive even more help than a poor farmer.

Why Farmers?

Insofar as farmers are actually poor, their case would deserve to be considered as part of overall distribution policy designed to help poor people. A policy designed to provide minimum incomes to *all* poor people would presumably provide for poor farmers, and at far less cost to the community than any policy designed to assist all farmers.

The chief reason that farm policy was *not* conceived simply as part of an overall income-distribution policy was the historical context of its development. During the 1920s farm prices and incomes had been falling and farmers had become worse off *relative to others* in the economy. Agricultural policy was an attempt to restore the original relationship. The policy of supporting prices stressed the fundamental notion of "parity"—the ratio of farm to other prices that happened to exist just prior to World War I—and all supports were fixed relative to the parity price. Such a policy necessarily implied that the rich farmer who had become less rich was to be restored to his original relative position, along with the poor farmer who had become even poorer.

Two additional arguments have also been made in favor of a special policy toward farmers. One is national security, the argument that the country should preserve farm capacity against the possibility of imported supplies being cut off. This argument is not special to agriculture, however, and almost every sector of the economy uses it when seeking special treatment.

The second argument is that of preserving rural life. While this has a considerable sentimental element, there are genuine externalities involved. City dwellers, for example, *do* gain something from seeing farms and crops along the highways, and are quite likely willing to pay something for this.

Only this last argument seems to provide a case for treating agriculture differently from other sectors. However, attempts to preserve rural society, especially in the versions that generate the most nostalgia, are not necessarily the answer to guaranteeing incomes sufficient to keep people on the land.

Recap Subsidization of agriculture (as opposed to stabilization, in which prices are evened out over good and bad years) is a redistributive policy. As such, it should be considered in an appropriate context. If the aim is to raise the incomes of poor farmers, it may well be more efficient to do this directly than to subsidize prices that also increase the incomes of rich farmers.

Exercises

1. If the elasticity of demand for farm products is −.8, by what percentage must output be restricted in order to increase farm incomes by 50 percent? By what percentage will farm prices change?

2. Suppose productivity per worker rises by 6 percent annually in agriculture and 2 percent elsewhere. If labor is the only input in all industries, by what percentage will farm production increase if the farm labor force remains unchanged?

3. Using the data in question 2, what will be the annual rate of change in farm prices, and in what direction, if the elasticity of demand for agricultural products is −.5?

4. Again, using the data in question 2 and the information that the labor force outside agriculture is ten times the farm labor force, by what percentage annually must the output of farm products rise if the output of farm products is to remain constant *and* all workers are to find jobs either on or off the farm? (Assume full employment in both sectors to start with.)

For Thought and Discussion

1. Suppose all farmers rent their land from absentee landlords, rents being fixed for only a year at a time. What would you expect to be the effect of a price-support program on farm rents, and on the distribution of income between landlord and farmer?

2. Farmers can grow either wheat or corn on their land. Price supports are introduced for wheat but not for corn. What will happen to the price of corn?

3. People are starving in some countries, while farmers are being paid to keep land idle in the United States. What arguments could be used *against* a proposal to pay American farmers to produce (rather than not produce) and to ship the output to famine areas where it would be distributed free?

4. By price support, rich farmers receive a much greater subsidy than poor farmers. Should the price-support system be replaced by transfer payments to poor farmers?

5. Should farmers be paid to leave the farm, or to stay on the farm? Why?

Part 4
Distribution

This part, consisting of Chapters 15 through 18, is concerned with the division of society's output among its members. In most societies, including socialist ones, the allocation of income among the various available goods is left to the individual. Thus, our primary concern is with the way in which income is distributed among individuals in society. In Chapter 15 we examine the general determinants of income. Chapter 16 considers the special features in the determination of labor incomes, and Chapter 17 discusses these features for nonlabor incomes. Finally, in Chapter 18, we consider the possible aims of distributional policy and the ways government intervention in the economy can alter distribution.

Chapter 15
Distribution and the Price System

Terms and Concepts

Distribution
Transfer payment
Factor market
Derived demand
Marginal product of labor
Value of the marginal product
Marginal revenue product
Prices as signals
Redistribution of wealth
General poverty
Distributional poverty
Transfer income

Distribution	How output is distributed
and the Market	among members of society
	in a market economy

Distribution is concerned with how goods and services are allocated among consumers, that is, with *who gets how much of what*.

It would, of course, be possible to distribute an economy's entire output directly without the use of a market. Everyone could simply be issued so many sacks of flour, so many bars of soap, etc., in such a way that the quantities involved would equal the available output of each good. Such a system of distribution actually exists in certain special sub-societies, such as the kibbutzim in Israel. In complex societies, however (including those characterized by socialist economies), distribution is carried out through a system in which consumers receive incomes that are spent on goods provided through the market.

There will inevitably be some goods that are not distributed in this manner. True public goods, for example, *must* be distributed in some other way. Indeed, there are numerous government services that are commonly distributed without reference to income, including many that *could* be distributed through the market. Apart from basic police protection and national defense, services supplied outside the market include education in virtually all countries and health care in many.

The Role of Incomes

For those goods that are distributed through the market, consumers are free (in the absence of rationing or other special restrictions) to choose their most preferred collection of goods within their respective budget constraints. The ultimate distribution of market goods is thus determined by:

1. the relative prices of different goods,
2. consumer preferences, and
3. the distribution of incomes.

Having previously discussed the relationship among prices, preferences, and consumer choice, we shall now focus our attention on the distribution of incomes.

The primary way in which consumers obtain income is from the sale of their personal services—labor income in the broadest sense. Approximately three-fourths of personal income in the United States is obtained from the sale of labor services to employers or from the implicit sale of proprietors' labor services to their own professions or businesses.

But labor is not the only major resource in the economy. There are others, such as land and capital, whose employment yields their owners rent and interest payments. Such income derived from *wealth* accounts for about one-eighth of total personal income in the United States.

After a firm has paid for all the inputs it uses—intermediate goods, labor, land, and capital—it may be left with a *residual profit,* an excess of total revenue over total cost. Just how this residual is distributed depends on the prevailing structure of legal and social institutions. In a *private-enterprise* economy, such as the United States, this residual is normally distributed to persons holding *claims* to specific shares of the firm. Corporate claims usually assume the form of transferable corporate *stocks,* and the residual profit is distributed in the form of *dividends* to the stockholders.

In socialist countries, the income from property (whatever it may be called) accrues primarily to the government which can either use it to offset otherwise necessary taxes or redistribute it as it chooses.

Transfer Payments

Finally, some consumers obtain income in the form of *transfer payments.* Through a variety of social service and similar arrangements, they are *given* incomes even though they neither sell labor services nor derive income from wealth. These are transfer payments in the sense that they are obtained not through the market mechanism but from the government that taxes certain consumers and transfers the tax proceeds to other consumers. Hence, transfer incomes, which are almost twice the size of dividend incomes in the United States, are directly determined by social policy rather than by the working of the economy.

Market Incomes and Factor Prices

The income a consumer receives from the sale of a given service depends on two things: (1) the price received for it, and (2) the quantity of it available for sale. *The distribution of income among consumers thus depends on the prices of the different types of services consumers have for sale and the initial distribution of salable services among consumers.*

In a market economy (excluding transfers), we thus have the relationship:

$$\text{market income of an individual} = \text{salable factor services of labor or wealth} \times \text{price of factor services}.$$

The endowment of potential labor hours (available time) is distributed more or less evenly throughout the population. But the distribution of special abilities and training (human capital) that account for different types of labor services is not uniform. Moreover, the distribution of wealth (ownership of resources other than labor) depends on the history and the socioeconomic structure of the country, and may take virtually any form. Thus, most economists are primarily concerned with the determination of factor prices.

Recap In virtually all advanced economies, output is distributed primarily through the market. The final distribution of goods is thus determined by the combined effects of income distribution, the prices of different goods, and personal preferences. Because incomes are obtained primarily from selling the services of either labor or wealth, the basic distribution of market income is determined by relative factor prices and the distribution of factor ownership. This income distribution may be altered if the government provides incomes to certain individuals in the form of transfer payments.

Capsule Supplement 15.1   **Measuring the Inequality of Income**

It is easy to recognize an equal income distribution. But if a distribution is not equal, just exactly *how* unequal is it? One simple measure is to take the richest population group—say, the top 5 percent of income recipients—and see what proportion of total income it receives. If income were distributed equally, the top 5 percent (or any 5 percent, since there would be no top) would receive exactly 5 percent of total income. If, on the other hand, income were distributed with the maximum possible degree of inequality, in which case the richest individual would receive it all, then the top 5 percent would obviously receive 100 percent of total income. All real-world income distributions necessarily lie between these two extremes, and the smaller the share of the top 5 percent, the closer to equality a given income distribution will be.

Statistics for the share of total income received by the top 5 percent of the population are widely available and thus useful for comparisons over long periods. For the United States, such figures go back to 1917, at which time the top 5 percent received almost 25 percent of total income. The share of the top 5 percent more or less held its own until the 1940s, when it began to fall. By 1948, it had fallen to 18 percent, and by 1977, it had fallen to 14 percent, just over half of what it had been at its peak in 1932.

Thus, the general trend in the United States has been toward *decreasing distributional inequality,* and the same trend has been evident in most of the world's highly developed countries. Distributional inequality is generally greater in poor countries than in rich countries. A recent United Nations' report estimated, for example, that, while the top 20 percent of income recipients in the United States obtained about 40 percent of total income, the top 20 percent of income recipients in Latin America obtained more than 60 percent.

A simple measure like the share of total income received by the richest population group cannot adequately describe the full properties of the income distribution. Even though we may know that the top 5 percent receive, say, 20 percent of total income, this tells us nothing about how the remaining 80 percent is distributed. It might all go to the *next* 10 percent of income recipients, or it might be equally divided among the remaining 95 percent.

Percent of total income received by
each one-fifth of U.S. families, 1977

Families	Income
Lowest fifth	6
Next lowest fifth	12
Middle fifth	17
Next highest fifth	24
Highest fifth	41

Lorenz curve depicting
data from the table

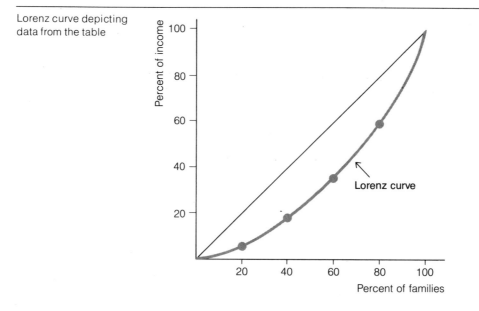

The table shows the percentage of total income received by the lowest fifth of
the U.S. population, the second lowest, and so forth, in 1977. By plotting this information on a graph we can obtain what is known as a *Lorenz curve*. Comparing this curve with the curve of complete income equality (actually a straight
line) permits us to visualize the existing degree of distributional inequality.

By using measures such as Lorenz curves, it is possible to compare the income
distributions of different population groups. For the United States we find, not
unexpectedly, that wage and salary income is less unequally distributed than
income from property and business. Income from rent is the least unequally
distributed form of property income, and income from dividends is the most
unequally distributed—the top 5 percent receiving almost 70 percent of total
dividend income. As between population groups, we note that the distribution

of income among blacks is more unequal than that among the white population, and that the distribution of income is more unequal in some geographical
regions than others, being greatest in the South, and least in the Midwest.

Factor Markets

**The general character
of factor markets**

The markets for factor services are essentially the same as the markets for
goods, and thus depend on conditions of demand and supply. Demand
conditions for all factors are determined by the same general considerations. There are, however, major differences among factors on the supply side that are sufficient to justify their individual treatment later.

Derived Demand

All factors share the common property that the demand for their services is
a *derived demand.* Consumers ultimately want goods. Hence, factor services are demanded only to the extent that they are required to produce
these goods. The more *specific* a factor is to the production of a particular
good, the more its demand depends on the demand for that good. If there
were no demand for tombstones, there would be no demand for
tombstone-makers, tombstone-making machinery, or land containing stone
suitable for tombstones.

We have already shown (in Chapter 7) that the firm's demand curve for a
variable input will be downward sloping like a demand curve for goods.
Because the supply curve for a factor will typically slope upward (although
this is less certain than in the case of goods), a perfectly competitive factor
market can be depicted by a diagram quite similar to that illustrating a
goods market.

Market Circumstances

Demand curves for factors, like those for goods, relate quantities to prices
under *given market circumstances.* For a given good, the relevant circumstances that affect demand were shown to be such things as consumer
incomes and the prices of other goods. For a given factor, the following
circumstances affect the demand for its services:

1. The demand conditions for the goods that use the factor in their production, specifically, the *prices* of such goods when their markets are perfectly competitive, and the *entire demand schedules* for such goods when
   their markets are imperfectly competitive.

2. The technology that determines what combinations of factors will be used to produce each level of output.
3. The price of other factors, because the choice of the least-cost process depends on relative factor prices.

We assume that these circumstances are constant when we draw a specific demand curve for a factor. If any circumstances change, then the demand for the factor and hence the demand curve will also change.

Recap Factor markets are markets for factor services. These markets do not differ, in principle, from goods markets, and may be either perfectly or imperfectly competitive. The demand for the services of a given factor is derived from the demand for those goods that employ these services in their production.

Perfectly Competitive Factor Prices

Determination of factor prices under perfectly competitive conditions

In Chapter 7 we briefly investigated the way in which a firm's demand for a variable input is determined. Here our analysis will show that, if factor markets themselves are perfectly competitive, that is, if firms are all sufficiently small that the actions of none affect the price of inputs, the demand for a factor stands in a clearly defined relationship with:

1. the production technology,
2. the quantities of fixed factors, and
3. the demand for the product.

Given the conditions of factor supply, factor prices are then determined by the interaction of demand and supply, as goods prices are.

To determine the firm's demand curve for a typical input (let's say labor), we must investigate how much labor the firm will plan to hire at each wage rate, given the firm's stock of capital equipment, its technology, and the market conditions for its product.

From the viewpoint of a profit-maximizing firm, an additional man-hour of labor will be used if it increases profits, but not otherwise. Hiring an additional man-hour does two things to the firm's profit position—it adds the additional wage paid to costs, and it adds the resulting increase in output to revenue. While the additional cost is simply the wage rate, what is the additional revenue? To find out, we must first determine how much additional output can be produced by using an additional man-hour, then determine how much is added to total revenue from selling this increased output.

The *marginal product of labor* (*MPL*) is the addition to total output that results from using one additional man-hour of labor. If the firm is selling in a perfectly competitive market, each unit of output produced will sell at the going price (P), so the value of an additional man-hour to the firm is $P \times MPL$. If the firm is selling in an imperfectly competitive market, additional units of output would not bring in revenue equal to the price, but (as explained in Chapter 9) something less than this because additional units could be sold only by offering all units at a slightly lower price. The addition to revenue obtained from selling an additional unit is the marginal revenue (MR), and the net effect on revenue of using an additional man-hour will be $MR \times MPL$.

Because each man-hour adds an amount equal to the wage (W) to total cost, and an amount equal to $MR \times MPL$ (called the *marginal revenue product of labor*) to total revenue, the firm will add man-hours as long as the marginal revenue product of labor *exceeds* the wage and will stop as soon as the excess disappears. In other words, the firm will optimally use that amount of labor for which the revenue from the marginal man-hour is just equal to its cost, or to where we have

$$MR \times MPL = W.$$

A firm that is perfectly competitive in its output market (we are assuming perfect competition in its input markets) will have $MR = P$, and the desired quantity of labor will be such that

$$P \times MPL = W.$$

The product $P \times MPL$, which is simply the special value of the marginal revenue product of labor when there is perfect competition in the output market, is often called the *value of the marginal product* of labor.

We have shown how the firm determines the quantity of labor it will use at a specific wage, W. The firm's demand curve for labor can thus be derived by establishing the profit-maximizing level of labor use at each different wage. This demand curve will be defined in terms of specific quantities of other inputs and a specific output market. Consequently, it will be expected to change if the quantities of other inputs change (capital equipment, for example), or if the price of the product (under perfect competition) or its demand curve (under imperfect competition) should change.

An Example

Using a numerical example, we can demonstrate how a demand schedule for labor is derived from the conditions of production (as represented by a marginal product of labor schedule) and output demand (as represented by marginal revenue data). In Table 15.1, the marginal product of labor (labor assumed to be the only variable factor) is shown (in column 2), opposite the relevant quantities of labor (in column 1). These data are presented graphically in Figure 15.1. Note that constant returns to scale prevail up to the

Table 15.1
Demand Schedule for Labor,
Basic Technical Data

(1) Quantity of labor (man-weeks)	(2) Marginal product of labor (MPL) (tons per man-week)	(3) Value of PxMPL for P = $10 per ton ($ per man-week)	(4) P = $20 per ton
Up to 9	20 constant	200	400
10	20	200	400
11	18	180	360
12	16	160	320
13	14	140	280
14	12	120	240
15	10	100	200
16	8	80	160
17	6	60	120
18	4	40	80
19	2	20	40
20 and above	0	0	0

Marginal product measured in tons per man-week.
Technology and quantities of other factors are constant.

Figure 15.1
The marginal product curve for a variable
input (based on data in Table 15.1).

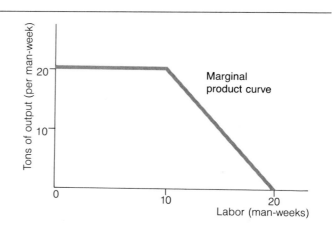

point at which ten man-weeks of labor are hired. This implies that the
capital constraint becomes effective at that point.

We'll assume that the firm's output market is perfectly competitive so
price and marginal revenue are equal. Consequently, the firm's marginal
revenue product is identical to the value of the marginal product. For each

employment level, the value of the marginal product is obtained by multiplying the marginal product of labor by the price of the output. Two hypothetical output prices, $10 per ton (column 3) and $20 per ton (column 4), are shown.

Let's first consider the case in which the output price (which the perfectly competitive firm cannot influence) is $10 per ton. How many man-weeks of labor will this firm seek to employ at each wage level? To find out, consider the specific wage of $80 per man-week and look down column 3, which lists the value of the marginal product at various employment levels when the output price is $10 per ton. We see that the figure of $80 per man-week corresponds to sixteen man-weeks of labor (from column 1). At sixteen man-weeks, then, the wage ($80 per man-week) and the value of the marginal product of labor ($80 per man-week) are equal, so this must be the most-profitable amount of labor for the firm. At a wage of $120 per man-week with the output price still at $10 per ton, we look down column 3 for the figure $120, observe that it occurs at an employment level of fourteen man-weeks, and conclude that the firm will wish to employ fourteen man-weeks of labor at a wage of $120. We can perform this operation for any wage (within the limits of our table) and find the firm's demand for labor at that wage.

If the demand conditions for the firm's output should change, so will its demand for labor at any given wage. Suppose, for example, the product price rose to $20 per ton, making the data in column 4 relevant to the firm's decisions. At a wage rate of $80 per man-week, we can determine the quantity of labor demanded by using column 4 figures instead of those in column 3, as we did previously. The demand for labor at an $80 wage will now be eighteen man-weeks, instead of sixteen man-weeks as it was when the product price was only $10 per ton. As we would expect, *an increase in the price of the product will normally increase the demand for labor by firms making that product.* Table 15.2, which shows the full demand schedules for labor at the two different output prices, illustrates clearly how the demand for labor is greater at the higher output price. Figure 15.2 shows the same information in the form of demand curves.

By relabeling the vertical axis, we can proceed directly from the marginal product curve to the demand curve for the input, as in Figure 15.3. Here we've drawn the marginal product curve as usual, with the quantity of labor measured horizontally and its marginal product measured vertically. The vertical measures can then be converted to the values $P \times MPL$ simply by multiplying by price (in this case $P = \$10$). By regarding these measures as the wage (to which they will be equal), the marginal product curve doubles as the demand curve, and is identical to the marginal product curve derived by the method above.

For a firm facing an imperfectly competitive *output* market, we can derive the demand curve for labor (or any other variable input) in the same way, except we would multiply marginal product by marginal revenue to

Table 15.2
Demand Schedule for Labor,
Actual Schedules

(1) Weekly wage ($)	(2) Quantity of labor demanded at $P = 10 per ton (in man-weeks)	(3) $P = 20 per ton (in man-weeks)
0	20	20
40	18	19
80	16	18
120	14	17
160	12	16
200	10	15
240	0	14
280	0	13
320	0	12
360	0	11
400	0	10
440	0	0

Derived from basic technical data of Table 15.1.

obtain the scale for the vertical axis. In this case, marginal revenue would vary with the level of output and thus with the marginal product.

Aggregate Demand and Supply

The *industry* demand curve for a factor (when the input market is perfectly competitive) is derived by adding the quantities demanded at each factor price for all firms in the industry. If the factor is used in more than one industry, we can add quantities demanded at each factor price and obtain the *economy's* demand curve for the factor. In full equilibrium, the relationship *marginal revenue product equals factor price* will hold for every industry that actually uses and is free to vary the factor.

Certain aspects of the supply of factors will be examined in more detail in later chapters. Here we take up only a broad description. Usually, we can assume that any one factor is used in several or all industries, so the supply in which we are interested is the *supply to the economy as a whole*.

In the short run, the quantities of certain factors (such as land and capital), remain fixed. Their supply curves are thus *inelastic*. We can generally assume that the supply of land is inelastic even in the long run, while the supply of capital is inelastic in the short run but not in the long run, since more capital can be produced in time (or the existing stock reduced by not replacing worn-out equipment).

Figure 15.2

The demand curve for labor at two different product prices.

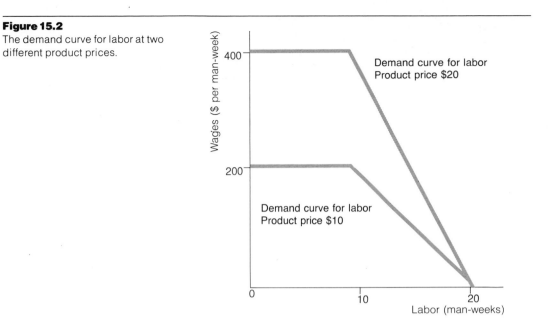

Figure 15.3

How the marginal product curve for an input can be turned into the demand curve by relabeling the vertical axis.

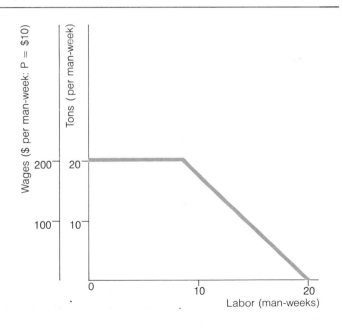

Figure 15.4

If factor markets are perfectly competitive, factor prices are determined in exactly the same way as product prices.

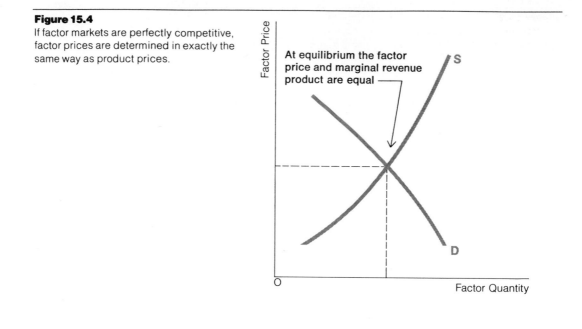

While the *population* is fixed at any given time, the supply of labor is not. We can generally assume that higher wages will both induce more people to work and induce those already working to work longer hours. Thus, the supply curve for labor is usually upward sloping. Under certain conditions the supply curve may have other slopes (possibly even a downward slope), but we shall ignore these for the moment.

Market Equilibrium

Thus, we can generally expect *normally sloped* supply and demand curves for factors under perfect competition, and an equilibrium price and quantity that are determined in the same way as in other competitive markets, as shown in Figure 15.4. The question of whether such an equilibrium is actually *reached* in every factor market (especially the labor market) requires special consideration, and will be discussed later.

We shall defer discussion of *imperfectly competitive* factor markets until the next chapter because this discussion is most relevant to the labor market.

Recap The demand for factor services by a firm is determined by the relationship between the marginal contribution of those services to output (their marginal product) and the contribution of additional output to revenue (marginal revenue). The firm will use only as much of a factor as will make its marginal revenue product equal to its unit cost. If there is perfect competition in the firm's output market, equilibrium will be reached where output price times the marginal product of the factor is equal to its unit cost. The firm's demand curve for a factor can be derived from these relationships; industry or economywide demand curves can be derived by aggregating individual firms' curves. Given supply conditions, equilibrium price can then be determined in the same manner as for goods markets.

Economic Efficiency and Income Distribution	**A look at the true function of factor prices in the economic system**

Given an initial distribution of wealth and preferences, and the absence of such complicating influences as indivisibilities, public goods, and public bads, perfectly competitive equilibrium will provide prices for both goods and factors. Because the distribution of factor ownership is predetermined by institutional considerations, the equilibrium prices will dictate the distribution of income because each person's income is the revenue from the sale of the factor services he or she possesses.

As we demonstrated in Chapter 8, a perfectly competitive equilibrium is optimal from the standpoint of efficiency because no reallocation of goods or factor inputs can make anyone better off without making someone else worse off. Hence, it might seem that the associated income distribution is optimal as well. Such reasoning is false, however, and it is important that we dispel this fallacy.

Wealth Distribution

First, the distribution of wealth is independent of efficiency in the economy. Indeed, an efficient competitive equilibrium exists for each possible wealth distribution. Hence, the criteria that establish an efficient resource allocation and an optimal output mix within a given wealth distribution contribute nothing to the judgment of whether one wealth distribution is better or worse than another. This is because any given redistribution of wealth will necessarily make someone worse off even though it may make society as a whole better off. The initial distribution of wealth can be quite arbitrary. Therefore, any argument that the distribution of income associated with a given distribution of wealth is "ideal" in any ultimate sense is obviously invalid, even though competitive equilibrium may prevail.

The Role of Prices

While it's true that competitive equilibrium prices (including factor prices) have important optimal qualities, we must be careful not to ascribe qualities to such prices that they do not possess. Under universal perfect competition, the relationship

factor price = value of the marginal product

will hold for all factors in all uses if there is general equilibrium. The real economic content of this relationship is simply that the *allocation of factors* among alternative uses is optimal under whatever circumstances exist because a movement of one unit of a factor from one use to another could not increase the value of society's output.

We can thus summarize the role of equilibrium prices (including factor prices) as follows:

1. *Equilibrium prices are signals, devoid of any moral content, that if followed correctly, will yield an optimal allocation in the economy.*
2. *A competitive equilibrium both generates optimal prices and ensures that, as signals, they are correctly followed.*

The Absence of Ethical Content

There is no reason to attach any notion of "fairness," "appropriateness," or even "inevitability" to the distribution of income that emerges from competitive equilibrium under some initial distribution of wealth. The contribution of the economist is to note that, given the existing distribution of wealth, the appropriate *signals* should be left undisturbed if the economy is to do as well as it can, *given that existing distribution.*

Assuming the existence of a competitive equilibrium, suppose we wish to increase the income of those selling labor services only. To do this by establishing a minimum wage higher than the competitive level will lead to economic inefficiency, and may be partly self-defeating. Such a minimum wage will lead to excess supply in the labor market and thus unemployment, as shown in Figure 15.5. In addition, the prices of labor-intensive goods will rise relative to those of capital-intensive goods, and the whole allocation of resources and choice of output mix will move away from the optimum.

Imperfect Competition

The optimality of factor prices holds only for a perfectly competitive equilibrium. If there were widespread imperfect competition, market prices would no longer represent signals pointed to efficiency.

Suppose, for example, the economy produced two goods, one under monopoly, the other under competition. The monopolistic output would be lower than that under competitive conditions. If the monopolistic industry were labor-intensive relative to its competitive counterpart, the market wage would also be lower than it would be under competitive conditions because the monopolistic industry, which uses relatively more labor, would

Figure 15.5
The effect of a legal minimum wage on the labor market.

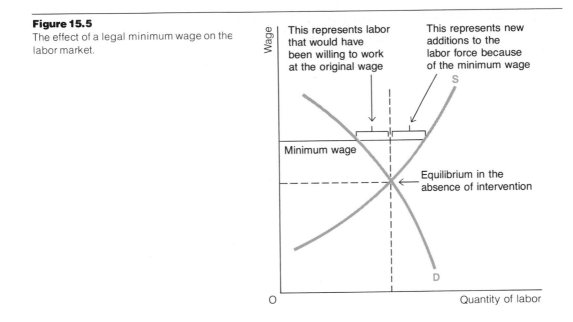

be operating below the competitive equilibrium level. The United States is characterized by extensive imperfect competition in both goods markets and factor markets, so actual factor prices cannot be considered reliable allocative signals.

Recap In perfectly competitive equilibrium, factor prices represent signals to which users of factors should respond in order to ensure an efficient allocation of resources. However, this does not imply fairness in the resulting distribution of income. Moreover, when extensive imperfect competition exists, as in the United States, factor prices should not be taken as reliable guides to allocative efficiency.

Capsule Supplement 15.2   **Incentives or Rewards?**

In the economist's idealized competitive model, prices are signals that serve to induce decision-makers in the economy to behave in a way that is "best" for society as a whole. As such, prices are *forward-oriented,* providing *incentives* for appropriate future behavior rather than *rewards* for past behavior. Thus, if a particular skill or factor service carries a high price compared with other skills or services, this price is not a reward to the existing supplier so much as an incentive for others to supply this resource. Indeed, the more successful suppliers are in reducing the relative scarcity of some resource, the lower will be the price they receive for it—in other words, the greater the degree to which individual suppliers fulfill social needs, the less they will be paid. This makes sense if factor prices are incentives, but nonsense if they are considered rewards.

The same considerations apply to interest payments and profits. High interest payments, for example, serve to induce investors to forgo immediate consumption and supply funds to business enterprises. On the demand side, such interest payments provide an incentive for firms to use less capital.

Profits—the residuals remaining for the firm after payment is made for resource services—also function as incentives. If the market is close to perfect competition, the existence of high profits in an industry is both a signal for the need for more firms to enter that industry, and an incentive for them to do so. Under imperfect competition, however, profits do not necessarily act as incentives for movement toward an optimal position. Indeed, they may act as incentives to monopolize, and thus to move away from optimality.

As with factor returns, the more efficient profits are as incentives, the smaller they will turn out to be as rewards, because the rapid movement of new firms into industries whose profits rise above normal levels will quickly bring those profits back to normal.

General Equilibrium Effects

How changes in the ownership of wealth can be expected to change the whole equilibrium pattern of an economy

Factor prices and goods prices are determined together as part of the general equilibrium of the economy. Thus, factor prices, as goods prices, depend on the available technology, resource supplies, consumer preferences, and the existing distribution of wealth.

An Example

In order to understand how a change in one of the underlying determinants of general equilibrium can affect all goods and factor prices, let's consider a simple example in which we can focus on the effects of a *redistribution of wealth*.

Suppose we have a society composed of two groups of equal size, country folks and city slickers. Two things are produced in the economy, "garages" and "massages." All country folks have identical preferences and consume only garages, while city slickers also have identical preferences but consume both garages and massages. Country preferences are therefore garage-oriented relative to city preferences, while city preferences are massage-oriented relative to country preferences.

The economy has two resources, labor and capital. Both are required to produce garages, but massages are produced with labor alone. Accordingly, garages are capital-intensive relative to massages, and massages are labor-intensive relative to garages. We assume that everyone works, regardless of how much wealth (capital) is owned, and that everyone receives the same wage. Thus, labor income is distributed evenly over the population. But we assume that wealth—and thus *interest,* the income derived from capital services—is not evenly distributed. Let us compare the equilibrium we would expect if all wealth were owned by country folks with that we would expect if all wealth were owned by city slickers.

If the wealth were owned by country folks, they would receive, in the aggregate, more income than city slickers, because wages would be the same for both groups and country folks would receive interest payments in addition. A unique equilibrium would exist in the economy, with associated equilibrium price levels for garages, massages, labor, and capital.

Now, suppose ownership of the wealth were transferred to the city. Aggregate city income could then exceed aggregate country income. Moreover, the rise in city income relative to country income would mean a rise in the incomes of massage-oriented consumers relative to those of garage-oriented consumers. Consequently, the demand for massages would rise, and the demand for garages would fall. Thus, we would expect an increase in massage output, a fall in garage output, and a rise in the price of massages relative to garages.

Because massages use labor only, increased massage output would draw labor out of garage production, which is declining anyway because of lower demand. But garage production uses capital as well as labor, and the decline in garage output would release capital, which the massage industry does not need. The excess supply of capital would cause a fall in its price—resulting in the excess capital eventually being used up by a switch to processes using a higher ratio of capital to labor in garage production. The result of the new allocation of resources on the factor markets, therefore, would be to lower interest payments relative to wages. (There is an interesting point here—interest payments are higher when the owners of wealth are oriented toward capital-intensive goods than when they are oriented toward labor-intensive goods.)

Thus, if wealth were owned in the city rather than the country, we would have a different equilibrium with:

1. a higher price of massages relative to garages,
2. a higher wage rate relative to the interest rate, and
3. a higher ratio of total wage income to total interest income in the economy.

In general then, each distribution of wealth will tend to be associated with a unique equilibrium, with unique prices for both goods *and* factors, and with a unique distribution of income between labor and the owners of wealth. If the economy is competitive, the equilibrium associated with any given wealth distribution will be just as "ideal" as that associated with every other wealth distribution. Nevertheless, we cannot move from one wealth distribution to another without making some members of society worse off.

Recap The way in which both goods and factor prices are linked together in general equilibrium can be illustrated by considering a hypothetical distribution of wealth. If this wealth is redistributed in such a way that the new owners of capital have different preferences than the old, we can show how relative goods prices, relative factor prices, relative amounts of different goods produced and the distribution of income will all change.

The Causes of Poverty

Why a market economy is likely to leave some people poor

There is no absolute definition of poverty. Economically, it can only be defined in terms of family income relative to some arbitrary standard that is regarded as minimally acceptable, a standard that necessarily varies among societies and over time within a given society.

General Poverty

The total output of an economy may be so low that, if it were divided equally among the population, everyone's income would lie below the accepted poverty level. For such an economy, widespread poverty is inevitable, and the most any redistribution could accomplish would be to give some an income above the poverty line at the cost of making everyone else very poor indeed. Such general poverty exists in many—perhaps most—of the less-developed countries of Asia, Africa, and Latin America.

Distributional Poverty

But poverty is also prevalent in highly developed countries like the United States, where the output of consumer goods per capita far exceeds a generously defined level of poverty. What accounts for such poverty? It's simply that the prevailing *distribution of income* in these countries is such that certain individuals are left with very little even though average income levels are quite high. We can thus regard such poverty as *distributional poverty* because income could theoretically be redistributed in a way that would leave no one below the poverty line.

In a market economy, distributional poverty essentially affects two groups: (1) those who have no labor services to sell, and (2) those who find little or no demand for the services they have to offer. The first group includes the aged, the sick, and mothers with young dependent children—

individuals constrained by their own physical condition or social tradition from offering labor services. The second includes those with inadequate education or training to offer anything but raw unskilled labor, for which the demand is very likely low in a technologically advanced economy.

It's inevitable that some members of society will grow too old to work, even in the absence of compulsory retirement, and that some will become physically disabled. Consequently, many of the old and sick are destined to be poor in a pure market economy unless some form of income transfer exists. The only market mechanism available for averting poverty under these conditions is the prior accumulation of wealth or purchase of insurance. In either case, individuals must have made the appropriate decisions while they were working and must have received sufficient income during that period to make such decisions while maintaining an adequate level of immediate consumption.

Poverty among those with labor services to sell is not inevitable in a market economy, but neither is there any mechanism to prevent it. Poverty due to unemployment can be regarded as stemming from the improper working of the system. Unemployment represents an excess supply of labor at the existing wage, and thus indicates a lack of equilibrium in the market. On the other hand, the excess supply implies that equilibrium, if ever reached, would be at a wage below the current level. Thus, equilibrium in the market for unskilled labor might result in employment for all, but at a wage insufficient to bring unskilled workers above the poverty line. The resulting income distribution would very likely result in a large number of poor unskilled workers rather than some (who presently have jobs) less poor with the remainder (who are presently unemployed) very poor. Wages for various types of labor will reflect the relative demand and supply for these types under a pure market system and will bear no necessary relationship to socially accepted standards of poverty or a ''fair'' wage, unless there is some intervention in the market.

Income Transfers

Because a pure market economy will generate no incomes to those with no factor services to sell, and because some individuals will inevitably fit into this category, nonmarket institutions are obviously required if poverty is to be alleviated. Moreover, any income received by those who contribute no factor services and have no claim on profits must be taken from those who do. This is why income unrelated to the sale of factor services is called *transfer income*—it is transferred, either voluntarily or through taxation, from those receiving market incomes to those who do not.

Although often backed by strong social sanctions, transfers originated as voluntary payments. The old were cared for by their own families through voluntary intra-household transfers. Children continue to be supported in this way almost everywhere. Other social institutions, particularly religious bodies, organized transfers from their nonpoor members to those who did not fit into the family transfer system (orphans, for example). Nonvoluntary transfers backed by the government's power to tax have a long history as well (Elizabethan England, for example, possessed a crude transfer system of this kind).

In a rich society like the United States, the existence of distributional poverty can be partly blamed on the faulty working of the market. Given the inevitability of a transfer system, however, most must be ascribed to inadequate or inefficient transfer policies.

Recap Poverty in a pure market economy is almost inevitable, even in those few rich countries in which an equal distribution of income would bring everyone above the poverty level. The operation of the market leaves individuals poor because they have no salable resources (the old), have resources that they cannot sell (the unemployed), or receive very low prices for what they have to sell (rural migratory workers). There is no provision within the market mechanism for assisting the poor. Such provision, therefore, must be made by transferring income from those receiving it through the market to those who do not.

Exercises

The table below presents production data for a hypothetical firm.

Number of workers	Total output (tons per week)	Marginal product of labor (tons per worker per week)
2	28	12
3	39	11
4	49	10
5	58	9
6	65	7
7	70	5
8	72	2
8+	72	0

1. If the firm is in a perfectly competitive market for its output, calculate the value of the marginal product for each level of employment:
   a. when the output sells for $5 per ton.
   b. when the output sells for $9 per ton.
2. Draw the firm's demand schedule for labor when the output price is $5 per ton, and also when it is $9 per ton. Draw the demand curves in each case.
3. The industry consists of 1,000 firms, all with production conditions iden-

tical to those given in question 1. The labor used is highly specialized—it is not demanded by any other industry, nor can this industry use any other kind of labor. If there are exactly 6,000 workers of this kind, all of whom will take whatever wage the market offers, what will be the equilibrium wage if the industry's output sells for $5 per ton?

4. Under the conditions given in question 3, what will happen to (a) the wage rate, (b) the total output of the industry, if the price of the product rises to $9 per ton?

5. How many workers, if any, would be unemployed under the general conditions of the two previous questions if:
   a. the minimum wage is set at $50 per week when the product price is $5 per ton?
   b. the minimum wage is set at $50 per week when the product price is $9 per ton?

6. Continuing with the same production data and the same 1,000 identical firms, what will the equilibrium wage be when the output price is $5 per ton and there are 7,000 workers in the labor force instead of 6,000?

7. Under the conditions in question 6, how many workers will be unemployed if the minimum wage is set at $50 per week?

8. With the same circumstances as those of questions 6 and 7, calculate the total wages received by all workers together
   a. under a free labor market.
   b. with a $50 minimum wage.
   Do your results surprise you? Would the relationship between the two totals generally be the same as here, or would it depend on exact data for specific industries?

For Thought and Discussion

1. Why is redistribution of income more readily accepted than redistribution of wealth?

2. If all profits were subject to a special income tax of 90 cents for each dollar of profit, would the signal and incentive effects of profits still be able to function?

3. Would it be possible to abolish poverty in the United States by manipulating *prices* (including factor prices) alone, without making direct transfer payments? Manipulating prices can be taken to include price controls and supports as well as taxes and subsidies.

4. If the government supports the old, the young will probably cease to make their own provisions for retirement. Do you think this would lead to important economic consequences, either good or bad?

Chapter 16
Labor Income

Terms and Concepts

Labor income
Personal income distribution
Skill differential
Wage differential
Human capital
Labor-leisure choice
Participation rate
Labor union
Closed shop
Bargaining
All-or-nothing offer
Lockout
Strike
Exploitation
Monopsony
Real wages
Productivity
Wage-price policy

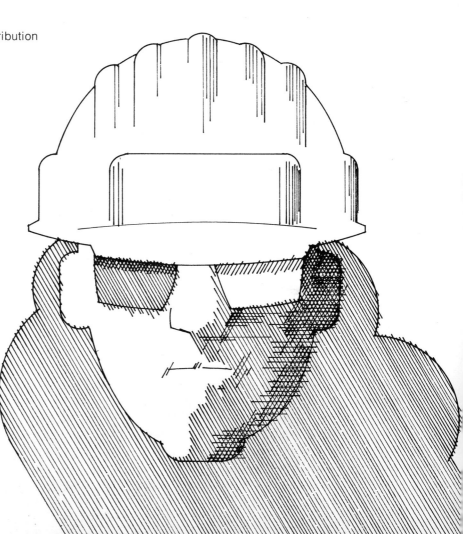

The Importance of Labor Income

Why the overall distribution of income is dominated by the distribution of labor income

We shall use the term *labor income* to mean all income derived from the sale of personal services, that is, all income typically classified as *earnings*. In this sense, the salary received by the president of the United States is just as much labor income as the wage of a stoop laborer in Southern California. Fees paid to entertainers and professional people for their personal services are also labor income.

Labor—The Prime Source of Income

Contrary to popular mythology, labor income in the form of wages and salaries is not only the predominant source of income at all income levels, but actually represents a greater proportion of income at higher income levels than at lower levels. This is because transfer payments (such as Social Security benefits, welfare payments, or unemployment compensation) are the major source of nonlabor personal income in the United States, and these are made mostly to individuals in low-income groups.

About 90 percent of U.S. families received labor income in 1977. The 10 percent with no labor income were primarily low-income families that received transfer incomes. This is shown by the very low median income of families with no labor income ($4,500) as compared with the median income of all families ($14,000). The "idle rich," those families without labor income but with incomes of $15,000 or more, represented less than one-tenth of one percent of all U.S. families.

Many families have both labor and nonlabor ("unearned") income—about half of the families with any labor income. In general, those with higher labor incomes are more likely to have nonlabor income to supplement their earnings than those in the lower labor-income groups. Even in the $50,000-plus income group, however, there were still 15 percent who had no income other than labor income. Thus, it is quite clear that in the United States today, and increasingly in other industrialized economies, *the overall distribution of income, excluding government transfer payments, is determined primarily by the distribution of labor income.* Even though this may not seem very surprising, it represents something of a revolution in economic thinking that has taken place only in the last twenty years or so.

The Traditional Class View

For almost 200 years, economists viewed income distribution as a *class* phenomenon. This view was based on the following two assumptions once relevant to the industrial and immediate preindustrial economies of Europe and North America:

1. Individuals either had property and received income entirely from selling property services, or had no property and received income entirely from the sale of personal services.
2. The range of prices for different personal services (wage and salary rates) was relatively narrow.

Based on these assumptions, economists concluded that the distribution between total labor income and total nonlabor income (*financial income distribution*) explained the distribution of incomes among individuals (*personal income distribution*). The general presumption was that a lower ratio of labor income to nonlabor income would be associated with greater inequality of distribution because workers were poor and property owners, rich.

Neither of these two assumptions is relevant to modern industrial society. Those who sell personal services and those who sell property services are not two mutually exclusive groups of individuals but predominantly the same people. The dispersion of wage rates in the United States, from about $3,000 to $200,000 and more per year, is enormous. Property ownership is still concentrated in the sense that a high proportion remains in the hands of a relatively few people, but it is *dispersed* in the sense that *some property* is owned by a very large number of people.

This is not to say that we are not interested in the relationship between labor and nonlabor incomes, or in that between the general wage level and the profit rate, the interest rate, and so on. Rather, it is to emphasize that, in our study of labor income, we must avoid the idea of a "single wage rate" and recognize the great differentials in compensation that exist from occupation to occupation.

Recap In modern industrial societies, and especially in the United States, income from labor (in the proper, broad sense) is the predominant source of income. This is true for the rich as well as the not so rich. The inequality in income distribution is thus due primarily to inequalities in labor income rather than to differences between labor income and income derived from property.

Wage and Salary Differentials

Why wage rates differ among occupations

"Raw labor," in the sense of pure muscle power, is only one of the many personal services that people can provide. Raw labor is still a major salable resource in certain parts of the world, although its importance is declining. In the United States, plain brawn is not too important. Even if we assume that all persons classified by the Department of Labor as farm workers or nonfarm laborers supply no skill, these accounted for less than 8 percent of those working in 1977. Furthermore, this percentage has been declining rapidly; in 1950 this minimum-skill group represented 18 percent of those working.

A majority of workers in all industrial countries, and an overwhelming majority in the United States, supplies personal services that embody a greater or lesser element of something other than, or in addition to, simple muscle power. We refer to this "something" broadly as *skill*, which can mean anything from the manual dexterity required to fashion a clay pot to the mental dexterity required to plot a trajectory for an experimental spacecraft.

The Importance of Skill

Certain skills, like the ability to wiggle one's ears, depend solely on inborn talents and can be exercised without any development or training. Because these are rare, however, we are not far amiss if we assume that *all* skills are either (1) obtained wholly from training or experience, or (2) innate, but realized only after having been developed by training or experience. A great violinist must have some innate musical skill, but must also have undergone a great amount of training and practice. Raquel Welch and Kareem Abdul Jabbar have certain obvious physical assets that play a role in their respective livelihoods. Neither would be as successful, however, without training and experience. Even the less-skilled forms of criminal activity (say purse-snatching) require some training and experience, and the more-skilled forms (safecracking and counterfeiting, for example) require much.

For the moment, rather than discuss how training and/or experience is actually acquired, we shall simply assume that there exists a supply of individuals who possess various skills for which there is some demand. How will the wages of skilled workers relate to those of the unskilled, and how will the wages for various types of skills relate to each other? We can derive a general principle from a relatively simple analysis.

The Market for Skills

Consider the case in which there are only two types of labor, "skilled" and "unskilled," which are regarded as totally different inputs to production. Like any two inputs, we assume some degree of substitutability between them due to alternative production processes employing different ratios of skilled to unskilled labor. Thus, the demand curves for the two types of labor can be devised in the ordinary way, and will have no unusual properties.

On the supply side, however, there is a special asymmetrical relationship between the markets for these two types of labor; namely, all skilled workers can also perform unskilled jobs, but unskilled workers cannot perform skilled jobs. Let's assume that the total supply of labor is perfectly inelastic (all workers will accept work for whatever wage they can get), and that the number of skilled workers in the total labor force is also fixed.

We shall refer to the number of unskilled and skilled workers as U and S, respectively; the supply curves for unskilled and skilled work as S_u and S_s; and the wages and demand curves for unskilled and skilled labor as W_u, W_s and D_u, D_s.

Because skilled workers can also perform unskilled jobs, they operate (potentially at least) in both markets. Their opportunity cost in skilled employment is W_u, so the supply curve in the skilled market will be horizontal at wage W_u out to S, then it will be vertical because S is the number of skilled workers. This is shown in Figure 16.1(a), where the equilibrium is given at W_s with demand curve D_s.

In the unskilled market, the supply curve will be vertical at employment U up to wage level W_s. At this wage, skilled workers will enter the unskilled market, so there will be a horizontal section of S_u out to $U + S$ (the total work force), at which point the supply curve will become vertical. This is shown in Figure 16.1(b), with equilibrium wage W_u under the given demand conditions represented by D_u.

Skill Differentials

The unskilled wage, in this simple case, puts a floor under the skilled wage because no workers will accept skilled employment at less than the unskilled rate. But the skilled wage does not have the same effect on the unskilled wage because unskilled workers cannot enter the skilled market. Thus, the skilled wage cannot be less than the unskilled wage. The usual case will be as shown in the two figures, where the difference in wages between the two markets represents a *skill differential*.

This differential will tend to diminish over time, and will even disappear if it is relatively easy to obtain the required skill (assuming demand does not change) because the differential will provide an incentive for the unskilled to become skilled. If the skill can be obtained only by long and difficult (or costly) training, the equalizing effect will be small. It will also be small or nonexistent if the skill requires some aptitude not widely distributed over the population.

In a dynamic world, skill differentials may remain wide even if the skills can be acquired by all (although only with training), and may even grow wider. This is because the *demand* for skilled workers may increase even more rapidly than the supply.

Those who already possess skills may attempt to maintain or widen existing skill differentials by increasing the difficulty of obtaining the skills they possess or by raising the "amount" of skill required. The latter arrangement is usually accompanied by a "grandfather clause" to ensure that those initially classed as skilled are not removed from the group. Such

Figure 16.1

How wage differentials arise when skilled workers can also perform unskilled jobs, but unskilled workers cannot perform skilled jobs. The skilled wage will generally exceed that of the unskilled.

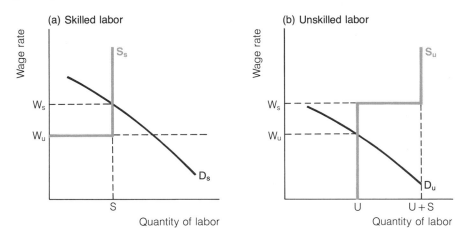

(a) Skilled labor

(b) Unskilled labor

action requires the skilled workers to act as a group, say, through a labor union or professional association, and to force their requirements on employers either by strike threats or legal sanctions. A strong union or professional association can even create a "pseudo-skill differential" by making membership both difficult to obtain and a requirement for getting employment in a certain industry or profession.

The Variety of Skills

In reality, labor services are not simply divisible into two groups, unskilled and skilled, but comprise an enormous number of different skill levels and types.

Skills can sometimes be differentiated by ordering them so each successive skill is "higher" than the preceding one in the straightforward sense that a person with the higher skill can do the work of the person with the lower, but not vice versa. In an office, for example, a pool stenographer could also do copy typing, and a private secretary could also act as a pool stenographer. In such a skill hierarchy, the higher skills will have the same kind of relation to the lower that "skilled" had to "unskilled" in our simple market analysis, and the wage level will be expected to increase as we move up the hierarchy.

But different skills need not bear a hierarchical relationship. Economics professors and aircraft mechanics are in two different skill groups (sometimes called *noncompeting groups*), with neither able to do the work of the

Figure 16.2
Especially negative aspects of unskilled work or positive aspects of skilled work may result in a *wage premium* (P) that skilled workers would require in addition to the available skilled wage to accept unskilled work. As shown in the diagram, such a premium may lead to a lower wage for skilled jobs than for unskilled jobs.

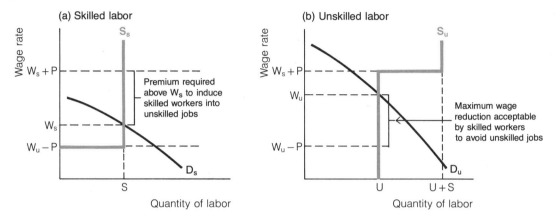

other. We generally expect both types of workers to receive a differential with respect to unskilled occupations, but the wages of the professor and those of the mechanic may bear any relationship. In a market economy, each wage will be determined in its own separate market. Hence, the mechanic may earn either more or less than the professor, depending on the respective market conditions for each.

Other Wage Differentials

Thus, skill differentials are not the only cause of wage and salary differentials. Occupations with exactly the same skill requirements may exhibit wage differentials because of special features inherent in them. One occupation may be so dirty, dangerous, or smelly that no one will choose to work in it for the same pay available in an alternative occupation. The supply of labor will consequently be zero in this occupation at wages equal to those in other occupations requiring comparable skills, unless there is excess supply in the overall labor market because of, say, a legal minimum wage. We might thus expect such unpleasant occupations to carry a positive wage differential.

Likewise, it's possible to contemplate a *negative* differential when an occupation has features other than the pay that are generally considered attractive. Indeed, certain less-skilled white-collar occupations are observed to carry a negative differential in relation to comparable blue-collar occupations for this very reason. This is illustrated in Figure 16.2(a) and (b).

Recap Labor has many characteristics, of which simple muscle power is only one. The characteristics of a particular type of labor, other than pure muscle power, are collectively known as skill. In a simple analysis, it can be assumed that skilled workers can also sell unskilled (muscle-power) labor. There will normally be no supply of skilled labor at less than the unskilled wage, which acts as a floor under the skilled wage. The skilled wage will thus generally be higher than the unskilled wage, the difference constituting a skill differential. Wage differentials may also develop because of the relative pleasantness (or unpleasantness) of job conditions.

Capsule Supplement 16.1   **Personal Rents**

The extreme case of skill differential occurs when only one person possesses a particular skill or talent. There may be only one surgeon who can perform a particular operation, or one attorney who can successfully defend a particular client. Even better examples are entertainers and sports figures, like Barbra Streisand and Reggie Jackson, each of whom possesses the inimitable skill of simply being themselves.

Because there is only one person providing such a skill, its supply is perfectly inelastic (except to the extent that the individual is more or less willing to give up leisure) above a certain wage. This wage floor is defined by the person's next-best alternative to providing his or her particular skill, and thus represents the minimum that would be accepted to contribute this special skill. (Of course, the person might actually be willing to pay a premium to supply such a skill if he or she derives other than monetary satisfaction from doing so.) For many entertainers, the best alternative occupation may carry quite a low wage. While a movie star may earn $1 million annually, he or she might not be able to earn more than, say, $15,000 in another occupation. The difference between what such a person actually receives and the value of the best alternative ($1,000,000 less $15,000 in our example) is often called *personal rent*. The term *rent* is used because the person presumably would have been willing to provide his or her special skill for anything more than $15,000, just as land receives rent because it remains available even if it is not actually used.

Why then is the movie star paid $1 million? Because of demand conditions. A movie studio may estimate that a film starring Jack Nicholson will make at least $1 million profit after paying other expenses. If the studio could hire him for, say, $20,000, it certainly would. But *other* studios would make the same calculation and be willing to offer him something up to $1 million. Consequently, if a particular studio is to obtain his services, the high wage must be paid. The exact upper limit for such personal rent is set by the potential value of such individuals' skills to their most eager potential employers. Personal rents exist even in nonmarket economies, primarily to preserve status. Stars of the Bolshoi Theater in Moscow, for example, receive such rents in both salary and services.

The general idea of a personal rent component in wages and salaries can be expanded to all cases in which individuals are actually paid more than the minimum for which they would be willing to perform their particular jobs. One could undoubtedly find examples of business executives and college professors, not to mention garbage collectors and truck drivers, who receive personal rents in this sense despite whatever special skills they may or may not possess.

Human Capital

The economic theory of acquired skills

In a complex modern economy, most labor services involve the application of skills that are either acquired or nurtured by training and experience. Obtaining or developing a skill involves using *resources* (the time and effort expended by the student or trainee, plus the costs of support and losses of earning opportunities that accrue to the trainee, his family, his employer, and/or society as a whole). Once these resources have been incorporated into the training, however, the skills developed are available to the individual and thus to society throughout the individual's productive working life.

Training as an Investment

There is an analogy between skill development, in which resources are "invested" in training and from which output (in the form of skilled services) accrues over many years, and investment in physical capital, in which there is also a large initial input of resources and from which output is forthcoming over a long period. This analogy has led to the common use of the term *human capital* in reference to the skills incorporated in people through training, education, and experience. This term can be extended to cover any resources (such as health services) that are "invested" directly in people. In our discussion, we shall concentrate on training and education.

The analogy between physical and human capital extends to the way in which human capital can be analyzed in a market economy. We can estimate both the *cost* of the initial investment by calculating the training costs (including forgone earnings during the training period), and the *return* on this investment by calculating the wage differential that can be ascribed to the training, adjusted for the length of time over which the differential will be received.

Nontransferability

There is, however, one crucial difference between human capital and physical capital—at least in a nonslave society:

Human capital necessarily belongs to the person in whom it is embodied. That person, therefore, can sell the services of accumulated skill, but not the "stock" of skill itself. Alternatively, the owner of physical capital not only can sell its services, but can transfer ownership of the capital stock itself.

Refugees from Hitler's Germany, for example, while commonly stripped of their property before they were allowed to leave, could not be deprived of the human capital embodied in them. Germany's resultant loss of important economic resources in the form of the human capital was enormous, and the gain to other countries (including the United States) was considerable. Rather less dramatic, but still of economic importance, is that on-the-job training and experience given to workers at a firm's expense represent an investment over which the firm has no ultimate control—although it may contractually arrange to "employ" the developed skill for a specified period of time.

Important consequences for the distribution of income follow from the impossibility of directly transferring human capital from one person to another. The most obvious is that there is a limit to the amount of human capital that can be embodied in a single person. There also is a limit (time) on the individual's ability to supply services. Although one individual may accumulate property without physical limit and thus obtain a large share of society's total property income, such concentration is not possible with human capital or the income derived from it.

Aside from certain innate abilities that are genetically transferable, human capital, unlike physical capital, cannot be *directly* inherited. Nevertheless, there can be considerable indirect inheritance. Parents with high education levels or particular skills can pass on at least part of them by providing specific or background training to their children. Moreover, such parents are generally more able to pay any costs involved in their children's training.

Policy Implications

The most important property of human capital investment from the viewpoint of distributional policy is that the returns accrue to the individual, regardless of who pays for the investment. This suggests a means for influencing long-term income distribution. While a policy of giving valuable physical property to individuals would surely be a political impossibility in a country like the United States, a policy of giving valuable human capital (through free education and training) is not only politically feasible, but an accepted tradition.

However the access to investment in human capital is distributed among individuals, and whatever the relationship is between the returns to one's particular skills and the costs of acquiring them, human capital is a *social resource* of great importance. One famous study of the factors influencing growth in the United States (E. F. Denison, *The Source of Economic Growth in the United States,* Committee for Economic Development, 1962) concluded that increases in education levels accounted for almost 30 percent of the growth in output per person from 1909 to 1929, and more than 40 percent from 1929 to 1957. These results suggest that the increase in human capital was as important as the increase in physical capital during the period 1909–29, and much more important during the period 1929–57.

Recap Most skills are acquired by training. Training involves the use of resources—the time of both the instructor and the trainee at a minimum—but the acquired skill can be used over a long period. Because of the analogy to investment in physical capital, the skills acquired through training are referred to as human capital. Unlike physical capital, human capital cannot be separated from the individuals in whom it is embodied. People can sell their services, but not their "stock" of skill. This has profound consequences for income distribution. Human capital is a social resource of the highest importance.

Capsule Supplement 16.2   **Education and Earnings**

While it's no surprise that a higher level of education is generally associated with higher earnings, the *extent* of this association came as something of a surprise to investigators in the 1950s and 1960s, who first analyzed the relationships in depth. The general pattern for the United States is shown in the table. In the table, mean family incomes are related to level of education attained by the primary breadwinner. The data are for 1976.

If we calculate the difference between the *lifetime earnings* of high-school graduates and those completing four or more years of college, a calculation that considers the shorter number of working years of the college graduate, the difference is almost $300,000—a high return indeed for investment in a college

Highest schooling level of household head	Mean family income
Incomplete elementary	$ 8,169
Complete elementary	$10,267
Incomplete high school	$11,710
Complete high school	$14,938
Incomplete college	$16,647
Complete college or more	$23,373

education. Moreover, the available evidence suggests that the differential in favor of college education has been increasing, as has the proportion of college graduates in the total population.

But we must be careful in interpreting the causal relationships involved in the link between education and earnings. The higher earnings may be a consequence of more education as such, abilities that are reflected in the attainment of higher education, socioeconomic backgrounds leading to higher educational levels, or simply the use of diplomas reflecting high education levels as entrance tickets to reduce supply in the best-paid occupations.

However, increased earnings do not represent the *full* differential represented by more education. A 1971 report by the Carnegie Commission on Higher Education showed that 89 percent of those with a college degree rated their jobs as ''enjoyable,'' compared with only 70 percent of those who had not attained a high-school diploma. Perhaps even more significant were marriage ratings; 60 percent of college graduates rated their marriages ''very happy,'' compared with only 38 percent of those who had not finished high school.

The Labor-Leisure Choice

How the amount of leisure time is influenced by the wage rate

Labor services, whether those of Washington lawyers or Oregon sawyers, can be acquired from individuals only insofar as they are willing to relinquish their *time*. Time is not given up merely in a passive sense, of course, because work of any kind requires some physical or mental *effort*, even if only the patience required to watch a console full of dials to ensure that a machine does not malfunction. We shall, however, assume that the relationship between time and effort is built into the occupation, and concentrate on the time element alone.

To the extent that people are free to choose the amount of time they work, they make a *labor-leisure choice*, where leisure is defined simply as the time individuals do not work and during which they are free to do as they wish.

The Real Choice Is Leisure versus Goods

As pointed out in Chapter 6, this choice is not really one between labor and leisure. If this were the case, almost everyone would choose to maximize leisure. Rather, it is a choice between leisure and the goods that can be bought in the market with the income earned from labor.

Analysis of this choice is basically the same as the analysis of any consumer choice in a market economy. The consumer has a fixed ''budget''— the number of hours of potentially available time to be allocated between work and leisure. For the sake of simplicity, let's assume that twelve hours are available daily, the remainder of the twenty-four being required for essential activities, such as eating and sleeping.

Consumers have a choice between "selling" any part of their time as labor or retaining it for personal leisure. We shall assume that the proceeds from selling labor time are used to buy a generalized good we shall call "consumption." The "price" on which the choice is based is the number of units of consumption that can be purchased by selling one hour of labor time. This is equal to the product of:

1. *the number of units of consumption that can be purchased with one dollar.* This is equivalent to the reciprocal of the price of consumption—if this price were to increase by 10 percent, then consumption per dollar would fall by 10 percent, and
2. *the number of dollars that can be obtained from the sale of one hour of labor time.* This is the *wage rate,* in dollars per hour, for the relevant type of work.

The product of these two items is often referred to as the *real wage* because it reflects the quantity of consumption that can be purchased with the proceeds from one hour of labor, regardless of the price of consumption.

The Analysis of Choice

Let's suppose that the real wage is two consumption units per hour. We can then draw a budget line, like *AB* in Figure 16.3, which shows that the individual can have twenty-four units of consumption and no leisure by working all twelve hours (point *B*), no consumption and twelve hours of leisure by not working at all (point *A*), and various points along *AB* by working part of the twelve hours.

Because consumption goods and leisure are both desirable, we cannot predict exactly what combination of leisure and consumption will be chosen. Rather, individuals will have their own preferences among the collections available. In Figure 16.3 we show an individual choosing point *L*—eight hours of work (giving sixteen consumption units) and four hours of leisure.

Now, suppose the wage rate rises with no change in the price of consumption, to give a new real wage of three consumption units per hour. The budget line will obviously change—to *AB'*. A new choice will be made, one possibility being that shown by *L'* in the diagram.

If the real wage rises, individuals can obtain more consumption with the previous work time, and more consumption even with slightly less work time, meaning that they can obtain both more consumption *and* more leisure. Thus, we might well expect, as shown in our example, that a higher real wage will result in more leisure being desired and thus less labor time being offered. As in ordinary demand theory, we cannot predict with cer-

Figure 16.3
Adjustment to a change in wage rates involves a choice between different combinations of consumption and leisure.

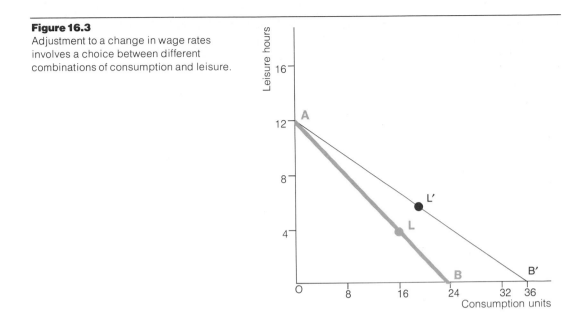

tainty that a higher wage will result in more leisure being demanded—it all depends on the resulting combination of *income* and *substitution* effects—but we would expect this to be the "normal" case at sufficiently high wage levels.

At very low wage levels, it is likely that the need for more consumption goods (such as food) will dominate other considerations, so individuals will work the maximum possible and view small increases in the wage rate purely as a means of increasing their level of consumption.

Recap Providing labor services, whether skilled or unskilled, takes up time for which workers have alternative uses—leisure. The effect of a change in the wage rate on the number of work hours offered can be analyzed in the same way as the consumer's choice of goods subject to a budget constraint. Whereas a "wrong-sloping" supply curve for a good would be regarded as very unusual, a "wrong-sloping" supply curve for labor (less supplied at a higher wage) may actually be expected above sufficiently high wage levels.

The Supply of Labor

The factors that influence the supply of labor

We normally measure labor input in terms of *man-hours*. This reflects the fact that the quantity of labor available at a given wage (assuming, for the moment, that all labor is the same) depends on the number of people willing to work at that wage (the size of the *labor force*) and the number of hours they are willing to work. Having already discussed the factors that influence the number of hours of work, we shall now concentrate on the determination of the size of the work force.

The Labor Force

The size of the labor force ultimately depends on the overall population. But the ratio of the labor force to the total population can and does change. In 1890, the labor force in the United States represented 35 percent of the population, a proportion that rose to 46 percent in 1977. The ratio of the labor force to the total population reflects several, quite different influences. One of these is the *age composition* of the population. Because the very young and the very old generally do not work, the labor force is influenced by the proportion of these age groups in the population. The proportion of those under ten in the population fell from 24 percent in 1890 to 19 percent in 1977, and the proportion of those over sixty-five rose from 4 percent to 11 percent.

The Labor Force Participation Rate

We normally concentrate on that part of the population old enough to work and not yet at the standard retirement age—the segment from 16 to 65 in the United States. The fraction of this population group that belongs to the labor force is called the *labor force participation rate*. This rate, which provides an index of the overall supply of labor, has exhibited an upward trend over the last twenty-five years (and is expected to continue rising in the immediate future) after having shown little overall movement during the previous fifty years.

   The participation rate is influenced by a wide variety of social and institutional factors, such as the age at which compulsory schooling ends and the social acceptability of careers for married women. Because there have been long-time socioeconomic pressures on men to work, the participation rate for men in the prime working years has remained close to 95 percent for the last eighty-five years. For married women, however, there has been a great increase in the participation rate over the same period—rising from 5 percent in 1890 to 47 percent in 1977. Somewhat less dramatic, but still significant, was the rise in the participation rate for single women, from 37 to 50 percent over the same period.

   The change in the participation rate for women generally, and married women in particular, has been influenced by a wide variety of socioeconomic factors. One of these has been the changing technology of household consumption. The household, viewed as a "firm" producing outputs for its members, has moved to less labor-intensive production methods, increasing the time married women can distribute between selling their services in the labor market and personal leisure. Another has been the rise in wage rates of women toward equality with those of men.

The Supply of Specialized Labor

So far we've discussed the supply of labor as if it were of only one kind. As we saw in previous sections, however, there are many different types of labor associated with various types and degrees of skill. The supply of a *particular kind* of labor is determined within the context of the overall labor supply by the interplay of incentives and requirements relating to it specifically.

Most of the factors that influence the overall supply of labor are of a long-term nature. Participation rates change, but only gradually over time. Consequently, we are usually justified in assuming that the overall labor supply curve is almost vertical, year-to-year changes in supply being attributed primarily to long-run influences.

In small subdivisions of the market, however, the supply curve for labor may be more elastic. A local labor market may experience a fairly rapid change in the amount of labor supplied as a result of migration or access to commuting facilities, the extent of the change being heavily influenced by the wage rate. Similarly, as some occupations differ little in skill from certain others, inter-occupational movement may be sensitive to wage differentials in the absence of labor unions or other barriers to entry.

Recap The number of persons available for work (the labor force) is determined by the total population and the proportion of those in the population who wish to work (the participation rate). Both of these are subject to complex social and institutional influences, as well as economic ones. In the short run, the overall supply of labor is relatively fixed.

Capsule Supplement 16.3   **Discrimination and Wages**

Does racial discrimination necessarily lead to lower incomes for those discriminated against? The 1976 data presented in the table certainly tend to confirm this.

Racial discrimination has a variety of meanings. It can mean simply that whites, for example, will not associate with blacks. Unless there are additional influences at work, however, such discrimination does not necessarily lead to lower incomes for those discriminated against. A group of whites who refuse to work on a job if blacks are also employed might themselves actually receive lower wages than average because the employer could use the threat of hiring blacks as a bargaining weapon to keep white wages low. Moreover, segregation

| Highest schooling level | Mean family income | |
of household head	White	Black
Incomplete elementary	$ 8,455	$ 7,112
Complete elementary	10,470	8,302
Incomplete high school	12,210	8,960
Complete high school	15,340	10,880
Incomplete college	16,997	12,816
Complete college or more	23,652	19,021

would presumably lead to all-black and all-white enterprises, in which case there would be no reason, at least in principle, for wages to be lower in all-black firms.

Thus it is not discrimination in the form of segregation that matters, but rather the "additional influences" mentioned. These influences derive from the one simple and basic fact—that whites and men constitute "in-groups." Dominating in all but a few occupations, whites and men discriminate from positions of relatively greater power. Many men will work with women, for example, but only if the women occupy positions at a lower level in the hierarchy. Thus, we find a systematic blocking of the entry of blacks and women into skilled trades that have high pay rates and, of even greater importance, discrimination against blacks and women in matters of promotion, overtime, and job security. A detailed breakdown of pay by job categories may well show the rates to be the same for all; but with the slightest degree of aggregation, the incomes of men and whites loom larger simply because a higher proportion of them are in the better-paid categories.

Labor Unions

The effects of unions on labor markets

A labor union is designed to exert a monopoly influence on behalf of the labor supplied by a specific occupational group or to a specific industry. Unlike a business monopoly, however, its objectives cannot be measured simply in terms of a single variable, like profits. A union's objectives are normally stated in terms of broadly defined benefits to its members. However, it is possible for a union (like a large corporation) to operate primarily in the interests of its management, subject to providing enough benefits to keep its members satisfied.

In some cases, a labor union may actually have a formal monopoly over the supply of labor through an agreement that only its members may work in some given firm or industry. This arrangement, common outside the United States, constitutes a *closed shop*. In the United States, however, the

Figure 16.4

In a competitive industry, labor unions can increase wages above the equilibrium level only at the expense of increased unemployment.

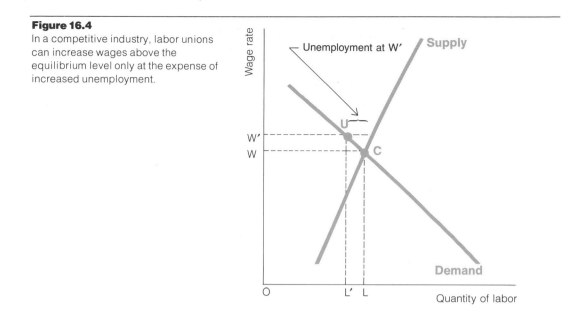

typical union controls only part of the labor supply, but so large a part that its withdrawal would bring the firm or industry to a virtual standstill. Direct control may be supplemented by moral coercion (picket lines, or threats of social ostracism) or even physical coercion (rarely used today) that effectively gives the union complete control over the labor supply in the short run, and thus during the course of a potential strike.

Let's first consider the effect of a labor union in a *competitive industry*. Given the availability of other productive inputs, like capital, and the demand conditions for the product, there is a determinate demand curve for labor in the industry, as shown in Figure 16.4. In the absence of a union, there is also a determinate supply curve for labor in the industry. Hence a competitive equilibrium will occur at point C with wage (W) and quantity of labor (L).

Now, suppose the workers in the industry form a trade union, and seek to raise the wage to W'. The point on the demand curve corresponding to this wage is U, indicating the quantity of labor at L'. Thus, the attainment of wage W' will mean that employment in the industry will decline by the distance $L'L$. Because it is a *competitive* industry, any attempt to force employers to both pay wage W' and employ L workers will drive the firms into other industries. This is the basic trade-union dilemma—wages can always be driven up, but typically at the expense of employment. The union will naturally try to ensure that this loss of employment falls on nonmembers.

The more inelastic the demand curve for labor is, the smaller is the effect on employment that results from a wage increase. Early trade unions, which were developed within the context of competitive industry, were most successful in representing individuals in occupations requiring specialized skills whose wages were a very small component of costs but whose services were essential to the operation of the industry.

Imperfect Competition

Labor unions have considerably greater scope for increasing the returns to their members above the nonunionized wage level when they operate in imperfectly competitive industries where monopoly profits can be dug into. Indeed, a large firm and a strong union might be considered natural partners.

A monopolist's demand curve, for simplicity assumed to be a straight line, is shown in Figure 16.5 together with its associated marginal revenue curve (MR). Suppose, again to simplify the arithmetic, that the average product of labor is one ton per man-hour and constant so the marginal product of labor is also constant and equal to one ton per man-hour. The quantity of labor used (in man-hours) is thus numerically equivalent to the level of output (in tons), and both can be shown on the horizontal axis of Figure 16.5. Because labor is the only input, the marginal cost of producing an extra ton is the cost of the additional labor, and because the marginal product of labor is one ton per man-hour, the marginal cost is equal to the hourly wage. Thus, the vertical axis of Figure 16.5 can measure both prices (dollar per ton) and wage rates (dollar per man-hour).

Suppose the total supply of the kind of labor the monopolist requires (which is not in demand elsewhere) is L man-hours, shown in the diagram. What will the wage rate be without a union? Due to the arithmetic coincidences for our example, L man-hours will produce exactly L tons, and the marginal revenue associated with L tons is the vertical height to the point A in the figure. If this amount of labor is to be the most profitable for the firm to employ, the marginal cost must equal the marginal revenue at A. Because the marginal cost is simply the wage rate per man-hour, the nonunion wage rate would be W, and equal to the marginal revenue associated with an output of L tons.

Bargaining

Because the wage level would be W even without a union, this represents the minimum wage that can be achieved. But suppose the union wants a higher wage, say that represented by W' in the diagram. If it simply wanted to attain that level of wages and nothing else, it could restrict its membership so as to offer only L' man-hours, corresponding to the point D on the firm's marginal revenue curve. To achieve this wage *and employment of all its members,* however, it must resort to *bargaining*.

Figure 16.5

In an imperfectly competitive industry, the labor union can divert part of the monopoly profit to its members and thus increase wages without reducing employment.

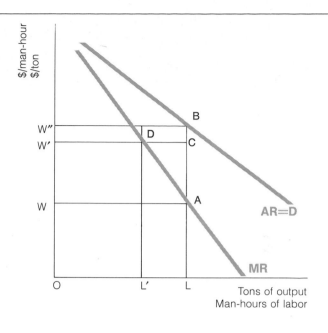

The typical bargaining procedure would be for the union to demand that the monopolist pay wage W' and employ L man-hours of labor, lest the union withdraw all labor from production. The union, in effect, offers a *point supply*, the point C in the diagram, rather than a perfectly elastic supply curve at wage W'. Such a bargaining move is called an *all-or-nothing offer*.

Will the monopolist accept the union's demand? By doing so, it certainly will not maximize profits, because marginal cost will exceed marginal revenue. The firm would obviously prefer to pay wage W for employment L, or offer employment L' for wage W'. Nevertheless, it would still make some profit (BC per unit) if it were to accept the union demand. This would certainly be preferable to closing down and making no profit at all.

The outcome of such bargaining, however, will depend on additional factors. For example, the firm might choose to close down temporarily (initiating a *lockout* or accepting a *strike*) in the belief that ceasing all wage payments would eventually cause the union to reduce its demands.

The highest wage the union could obtain and still have all its members employed, however strong its bargaining power, would be W'' in the diagram. At this wage rate, the total wages paid would equal the total revenue from selling the product as long as the firm is required to use L man-hours. At any higher wage, the firm's revenue would be insufficient to pay the wage bill, and it would be forced to reduce employment or eventually go bankrupt.

In summary, then, the union could potentially obtain a wage anywhere between W and W'' (the exact level depending on its bargaining strength relative to that of the firm), while keeping all its members employed.

Evidence in the United States bears out the general presumption that labor-union activity is most prevalent in those industries exhibiting a high degree of imperfect competition. Union membership accounts for 30 percent of all workers in nonagricultural occupations, but it is noticeably higher than this average in monopolistic and oligopolistic industries, such as telecommunications (68 percent) and automobiles (83 percent). It is only slightly higher in the more competitive clothing and textile industry (50 percent), and noticeably lower in industries with extremely weak forms of imperfect competition, such as retail trade (3 percent).

The Impact of Unions

The overall impact of unions on the distribution of income between labor and other factors is difficult to assess. There is even some doubt that unions have had much impact on wage levels as a whole because wage rates, over the years, have risen as fast in many occupations having no perceptible union influence as in those with strong union influence. The broad evidence to date is regarded as inconclusive in either direction.

Unions have probably had more effect on nonwage conditions of employment (such as hiring, firing, and promotion) and on the division of the total payment to labor between direct wage payments and indirect payments (such as pensions) than on average wage rates as such. Moreover, they have succeeded in having workers share in the monopoly profits of imperfectly competitive industries, and have had a great influence in determining entry into certain skilled and pseudo-skilled occupations.

As to the overall distribution of labor income among individuals, the net effect of labor unions may well have been to exaggerate inequalities. By restricting entry into skilled occupations, unions raise skill differentials indirectly by keeping the pool of unskilled workers larger than it would be ordinarily, the effect being to hold the unskilled wage down. The extent of this effect, however, is uncertain.

A labor union, even when it cannot change the wage level much from what would be achieved under market conditions, can nonetheless prevent the *simple exploitation* of individuals or small groups. That is, it can prevent individuals from being paid *less* than the market wage through ignorance of market conditions or through employer coercion. The union can also be effective in a *monopsony* situation—where a single firm is the only employer of labor in an area—by demanding for its members a wage that would otherwise prevail under competitive conditions.

Recap Labor unions act as monopolies or near monopolies in supplying labor to particular occupations or industries. In a perfectly competitive industry, a union may determine the minimum wage, but it cannot determine both the wage and the level of employment. Higher wages in such an industry will normally be achieved only at the expense of lower employment. In an imperfectly competitive industry where there are monopoly profits, a union may be able to bargain for both a specified wage and a given level of employment. Economic factors set limits within which a bargaining agreement will be reached, but cannot guarantee the exact outcome of a bargaining situation. The overall effect of unions on wages is unclear. There is conflicting evidence about whether overall wage rates would have followed the same historical course in the United States in their absence. Unions, however, have had a positive influence on such nonwage factors as working conditions and fringe benefits.

The General Wage Level

How the overall level of wages in the economy is constrained by society's productivity

Up to this point, we have been concerned primarily with wage differentials that accrue to different types of labor. Given the initial wealth distribution, such differentials constitute the most important single factor in determining income distribution. We shall now turn to the question of general wage levels over the economy as a whole. In so doing, we shall act as if there were a single homogeneous type of labor.

In discussing changes in the general wage level, we must make adjustments for the price level. In discussing wage differentials, we can legitimately compare a current hourly wage of $5 in one occupation with a current wage of $4 in another because prices are fixed at a given point in time. However, we cannot compare a general wage rate of $5 in one year with a rate of $4 in some previous year without allowing for the change in the price level between those two years.

Real Wages

When taking a broad view of wages, we must look at *real wages,* that is, money wages after adjusting for changes in the cost of living. Constant real wages imply an unchanging amount of goods and services purchased from one year to the next, while a 5 percent increase in real wages implies that 5 percent more of everything purchased in the first year can be purchased in the second.

Although money wages accruing to a particular occupation theoretically have no upper limit, average real wages over the economy as a whole have a very clear upper limit. Specifically, because total real wages cannot exceed the total goods and services produced, average real wages cannot exceed the average output per worker over the economy. We measure this average output, like wages, in *real* terms, so a 5 percent increase in real output means a 5 percent increase in the actual quantities of goods and services produced.

In a growing economy, like that of the United States, increases in average real wages are almost entirely due to increasing average output. The *proportion* of total output going to labor (in the broad sense) has changed over time, but comparatively little. Indeed, relative to the large long-run changes predicted by the nineteenth-century economists (notably Karl Marx), the proportion of total output going to labor over time has remained relatively constant.

Wages and Productivity

In the period from 1950 to 1976, real *output* per employee man-hour over the economy as a whole rose by 95 percent. Over the same period, the real wage (total compensation per man-hour, including such things as pension contributions) rose by 100 percent. Hence, 95 percent of the increased real wage was due to increased output per man-hour (*productivity*), with only 5 percent due to an actual change in the share of output going to labor.

Although real wages *in a given industry or occupation* may increase faster than the average, and even faster than real output, this cannot occur over the economy as a whole. The money wage of musicians, for example, might rise by 20 percent in one year. While this would increase the cost of activities using musicians, and hence the prices of such events as Broadway musicals and symphony concerts, the repercussions over the economy as a whole would be small. Musicians would find little change in the overall cost of living, and thus would experience a *real wage* increase of 20 percent.

But suppose that *all* workers demanded, and received, a 20 percent money wage increase during a year in which productivity did not change. There would be two effects:

1. Because labor represents a high proportion of costs everywhere, costs would rise in all industries.
2. Because labor income is a large proportion of total income and because workers would receive 20 percent more money income, total incomes would increase and so would the demand for most goods.

The combination of increased production costs and increased demand would put severe upward pressure on prices, which would rise. Eventually, most, if not all, of the increase in the money wage would be balanced by increased prices resulting from *inflation* so the *real wage* would have changed little.

Thus, the upper limit placed on real wages by the available quantities of output will be maintained through price inflation, regardless of how much the general *money wage* may rise.

Because a rate of increase in the general wage level that exceeds the rate of increase in overall productivity is likely to lead to inflation, it follows that one possible policy to *prevent* inflation would be to have the general wage level move in step with productivity increases. A measure of this kind is called a *wage-price policy*. While difficult to carry out in an economic system in which the labor market is broken into numerous segments with independent wage determination, such policy is accepted in the United States as one method available to counteract inflation. Wage-price policy is discussed fully in Chapter 26.

Recap To discuss the general level of wages, as opposed to the level of wages in a specific occupation, we must adjust for price changes and consider real wages. Total real wages cannot exceed the total level of goods and services produced in the economy, and the rate of increase in the average real wage is predominantly influenced by the growth of productivity in the economy. Although the real wage in a particular occupation might rise by 100 percent during a given year, the average real wage could not possibly rise by this much—even if all income went to wage earners. If overall money wages were to rise by 100 percent, prices would rise sharply to keep real wages at a level consistent with the economy's overall level of productivity.

Exercises

1. Hypothetical demand schedules for skilled and unskilled labor are given in the tables that follow.

Skilled Labor		Unskilled Labor	
Wage ($/week)	Number employed	Wage ($/week)	Number employed
100	12,000	100	26,000
120	11,000	120	24,000
140	10,000	140	22,000
160	9,000	160	20,000
180	8,000	180	18,000
200	7,000	200	16,000
220	6,000	220	14,000
240	5,000	240	12,000
260	4,000		

What will be the lowest weekly wage for skilled labor if the total labor force (skilled and unskilled) is 24,000 and skilled workers will work in whatever job brings the highest pay?

2. With the same data as used for question 1, find both the skilled and the unskilled wage in each of the following cases:
   a. 4,000 of the total labor force are skilled.
   b. 6,000 of the total labor force are skilled.
   c. 8,000 of the total labor force are skilled.

3. Would any of the wage rates found in question 2 be changed if skilled

workers refused to accept unskilled work under any circumstances? If so, what would be the wage rates under these circumstances?

4. A monopolist uses one special kind of labor as its only input, and the marginal and average products of labor are constant and equal at five tons per man per week. The firm's demand conditions are such that it can sell exactly 5,000 tons weekly at a price of $120 per ton, and the marginal revenue associated with this level of sales is $80 per ton. There are 1,000 workers who have the skill required by the firm, and they are organized into a union.
   a. What would be the wage if the union were totally ineffective?
   b. What is the maximum wage the union could extract by bargaining, if it were to ensure employment for all its members?

5. Take the data used in question 4 and assume that bargaining takes place annually with each year's contract depending only on the bargaining of that year. By striking, the union can obtain the basic nonunion wage plus $40 per week extra for each month the strike lasts (up to the maximum the firm can pay) as its new contract. Workers receive no pay when on strike, and the new contract lasts only for the remainder of the year after the strike ends.
   a. If the strike lasts long enough to obtain the maximum possible wage, what will be the total income of each union member over the year?
   b. See if you can discover the length of strike that gives the maximum annual income to the union members. (You can do this by working out all the numbers, or by calculus.)

For Thought and Discussion

1. If everyone had the same innate abilities, perfect foresight, complete information, and free access to training for any occupation, would you expect labor incomes to be equalized? What about wage rates for different occupations?

2. Would it be in the interest of trade unions to advocate rigorous antitrust policies designed to achieve universal perfect competition?

3. Should the prediction of long-run population changes be a job for economists?

4. If it is known for certain that average productivity is rising at no more than 3 percent per annum for the economy as a whole, should it be illegal for *any* wage rate to rise by more than 3 percent annually?

Chapter 17
Nonlabor Income

Terms and Concepts

Nonlabor income
Opportunity cost
Rent
Interest
Residual profit
Capital gains
Locational property of land
Differential rent
Return to capital
Quasi-rent
Shadow price of capital
Dynamic profits
Monopoly profits
Dynamic entrepreneurship

Sources of Nonlabor Income

The classification of nonlabor incomes

Nonlabor income is income derived from sources other than the sale of personal services, that is, income typically classified by official publications as "income other than earnings." A considerable proportion of this income in most Western economies consists of government transfer payments. Because these are not determined in conventional factor markets, however, we shall ignore them in this chapter; they will be discussed as part of overall distributional policy. We shall confine our present discussion to nontransfer, nonlabor income—specifically income derived from the *sale of property services* and *residual profits*.

Mixed Incomes

Income derived from the sale of personal services is not confined to wages and salaries. Indeed, the sale of such services is often combined with the sale of other factor services. Taxi drivers who own as well as drive their cabs sell a combination of their own labor as drivers along with the services of their property. Combinations of this kind are the rule in small-scale farming, the professions, and small businesses, but the *personal service* component in each should be regarded as labor income.

In principle, the two components of a combination income can be separated by using the *opportunity cost* concept. The labor income of a taxi driver-owner, for example, could be computed as the earnings he would receive for the same work as an employee. For many small businesses we find that the labor component, computed this way, actually *exceeds* total income—a delicatessen proprietor may work twelve or more hours per day for less income than she could earn as an employee, accepting the loss from her "property component" presumably because working for herself brings "psychic" benefits over and above money income. Henceforth in our discussion, we shall assume that we can separate labor from nonlabor income.

The Primary Sources of Nonlabor Income

From the viewpoint of the individual, nonlabor income may be derived from any of the following sources:

1. The services of land or other natural resources.
2. The services of physical capital, like buildings and machinery.
3. Financial assets, like stocks, bonds, or savings bank balances.
4. The residual profits accruing from business activity.

As we shall see in the next section, income from financial assets represents the transfer of income ultimately derived from the services of physical capital through a variety of intermediaries to those who have lent funds for the purchase of that capital, or from residual profits earned by corporations for their stockholders.

For the economy as a whole, we do not consider income from financial assets, but concentrate on the real source of this income—the services of physical capital or land, or residual profits.

Nonfinancial Sources of Nonlabor Income

Thus, we shall concentrate on three basic types of nonlabor income:

1. The return to land, or *rent*.
2. The return to physical capital, or *interest*—so called because this income generally takes the form of interest transferred to those who have lent funds to buy the capital.
3. *Residual profits*.

Just as there are frequent problems in separating labor and nonlabor income, there are also problems—usually much greater—in separating the various types of nonlabor income. "Rent," in the commonly accepted sense, usually refers to a mixture of pure rent from land (the economist's "rent") and a return from the services of physical capital in the form of buildings. It may even include receipts from other economic activities, such as the provision of heat and janitorial services. Corporate "profit," in the usual sense, normally refers to a mixture of the return to the physical capital owned by the corporation and the residual profit from business operations, only the profit from business operations being truly a "profit" to the economist.

Recap The sale of property services is often mixed with the sale of labor services, as in the case of a taxi owner-driver. We assume that all labor income is removed before we examine the nonlabor component of income. Nonlabor income is derived from the sale of the services of natural resources such as land (rent), the sale of the services of physical or financial capital (interest), and the residual profits of firms. In common usage, these terms represent mixtures. "Rent," for example, usually refers to a combination of the return from land, the return from physical capital (buildings), and sometimes the sale of janitorial and other services.

The Channeling of Property Income	**Why it is often difficult to establish the ultimate source of nonlabor income**

The simple analysis of property income is straightforward enough. An individual owns a certain amount of property and sells its services at the market price. The income is the product of the quantity of services sold (which is directly related to the quantity of property owned) times the price per unit of services. In a complex modern economy, however, the relationship between the sale of property services and the eventual receipt of income generated by these services is indirect and often quite circuitous. Let's look at an example.

The Division of Property Income

Consider a machine that costs $10,000, never wears out, gives 2,000 hours of service per year, and yields a market return of $.50 per hour. An individual who fully owns such a machine and sells its services will obtain a property income of $1,000 per year.

But suppose the machine is owned in a legal sense but was purchased with a savings bank loan of $10,000 at 6 percent interest. The bank, in turn, has simply lent the owner funds that were lent to it by depositors for 5 percent interest. While the sale of machine-hours still brings in $1,000, the owner must pay $600 interest to the bank. The bank, in turn, must pay $500 interest to depositors. Thus, receipts from the same resource services as before now appear as $400 income to the owner, $100 to the banker, and $500 to depositors, assuming no costs in the banking operation.

If we like, we can consider the "real" ownership of the machine to be held by the individual who physically possesses it, the banker, and the bank depositors in the ratio of 40 percent, 10 percent, and 50 percent. Or we can simply regard the physical possessor as a firm selling an output of $1,000 and buying financial "resources" for $600; and the bank as another firm selling financial resources worth $600 and buying inputs for $500. We can even think of the depositors as the "real" owners of the machine, paying the physical possessor and the bank to act as *intermediaries* in a complex transaction to turn their money savings into real resources.

Now, let's revert back to the case in which the owner did not need to borrow to buy the machine. Obviously, this individual must have had $10,000 to start with. This money could have been lent to the bank at 5 percent interest, rather than used to buy the machine. Thus, there is an *opportunity cost* of $500. We may consider the income from the sale of machine services as made up of $500 in *imputed interest*, with the remainder of the $1,000 as income from entrepreneurial services.

However the income from the machine is distributed, the total is always the same. Subject to some slight modification, we can therefore state that:

All property income is ultimately derived from the sale of real resource services. The existence of financial intermediaries (like banks) may affect the distribution of the property income among its ultimate recipients, but not its total amount.

Modification is necessary if the operations of financial intermediaries themselves require real resources (as they do). In this event, the total return would be somewhat less, reflecting the fact that resources were expended in channeling funds from "investors" to those who actually acquired the capital. The willingness of other parties to pay for these resources is itself an index of their usefulness. While depositors could theoretically lend directly to machine buyers, they generally know neither how to contact them nor the potential risk of default, hence the need for banks and other financial intermediaries. In the United States, the overall contribution of financial intermediaries to national product (measured in terms of the real resources employed in the financial sector) is about 3 percent of GNP.

Corporations

The distribution of income derived from the sale of property services is even more circuitous when we consider the effect of corporations. A corporation is itself a kind of financial intermediary in the sense that it owns resources, and stockholders "own" it.

Let's suppose that our machine is owned by a corporation, which, in order to acquire it, sold 10,000 shares for $1 each. The corporation then receives an income of $1,000 annually. If it distributes all this income as dividends ($.10 per share), the situation is quite simple; it is as if all stockholders owned a share of the machine proportional to their stockholdings. But the corporation may distribute less than its income—say $.05 per share—keeping $500. With this $500 it buys a small machine, but one that can earn the same ratio of income to capital value (10 percent) as the big machine. The stockholders, although receiving only $500 income in dividends, now own machines that generate $1,050 in income instead of $1,000. This increase in the value of their assets is a *capital gain*. Corporate stockholders thus receive returns both in the form of actual dividends and in the form of capital gains. The gains are not realized, however, until the stock is sold.

Residual Profits

After paying for all labor and nonlabor resource services, a firm may be left with a *surplus* or *residual profit*. As we've seen, in the long run a perfectly competitive firm under constant returns to scale will have no residual profit, but an imperfectly competitive firm, and even a competitive firm under certain conditions, will be expected to yield such a surplus.

Some economists have attempted to treat "profit" as a return to "entrepreneurship." But because of the difficulties involved in identifying and measuring the entrepreneurial component of production, this approach has not become generally accepted. The right to receive the surplus resulting from a business operation, in reality, is primarily a legal, rather than an economic, prerogative. The particular contractual arrangements of the firm generally determine who possesses a claim to the residual profit. It might be the owner or financier of the capital equipment used (the "capitalist"), the effective organizer and manager of the business who may have borrowed or rented all the capital used (the true "entrepreneur"), or even the main labor supplier (as in the case of small businesses, farms, and professional enterprises). In the case of corporations, it is the stockholders who possess the ultimate claim on profits even though the corporation may retain them for internal use.

Recap All property income is derived from the sale of real resource services. The division of this income, however, may be complex if there are financial intermediaries. While financial services can add to real economic output, their primary effect is simply to redistribute a given amount of property income.

Capsule Supplement 17.1   **How to Become a Millionaire**

Although difficult, it is possible for you to become a millionaire from the sale of personal services. All you have to do is write a best-seller, quarterback an NFL contender, or record a couple of "platinum" LPs. Lacking the personal resources of the likes of Harold Robbins, Ken Stabler, or Joni Mitchell, however, you might prefer to make your million by investing $1,000 at 6 percent interest, compounded quarterly—and waiting 116 years. If, on the other hand, you aspire to become one of America's 200 thousand millionaires in a hurry, you'll most likely have to locate some property—preferably real estate or corporate stock—whose services are about to command a much higher price than they do now, *but whose present owners do not know this.*

Suppose the property you "discover" currently provides services worth $50 annually, but they will soon bring $100. If the current average rate of return on investment is 5 percent, the present owner will probably take $1,000 for it because $50 is 5 percent of $1,000. At that price, you'll be receiving a return of 10 percent when the price for the service goes up. In effect, you'll have transferred a potential future income of $100 per year from the previous owner to yourself in the process of paying for what he believes to be the rights to only $50. Given the existing 5 percent return, the property would be valued at $2,000. However, to sell it for this amount immediately, you will have to convince a potential buyer that the income from it is really going to be $100 per year. If you are skillful, you may be able to do better and convince the buyer that the income will be, say, $150, and not the $100 you actually expect. If you can do this, you can resell the property for $3,000, tripling your original $1,000 investment in a short time.

If you are successful in these transactions, you will have transferred wealth to yourself from both the person who originally sold the property to you and from the person to whom you have sold it. Assuming your predictions were correct, the original seller will have transferred the right to the $50 increase over the old return that he would have received had he retained it or, alternatively, the additional $1,000 he could have gained from the sale had he waited. The person to whom you sold the property paid you $3,000, but she will be able to sell it for only $2,000 when the true income becomes established, so she will have also transferred $1,000 to you.

This, then, is how you can become a millionaire—by buying property from those who underestimate its future returns, then selling to those who overestimate those returns. There is, of course, a catch. You must be the one who makes the right judgment, not one of those who under- or overestimates.

In the kind of transaction described above, you will have neither contributed anything to the operation of the economy, nor hindered it in any way. You will have simply transferred wealth from others who are trying to do the same as you, but have judged incorrectly. You *could*, however, have performed a socially useful function had you been responsible for the actual increase in income from the property by, say, taking it from a less-productive use and putting it to a more-productive use. Alternatively, you could have hindered the operation of the economic system had your overselling moved resources into sectors in which they proved less productive than you had led everyone to believe.

Income from Land

The specific features of income from land

Prior to the historical evolution of capitalism, land was the chief source of nonlabor income. Furthermore, the social and political stratification of society was largely determined by the distribution of income from land. Today, however, rental income, as defined in the U.S. national accounts—which includes the return on houses as well as on land *per se*—constitutes only about 10 percent of total nonlabor income in the United States.

Supply Effects

The special feature of land, viewed simply as *space,* is its totally inelastic supply. If all land were equally adaptable to all uses, the overall market for land would have a vertical supply curve as shown in Figure 17.1.

Thus, the return for land services would have no effect on the total quantity of land available. In this sense, land is unique. If the price of capital services were to rise, the increased return to capital, appearing as higher interest rates and/or higher profits, would result in the production of more capital goods, and thus an increase in the quantity of capital services. Similarly, if wages were to rise, we would expect changes in the hours of work offered per worker, and perhaps in the size of the labor force over the long run. But regardless of whether the price of land services rises or falls, the amount of land will remain essentially unchanged.

Figure 17.1
Even though the quantity of land may be fixed, there is still a market rent at which the quantity of land demanded exactly equals the quantity available.

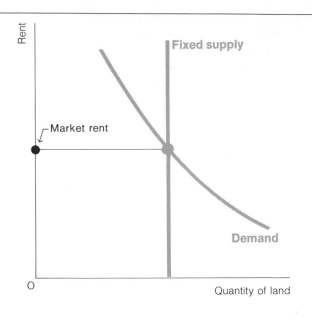

Allocation Effects

This does *not* mean that rent, regarded as a price, performs no function in a market economy. Although the level of market rent will not affect the *aggregate* quantity of land available, it will still affect the allocation of land among alternative uses and the choice among processes requiring different mixtures of land and other factors.

If rents rise relative to other factor prices, firms will shift to processes that use less land per unit of output, and thereby "substitute" other factors for land. As inner-city land rents rise, owners will provide more dwelling units per acre of land by building high-rise apartment buildings. Such structures represent a means by which dwelling space can be provided with more capital and less land per dwelling unit than, say, single-family houses.

With fixed supply, the level of rents is determined entirely by demand. As with any resource, this demand depends on the role of land in various production processes, relative demand for products requiring different amounts of land inputs, and the existence of substitutes.

If, for example, there were a shift in a country's trading relationships such that it began to export manufactured goods rather than farm products, we would expect the demand for land to fall because less land is used per dollar of manufactures than per dollar of farm products—assuming, of course, that other things in the economy were not changed. Such a reduction in the demand for land, as illustrated in Figure 17.2, would lead to a decline in rents.

Figure 17.2

With fixed supply, the level of rent depends only on demand. It rises or falls with an increase or decrease in demand.

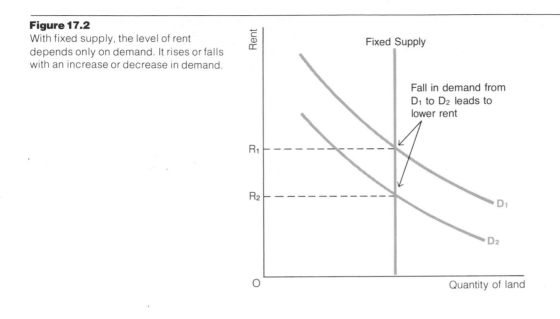

Fall in demand from D_1 to D_2 leads to lower rent

Land Has Many Characteristics

Land is not homogeneous but has several characteristics. A given unit of land is, first of all, *space*. But it is space in some particular place; that is, it has *location*. Moreover, land embodies a variety of *natural resources*— fertility, oil and minerals, forests, and water. Thus, it is primarily the spatial and locational aspects that are absolutely fixed, though even space can be expanded, as the Dutch have demonstrated in their reclamation of IJsselmeer (Zuider Zee). While certain natural resources (like oil) are subject to depletion in the long run, others (like timber) can be restored or augmented.

Just as space in the aggregate is fixed to the economy as a whole, so is space fixed in a particular location. Consider, for example, the Wall Street area of Manhattan. As the available "acreage" in this area cannot be changed, the associated return to land is determined exclusively by demand, an increase in which will simply cause rents to rise.

Differential Rent

The demand for land, either as a whole or in a particular location, depends on the value of using that land (its marginal product in value terms). This value depends, in turn, on the existence of substitutes. As far as the *locational property of land* is concerned, parcels of land in different locations are potential substitutes. At some inconvenience, a Wall Street firm could certainly move to the Bronx or, for that matter, Des Moines. The value to the firm of remaining on Wall Street compared with moving elsewhere is a measure of the maximum difference the firm will pay between rent on Wall Street and rent in an alternative location. The desirability of a particular location is thus measured by *differential rent,* the difference between the rent in the preferred location and that associated with the next-best alternative.

In an agricultural context, land may differ in fertility, even in the same general location. Because more fertile land will yield more output per acre than less fertile land, differential rents will again be expected to occur, even though fertility is a less-permanent feature of land than space or location.

Policy Implications

Rents accruing to the spatial and locational properties of land provide no supply incentives because these properties are fixed. This suggests that pure rents could be socialized or heavily taxed without affecting the operation of the economy. Certainly, at least in simple cases, the existence of land is unaffected by the way in which rental income is distributed or to whom it goes—as compared with capital, on which a heavy tax would ultimately lead to a decrease in supply.

There are two important points we should note with respect to this argument. The first is that even if land were socialized, it would still be desirable to charge users market rents. For while pure rents may have no incentive effect on supply, nonetheless they determine resource allocation among alternative uses. Because of the locational desirability of land in Manhattan, rents there are high. But these high rents lead to the efficient use of a scarce resource by encouraging (1) its intensive use (high-rise buildings), (2) its use by those for whom the location has the greatest advantage, and (3) the development of alternative locations.

The second is that "rent" in the everyday sense covers many things other than the payment for the pure space-location properties of land. Rent for office space includes payment for other services, such as heating, and for the use of capital in the form of the building erected on the land. Thus rent for office space is only partly for the use of the land on which the office building stands. The difficulty of separating the "pure" space-location elements (the only ones to which the above argument applies) from other rent elements is an important reason why simple tax schemes based on taxing pure rents have proved relatively unsuccessful.

Externalities

Among the various distributional problems that arise in the case of rents, the greatest is perhaps due to certain externalities deriving from location.

Suppose a city builds a subway line through a particular area. This alters the locational properties of land near the subway, presumably making this land more desirable. This desirability, a social benefit, will make people willing to pay higher rents for locations near the subway than they would have previously paid. In a market economy, these rents will be reflected in increased incomes to landowners along the route—either in the direct sense or through capital gains. Thus, actions taken by the city will result in landowners being subsidized by consumers. Rents in a market economy often reflect such a transfer of social benefits from those for whom they were created to those who own land.

Various schemes have been suggested to prevent (or retrieve) some of this transfer. Among these are "betterment" taxes or levies related to increases in real-estate values (and thus increases in future rents) resulting from public action.

Recap The most prominent feature of land (viewed simply as space) is that its supply to the economy as a whole is fixed. Thus rent, the return to land services, cannot have any incentive effect on the supply of land, though it does affect the allocation of land among alternative uses. This leads to some special conclusions about the taxation of rents from land. Rents can also result in social benefits from certain externalities of location being converted into private benefits.

The Return to Capital

Special features of the return to capital

As we've noted, the income received from business activity usually represents a return to capital mixed with a smattering of residual profits, rent, and (in the case of small businesses) payments for labor services.

The return to capital proper is that part of business-derived income ascribed exclusively to the use of capital services. The *pure return to capital* is equivalent to the business income that would be received if the firm had no activity other than "renting out" its equipment for use elsewhere at market prices. In other words, if we were to imagine the firm being divided into two parts—a capital-owning part and an entrepreneurial part—with the entrepreneurial part hiring capital services from the capital-owning part at market prices, the payments made for those services would constitute the pure return to capital.

The Market Price of Capital

In principle, if there are perfectly competitive factor markets, the price of capital services is determined by ordinary supply and demand considerations. As with any factor, the demand for capital is determined by the existing technology, relative demands for products using varying amounts of capital, and market conditions for other factors. The conditions that affect the supply of capital are of a special kind, however, and differ greatly between the short run and the long run.

The Short Run

At any point in time, the capital stock can be taken as fixed because increasing it takes time and reducing it—which can only be accomplished by not replacing machines as they wear out—takes even longer. Suppose there is a sudden increase in the demand for oil tankers. Because the supply of tankers is fixed in the short run, the price of tanker services will rise sharply. This price increase will induce the production of more tankers. But as these will not be immediately available, the price of tanker services will be high in the short run, and fall only after the newly produced tankers become available. These high short-term returns to capital are due to the slow rate of adjustment in the capital stock. The excess of the short-run price of capital services over their long-run price is sometimes called a *quasi-rent*—"rent" because it is derived from a fixed capital supply, like land, and "quasi" (meaning almost) because, *unlike land rent,* it will disappear as a result of long-run adjustments.

Classical Capital Theory

The determination of the return to capital in the long run is much more complicated. The classical analysis of the past went something like this:

Capital accumulation is financed by saving, the rate of interest on financial assets being ultimately determined by the rate of return on physical capital. Too high a rate of capital accumulation will increase the amount of capital available relative to other factors, and lead to a fall in the return to it. The consequent fall in interest rates will discourage saving and thus reduce the funds available for investment. In turn, these will fall, slowing the rate of capital accumulation. Conversely, too low a rate of capital accumulation will lead to higher interest rates, more saving, and thus more investment. All the while, the ratio of capital to other factors is constantly rising so the rate of return and the rate of interest are constantly falling. Eventually, the economy accumulates as much capital as it can use, and investment falls to zero.

Modern Doubts

This analysis ignores many important elements, especially technological change, that prevent the return to all factors (including capital) from falling steadily. Economists today doubt that investment is as sensitive to the rate of return as suggested in the classical analysis, and even more that the rate of saving is influenced by the rate of interest. Some economists even doubt that long-run capital accumulation and the rate of profit can be analyzed in terms of market behavior, and offer social or political explanations about why capital has tended to accumulate rapidly in some societies or in some periods, and slowly in others. In any event, these long-run theories are primarily designed to explain the transformation of economies over decades or centuries, rather than provide a basis for short- or medium-run policy decisions.

Allocative Effects

As a price, the return to capital provides the same allocative function as any other price. However, its usefulness in carrying out this allocation is severely diminished because most capital services are derived from capital that is owned outright and therefore does not pass through the market. To the extent that a firm's capital costs are fixed, the allocative function of price is blurred.

From the viewpoint of economic efficiency, it wouldn't matter if capital were privately owned (as is typical in Western economies) or publicly owned (as is typical in socialist economies) provided the allocative function of price were preserved. Thus, to ensure efficiency, a socialist country should charge each productive enterprise for the use of capital so those factories that could get along with less capital are not tempted to waste it simply because it does not appear as a charge against them. For maximum efficiency, the appropriate *shadow price of capital* charged to such factories would be the same as if the economy were *perfectly competitive*.

In spite of the common association of the terms *capitalism* and *free enterprise*, there is no reason, in principle, why entrepreneurs should actually *own* any capital, and no reason why the incomes from the sale of capital services should go to entrepreneurs or any other specific group. The economist's ''ideal'' model of the perfectly competitive economy would actually work *better* if entrepreneurs hired capital services as needed—the capital (wealth) could be owned by the government, workers, or anyone, so long as its services were freely offered on the market to all comers at the going price.

The proportion of the population that receives some of their income from returns to capital has been increasing in most non-socialist countries. Indeed, nearly one-half of U.S. income recipients obtained some direct income from nonlabor sources in 1977.

Recap The return to capital is that part of business income that can be ascribed specifically to capital services. It is the income a firm would obtain by renting its capital to someone else, rather than using it in its own business. In the short run, because the amount of capital is relatively fixed, the return to it has some of the properties of rent and is often referred to as quasi-rent. In the long run, however, a high rate of return can be expected to increase the supply of capital equipment, and a low rate of return to decrease it. Thus, in the long run, the return to capital has both the incentive and allocation effects of price.

Residual Profits

The role of residual profits in the economy

Residual profits are the only form of income not related to the *price* of some factor, the term *profits* covering a mixed bag of incomes arising from rather different aspects of economic activity. By stressing the *residual* nature of these payments, we are making it clear that we have already removed those elements that represent returns to specific factors.

Residual profits are the excess of total revenue over total cost (including the opportunity cost for owned capital and the entrepreneur's own labor). Such a residual need not exist, but when it does, it may be for more than one reason.

Perfect Competition

There are no residual profits under perfect competition in a long-run stationary equilibrium. Under these circumstances, price equals minimum average cost everywhere. Consequently, total revenue (price × quantity) is equal to total cost (average cost × quantity), and there is no residual. If, as is often useful, we regard residual profit as a return to "entrepreneurship," it's easy to see why there is no return. Entrepreneurship in this case contributes nothing. Given that we have a stationary equilibrium, technology and factor prices are constant so the optimal process already chosen remains in use. Furthermore, because prices are constant, there is no output decision to be made. Production simply continues at an established level using established methods, and no entrepreneurial art is called for.

While the situation just described is completely hypothetical and never likely to exist, it provides a base point for discussion: *Residual profits exist primarily because the economy is* not *in a stationary, perfectly competitive, long-run equilibrium.*

Specifically, residual profits arise for one of two main reasons:

1. because the economy is not in a stationary, long-run equilibrium, in which case there are *dynamic profits*.
2. because the economy is imperfectly competitive, in which case there are *monopoly profits*.

Dynamic Profits

Typically, dynamic profits arise when entrepreneurs perceive that a new technique will enable them to produce at a lower cost than other firms in the industry. By selling at the going competitive price they can thus make a profit. Eventually, their success will motivate other firms to adopt the new technique until costs are the same everywhere. Finally, competition will force the industry price down to the new minimum average cost level, and dynamic profits will cease.

The prospect of dynamic profits encourages entrepreneurs to enter industries that are below optimal size, to adopt new techniques, and to perform other functions that move the economy either toward equilibrium or toward greater efficiency. We can thus regard dynamic profits as the *return to dynamic entrepreneurship*.

Unfortunately, the price effects of dynamic entrepreneurship are often short-circuited because the resulting profits may accrue to the suppliers of capital rather than to the entrepreneur. In a large corporation, for example, there is considerable separation between the ownership of capital and the control of corporate activities. Thus, it may be difficult for corporate management, lacking direct access to capital, to properly exercise its entrepreneurial prerogatives.

When reference is made to the "profit incentive" as an important force in economic progress, *dynamic* profits are being described. These profits, it should be noted, are self-liquidating—once the economy reaches its ideal configuration, such profits automatically vanish.

Monopoly Profits

Monopoly profits are something else. As we have noted in previous chapters, their existence is an index of the economy's divergence from its optimal configuration. Unfortunately, we cannot separate "good" dynamic profits from "bad" monopoly profits in the United States and other Western economies. Therefore, it is virtually impossible to reach any conclusions about the degree of divergence from the optimum merely by looking at profit levels in various industries.

Recap Residual profit is the income that remains after returns to land, capital, entrepreneurial labor, and other resources are paid. In a long-run stationary equilibrium under perfect competition, there would presumably be no such residual. Residual profits are therefore derived either from dynamic factors or from the existence of imperfect competition. Dynamic profits arise where there is a possibility for technological innovation or an increased number of firms, and actually serve to promote rapid technological progress and the movement of entrepreneurial talent into areas where expansion is called for. Monopoly profits, on the other hand, indicate a divergence from economic efficiency.

Capsule Supplement 17.2   **Corporate Profits**

Although corporate profits in the United States are simply residual profits mixed with a return to capital, they possess two special features that dictate a brief discussion. These features are, first, that they are taxed, and, second, that a considerable proportion of corporate profits is typically reinvested without ever being paid out to stockholders.

Let's first consider the tax on corporate profits. Revenues from this tax, whose rate reaches 48 percent, represent nearly one-fourth of the total tax receipts of the federal government. But is this really a tax on profits, or a form of sales tax on consumers? This question has been debated repeatedly but has never been resolved.

The case for regarding the profit tax (which is independent of the income tax on dividends paid by stockholders) as a kind of sales tax is as follows: In order to raise capital and maintain its operation over the long run, a corporation must guarantee an acceptable return on capital, either directly in the form of dividends or indirectly in the form of capital gains from undistributed profits. This return must be paid from profits *after taxes.* Thus, the corporation's profits *before taxes* must be large enough to pay *both* the tax *and* the return to capital. Insofar as the corporation can and will vary its ratio of profits to sales, it will act to increase this ratio because of the tax. Consumers who buy the goods produced by the corporation will thus pay prices that are higher because of the tax. In effect, the corporation will essentially collect a kind of sales tax on behalf of the government.

However, if the corporation is a true profit maximizer, extracting the maximum possible profit whatever the tax, it will charge prices at the same ratio to cost whether there is a tax on profits or not. Under these circumstances, the tax does *not* affect the consumer directly and is a true tax on profits. But, in view of the increasing belief by economists that corporations are not true profit maximizers, there is a case for regarding at least part of the corporations' profits taxes as a kind of sales tax. We say that some of the tax is *shifted* from the corporation itself to consumers.

Thus, the corporate income tax has mixed effects. It is, at once, a sales tax with the corporation acting as agent for the government, a tax on the monopoly profits, and a tax on property income over and above the ordinary income tax.

Any scheme for a massive redistribution of income based on a "universal dividend" paid from corporate profits must take into account the large receipts from corporate taxes. Furthermore, maintaining the rate of increase in the capital stock that is sustained by the direct reinvestment of profits would require voluntary or compulsory saving of a similar amount by consumers. Thus, only dividends could be legitimately regarded as income available for redistribution—and dividends in 1977, divided equally over the whole population, would have amounted to about $150 per person. Universal distribution of corporate profits, therefore, would provide no bonanza to the average citizen. Those who grow rich on corporate profits do so, not because the total is so great, but because they receive a large share of the available total.

Exercises

1. Max has a newsstand he operates without help from 8:00 A.M. to 5:00 P.M. every day, including Sunday. His net receipts come to $600 per week, after paying for his papers and magazines but not the expenses of operating his stand. If he pays $100 per week rent for the stand, and he could work the same hours with a large stationery store at $3 per hour, what part of his total income should be regarded as labor income? What is his net nonlabor income?

2. The demand schedule for land on a small island is:

Rent ($ per acre)	1,000	1,500	2,000	2,500	3,000
Acres demanded	400	300	200	100	0

   a. The island has an area of 200 acres, and all land is equally valuable. What will be the market rent?
   b. A land tax of $500 per acre is levied on all landowners. What will happen to the level of rents?
   c. A land boom causes a large increase in demand, and the quantity demanded at every rent level is exactly doubled. What will be the new level of market rent, assuming no land tax?

3. Consider your own income, including any scholarship or remission on fees you may be receiving. How much of this is labor income? How much is derived from property income? How much is a transfer payment, either private or public?

For Thought and Discussion

1. Does it make any difference to the actual performance of the economy exactly *how* property income is divided? Why?

2. Reread the discussions of arbitrage and speculation in Chapter 5. Do these suggest a useful social purpose for some types of stock-market activity?

3. It might be argued that because landowners contribute nothing to the supply of land, all rents are generated by society as a whole and should accrue to society as a whole. Is this argument too simplistic? Explain.

4. Apply the same argument as in question 3 to the case of the popular singer whose voice constitutes a natural endowment. How do your conclusions differ from those you reached in the land case?

5. Some would claim that receiving "unearned" (usually meaning non-labor) income is immoral. In this respect, compare: (a) residual profits, (b) transfer payments (welfare and similar forms of income), and (c) royalties from the sale of phonograph records.

Chapter 18
Distributional Policy

Terms and Concepts

Income tax	Meritocracy	Indirect taxes
Transfer payments	Income replacement	Social dividend
Disposable income	Income support	Negative income tax
Pareto criterion	Lump-sum tax	Intertemporal decision
Minimum base	Wealth tax, property tax	Interpersonal decision
Subsidiary equalization	Proportional tax	
Primary equalization	Progressive tax	
	Regressive tax	

The Inevitability of Distributional Effects

Why distributional questions cannot be avoided

Before discussing those policies specifically designed to attain distributional objectives, it should be noted that virtually all economic policies have distributional effects, even when such effects are not among a given policy's stated goals. Furthermore, a policy designed to achieve a specific distributional objective may have indirect distributional effects that should not be ignored. A farm-price-support policy, for example, may be regarded by its proponents simply as a way to raise farm incomes. Its probable effect, however, will be to raise farm prices. And, because low-income consumers spend a greater fraction of their incomes on food than the rich do, the policy's overall effect may well be to redistribute income away from the poor rather than away from those who are more capable of subsidizing the farm sector.

Microeconomic Policy

Virtually all microeconomic policies have distributional effects, even though these effects aren't always obvious. Vigorous antitrust policy may reduce monopoly profits and thus have clear distributional implications. But it may also reduce employee compensation in the affected industry insofar as the union representing the industry's workers has been able to extract a portion of these profits through premium wages. Moreover, the resulting lower prices and greater output of the regulated industry will represent a gain to consumers. The question of which consumers will actually gain, of course, will depend on the particular goods involved. Antitrust enforcement in the pharmaceutical industry will most benefit the old and the sick, while antitrust enforcement in the sports-car industry will most benefit the young and the affluent. Antipollution policies will generally have a greater positive impact on the poor, who cannot afford the rental premiums necessary to live in less-polluted areas, than on the rich, who are already protected in their suburban enclaves. Expanding the supply of public goods will also usually represent a redistribution in favor of the poor because the rich can often afford club goods that provide similar benefits.

Macroeconomic Policy

While macroeconomic policy is discussed in detail in Chapters 29 through 32, we can briefly preview some of the distributional effects of such policy at this stage. One major choice governments perennially face is between inflation and unemployment—less unemployment with more inflation, or more unemployment with less inflation. Unemployment has obvious distributional effects. It hurts both those who are unemployed and wage earners in general because of the implied excess supply in the labor market. But inflation has distributional effects as well. Those with fixed money incomes (such as pensions) find that rising prices erode the real value of their incomes. Because less-skilled workers (who are most affected by unemployment) and the aged (whose pensions are most affected by inflation) are both typically on the bottom rung of the income ladder, the distributional effects are complex. Consequently, it's no simple matter to choose between unemployment and inflation on the basis of their relative effects on the poor.

The various means used to achieve macroeconomic policy objectives also have distributional effects. If the economy faces a slump, there are essentially two ways to stimulate a recovery. One (fiscal policy) is to increase government expenditures or cut taxes; the other (monetary policy) is to reduce interest rates and thereby stimulate business investment. The distributional effects of fiscal policy will depend on how the government chooses to make its extra expenditure—increased expenditure on missile systems will most benefit skilled workers, defense firms, and towns near missile sites and aerospace factories, while increased expenditure on urban swimming pools will most benefit construction workers and urban residents. Monetary policy will generally have a broader impact than fiscal policy, but will tend to increase profits more than wages.

In summary, if income redistribution is an important policy objective, the government must consider the distributional aspects of *all* its policies, not simply of those specifically labeled "distribution."

Recap Virtually all economic policies have important distributional effects regardless of whether or not they are primarily concerned with distribution. A decision to permit the economy to move into a mild recession, for example, will cause a different distribution than a decision to permit mild inflation. Thus, distributional questions can never be avoided in formulating economic policy.

The Tools of Distributional Policy

The main policy instruments for influencing distribution

The total benefits received by an individual are the sum of the benefits from

1. those things purchased with whatever income is received,
2. those things received for which income is not exchanged, such as free goods, public goods, and the like (less the negative benefits from public bads), and
3. the net effect of any consumption externalities arising from the actions of others.

In principle, distributional policy should be concerned with the distribution of total benefits. But many benefits, especially externalities, are so local and specialized that it is impractical to consider them in the broad picture. Consequently, actual distribution policy focuses on income distribution, modified when feasible to include the effects of public goods and free goods. The primary tools of distributional policy are thus generally those that affect income.

Before discussing the techniques available for altering the actual distribution of income, we should note that the distribution of *benefits derived from income* can be changed without directly affecting money incomes *per se*. Intervention in the price system can achieve benefit redistribution of this kind. For example, a subsidy on food prices paid for by a sales tax on fur coats would tend to redistribute benefits from the rich to the poor without any direct redistribution of income.

An individual's market-derived income arises from the sale of productive services—those of labor and property resources—and thus depends on the quantities and prices of these services. Income distribution can therefore be influenced by changing the *distribution of wealth* and/or by changing *factor prices*. In general, only two types of policy measures are used—even in socialist countries—to influence the distribution of wealth: free education (to provide human capital to those with no other source of income) and estate taxes (to reduce the amount of property handed down from one generation to another). Direct influence over factor prices is more common and is apparent in such measures as minimum-wage laws and profit taxes. (Profit taxes reduce the net price received by those selling capital services.) In command economies, wage rates can be specifically set to reflect distributional goals.

Taxes and Transfers

The most important tools for affecting major changes in the distribution of income are *income taxes* and *transfer payments*. All governments provide extensive services that are not sold, but whose costs are covered by taxes and other government revenues. Once a government decides to raise a given sum in taxes, it must decide how the burden of these taxes is to be distributed over the population. This choice is a matter of distributional policy. One of the most important and widely used taxes is the income tax; the amount paid by each individual depends on income. The benefit a person derives from his or her income depends on how much remains after paying income taxes—this remainder constitutes *disposable income*. The distribution of benefits among different income groups can be changed by differentiating the amount of tax paid by persons at different income levels. If the benefits provided by government services are more or less evenly distributed over different income groups, while the tax system imposes a larger burden on the rich than on the poor, there will be a net redistribution of benefits from the rich to the poor.

The second major device for changing the distribution of income is the use of transfer payments. A payment constitutes a *transfer* if it is *not* offered in exchange for labor or property services. Wages paid by the government are not transfer payments because they represent payments for labor services received. Social Security and welfare benefits, on the other hand, do constitute transfer payments because recipients supply no services in return. In Chapter 15 we pointed out that transfer payments have always been a necessary feature of society because the very young, the very old, and the disabled cannot usually provide factor services. A fundamental development of the last half-century has been the government's assumption of responsibility for such transfers, a responsibility that traditionally fell on family members and various religious and social institutions.

Transfers may take the form of goods and other nonmonetary benefits; therefore public goods can be regarded as direct transfers to society of the benefits they provide. While private transfers in the past were typically in the form of goods—the provision of food and lodging to elderly relatives, for example—government transfers today are typically in the form of direct cash payments. Such transfer payments thus add to whatever disposable income the recipients may already have.

The net effect of governmental distribution policy depends on the combined effects of taxes and transfers. The basic relationship is:

$$\text{disposable income} = \text{market-determined income}$$
$$- \text{ taxes paid} + \text{transfer payments received.}$$

Note that a transfer payment plays the same role as an income tax, but in the opposite direction. Thus, a transfer can be thought of as a negative tax. Under a distributional policy designed to make disposable incomes more equally distributed than basic, market-determined incomes, those with high market incomes will pay relatively high taxes and receive relatively few transfers so their disposable incomes will be less than their market incomes. Those with low or zero market incomes will pay relatively few taxes and receive relatively more transfers so their disposable incomes will exceed their market incomes.

Recap The distribution of goods and services is determined both by prices and the distribution of income. The government can influence this distribution by supplying goods free or intervening in the market system, as well as by directly redistributing market-determined income. The most important instruments for direct redistribution are income taxes and transfer payments.

The Aims of Distributional Policy

Problems in formulating the objectives of distributional policy

The major aim of distributional policy is to influence the distribution of goods and services among members of society in a particular way. In general, we shall adopt the traditional view that distributional objectives are ultimately a matter of social or political choice toward which the economist should remain neutral. This does not, however, preclude us from examining plausible models of social interaction that suggest particular patterns of distribution, or from stressing those distributional objectives that reflect broadly accepted social-welfare criteria. Moreover, while economists may view alternative distributional policies with an unprejudiced eye, one of their basic responsibilities is to point out the respective economic consequences of each policy.

The Arguments for Equality

At one stage in the development of economics, when it was heavily influenced by such nineteenth-century utilitarian thinkers as Jeremy Bentham and John Stuart Mill, economists considered individual "utility" or "welfare" to be both measurable and directly comparable among persons. Furthermore, they accepted the hypothesis of *diminishing marginal utility*—that the increment in utility associated with each additional dollar of income grows less as income increases. According to this hypothesis, a person gains more utility from an increase in income from, say, $3,000 to $4,000 than from an increase from $10,000 to $11,000. In the simplest version of this approach, in which the "amount" of utility associated with any given level of income is assumed to be equivalent for all individuals, we would conclude that an additional $1,000 would benefit a person with an income of $3,000 more than one with an income of $10,000. It follows that only an equal distribution of income would maximize "social welfare" (in this case, the simple sum of individual utilities) for a given aggregate income.

While many economists still accept the hypothesis of diminishing marginal utility, the notion that the utility gained by different persons is directly comparable is no longer accepted. The equal distribution argument, as given above, must therefore be rejected. This does *not* mean that economists regard an equal distribution as necessarily "bad," or that none would accept such a distribution as a desirable goal. It simply means that an equal distribution cannot be *proved* to be better or worse than any other.

In the simple economic models from which we reached conclusions about economic efficiency and the optimal composition of output (in Chapters 8–10), we viewed society as consisting of individuals whose welfare depended only on "income" in the broad sense of the goods and services available to each one. And in discussing economic efficiency, we assumed that anything that made *someone* better off and *no one* worse off constituted an improvement in social welfare. Unfortunately, this criterion, known as the *Pareto criterion* (after Vilfredo Pareto, 1848–1923, an Italian economist and sociologist), does not help us analyze those problems of distribution in which we are concerned with making some group (the poor, for example) better off at the cost of making some other (the rich, perhaps) worse off. If we assume welfare *interdependence*, however, the situation is changed.

Interdependence

An individual's "welfare" may be affected by the apparent welfare of others. In a purely compassionate society, for example, a given individual's welfare would presumably be increased if any other member of society were made better off materially, even if the individual were not. More realistically, we might assume that individuals gain welfare only from an increase in the incomes of those *below* them on the income scale. This would imply that those with higher incomes would be willing to give up *some amount* of their own income to those with lower incomes, while still considering themselves just as well off—the loss of personal incomes being compensated by the satisfaction of seeing others better off. Because the poor would then be *better off*, such a redistribution would improve social welfare in the simple sense that some members of society would be made better off, and none worse off. The resulting redistribution would be toward a greater equality of incomes, though representing only a partial step in that direction.

The strict interpretation of this "compassionate interdependence" model is that *voluntary private transfers* can generate an optimal redistribution because both donors and recipients would gain from them. Because such voluntary transfers, in the form of charitable donations, actually take place when no other transfer system operates, some confirmation is given to this model's underlying assumptions.

Analysis of this kind suggests that more can be said about income distribution from economic models than is often supposed. Indeed, the particular model just described indicates that an optimal redistribution may well be in the direction of greater equality.

Typical Aims

To arrive at more specific objectives of distributional policy, we must draw on moral, political, and social values. Among the distributional aims drawn from these sources and commanding apparent support in most Western economies are the following:

1. *The minimum base*. Here the aim is to ensure that a minimum standard of living is achieved by all members of society, whether old or young, disabled or healthy. This may be modified to the *conditional minimum base*, in which the aim is to provide a minimum living standard conditional on individuals making whatever "contribution" to society is feasible for them. The conditional minimum base would typically not provide a base income to a healthy, working-age individual for whom a job was available. The United States and most relatively rich economies include some version of the conditional minimum base among their distributional objectives, although this aim generally constitutes a luxury most poor economies cannot afford.

2. *Subsidiary equalization*. This aim requires that any policy whose primary objectives are not distributional in nature, but that has distribu-

tional consequences, should be formulated so as to increase equality. The progressive income tax, one of the best-known distributional policies in the United States, provides an example of subsidiary equalization. The income tax is essentially an instrument for raising revenue, not for bringing about redistribution. Once the government settles on how much revenue is to be raised, however, the tax is implemented in a manner that will increase the equality of disposable incomes.

3. *Primary equalization*. We can apply this term to any policy whose primary objective is to induce a greater equality in disposable incomes. If we could pair government transfer payments with the part of the general tax revenue designed to finance them, the resulting tax-transfer package could be regarded in this light. However, because there is no *official* pairing of transfers with any particular source of revenue, this would reflect an arbitrary division of overall policy.

4. *Promotion of a meritocracy*. The aim of this type of policy is to promote "equal opportunity" with respect to access to human capital and/or property wealth, and then accept the resulting market-determined income distribution. Its primary concern is thus with the distribution of resources rather than with that of income *per se*. Typical policies that incorporate the meritocratic principle (which constitutes an important part of the American ethos) are free education and estate taxes.

These four aims are not mutually exclusive. Distributional policy, for example, could be *meritocratic* with a *conditional base* modified by *subsidiary equalization*. This combination is, in fact, a fair description of the overall direction of U.S. distributional policy, except that private property is treated with rather more respect than implied by a strict meritocratic aim.

Recap The objectives of distributional policy can be extremely varied. Typical aims include: diminishing income inequality; ensuring that everyone, or at least everyone conforming to certain patterns of social behavior, receives a minimum income; and equalizing access to certain private means of acquiring income.

The Distributional Unit

To whom or to what groups do we want to distribute?

While most simple economic analysis focuses on the "individual" as the basic unit in matters of distribution, real distributional policies are typically based on the "family" or "household." For philosophical as well as practical reasons, the distribution *within* the family is not generally considered to be a matter for public policy, except in special cases such as the maltreatment of children, family separation, or property division.

In the United States, the basic unit generally considered in policy matters is the "primary family." This term refers to family members actually living together. Approximately 93 percent of the U.S. population is divided among nearly 60 million such families, with more than 15 million additional individuals living separately as "primary individuals" (in effect, one-person families). Policy need not be confined solely to the distribution among families, however, because we may be interested in the distribution among more-comprehensive groups designated on the basis of such criteria as race, occupation, or geographic residence.

The Individual Is Always Counted

Even though we may focus our attention on distributional units larger than the single individual, we still retain implicit recognition that the individual is the ultimate base unit. We do this when considering relative family sizes in comparing family incomes. For example, a situation in which a family of ten has the same income as a family of two would not usually be viewed as representing an equal distribution of income. For practical reasons, we may regard multiperson families as having the same size *on average*, but certainly differentiate them from one-person families. And when considering units larger than the family, we always compare average, as opposed to aggregate, incomes of the groups involved.

The Status of Groups

There are several reasons for considering intergroup distribution. One is that incomes for all members of a particular group may be determined in a similar way, which differs from that of other groups. This is certainly true in the case of farmers and, to a lesser extent, the inhabitants of depressed regions like Appalachia. Primarily, however, intergroup distributional policy represents a simplified approach to the solution of complex distributional problems. If, for example, nonwhites are much poorer than whites on the average, then equalizing the white-nonwhite income distribution will be expected to equalize incomes in general.

There are considerable dangers, however, in concentrating unduly on intergroup distribution. The overall distribution among *individuals or families*, which should be our ultimate concern, may be changed little by a policy that affects intergroup distribution. Agricultural price supports, for example, may succeed in raising average farm incomes relative to nonfarm incomes, but only by making rich farmers even richer, while providing little or no gain to poor farmers. While the inequality among groups would fall in this case, that among individuals would actually increase.

Recap Economists have traditionally focused their thinking about social welfare on the individual. The real basic units of society, however, are families or households, a fact that may pose problems in devising distributional policy. Moreover, it is often desirable to consider the distribution among groups defined geographically, socioeconomically, or racially.

Transfer Payments in the United States

Typical arrangements for income transfers

The most straightforward way to distribute income to the poor is to provide them with outright cash grants. Because such grants do not represent compensation for current resource services, they are appropriately referred to as *transfer payments*.

Note that the typical pension qualifies as a transfer, even though it represents a payment for *past services*. (For a payment to be classified as current income, as opposed to a transfer, it must be paid out of receipts from the sale of current output.) However, if the *right* to a future pension was part of the original compensation for resource services, we usually consider the individual with a *private pension* to have accumulated *wealth* (his share of a pension fund), in which case the pension may be regarded as current income derived from that wealth.

While transfer payments through private charities and modest government grants at the local level have a long history, extensive transfers from public funds are a relatively recent development. Government transfer payments represented less than 2 percent of total personal income in the United States in 1929, and rose to only 4.5 percent in 1933, when unemployment reached its peak of 25 percent. The social and political consequences of the Great Depression ultimately resulted in major increases in unemployment benefits and other transfers, however, and the post–World War II period saw the development of a full-scale federal Social Security program. Government transfers represented a full 6 percent of total personal income in 1946, and had risen to more than 13 percent of personal income by 1977.

The largest component of total transfer payments (approximately 50 percent in 1977) is Social Security, primarily payments to recipients over 65. Transfer payments to retired and disabled persons, their dependents, and surviving dependents have always dominated the transfer system—this category constituted almost 80 percent of the total in 1977 and accounted for 45 percent even in 1933, when poverty among the ablebodied was widespread.

Types of Programs

Programs providing transfer incomes to the retired and disabled are sometimes referred to as *income replacement* programs because they replace incomes from other sources that have stopped for some reason. While *unemployment payments* are classed by the government in this category, they could just as appropriately be considered *income support* programs. These programs are designed to supplement other income sources (which may be zero) for persons who are neither retired nor physically disabled.

Social Security

The most important income replacement program in the United States is *Social Security*, a program that originated in 1935 and reached its present form after World War II. Social Security covers about 90 percent of employed persons in the country. It provides benefits to retired and disabled persons and also to their survivors, with retirement pensions and pension supplements representing about two-thirds of total dispersements. Payments are made to about three-fourths of all individuals over age 65. Social Security benefits depend partly on the length of an individual's employment in a covered occupation prior to retirement (or disability), but have upper and lower limits.

There are special income replacement programs other than Social Security for government employees, veterans, and railroad employees. For many years there were no income replacement programs for farmers, self-employed persons, or others who were not employees, but recent legislation has brought them into the Social Security program.

Considered as a policy whose aim is to provide a minimum base income, the American Social Security program has not been unduly generous. The average monthly payment for a retired husband-wife family from Social Security in 1977 was significantly below the officially defined poverty level.

Support Programs

Income support programs, from which payments to "ablebodied" members of the community accrue, can be divided into those providing unemployment compensation and those addressing pure "need."

Unemployment benefits in the United States are administered under a joint federal-state system whereby the federal government stands behind the programs to prevent their collapsing from lack of funds (as they did, when most needed, during the 1930s). These payments are *not* generally related to income—the president of a large corporation can draw them even after he has already received, say, $150,000 during the first half of the year, provided he has lost his job and cannot find another. The average *weekly* payment per person in 1977 was about one-third of the average weekly wage but well above the official poverty line for a single individual.

The remaining income support programs vary widely, but are primarily need-oriented. These transfer payments are made to persons simply because they are poor. Virtually all such programs are administered by state or local governments, but are usually financed in part by federal grants. Because of their local nature, benefits tend to vary widely, being as much as eight times as great in some states as in others. A high proportion (about half) of "need" payments go to supplement incomes of the aged or the disabled whose Social Security payments are insufficient for support. The remainder is primarily that of the kind known as "Aid to Families with Dependent Children" (AFDC)—commonly called "welfare."

There has been considerable objection to making transfer payments, other than simple unemployment benefits, to families containing able-bodied male members. Under some local rules, a family whose head is employed but receiving a very low wage or is unemployed but ineligible for unemployment compensation, faces particular difficulties. Indeed, such a family may be "encouraged by the system" to increase its income by separation that leaves the unsupported spouse eligible to receive AFDC or similar benefits.

Despite the strong emotions aroused by "welfare," total transfer payments to persons who are neither aged nor physically disabled constitute an extremely small fraction of total income in the United States—less than 1 percent of total personal income in 1977. The average monthly payment per recipient family in 1977 was $238, and the average per family member was $77.

Recap The variety of existing transfer programs in the United States is enormous. It is convenient to divide these programs into income replacement programs, designed to make up for a complete loss of income due to age, disability, or unemployment, and income support programs, designed to supplement other, inadequate income sources. Most programs in the United States are of the income replacement kind, such as Social Security. Income support programs tend to be uneven in their operation, and fail to cover many categories of persons.

Capsule Supplement 18.1   **"Welfare" and Incentives**

Public assistance or "welfare" benefits, primarily in the form of Aid to Families with Dependent Children (AFDC), equaled only 0.6 percent of GNP in 1977 and represented only slightly more than one cent out of every tax dollar. Yet these benefits continue to generate social and political controversy far out of proportion to their small impact on the general economy. Much of the political heat stems from the fact that families on welfare are heavily concentrated in a few areas (especially urban ghettos), so transfers constitute a significant portion of large-city budgets. The enormous variation in benefits (and conditions for receiving them) also leads to the belief that potential welfare clients migrate from one locality to another in the quest for higher benefits, further concentrating the problem. Whether or not this belief is justified by the facts, it generates controversy.

While few appear to object to the principle of a conditional minimum base income, there is a broad diversity of opinion about what the conditions should be. Whether this is due to the so-called Puritan work ethic or simply to pressure from low-income workers, legislators have an almost pathological fear of being held responsible for a program that gives some people more income for doing nothing than others receive from hard work. There is, of course, a genuine *incentive* problem that is certainly economic. If individuals are paid from welfare or unemployment benefits as much as they could normally earn, they will tend to withdraw from the labor force. This reduces the resources and output of the economy *unless they are allowed to keep at least part of what they earn by working*. This is one problem that most economists' "ideal" transfer schemes, like the negative income tax, are designed to handle.

Many of the problems that arise from welfare stem from the structural and administrative properties of specific programs. If emphasis is placed on the prevention of "cheating," for example, extensive information must be collected on beneficiaries. This may lead to high administrative costs and an unpleasant program atmosphere, both of which would tend to reduce the true social benefits derived from a given outlay. It would, however, make for financial savings insofar as potential beneficiaries would prefer to live in poverty rather than become involved with the programs. The typical structure of AFDC programs has been accused of leading to great social disruption. If a husband leaves his family, the family may obtain benefits for which it would otherwise be ineligible. Insofar as family preservation is considered to be an important social goal, it is a poor economic policy that provides such strong incentives for separation.

Taxes and Distribution	The use of taxes to change the distribution of income

All taxes affect distribution. Consequently, the overall impact of the tax system can be truly measured only when all taxes are taken into account. The income tax nevertheless has the most clearly defined effect on distribution and thus provides the starting point for our discussion.

As its name implies, an income tax is a tax levied in relation to the level of income on either an individual, a family, or a corporation. Just what kinds of taxes can and cannot be considered income taxes? A *lump-sum tax*, like the defunct poll tax, is not an income tax because the amount of such a tax is completely independent of income. Nor is a *wealth* or *property tax* that varies only with the value of the wealth or property being taxed rather than with the amount of income that may be derived from it. On the other hand, there are some taxes that do qualify as income taxes, even though they may be called by another name. The most obvious example in the United States is the *Social Security contribution* paid by individual employees. This contribution constitutes a tax on labor income that varies with the level of income up to a stipulated maximum level ($17,700 in 1978).

An income tax brings about a divergence between each individual's gross or pretax income and his or her disposable or after-tax income. Consequently, it affects the relationship between the market distribution of incomes and the distribution of disposable incomes that determines the real distribution of benefits. In other words, an income tax redistributes these benefits. Most income-tax systems do, however, take other things than

Table 18.1
Federal Income-Tax Rates, United States,
1977 (for a single individual
taking the standard deduction)

Income	Tax	Average tax rate (tax as a percent of income)	Marginal tax rate (percentage payable in tax from additional dollar of income)
$ 5,000	$ 283	5.7	17
10,000	1,227	12.3	24
20,000	3,999	20.0	34
50,000	18,420	36.8	60

pure income levels into account. Some countries, for example, tax income derived from wealth at a higher rate than labor income. Moreover, most countries, including the United States, tax large families less than small families and people over sixty-five at a lower rate than individuals of prime working age.

Tax Progression

We classify the degree of progression of a tax by the way in which the *average tax rate* (the amount of the tax as a percentage of income) changes as income changes. If the average tax rate is *constant* at all income levels, the tax is said to be *proportional*. If the average tax rate *increases* as income increases, the tax is called *progressive*, and if the average tax rate *decreases* as income increases, the tax is said to be *regressive*.

To say that a tax is progressive does not simply mean that the *amount* of tax increases as income rises (all proportional and most regressive taxes have this property), but that the *proportion* of income paid in taxes increases with income. Table 18.1 shows the rates of U.S. federal income tax for various levels of income for a single individual taking standard deductions. A taxpayer with a gross income of $10,000 would pay 12.3 percent of his or her income in taxes, compared with only 5.7 percent for a taxpayer with an income of $5,000. Hence, the federal income tax, like almost all modern income-tax systems, is progressive.

A strictly proportional income tax results in disposable income being distributed in an identical proportion to the original gross income. Suppose that the economy consisted of 80 million poor taxpayers with incomes of $5,000 and 20 million rich taxpayers with incomes of $20,000, so the total income is $800 billion with $400 billion (50 percent of the total) going to the rich 20 percent. If there were a proportional tax of, say, 15 percent, the poor would each pay $750 and the rich would each pay $3,000. After deducting these taxes, total disposable income would be $680 billion, of which the rich would receive $340 billion or 50 percent of the total, the same as before the tax. A proportional tax is therefore *neutral* with regard to distribution.

Now consider the same economy, but with progressive taxes at U.S. rates, from Table 18.1. The 80 million poor taxpayers would each pay $283 and be left with disposable incomes of $4,717. The 20 million rich would each pay $3,999 and be left with disposable incomes of $16,001. Under these tax rates, we find that total disposable income is now $697 billion, and that the rich 20 percent receive 46 percent of it—a lower proportion than before the tax. A progressive tax thus reduces inequality in the distribution of income.

We can determine whether a tax system is progressive or not by comparing the marginal tax rate (the tax payable on an additional dollar of income) with the average tax rate at each income level. If the marginal tax rate exceeds the average rate, the tax structure is progressive; if it equals the average rate, the tax is proportional; if it is below the average rate, the tax is regressive. Note that in Table 18.1 the marginal federal income-tax rate is higher everywhere than the average rate.

Limits of Redistribution

A progressive tax can never equalize disposable incomes unless it reaches a confiscatory marginal rate of 100 percent, taxing away the entire marginal income above the equalizing level. Furthermore, as the marginal tax rate becomes quite high—say, 70 percent—the potential gains from tax avoidance become very large. Several studies have shown that those receiving the highest incomes in the United States (those in the million-dollar class) pay fewer taxes than those with significantly lower incomes. This is due to the incentive of the very rich to adjust their financial affairs with tax-avoidance techniques devised by their accountants and lawyers.

Because a regular income tax can only affect redistribution insofar as it increases the tax rate on high incomes and reduces the tax rate on low incomes, the extent of redistribution is limited both by the highest marginal rate that can be effectively collected and by the general level of taxes. If total income-tax revenue represents only a small proportion of total personal incomes, the potential for a substantial redistribution is small. Redistributive possibilities are enormously increased if persons below some basic income level actually *receive payments* (that is, "pay" negative taxes) in relation to the gap between their income and the basic level. A detailed discussion of the so-called *negative income tax* is presented in the next section.

The Overall Tax System

Although income taxes are the only taxes specifically tied to individual incomes, there are many other taxes whose effects tend to vary systematically with income level. Attention has already been drawn to Social Security contributions in the United States. These are proportional to labor incomes up to a maximum income level (6.05 percent of income up to $17,700 in 1978), above which no further contribution is extracted. In effect, these contributions are proportional taxes for incomes below $17,700 and regressive taxes for higher incomes. Because Social Security contributions are fairly large compared with the income tax proper, except at high-income levels, the effect of the income tax together with these contributions is much less progressive than that of the income tax alone, especially at middle-income levels.

The incidence of *indirect taxes*, like sales and property taxes, is difficult to assess. Although such taxes are not directly related to income (hence the term *indirect*), each is related to some item of expenditure that is a predictably larger or smaller proportion of income at different income levels. Taxes on real estate, for example, are reflected in rents and costs of home ownership, and generally represent a greater fraction of total expenditure for low-income groups than for high-income groups. Consequently, such taxes tend to be *regressive*.

The total tax structure of the United States consists of state and local, as well as federal, taxes. These taxes vary greatly in their degree of progression, state income taxes tending to be proportional or progressive, state sales taxes tending to be regressive. A special study, conducted by the President's Council of Economic Advisers on the basis of 1965 data, found that when all taxes are taken into account, the overall U.S. tax system is actually regressive at low-income levels. Individuals whose incomes were less than $2,000 paid 44 percent in total taxes, compared to 27 percent paid by those with incomes between $2,000 and $15,000, and 38 percent paid by those whose incomes were more than $15,000. This pattern was attributed to the regressive character of most state and local taxes, which collectively tended to offset the progressive federal income tax.

Recap Taxes affect the distribution of income if they are not proportional, that is, if the proportion of income paid in taxes varies with the level of income. Taxes are said to be regressive if the poor pay a higher proportion of their incomes in taxes than do the rich, and progressive if the reverse is true. Income taxes in the United States, as in most countries, are designed to be progressive. But because most sales taxes and many other taxes are regressive, the U.S. tax system as a whole is regressive at low-income levels.

The Overall Tax-Transfer System

The net effect of combining taxes and transfers

Because it is the combined impact of taxes and transfers that really matters, a comprehensive distributional policy must be formulated in terms of the tax-transfer system as a whole. In the last section we saw that the overall U.S. tax system is regressive. However, the *combined* effect of taxes and transfers is progressive. Viewing transfers as negative taxes, the same 1965 study previously cited showed the tax-transfer rate on incomes below $2,000 to be −82 percent (transfers exceeded taxes by 82 percent of basic income). This rate became +16 percent (taxes exceeding transfers) in the $2,000 to $3,900 bracket, and rose gradually through successive income brackets to +37 percent when income was more than $15,000. Details are given in Table 18.2.

These figures do not necessarily imply that all individuals are subject to the same mix of taxes and transfers. In the under $2,000 bracket, for example, some may pay taxes but receive no transfers, while others may receive transfers but pay few taxes. (While government transfers are not generally subject to income taxes, transfer recipients will still normally pay sales and other indirect taxes.)

"Ideal" Schemes

Most "ideal" distributive schemes devised by economists (of which there have been many) envision the tax-transfer system as a whole. Two types of programs, which illustrate alternative new approaches, are the *social dividend* and the *negative income tax*.

The social dividend takes a direct approach to the problem of providing a basic minimum income level. Such a level could be assigned on an individual or a family basis—for the United States, the rock-bottom minimum might be $2,750 per family (half the poverty line for a family of four in 1976). This amount would then be paid as a social dividend to *every* family (including one-person families). It would, however, be treated as taxable income, so the rich would pay most of it back in income tax while the poor would retain it all. Proper adjustment of tax rates would ensure that *everyone* received a minimum income. An important advantage of this type of scheme is that, unlike many existing welfare programs, it would provide no disincentive to earn market income.

A negative income-tax program would involve both positive *and* negative taxes. Again we would specify a basic minimum income level. Anyone with an income below this level would be granted *part* of the deficiency according to a negative income-tax scale—either a constant proportion of the gap, or a proportion increasing with the size of the gap (giving a progressive negative income tax). Individuals with incomes above the basic level would pay positive income taxes. Like the social dividend, this scheme would

Table 18.2
The Tax Transfer Structure,
United States, 1965

| Income class (in $1,000) | As proportion of pretransfer income (%) | | | | Taxes less transfers |
	Federal taxes	State and local taxes	Total taxes	Transfers	
under 2	19	25	44	126	−82
2–4	16	11	27	11	16
4–6	17	10	27	5	21
6–8	17	9	26	3	23
8–10	18	9	27	2	25
10–15	19	9	28	2	26
over 15	32	7	38	1	37

Source: *Economic Report of the President,* 1969.

provide each family with a minimum income, avoid the necessity of personally inspecting prospective recipients to determine whether or not they "need" or "deserve" assistance, and provide incentives for low-income individuals to obtain other earnings.

Programs of this kind differ most from existing tax-transfer systems primarily in that they aim at *unconditional* minimum income levels—not necessarily for moral or social reasons, but largely on the grounds that the social costs (direct and implicit) of administering conditional systems represent an immense waste of society's resources.

Recap To consider the overall effects of distributional policy, we must consider taxes and transfers together. Economists' "ideal" schemes, such as the social dividend and the negative income tax, represent attempts to devise a unified policy in which taxes and transfers are considered together.

Distribution in Kind

Redistribution without changing nominal incomes

The direct provision of certain goods and services to households in accordance with some criterion other than income will generally result in a redistribution of real income. Public goods, of course, *must necessarily* be distributed in this manner, but our interest here lies in goods that *could* be distributed through the market but for which a deliberate policy choice is made to distribute otherwise.

The oldest and most common example of distribution outside the market is education. Obviously, education could be supplied exclusively by private schools in return for fees. In this case its distribution would be determined by the distribution of income and individual preferences (of the parents, not the children).

Education

Education possesses several special features that make it suitable for non-market distribution. Among these features are:

1. There are no major allocation problems—everyone needs and (at least in principle) can be given the same ''amount'' of schooling up to some predetermined level.
2. Subsidiary trading cannot destroy the original allocation—the rich cannot bribe the poor to give up their places in the classroom so rich children can receive ''more'' education.
3. It is considered socially desirable that everyone receive some minimum amount of education.
4. There is considerable doubt that unconstrained action in accordance with individual preferences is optimal, because:
   a. The education decision is a long-period *intertemporal decision,* and thus is largely irreversible. A child must be educated early. Costs come at the time of schooling (if fees must be paid), but benefits come only years later. Such decisions, to be optimal, require foresight of a high order.
   b. Education is also an *interpersonal decision* because the costs fall on the parents, while the benefits (or their absence, if the decision is to forgo schooling) accrue to the child.

Of course, the rich can still presumably obtain better education than the poor, if they choose, by paying for private schools even when universal free education is available.

Health Care

The factors favoring the distribution of education outside the market can also be applied to health services:

1. The allocation can be based on objectively determined need.
2. Subsidiary trading is not possible (except in drugs and supplies).
3. Such services are considered socially desirable.
4. Individuals are prone to make poor choices—even in their own self-interest—when given the option of spending income on preventative medical treatment or on other things.

Nonmarket distribution of medical services is common in virtually all of the richer countries except the United States. In these countries, the fiction of a market system is sometimes preserved in the guise of compulsory health "insurance" and the payment of "fees" to doctors by the government. Regardless of whether or not doctors are regarded as government employees, however, the *distribution* of services is made independent of income. As in the case of education, of course, the rich can choose to pay more and have additional luxuries such as appointments and access to selected specialists.

"Free" education and health services are actually free only from the viewpoint of the individual. The resources used to provide these services must be paid for either out of general tax revenue, specifically earmarked tax receipts (such as "insurance contributions"), or a mixture of the two. The distributional impact of moving from a system of market-provided medical services to some form of public health care can be predicted only when the nature of financing is established.

A Contrasting Case

Consider the hypothetical case in which an *automobile* is directly provided to every household in the United States. The problem isn't that the U.S. economy can't provide an automobile for every household—it can, and very nearly does, through the market system. Rather there is no reason why a household shouldn't be left free to decide whether it wants to spend the money-equivalent of an automobile on the automobile itself or on something else. With direct distribution, subsidiary trading would certainly develop, with those receiving automobiles but preferring other things exchanging the automobile for something else.

Consequently, when households can be presumed to be the best judge of their own requirements, and when there is no major divergence between social and private evaluations of these requirements, economists agree that distributing *money income* is superior to distributing goods in kind.

Recap By intervening in the market it is possible to redistribute incomes without changing total incomes. Subsidizing the prices of goods that represent a large share of the budgets of the poor (food, housing) can achieve some redistribution, as can direct government provision of certain goods. The most widespread examples of direct government-provided goods are education and health services.

Capsule Supplement 18.2   **Medicare and Medicaid: A Case Study in Distribution**

America's first step toward a national health-care policy was the enactment of Medicare and Medicaid legislation in 1965. This legislation was designed to increase the availability of medical services to certain groups of individuals unable to afford full medical care through the market. Specifically, Medicare was established to provide federally subsidized health care to persons over 65 on Social Security (who are required to pay regular "insurance" premiums), while Medicaid was set up as a mixed federal, state, and local program to provide free or subsidized health care to low-income families under conditions that vary from state to state.

What happens when programs like these are instituted? Are benefits distributed as originally planned, or do they accrue in part to individuals for whom they were not intended? How are the costs and benefits of such programs allocated among various population groups? These are the types of questions we must answer if we are to learn how to formulate effective distributional policies. In the case of Medicare and Medicaid, many such answers have been provided by a 1971 study carried out by the Michigan Department of Social Services.

This study considered the impact of these programs on three broad population groups: the recipients of benefits from these programs (households either obtaining or eligible for benefits), nonrecipients (households not obtaining or eligible for benefits), and physicians. Because these programs were intended to be distributional, recipients were meant to (and did) gain at the expense of nonrecipients—but a considerable gain went to physicians even though this was not the original intent of the program. The net results of the study are shown in the accompanying table.

The provision of subsidized health care to those unable to afford full health care at market prices led, inevitably, to an increase in the total demand for physicians and other health services in the economy as a whole. Because the supply of health services could not be increased overnight, the normal operation of the market resulted in upward pressure on the price of health services. The Michigan study estimated that physicians' fees rose almost 7

Distributional Effects of the Medicare-
Medicaid Programs, 1967–68
(All figures in millions of dollars)

Population group	Benefit to group[a]	Cost to group[b]	Net benefit[c]
Recipients	9.25	4.13	5.12
Nonrecipients	3.67	8.80	−5.13
Physicians	0.86	0.26	0.61

[a] Estimated benefits after adjustments of various kinds. Benefits to nonrecipients include higher incomes of physicians and other health-care workers, reduction in payments for programs and charity replaced by Medicare-Medicaid.
[b] Contributions or tax payments to support the programs.
[c] Benefit to group *less* costs to group.

Source: Michigan Department of Social Services, *Health Care and Income,* Research Paper No. 5, April, 1971.

percent more than they would have risen without the two programs, and that the price of hospital care rose more than 14 percent as a result of their impact.

The rise in the price of health services meant that the real benefits to recipients fell below the dollar value of payments made, while physicians' incomes rose with no increase in effort. In other words, there was a partial redistribution of income from nonrecipients to physicians rather than to the planned beneficiaries. This diversion was estimated at almost one-eighth of the total benefits distributed. It should be noted that not all the gain to physicians was due to increases in the level of fees actually charged. Prior to the institution of these programs, physicians had traditionally provided some services free to their poorer patients, the resulting lack of compensation being offset by high fees charged to others. Medicare and Medicaid thus enabled physicians to charge market prices for services originally provided free, without any counterbalancing reduction in fees charged to patients who could afford to pay.

One of the lessons of the Medicare-Medicaid experience is that, if a policy is designed to enable part of the population to buy something it has not hitherto been able to afford, steps should be taken to ensure that the supply is increased at the same time lest price increases erode many of the planned benefits.

Exercises

1. A society levies an income tax according to the simple formula that the tax is equal to 10 percent of the amount by which income exceeds $5,000.
   a. Calculate the tax and the average rate of tax for gross incomes of $1,000, $5,000, $10,000, $20,000.
   b. Is the tax proportional, progressive, or regressive?

2. Assume that 25 percent of all persons have incomes of $1,000, 25 percent have incomes of $5,000, 25 percent have incomes of $10,000, and the remaining 25 percent have incomes of $20,000.
   a. What proportion of total pretax income is received by the richest 25 percent of the population?
   b. What proportion is received by the poorest 25 percent?

3. With the income tax of question 1 and the income distribution of question 2,
   a. what proportion of total after-tax (disposable) income goes to the richest 25 percent?
   b. what proportion goes to the poorest 25 percent?

4. If the income tax is 50 percent of income in excess of $5,000, instead of 10 percent as in question 1, and the income distribution is that of question 2,

a. what proportion of total disposable income goes to the richest 25 percent of the population?

b. what proportion goes to the poorest 25 percent?

For Thought and Discussion

1. "If we simply give people money, they'll stop working and the economy will collapse." Discuss this common argument against unconditional transfer payments.

2. Analyze carefully the difference in distributional effects between manning the armed forces by:
   a. a low-paid draft army.
   b. a highly paid volunteer army.

3. Suppose it was decided that $4,000 should be the basic income level at which as many people as possible should be supported. Compare the likely effects on incentives to earn other income of the following two schemes:
   a. a social dividend of $4,000 paid to everyone with a proportional income tax on total income including the dividend.
   b. a negative income tax on incomes below $4,000, so all in this group receive a fixed proportion of the difference between their earned income and $4,000, with a regular, positive proportional tax on the excess of earnings above $4,000.

4. Many people "cheat" on welfare by hiding assets or sources of income from social workers. Does this mean we need better enforcement of conditions for making welfare payments? A different system of transfer payments? A tightening of the "moral fiber" of the community?

5. What rationale do you suppose lies behind a government's decision to provide public assistance in the form of food stamps as opposed to cash transfers of equivalent value?

Part 5
Macroeconomics

This part, Chapters 19 through 22, provides the theoretical foundation for the study of problems and policy at the macroeconomic level. Chapter 19 gives the general basis of the macroeconomic approach, and Chapter 20 outlines the formation of the national income accounts. Chapters 21 and 22 provide an analysis of the economy as a macroeconomic system.

Chapter 19
Thinking in Aggregates

Terms and Concepts

Macroeconomics
Gross national product
Economic weights
General price level
Current dollars
Constant dollars
Index numbers
Consumer price index
Wholesale price index
GNP deflator
Index of industrial production
Aggregation
Consumption function
Mechanistic models

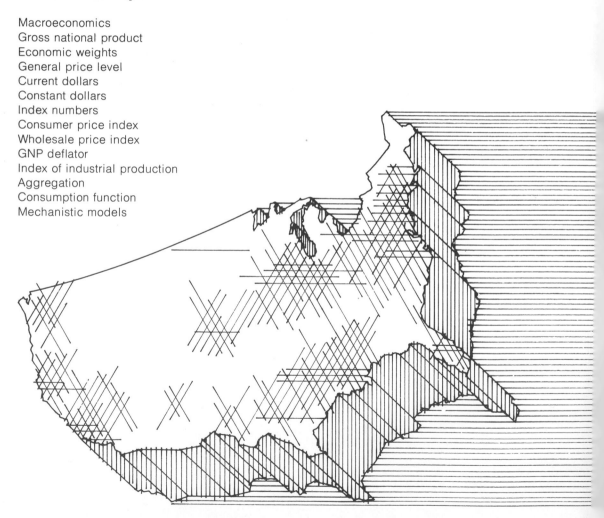

An Introduction to Macroeconomics

Why there is a macroeconomics as well as a microeconomics

If the economy produced a single good—say corn—there would be no problem assessing its overall performance. Given the existing technology, the available resources, and predictable weather conditions, we could estimate the *capacity output* of the economy simply as so many tons of corn. Society's production possibilities would have only a single dimension, the upper limit of which would be this capacity output.

If actual production were below capacity, we would know immediately that the economy was performing below par, and by how far it was falling short of its possibilities. Naturally, we would want to know why. Presumably it would be because certain resources were not fully employed. There might be unemployed labor, for example. If so, we would again want to know why. For only with such knowledge could we devise an appropriate policy for promoting full employment.

In this simple world there would be no problem measuring *economic growth*. Whether in terms of capacity or actual output, we could compare the quantity this year with the respective quantity last year and determine whether capacity or actual output had increased or decreased (and by how much), or if it had remained stationary.

Allocation

Although corn is the only output in our example, it has at least two different uses. It can be used either as food—*consumption*—or as seed to grow next year's crop—*investment*. By simply noting the quantity devoted to each use, we could measure the allocation of corn between consumption and investment.

But just how should corn be allocated between these two uses? This would depend on how the economy was organized. Other things being equal, people presumably would want to consume as much corn as possible. On the other hand, because the size of next year's crop depends, in part, on this year's investment in seed, the higher the investment, the higher next year's consumption.

A centralized system might simply decide on the level of investment required for output to grow over time at a certain desired rate, then allocate the rest to consumption. A decentralized system, with thousands of firms, might let each individual producer reach a decision about investment, and each individual consumer reach a decision about consumption. This introduces the possibility that the total amount of corn these many decision-makers collectively plan to invest and consume will not equal the total amount of corn available, in which case it is obvious that something will have to give.

Price

Finally, let's suppose that it is inconvenient to lug around one's stock of corn, so we have *money* that is carried about and exchanged for corn as needed. Consequently, we shall have *exchange,* and thus a price for corn in terms of, say, dollars.

Given a price, we can measure the economy's output in money terms, as well as in real quantity terms. If output were 1 million bushels at a price of $5 per bushel, the value of the economy's output would be $5 million. If we were told that the value of output rose from $5 million to $6 million, we could not tell whether society's *real output*—the quantity produced—had risen or not. We could determine this only if we were given either the actual quantities or both the output values and the prices in the two periods. If the price of corn had risen from $5 to $6 per bushel, the increase in the value of output from $5 million to $6 million would not have represented a change in real output. This quantity would necessarily have remained constant at 1 million bushels.

Many Goods

Obviously, real economies produce more than one good. They produce thousands of different goods. Consequently, there's not just one price, but thousands of different prices. Moreover, investment and consumption do not generally constitute alternative uses of the same good. Rather, investment typically involves things like machines and buildings while consumption typically involves things like food and clothing—quite different sets of goods.

In *microeconomics* we concentrate on the diversity of things, on differences between the prices and quantities produced of different goods. While this provides us with an overall description of the economy, it may be so complex that we cannot easily view the economy's performance as a whole. In short, we often cannot see the forest for the trees.

In *macroeconomics* we seek a broad picture in which the sum of the economy's operations, rather than its internal divergences, are made apparent. To do this, it is convenient to view the economy *as if* it produced one good. We call the money value of this good *total output* or gross national product (GNP); its price, *the general price level* or simply *the price level;* and its quantity, *real output* or *real GNP*.

The questions posed in basic macroeconomics are identical to those we just asked in reference to our one-good economy. What is the capacity level of output? Is the economy operating at this level and, if not, why not? Does the sum of individual demands match available quantities? How is output divided between consumption and investment? What determines the price level?

Macroeconomics is essentially *practical*. It is concerned with deriving the *least-complex view* of the general operation of the economy that is satisfactory for one or another purpose, such as developing a policy to promote full employment.

There is no *single* view of the overall working of the economy that is both simple and suitable for every purpose. For this reason, economists work with a variety of representations or *models* of the economy.

Recap If the economy produced only one good, we could easily judge its overall performance by directly measuring the output of this good and noting whether the economy was producing at capacity, whether its output had increased since last year, and so on. Because a real economy produces thousands of different goods, measuring and analyzing its overall performance is extremely difficult. Macro-economics is a simplified way of viewing the economy as if it produced only one good, total output.

Aggregating Things

The problems of reducing collections of many goods into single aggregates

Now imagine an economy with two goods, corn and cotton, in contrast to the single-good economy described in the preceding section. We wish to take a macroeconomic view of this economy—specifying a single output and a single price level—rather than focus on the differences between the corn and cotton markets. We'll assume that the economy uses money, so dollar prices exist for both corn and cotton.

If output consists of 1 million tons of corn and 250 thousand bales of cotton, we certainly cannot aggregate these quantities into a single "output" by adding them directly, because they are not even expressed in the same units. We could, of course, weigh the cotton to obtain its quantity in tons and thus measure both in the same units. But, we still could not meaningfully add them directly for economic purposes.

Economic Weights

The economic uses of corn and cotton are quite different. There is no reason why society should consider a ton of corn as being "equivalent" in any sense to a ton of cotton. As *physical weights,* a ton of corn and a ton of cotton are equivalent, but as *economic goods* they are not.

The only reasonable measure of equivalence from the economist's point of view is some kind of *relative price.* If a ton of cotton is bought and sold for $200, while a ton of corn is bought and sold for $100, there is evidence that people in the economy value one ton of cotton the same as *two* tons of corn. An appropriate way of aggregating the outputs of corn and cotton would thus be to multiply the number of tons of cotton by two and add the number of tons of corn. We would give a ton of cotton twice the *economic weight* of a ton of corn, because market prices suggest that the community *values* a ton of cotton at twice as much as a ton of corn. For an output of 1 million tons of cotton and 500 thousand tons of corn, our aggregation would give us 2.5 million of what we might call "corn-ton equivalents."

Note that we could have worked from the other end, halving the number of tons of corn and adding the number of tons of cotton, to obtain a measure (1.25 million) in "cotton-ton equivalents." With thousands of different goods in a real economy, there is no "natural" choice for a single good in terms of which to calculate such "equivalents." Hence, we avoid a measure that stresses the role of any one good.

Value Measures

A straightforward way to avoid using one good or another as a reference is to use the *value of output* as our basic measure, multiplying the quantity of each output by its dollar price, and adding the products. For an output of 1 million tons of cotton and 500 thousand tons of corn, at prices of $200 and $100 per ton, respectively, the *value of output* of the economy would be $250 million [= (1,000,000 × $200) + (500,000 × $100)]. But the use of value as our measure introduces a new problem. While a ton of cotton (or corn) means much the same thing from year to year, a dollar does not because prices may change.

Suppose the outputs of cotton and corn each rose by 20 percent, from 1 million tons and 500 thousand tons to 1.2 million tons and 600 thousand tons, respectively, and the prices of cotton and corn remained unchanged at $200 and $100 per ton. If we calculate the various measures, we find that the "corn-ton equivalent" has risen by 20 percent to 3 million (2.5 + 0.5), the "cotton-ton equivalent" by 20 percent to 1.5 million (1.25 + 0.25), and the value of output by 20 percent to $300 million [= (1,200,000 × $200) + (600,000 × $100)]. All measures show a 20 percent increase.

But if, in addition, both prices had risen by, say, 10 percent, to $220 per ton for cotton and $110 per ton for corn (the *relative* price of cotton compared to corn remaining unchanged), the "corn-ton" and "cotton-ton" equivalents would both still show a 20 percent increase, while the value of output would show a 32 percent increase to $330 million [= (1,200,000 × $220) + (600,000 × $100)].

The Price Level

The value measure differs from the quantity measures because the prices of both goods have risen by 10 percent. The dollar is no longer worth what it once was. It now takes $1.10 to buy the same amount of corn *or* cotton *or* any mixture of corn and cotton that could formerly be purchased with $1.00. We can therefore unambiguously refer to a 10 percent increase in the *general price level*.

By allowing for the change in the general price level, however, we can ascertain the *real* change in output from the change in money value. The value of output has risen by 32 percent because the current value is 132/100 of the previous value, while the current price level is 110/100 of the previous price. Dividing the value ratio by the price ratio, 132/100 ÷ 110/100, gives us 132/110 = 1.20 = 120/100, so real output has increased by 20 percent. This is the same as measured by the "equivalents," and is equal to the actual change in the production of both corn and cotton.

Even though we can extract the *change* in real output from changes in the value of output and the price level, we still face the problem of deciding what to call the "units" in which real output is measured.

In the example given, suppose the initial figures refer to 1975, and the later figures to 1976. Previously we took the change in value and adjusted for the change in price. Instead, take the actual value for 1976 ($330 million) and divide by the ratio of 1976 to 1975 prices (by 110/100). The answer is $300 million (= 330 × 100 ÷ 110). This is precisely the figure we obtained for the value of the 1976 output *when prices were the same as in 1975,* and shows a 20 percent increase over the *actual* value of production in 1975 ($250 million).

Thus, if we take the actual value of output in 1976 and divide by the ratio of 1976 to 1975 prices, the result we obtain is the value that would have been associated with 1976 output had that year's *prices* been those of 1975. Therefore, the figure of $300 we obtained can be described as being expressed in *1975 dollars,* because it is based on 1975 prices. Thus, the "units" in which real output is measured in our example are the 1975 dollars.

The second year in our example need not be 1976, but might be 1979, 1968, or any year at all. If we adjust everything by the price ratio between the year in question and 1975, we refer to 1975 as the *base year* in our calculations.

The "As If" Approach

For macroeconomic purposes, therefore, we proceed *as if* the economy produced only a single good.

1. The value of its output (GNP) is the total value of all goods produced in the economy. This value is expressed in dollars, at prices for the period in question. We refer to these as *current dollars* if emphasis is needed.

2. The price of this good is the *general price level,* measured as an *index* relative to the price level in some *base year,* as in the example above.

3. The quantity of this good (*real output* or *real GNP*) is typically measured by adjusting the value of output for the change in the price level relative to the base year. This is expressed in terms of dollars for a particular year, such as *1975 dollars* if 1975 is the base year, or *constant dollars* in nonspecific contexts.

For example, suppose the value of the output of this "single good" was

$270 million in 1975 and $336 million in 1978, and the general price level in 1978, with 1975 = 100, was 112. For 1978, we would then have:

$$\text{output (GNP) in current dollars} = \$336 \text{ million},$$

$$\text{real output (real GNP) in 1975 dollars} = \frac{\$336 \text{ million} \times 100}{112}.$$

Thus, although output in *current dollars* rose from $270 million to $336 million (24 percent), real GNP in *1975 dollars* rose from $270 million to only $300 million (10 percent).

In the examples used in this section, we confined ourselves to cases in which the quantities of all outputs changed in the same proportion, and in which prices, if they changed, also changed in the same proportion. There were no ambiguities at any time: real output and output measured by corn or cotton equivalents all changed in the same proportion. Under such conditions, the following relationship holds exactly:

$$
\begin{array}{l}
\text{output in constant dollars} \\
\text{of base years (real output)}
\end{array}
=
\begin{array}{l}
\text{value of output in current year} \\
\text{divided by index of current year's} \\
\text{price level relative to base year.}
\end{array}
$$

The next section is devoted to the problems that arise when quantity and/or price changes do not all occur in the same proportion.

Recap Because the economy produces a large number of different goods, we can treat it as if it produced one good only if we can aggregate all goods produced into a single measure. Because the price of a good is a representation of its value to the economy, aggregate output can be calculated by weighting the output of each good by the price of that good. Prices change from year to year, however, so we must specify which prices are being used as weights. The value of output is thus said to be expressed in "1975 dollars" or "1978 dollars" depending on whether the prices used in its calculation were those of 1975 or 1978. We can compare outputs in different years directly only if they are measured in terms of the same prices.

Index Numbers

How aggregates are expressed as index numbers, and why these can never be perfect

If the prices of corn and cotton both rise by 20 percent from 1978 to 1979, and these are the only two goods in the economy, there's no doubt that the general price level will also rise by 20 percent.

But what can be said about the general price level if the price of corn rises by 10 percent from 1978 to 1979 and the price of cotton increases by 20 percent? It's obvious that we should consider the general price level to have risen by at least 10 percent because the price of everything has increased by *at least* 10 percent, but by *no more than* 20 percent because nothing has risen by a greater percentage.

Simple Averages

The index of the general price level ought to show a change somewhere between 10 and 20 percent in this case, that is, somewhere between the least and the greatest percentage change in individual prices. One way to obtain a general price index with this essential property would be simply to take the *average* of these two percentage changes—15 percent in the corn-cotton example.

But a simple average is potentially misleading. Suppose people spend 90 percent of their budget on corn, and only 10 percent on cotton. A 10 percent rise in the price of corn will then have more effect on what can be bought with a given budget than will a 20 percent rise in the price of cotton. Given a budget of $100 at the original prices, $90 will be spent on corn, $10 on cotton. To buy the same amount of corn at the new prices will cost $99, to buy the same amount of cotton will cost $12. Thus, it will cost $111 to buy the same things at the new prices that $100 bought at the old. This is an increase of 11 percent, which is between 10 percent and 20 percent, but much closer to 10 percent because corn is more important in the budget.

Weights

A simple average of two things is obtained by halving each of the things and adding. The simple average of 10 percent and 20 percent is $(\frac{1}{2} \times 10\%) + (\frac{1}{2} \times 20\%) = 15\%$. In a simple average we give equal weights ($\frac{1}{2}$ and $\frac{1}{2}$) to both things. In a *weighted* average, we do not necessarily give equal weights, although the sum of the weights must always add up to one, as do $\frac{1}{2}$ and $\frac{1}{2}$. The obvious choice for computing a price-level change would thus be to take a weighted average of the price changes of the individual goods, with weights expressing their relative importance. In the corn-cotton example we would give corn a weight of 9/10 (because it is 90 percent of the budget) and cotton a weight of 1/10. A weighted average of the two price changes would then be $(9/10 \times 10\%) + (1/10 \times 20\%) = 11\%$. This is the same percentage by which the dollar cost of purchasing the original quantities of corn and cotton has increased.

A weighted average can easily be extended to cover any number of goods, with the weights always adding up to unity.

Index Numbers

It's common practice to compute a weighted average of this kind in a slightly different way. Instead of concentrating on percentage changes, we concentrate on relative *levels*. Denote all prices for 1975 (the base year) by 100. The 1976 price of corn is then 110 in these same units, and the 1976 price of cotton is 120. By taking a weighted average of the two price levels in 1976, we obtain $(9/10 \times 110) + (1/10 \times 120) = 111$. The result of this computation is an *index number* or, specifically in this case, a *price index*. It shows the 1976 price level to be 11 percent higher than that of 1975. When we refer to a *price level* in economics, we are normally referring to an index number for prices computed in this manner.

A price index may not cover *all* prices. Many price indexes are computed this way for a group of prices covering only part of the economy. The best known is the *consumer price index* (or "cost of living" index). This index of prices of consumer goods uses weights corresponding to *relative household expenditures* on these items. There is also a *wholesale price index,* covering raw materials, farm products, and some manufactured goods weighted according to their importance to the overall economy, not simply to households. Several indexes of stock market prices also exist, each of which attempts to summarize the general level of prices of thousands of corporate stocks.

The price index that attempts to represent the general level of *all* prices in the United States is known as the *GNP deflator*. It is an index applied to GNP in current dollars to obtain real GNP, or GNP in constant dollars.

The Index-Number Problem

Any index is only a "best" indicator of the events it is attempting to chart. There is no *perfect* index number.

The greatest problem with index numbers is that they depend heavily on the properties of the base year to which they refer, and the inferences to be drawn may vary if that base is changed. This is especially true if prices or quantities of different goods change in markedly different proportions from year to year.

Consider an economy producing two goods, apples and bananas, for which quantities, prices, and values of output are as shown in Table 19.1 for each of the three years 1950, 1960, and 1970. In 1950, because the value of outputs of the goods are equal, an index with base 1950 will weight both prices equally. Because prices are the same in 1970 as in 1950, and because the index for 1960 is given by $(\frac{1}{2} \times 80) + (\frac{1}{2} \times 120) = 100$, the price index with base 1950 is 100 in every year.

Now, compute the price index with 1960 as the base year. Outputs of the two goods in 1960 were valued at $4 million and $24 million, giving total 1960 output of $28 million and weights of $\frac{1}{7}$ ($= \frac{4}{28}$) and $\frac{6}{7}$ ($= \frac{24}{28}$). The computation is shown in Table 19.2.

Finally, compute the price index with 1970 as the base. The weights will be $\frac{4}{5}$ and $\frac{1}{5}$, and the index will obviously be 100 for 1950. For 1960, the prices of the two goods, with $1970 = 100$, are 80 and 120, giving the price index for 1960 as $(\frac{4}{5} \times 80) + (\frac{1}{5} \times 120) = 88$.

Table 19.1
Price-Quantity Data

Year	Quantities (thousands of tons)		Prices ($ ton)		Value of output ($ millions)		
	Apples	Bananas	Apples	Bananas	Apples	Bananas	Total
1950	100	100	100	100	10	10	20
1960	50	200	80	120	4	24	28
1970	200	50	100	100	20	5	25

Table 19.2
Price Index with 1960 Base.
Prices, relative to 1960 = 100

Year	Apples	Bananas	Index value
1950	125	83.3	$(1/7 \times 125) + (6/7 \times 83.3) = 89.3$
1960	100	100.0	$(1/7 \times 100) + (6/7 \times 100) = 100$
1970	125	83.3	$(1/7 \times 125) + (6/7 \times 83.3) = 89.3$

Table 19.3
Comparison of Price Indexes

Year	Price index with base		
	1950	1960	1970
1950	100	89.3	100
1960	100	100.0	88
1970	100	89.3	100

We can now assemble all three price indexes in Table 19.3. Immediately we see the inconsistent results. Price indexes with base 1950 show no change in the price level, price indexes with base 1960 show the price level *higher* in 1960 than in 1950 or 1970, while price indexes with base 1970 show the price level *lower* in 1960 than in 1950 or 1970. Note that, when the prices are the same, as in 1950 and 1970 (or change in the same proportion), the change of base has no effect on the relationship of the indexes for those years.

Generally speaking, there is nothing we can do about such inconsistencies. In a particular case we might argue that a specific base year was an inappropriate choice, perhaps because the economy was known to be in an unusual situation, but the general problem is always with us. As these inconsistencies between indexes with different bases diminish, there is less variation occurring in relative prices or relative quantities from year to year. If either the quantities or prices consistently change in the same proportion, the inconsistencies disappear. In using price indexes at the conceptual level, we assume that the variations in the relative prices or quantities are small enough to eliminate inconsistency problems.

Quantity Indexes

Although we have concentrated on price indexes, it is possible to construct *quantity indexes* as well. In these we weight *quantities* relative to base year values of 100 instead of prices. For the example just given (see Table 19.1), we could compute quantity indexes with base 1950 and would find indexes of 125 [= (½ × 50) + (½ × 200)] for 1960 and 1970. A well-known quantity index is the *index of industrial production,* which measures output in mining and manufacturing and is computed this way.

There are two main methods for computing changes in real output. One is to take the value of current output and divide or *deflate* this by an appropriate price index to find the value of output in base-year dollars. The other is to compute a quantity index in terms of base-year weights.

In our previous example, we can compute the value of output in 1950 dollars (see Table 19.1). Because the price index with base 1950 happens to remain unchanged, values in 1950 dollars and current dollars are the same—$20 million for 1950, $28 million for 1960, and $25 million in 1970. Thus, on this computation, real output rose from 1950 to 1960, then fell from 1960 to 1970. Quantity indexes with base 1950 are 125 for 1960 and 125 for 1970. Using this computation, output rose from 1950 to 1960, but did not change from 1960 to 1970.

This is the same type of inconsistency that gives different results for different base years, even though both quantity and price indexes are to the same base. The reason is that the *value of output* for a given year *reflects both prices and quantities* for that year, but the *price index* reflects only *prices* for that year, and the *quantity index* only *quantities*. From 1960 to 1970, the value of output fell because the fall in the price of bananas reduced the value of banana output by more than the rise in the price of apples increased the value of apple output. The quantity index registers no change, of course. The price index shows no change over this period because the shares of the two goods in total output value *in the base year* resulted in the two opposite price changes canceling each other out.

Economists have lived with index-number problems for a long time. While we usually assume that changes do not introduce major inconsistencies, we must be wary of index numbers over periods in which major changes in the structure of the economy have taken place.

Recap If prices of different goods change in different proportions, what can we say about the "general" change in prices? The normal method is to compute a weighted average of individual price changes, giving greater weights to those goods representing a higher proportion of total expenditure than to those representing a lower proportion. The result is a price index that is always expressed with reference to a base year—the year whose expenditures provide the weights for the index. Quantity indexes can be derived in the same way. The fact that indexes with different bases will generally give different results (unless all prices or quantities change by the same percentage) represents an irreducible degree of imprecision with which we must live.

Capsule Supplement 19.1 **Index Numbers in the United States**

Two of the best-known price index series in the United States are the indexes of *consumer prices* and *wholesale prices*. Both are currently computed with 1967 as base—written 1967 = 100. These series antedate 1967, of course. Prior to the most recent revision, the base was the average of prices from 1957 through 1959. Because confidence in any index-number series declines the greater the difference between the structure of the economy in the base year(s) and the year under consideration (most often the current year), series are revised periodically to new bases. These revisions usually include other improvements, such as increasing the number of goods covered.

The consumer price index has been calculated successively on bases 1917–19 (from 1913 through 1935), 1934–36 (1936 through 1949), 1947–49 (1950 through 1963), 1957–59 (1964 through 1970) and 1967 (1971 to date) with some shorter intermediate revisions. When a series is revised, the new series is joined to the old. The consumer price index for 1965 is given in terms of the 1957–59 base, for example. To join this to a series based on 1967 prices, we calculate the 1967 index using base 1957–59, then divide the entire 1957–59 series (including 1965) by this index to obtain a continuous series. Subindexes for various commodity groups are also published. There are, for example, consumer price subindexes for such groups as food, housing, and transportation.

Institutional constraints may keep an index in an antiquated form. The official index of prices received and paid by farmers is still computed with base 1910–14 because various agricultural acts mandate that price supports be based on relative price ratios in these particular years.

One of the best-known price indexes is the "Dow-Jones." This is a relatively unsophisticated index of the prices of a fixed selection of common stocks on the New York Stock Exchange. While a more sophisticated index with far greater coverage is published by the New York exchange itself, the Dow-Jones retains its popularity because most people are used to seeing it and can detect immediately from it whether stock prices are high or low relative to average levels or to their expectations.

Among quantity indexes, the best known is the Federal Reserve Board's Index of Industrial Production. This index is closely scrutinized for any signs of recession in the economy because it is available before the more complete statistic—real GNP—becomes available.

Aggregating Decisions

The greatest aggregation problem is that of aggregating decisions

Aggregating prices and quantities, with the associated problems of index numbers, is only one dimension of the simplification that characterizes macroeconomics. Another is the simplification that results from considering relationships among large aggregates (national income, total investment, total consumption, and so on) as opposed to relationships among variables relevant to individual decision-makers.

Such relationships among aggregates are *artificially constructed* by economists. Over the next few chapters, for example, we shall proceed as if households collectively determine their total consumption expenditure in relation to aggregate household income. In actuality, of course, households determine their consumption expenditures individually on the basis of their own respective incomes. Households as a group are not even aware of what aggregate household income and total expenditure are. Indeed, without the statistical-gathering efforts of the U.S. Department of Commerce, *no one* would know the values of these aggregates—and no one *did* know these values until the 1930s.

The Aggregation Problem

How do we aggregate *decision processes?* This question lies at the heart of what is known as the *aggregation problem.* If we know exactly how the individual expenditures for each of 1,000 individuals will change when their respective incomes change, can we predict how the *aggregate expenditures* of these 1,000 people will change when their aggregate income changes?

The answer, which may seem surprising, is that we generally cannot. This is because the same aggregate income, *distributed in different ways,* would lead to different expenditures. Consider a population of two people: Peter, who spends exactly half of whatever income he receives, and Paul, who spends all of his income. An aggregate income of $1,000 will lead to an aggregate expenditure of $500 if it all goes to Peter, $1,000 if it all goes to Paul, $750 if it is divided evenly, with various expenditures between $500 and $1,000 for intermediate distributions. For the same reason, a given total expenditure may be associated with a variety of aggregate incomes—a $750 expenditure can come from $1,000 aggregate income divided evenly, from

$1,500 aggregate income distributed all to Peter, or from $750 income distributed all to Paul.

Note that if both Peter and Paul behaved in the "same" way (spent 75 percent of their income), distribution would not matter, and there would be no aggregation problem.

Thinking in Aggregates

When macroeconomic analysis first appeared, economists had considerable knowledge of individual behavior patterns and, naturally enough, attempted to establish aggregate patterns by inference from individual patterns. The aggregation problem thus caused much concern initially.

Modern macroeconomists, by contrast, recognize that there is no easy way around the aggregation problem and choose to ignore it by *thinking in aggregates* from the outset, and *using empirical investigation* to derive relationships among these aggregates. These procedures are greatly facilitated by the statistics we now have available on such things as aggregate household income and aggregate household expenditure. From these, the aggregate relationship between household expenditure and income (known as the *consumption function*) is determined by comparing the actual values for the two aggregates under as many differing circumstances as we can.

The microeconomic theory of the individual household or firm is still used as a *guide* to the types of relationships that might be expected to exist among aggregates, but only as a guide. In the final analysis, relationships among aggregates are established *on their own terms* by empirical methods.

Recap Individual households make individual decisions about what to do with their incomes. In macroeconomics we proceed as if households in the aggregate make a single decision about what to do with aggregate household income. The justification for this is essentially empirical and practical—we compare aggregate household expenditure and aggregate household income under alternative circumstances and develop models of macroeconomic behavior on the basis of the relationships we observe.

Capsule Supplement 19.2   **The Forest and the Trees**

Prior to the beginning of modern macroeconomics in the late 1930s, it could be said that policy-makers could scarcely see the forest for the trees. Economists were micro-oriented, content to look at the economy as a collection of small units and examine the behavior of individual markets. Only the occasional monetary theorist looked at the economy as a whole, and then only because the effects of money on the economy were essentially dispersed and not concentrated in any one industry or market. Indeed, when the Great Depression hit, there were really no reliable data on the overall operation of the economy.

Macroeconomics, of course, is the technique of looking at the forest rather than the individual trees. Perhaps ironically, it is now so well developed as an analytical basis for policy that many policy-makers never look at the trees anymore. This can bring on its own distortions and dangers in policy-making, just as the earlier failure to take an overall look at the economy did in its time. In 1949, for example, the overall unemployment rate for the United States was 5.9 percent; in 1963 it was 5.7 percent, close to the 1949 level. Taking an entirely macro view and looking only at aggregate unemployment rates, we would conclude that unemployment was high in both years but that the situation was slightly better in 1963 than in 1949. But if we take a more micro view, we see an important difference between the two years in that the unemployment rate for *nonwhites* was 8.9 percent in 1949—high enough—but was an even higher 10.8 percent in 1963 even though the overall unemployment rate was slightly lower than it had been in 1949. Would we necessarily conclude that 1963 was a better year than 1949?

Identical values for economic aggregates may hide great disparities in the distribution of income, in the impact of unemployment on different groups of persons or regions of the country, in the division of national production between weapons systems and improved urban housing, and in the relative outputs of polluting and nonpolluting industrial processes.

The current trend in both economic theory and economic policy is toward a meaningful synthesis of micro and macro approaches. Without the simplifications of macroeconomics, we would lose track of the overall picture, but within that overall picture we cannot avoid looking at vital details. All policy is ultimately connected—all macro policy affects the distribution within the aggregates as well as the level of the aggregates, and all policy directed at the distribution will affect the totals. The art of providing the economic background for policy decisions is to be able to show all the effects without making the story so complex that it cannot be followed by those responsible for policy. We cannot look simultaneously at the forest and all the trees and make clear sense of what we see. So we look separately at the aggregates and the details, and ultimately try to produce a synthesis of the overall picture plus a few appropriately selected details.

The Economy as a Machine

Why it's useful to treat the economy as a machine, and why this can be consistent with nonmechanical behavior by individuals

Macroeconomic simplifications of the economy (which we call macro-models) are predicated on relationships among aggregates and do not take individual behavior into direct account. They are essentially *mechanistic* in character. For example, the economy may be represented by a machinelike model in which, by figuratively turning the knob marked "tax rate" to different values, different levels of output are generated. Some early macromodels were indeed represented by physical machines (Professor A. W. Phillips devised a hydraulic machine for this purpose in the 1950s). Now such representations are provided by programmed computers. Although the economy itself is not a machine, the growing success of macromodels suggests that it can be meaningfully represented by a machinelike model for many purposes.

A basically predictable and mechanical relationship among aggregates in the economy could be due to basically predictable and mechanical behavior on the part of individuals in the economy. Indeed, it may be that people are more like sheep than many humanists and social scientists would like to think, but it doesn't have to be so.

Individual Variety

It is quite possible for individuals to behave in a variety of ways, and yet maintain relatively stable relationships in the aggregate, provided their individual eccentricities are independent of each other.

Suppose, for example, all households spend 90 percent of their income for sure, then toss a coin to see whether they will spend or save the remaining 10 percent. With 70 million households in the United States, we would expect that the number of households who will decide to *spend* the remaining 10 percent will be very close to 35 million. In terms of probability theory, in fact, we would expect the number of such households to lie within 50 thousand either side of 35 million 9,999 times out of 10,000.

If all households have the same income, aggregate expenditure will be within 94.99 percent and 95.01 percent of aggregate income to the above degree of probability. It can be shown that this result holds very closely even if incomes are not distributed evenly, provided the income distribution is unrelated to the decision process.

Hence, although we cannot predict the behavior of any individual household (beyond predicting that it will spend *either* 90 percent *or* 100 percent of its income), we know that the ratio of aggregate expenditure to aggregate income will be stable, for all practical purposes, at 95 percent.

The economy as a machine provides a very workable model, but we may have to go beyond the aggregates and their relationships to assess the specific impact of a given event. A 5 percent decline in aggregate income, for example, might be predicted by the model if a certain policy is adopted. However, a 5 percent decline in aggregate income could mean that *everyone's* income falls by 5 percent, or, alternatively, that 5 percent of the population loses *all* its income while 95 percent of the population remains unaffected. While the human consequences are clearly quite different in the two cases, the model may make no distinction between them.

Ultimate judgments about the desirability of particular policies will thus often require that we look beyond the information provided by a mechanistic macromodel.

Recap Macromodels of the economy are essentially mechanistic. This is not inconsistent with unpredictable behavior by individuals because the random variation among individuals will cancel out over a large population.

Exercises

All questions are based on the following data for an economy in which clothing and food are the only products.

	Price of		Production of	
	Clothing ($/pound)	Food ($/ton)	Clothing (pounds)	Food (tons)
1960	10	80	800	500
1970	8	100	1,000	160

Calculate the following:

1. The value of output in 1960 in current dollars.
2. The value of output in 1970 in current dollars.
3. The percent change in output in current dollars from 1960 to 1970.
4. The price index for 1970 with base 1960.
5. The real output in 1970 expressed in 1960 dollars.
6. The price index for 1960 with base 1970.
7. The real output in 1960 expressed in 1970 dollars.
8. The percent change in real output from 1960 to 1970 in terms of 1960 dollars.
9. The percent change in real output from 1960 to 1970 in terms of 1970 dollars.

For Thought and Discussion

1. The Soviet Union's industrial production index was weighted for many years by relative prices of the various goods at the very beginning of its industrial development. Many Western economists maintained that the index so constructed necessarily exaggerated the extent of Soviet industrial growth. From your knowledge of index numbers, what would you expect to be the basis of this criticism?

2. Should the government watch only the aggregates in the economy and ignore individual industry and sector changes? Why?

3. In the mid-1960s, the Netherlands and Czechoslovakia had about the same population and about the same aggregate output (measured in terms of U.S. dollars). Should the economies be regarded as equivalent? Why?

Chapter 20
The National Accounts

Terms and Concepts

National income accounts
Double counting
Value added
Gross national product
Depreciation
Capital consumption allowance
Net national product
National income
Disposable income
National expenditure
Circular flow of income

The Development and Use of National Accounts

Why we construct and use national accounts

While economy-watchers have long had many indicators to tell them whether economic activity is on the upswing or the downswing, a true measure of the overall output of the economy did not exist until the development of the *national income accounts* in the 1930s.

National income accounting represents an attempt to evaluate the total output of the economy in a meaningful way, using measures that are independent of institutional changes having no effect on the ultimate flow of goods. If, for example, two firms merged, but the composite firm produced exactly what the component firms once produced separately, there should be no change in the measure of total output. The primary aim of the national accounts is to estimate the value of total output as accurately as possible.

In the process of collecting the data required to measure total output, information is obtained regarding such things as (1) the value of output from the various productive sectors (agriculture, manufacturing, retail trade, etc.), (2) the allocation of output among users (households, governments, firms, etc.), and (3) the distribution of output among different types of income-earners (laborers, property owners, etc.).

The national accounts, therefore, consist of a measure of total output, accompanied by a variety of tabulations showing where this output originates and how it is allocated. Moreover, total output may be classified in terms of broad types of goods (consumer durables, consumer nondurables, capital equipment, buildings, etc.), or in a variety of other ways. Different breakdowns are useful for different purposes. An elaborate national accounting system like that of the U.S. Department of Commerce provides many such breakdowns.

The fact that macroeconomic models are built around the national accounts is important for our purposes. It is the total output measured in the national accounts that we regard as the "good" produced by the economy, and it is the various broad items included in the accounts, like "consumption" and "personal income," among which specific quantitative relationships are presumed to hold.

Recap The national accounts represent an attempt to calculate the total value of the economy's output and to describe where this output originates, the broad purposes to which it is put, and how it is divided among different categories of income recipients.

Avoiding Double Counting

Overcoming the chief problem in constructing the national accounts

It would seem that the most straightforward way to ascertain the total value of society's production (GNP) during a particular year is to contact every firm that produced anything during that year, determine the value of what each produced, and sum these values.

This kind of procedure provides a conceptual basis for determining GNP but it cannot be used in the simple manner described because of *double counting*.

The Danger of Duplication

A firm will normally regard the value of its output to be the total receipts obtained from its sales. A food processor who sells 100 thousand packages of frozen peas at $1 per package will count sales as $100,000. But this figure is not a true measure of output because growing the peas was not part of the processor's operations.

Suppose the processor is supplied with fresh peas by a farmer who delivers the amount required for 100 thousand packages of frozen peas at a total cost of $70,000. For the moment, we'll assume that the farmer sells his entire output to the processor.

Now, in conducting our census of total output, we'll send forms to *both* the farmer *and* the food processor, asking each to specify output. If each reports the value of total sales, the farmer will put down $70,000 and the processor $100,000. Thus, $170,000 will be associated with peas whose final value is only $100,000. We would count the value of these peas *twice,* once as the output of the farmer, and once as the output of the processor.

The Elimination of Double Counting

One way to avoid double counting is to count the value of the peas only in the *final stage* of production—to eliminate the farmer's output altogether. This would create a problem, however, if the farmer also sold fresh peas directly to consumers. If we eliminated the farmer's output from our count, we would exclude the value of these fresh peas from GNP. If we added the farmer's total sales to the processor's, we would include the value of the fresh peas but also double count the frozen ones.

The easiest way to illustrate the appropriate method for eliminating double counting is to look at the *complete accounts* for both the farmer and the processor. Let's assume that the farmer has sales of $90,000, of which $70,000 comes from the processor and the rest from final consumers, and that his only expense is labor, which costs $75,000. The processor has sales of $100,000 and two payments—$70,000 for the raw peas and $15,000 for

Table 20.1
Current Accounts of Two Firms

I The Farm

Expenditures		Receipts	
Wages	$75,000	Sales to processor	$70,000
Profit	15,000	Sales to consumers	20,000
Total	$90,000	Total	$90,000

II The Processor

Expenditures		Receipts	
Materials	$ 70,000	Sales to consumers	$100,000
(peas from farmer)			
Wages	15,000		
Profit	15,000		
Total	$100,000	Total	$100,000

labor. In each case, the surplus of receipts over expenditures will be regarded as a profit accruing to the proprietor.

The simple current accounts for these two firms are given in Table 20.1. Note that those peas in danger of being double counted actually appear *three times* in these accounts—as a sale by the farmer, as a purchase by the processor, and as incorporated in the processor's sales to consumers. Two of these three times, they appear in counterbalancing transactions—the sale by the farmer that is also a purchase by the processor.

We can thus eliminate double counting by deducting from the sales of a firm any purchases of raw materials from other firms.

If we do this here, we count the *full* sales of $90,000 by the farmer (who has not bought materials or anything else from other firms). But for the processor we count sales *less* purchases from other firms, or $30,000 (= $100,000 − $70,000). These two amounts total $120,000. This is exactly equal to total pea sales to consumers ($20,000 fresh from the farm plus $100,000 in frozen form), and also equal to total incomes ($90,000 in wages for both firms plus $30,000 in profits for both firms), a relationship that is not accidental.

Value Added

The value of a firm's sales less the value of raw materials and other current purchases from other firms is known as *value added*. This concept is nicely illustrated by the processing firm in our example—it has taken peas worth $70,000 and converted them into frozen peas worth $100,000, adding $30,000 to the value of the original peas by the processing operation.

We assumed that the farmer in our example used no inputs obtained from other firms. Had he purchased, say, fertilizer and insecticide, the value of these would be deducted from sales to obtain his gross value added. Purchases from other firms are typically things like raw materials and component parts, although they may also be services like communications or transportation. We *do not deduct* direct payments to persons in the form of wages or profits.

Because it measures the difference in value between the things coming into the firm and those going out, value added shows how much production is carried out within the firm.

Computing GNP

By treating the gross value added as the output of each firm, we completely avoid double counting because every potentially double-counted item will appear as a purchase from some other firm and, as such, will be eliminated.

GNP in a closed economy (an economy that has no transactions with the rest of the world) will be equal to the sum of gross values added by all firms.

In our example, the sum of the values added is also equal to the value of *final sales* (sales to consumers, assuming there is no government) because all other sales must be to firms, and these are canceled out. Hence, in a simple closed economy with no government:

$$\text{GNP} = \text{value added} = \text{value of final sales to consumers.}$$

Recap To measure the value of the national product, we cannot merely add up the value of everything produced in the economy because some materials and components would be counted more than once. We eliminate double counting by subtracting the value of purchases from other firms from the value of output of each firm to obtain value added. The sum of all values added is equal to the sales of goods and services to final consumers and constitutes the gross national product.

Capsule Supplement 20.1   **Instant GNP**

To make the collection of national income accounts practical, many arbitrary decisions about what to include and what to exclude had to be made in the early stages of their development. The results of these early decisions are frequently found to be inappropriate in light of changing social and economic patterns, as illustrated by the following recipe for "Instant GNP."

Let every man whose wife, mother, or daughter keeps house full time formally employ her as a housekeeper at 50 percent of his income, with each paying half of the expenses of the joint household. The man could become a bona fide employer by obtaining an employer identification number from the Internal Revenue Service and paying an employer's Social Security contribution on her behalf. Under standard statistical procedures in the United States, her pay would be treated as wages and added to the income side of GNP, increasing it by about 35 percent. The equality of aggregate incomes and expenditures would be maintained by counting his payment as the purchase of personal services. Half of *his* former expenditure on household goods and services would consequently appear as *her* personal consumption expenditure.

Without any change whatsoever in the *actual* goods and services produced in the economy, there would be a huge increase in statistically recorded GNP. This increase would result because the national income accounts normally do not include services performed by housewives in the home, even though the equivalent services performed by paid domestic workers are included.

There would be other statistical changes as well. The labor force would increase by about 45 percent, and the unemployment rate would be cut by one-third. There would be real changes in the economy, as well as statistical ones. Under existing income-tax rules, while the woman's pay would be taxable income, the man's payment would not be tax deductible as an expense. The household would thus be taxed on 150 percent of the man's income; more taxes would be paid and there would be less disposable income. This redistribution of income from the private to the public sector could potentially lead to major changes in the operation of the economy and in society's ultimate "output mix."

Capital Equipment, GNP, and NNP

Why capital items require special treatment

To calculate GNP we must be careful to exclude the value of components and materials sold by one firm to another. Like the farmer's peas in our example, we assume that such "intermediate goods" are physically transformed or used up in the production process.

If all interfirm sales are of components and materials, then aggregate sales minus aggregate interfirm sales equals total value added and thus gross national product. A special case arises, however, when a machine or some other piece of capital equipment is sold. Because such items are sold by firms, and nearly always purchased by firms, capital equipment sales are primarily interfirm sales.

But, if an airline buys a new jumbo jet on January 1, 1979, its production of travel services during 1979 does not "incorporate" the aircraft, because the jet will still be in existence at the end of the year. On the other hand, an aircraft that has been used for a year is different from, and has less value than, a new aircraft.

What has been incorporated into the airline's production is not the aircraft itself, but its *services* over the year. However, this does not alter the fact that the aircraft manufacturer sold the jet itself. An interfirm transaction of some kind has been involved—and one we need to sort out.

Current and Capital Transactions

We referred to the simple accounts in the preceding section as *current* accounts. The term *current* means that all items included can be *fully assigned* to the operations of the year to which they refer. Obviously, the entire cost of a jumbo jet, which will be used for several years, cannot be fully assigned to the operations of any one year.

So, while the value of the aircraft does not appear in the current account of the airline, it does appear in the current account of the aircraft manufacturer as part of that firm's sales the year it is sold. Thus, when we compute GNP by summing values added, the value is *not* canceled out, as it would be for items like fuel or raw materials.

Sales of capital equipment, even to other firms, are not canceled in computing GNP. They count as final sales.

Thus, the term *final sales* in the national accounts refers to all sales other than interfirm sales on current account. For a closed economy, final sales includes sales to (1) households, (2) firms, and (3) the government.

Although the initial cost of capital equipment is not "incorporated" into output of the first, or any one year, the *decrease in value* resulting from its use over any given year can clearly be assigned to that year's operations. If an aircraft costs $3 million and will last for fifteen years, we can expect its value to decline by something like $200 thousand per year. This decline (known as *depreciation* or *capital consumption*) represents the value of capital "used up" producing current output, and should, therefore, appear in the current accounts. If we deduct only currently used materials and components from a firm's sales, we obtain *gross value added,* as in the preceding section. By deducting capital consumption for the year as well, we arrive at *net value added.*

Computation of NNP

The sum of gross value added over the economy is GNP. The sum of net value added is known as *net national product* (NNP). In principle, we should measure the total output of the economy by NNP rather than by GNP, because this takes into account the fact that the economy uses up a portion of its capital stock during the year.

In practice, however, it's difficult to accurately estimate "true" capital consumption over a year. Actual depreciation allowances made by firms are determined by accounting conventions and income-tax rules, and are not generally consistent with the procedures economists consider most

Table 20.2
Current and Capital Accounts—
Utopia Airlines Corporation

I Current Account

Expenditures		Receipts	
1. Fuel and supplies	$ 20,000	5. Passenger receipts	$100,000
2. Wages	50,000		
3. Profit paid to owner	10,000		
4. Depreciation to capital account	20,000		
Total	$100,000	Total	$100,000

II Capital Account

Assets	Dec. 31, 1978	Dec. 31, 1979
Aircraft	$300,000	$280,000
Depreciation funds accrued	—	20,000
Total	$300,000	$300,000

Gross value added: $80,000 (item 5 less item 1).
Net value added: $60,000 (item 5 less items 1 and 4).

appropriate. *Although we can actually measure GNP, but can only estimate NNP, we normally use GNP as our basic measure of output.*

Even though a firm does not include the purchase of capital items in its current account, it could maintain a separate capital account for this purpose to note the value of such items at the end of each period. The firm could keep the actual value of its capital intact by transferring depreciation funds (kept as securities) from the current account to balance the decline in value of its capital from year to year. Hence, when a piece of equipment finally wears out, these funds, in an uncomplicated situation, would be just sufficient to replace it. Table 20.2 shows hypothetical current and capital accounts for a newly established, one-aircraft airline.

We can now summarize, for a closed economy, the relationships among GNP, NNP, final sales, and capital equipment:

GNP = the sum of gross values added over the whole economy
 = total final sales.
NNP = the sum of net values added over the economy
 = GNP less capital consumption allowances.

Recap Although items of capital equipment are usually sold by firms to other firms, their value is included in the calculation of "gross value added" because they are not completely "used up" in production, like raw materials and components. Hence, all sales of capital equipment are treated as final sales and counted in national output. In principle, we acknowledge that capital is partly "used up" over the period of our accounts. In practice, however, the measurement of capital consumption is difficult, so we conventionally measure output as gross national product (GNP) from which capital consumption is not deducted. If we deduct capital consumption from GNP, we obtain net national product (NNP).

National Income

The concept of national income
and its relationship
to national output

National income is the sum of all incomes derived from the operation of the economy over a year. Let's assume, for the moment, that the economy's capital does not depreciate so gross and net value added are equal everywhere, making GNP equal to NNP. We shall refer to total output under these conditions simply as *national product*.

To produce goods, a firm uses resources that are purchased directly in a market economy. During the course of a year, a firm makes wage, interest, and rental payments that represent incomes to their recipients. The residual—the difference between the receipts from the sale of output and payments for materials, labor, and the use of property—is profit, and represents part, if not all, of the income received by the firm's "owner."

Thus, the value of a firm's total output is necessarily equal to the sum of the dollar values of:

1. purchases (of raw materials and components) from other firms;
2. payments (such as wages, interest, rent, royalties, and so on) for the use of resources; and
3. the residual profit, equal to total receipts less purchases and payments.

Purchases are the interfirm transactions that are subtracted from the value of the output to give "value added." Payments and the residual profit comprise the incomes received by those involved in the firm's operations; therefore, these accounts must sum to the firm's value added.

Defining National Income

In an economy with no government in which all resources are privately owned by households, all incomes are derived from the sale of resource

Table 20.3
National Accounts of a Two-Firm
Economy

Aunt Mabel's Manufacturing Company
(Figures in billions of dollars)

Sales to households	80	
Sales to agriculture (interfirm)	20	
Total sales (= value of total output)		100
Materials purchased (from agriculture)	50	
Wages paid	35	
Total payments		85
Residual profit (sales less payments)		15
Total sales	100	
Less purchases from other firms	50	
Value added		50
Wages paid	35	
Profits	15	
Income from firm's operations		50

services to firms or from residual profits. Thus, the sum of resource payments and profits over the economy must equal the total of all incomes received by households, that is, *national income*. But the sum of these items within each firm is equal to the firm's value added. Consequently, the sum over all firms is equal to the sum of the values added over all firms, or *national product*. Hypothetical accounting relationships for an economy with two firms are shown in Tables 20.3, 20.4, and 20.5.

Therefore, in a simple economy with no capital consumption or government:

National income = the sum of all factor payments plus the sum of
all residual profits
⇒ the sum of values added over all firms
= national product.

What happens if we introduce capital consumption allowances? The answer is relatively simple because such allowances *generate no income*. If we refer back to Table 20.2, we see that the incomes generated by the airline consist of wages plus profits, or total sales less materials purchased from other firms *less depreciation allowances*. In other words, if capital consumption occurs, the sum of incomes would be equal to *net,* not gross, *national product*.

Table 20.4
National Accounts of a Two-
Firm Economy

Uncle Shorty's Farm
(Figures in billions of dollars)

Sales to households	100	
Sales to manufacturing (interfirm)	50	
Total sales (= value of total output)		150
Materials purchased (from manufacturing)	20	
Wages paid	90	
Total payments		110
Residual profit (sales less payments)		40
Total sales	150	
Less purchases from other firms	20	
Value added		130
Wages paid	90	
Profits	40	
Income from firm's operation		130

Table 20.5
National Accounts of a Two-Firm
Economy

Aggregation of Both Firms
(Figures in billions of dollars)

National product = sum of values added = 50 + 130 = 180
= sales to final buyers (households) = 80 + 100 = 180
= total sales less interfirm sales = 250 − 70 = 180
= total wages plus total profits = 125 + 55 = 180
= national income

Note that there is no depreciation of capital in this economy, so gross and net outputs are equal. All payments for the use of resources are in the form of wages, so wages and profits are the only forms in which incomes are received. There are no government nor foreign economic transactions.

Of course, if and when the airline *replaces* the original aircraft, or buys an additional one, income will be generated within the airline industry. In any event, for an economy with capital consumption but no government:

National income = the total of all incomes paid
= the sum of *net* values added over the economy
= NNP.

Recap The value added by a firm is equal to the incomes paid out by the firm, including the profits of its owners. Consequently, in a simple economy, with no government, national income (the sum of all incomes paid out) will equal national product. This outcome must be modified if there is capital consumption.

The Government Sector

How the government sector complicates things

If the government did nothing more than operate the post office to just break even, we could fit the government sector into the accounts in the same way we fit an individual firm.

The market value of the post office's services represents its output, the same as for a private firm. To produce this output, materials and components purchased from firms, as well as the services of privately owned resources, are used. As with a private firm, the cost of materials and components is deducted from the value of output to give the value added by the post office. This amount is added to the total value added in the private sector to give national product.

Government Value Added

Given our assumption that the post office breaks even, its value added is exactly equal to wages, rent, and interest paid to individuals. Hence, the addition of these to the sum of incomes paid out by the private sector gives national income, which is equal to national product.

Because postal services are "sold" to firms as well as to households, some of the post office output might be used in private-sector production. But because the value of this output would already have been deducted in determining the value added by private firms, there would be no double counting.

Nonmarket Output

Let us now expand our discussion to include other government activities—the provision of defense, police, education, etc. Because the "output" of each such activity is not sold in any market, we must decide how to attach a value to it. It is common practice to value such output in terms of the materials and factor services that have gone into it.

Thus, the value added by police services is represented by the wages of police officers, rents paid for police stations, etc., and is simply summed with the total value added in the private sector to determine national product. Moreover, such wages and rents are added to factor payments that originate in the private sector to determine national income. Because the addition to national income is equal to the addition to national output, it would seem that the private-sector accounts remain unaffected by the government's operations.

The Type of Tax Is Important

In fact, the private-sector accounts may be affected in a variety of ways, depending on *how* the government collects the revenue to finance its operations. Let's suppose the private sector produces output worth $100 billion annually. Assuming no capital depreciation, national product and national income are both $100 billion. A government suddenly comes into existence and hires workers for wages of $5 billion. We'll assume that these workers produce services valued at cost ($5 billion), and that they were previously unemployed so private sector output is unaffected. The addition of government activity thus causes national income to rise from $100 billion to $105 billion.

But the government must somehow raise $5 billion to pay its wage bill. Among the various ways of doing this, two illustrate contrasting impacts on the national income accounts:

1. Imposing a 5 percent sales tax on the final output of the private sector.
2. Imposing income taxes on all incomes just sufficient to bring in the needed amount.

In the first case, assuming no change in the real output of the private sector, *the effect of the sales tax is to increase the market price of all privately produced final goods by 5 percent.* The $5 billion increase in the value of private output (at market prices) will be paid to the government as sales tax, leaving $100 billion to be distributed as incomes, just as before. Because the government operations themselves add $5 billion to both national output and national income, national output will equal $110 billion, but national income will equal only $105 billion.

In the second case, the market value of private output is unaffected. National output will be $105 billion and national income *before tax* will be $105 billion. But individuals will pay $5 billion in income taxes, so their *disposable income* (that remaining after the payment of personal taxes) will be only $100 billion. These two cases are presented in Table 20.6.

Price Effects

Even though the economy produces *exactly the same goods and services in both cases,* national product is $110 billion in one case and only $105 billion in the other. Because the same outputs are valued at $110 billion in one case and $105 in the other, the discrepancy must be due to a *difference in market prices.* This difference, of course, comes from the sales tax in the first case.

Some countries (not the United States) report their national accounts

Table 20.6
Comparison of the National Income
Accounts by Government Financing
Methods
(Figures in billions of dollars)

	Government expenditure financed by	
	Sales tax	Income tax
1. Private output at market prices	105	100
2. Less sales tax	5	—
3. Incomes from private sector	100	100
4. Value added (= income generated in government)	5	5
5. National product (line 1 + line 4)	110	105
6. National income (line 3 + line 4)	105	105
7. Less income tax	—	5
8. Disposable income	105	100

with two figures for national product: *national product at market prices* (including sales and similar taxes), and *national product at factor cost* (excluding these taxes). In our example, national product at factor cost is $105 billion in both cases.

To complete our comparison, let's look at the relationship between income and expenditure. In both cases there is private output worth $100 billion at *pretax prices* to be purchased out of income, and $5 billion in government services *provided free*.

In the sales-tax case, individuals in both sectors received $105 billion in income, all of which they were free to spend, and there was $105 billion of private output at market prices including the tax. For their $105 billion, consumers received private goods worth $100 billion at factor cost, plus government services worth $5 billion.

In the income-tax case, individuals in both sectors received $105 billion in income, but only $100 billion of their income was disposable income that could be spent on private goods. The output of private goods was $100 billion, with market prices remaining at pre-government levels, and the output of free government services was $5 billion.

Real Flows the Same

Thus, the flow of "real" goods and services is unaffected by the method of finance. If we (1) take disposable incomes, (2) adjust them for price differences, and (3) add free government services, we obtain the same *"real" effective income* in both cases, as shown in Table 20.7.

Table 20.7
Further Comparison of the
National Income Accounts
by Government Financing Methods
(Figures in billions of dollars)

	Sales tax	Income tax
1. Disposable Income	105	100
2. Price change	+5%	—
3. "Real" disposable income		
(line 1 adjusted to original prices)	100	100
4. Free government services	5	5
5. "Real" effective income	105	105

Line 5 represents the value of goods and services received by members of the economy at pre-government prices, whether purchased in the market or provided free by the government.

These figures are derived from Table 20.6. For the price change, see the text.

In actual national income accounts, sales taxes and similar "indirect" taxes are excluded from national income because they do not represent anyone's income at any stage. Alternatively, we do not exclude income taxes because individuals normally include these taxes in their view of income. This distinction is merely convention because one's income (in the sense of the amount available to spend without using up wealth) is really *disposable income*. It is disposable income after adjustment for prices (*real disposable income*) that remains the same regardless of how the government finances its operations.

Whatever the logical merits of this convention, it remains that GNP, as measured by the United States, contains both capital consumption allowances and indirect (sales-type) taxes. Accordingly, from GNP, we subtract capital consumption allowances to obtain net national product, then indirect taxes to obtain national income.

Not all national income goes directly to individuals. For example, *undistributed corporate profits*, while nominally owned by stockholders, remain under the control of corporations. Similarly, *taxes on corporate profits* are deducted from corporate accounts before payments are made to individuals, and thus do not form part of personal incomes. In the United States, *Social Security taxes* are treated as beyond the control of the individuals who may later receive benefits from them. Like undistributed corporate profits, they are excluded from personal incomes. On the other hand, *transfer payments* from the government to private individuals are included in personal income, but not in national income because they do not represent payments for current productive services. Thus, we obtain *personal income* by subtracting undistributed corporate profits, corporate taxes, and Social

Figure 20.1
Relationship of the major components of the national income accounts for the
United States in 1977, including gross national product, net national product,
national income, personal income, and disposable personal income.

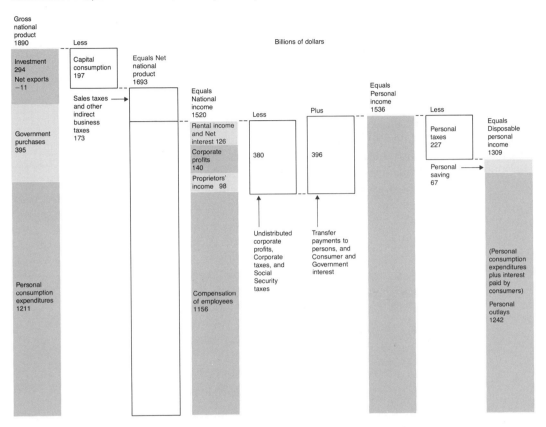

Security taxes from national income, and adding transfer payments received by individuals.

If we then subtract personal income taxes from personal income, we
obtain *disposable personal income,* that part of society's total income over
which individuals have final control. Figure 20.1 shows the relationship
among the main components of the national income accounts for the United
States in 1977.

Recap The government sector buys resources on the market, then supplies its
output to the economy "for free." This introduces complications into the national
income accounts, some of which change depending on whether the government
finances its operations by sales taxes or income taxes. These complications arise
from the conventional treatment of these taxes in the accounts.

Output, Income, and Expenditure

**How we can view the accounts
in three different ways
and visualize total income
as a circular flow**

Now that we've examined the relationship between national product and national income from the production side, we can gain an even better understanding of the economy's performance by looking at this relationship from the expenditure side.

Every good that passes through the market has both a buyer and a seller. So far we've focused our attention on transactions from the viewpoint of the seller, from whose receipts the factors of production are paid.

Instead of computing national product by summing the respective values added by sellers, we can look at things from the buyer's side. Specifically, we can compute national expenditure by summing the value of purchases for final use by all firms and individuals (omitting purchases of materials and components).

For a closed economy with no government sector, we would have the following relationships:

	Output Approach		Expenditure Approach
Take:	Value of total sales	=	Value of total purchases
Subtract:	Sales of materials and components	=	Purchases of materials and components
To obtain:	National product (Final output)	=	National expenditure (Purchases for final use)

Purchases for *final use* are relatively easy to identify. All purchases by *households* (consumption) are for final use, as are all purchases of *new capital equipment* (investment) by firms. All purchases by firms other than capital equipment are presumed to be for use in production, not for final use. Thus, we can determine *national expenditure* (and thus national output) by adding *personal consumption expenditure* and *investment expenditure by private firms*.

The Government as a Purchaser

But what if there's a government sector? Typical government services are not sold on the market, and thus do not correspond to any expenditure by members of the economy. In fact, such services are free to individuals. On the other hand, because the government must buy goods and factor services to produce its output, the services are not free to society as a whole.

We can solve the problem of the government sector by regarding the government as a *final purchaser*. This is equivalent to assuming that the government purchases its own output *on behalf of* households. Because the value of the government's total output is considered to be equal to that of the goods and services it uses to produce the output, we obtain total national expenditure by adding government expenditures on goods and services to personal consumption and business investment expenditures.

Foreign Trade

If the economy engages in foreign trade, there's a potential difference between national product and national expenditure that does not arise in a closed economy. Although everything represented by a sale must also be represented by a purchase, the seller may be in the United States and the buyer in Brazil. Similarly, some of the purchases made by United States residents may correspond to sales in Italy. Thus, although *world product* must equal *world expenditure, national product* (the value of production and sales by firms in a particular country) need not be equal to *national expenditure* (expenditure by the country's residents).

For most countries most of the time, however, total sales abroad (exports) are very nearly equal to total purchases abroad (imports). If the two are identical, the output sold abroad is equal in value to the expenditure on foreign goods, and the two accounts cancel each other. Some countries—those receiving massive foreign aid, for example—have national expenditures that exceed their national products, while others have national products that exceed their national expenditures. At the peak of its foreign-aid program (1947), the United States' national product exceeded its national expenditure by $12 billion (4 percent of GNP).

The Circular Flow of Income

Given the agreement between sales and purchases, between the value of output and the payments for resources and materials used in that output, and between expenditures and incomes, it's convenient to think of income as *flowing in a circuit* through the economy.

By imagining a simple closed economy with no government sector, in which no capital goods are produced and all existing capital lasts forever, we can visualize output as generating income of equal value, which becomes expenditure sufficient to buy the output. This movement completes the circuit as in Figure 20.2.

If there is a government that collects taxes and spends these to provide free government services, then there is an additional loop in the circuit, as in Figure 20.3. Part of the income flows to the government (via taxes) then flows on to join consumers' expenditures to give total expenditure equal to total output.

Income doesn't *really* flow in this simple circular fashion. At each stage in the process, *decisions* are made. Furthermore, *time* is involved. The

Figure 20.2

The circular flow of income for a simple economy with no government, capital, or foreign sectors.

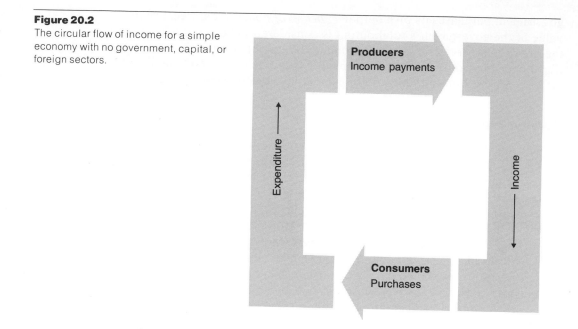

output "sold" on a particular day is purchased by expenditures determined not by the income paid out on that day, but by income paid out previously. Many problems arise in the operation of the economy because the flow is *not* an automatic, continuous circuit. The study of how the circuit is interrupted, and how it divides into separate branches that do not match automatically, is the primary topic of the next few chapters.

Recap Because every sale has its counterpart in a purchase, we can approach the national income accounts from the expenditure side. Total sales of final output must equal total purchases of final goods, with some modifications for the effects of foreign trade. For illustrative purposes, it's useful to visualize national income as flowing through the economy and becoming the expenditure that ultimately pays for national output. In truth, this flow is anything but simple and automatic.

National Product and Material Welfare

Some deficiencies of GNP as an index of social welfare

Because GNP is a measure of the economy's total output, presumably, it should be a reasonable index of society's material welfare.

To employ GNP meaningfully as such an index, we would need to deflate it by a price index—as discussed in Chapter 19—to obtain *GNP in constant*

Figure 20.3
The circular flow of income for an
economy with a government sector.

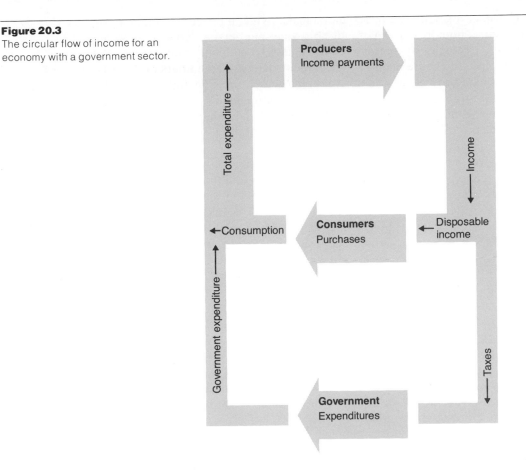

dollars. But even after adjusting for prices (and population changes), many
practical and conceptual problems remain. For example, GNP does not
reflect income distribution—and is not adapted for that purpose. Moreover,
even though public goods are included in GNP (at cost, and thus not necessarily with a weight reflecting their true social value), public bads are not
subtracted.

Costs or Benefits?

The problem is well illustrated by output devoted to defense. Does the
existence of a large defense capability represent a positive benefit to social
welfare, or does it simply represent a cost of maintaining the economic
system from which society's true benefits are derived? If it is the latter,
defense-related output should be omitted from any total valuation of benefits if we are to avoid double counting.

Consider a small tribe of 100 individuals, living in peaceful simplicity by producing annually one ton of fudge brownies per person. Now suppose the tribe is threatened by aggressive strangers who suddenly appear over the mountains. To ensure maintenance of their society, 20 members of the tribe are taken off brownie production to form a guard unit. The unit successfully keeps the strangers away, but brownie production falls by 20 percent. Is the tribe worse off, in some sense, than before? Indeed, most of us would consider the tribe worse off, and the 20 percent fall in brownie production to be a reasonable indicator of the decline.

However, conventional GNP statistics would not show this. Suppose the tribe's economy were monetized, brownies were sold through the market at 10 cents a pound, and each tribe member received an annual income of $200, the value of the individual's output. GNP would be $20,000, computed as either 100 tons of brownies at 10 cents a pound, or as 100 incomes of $200. When the tribe is threatened, suppose the guards are paid the going wage ($200) and defense costs ($4,000) are financed by a 20 percent income tax. GNP remains at $20,000 ($16,000 in brownie incomes plus $4,000 in guard incomes), and the tribe is apparently no worse off than before. The result occurs because the guards are counted as contributing benefits equal to their collective wages. Their wages, in turn, equal the value of the brownies they *would have produced* had they been otherwise employed. This is precisely how the matter is treated in the national income accounts.

Of course, we could argue that the tribe is better off *after the external threat* with its defense than without. But the statistics show it to be just as well off as in peaceful times, even though subject to external threat *and* reduced brownie consumption.

To take an example closer to home, U.S. GNP (in 1958 dollars) *fell* from $361 billion in 1944 to $310 billion in 1947, with the ending of World War II. On the other hand, GNP *less defense expenditure* actually rose from $218 billion to $293 billion over the same years. Was the United States better or worse off in 1947 than in 1944?

Environmental Depreciation

Another current problem is environmental depreciation. While depreciation on private capital used in business is thoroughly accounted for and deducted from taxes because it is a private cost, depreciation on other resources rarely receives such loving attention. This is true of human capital, and it is true of the environment. Environmental depreciation costs are essentially public rather than private, and payments can be deferred to later generations—two factors that easily lead to neglect.

The effect of economic activity on the environment is twofold—certain items are taken away from the environment and others are added to it. Certain costs of environmental depletion, such as using mineral resources, appear as private costs because the rights to the minerals are privately owned and, consequently, are sold on the market. But these private costs may diverge widely from the true social costs for several reasons. The most important reason is that the depreciation taken by the mining enterprise is related only to the price paid for the mineral resources—the long-run social value may be much different. In addition, the private costs may fail to reflect the true degree of depletion or true social costs. The cheapest (least *private cost*) way to mine shallow coal is simply to rip off the topsoil, shovel the coal, then proceed, leaving large, ugly gashes in the landscape. Obviously, the depreciation of the environment is greater than the simple value of the depletion of coal reserves, and can be accurately measured only by including the cost of reclaiming the land.

Items added to the environment—such as air and water pollution—are even less likely to be reflected in private costs, and typically have the characteristics of public bads. The real problem with environmental depreciation is not simply that the costs are social rather than private, but that *the costs go unpaid and uncounted*.

The United States and all other industrial countries have degraded the environment for centuries, and with increasing rapidity in recent decades. If ordinary capital were depreciating similarly without repair or replacement, we would *deduct* the value of this depreciation from GNP to obtain a true estimate of net output. Because this has not been done with respect to the environment, we have been overstating our net output. We have, in effect, been stealing output from future generations and counting it as our own.

Recap GNP in constant dollars is a measure of society's material output. However, it has conceptual and practical deficiencies as an index of material welfare. Defense expenditures, for example, appear as a net addition to society's benefits, yet they may simply represent a cost of running society. Moreover, environmental depreciation is generally not counted in estimating net output, thus leading to an overstatement of current production.

Exercises

The following data apply to a hypothetical economy in 1980 (figures are in millions of units of that country's currency):

Wages 100
Income taxes 20
Capital consumption allowances 25
Income other than wages 40
Indirect taxes 10

In addition, the following facts are known: There are no corporations, and all income is paid directly to persons. There are no transfer payments, and government expenditure is exactly equal to taxes (balanced budget). Government expenditure is made exclusively to provide government services to the economy.

Calculate each of the following:

1. Gross national product
2. Net national product
3. National income
4. Personal income
5. Disposable personal income
6. Government sector gross output
7. Private sector gross output
8. Consumption expenditure, if investment is 35.

For Thought and Discussion

1. Suppose the economy consisted only of a private sector with no government or foreign transactions. What would the national accounts look like if business as a whole suffered net losses? (This happened in the United States in 1932.)

2. Think of as many goods and services as you can that are produced by households for their own use, but that could be purchased commercially or produced with labor employed by the household. Do you think GNP is *seriously* understated by omitting these households' own production?

3. For the United States, national output and national expenditure are almost equal. For a few countries, the two differ markedly. Without worrying about how it could happen, do you think a country would be "better off" if:

   a. its national output were $100 million and national expenditure $80 million, or
   b. its national output were $80 million and national expenditure $100 million.

4. What would happen to the "circular flow" if those receiving incomes decided not to spend these incomes entirely?

Chapter 21
Income-Expenditure Analysis

Terms and Concepts

Withdrawal
Injection
Keynesian scenario
Monetarist scenario
Income-consumption loop
Balance condition

Introduction

What income-expenditure analysis seeks to explain

What caused real GNP in the United States to fall by almost 30 percent from 1929 to 1933, even though there was no decline in real resources? Were special historical factors to blame, or factors inherent in the operation of the economic system? Could such events recur? Can we prevent the recurrence of another severe depression?

Can we predict the level of real GNP in some future period? Is it completely predetermined or can we influence the real GNP level? If we can influence it, what must we manipulate in order to do so? How will real GNP be affected by increased taxes? By a sudden burst of business investment? By changes in government expenditures? Will the economy grow naturally over time, or must it be given a push?

These are a few of the questions considered by income-expenditure analysis, which is essentially macroeconomic. Accordingly, we do not attempt to discover why the economy is operating below full capacity by separately investigating why industry 1 is operating below full capacity, then industry 2, and so on. Rather, we presume that the problem pervades the economy as a whole and cannot be attributed to the specific problems affecting any one market. Thus, we proceed along conventional macroeconomic lines, treating the economy as if it produced a single good called real output or real GNP. We recognize that this output has different uses and that the demand for it may come from different sectors of the economy for different reasons.

Recap Income-expenditure analysis is a study of the economy from a macroeconomic point of view. It is designed to answer such questions as why there are recessions, and how changes in government expenditure, taxation, and investment affect the level of output.

Withdrawals and Injections

How the "circular flow" of income can be broken and restored

Let's begin our discussion with a simple economy whose annual output is purchased exclusively by consumers and is valued, at the current price level, at $100 million. Assuming no depreciation or taxes, the entire $100 million received by firms from the sale of output is paid out in the form of *personal income*—wages, payments for nonlabor factor services, and profits—as described in the last chapter. If consumers plan to spend their entire incomes, the $100 million they collectively receive will obviously generate $100 million in expenditures.

Figure 21.1
The circular flow of income at equilibrium.

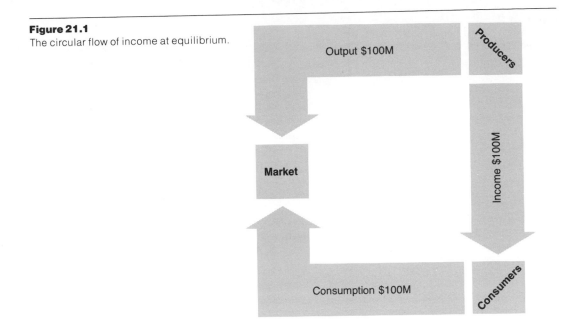

Equilibrium

In this case, the value of current output is equivalent to the value of planned expenditures, with income forming the link between the two. We can visualize the $100 million as an undisturbed *circular flow*, as in Figure 21.1. The sale of output generates receipts of $100 million, which are paid out as incomes totaling $100 million. From these incomes, expenditures of $100 million are generated, which lead to further sales of $100 million, and so on.

In the absence of anything that might lead producers to change the level of output or cause consumers to spend an amount other than their total incomes, this sequence of events will persist indefinitely. It is an *equilibrium* situation.

Withdrawals

But what if consumers plan to spend *less* than their total incomes on goods produced in the economy? For example, suppose consumers decide to spend part of their incomes in *another* economy. Specifically, let's assume that incomes are paid in gold, which is acceptable anywhere in the world, and that consumers annually take vacations abroad during which they collectively spend $10 million.

Now if $10 million is spent abroad, only $90 million of the $100 million income remains available for purchasing domestic output. If producers continue to produce as before, they will find that they can no longer sell

Figure 21.2
Withdrawal from the income flow leading
to disequilibrium.

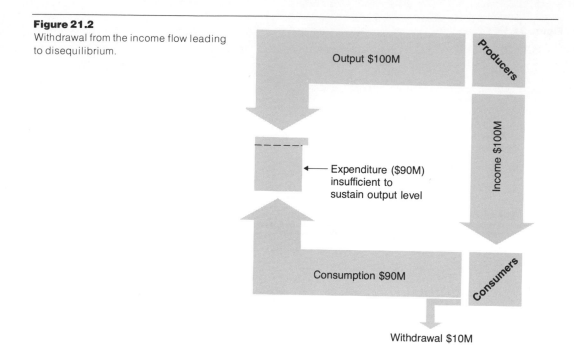

$100 million worth of output because buyers will spend only $90 million.
The simple circular flow has been broken, as shown in Figure 21.2. Between the receipt of income and the generation of expenditure, $10 million
has dropped out of circulation in our domestic economy. We refer to this
$10 million as a *withdrawal* from the income-expenditure flow.

Injections

Now, suppose some other country—it may or may not be the same country
in which our people spend their vacations—wants some of our domestic
output. In particular, suppose this country is willing to exchange gold for
$10 million worth of our domestic output. Such an expenditure, originating
outside the primary income-expenditure flow, is referred to as an *injection*
into this flow.

This injection adds $10 million to the total expenditure on domestic out-
put, just sufficient to offset the $10 million withdrawal. Output of $100
million now generates $100 million in income: $10 million "leaks" out of
the system and $90 million is used to buy domestic output. To this $90
million is added the $10 million in injections. Thus, total expenditures on
domestic output are $100 million—exactly enough to buy the current out-
put. Although the circular flow is broken, the losses from it (withdrawals)

Figure 21.3
Equilibrium sustained by injection equal to withdrawal.

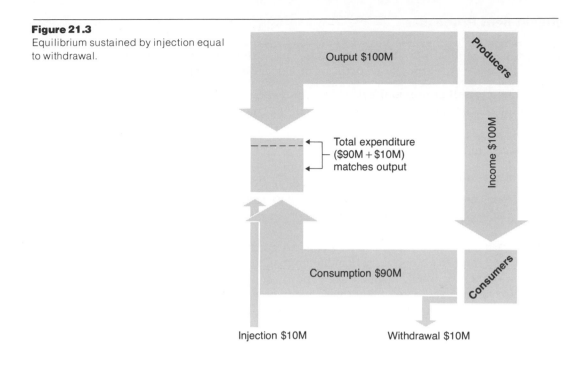

are exactly balanced by the gains to it (injections), and the existing level of output can be maintained as long as there are no changes in withdrawals or injections. This is illustrated in Figure 21.3.

The Balance Condition

We can now state the fundamental proposition of income-expenditure analysis:

The economy's equilibrium level of output can be sustained if total withdrawals are exactly balanced by total injections.

But what if injections totaled $5 million rather than $10 million? From an output of $100 million, we would have $100 million in domestic incomes generating expenditures of $90 million. Adding the $5 million injection, total expenditure would be $95 million—less than the $100 million current value of output.

It is the relationship *between injections and withdrawals* that counts. If withdrawals exceed injections, the loss from the income-expenditure flow is not balanced by outside gains. Thus, total expenditure, including injections, is less than total income (which is equal to the planned value of output). Expenditure is not enough to buy the planned output, and something must change.

Adjustment Processes

If buyers spend only $95 million on goods worth $100 million at current prices, there are two types of adjustment producers might make:

1. Continue to sell at previous prices but cut *real output* by 5 percent.
2. Continue to produce the same real output but cut *prices* by 5 percent.

Cutting prices implies that *all* prices, including factor prices and thus *wages,* must fall by 5 percent. While some combination of reduced real output and lower prices is also possible, we usually concentrate on these two extremes. Whether the outcome is reduced real output or lower prices, or both, we can unambiguously state that if expenditures are less than output, the resulting influences will create *downward pressure* on the economy.

In our example, if injections had exceeded withdrawals (say, the outside demand for domestic output was $10 million but only $5 million of domestic income was spent abroad), planned expenditure would have *exceeded* output at current values. There would then have been *upward pressure,* and a tendency for real output, the price level, or both, to increase.

An excess of withdrawals over injections exerts downward pressure on the economy. An excess of injections over withdrawals exerts upward pressure.

Recap The economy can remain in balance or equilibrium only if the existing income generates sufficient expenditures to purchase the output from which the income is generated. Any part of income that is not spent on this output (spent abroad, for example) represents a withdrawal from the income-expenditure flow. Expenditures (purchases by foreigners, for example) that do not depend on the level of income represent injections into the flow. The economy can be in equilibrium only if withdrawals are equal to injections. There will be downward pressure (on prices, real output, or both) if withdrawals exceed injections, and upward pressure if injections exceed withdrawals.

Keynesian and Monetarist Scenarios

The two different scenarios of macroeconomic adjustment

We have shown that if withdrawals exceed injections, there will be downward pressure on the economy in the form of reduced real output, reduced prices, or both. We were careful not to say exactly what form this downward pressure will take simply because there is disagreement among economists about how much emphasis should be given to each of these two basic types of adjustment.

Scenarios, Not Theories

The differences between the two types of adjustment can best be characterized in the context of alternative scenarios that are commonly used to describe the adjustment process. One of these scenarios is the *Keynesian*, named after John Maynard Keynes whose work in the 1930s underlies all income-expenditure analysis. The Keynesian scenario emphasizes the downward effect on *real output*. The assumption is that in the actual economy prices will adjust little, or at least very slowly, and that adjustments must be made by cutbacks in production (leading to layoffs and unemployment).

The alternative scenario reflects the so-called *monetarist* point of view. This is the original, pre-Keynesian scenario, revived in the 1960s by Milton Friedman, a contemporary American economist. The monetarist scenario emphasizes *price flexibility*. The basic assumption is that downward pressure will ultimately lower prices rather than real output—although real output may decline temporarily while the price adjustment process is in operation. As their name suggests, the monetarists stress the relationship between the income-expenditure flow and the stock of money. Keynesians are more interested in how withdrawals and injections relate to income.

An Example

To illustrate the differences between these two scenarios, let's continue with our previous example. The economy produces output that sells for $100 million, its residents take vacations abroad worth $10 million, and a third country spends $5 million on domestic output. The domestic output of $100 million generates $100 million in incomes, which, in turn, generate $90 million in expenditure from domestic sources. Adding the $5 million expenditure injected from abroad, total expenditure is $95 million—not enough to sustain output at $100 million. Consequently, there is downward pressure. Regardless of whether this reduces real output or prices, we cannot reach a balance as long as withdrawals remain at $10 million and injections only at $5 million.

Now suppose that, by reducing real output, prices, or both, the *value* of output drops to $95 million. This will generate income of only $95 million. If withdrawals persist at $10 million, expenditure from domestic sources will then be only $85 million. Given the injection of $5 million, total expenditure will be $90 million—still not enough to sustain even the new lower output of $95 million.

If nothing happened to change the relationship between withdrawals and injections, the value of output in the economy would eventually decline to zero. Each reduction in the value of output would cause an equivalent reduction in income, and the excess of withdrawals over injections would

Figure 21.4

A simplified Keynesian scenario showing the effect of a fall in
planned expenditure.

Simplified Keynesian scenario

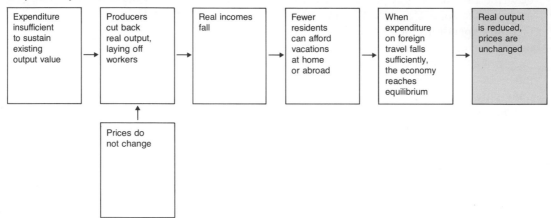

remain unchanged, exerting still further downward pressure. With the
faintest touch of realism, we would expect the process to be stopped, of
course, by some induced change in withdrawals or injections. At this point
we can indicate the differences between the two scenarios.

The Keynesian Version

If the adjustment is along Keynesian lines, real output will decline. That is,
if producers anticipate expenditures of only $95 million, they will reduce
their output to this level, while holding prices constant. We know a decline
in real output means a decline in the quantity of real goods and services
available to consumers. Interpreted alternatively, people's money incomes
decline (to $95 million) while prices do not, so consumers are poorer in
terms of the real goods and services they can afford. As they become
poorer, foreign travel will be cut in favor of more essential things like food.
The decline in real incomes will thus reduce expenditures on foreign travel,
so withdrawals will decline.

Eventually, expenditures on travel will fall to $5 million and be exactly
balanced by injections (assumed to be unaffected by events within the
domestic economy). The level of real output at which this happens can
therefore be sustained indefinitely. If we could predict the exact level of
income at which the demand for foreign travel would equal $5 million, we
could predict the equilibrium level of real output. For example, if foreign
travel were $5 million at an income level of $75 million, this $5 million

Figure 21.5

A simplified monetarist scenario showing the effect of a fall in planned expenditure.

Simplified monetarist scenario

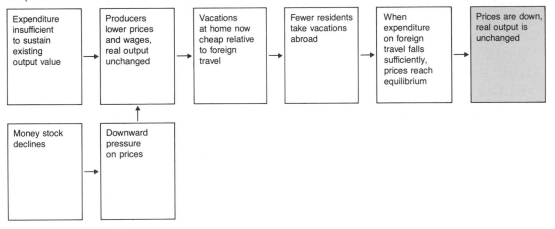

withdrawal would be balanced by the $5 million injection, yielding a total expenditure of $75 million, and thus an equilibrium situation. Figure 21.4 illustrates this case.

The Monetarist Version

The monetarist story would differ significantly from this. First, the monetarist assumes that when withdrawals exceed injections, $10 million of the country's money stock (gold) is withdrawn from the economy, while only $5 million is injected. In other words, unless the money stock is being expanded simultaneously by using substitutes for gold, it is declining. Thus, the monetarist would attribute the downward pressure to an inappropriate relationship between the declining money stock and the level of transactions. Note that the *actual effect,* downward pressure, is the same as in the Keynesian scenario.

The monetarist believes the falling price level is the primary adjustment. Even though money incomes fall, the price level (cost of living) falls in step. People's *real incomes* do not fall in terms of the domestic price level because they can buy the same things as before if their purchases are confined to the domestic market. Prices abroad, however, are presumably unchanged, and those vacations abroad, still costing $10 million, must now be paid for from a *smaller money income.* If incomes fall to $90 million, even though domestic prices will have fallen in proportion, it will now take more than 11 percent of income to buy the same overseas vacations that could formerly be obtained for 10 percent. Consequently, people will start cutting back on vacations abroad—not because they are becoming markedly poorer in real terms, but because the *relative* price of domestic goods and services is falling relative to those elsewhere. More can be obtained per dollar by spending income at home. Eventually, expenditures abroad will fall to the level at which they are balanced by injections, the money stock will cease to decline, and a new equilibrium will be reached. This process is illustrated in Figure 21.5.

The End Results

The variations in the adjustment mechanisms of the two scenarios lead to two quite different pictures of the ultimate state reached by the economy.

According to the Keynesian framework, the economy will contract into a *recession* or *depression* with the level of real output below the capacity of the economy. This is presumably accompanied by unemployment. According to the monetarist framework, real output will remain unchanged, but the price level will be lower. There will be some loss to consumers, who cannot afford as many vacations abroad and presumably will settle for Disney World and Sun Valley. This loss, however, is relatively small compared to that predicted by the Keynesian analysis.

Both scenarios, as presented in terms of such a highly simplified economy, contain an element of caricature. Nonetheless, they illustrate the difference in *emphasis* between the two approaches, which can be summarized as follows:

The Keynesian analysis emphasizes:

1. the effects of withdrawals from and injections into the income-expenditure flow, rather than the relationship of money balances to income and expenditure;
2. relative inflexibility of prices so adjustments take place primarily as variations in real output; and
3. the possibility that the economy will decline to and remain at less than capacity output in the absence of a counteracting policy.

Those who accept the Keynesian view emphasize policy approaches based on direct manipulation of withdrawals and injections.

The monetarist analysis emphasizes:

1. the effects of changes in the relationship between the money stock and the overall level of transactions, rather than the effects of withdrawals and injections as such;
2. relative flexibility of prices (including wages), at least beyond the very short-run period, so adjustments are assumed to take place as variations in the price level; and
3. the likelihood that price flexibility and the effects related to the real level

of money balances will prevent the economy from remaining below its capacity level of real output in the long run.

Those who accept the monetarist view emphasize policy approaches based on direct manipulation of the economy's stock of money.

Which Is Relevant?

The monetarists, who are more optimistic than the Keynesians about the economy's possibilities for self-adjustment out of below-capacity situations, have to face the fact that the depression of the 1930s *did* occur. In fact, it was the Great Depression that led to the development of Keynesian analysis, and consequently to the thirty-year eclipse of the monetarist approach. Modern monetarists, however, point to recent empirical findings that, they contend, demonstrate that the persistence and depth of the Depression was due to *inappropriate monetary policy*. Even so, many economists remain unconvinced or at least question the *speed* with which the monetarists' adjustment process works.

Whether the Keynesian or the monetarist approach is most relevant to the analysis of actual economic conditions depends on the answer to the question: Does adjustment primarily take the form of real output changes or price and wage changes? Few economists doubt that real output changes occur. But monetarists tend to view these as *short-term* component changes in the total adjustment process, and assert that output will readjust once prices (or real money balances) finish changing. In this view, both scenarios are relevant, and most actual adjustments represent a mixture of the two.

We shall regard the Keynesian approach as being valid in the short run. The point at issue is whether it is relevant to long-run problems. Our Keynesian scenario showed that the economy would reach a balance between withdrawals and injections at a real output level of $75 million at constant prices rather than at the full employment level of $100 million. Consequently, it represents a relevant analysis. But to imply that the economy necessarily becomes "stuck" at such a level unless there is a deliberate manipulation of withdrawals and injections may not be justified.

Upward Pressures

When the pressure on the economy is *upward* rather than downward—if injections in our example had been $15 million, $5 million in excess of withdrawals—the monetarist scenario remains the same except that the direction of the changes is reversed. Our hypothetical economy would have gained gold and thereby would have experienced an increase in its money stock, leading to an increase in the price level. Vacations abroad would have become cheaper relative to domestic prices, expenditure on foreign travel would have increased, and withdrawals would have risen. Once reached, the new equilibrium would have been at a higher price level than before.

If the economy is not initially at capacity, but starts from a position of recession, the Keynesian adjustment mechanism also works in the manner previously described with the directions reversed. Real output will rise, consumers will receive larger incomes and will spend more on foreign travel, and withdrawals will rise until they balance injections. The new equilibrium will be at a higher real output level with lowered unemployment.

However, if the economy is *already producing at maximum capacity,* the Keynesian mechanism cannot operate in the upward direction because real output is already at its maximum level and cannot increase any more. Any adjustments that occur must be in prices, not in real output. Under these circumstances, Keynesians would accept the general outlines of the monetarist scenario. Further discussion of the effect of upward pressure on an economy operating at capacity is given in Chapter 25, which considers inflation.

Recap There are two different scenarios for the adjustment process when the economy is unbalanced and subject to upward or downward pressures. The Keynesian scenario emphasizes adjustment by change in real output levels and employment, while the monetarist scenario emphasizes adjustment by changes in prices and wages. While actual adjustment processes contain elements of both scenarios, the Keynesian scenario is probably the most relevant to short-run changes.

Capsule Supplement 21.1   **Monetary Theory:**
A Brief Preview

Because the role of money in the economy is not discussed in detail until Chapter 26, we shall preview some of the important properties of money at this time. By money, we specifically mean the *stock* of money generally considered to consist of the cash (coins and paper currency) and checking-account balances held by the public. Why checking-account balances? Because payments are just as easily made by check as by cash for most transactions (and more easily for many). Thus, in terms of how it can be used, a checking account containing $100 can be treated as virtually identical to $100 in dollar bills.

In common usage, "money" is often confused with what is more properly termed "income" or "expenditure." In referring to the demand for money or the desired quantity of money, we do not mean the demand for expenditure, but for the money stock individuals collectively desire to hold *unspent.* While we might presume that everyone would like more income or more expenditure (if it involved giving nothing up), it does not follow that everyone wants to hold more money. Thus, while the demand for expenditure or income by individuals may be insatiable, their demand for unspent money balances is finite and can be determined on the basis of their particular circumstances and desires.

People *hold* money primarily because they need a reserve capability to make future payments, both expected and unexpected. This is why people keep balances in their bank accounts and cash on their person. Because anticipated payments tend to be roughly proportionate to general levels of expenditure, which, in turn, are more or less proportionate to incomes, we can expect people will desire to hold money balances that stand in some determinate ratio to their incomes. If incomes rise, people will wish to hold more money; if incomes fall, they will prefer to hold less.

What happens then if individuals have more in their bank accounts than they desire to hold in that form? They will reduce their balances by *spending* the excess, increasing their regular expenditures until the surplus has been used up. If, on the other hand, they have less in their account than they need, they will reduce spending until their balances have built up. Thus, if the economy is such that all individuals are holding exactly the amount of money they want and the quantity of money in the economy is increased (which, as we shall show later, can be done through the banking system), spending will be expected to rise. If real output is fixed, say because the economy is operating at full employment, the increased expenditures will be expected to push prices up. Thus, if the real quantities of goods and services in the economy are relatively fixed, an increase in the quantity of money can be expected to increase prices. On the contrary, a reduction in the quantity of money will be expected to cause the general price level to fall.

An extreme form of this reasoning is known as the *quantity theory of money*. It holds that the general level of prices will change exactly in proportion to the change in the total stock of money, so a 10 percent increase in the quantity of money would cause a 10 percent increase in the general price level. Most economists accept the existence of *some* relationship between the quantity of money and the price level when the economy is at full employment, but not necessarily when it is operating at less than capacity, as during a recession. Only the so-called monetarists, and not even all of them, accept the quantity theory as applicable to more than a restricted set of economic circumstances.

The Income-Consumption Loop

Expansion of income-expenditure analysis to cover internal withdrawals and injections

In the preceding discussion of withdrawals and injections, we used an example in which withdrawals and injections were both attributed to transactions with other economies. This is the simplest and clearest way to show the effect of withdrawals and injections.

But if this were the only context in which we could use the withdrawal-

Figure 21.6
The income-consumption loop.

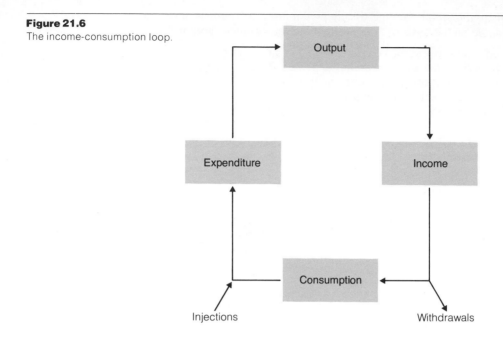

injection approach, our analysis would be useful only for discussing problems resulting from an economy's relationships with the rest of the world. The analysis would throw no light on the internal problems of an open economy that do not come from external withdrawals and injections. Fortunately, however, we can easily expand this approach to cover *internal* withdrawals and injections.

The Importance of Consumption

The largest component of total expenditure in all economies is *consumption*, the expenditure by households on newly produced goods and services for final use by consumers. Furthermore, the major determinant of the level of consumption is the level of income itself. Thus, the most important flow in the economy is the *flow from income to consumption*, then *to output* and around again *to income*. In our previous example, we assumed this to be the *only* flow entirely within the domestic economy.

To generalize withdrawal-injection analysis, we concentrate on this flow—the *income-consumption loop*. A *withdrawal* is any diversion of income *out of this loop*, and an *injection* is any expenditure coming *from outside this loop*, that is, any expenditure not determined by the level of the income flow itself. This flow is illustrated in Figure 21.6.

Types of Withdrawal

A withdrawal is *any* use of income other than as consumption expenditure on current domestic output. Among the uses to which income may be diverted are the following:

1. Increases in money balances, accomplished either by stashing cash under the mattress or allowing bank balances to accumulate.
2. Deposits in savings accounts or purchases of government bonds or corporate securities because they are not expenditures on currently produced goods and services.
3. Payments to the government in the form of taxes, because expenditures from taxes are not under the control of the income recipients.
4. Expenditures abroad or expenditures on goods produced abroad (imports), as in our previous example.

For the sake of simplicity, we usually lump the first two uses together as *saving,* and make no distinction between expenditures actually made abroad and expenditures on goods produced abroad.

Therefore, *the main forms of withdrawal from the income-consumption loop are saving, taxes, and imports.*

Types of Injection

An injection is any expenditure on domestic output that does not result directly from consumer income-expenditure decisions. The chief sources of injection are the following:

1. Expenditures by firms and businesses on currently produced goods, other than those materials and components eliminated in calculating value added in the economy, that is, investment expenditures on *capital items* like machinery and new buildings.
2. Expenditures by the government on goods produced within the economy.
3. Purchases of domestic goods by foreigners (exports).

Therefore, *the main forms of injection into the income-consumption loop are investment, government expenditure, and exports.*

Figure 21.7 illustrates the income-consumption loop as complicated by the withdrawals and injections described above.

The Balance Condition Restated

As already pointed out, the important element in income-expenditure analysis is the balance between *total* withdrawals and *total* injections. Suppose the value of output, and hence income, at current prices is $100 million, of

Figure 21.7
The basic structure of the Keynesian model.

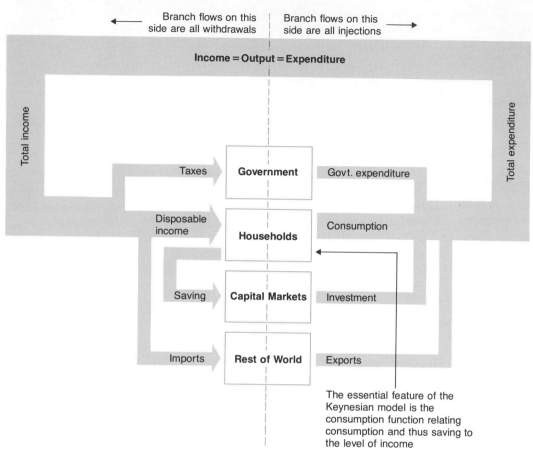

Branch flows on this side are all withdrawals ←   Branch flows on this side are all injections →

Income = Output = Expenditure

Total income

Total expenditure

Taxes → **Government** → Govt. expenditure

Disposable income → **Households** → Consumption

Saving → **Capital Markets** → Investment

Imports → **Rest of World** → Exports

The essential feature of the Keynesian model is the consumption function relating consumption and thus saving to the level of income

which households spend $5 million on imports, pay $12 million in taxes, and save $11 million. Withdrawals total $28 million, and consumption expenditure is $72 million. Now suppose exports total $7 million, government expenditure is $13 million, and investment $8 million. Total injections come to $28 million. The economy is in balance because total expenditure, consisting of consumption ($72 million) plus injections ($28 million), is exactly equal to output at current prices, and thus to income before withdrawals.

If investment were to fall to $7 million, with the other items unchanged, withdrawals and injections would no longer balance. Total expenditure would then equal consumption (still $72 million) plus injections of only $27 million—a total of $99 million. This would not be enough to buy the current output of $100 million. There would be downward pressure on the economy unless something were done. One option would be to increase government expenditure by $1 million, to $14 million, bringing total injections back up to the original level of $28 million and thus restoring balance. This is the key to basic Keynesian economic policy.

The economy can be kept in equilibrium when there is a change in the level of any form of injection or withdrawal by a counterbalancing change in any other injection or withdrawal designed to ensure that total injections remain equal to total withdrawals at the existing output level.

Special Linkages

Although the relationship between total withdrawals and total injections is important in income-expenditure analysis, there are certain noteworthy links between particular types of withdrawals and particular types of injections.

The most important form of saving, for example, is the purchase of new corporate securities—either directly by consumers, or indirectly when pension fund contributions or increased bank balances are used for this purpose by the institutions to which this money has been entrusted. The sale of such securities is an important source of funds by which firms finance investment expenditures. Thus, there is a link between *saving and investment*. While this does not necessarily mean that these will be equated, it suggests that there is sufficient reason to focus on the relationship between the two.

A similar link exists between government expenditure and taxes, taxes being the predominant way to finance expenditures. Again, the two need not be equal—the government can have a *deficit* (an excess of expenditure over current tax revenue), a *surplus* (an excess of tax revenue over expenditure), or a *balanced budget* (equality of the two)—but expenditure cannot be planned in complete ignorance of revenue.

Finally, exports and imports are linked through the operations of the rest of the world. Most of our basic analysis will be done in terms of a closed economy. A detailed study of the export-import link appears later.

Recap We carry out basic income-expenditure analysis by considering withdrawals from and injections into the main flow within the domestic economy—from income to consumption expenditure. The primary withdrawals from this income-consumption loop are expenditures abroad (imports), saving, and taxes. The main injections are expenditures originating outside the economy (exports), investment expenditures by firms, and government expenditures. The economy will remain in balance if a change in any form of withdrawal or injection is met by a counterbalancing change in some other withdrawal or injection.

Capsule Supplement 21.2   **Variations in
Injection Sources**

In 1977, the primary source of injections into the income-consumption loop of
the U.S. economy was the government, with total government expenditures
comprising 21 percent of GNP. Private investment was second, comprising 15
percent of GNP, while exports ran a poor third, at 9 percent of GNP. The relative
importance of these various sources of injections has not always been the
same, however, and varies today among nations.

Except during the major war periods, private investment, rather than government expenditure, constituted the most important source of injections up to
the 1950s. If we go back to 1901, government expenditure was a mere 3 percent
of GNP (most of this, local government expenditure), while private investment
was 23 percent of GNP. Over the three-fourths of a century since then, private
investment, despite many ups and downs, has followed a downward trend as a
proportion of GNP, while government expenditure has risen more or less steadily as a proportion of GNP.

Even exports, now the least significant item among injections, were more important than government expenditure in 1901—in fact they were more than
three times as important. It wasn't until after World War I that exports yielded
second place to government expenditure. In the United States at present, exports play a very minor role in total injections; exports are much more important in most countries and for some they are the dominant injection. Australia
has a more typical pattern of injections than the United States, although the
relative significance of injections is the same. For Australia, government expenditure is 23 percent of their GNP, private investment is 17 percent, and exports are 15 percent.

It should be noted that the growth in importance of government expenditure
relative to other injection sources has been a universal and long-run trend and
was apparent *before* Keynesian economics made its appearance. Although
Keynesian economics has emphasized the policy importance of appropriate
manipulation of government expenditure and has certainly been a factor in the
growth of government expenditure relative to GNP, it has certainly not been the
primary cause. Indeed the causal sequence may very well be the other way
around. The suggestion that the economy could be stabilized by variations in
government expenditure when these were a mere 3 percent of GNP (as in 1901)
would have appeared ridiculous. But it was the large proportion of government
expenditure in total injections during the 1930s that made Keynes's remedies
practical.

Exercises

1. The existing output of an economy is $1,200 million. Planned saving is
   $100 million, the government will levy taxes of $200 million, and
   businesses will invest $250 million. If there are no international transac-

tions, what level of government expenditure will balance the economy at its existing output level?

2. Suppose the figures are as given in question 1, except that the economy has exports of $20 million and imports of $16 million. What will now be the balancing level of government expenditure to maintain existing output?

3. In the economy of question 1 (no international transactions), government expenditure balances the economy at its original output level of $1,200 million. The tax system is such that every dollar of additional output beyond $1,200 million will increase taxes by 50 cents. If the levels of saving and investment are unaffected by the level of output, by how much will the output rise if government expenditure rises by $1 million?

For Thought and Discussion

1. Which of the following transactions by a household represent withdrawals from the income-consumption loop?
   The purchase of General Motors stock, the purchase of a new car, the purchase of a used car, a down payment on a new house, a cash gift to a relative in the United States, a cash gift to a relative abroad, the payment of a parking fine, the sales tax on a purchase, the payment of a restaurant check

2. Which of the following transactions represent injections from outside the income-consumption loop?
   The purchase of a new car by a household, the purchase of a new car by a firm, the purchase of a new car by a foreign visitor, the purchase of a new car by a government agency

3. One of the examples given in the text concerns the excess of withdrawals over injections when residents of one country spend $10 million abroad and foreigners buy $5 million of domestic goods. Suppose "abroad" is the only other country in the world. What can we say about the relationship between withdrawals and injections in that other country?

Chapter 22
The Basic
Keynesian Model

Terms and Concepts

Consumption function
Marginal propensity to consume
Average propensity to consume
Saving function
Marginal propensity to save
Average propensity to save
Equilibrium level of income
Capacity
Money illusion
Phillips curve
Multiplier
Fiscal policy
Macromodels

The Starting Point

The basic structure of Keynesian analysis

The Keynesian model is a macroeconomic view of the economy based on income-expenditure relationships with special reference to withdrawals from and injections into the income-consumption loop. In the simplest Keynesian model, the only withdrawal is *saving* and the sole injection is *investment*. Adjustments in the economy are presumed to conform to the "Keynesian scenario" discussed in the last chapter, that is, to consist of changes in real output and employment (unless constrained by capacity) rather than in prices.

The Consumption Function

Central to the Keynesian model is the division of disposable household income between consumption and saving. Specifically, it is assumed that the level of consumption is determined entirely by the level of disposable income. It is further assumed that the only withdrawal is saving, which necessarily equals the difference between income and consumption. Thus, the decision to consume a certain fraction of income implies a simultaneous decision to save the remaining fraction.

In the basic Keynesian model, the relationship between consumption and income is taken at face value, that is, the level of consumption in any given period is determined by the level of income in that period. As we shall observe later, more sophisticated macroeconomic models also consider the effect of *past* income levels on a given period's consumption expenditure.

When expressed in exact terms, the relationship between consumption and income is called the *consumption function*. Keynes introduced his view of this relationship with the following observation: "The fundamental psychological law, upon which we are entitled to depend with great confidence both *a priori* and from our knowledge of human nature and experience, is that men are disposed, as a rule and on the average, to increase their consumption as their income increases, but not by as much as the increase in income." In fact, while this assertion bears little resemblance to any "fundamental psychological law," it constitutes a shrewd empirical summation.

Since the original work of Keynes in the 1930s, the relationship between aggregate income and aggregate consumption has been the object of substantial empirical research. This research clearly bears out the fundamental Keynesian premise that the level of consumption can be explained, in a determinate and predictable fashion, by the level of income—although, as we have indicated, not necessarily by the level of *current* income alone.

Injections

Injections, generally restricted to investment expenditures in the basic Keynesian model, are assumed to be independent of income. This does not mean that we regard investment and other potential injections as being randomly determined or unrelated to *other* factors in the economy. It simply means that, when focusing on income-expenditure relationships, we take the level of such injections as *given* or *autonomous,* meaning only that they are not influenced by the level of current income.

The operation of the basic Keynesian model is actually quite simple. Investment is given. The economy can be in balance only when withdrawals equal the level of this investment. The only withdrawal is saving, the level of which depends on the level of income. Thus, the only sustainable income level is that at which saving is equal to investment (or total injections, if there are other forms).

Before presenting a formal analysis of this model, we need to examine the income-consumption relationship in more detail.

Recap The Keynesian model is a macroeconomic representation of the economy in which the income-consumption loop is central. The primary withdrawal in this model is saving (the only withdrawal in the simplest version), which is assumed to be determined entirely by the level of income—the relationship being called the consumption function. The primary injection in this model is investment, but all injections affect the model in the same way.

Capsule Supplement 22.1   **John Maynard Keynes, 1883–1946**

Like many revolutionaries, John Maynard Keynes (pronounced "Kainz") possessed "establishment" credentials. Unlike some, however, he never relinquished these credentials. Thus, he was able to change the course of economic thinking and the direction of economic policy by a palace revolution, never having to storm the gates or wait long years in exile.

His father was John Neville Keynes, a noteworthy philosopher and economist himself, who lived to attend (at age 93) his more famous son's funeral. Maynard, as the younger Keynes was always called, acquired his establishment credentials by going to Eton and then on to King's College at Cambridge. He was an outstanding scholar at both, and it's said that Alfred Marshall himself begged Keynes to choose economics as his major discipline. But he chose mathematics as his major academic field and the civil service as his profession. After spending two years in the India office, he wrote *A Treatise on Probability,* then returned to teach at Cambridge—as an economist. Again he was a success, becoming editor of the *Economic Journal,* then and still the most prestigious publication on economics in Britain.

His brief tenure with the English bureaucracy that ruled India launched him on the path toward "Keynesian" economics. His time in India resulted in the publication of *Indian Currency and Finance* (1913) as well as in an appointment to a royal commission to investigate Indian monetary problems. From that time on, Keynes steadily developed his views on what we now call macroeconomics.

By the time World War I ended, Keynes was a famous and extremely versatile man, with academic publications in mathematics and economics, political writings, high public-service experience, contributions to journalism (with the *Manchester Guardian*), and a deep involvement in art, literature, and the theater. He belonged to the "Bloomsbury Circle" (the intellectual in-group that included Leonard and Virginia Woolf, E. M. Forster, and Lytton Strachey). Keynes possessed major collections of art and rare books, and managed to round off his connections with the world of culture by marrying Lydia Lopokova, a prima ballerina with Diaghilev's Ballet Russe. He soon became a millionaire by the most risky route possible—speculating in foreign currencies—and used the same financial talents to increase the funds of King's College at Cambridge (of which he was bursar) more than tenfold.

During the 1920s, Keynes continued to develop his ideas about the overall operation of the economic system. His *Tract on Monetary Reform* (1923) was an attack on gold fetishism in international monetary arrangements—then more revolutionary than it seems now. It remains famous for the single phrase, given in response to the argument that the economic mechanism would work out in the long run: "In the long run we are all dead." By 1930, he had finished his *Treatise on Money,* a work that analyzed the ups and downs of the capitalist economy in terms of relationships between savings and investment. Although the *Treatise* is a major contribution in itself, Keynes saw beyond it almost as soon as it was published, and it came to be completely overshadowed by his ultimate masterpiece, *The General Theory of Employment, Interest and Money,* published in 1936, but influential in draft form before that.

The *General Theory* (as it is typically referred to) is a very closely argued book, but the major substantive points are easily stated: (1) The capitalist system will not necessarily return to full employment from a depressed state automatically through self-generated forces within the system. (2) The capitalist system, however, can be moved to full employment by government policy that supplies a sufficient level of injections to make up for any deficiency left by the operation of the private sector.

These two ideas represented a true revolution in political economics. There had been others before, including Marx, who had suggested the capitalist system might not be a self-righting ship, but none had argued along lines close enough to conventional economic thought to make the idea an acceptable one. Keynes produced the right reasons. More importantly, Keynes did not simply write of necessary doom for the capitalist system, as Marx did, but showed the way out. After the *General Theory,* the responsibility for the ultimate health of the capitalist system was squarely placed on government rather than on the businesses and banks that had been considered before to have that responsibility.

Only one year after the *General Theory* was published, Keynes was forced into semiretirement by illness. He emerged during World War II to become one of the chief architects of the international monetary system that operated remarkably well for the first quarter-century after the war ended. He also foresaw some of the modern problems of inflation and the eventual necessity of an international money that could be created at will like domestic paper money. But the *General Theory* remained the climax of his career. Honors came in the later years—he received a peerage in Britain as Baron Keynes of Tilton and, better still, saw his economic principles embodied in formal statements of commitment to full employment by the major governments of the world.

| The Simple Consumption Function | The relationship between consumption and income |

The exact relationship between aggregate consumption (household expenditure) and its various determinants is known as the *consumption function*. The simplest view of the consumption function comes directly from Keynes's original work: aggregate consumption over a given year depends only on that year's aggregate income. According to this view, consumption expenditures in 1978 were completely determined by the level of household income in 1978. Of course, there was only one level of income and one level of consumption actually attained in 1978, so the consumption function for that year, which specifies the levels of consumption that *would have been* associated with different levels of income, is purely hypothetical. We simply assume that households knew what they would have done had their incomes in 1978 been higher or lower than they actually were.

A Typical Example

Information about the levels of consumption associated with different levels of income may be presented in a table to show the general properties of the consumption function. Table 22.1 contains information about the collective behavior of households at various income levels in an imaginary economy.

If income were $40 billion, consumption and income would be equal. If income were to rise to $50 billion, consumption would rise to $47.5 billion—an increase of $7.5 billion in consumption for an increase of $10 billion in income. If income were then to rise to $60 billion, consumption would rise to $55 billion—another increase of $7.5 billion in consumption for an increase of $10 billion in income. Conversely, if income were to fall from $40 billion to $30 billion, consumption would fall by $7.5 billion to $32.5 billion.

For the income-consumption relationship given by the data in this table, there is a $7.5 billion change in consumption for every $10 billion change in income. This is consistent with the Keynesian hypothesis that people tend to vary their consumption expenditures directly with income, but by less than the variation in income.

Table 22.1
Consumption Function for Lunar Colony
Clavius, 2001.
(Figures in billions of Clavian dollars)

If disposable income in 2001 is	Consumption expenditure will be
20	25.0
30	32.5
40	40.0
50	47.5
60	55.0
70	62.5
80	70.0
90	77.5
100	85.0
110	92.5
120	100.0

The Marginal Propensity to Consume

We can now introduce a very important term, defined as follows:

When income changes by a small amount, the ratio of the change in consumption to the change in income is known as the marginal propensity to consume (MPC).

In Table 22.1, because every $10 billion increase (decrease) in income is associated with a $7.5 billion increase (decrease) in consumption, the marginal propensity to consume is 0.75 or ¾. Even though the marginal propensity to consume need not be constant over all levels of income, as in this example, it is often assumed to be so.

The Average Propensity to Consume

We shall now introduce another important term.

At any income level, the ratio of total consumption to total income is the average propensity to consume (APC).

At the income level of $40 billion in Table 22.1, the average propensity to consume is 1.0 (= 40/40), while at an income level of $50 billion it is 0.95 (= 47.5/50). Note that for the data in this table, the average propensity to consume *changes* (becoming smaller as income increases) even though the marginal propensity to consume remains constant.

Theoretically, it would be possible for both the average and the marginal propensity to consume to remain constant. This would occur, however, only if consumption were a constant proportion of income at all levels of income.

Figure 22.1
The consumption function derived from data in Table 22.1.

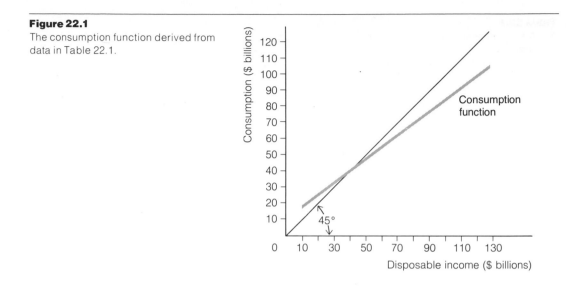

Drawing the Consumption Function

The simple consumption function is often depicted in graphic form as in Figure 22.1, which illustrates the data presented in Table 22.1. (It is standard to measure income on the horizontal axis and consumption on the vertical axis.) The basic features of this graphic representation of the consumption function can be summarized as follows:

1. The slope of the consumption function at any income level is a measure of the marginal propensity to consume at that income level.
2. The slope of the line joining the origin to any point on the consumption function is a measure of the average propensity to consume at the income level corresponding to that point.
3. The saving corresponding to a given income level is found by the vertical distance between the consumption function and a 45° line (whose height equals the level of income measured horizontally) at that income level.

The Saving Function

Because the consumption function shows the level of consumption planned for each possible income level, it also shows the level of saving (income less consumption) planned for each income level. Instead of showing consumption for each income level, we could modify the consumption function to show saving for each income level. Such a *saving function* is illustrated in Figure 22.2.

Figure 22.2
The saving function derived from the consumption function in Figure 22.1.

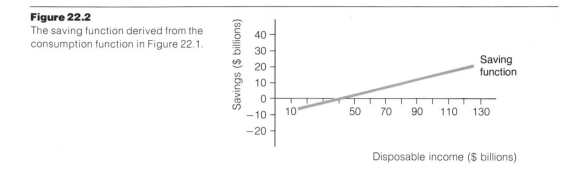

Table 22.2
Consumption and Saving Functions for Lunar Colony Clavius, 2001 (data from Table 22.1).
(Figures in billions of Clavian dollars)

Income	Consumption	APC	MPC	Savings	APS	MPS
20	25.0	1.25		− 5.0	− .25	
			.75			.25
30	32.5	1.08		− 2.5	− .08	
			.75			.25
40	40.0	1.00		0.0	0.0	
			.75			.25
50	47.5	.95		2.5	.05	
			.75			.25
60	55.0	.92		5.0	.08	
			.75			.25
70	62.5	.89		7.5	.11	
			.75			.25
80	70.0	.87		10.0	.13	
			.75			.25
90	77.5	.86		12.5	.14	
			.75			.25
100	85.0	.85		15.0	.15	
			.75			.25
110	92.5	.84		17.5	.16	
			.75			.25
120	100.0	.83		20.0	.17	

The ratio of total saving to total income at any income level is the *average propensity to save* (*APS*). If income changes by a small amount, the ratio of the consequent change in saving to the change in income is the *marginal propensity to save* (*MPS*). Because income is either saved or consumed, the average propensities to save and to consume must sum to unity, as must the two marginal propensities. This is only true, however, in a case like the present one in which saving is the only withdrawal.

Table 22.2 contains the basic data of Table 22.1, along with the same information expressed as a saving function. Note that the average propensity to save is *negative* at low-income levels, because saving is negative at those levels.

Recap The consumption function is the relationship between income and the consumption expenditure corresponding to it. It can be depicted as a table, with incomes in one column and corresponding consumption expenditures in another, or as a graph. To describe the income-consumption relationship, we use the term "propensity to consume." The marginal propensity to consume is the increase in consumption expenditure per dollar increase in income; the average propensity to consume is the ratio of total consumption to total income. The marginal propensity to consume is less than unity. Because what is not consumed is saved, the consumption function indicates saving at each level of income, and can be transformed into a saving function.

Predicting the Level of Output

How the level of output
is determined from
the consumption function
and the level of investment

Given the consumption function and the level of investment (or total injections, if there are injections other than investment), we can predict the unique level of output that can be sustained in the economy.

We can do this simply by checking our consumption function (or saving function), locating the level of saving equal to the already specified level of investment, and finding the income level to which this corresponds. In our simple model, the levels of disposable income, national income, and hence total output are all equal. To avoid confusion we'll refer to this level simply as "income."

An Example

Let's do this for our hypothetical economy whose consumption and saving functions are given in Table 22.2. Suppose planned investment is $10 billion. We look down the savings column of the table and locate $10 billion. This corresponds to an income (and thus output) level of $80 billion, which is thus our predicted output level for investment of $10 billion.

To check this, we note that an output of $80 billion will give an income of $80 billion. From this level of income, households will withdraw $10 billion in savings, "passing on" $70 billion in consumption expenditure. Investment of $10 billion will be injected into this, bringing total expenditures up to $80 billion, exactly equal to total output.

We could carry out the same process for any other level of investment that came within the bounds of the table. Note that if $100 billion were the capacity output for this economy, we could not find savings to match any

Table 22.3

Predicted Income for the Lunar Colony
Clavius, 2001. (Capacity output
$100 billion, figures in billions
of Clavian dollars)

Planned investment (per year)	Predicted income (income = output)
0.0	40
2.5	50
5.0	60
7.5	70
10.0	80
12.5	90
15.0	100

level of investment higher than $15 billion—above this level, our simple model could not be applied because real output could rise no further to balance savings with investment. An attempt to make an investment expenditure greater than $15 billion, without some other change in the system, would lead in fact to *inflation* and a different type of analysis.

Table 22.3 shows the various levels of income (output) that would be predicted for various levels of investment, assuming that the economy has the same consumption function as in Tables 22.1 and 22.2, and that capacity output is $100 billion.

Table 22.3 is derived directly from the consumption function data by putting the savings figures from Table 22.2 in the investment column of Table 22.3. The corresponding income figures from Table 22.2 are put in the "predicted income" column of Table 22.3.

The Analysis in Graphic Form

The foregoing analysis can be nicely illustrated by a diagram, Figure 22.3. As before, we measure income along the horizontal axis and consumption and other expenditures along the vertical axis. First, we draw the consumption function, C. We then add the "45° line," Y, which joins points representing equal quantities on the vertical and horizontal axes. (This line is at 45° to the axes only when the scales have the same intervals on both axes.)

The vertical distance at any income level between the consumption function and the 45° line is the difference between actual planned consumption at that income level and what planned consumption would be if all income

Figure 22.3
Determination of the equilibrium level of income.

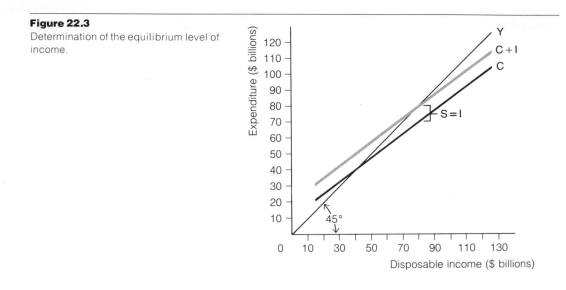

were consumed (shown by the 45° line). This difference represents planned withdrawals from the income-consumption loop at that income level, assumed here to consist entirely of saving.

Given a specific level of planned investment (the only injection), say $10 billion, planned total expenditure would equal planned consumption plus planned investment. The consumption function already shows planned consumption at all income levels. To show planned total expenditure, we measure $10 billion vertically above this curve at every income level. Drawing this new curve, $C + I$, is equivalent to shifting the consumption function vertically by an amount equal to $10 billion on the vertical axis. Any point on the new curve shows planned total expenditure corresponding to each income level.

Equilibrium income is given by the intersection of this total expenditure curve with the 45° line, because at that point, predicted income (Y) is equal to planned expenditure ($C + I$, where C is consumption and I is investment). Because the vertical distance from the consumption function to the 45° line is equal to S (for saving, the only form of withdrawal in the example), and the vertical distance from the total expenditure curve to the income-consumption curve is equal to I (the only injection in the example), when the total expenditure curve intersects the 45° line, we have injections (in this case I) equal to withdrawals (in this case S).

Summary

Thus, we have seen that the level of real output can be predicted, in the simple Keynesian model, from (1) the *consumption function* and (2) the *level of investment*.

Because we can take the consumption function to be given for a particular economy at a particular time, we can state the relationship somewhat differently:

For a specified economy, the level of output will be determined by the level of investment. Because a consumption function can be expected to show higher saving associated with higher income, the level of output will rise or fall as the level of investment rises or falls. This will hold, even in the simple model, only for investment within the limit set by the saving level at capacity output.

Although we expect this kind of relationship to hold in complex models, such as those designed to simulate the real economy accurately, we cannot generally expect to predict output from a knowledge of the level of investment *alone*. What we have set out here is the most simplified version of the Keynesian model.

Recap The consumption function specifies the level of saving associated with each level of income. Because saving is assumed to be the only form of withdrawal, the economy can be in balance only when injections (investment in simple versions) equal planned saving. Given a specific injection level, we find the equal saving level from the consumption function. The income (output) to which this level of saving corresponds is then the predicted income associated with that level of injection. The analysis holds only if the predicted income lies within the capacity of the economy.

Capsule Supplement 22.2   **Saving Is Not Always a Luxury**

The simple Keynesian model is based on a consumption function which assumes that saving increases as a fraction of income as income rises (increasing APS). In other words, saving appears in the Keynesian system as a *luxury* (something people tend to spend a higher proportion of their income on as they grow richer) rather than a *necessity* (something people spend a lower proportion of their income on as they grow richer).

Generally speaking, saving can be regarded as a luxury. However, there can be exceptions in the short run, at least with respect to certain kinds of saving; 1971 was a boom year for savings account deposits although the economy was moderately depressed. The saving boom, which was somewhat unexpected, was attributed to "uncertainty" by the official commentators.

There are good reasons why saving might *increase* in the short run when incomes fall, or are expected to fall, instead of *decreasing* as predicted by the consumption function. These reasons can be summarized as precautionary measures in the face of uncertainty. If the economy is depressed, workers realize that their chances of becoming unemployed are rising, just as the proprietors of small businesses realize that the chances of their profits falling or disappearing are increasing. As a precautionary measure to tide such individuals over a presumably temporary bad period or to finance them while they search for new jobs, many will decide to build up their savings account balances beyond the level they would normally keep if they felt certain their present incomes would continue.

Such precautionary measures benefit individuals but not the economy, because increased saving when the economy is depressed only adds to the downward pressure on the economy and thus tends to worsen the situation. This is one of the many examples in the operation of the economy (and of the social system generally) of the *fallacy of composition*—that what is good for individuals separately is not always good for these same individuals as a group.

Note that, if the worst fears of individuals taking precautionary measures should come about, then savings will fall as their incomes fall—just as predicted by the consumption function. Indeed, the very purpose of precautionary saving is to provide for a period of consumption in excess of income (negative saving), which is certain to follow a sufficient reduction in income.

Unemployment in the Keynesian Model

How too low an injection level creates unemployment

The Keynesian model assumes that adjustments take the form of variations in real output. Thus, our predictions of equilibrium levels of income (or output) refer to *real* income (or output). However, it is obvious that there will be an upper limit on output. Above this limit no further adjustment can be made; below this limit some resources will not be used. This upper limit is called the *capacity* or *full employment level* of output. We assume this level to be given in the economy, determined independently of the consumption function and the level of injections and withdrawals.

Specifically, the economy's capacity to produce is determined by its technology and its stock of available resources. In reality, machines can be operated a little faster or a little slower, and labor can be employed more or less efficiently. Hence, capacity may be appropriately thought of as a zone, rather than an abrupt barrier, within which the economy is able to expand or contract marginally.

In the long run, given sufficient time to choose the appropriate processes under conditions of relatively unchanged resource availability, the economy will employ all resources fully if it is truly at capacity. However, when resources are changing constantly—as in most economies—adaptation to appropriate processes may be incomplete. One resource, labor for example, may be fully utilized while machines remain idle.

Capital Sufficiency

A working assumption to which we shall adhere in the following discussion is that advanced industrial economies normally have sufficient capital to ensure that the available labor force can be fully employed with the production techniques in actual use. We must stress that it is a question of *fact* whether this assumption is borne out in specific cases. There are fairly clear examples of regions (such as the southern part of Italy) in which capacity is reached with all capital fully employed, but with considerable surplus labor. By contrast, major unemployment of labor in the United States and Britain during the past century has occurred only when there has also been major unemployment of capital.

It is common, therefore, in discussing income levels in the United States and most advanced industrial economies, to refer to the capacity level of output as the *full employment level*, and to consider the level of unemployment (of labor) as the most important index of underutilization of economic resources.

Unfortunately, the term *full employment*, like *capacity*, is not always precise. In an economy in which people are always moving between jobs, for example, unemployment is never zero, even though employers might be willing to take on more workers. The actual unemployment percentage considered to represent full employment varies from one economy to another, depending on such factors as the method of collecting labor statistics and the general level of labor mobility. In recent years, official sources in the United States have considered 4 percent unemployment (a figure on the high side) to constitute "full employment."

Any given economy at any given time will be characterized by a level of potential real output usually called *potential GNP, capacity GNP,* or *full employment GNP,* expressed in some real output measure, such as "1972 dollars."

Capacity and Prediction

Given the consumption function and the level of investment, we can predict the equilibrium level of real output that will be sustained in the economy. If this level is *higher* than capacity, we must discard the prediction because the fundamental assumption of Keynesian analysis—that adjustments are made by variations in real output—cannot hold then. Hence, the Keynesian model, unless specifically modified for the purpose, applies *only* to real output at or below capacity. Analysis of the economy for cases in which predicted output is above capacity is the subject of Chapter 25, Inflation.

If the predicted equilibrium level is below capacity, the economy is destined to operate at less than full employment. There will be a *gap* between actual and capacity GNP, representing unrealized potential output in the economy.

Consider, for example, the hypothetical economy we have been analyzing. Assume that capacity GNP is $100 billion. From the data in Table 22.3, we can determine the gaps between actual and potential GNP associated with various levels of investment. These are listed in Table 22.4.

Table 22.4
Actual and Potential GNP for the
Lunar Colony Clavius, 2001. (Capacity
output $100 billion; all figures
in billions of Clavian dollars
at constant price level)

Investment	Output	Gap between actual and potential output	Percent below capacity
0.0	40	60	60
2.5	50	50	50
5.0	60	40	40
7.5 ·	70	30	30
10.0	80	20	20
12.5	90	10	10
15.0	100	0	0

Unemployed Labor

While the gap between actual and potential GNP represents unused resources of many kinds, machines as well as people, it is unemployed labor
with which we are primarily concerned.

The greater the gap between equilibrium (or actual) GNP and potential
GNP, the higher the level of unemployment will be, other things being
equal. We would expect the percentage of unemployment and the gap
between potential and actual GNP, expressed as a percentage of potential,
to vary directly, and they do, though not necessarily in proportion.

Over the period from 1955 to the present, unemployment in the United
States has exhibited a tendency to change by approximately 1 percentage
point for every 3 percentage points change in the GNP gap, with 4 percent
unemployment at zero gap. Thus, a 9 percent GNP gap corresponded to 7
percent unemployment ($\frac{1}{3} \times 9 + 4$), while a 3 percent GNP gap corresponded to 5 percent unemployment ($\frac{1}{3} \times 3 + 4$).

This relationship, with employment being reduced by only one-third of
the proportion by which output falls below potential, does not necessarily
hold for major GNP gaps that persist for a long time. Between 1929 and
1933—during the Great Depression—output fell by 29 percent while unemployment rose from 3.2 percent to 24.9 percent—more than double the
increase in unemployment that would have been predicted from the relationship just described.

Recap A particular economy at a particular time has a capacity or full employment level of output that is the maximum level of output the economy can produce
with its existing labor force, capital stock, and technical knowledge. The output

level predicted by the Keynesian analysis cannot actually be attained unless it is at or below this full employment level. On the other hand, if the predicted output level is less than the full employment level, there will be unused resources, particularly unemployed labor.

The Persistence of Unemployment

The possibility of sustained high unemployment

The analysis of the preceding section leads us to a very important conclusion. In the Keynesian scenario, prices and wages are viewed as relatively inflexible. Consequently, if the level of injections produces real output below the full employment level, this output will persist as long as neither the level of injections nor the consumption function change. That is, the level of real output predicted from the Keynesian model is an *equilibrium level* that will be sustained until some externally motivated change occurs.

Price Flexibility

Monetarists, on the other hand, would generally regard the level of real output predicted by the Keynesian analysis as that characterizing the short run only. In the long run, according to the monetarists, market forces would lead to *price changes* and the ultimate adjustment of real output back to capacity.

The key to price flexibility is wage flexibility. If wages remain constant, production costs (and thus prices) cannot change much because wages generally constitute the dominant component in production costs over the economy as a whole. If production costs remain fixed, there can be small price changes associated with variations in profit margins, but not true price flexibility.

By wage flexibility we mean variations in the money or nominal wage rate, rather than in the real wage rate. The extreme monetarist analysis would predict a decline in both money wages and the price level. Hence, although the dollar wage rate would fall by, say, 5 percent, the price level (and cost of living) would also fall by 5 percent, so the wage earner could buy the same real goods and services as previously—the *real wage* remaining unchanged.

Keynes maintained that the real economy would be characterized by wage inflexibility in the *downward* (but not upward) direction. His reason was that both individual wage earners and labor unions would strongly resist attempts to reduce money wages, even if there were considerable unemployment and even if they were convinced that the cost of living would keep in step with any change. Unwillingness to accept a reduced money wage, even if prices would follow and leave the real wage unchanged, is sometimes referred to as *money illusion*. It is an illusion only in the abstract and aggregate sense. To the individual wage earner, a wage cut is an immediate, definite event. A change in the cost of living, on the other hand, is an uncertain possibility that depends on the economy as a whole and is quite beyond the individual's control.

The monetarist argument is that unemployment, like excess supply in any market, must lead to downward pressure on the price—in this case the money wage rate—despite individual and labor union resistance.

The Phillips Curve

Whether wages are flexible downward or not is ultimately a question of fact, not speculation. Determining the facts in the context of an economy in which large numbers of different and often counteracting influences are simultaneously at work is not easy. The major attempt to answer this question factually was made by A. W. Phillips, a British economist. Phillips examined the historical relationship between the rate of wage change and the level of unemployment in Great Britain over a period of almost a century. The results of his study are embodied in the *Phillips curve*, which has the general shape shown in Figure 22.4.

This curve shows that the rate of wage change varies inversely with the level of unemployment. Note that it is much steeper *above* the line showing zero wage change than below it. Point *A,* at which the curve crosses this line, shows the level of unemployment at which wages neither rise nor fall. It is not at zero unemployment, but something higher.

The bottom tail of the curve (below *A*) is relatively flat and shows that wages fall, but very slowly, as unemployment becomes higher and higher. This seems to be the closest we can get to answering our question about downward wage flexibility—indeed wages do fall when unemployment is sufficiently high, but fall relatively slowly, with the rate of decline rising very little as unemployment increases.

The top portion of the Phillips curve shows that wages will *rise* very rapidly at low levels of unemployment. This has important implications for policies designed to maintain full employment without inflation, which we shall discuss later.

The evidence thus shows high unemployment levels associated with slow rates of downward wage movement, if not actual rigidity. A state of depression in the Keynesian model may not be a true equilibrium state, but an "automatic" adjustment may take years. This suggests that from a policy point of view, we need to act and not wait for adjustment. The Phillips curve may not represent an unchangeable economic law, but it is something we must always take into account.

Recap An important difference between the Keynesian and monetarist scenarios relates to the likely persistence of unemployment. Monetarists emphasize that although low injections may result initially in high unemployment, this will result in

Figure 22.4
The Phillips curve.

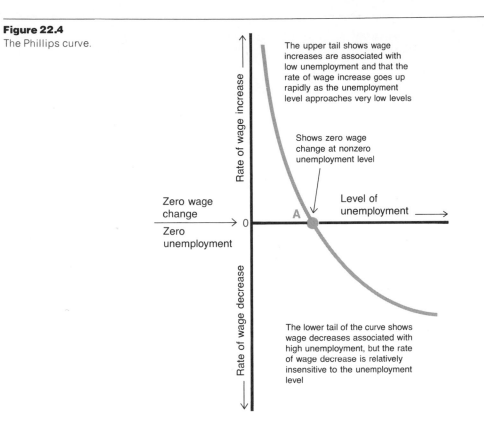

Rate of wage increase ———>

The upper tail shows wage increases are associated with low unemployment and that the rate of wage increase goes up rapidly as the unemployment level approaches very low levels

Shows zero wage change at nonzero unemployment level

Zero wage change
Zero unemployment

0

A

Level of unemployment ———>

Rate of wage decrease ———>

The lower tail of the curve shows wage decreases associated with high unemployment, but the rate of wage decrease is relatively insensitive to the unemployment level

downward pressures on wages and prices, ultimately leading to expanded expenditure. The chief empirical evidence on the relationship between unemployment and wage changes is expressed in the Phillips curve. It suggests that there is little downward movement of wages when unemployment is high, but considerable upward movement when unemployment is low. The Phillips curve suggests that unemployment might persist for long periods, and that rapid recovery through wage rate changes is improbable.

The Multiplier Effect

How a million-dollar increase in injections will raise output and income by more than a million dollars

So far our interest has focused on the level of income, and thus on the level of output, associated with a particular level of total injections for a given consumption function. We shall now examine the relationship between a

Table 22.5

The Multiplier Effect for the Lunar Colony Clavius, 2001. ($ represent billions of Clavian dollars per year)

Planned rate of investment ($)	Output and income ($)	Increase in investment rate ($)	Increase in output and income ($)	Ratio of increase in investment rate to increase in output
0.0	40			
2.5	50	2.5	10	4
5.0	60	2.5	10	4
7.5	70	2.5	10	4
10.0	80	2.5	10	4
12.5	90	2.5	10	4
15.0	100	2.5	10	4
17.5	110	2.5	10	4
20.0	120	2.5	10	4

change in the injection level and the consequent change in the equilibrium level of output.

An Example

Let's first examine the effect of a change in investment on the equilibrium level of output for the numerical example developed previously. Table 22.5 shows the data for the same economy as Table 22.3, but has additional columns that show changes in investment and in income (or output), and the relationship between these changes. Here we assume that capacity output is at least $120 billion, so real output is capable of attaining all the values given.

Note that the increase in output at each step is *greater* than the increase in investment that brings it about. If investment is $5 billion, output is $60 billion. If investment is increased by $5 billion to $10 billion, output will increase by $20 billion to $80 billion. An increase of only $5 billion in investment will result in a $20 billion increase in output—*four times* the amount by which investment was increased.

An increase in investment thus has a *multiplicative* effect on the level of output. The ratio of the increase in output to the increase in investment necessary to bring it about is known as the *multiplier*. For the data given, the multiplier is constant at a value of 4.

The Multiplier Process

What causes this multiplier effect? What determines the value of the multiplier? Obviously, it must be related to the *consumption function,* which determines what level of output will be associated with each level of investment.

The easiest way to obtain an understanding of the multiplier effect is to consider a typical Keynesian process by which the economy might move from the output appropriate to one level of investment to the output appropriate to another. Because the scenario is Keynesian, we shall proceed by income-expenditure analysis, and assume that all adjustments occur in terms of real output levels.

Consider the economy represented by Table 22.5, which we'll assume is initially in balance at an output level of $60 billion, including $5 billion investment and $5 billion saving. Now suppose that businesses, for some reason, decide to increase investment by $10 billion.

Initially the economy was in balance with withdrawals (saving) equal to injections (investment). Now injections have risen by $10 billion without a corresponding change in withdrawals. Planned expenditure is $70 billion ($55 billion consumption plus $15 billion investment), while output is $60 billion. There will be upward pressure on the economy that will increase real output by $10 billion to meet the increased demand.

The Generation of New Expenditure

But a $10 billion increase in output will not suffice to bring about a balance in the economy. The increase in output will result in increased employment, and will generate an increase in income of the same amount. Households will receive $10 billion more in incomes, and will thus plan to spend more. How much more? This will be determined by the *marginal propensity to consume,* which is constant in this economy at 0.75 for all income levels (see Table 22.2). Consequently, households will increase consumption by an amount equal to 75 percent of their increased incomes.

Thus, the $10 billion increase in income will generate $7.5 billion in new consumption expenditure, over and above the existing consumption expenditure, and add to the total investment expenditure. Total planned expenditure will now be $77.5 billion—the original $60 billion plus the $10 billion increase in investment plus the $7.5 billion in additional consumption resulting from the first increase in output. Consequently, though output has increased to $70 billion, it is insufficient to satisfy planned expenditure. Upward pressure on the economy continues, although it is diminishing because planned expenditure now exceeds output by only $7.5 billion instead of $10 billion, as before.

As output increases by $7.5 billion to meet the new planned expenditure, another income increase is generated—this time of $7.5 billion. Consumers will increase planned consumption by 75 percent of this—$5.625 billion. Planned expenditure still exceeds output, although the gap is down to $5.625 billion. As output increases in an effort to close this gap, income will rise again, by $5.625 billion, generating additional consumption expenditure equal to 75 percent of $5.625 billion. Note that with each successive "round" of increased output, the additional expenditure generated decreases. First it was $10 billion (the basic increase in investment), then $7.5 billion (the first round of induced consumption), then $5.625 billion, and so on. The additional expenditure will continue to decline by 25 percent on each additional round (because only 75 percent of each increase in income becomes an increase in consumption) until it eventually becomes small enough to be ignored.

The Final Result

Of course, we already know what the *ultimate* output level must be. Specifically, from Table 22.5, we know that the economy is in balance at an output of $100 billion when investment totals $15 billion (the initial $5 billion plus the $10 billion increase). The successive output levels after each round of adjustment are:

$60 billion (initial)
$70 billion
$77.5 billion
$83.125 billion ($77.5 + $5.625 billion)
$87.34375 billion ($83.125 + 75% of $5.625 billion)

These figures are moving toward the final value of $100 billion, though increasingly slowly. If the adjustment process were as described, it would admittedly take many rounds to come close to $100 billion—but if a round took, say, only a day, the *time* required could be relatively short.

It is important to remember that even after one round, the increase in output exceeds the increase in investment that caused it. The reason for this is that the increase in investment causes an increase in income, which, in turn, causes an increase in consumption. The ultimate increase in output thus reflects not only the original increase in investment, but also the increase in consumption *induced* by the consequent increase in income.

When investment rises from $5 billion to $15 billion, output rises by $40 billion; $10 billion represents the *direct* increase in investment expenditure, and $30 billion represents an induced increase in consumption expenditure. This result is illustrated in Figure 22.5.

Recap If injections rise, so will the level of output, provided the economy is not already producing at capacity. Output will increase by more than the original injections. This is because the injections increase income by an equivalent amount,

Figure 22.5
The multiplier effect. An increase in investment from $5 billion to $15 billion results in an increase in the equilibrium level of income from $60 billion to $100 billion.

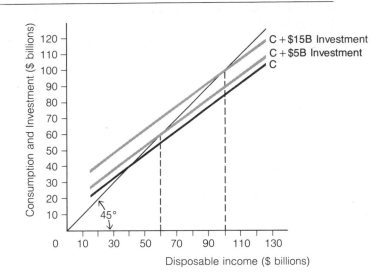

which, in turn, generates additional consumption expenditure. This is known as the multiplier effect. The multiplier is the ratio of the increase in output to the increase in injections that causes it.

The Value of the Multiplier

How the value of the multiplier can be determined from the consumption function

In the preceding section, we showed that an increase in investment (or any injection) ultimately results in an increase in output that is a multiple of the original increase in investment. Moreover, we saw that the nature of the consumption function, specifically the value of the marginal propensity to consume, is crucial to the multiplier process.

An Algebraic Derivation

We'll now formally analyze the multiplier process and show how the value of the multiplier is derived from the value of the marginal propensity to consume.

Denote the initial level of output (=income) in the economy by Y (its standard symbol in economics) and the level of investment that sustains this by I. If the initial level of consumption is denoted by C, we then have the relationship

$$Y = C + I,$$

that is, output is equal to total expenditure.

Let's now consider the economy at a new state of equilibrium, after investment has increased. Increases will be denoted by ΔI ("delta I"), ΔY, and ΔC, where Δ is the standard mathematical notation for incremental change.

If the economy is initially in balance, with expenditure equal to output, and moves to a new equilibrium position, also with expenditure equal to output, then the *increase* in expenditure must be equal to the *increase* in output.

The increase in expenditure is necessarily the sum of the increase in investment expenditure and the increase in consumption expenditure. That is, it is necessarily equal to

$$\Delta I + \Delta C.$$

Because the increase in output is ΔY, we thus have

$$\Delta Y = \Delta I + \Delta C.$$

Now the increase in consumption, ΔC, is not arbitrary, but determined by the consumption function. By definition, the ratio of an increase in consumption to the increase in income causing it, for a particular consumption function, is the marginal propensity to consume, MPC. That is,

$$\text{MPC} = \Delta C / \Delta Y,$$

which can be restated as

$$\Delta C = \text{MPC} \times \Delta Y.$$

If we insert this in the relationship above between ΔY, ΔI, and ΔC, we obtain:

$$\Delta Y = \Delta I + (\text{MPC} \times \Delta Y).$$

Moving all terms involving ΔY to the left-hand side, we obtain:

$$\Delta Y - (\text{MPC} \times \Delta Y) = \Delta I,$$

or

$$(1 - \text{MPC}) \times \Delta Y = \Delta I.$$

Dividing both sides by ΔI, then by $(1 - \text{MPC})$, we finally obtain:

$$\Delta Y / \Delta I = 1/(1 - \text{MPC}).$$

The left-hand side is now the ratio of the increase in income to the increase in investment that caused it—in other words, the multiplier. The right-hand side consequently denotes the value of the multiplier in terms of the marginal propensity to consume.

The value of the multiplier in the basic Keynesian model is equal to 1 divided by 1 minus the marginal propensity to consume. If saving is the only form of withdrawal, this value is equal to 1 divided by the marginal propensity to save.

Some Numerical Relationships

Note that, if the marginal propensity to consume is zero (if consumers save all of any increase in income), the multiplier is $1/(1 - 0) = 1$. Thus, the multiplier is greater than unity only if the marginal propensity to consume is greater than zero. And only when the multiplier is greater than unity will there be a true multiplier effect with output increasing by more than investment.

The value of the multiplier increases as the marginal propensity to consume increases. For an MPC of 0.5, the multiplier is 2; for an MPC of 0.75, it is 4, as in our numerical example in the previous section. With an MPC of unity, the economy cannot achieve balance until income reaches a level with a lower MPC. This is because unitary MPC implies that no savings are generated to offset the change in injections that initiated the process.

Multipliers in Complex Models

In more complex macromodels, such as those actually used for forecasting and policy, the determination of the multiplier is more complicated. Values determined for multipliers in such models are typically *less* than we would obtain from simple formulas. For one well-known model (the Wharton model), the marginal propensity to consume exceeds 0.9. This would be expected to give a simple multiplier of 10 or more, but if we ask the computer for the effect of a $1 million increase in government expenditure in this model, the answer is an increase in GNP of about $2 million— indicating a multiplier of 2.

The reasons for the true multiplier being less than that computed from the marginal propensity to consume are many and complex, but some of the factors are easy to understand. One is that, because income taxes increase with incomes, there are additional withdrawals in the form of taxes that lower the amount of expenditures as incomes rise. Imports, another form of withdrawal, also tend to rise with income, further diminishing the expenditure effects.

Recap In the basic Keynesian model in which saving is the only withdrawal and is determined entirely by the consumption function, the value of the multiplier is equal to $1/(1 - MPC)$, where MPC is the marginal propensity to consume.

Policy Implications of the Keynesian Model

The Keynesian model carries clear implications for macroeconomic policy

Although we shall consider the problems of macroeconomic policy later, now is a good time to briefly review the general policy implications of the simple Keynesian model. The basic principle is illustrated in Figure 22.6.

Given the consumption function and the absence of withdrawals other than saving, the level of real output (within the limits of capacity) is determined by the level of injections. In developing the model, we have assumed the primary injection to be investment. But the level of real output ultimately depends on the *level* of injections, not the type or source.

Fiscal Policy

Thus, the general policy implications are quite simple. If the planned level of investment leads to a level of real output below capacity, the output can be raised to capacity by making an *additional* injection equal to the difference between the level of injection needed to reach full employment and the planned level of actual investment. Suppose the full employment output of the economy in our numerical example is $120 billion, and planned investment is $15 billion. This level of investment will give output of only $100 billion (see Table 22.5). Full employment requires a total injection of $20 billion. Consequently, a policy injection of $5 billion (say, from added government expenditures) is needed to make up the difference. If this injection is made, the full employment level of output will be attained. Such manipulation of government expenditure (or taxes) is known as *fiscal policy*.

We can look at this from a slightly different point of view, using the multiplier. In the absence of specific policy measures, the real output of the economy will be $100 billion—$20 billion short of full employment. In this range of output, the multiplier is 4, implying that every additional dollar of injections will raise output by $4. Hence, it takes $5 billion more injections to raise output by the $20 billion needed to produce full employment.

Indirect Policies

An alternative to introducing additional injections from a new source, such as government expenditure, is to increase planned investment itself. We have assumed in this chapter that the level of investment is *exogenously determined* (determined outside of the economy), but this does not mean that we have assumed investment to be insensitive to all economic influences. Within limits, we can expect investment to be sensitive to such things as the rate of interest, tax treatment of investment expenditure, and so on. By manipulating these things, we may be able to induce businesses

Figure 22.6

Economic policy in the Keynesian model.

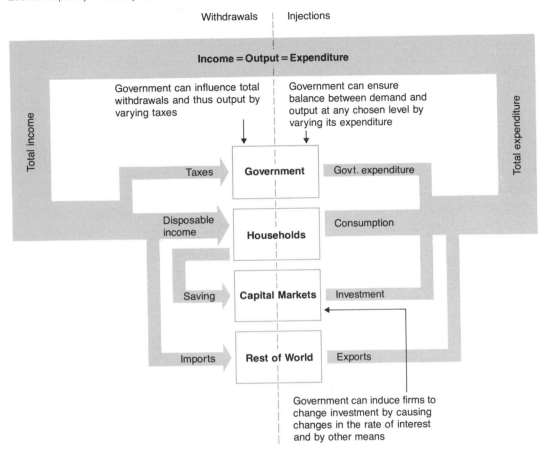

to increase investment by the amount needed to ensure full employment. In this indirect case, it is more difficult to predict the policy change required than when a direct injection is made by the government. We need to know how much the interest rate, for example, must be changed in order to achieve the desired increase in investment.

If the economic problem is one of too much upward pressure rather than of unemployment, the same general policy measures can be used in reverse. The government can reduce total injections, if they tend to exceed withdrawals, by reducing its own expenditure or by inducing firms to reduce the level of their investment.

In the simple model, saving is the only form of withdrawal. In the real economy, taxes represent an important withdrawal item that is controlled by the government. Policy can thus be carried out by varying withdrawals (taxes) rather than, or in conjunction with, varying injections. Because most taxes are related to income or expenditure, policy involving tax manipulation requires a special discussion, deferred until Chapter 30.

Recap Given the consumption function, the level at which the economy operates (within its capacity limits) is determined by the level of injections. Because the source of injections is unimportant, any tendency of the economy to operate below capacity because of too low a level of investment can be counterbalanced by an injection of government expenditures equal to the difference between planned investment and the level of total injections required to give the desired output level. As an alternative to varying government expenditures, the government may use policies (variations in interest rates, for example) designed to induce changes in private investment.

Macromodels for Practical Use

For practical policy purposes, our models are necessarily more complex than the basic Keynesian model

The basic model we've been discussing is far too simple to be used in practical policy applications. It illustrates the general working of the economy under conditions in which the key features of the Keynesian model—a stable consumption function and adjustment by variation of real output—are reasonable approximations to reality.

Several types of modification are called for in developing more realistic macromodels. Among these are

1. the specification of a consumption function that involves more variables than the income of a single period,
2. the inclusion of important economic variables left out of the simple model (money, interest rates, tax policies),
3. the determination of investment within the model instead of it being given, and
4. the explicit treatment of the relationship between output and employment.

The Consumption Function

Because consumption levels are influenced by households' previous experiences, we need to relate current consumption to past consumption as well as to current income to obtain a realistic consumption function. Such influences as the average income anticipated over a long period are also important—a household that temporarily loses income because of short-term illness will not be expected to behave the same as a household whose income is permanently lowered, for example. Moreover, a household with a large bank balance and/or large stock holdings will react less to short-term changes in its income than will a household with few assets. Thus, we should allow for long-run average income (''permanent income'') and for wealth (including money balances) in the consumption function, as well as for short-run changes in income (''transitory income''). Once wealth appears in the consumption function, the possibility of changes in consumption expenditure due to changes in money holdings becomes apparent— enabling us to reconcile the Keynesian and monetarist approaches, at least partially.

It's also useful to break the consumption function into several different functions. The relationship between income and expenditures on automobiles, for example, need not be the same as that between income and expenditures on nondurables (food and clothing). This is one example of the kind of disaggregation characteristic of the more complex models.

Large Models

Modern research methods and computational techniques permit the development of extremely complex models whose properties cannot be illustrated in simple diagrams or examples. Nevertheless, such models have been developed from the basic Keynesian model by subdividing the aggregates and adding further determining variables to the basic model.

By the use of econometric techniques, exact numerical relationships among the variables included in the model can be estimated, using historical data. Such models are thus capable of providing quantitative predictions about what will happen when a specified policy or other change is made. Such predictions are not simple—say, showing how much real GNP will change if taxes are changed by a specific amount—but are typically in the form of a long-term series showing the effects of the tax change in each of a succession of future time periods.

Some Important Models

Because *the* macromodel of the United States does not yet exist, there are several different models, each known by the names of those primarily responsible for its development (the *Klein-Goldberger* model) or by the institution(s) that sponsored the work on it (the *Brookings-SSRC* model, the *Wharton* model, and the *Federal Reserve Board-MIT* model).

All such models are constructed in basically the same way. The subsectors that together determine aggregate demand are chosen. These will be various subdivisions of the basic consumption, investment, government, and foreign sectors. The form of the consumption or investment function for each subsector is chosen either from considerations of theory or by trying out many different forms and choosing the one that seems to best fit past data. Other aspects of a complete macromodel that we have not yet discussed, such as wages, employment, and price-level determination, are also typically included. Numerical values expressing the various relationships among significant macroeconomic variables are estimated on the basis of data from past periods, giving a fully quantified model.

Models differ in emphasis, complexity, and their basic time frame (whether they are revised on an annual or a quarterly basis). The simplest of the modern macromodels is the Klein-Goldberger model. This is the outgrowth of a pioneer quantitative macromodel, first developed by Laurence Klein over the period from 1946 to 1953, with some further development and expansion since. It is the closest of the large models to the basic Keynesian framework. It contains sixteen *structural equations,* quite a small number compared to later models. Because its basic time period is the year rather than the quarter, this model is generally considered too ''coarse'' for most policy applications.

The most complex model, and the most elaborately devised, is the Brookings-SSRC model. Assembled by a large number of workers with individual teams working on different sectors, this model contains no fewer than 150 structural relationships, exhibiting almost a hundred times the complexity of the Klein-Goldberger model (complexity increases as the square of the number of structural equations). It is a quarterly model.

Economists with a special interest in monetary policy felt that the Brookings model, despite its great complexity, treated monetary aspects inadequately. Thus, the Federal Reserve Board–MIT model was created. It contains more monetary detail than the Brookings model, but possesses less detail elsewhere. It contains seventy structural relationships.

The Wharton economic forecasting model was designed for general purpose forecasting and policy study. It is quarterly, with forty-seven structural relationships.

For comparison, the basic Keynesian model described in this chapter contains only *one* structural equation—the relationship between consumption and income.

Recap For practical applications to macroeconomic prediction and policy, models need to be more complex than those discussed previously. Although these models are based on the simple Keynesian model, they have more sophisticated consumption functions, specify more types of withdrawals and injections, and divide the economy into more sectors. By "fitting" such models to past data, relationships among the many macroeconomic variables can be quantitatively estimated. No single model has emerged as the most suitable for all purposes.

Exercises

An economy has a consumption function with the following properties:
   a. Marginal propensity to consume = 0.80 at all income levels.
   b. At an income of $1,000 million, saving is $100 million.

1. Prepare a table showing consumption and saving at income levels of $500 million, $600 million, $700 million, $800 million, $900 million, $1,000 million, $1,100 million, and $1,200 million.

2. What will be the equilibrium level of income for the economy when injections total $80 million, saving being the only withdrawal?

3. Suppose the capacity output of the economy is $1,100 million and investment totals $110 million. Would the economy be operating at capacity assuming investment to be the only injection and saving to be the only withdrawal?

4. If the economy is below capacity in the circumstances of question 3, what additional injection will the government need to make or induce to bring the economy up to capacity?

5. What is the value of the simple multiplier in this economy?

For Thought and Discussion

1. Would a multiplier effect occur if the government simply paid the unemployed a wage without requiring them to perform any work?

2. Would a multiplier effect result from government expenditure in a socialist economy?

3. Conservatives in the United States have often asserted that Keynesian economics introduces "socialism." Do you agree?

4. An alternative to increasing government expenditure or boosting investment when planned saving seems as if it will exceed planned injection would be to reduce planned saving. How would you try to achieve this?

Part 6
Applications of Macroeconomic Analysis

This part, consisting of Chapters 23, 24, and 25, applies the macroeconomic analysis developed in Part 5 to the three main problem areas of the modern economy. Chapter 23 discusses economic fluctuations, Chapter 24 covers economic growth, and Chapter 25 analyzes inflation.

Chapter 23
The Fluctuating Economy

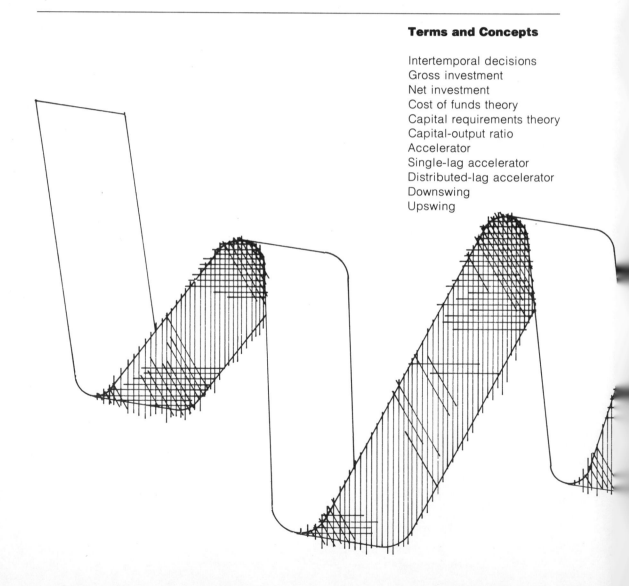

The Causes of Economic Fluctuations

Isolating the most important factors

In the previous chapter, we demonstrated that if the consumption function is stable, the existing level of income will be sustained as long as withdrawals balance injections. Moreover, we showed that this level of income need not be associated with full employment. Our concern in this chapter, however, is not why the economy may remain steady at, say, 8 percent unemployment, but why the overall level of economic activity actually tends to fluctuate over time.

That the economy does fluctuate is clearly illustrated in Table 23.1, which charts the annual percentage change in real GNP from 1929 to 1977. Over this period the economy generally experienced growth, and most of the changes are positive, except during the early 1930s and certain other recession periods. In any event, the magnitude of these changes varies greatly over this forty-eight year period.

We can assume that the consumption function is relatively stable. Consequently, the level of saving would be relatively stable if income did not

Table 23.1
Annual Percentage Change in Real GNP
(1972 dollars), United States, 1930–77

Year	Percentage change from previous year	Year	Percentage change from previous year	Year	Percentage change from previous year
1930	−10	1946	−12	1962	+6
1931	− 8	1947	− 1	1963	+4
1932	−15	1948	+ 4	1964	+5
1933	− 2	1949	—	1965	+6
1934	+ 9	1950	+ 9	1966	+6
1935	+10	1951	+ 7	1967	+3
1936	+14	1952	+ 3	1968	+5
1937	+ 5	1953	+ 4	1969	+2
1938	− 5	1954	− 1	1970	—
1939	+ 8	1955	+ 8	1971	+3
1940	+ 8	1956	+ 1	1972	+6
1941	+16	1957	+ 1	1973	+5
1942	+13	1958	− 1	1974	−2
1943	+13	1959	+ 7	1975	−2
1944	+ 7	1960	+ 2	1976	+6
1945	− 2	1961	+ 2	1977	+5

fluctuate. Because the primary forms of withdrawal are saving and taxes, we can deduce that changes on the withdrawal side leading potentially to income fluctuations are primarily those arising from government taxation policy. The main forms of injection, remember, are investment and government expenditure.

Thus, the two most likely sources of economic fluctuations are government policy, which influences both withdrawals and injections, and private investment, which influences injections. In the 1930s, the size of government withdrawals and injections was relatively small compared with that of saving and investment. Thus, we should concentrate on private investment when analyzing the basic causes of the Great Depression. Although government withdrawals and injections have been large since World War II, we still focus on investment as the primary source of fluctuations in economic activity.

In the early 1930s, government policy was *not* appropriately used to counterbalance fluctuations in private investment. Since World War II, government policy has been used much more successfully, and economic fluctuations have been smaller in recent years.

As we demonstrated in the last chapter, changes in investment will cause multiplied changes in the level of GNP, so a $1 billion decline in investment will cause more than a $1 billion decline in GNP.

Why does investment fluctuate? That's the question which we will now consider.

Recap Because the economy would remain steady if withdrawals and injections remained in balance, we look for those withdrawals and injections that tend to vary. The primary forms of withdrawal, saving and taxes, tend to be steady if income remains steady and there are no changes in tax rates. Thus, fluctuations basically stem from changes in injections. Of the primary forms of injections, the level of government expenditure is a matter of policy. Consequently, it is variations in private investment that provide the basic cause for nonpolicy fluctuations.

Capsule Supplement 23.1 **The Great Crash and the Great Depression**

On October 24, 1929—"Black Thursday"—the stock market, which had begun to weaken on Wednesday afternoon, took its infamous downward plunge. Panic ensued, sales of shares reached unheard-of levels, and the Great Crash was under way. Even though some investors and stockbrokers *did* jump out of windows, the Crash, as devastating as it may have been, was really a minor event compared to the dismal years of the Great Depression, which were to follow. Even the suicide rates reflect this. In 1929, this rate was 13.9 per 100,000 population, only a fraction higher than it had been in 1927 or 1928. In 1932, it rose to its all-time high of 17.4 per 100,000. Those 1932 suicides were not the spectacular leaps of broken Wall Street financiers, but the desperate final solutions of those long without incomes, work, or hope of either. Of course, the vast majority of Americans carried on in the face of incredible hardship.

With the benefit of hindsight, it is difficult to sympathize with those who lost money in the Crash, because stock prices had obviously reached a level unjustified by any real economic performance. In the period from 1921 to 1929, stock prices had risen by 500 percent, although commodity prices had fallen slightly over the same period and GNP had increased by only 40 percent. However, the rise in stock prices had been so steady for so long that few foresaw the inevitable. Indeed, Irving Fisher of Yale University, who was perhaps the greatest economist of the period, spotlighted the fallibility of his profession by assuring the United States that stock prices would settle down at the then-current level—one week before the Crash.

But if the Crash was inevitable, the Depression was not its inevitable sequel. It was the result of the Hoover administration's refusal to regard the level of economic activity as a matter for government policy. What little policy was carried out proved to be, on balance, for the worse. The administration confined itself mainly to talk of "courage" and assertions that the economy had "turned the corner." The United States had no nationwide Social Security or unemployment schemes at the time, and the Hoover administration refused to introduce them. Instead, Hoover tried to organize a charity drive to help the unfortunate. But there were few Americans who didn't feel that *they* were the unfortunate, and the drive failed badly.

The downward spiral of the economy itself, as opposed to the fall in inflated stock prices, was due to a massive decline in investment and exports (investment was strongly affected by the Crash). The drop in expenditures signaled the need for a substantial increase in government spending to maintain the level of total injections. Expenditures of the federal government, however, were virtually kept at 1929 levels through 1930 and 1931. There was even a substantial federal *surplus* (excess of taxes over expenditures) in 1930. In short, the net effect of government policy was to push the economy farther downward.

United States GNP had been $204 billion in 1929 (measured in 1958 dollars). From this level it fell to $183 billion in 1930, then to $169 billion in 1932, and finally to $141 billion in 1933—a total decline of 31 percent in four years. Unemployment had reached 25 percent by 1933; almost 13 million unemployed people roamed the United States in search of jobs or any other means of support. The Hoover administration became wholly discredited by the end of its term, and the seeds of major political upheaval had been sown. Germany, the only other major industrial nation with an unemployment rate approaching that of the United States, turned to Hitler in 1933. Luckily for the United States, the presidential election fell in 1932.

The first Roosevelt administration was given an overwhelming mandate in 1932—and the New Deal period began. By the standards of modern macroeconomic policy, the New Deal was relatively modest in its operations. Its greatest impact was in distribution and agricultural policy rather than in macroeconomic policy proper, but at least its moves were in the right direction. Federal government expenditure had risen by about one-third from 1931 to 1932—even before the Roosevelt administration had come into office— reflecting the actions of the Democrats who had managed to obtain House control. Expenditures continued to rise as a result of the New Deal proper, and by 1934 had doubled from their 1929 levels.

Despite its successes, the New Deal failed to restore full employment (even though the worst of the Depression was over after 1933), and the rate of unemployment was still 14.3 percent in 1937 when another downturn took place. It was the second Roosevelt administration that failed to act appropriately this time. Government expenditure fell in 1937 and 1938 instead of rising as modern policy would dictate. The unemployment rate climbed back to 19 percent in 1938, but America was spared further disaster by injections originating from across the Atlantic as the European nations began to increase their arms expenditures in preparation for war. By 1939, the United States had finally regained its 1929 level of GNP.

The eventual entry of the United States into the war (in 1941) finally generated sufficient government expenditure to bring the economy to full capacity. World War II thus ended the most sustained and most severe period of economic depression in U.S. history.

The Nature of Investment

Two aspects of investment

Generally speaking, the investment process implies the creation or purchase of goods that bring benefits over a relatively long period of time. It is not like the consumption process that provides immediate benefits. Investment is also different from producers' purchases of materials where direct benefits cease as soon as the materials are incorporated into a finished product.

When we aggregate investment, only expenditure on *newly produced* capital goods is counted. A firm, of course, may "invest" in a used truck purchased from some other firm. But, from the viewpoint of the economy as a whole, because the truck was already part of the capital stock, the sale from one firm to the other merely transfers ownership within the economy without contributing anything new to the economy. For the same reason, we do not regard transactions in financial assets as investment. An individual may "invest" in stocks, but from the viewpoint of the economy as a whole, the purchase and sale of stock merely represent the transfer of claims over real assets within the economy. If a corporation builds a new factory with funds obtained by selling stock, the resulting investment, in the economist's sense, is the creation of the newly produced factory, not the transfer of ownership represented by the initial sale of stock.

The Two Sides of Investment

Investment can be viewed in two ways. It constitutes expenditure on *new goods;* and it represents additions to society's *capital stock,* and thus potential future benefits. Because the two are linked over time, investment decisions are called *intertemporal decisions* in which expenditures made in some initial period are balanced against benefits that do not appear until later.

We usually confine our attention to one side or the other. In income-expenditure analysis, for example, we are concerned only with the fact that investment represents current expenditure, and thus contributes to the *demand* for the economy's current output. The ultimate effect of investment on the *supply* of output is ignored because we conventionally assume the economy's output to be given for each period discussed. In analyzing economic growth, however, we are interested in investment both as a form of immediate expenditure and as an activity that adds to the potential output of the economy in later periods.

Not all of the investment expenditure contributing to aggregate demand results in the expansion of future output. Because capital wears out and must eventually be replaced, some portion of investment expenditure necessarily goes to replace worn-out equipment. This part of investment adds no new capacity; it merely keeps capacity at its original level.

Gross and Net Investment

The economy may possess an airline fleet of 1,000 planes, 100 of which become unusable every year. To keep the fleet at a constant level, 100 new aircraft must be produced every year for *replacement.* To *increase* the fleet by 100 thus requires a total of 200 new aircraft—100 for replacement and 100 for the increase.

From the viewpoint of income-expenditure analysis, the demand for newly produced aircraft is the *total* demand of 200, because an injection is an injection, from whatever source or for whatever reason. We refer to the total expenditure on new capital goods as *gross investment,* regardless of whether it is for replacement or for increase. From the viewpoint of growth of the economy's potential output of air transport services, it is only the *increase* in the number of aircraft that counts—the total number of new aircraft less those used for replacement. We refer to the expenditure devoted to increasing the capital stock as *net investment*.

In terms of our analysis we thus have

$$\text{gross investment} = \text{net investment} + \text{replacement}.$$

Sometimes we may prefer to focus on the decline in the value of the capital stock (capital consumption or depreciation) rather than on actual replacement. Then the following relationship results:

$$\text{gross investment} = \text{net investment} + \text{depreciation}.$$

Gross investment is the same in both formulas. Depreciation and replacement should be much the same over a period of several years, but may differ over short periods. These two definitions of net investment may thus yield different figures, especially over periods of a year or less.

Investment may take the form of a wide variety of capital goods and may be made by the government or by the private sector. Roads, bridges, and school buildings are clearly capital goods, but are typically paid for by governments. Expenditures on these therefore represent *government* or *public* investment. Industrial machinery, factory buildings, and most housing are normally paid for by firms, and thus represent typical forms of *private* investment.

We normally make no distinction (at least in simple economic models) between government spending on capital items like school buildings and on current items like teachers' salaries. All are considered *government expenditures,* so there is no special category for government investment.

Thus, when we use the term "investment" we normally mean *private investment.* We shall follow this tradition here.

Recap Investment has two aspects: it represents expenditure, which generates income, and it adds to the economy's future productive capacity. All purchases of new capital goods (gross investment) represent expenditure, but only the excess of new capital goods over old due for replacement (net investment) increases the economy's productive capacity.

Financing Private Investment

The channeling of funds into investment

Building and equipping a new factory involves a heavy initial expenditure on such things as labor, construction materials, and newly produced machinery. The benefits or *return* from this expenditure will normally appear quite slowly, however, over many years in the future. For this reason, private investment is typically financed by some form of *borrowing* in which the investing firm initially receives a large loan with which it pays for the investment expenditure. In return the firm makes a commitment to repay the loan in future years as the return on the investment appears.

Lending

Because virtually everyone would prefer to have $1,000 *now,* rather than $1,000 *later,* it will generally not be possible to borrow $1,000 in exchange for, say, ten periodic repayments of only $100. To induce a lender to part with $1,000 now, he must be promised *more* than $1,000 in the future. This excess repayment needed to induce an individual or firm to lend is *interest.*

The *interest rate* is the excess repayment expressed as so much per $100 lent for one year—as a percentage per annum.

Borrowing

Borrowing to finance private investment takes many forms. A firm may simply borrow from a bank, signing a contract to repay certain amounts by certain future dates; or it may sell bonds to the public, each bond being a firm contract to repay in a certain manner. Bonds are more typically used by governments and semigovernmental authorities than private firms.

Private firms may also borrow by selling new shares of stock to the public. A share of stock entitles its owner to a share of the firm's future profits (presumably higher because of the investment). The issuance of stock, however, can be regarded as an implicit form of formal borrowing, with expected dividends being comparable to interest payments.

The Channeling of Funds

Where do investment funds come from? It is clear that potential lenders can use whatever funds they possess to (1) purchase consumption goods, (2) maintain or increase their money balances, or (3) lend in order to obtain a return in the form of interest or dividends. Lending therefore competes with both consumption and the holding of money balances.

From the income-expenditure viewpoint, lending out of income constitutes a *withdrawal* because funds that are lent would have otherwise presumably been used for consumption. Consequently, the primary source of funds for financing private investment is that part of income not consumed, or *saving*. This does not mean that households lend funds directly to investors. Although they may indeed buy newly issued stock, they may also buy life insurance or contribute to pension plans (in which case insurance companies or pension funds lend the money for them), or keep savings accounts (in which case banks do the lending).

As already pointed out, the channeling of funds from the income stream through households into the hands of investors involves a choice by households among consumption, the acquisition of money balances, and lending. This choice is perhaps best viewed as a two-step process:

1. A decision between consumption and asset accumulation (saving in the broad sense).
2. A decision, given the level of saving chosen in decision 1, between holding money or acquiring interest- or dividend-bearing assets.

The Effect of Interest Rates

How the rate of interest affects these two decisions is very important in determining the usefulness of alternative economic models. A high rate of interest means that the *future* return from lending will be high. This may induce households to forgo some present consumption in order to increase their lending, hence their potential future consumption. The higher the interest rate becomes, the more willing households may be to forgo present consumption in order to increase future consumption by more than present consumption has been cut. A high rate of interest might also induce households to reduce money balances in order to increase lending. The households would increase their risk of being illiquid (having insufficient money balances to make emergency payments, necessitating the sale of other assets whose market prices may be low), but also increase their future return from interest-bearing assets.

Thus, it's plausible for the interest rate to affect both the consumption-saving decision and the money-lending decision. It is, of course, a question of *fact* whether either or both decisions are actually sensitive to interest rates.

Pre-Keynesian economists considered the consumption-saving decision to be sensitive to the rate of interest. Keynesian analysis, on the other hand, assumes that the level of saving (like the level of consumption) depends exclusively on the level of income, and therefore is independent of the rate of interest.

The Keynesian consumption function has been investigated extensively over the years, and the rate of interest has not been found to be important. Thus, there is general agreement among economists that the rate of interest plays an important role in the allocation of assets between money and loans, but not in the decision to consume or save.

Recap Investment requires using current resources whose benefits ordinarily do not accrue until future years. For this reason, private investment is typically financed by borrowing, the firm receiving funds in the present to acquire capital, but not repaying these funds until the returns from this capital become available. Because lenders will not normally permit their funds to be tied up in this way unless they receive some form of interest, the interest rate will influence the manner in which households choose to save.

The Level of Investment

Two main explanations about how the amount of investment is determined

In the preceding chapters we've taken the level of investment as given, and concentrated on the economic consequences of this given level. The time has come to examine those factors that influence the actual level of private investment.

Figure 23.1
The Keynesian view of how the level of investment depends on the rate of interest.

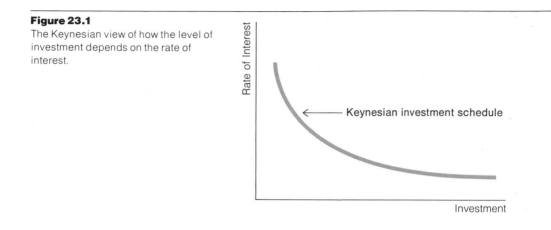

Keynesian investment schedule

Rate of Interest

Investment

The Cost of Funds

Businesses invest with the aim of making a profitable return on their capital. The actual earnings they expect per dollar invested in a particular project is determined by such factors as technology, the existing capital stock and expectations about the future of the economy. There are many projects that will provide relatively small earnings per dollar invested, and significantly fewer that promise a high return. Businesses finance their investment by borrowing, and must pay interest from their earnings. The return on capital therefore depends on the excess of earnings over interest, so the higher the rate of interest, the smaller the number of profitable projects. The level of investment, other things being the same, will thus depend on the *rate of interest*. Specifically, *high* levels of investment will be associated with low rates of interest and *low* levels of investment with high rates of interest. A graphic representation of the so-called *investment schedule,* as visualized in simple Keynesian analysis, is shown in Figure 23.1. This approach to investment constitutes a *cost of funds* theory in which the level of investment is assumed to depend on the cost of financing the investment.

Capital Requirements

Quite a different approach stresses the role of *capital requirements*. Instead of assuming the existence of a more or less stationary "pool" of investment opportunities from which a larger or smaller number will be chosen as the cost of borrowing changes, this approach concentrates on the way in which the size of the pool itself changes.

The simplest version of the capital requirements approach assumes a fixed relationship between the level of output for a given period of time and the amount of capital equipment required to produce this level of output. This relationship is usually expressed as the *capital-output ratio* that indicates the capital required to produce a given output per time period.

The numerical value of this ratio depends on the *time unit* over which output is measured. If $3 million in capital is required to produce $1 million in output per year, the capital-output ratio in terms of output *per year* is 3. How much capital would we need to produce $250,000 in output every quarter? Still $3 million, because production at the rate of $250,000 per quarter would require exactly the same initial equipment as production at the rate of $1 million over a full year. Thus, if we measured the capital-output ratio in terms of output *per quarter,* its value would be 12.

The capital-output ratio is almost always measured with respect to annual output. Hence, a capital-output ratio of 2.5 normally means that $2.5 million in capital equipment is needed to sustain output at the rate of $1 million per year, unless it is clearly stated otherwise. From this simple type of model, we can derive the *accelerator principle,* discussed later.

Modern Theories

Modern investment theories are usually mixed, involving both *cost of funds* and *capital requirements* elements. Because the relative importance of these elements varies for different types of investment, the investment sector in large forecasting models is usually separated into smaller sectors (residential construction, business plant and equipment, business inventories, etc.), whose behavior is explained individually.

Economists are much less certain about the determinants of investment than they are about the determinants of consumption. However, if only one of the two ''pure'' approaches were to be used, a majority of economists would probably prefer the capital requirements theory.

Recap The level of private investment is determined, in part, by the rate of return on particular types of investment. This rate will determine which investments are profitable at different interest rates. The effect of the interest rate on investment can be illustrated by an investment schedule. The level of investment at a given interest rate is also influenced by the economy's overall requirements for capital. If output is expanding, more capacity and thus more capital will be needed, increasing investment spending. If output is falling, less capital will be required, and investment will fall.

The Accelerator Principle

How investment is influenced by the rate at which output changes

In the late nineteenth century, economists began to note that the level of private investment fluctuated more than the level of overall economic activ-

Table 23.2
The Simple Accelerator—
A Hypothetical Example.
(Capital-output ratio = 3; capital in
millions of dollars; output in millions
of dollars per year)

Period	Output	Capital required	Capital available	Investment required	Change in output
1	100	300	300	0	
					4
2	104	312	300	12	
					6
3	110	330	312	18	
					0
4	110	330	330	0	
					10
5	120	360	330	30	
					5
6	125	375	360	15	

ity. This observation resulted in the development of the *accelerator princi-ple* by J. M. Clark in 1917.

Clark studied fluctuations in both railroad traffic and orders for new railroad cars. He noted that the level of car orders was more closely related to *changes in the level of traffic* than to the *level of traffic* itself. Because orders for new cars constituted planned investment by railroads, Clark's empirical study provided evidence for the simple accelerator principle or accelerator, which can be stated as follows:

The level of investment will vary with changes in the level of output, rather than with the level of output itself.

An Example

The simple accelerator can be derived from the assumption of a fixed capital-output ratio. Table 23.2 sets out a numerical example that illustrates this. In this example, we assume that the capital-output ratio is 3, that is, that an annual production of $1 million in output requires $3 million in capital equipment. We also assume that the capital required to produce this planned level of output in every period is always readily available (by new investment, if necessary), and that this becomes the available capital for the next period.

The main feature demonstrated by the table is that, *although output never falls, the level of investment fluctuates both up and down.* A second feature is that the ratio of investment to the change in output is 3, the same as the capital-output ratio.

An Algebraic Analysis

The properties illustrated in the table can easily be shown algebraically. Denote output by X, capital by K (we avoid C so as not to confuse capital with consumption), and the capital-output ratio by a. The capital required to produce output X is given by the capital-output ratio. In other words, we have

$$a = K/X,$$

or

$$K = aX.$$

Because we need to compare values in successive periods of time (t) we *date* the variables, using X_t to represent output at some period t and X_{t-1} for output in the period immediately preceding t, with equivalent meanings for K_t and K_{t-1}.

If capital is exactly correct for the period ($t - 1$), we then have

$$K_{t-1} = aX_{t-1}. \tag{1}$$

If output rises to X_t in the next period, the capital required will be

$$K_t = aX_t. \tag{2}$$

Subtracting the first relationship from the second, we obtain

$$\begin{aligned} K_t - K_{t-1} &= aX_t - aX_{t-1} \\ &= a(X_t - X_{t-1}). \end{aligned} \tag{3}$$

Now $X_t - X_{t-1}$ is the *change* in output between the two periods. As usual with changes, we use the *delta notation,* introduced in Chapter 22, writing ΔX instead of $(X_t - X_{t-1})$. Because $K_t - K_{t-1}$ is the change in capital between the two periods, we also write it as ΔK. However, the increase in capital is necessarily equivalent to the purchase of *new* equipment, and thus to *investment,* so we have

$$I = K_t - K_{t-1} = \Delta K. \tag{4}$$

Inserting I and ΔX in place of $(K_t - K_{t-1})$ and $(X_t - X_{t-1})$, respectively, in equation 3 gives

$$I = a\Delta X. \tag{5}$$

The formal statement of the simple accelerator is:

Investment per period is proportional to the change in output per period.

The constant of proportionality (the ratio of investment to the change in output) is equal to the capital-output ratio. In general, this will be true only if the length of the period for which output is measured in defining the capital-output ratio is the same as the length of the period over which the accelerator process is measured.

In the example in Table 23.2, the level of output is assumed never to fall. In reality, of course, output does experience a decline sometimes. What happens to the accelerator relationship in this case?

The Asymmetry of the Accelerator

If output falls, the capital required will be less than the capital available. When the capital required is greater than the capital available, additional capital is provided by investment, that is, by the use of resources to provide the new capital. When there is a potential surplus of capital, however, there is no reverse process by which the excess capital can be converted back into resources (except for inventories of consumer goods that can be sold).

The accelerator is asymmetric. When output falls, it cannot work in the same way as when output rises.

In a real economy, the capital stock will be expected to decline over time, at least to a limited extent. This is because capital goods wear out and eventually need to be replaced. By not replacing capital when excess capital stock exists, the capital stock is reduced. Adding replacement to the model modifies the working of the accelerator somewhat, but does not change the underlying principle that investment will depend on the *change* in output.

Recap Because capital requirements vary with the level of output, any increase in output will call for more capital that must be supplied by investment. A decrease in output will call for less capacity and thus for a reduction in the capital stock— negative net investment. The level of investment is determined by changes in the required capital stock and thus by changes in income. If the level of investment is directly proportional to the change in output, we say investment follows the simple accelerator relationship. The term *accelerator* is used because a change from 2.5 percent growth of output to 5 percent growth would double the investment level, although output itself would rise by only 5 percent.

Qualifications to the Accelerator

Why the simple accelerator must be modified

In the preceding section it was implicitly assumed that investment in, say, 1980 would be determined by the change in output from 1979 to 1980. But investment plans cannot be put into effect immediately, so investment in 1980 could only be determined by the change in output over the same year if businesses were able to *forecast* output well ahead of time. This does not mean that the forecast for all of 1980 would have had to be made before the end of 1979. Real time is not divided into calendar years, and plans and forecasts can be made and revised continuously. Working macromodels are usually based on *quarters* rather than *years,* so plans for the third quarter of some year can be finally checked in the second quarter, requiring a forecast only three months ahead. But even quarterly forecasts can be wrong, so we would expect some variation in the relationship between actual investment and the actual change in income if planned investment were based on a forecast.

Lags

In contrast to a "forecast theory," it is often assumed that investment *lags* behind changes in income, that is, that investment for the third quarter (planned in the second quarter) is based on the *actual* change between the first and second quarters, rather than the *forecasted* change between the second and third quarters. Sometimes this view may be expressed differently, but equivalently: that investment is based on a forecast, but a forecast based on the experience of the last actual change. A simple accelerator that uses the actual change between the last two periods as the basis for current investment is called a *single-lag accelerator.*

As we saw in discussing replacement, it may be possible to increase capital stock quickly, but will normally take much longer for excess capital to decrease. Thus, it's appropriate to assume that business will be somewhat cautious about increasing the capital stock.

If output increases noticeably in one quarter, *but is expected to fall back to its old level in the next,* most firms will probably choose to maintain the capital stock at its existing level and make no net investment. In practice, output can usually be expanded temporarily without increasing capital, but at added cost. For example, labor can be employed overtime and equipment can be used without taking time out for routine maintenance.

However, if output increases *and is expected to remain at the new level or increase more,* we will expect net investment to occur.

Expectations about the future are based on many things, one of which is past experience. It would thus seem reasonable to suppose that expectations about the permanence of a new output level would depend, at least in part, on past experience of change. Rising output over this quarter, preceded by growth over the previous quarter and the quarter before that, would lead to a firmer expectation that the current growth is permanent enough to respond to than, say, current growth preceded by a history of rising and falling output.

For this reason, modern accelerator models usually incorporate changes over several past periods, in addition to the most immediate change, as determinants of current investment. The more recent the period, the greater the weight assigned to that particular period's change. We thus obtain an accelerator that depends on output changes for many past periods, but that assigns the greatest weights to the most recent changes. A model formulated in this way is called a *distributed-lag accelerator*. Practical formulations are almost always of this kind.

Business Outlook

The past is not the only source of information on which expectations are based. There is also a general "business outlook" (difficult to measure, and thus not popular with quantitatively oriented economists) that is clearly important. If the general business outlook is *optimistic,* firms will tend to view a given increase in output as permanent and thus be inclined to invest.

Capacity Limits

When rapid increases in output lead to high levels of planned investment, there are often physical limits on the rate at which actual investment can take place. The industries that produce investment goods (construction and equipment manufacturing) themselves have capacity limitations. They may simply be unable to produce immediately all the new capital equipment required to meet the spurt in output. Firms may have to spread the installation of the additional capacity they seek over several quarters (or even years).

This means that in the first quarter of 1980, for example, firms may still be carrying out capital expansion plans made in the first quarter of 1979. In addition, they may be carrying out other plans made in the second, third, and fourth quarters of 1979. We refer to these still uncompleted plans as a *backlog* of investment projects.

As a result, actual investment in any quarter may not depend simply on the plans of the previous quarter, but on plans made up to several quarters before. Thus, current investment may depend on *planned investment* over several previous periods. This gives added legitimacy to the distributed-lag accelerator.

There may also be limits on the rate of investment that are *internal to the investing firm*. As a practical matter, the firm may simply have an upper limit on its ability to absorb new capacity.

Such limits on the rate of investment will presumably cause a *spillover* in investment from one period to the next. Output may rise for a year, then remain more or less stationary. Instead of net investment being high for a year, then falling to zero, it may initially rise less rapidly than output (because it takes time to get things moving), but continue for a year or more after output has stopped increasing.

Funds and Finance

Firms finance their investment plans from either or both of two main sources of new funds:

1. Profits not distributed to stockholders (retained earnings) or their equivalent. These appear as *business savings* in the national income accounts.
2. Funds in the hands of the public. These may be obtained by issuing bonds, securing loans from banks or other financial institutions, or selling new stock.

There is considerable evidence that, other things being the same, businesses prefer to expand *internally,* using retained earnings. Generally speaking, while dividends tend to remain relatively stable, profits vary widely from year to year. Thus, retained earnings will increase sharply when profits rise, and decline sharply when profits fall.

Therefore, we could expect *profits* to be a factor in the determination of investment. With high profits, we would expect some investment to be undertaken that might be passed over when profits are low. In short, we would expect investment to vary directly with the profit level.

When a firm's internal funds are insufficient to finance its desired investment, it will secure funds from the public. These funds will have a direct *cost* to the firm in the form of interest or dividend payments. Thus, we expect *interest rates* to have some effect on investment. The higher the rate of interest, the less attractive investment will be.

Types of Investment

Because about three-fourths of the gross investment in the United States consists of *business plant and equipment,* we typically concentrate on this type of investment in discussing basic investment theory.

Nevertheless there are two other types of investment that are important and behave somewhat differently from investment in business plant and equipment. These are investment in *residential construction* and investment in *business inventories.* While residential construction is the more important component of total investment, business inventories are of considerable interest because they fluctuate more than other types of investment.

Investment in residential construction depends on many long-run factors, such as population changes and marriage rates, which are not immediately influenced by changes in total output. However, such investment *is* influenced by average income levels. Moreover, because mortgage interest is a major cost to both owner-occupiers and landlords, we would expect interest rates to play an important role in residential investment decisions. Buildings take a comparatively long time to produce (compared with, say, machinery), and are the most durable of all capital goods. Therefore, we would expect investment in housing to involve many lagged relationships.

Inventory investment lies at the other extreme of the time-scale from residential investment. Because inventories, which are held by businesses to even out deliveries and sales, consist of ordinary goods, they can be increased almost instantaneously (positive inventory investment) and decreased by simply selling them off (negative inventory investment). Whereas net investment in equipment can be negative only to the extent that worn-out machines are not replaced, gross investment in inventories can easily be negative. Because inventory investment can be both positive and negative, and because manufacturers and distributors will tend to keep inventories more or less proportional to sales, inventory investment fits nicely into the simplest accelerator model.

Recap Although the accelerator relationship appears to influence investment, the simple accelerator does not fit real economic situations. Investment will occur in response to predicted capital requirements and thus will usually depend on business conditions and the recent history of investment, as well as on current changes in output. In some cases, investment plans may have to be stretched over a longer time period because equipment firms are already operating at capacity—a circumstance that will cause actual investment to spill over from one period into later periods. There will also be financial influences, including the cost of funds. Profits are also likely to be a factor because businesses often invest from their own savings, which vary with profit levels.

The Anatomy of Fluctuations

What happens as the economy fluctuates

We have emphasized the point that economic fluctuations stem primarily from changes in private investment. Such changes serve to initiate a *process,* which can be analyzed best in terms of its effect on the various withdrawals and injections in the income-expenditure loop.

Suppose the economy's capital stock has been growing steadily for some time, but now this growth slows down or stops. A growing capital stock means a high rate of net investment. Due to the multiplier, a high rate of investment generates a high level of income. A slowdown in the growth rate of capital stock implies an actual *reduction* in gross investment. The lower investment level will generate a lower income level in the absence of a counteracting policy, such as an increase in government expenditure, and will thus cause an actual fall in the income level.

The Downswing

Thus, an economic *downswing* is initiated by the fall in income that results from a decline in investment. Let's see what happens to the various withdrawals and injections.

1. *Saving* will decline, of course, as incomes fall, in accordance with the consumption function. With a marginal propensity to consume of MPC, saving will fall by $(1 - \text{MPC})$ million for every $1 million reduction in income. If the only change in the economy were the initial reduction in investment, incomes would fall just enough to reduce saving by the same amount as the decline in investment.

2. *Taxes,* generally being levied in relation either to income (income taxes) or consumption (sales taxes), will normally fall as incomes fall. However, because taxes do not take all of either income or consumption, the reduction in taxes will be less than the reduction in income.

3. *Investment* may or may not be affected. Much depends on which economic variables businesses react to in making their investment decisions. A fall in investment was presumed to have started the downturn, and this fall occurred because businesses had attained their desired levels of capital stock. But these levels were based on high expenditure and activity levels. Now that incomes have fallen, the formerly desired capital stock is *too high*. Businesses may decide that they should reduce the capital stock by not replacing worn-out machines. This will cause a *further* fall in investment unless businesses believe the downturn to be minor and temporary, and decide to ignore it in their investment plans. Thus, we can expect investment to probably fall and certainly not rise.

4. *Government spending* remains a matter of economic policy. The government may choose to keep its expenditure at the existing level, or it may be institutionally constrained to do so because of previous commitments. However, because tax receipts are falling, the government will run into *deficit* if it had previously balanced taxes against expenditures. If the government is committed to a *balanced budget* (as the U.S. government was at the beginning of the Great Depression), it will be forced to *cut* expenditures as its tax receipts fall. However, a government with a strong commitment to full employment might choose to *increase* expenditure to counteract the fall in investment. While certain types of government expenditure, such as unemployment payments, will tend to rise automatically, there will be many political pressures to reduce spending.

In the downswing then, withdrawals and injections will both fall. In the absence of a full employment government policy, injections are likely to be pushed farther downward as businesses react to falling demand and governments become wary of allowing their deficits to grow too large. Thus, unless appropriate policy action is taken, an initial fall in investment may set up a downward process of considerable dimension. Figure 23.2 illustrates the process described.

Figure 23.2
The anatomy of economic fluctuations: events of the downswing.

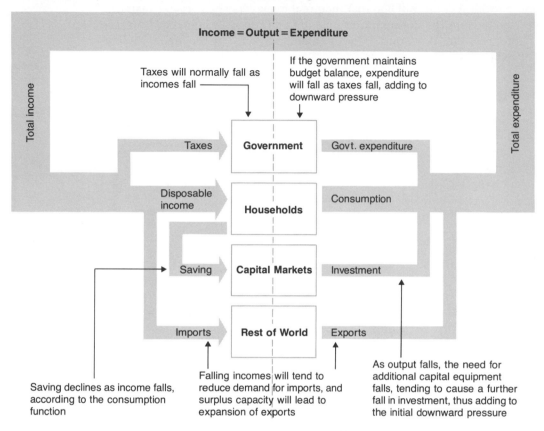

The Floor

Will the economy plunge continuously downward until its institutions collapse? No, because certain influences will eventually slow down the rate of decline. Even under a balanced budget philosophy, government expenditure cannot decline indefinitely because there are simply too many expenditures to which the government is committed. Even investment will eventually pick up because, as equipment wears out, the existing capital stock will become inappropriate even to a low activity level. Replacement will begin again, and this will represent an *increase* in investment compared with its lowest level. Moreover, in the absence of appropriate policy (or the presence of inappropriate policy), the downturn may go so far or last so long that political changes may occur.

Monetary factors will also tend to dampen the downturn process. In a prolonged downturn, prices can be expected to fall. If the money stock is not reduced, people will find that their real money balances rise, causing an upward shift in the consumption function and, thus, in influences running counter to the downturn. These influences may work quite slowly, however.

The Upswing

Once investment begins to rise with the return of replacement spending, it will have a multiplied effect on income. The resulting *upswing* will be similar to the downswing, but in reverse. However, there will be some subtle differences.

1. *Saving* will rise as incomes rise, in accordance with the consumption function. After a prolonged recession, however, there might be a temporary shift in the consumption function as consumers spend a higher proportion of their incomes than they plan for the long run, due to the relatively long period of low consumption.

3. *Investment* will rise somewhat, as predicted by the accelerator, as firms discover that their capacity is lagging behind the rising demand. If businesses believe that the future looks favorable, they may attempt to increase capacity ahead of current demand, further increasing investment.

4. *Government spending* is still a policy matter. Because tax receipts are rising, there will be strong political pressures to have government expenditure rise at least in step. This will be especially true if the economy has been in a recession, with lowered government expenditure, for some time. Much social capital—schools and roads, for example—may have depreciated over this period and will need to be replaced. These processes are illustrated in Figure 23.3.

In the upswing, injections are likely to rise more rapidly than they would fall in a downswing of equivalent dimensions. This leads us to expect that the upswing will require less time than it took for the downswing to move the economy to its depressed level.

At the Top

What will stop the upswing? It could potentially peter out below full employment if businesses invest only the minimum to keep up with capacity. However, during the upswing, a high level of government expenditure is virtually built into the economy. Combined with the generally optimistic long-run business view that results from modern government's commitment to maintain the economy at or near full employment, most upswings will reach capacity output.

However, attainment of capacity need not stop the upswing process.

Figure 23.3

The anatomy of economic fluctuations: events of the upswing.

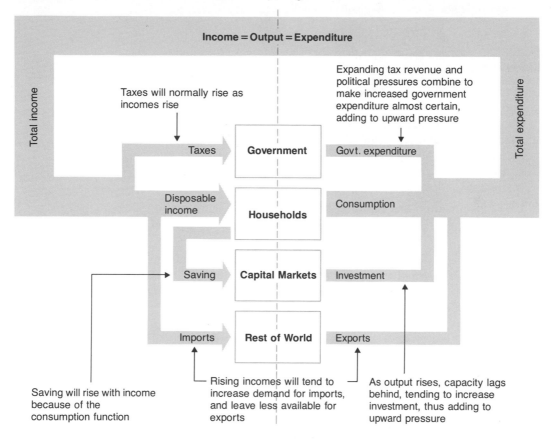

Although the maximum level of investment the economy can sustain is given by the level of saving at full employment income—assuming no budget surplus—firms may still attempt to increase investment. Under these circumstances, the upswing process will turn into an *inflationary process,* as discussed in Chapter 25.

Recap An initial decline in investment will set off a decline in income. The reduction in income, in turn, will affect the various withdrawals and injections in the economy. More importantly, it will reduce the economy's capital requirements, causing a further decline in investment, thus adding to the downward pressure. Falling taxes are likely to exert a downward influence on government expenditure, further reducing total injections. The economy will tend to continue moving on a downswing until either counteracting policy is adopted or built-in constraints stop the fall of investment and government expenditure. In a generally similar way, an increase in investment that raises income will tend to initiate a process that further increases incomes, bringing about an upswing.

Exercises

1. Suppose the multiplier is 4 and the government plans to rebuild its urban transit system at a total cost of $100 million. Assuming other planned injections remain constant and saving represents the only withdrawal, what will be the increase in GNP resulting from the transit project over each of the next five years if
   a. the expenditure on the project is all made in the first year?
   b. the expenditure is spread evenly over five years?

2. If $12,000 in additional capital will enable output to increase by $500 per month, what is the value of the capital-output ratio as traditionally measured?

3. If the capital-output ratio is 3 and GNP rises from $200 million to $212 million, by how much will we expect investment to increase assuming no depreciation? If the multiplier is 2, what will be the extra increase in GNP induced by the original rise of $12 million?

For Thought and Discussion

1. Suppose the consumption function is not stable, but shifts in a way that indicates that consumers are more cautious and save more when the economy moves downward, and indulge themselves and spend more when the economy moves upward. Would this tend to increase or decrease the fluctuating tendencies of the economy?

2. Do you think a fully planned economy would be exempt from economic fluctuations?

3. In most Western countries, the role of the very large, multiproduct corporation has been growing. Would you expect this trend to increase or diminish the volatility of private investment?

4. An important part of total expenditure in the economy is the expenditure by local governments. From your observations, do you think this expenditure tends to lessen or heighten the fluctuating tendency of the economy?

5. It has been asserted that without Keynesian economics, the Marxian prophecy would have been fulfilled, that capitalism would have collapsed as a result of its own ups and downs. What do you think of this assertion?

Chapter 24
Economic Growth and Development

Terms and Concepts

Economic growth
Economic development
Capital accumulation
Rate of GNP growth
Poverty cycle
Harrod-Domar growth model
Technological progress
Embodied technological progress
Disguised unemployment
Infrastructure of the economy

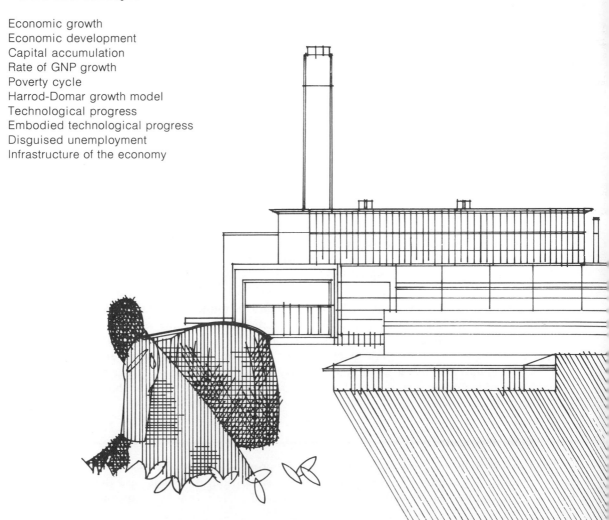

Growth and Development

Some introductory comments

Economic growth simply means a general increase in the quantity of goods and services available to society. Obviously, such growth does not require an increase in the output of *all* goods and services. Although real GNP in the United States has increased more than twentyfold over the past century, it has done so despite the decline and ultimate demise of sarsaparilla, buggy whips, and whalebone corsets. Indeed, it's precisely because the composition of goods and services remains in a constant state of flux that we generally regard growth as a macroeconomic phenomenon and monitor it in terms of changes in aggregate measures, such as real GNP.

We must be careful not to confuse the terms *growth* and *development*. Raising the GNP of a poor nation whose economy is based predominantly on peasant agriculture will typically require major structural change. Industrialization, urbanization, and the fostering of new economic institutions will all be involved. Such change, when brought about, constitutes *development*. Alternatively, an increase in the GNP of *any* nation at *any* stage of development, when brought about without significantly affecting its economic structure, constitutes *growth*.

Over a sufficiently long period of time, any economy is bound to undergo structural change. Hence, the experience of the United States over the past century reflects development as well as growth.

Growth and Fluctuations

We must be careful to distinguish between growth proper and cyclical upswings. Suppose an economy had an output of $500 million (in constant dollars), underwent a recession during which output fell to $400 million, then recovered to the original $500 million. Has this economy "grown" from the depth of the recession to $500 million? Not really, because potential output presumably remained unchanged at $500 million the whole time. The economy simply failed to achieve its potential during the recession. The movement back to this potential thus constitutes recovery, not growth. Accordingly, growth refers to changes in the economy with short-term cyclical movements taken out, either by considering potential output or by averaging outputs over periods long enough to eliminate the effect of short-term fluctuations.

GNP Per Capita

Even though the economy's output may be growing at, say, 5 percent per annum, population may be growing at the same rate, in which case the quantity of goods available for each member of society remains constant.

Consequently, it's possible to have growth in total GNP without growth in *GNP per capita*. Indeed, if population were growing at 6 percent per annum, we would have *declining* GNP per capita associated with growth in total GNP. Without growth in GNP per capita, a country may be growing "richer" in total output without its *people* growing any richer as individuals.

In investigating growth, we must carefully consider changes in both total GNP and GNP per capita.

Recap Growth and development differ mainly in that "development" is used when major structural change is involved. "Growth" is used when there is little change in structure. In assessing the growth performance of an economy, we should take out short-term fluctuations. Moreover, we should consider the growth in GNP per capita as well as in total GNP because GNP per capita reflects what is happening to the individuals within the society.

The Sources of Growth

The main factors that determine growth

The production of output requires the input of resource services. It follows that growth in total output can be achieved only by increasing the quantity of resources available or by securing more output per unit of resources used, that is, by increasing the economy's productivity.

The physical resources available to the economy are traditionally divided into the three broad categories: *land* (including minerals, water, climate, and other resources inherent in the natural environment), *capital* (in the physical sense of machines and structures), and *labor*. Resources classified as land cannot generally be increased, and some, like deposits of minerals or fossil fuels, are necessarily diminished with use. Of course, there are exceptions: the Dutch, for example, have increased their land mass by the application of capital and labor to reclaim the IJsselmeer. Moreover, natural resources may exist but remain undiscovered. While the tiny country of Kuwait possessed virtually no "known" natural resources fifty years ago, the subsequent discovery of oil transformed its GNP per capita into one of the world's highest.

Increases in Resources

In general, then, increasing a nation's physical resources means increasing its "stock" of labor and/or capital, because these are the only resources people control. An increase in population will certainly increase the potential labor force, but it will also increase the number of people who must share the potential increase in total output. An increase in the stock of capital, on the other hand, can increase total output without increasing population, and thus virtually ensures growth in GNP per capita as well as in total output.

While growth in GNP per capita is thus likely to be associated with increased physical capital, it is possible, nonetheless, to increase GNP per capita by increasing the amount of labor *if* this can be done without an equal (or greater) increase in population. Increasing labor resources at a greater rate than the total population is possible if the proportion of the population in the labor force can be increased. Among the factors that may accomplish this end are social changes that make it easier for women to work, advances in public health that reduce debilitating diseases (like malaria), and structural changes that allow unneeded members of peasant households (often called the "disguised unemployed") to move into other occupations.

Increases in Productivity

Increased productivity, historically, has been one of the most important sources of growth in GNP per capita, and certainly the most important source of growth in the United States over the past century. Although normally accompanied by increases in both capital and labor, increased productivity presents the possibility of raising output with constant levels of all resources. Productivity can increase as a result of several different factors.

1. *Increased efficiency* in the organization of the economy leads to a more efficient allocation of resources among alternative uses, and thus less resource waste. Much of the growth in Europe from the Middle Ages through the Industrial Revolution of the late eighteenth century stemmed from the development of the modern economic system and the increased efficiency with which existing resources and technology were used.

2. *Economies of scale,* derived from the ability to use production processes that require fewer inputs per unit of output but cannot be operated at low levels of output, become effective only as the economy grows. The ability to take advantage of such scale economies has been an important factor in the growth of American productivity.

3. *Increased effectiveness of human resources* results from the spread of education and the development of skills. Even though the size of the labor force may remain constant, its effectiveness can be increased by basic education (enabling instructions to be put in written manuals, for example) and by advanced training that promotes the understanding of complex production processes. The processes of training and education have been compared with the accumulation of physical capital—being regarded as a way to increase society's "human capital," and thus to increase its stock of

resources rather than its level of productivity. Human capital, in the context of income distribution, is discussed in Chapter 16.

4. Finally, there may be a *residual increase* in productivity in addition to that explained by the other factors. It is generally concluded that this "residual of ignorance" is due to the discovery of new production processes, new types of equipment, and new human skills and management techniques. We refer to it simply as *technological progress*. The available evidence suggests that technological progress has been the greatest single cause of productivity increase in the United States as well as in virtually all other industrialized countries. Despite its importance, we know comparatively little about the factors that influence the rate of technological progress. What little we do know is discussed later in this chapter.

International Considerations

In the remainder of this chapter, we shall discuss growth primarily in the context of an isolated economy. But we should note that, in principle, all the factors required for growth can be obtained from outside the economy. The labor force can be increased by immigration, capital can be obtained from imports, and other countries' natural resources can be purchased or acquired by political dominance. Other contributions to productivity growth can also be obtained—human capital by "brain draining" and technological progress by using production methods developed elsewhere. These possibilities can be crucial in stimulating the growth process in a previously poor or stagnating economy. Indeed, the United States has used all of them at one time or another.

Recap An economy can grow only by increasing its resources or by increasing productivity so more output is produced per unit of input. Resource growth is generally confined to increasing labor and/or capital because natural resources are relatively fixed. Productivity growth can result from increased efficiency in the allocation of resources, economies of scale, increased labor effectiveness through education and training, and technological progress through new discoveries. An individual country may be able to obtain increased resources and the "know-how" for technological progress from elsewhere in the world economy.

Capsule Supplement 24.1   **Malthusianism**

Because he is known as the "Reverend," and because he possesses a reputation of being a prophet of doom, Thomas Malthus (1766–1834) is commonly believed to have been a puritanical clergyman who dabbled amateurishly in economics. On the contrary, although he was indeed ordained as a minister,

Malthus is considered to have been the first true professional economist, and taught economics at a college for employees of the East India Company. Although he wrote one of the very first economics texts in 1820, *Principles of Political Economy,* his fame rests on his *Essay on the Principle of Population* (1798).

With some compound growth calculations, Malthus showed that if population doubled every twenty-five years—a quite-possible event if each family had between three and four children, born before the parents reached twenty-five, who all lived to the age of fifty—a single couple at year A.D. 0 would have produced enough descendants by the 1790s to populate the world to a density of four per square yard with enough left over to populate the rest of the solar system. (The actual population figure Malthus derived exceeded a trillion billions—actual world population even now is only slightly more than four billion.)

Why hadn't this happened, asked Malthus. Because, he answered, the means of subsistence had grown only slowly, at best, and population had been kept down by starvation and pestilence. As a consequence of his analysis, Malthus became the first to propose a population policy, and advocated the prevention of population reaching a crisis level at which famine would become the ultimate control. He was willing to have his own generation suffer by sexual abstinence, abortion, and even some starvation to prevent greater disaster to future generations. However, his *Essay* (originally published anonymously) was to be read by his own generation, which did not much care for what Malthus had proposed for it.

Malthus's model did not allow for the growth of output by accumulation of capital or by technological change. These factors made his dire predictions erroneous. The modern rebirth of Malthusianism is based on two things: (1) that capital accumulation and technological progress cannot increase the availability of pure space and exhaustible natural resources, and (2) that however much we can expand total output, we can increase output per person more if population grows less. Added to these factors is the problem that has emerged in recent years—disposal of the expanding wastes of economic activity into a relatively fixed environmental capacity.

Many of the poorer countries of the world remain near the Malthusian constraint, and a lower rate of population growth would make a huge difference to their present slow growth rates of output per person. From the mid-nineteenth to the mid-twentieth centuries, the rate of growth of *total* GNP was much the same for the less-developed countries as for those more advanced. But the rate of *population growth* was almost twice as high in the less-developed countries so the rate of growth of *output per person* was lower in the less-developed countries, widening the gap between the rich and the poor.

Policies to restrain population growth can touch some very sensitive nerves. Any ethnic or religious group whose population is growing at faster than the average rate can easily be made to feel (sometimes perhaps justifiably) that population policy is aimed at ensuring that they remain a minority within the population. Overeagerness of the rich countries to subsidize population control in the poor countries can easily bring suggestions that such policy is designed to be a form of subtle genocide. This is all reminiscent of Malthus, who suggested that it was the poor who should restrain their numbers, not the rich. International and intergroup suspicions, however, should not be allowed to hide the real problems that exist.

The greatest change since Malthus has been the development of techniques of population control (the birth-control pill, for example) that do not require the sacrifices Malthus urged on his generation.

Capital Accumulation and Saving	How capital accumulation involves intertemporal choice

Unless population is stationary or falling, a country's GNP per capita cannot rise without *capital accumulation* or *technological progress,* and as we shall note later, technological progress without capital accumulation is likely to be very slow or nonexistent. Consequently, increases in the capital stock play a central and crucial role in economic growth.

Let's briefly consider what happens to society's output when there is an increase in one productive resource while others remain unchanged. Suppose, for example, there is a 5 percent increase in labor with no increase in capital. As long as this additional labor can be used productively, total GNP will be expected to rise. But this additional labor will almost certainly require capital to work with. Because total capital is fixed, this requirement for additional capital must be met by reducing the amount of capital currently available to the existing labor force. In the absence of economies of scale and technological progress, the 5 percent increase in labor would increase total output by 5 percent *if it had the same amount of capital per person to work with as the rest of the economy.* But, because capital must be taken from the rest of the economy, the output there will decline somewhat. Thus, the new addition to the labor force cannot add more to total output than 5 percent of the original output. The output of the existing labor force will fall, so the *net* result of the 5 percent increase in the labor force will be an increase of *less* than 5 percent in total output. Similarly, we could argue that a 5 percent increase in capital with no increase in the labor force would increase output, but by less than 5 percent. To increase output by 5 percent would require *both* capital *and* labor (if these were the only two resources used) to increase by 5 percent.

A 5 percent increase in the labor force resulting from a population increase of 5 percent with no increase in capital (or a capital increase of less than 5 percent) will increase total GNP by less than 5 percent and thus cause GNP per capita to *fall*. On the other hand, a 5 percent increase in capital with no increase in population (or a population increase of less than

5 percent) will increase total GNP by less than 5 percent, but by more than the increase in population, so GNP per capita will *rise*.

Surely we would conclude from our analysis that capital accumulation cannot be anything but desirable, and the more of it the better. But we've not yet introduced the *cost to society* of increasing its capital stock.

The Cost of Capital Accumulation

Capital consists of machines, structures, and other such goods, all of which the economy must produce. The resources needed for producing new capital goods cannot be used simultaneously to produce other things. Consequently, if we wish to increase the production of new capital goods (*investment*), we must reduce the output of goods for immediate use (*consumption*). The increased capital will raise the level of output per person *in the future* and thus permit a higher level of consumption than is now possible, but the investment needed to bring about this future increase reduces consumption *now*.

Capital accumulation represents a distribution of economic welfare from persons in the present, whose consumption must be reduced in order to free resources for the production of capital goods, to persons in the future, who will have higher potential levels of consumption because of the increased future output of the economy.

An Example

We can illustrate this with a numerical example. Imagine a simple economy with an existing capital stock of $400 million. Current GNP is $80 million. The increase in total GNP that results from an increase in the capital stock beyond this level is $1 of GNP for every $5 of additional capital—a 1 percent increase in capital at the initial level giving a 1 percent increase in total GNP (and also in per capita GNP because population is assumed to remain unchanged).

Assume, for simplicity, that capital does not wear out, and that there is never a need for capital replacement. So investment of $20 million in new capital each year would mean that consumption is necessarily $20 million less than GNP each year. On the other hand, by not accumulating capital at all, the economy could consume all of its output. That is, consumption would equal GNP.

In Table 24.1, the first two pairs of columns show total GNP and total consumption each year under two sets of conditions: (1) that the economy does not accumulate capital; and (2) that the economy accumulates $20 million in capital each year for five years, then maintains total capital at $500 million. Each annual increment of $20 million in capital enables GNP to increase by $4 million.

Table 24.1
Consumption and Capital Accumulation.
(Millions of dollars)

Year	No Capital accumulation		Accumulation to 500 over 5 years		Accumulation to 500 over 10 years	
	GNP	C	GNP	C	GNP	C
1	80	80	80	60	80	70
2	80	80	84	64	82	72
3	80	80	88	68	84	74
4	80	80	92	72	86	76
5	80	80	96	76	88	78
6	80	80	100	100	90	80
7	80	80	100	100	92	82
8	80	80	100	100	94	84
9	80	80	100	100	96	86
10	80	80	100	100	98	88
11	80	80	100	100	100	100

The five-year accumulating economy has only $60 million available for consumption in the first year. Consumption rises by $4 million each year as a result of the increase in GNP. The non-accumulating economy has $80 million each year. For years 1 to 5, the accumulating economy is worse off, in the sense that the population has less available for its immediate consumption than the non-accumulating economy. From year 6 on, however, the level of consumption for the economy that has increased its capital over five years is higher.

The last pair of columns in the table shows the effect of growth at a slower rate than the middle pair, taking ten years instead of five for the economy's capital to accumulate to $500 million. Compared with the five-year rate, consumption is higher under this assumption for the first five years because of the lower rate of annual investment. Then consumption for the remainder of the ten-year period is lower because the economy is still accumulating capital. At the end of ten years, both accumulating economies have reached the same state. Thus, the distribution of consumption between time periods depends not only on whether or not growth is taking place, but on the rate of growth as well.

The faster the rate of capital accumulation (and thus the higher the level of required investment), the greater is the consumption loss in the present time period and the consumption gain in future time periods.

The production of capital goods generates income just as the production of consumption goods does. Hence, if we look at the growth process from the viewpoint of consumers, the consumption they must forgo during any period to guarantee that society's resources can produce capital goods represents *income not consumed* or *saving*. A faster rate of growth in the capital stock thus requires a higher rate of saving than a slower rate of growth in the capital stock.

Recap Capital accumulation plays a key role in economic growth. Without technological progress, an increase in labor alone will raise total GNP but will lower GNP per capita, while an increase in capital alone will raise both total GNP and GNP per capita. Increasing society's capital has its costs, however, because the resources used to produce new capital goods cannot be used to produce current consumption goods. Growth through capital accumulation thus involves an intertemporal decision because consumption levels in the present time period must be reduced so those in future time periods may be higher. The faster the rate of growth, the greater are the consumption losses at present and the consumption gains in the future.

The Rate of Growth

The factors that determine the rate of growth and how this rate can be influenced by policy

The rate of capital accumulation, and therefore the rate of growth in both total and per capita GNP, depends on the level of investment. In a fully employed economy, the level of investment depends, in turn, on the amount of GNP diverted from current consumption, that is, on the level of *saving*. In the absence of technological progress, therefore, the rate of growth depends on the level of saving—the higher the proportion of income saved, the higher the rate of growth.

Classical Growth Theory

Early versions of the growth process went something like this: saving is done by consumers, who are induced to defer consumption from the present to the future by being offered more at some later date than they are required to give up now—the "more" being interest. High interest rates will thus induce high levels of saving. Interest is the return to capital and is determined by the marginal product of capital. It will be high when the ratio of labor to capital is high and fall (due to diminishing marginal productivity) as capital is accumulated. A poor country with a relatively small capital stock will thus have high interest rates that will generate a high level of saving and thus a high rate of capital accumulation. As the country becomes richer, the rate of interest and hence its rate of accumulation will decline.

Although some rich countries (such as Britain) did indeed exhibit higher interest rates and faster growth rates during their early stages of industrialization than later, there is little evidence that this scenario is generally true. The main flaw in this model, which we now recognize, is that the *level of income* rather than the *rate of interest* constitutes the most important determinant of saving.

Modern Growth Theory

When saving is assumed to be determined by the level of income, the prediction is quite different. Poor countries have low incomes, little or none of which is saved. This situation results in a *poverty cycle,* so-called because low rates of saving lead to low rates of growth and the tendency for already low levels of per capita income to persist. Rich countries, having higher per capita incomes to begin with, tend to save more and grow faster.

Given the relationship between income and saving, and that between increases in capital and increases in output, it's easy to construct simple models that predict specific rates of growth under alternative economic circumstances.

Suppose the average propensity to consume is constant and therefore equal to the marginal propensity to consume at 0.90, so $10 is saved out of every $100 of GNP. We are assuming a very simple economy with no government and no capital depreciation, so disposable income equals the entire GNP. Suppose also the technology is such that a $4 addition to the capital stock is required for total output to increase by $1 per year. From this information we can easily calculate the economy's rate of growth in the following way. For every $100 of GNP this year, $10 will be saved and thus $10 worth of capital equipment will be produced and added to the capital stock. Next year's economy will have an additional $10 in capital for every $100 in GNP this year, and thus will be able to produce $2.50 (= $10/4) more output for every $100 produced this year, giving 2.5 percent more output than this year. Every $100 in GNP produced next year, in turn, will lead to $2.50 more output the following year, and so on. The rate of growth in GNP will thus be a steady 2.5 percent each year.

Different propensities to save and/or different technical relationships between output and capital requirements will obviously give different growth rates. The general formula is that the rate of growth equals the propensity to save divided by the capital-output ratio (the formal name for the amount of capital needed to generate an additional $1 of GNP). This quotient is then expressed as a percentage. In the example given, the propensity to save is 0.10, the capital-output ratio is 4, giving the growth rate of 0.025 (= 0.10/4) or 2.5 percent.

This simple growth model is commonly referred to as the Harrod-Domar model after two economists, Sir Roy F. Harrod and Evsey D. Domar, who wrote independent studies incorporating the general features we've outlined. Note that steady growth in this model requires that businesses and the government together plan to invest exactly what consumers plan to save. If planned investment is less than the saving generated by the presumed full employment level of GNP, there will be downward pressure on the economy that will consequently lead to a recession. Too high a level of planned investment, on the other hand, will lead to upward pressure and inflation.

Growth Policy

If we take the Harrod-Domar model at face value, it would seem that a capitalistic economy must either grow or die, because, unless planned saving is absorbed by planned investment (leading to growth), the excess of leakages over injections will cause depression and collapse. A century ago, Karl Marx arrived at a similar conclusion. But he felt that growth could do no more than defer the ultimate and predestined collapse of capitalism. In Marxian analysis, the constant pressure to prevent wages from rising is the factor that requires capitalists to change to more labor-saving methods of production and thus promote capital accumulation and growth. Both analyses ignore the possibility that the government may intervene to absorb savings by producing public goods that do not necessarily result in growth. Only when the government sector is negligible relative to the private sector must growth-generating investment equal saving.

Government policy can increase, as well as reduce, the rate of growth compared to that calculated in the simple model. It can undertake growth-generating investment and force an equivalent reduction in consumption by increasing taxes. All growth in Soviet-type economies is carried out this way, and similar policies are pursued in many mixed economies in which production is carried out by government enterprises as well as by private firms. Even in the United States, the government indirectly produces certain types of capital goods, like highways and public housing, by paying private contractors to act in its behalf.

The rate of growth can also be influenced indirectly by bringing about changes in the propensity to save. Because the rich usually save a higher proportion of their incomes than the poor, a redistribution of income in favor of the poor will tend to lower the overall propensity to save. A redistribution in favor of the rich will tend to raise saving. The effects of redistribution pose a particular dilemma for the poorer countries—to grow faster they need a higher propensity to save. This can generally be attained only by redistribution toward the rich; yet social justice suggests redistribution toward the poor, especially because the poor will normally be very poor indeed. For a rich country, where rapid growth is a less pressing issue, this dilemma remains, but it is much less acute.

Recap Classical growth theories predicted that the rate of saving and thus the rate of growth would be high when the rate of interest was high, and that the rate of interest would fall as capital was accumulated, leading to a declining growth rate. Modern theories emphasize income rather than the interest rate as the chief determinant of saving, and thus predict a low rate of growth in poorer countries and a higher rate in richer countries. Given the consumption function and the capital-output ratio, we can develop simple models of growth, such as the Harrod-Domar model, in which the equilibrium rate of capital accumulation can be changed only by changing the propensity to consume or the technology relating capital and output. This poses a potential policy dilemma in a poor country whose growth rate may fall if income is more evenly distributed. Simple growth theories ignore the ability of the government to manipulate the levels of saving and investment, and thus the rate of growth, through economic policy.

Capsule Supplement 24.2 **Karl Marx, 1818–83**

Karl Marx was characterized by intense dedication and, like the economic system he portrayed, contradiction. For eighteen years he spent his days, from 10 A.M. to 7 P.M., in the library of the British Museum writing his doomsday book against capitalism. Throughout this entire period he was supported by his friend and fellow revolutionary, Friedrich Engels, whose income was wholly derived from the profits of textile mills in England and Germany. In all, Marx lived in London for thirty-four years—half again as long as he had ever lived in Germany. He died and was buried there, yet no one has ever referred to Marx as an English economist. He remained always an exile, totally German in style and thought, never joining the English intellectual scene.

Marx was born in Trier, Germany, in 1818. His family was comfortably middle class. His father was a successful lawyer, a Jew who became a Christian as his practice grew. Young Marx entered the university, emerging as a philosopher in search of an academic career. He was a Hegelian philosopher, and the Hegelians were viewed as aesthetic radicals by the state, which ran the universities. When his academic sponsor was dismissed from his post, Marx was forced to abandon the idea of an academic career. He married the girl next door (who happened to be beautiful and aristocratic), edited a liberal newspaper for a while (it eventually proved that he was *too* liberal), then moved to Paris in 1844.

In Paris, Marx became reacquainted with Friedrich Engels, whom he had originally met at a meeting of young Hegelians in Berlin, and beginning in 1844 the two became lifelong friends and intellectual collaborators. Revolution was in the air of Europe in those days, and young revolutionaries were unwelcome. Marx was expelled from Paris in 1845 and moved to Brussels, but was forced to leave there when revolution actually occurred in 1848. After a brief return to

Germany, his last visit to his homeland, he moved to London in 1849 where he remained until his death.

The fruit of the Marx-Engels collaboration in Paris and Brussels was a small pamphlet that was sufficient to put both their names into the history books forever—it was *The Communist Manifesto*. The theme of the *Manifesto,* written after the revolutionary attempts of 1848 had petered out, was the *historical inevitability* of the final overthrow of the existing system.

In London, Marx set out to show in detail how the capitalist system would ultimately collapse as a result of its own internal working, thus proving the theme of historical inevitability. This project, while expected to be completed in less than two months, took eighteen years of Marx's long workdays in the museum. Indeed, only one of the four volumes of *Das Kapital* was published in Marx's own lifetime—in 1867. The messy manuscript required an enormous amount of editing (by Engels), and Volume 2 did not appear until 1885 (two years after Marx's death). Volume 3 was eventually published in 1893, and the final volume in 1910. The enormous expansion of the work from its initial conception to the completed version was a result of Marx's Germanic scholarship, which led him to read every book on economics then available and to argue, often in lengthy footnotes, with authors not worth the trouble. The wonderful directness and simplicity that characterized the *Manifesto* is completely missing in *Capital* (the usual English version of the title of his major work).

The broad line of argument in what we might regard as the macroeconomic section of *Capital* is that capitalists attempt to increase their profits by expanding output. In doing so, they increase the demand for labor and tend to bid up wages above the minimum or subsistence level. Because their profits are derived from the "surplus value" created by labor (the difference between what labor actually contributes to production and what is required to provide a subsistence wage), the rate of profit must fall as wages rise. To avoid declining profits, capitalists turn to labor-saving processes that require more machinery. This, in turn, causes unemployment, keeping wages down. As more capital is employed, however, the rate of profit falls, and eventually the system moves into a "crisis" in which there is widespread bankruptcy and unemployment. As a result of this crisis, both wages and the price of machinery fall to less than their true "value" (to Marx, value was the amount of labor required to reproduce the machinery). With lower wages and prices, production becomes profitable again, and the system begins another cycle. Marx's long-run prognosis was that such periodic crises, accompanied by a concentration of capital in the hands of fewer and fewer capitalists, would become worse and worse. Eventually unemployment would reach the level at which it would not disappear even in the boom, there would be revolution, and the capitalist system would collapse.

While his long-run predictions have not been borne out, Marx was the first to analyze the business cycle in terms of the internal working of the system. The real impact of Marx's work has been in the basic idea of the inevitability of capitalism's ultimate collapse. This gives his followers the wonderful feeling that, whatever their vicissitudes at any time, they are the wave of the future. Perhaps the ultimate contradiction in Marx's own work is that he should have devoted eighteen years to analyzing the collapse of capitalism, which he believed to be inevitable, but he did not hand down any guidelines about how capitalism's successor would work.

Technological Progress

Why there is little policy about one of the major determinants of growth

Technological progress involves the introduction of new production techniques that can produce a given level of output using less of one or more inputs, and no more of all others, than existing techniques. Because technological progress enables more output to be produced from a given stock of resources, it implies the possibility of growth in both total GNP and GNP per capita without capital accumulation or increases in other resources.

Invention and Innovation

New techniques don't just fall out of the sky—they must be discovered and developed. The *rate of innovation* requires some explanation because it has been virtually zero during certain stages of history and quite rapid during others. Like population growth, innovation is obviously influenced by economic variables, but economists haven't yet devised a simple, clear-cut theory about it.

Inventors of new technological devices must obviously devote some resources (at least their own time) to them. Because innovation involves experimentation and frequently considerable luck, we probably ought to include time spent in unsuccessful research, as well as in successful development, in ultimate technological successes. But even if we did this, it is clear that the return to society from the invention of, say, the steam engine is an astronomic multiple of the resources devoted to its original invention and later development. Indeed, if resources devoted to research and development could be guaranteed an average return based on past experience, every economy would probably choose to increase the proportion of resources devoted to this end. On the other hand, the process of innovation often involves a rather long sequence of events, and attempting to rush through this sequence may significantly increase research costs relative to results.

Embodied Technological Progress

The main reason why growth through technological progress is not as simple as it may seem is that most technological progress is *embodied*, rather than disembodied. By this we mean that to put new technology into practice requires either *new* physical capital or *new* human capital. That is, the new technology is contained "in" new machines or "in" new skills—hence the term *embodied*.

New, more efficient production techniques may thus exist "on paper," but cannot be used until new machines or specially trained workers (often both) are available. The rapidity with which new technology actually affects the level of the economy's output thus depends on the rate at which new equipment and skills are actually put in use.

In other words, the rate of growth through embodied technological progress depends on the level of *gross* investment, not just *net* investment, as in the case of growth through capital accumulation. Even if there's no net accumulation of capital, embodied technological progress, and hence economic growth, will occur if old worn-out equipment is replaced by equipment embodying the new technology. However, the rate of progress will clearly be faster, the higher the rate of capital accumulation, because then the additional capital, as well as the replacement capital, will embody this technology. Hence, with embodied technological progress, GNP per capita would increase faster if capital accumulation were at 5 percent per annum and population growth at 2 percent per annum, than if there were a stationary capital stock and an annual decline of 3 percent in population.

It can also be argued that a higher general level of education provides a labor force that is more quickly adaptable to new skills, and thus promotes a more rapid rate of embodied technological progress.

Further Consequences of Embodiment

Historically, the embodiment of new technologies has been one of the most potent sources of economic growth, development, and structural change. The discovery of new textile production techniques in the eighteenth century led to their embodiment in the factories and machines around which the Industrial Revolution developed, and that embodiment led to massive social, as well as economic, changes that spread throughout the world. The embodied technology of the railroad dominated the economic development of the United States in the second half of the nineteenth century, while that of the automobile dominated the first half of the twentieth. Embodiment of electronic computer technology may well be seen by future historians as having dominated the economic development of the United States and other technologically advanced countries in the second half of the twentieth century.

In a capitalist economy in which investment depends on private business decisions, and in which businesses periodically run out of ideas about where to expand next, technological change can provide the incentive for new investment because of the new capital needed for its embodiment.

Joseph Schumpeter (1883–1950), an Austrian economist who eventually migrated to the United States to teach at Harvard, thought the process of change in the capitalist system was reflected in the activity of those embodying new technologies as they arose, the system slumping as each cycle of innovation was completed.

In the Schumpeterian view, each upward thrust of the economy stems from the activities of a few great innovators. These aren't necessarily the actual discoverers of new technological devices and processes, but those who correctly perceive the role and importance of such discoveries in the marketplace. Henry Ford was such an innovator in the boom of the 1920s, as were the railroad magnates of the late nineteenth century. Once the central innovative thrust has been made, more obvious opportunities develop for less imaginative entrepreneurs who follow the innovators and invest in subsidiary activities. The cycle ends when the basic innovation is thoroughly established and the obvious opportunities have been thoroughly exhausted.

Despite the importance of technological embodiment, we know remarkably little about the determinants of technological change. While large corporations spend huge sums on research and development, they obtain most of their return from numerous minor innovations rather than from spectacular discoveries. Great technological breakthroughs may come from anywhere. Even though much of the initial work on transistors came from the laboratories of giant corporations (Bell Labs, in particular), the computer was actually developed by small firms. With computers, IBM played the role of the Schumpeterian innovator, taking something it had not invented but which it was especially well suited to appreciate.

Recap Empirical studies show technological progress to be one of the most important determinants of the growth rate. Economists have no clear idea about how the rate of technological progress can be increased. However, because most technology is embodied in new equipment, technological progress is usually assisted by a high rate of capital accumulation. A high rate of investment in education, by permitting quick adaptation of the labor required, also assists technological progress. The process of embodying new technology into new machines and equipment has had a dynamic effect on the growth of capitalist economies.

Can Growth Be Bad?   How an economy may be growing, but in the wrong direction

In recent years, the desirability of concentrating on rapid growth as a policy, and even the desirability of growth itself (at least in highly developed economies), has been the subject of much debate. Among the main issues raised by those who question the wisdom of growth are the following:

1. Finite stocks of natural resources such as oil and minerals are being used at ever-increasing rates, thus bringing the inevitable total depletion of these resources near enough to warrant immediate concern.
2. Modern technology is increasingly responsible for the production of public bads, such as pollution, and the sheer scale of operations in technologically advanced societies will inevitably result in a variety of ecological crises.
3. Many goods whose production is associated with rapid growth in rich countries (such as the automobile) are used primarily to overcome disadvantages of the life-style required in such societies (such as living in suburbs). These have major disadvantages of their own (pollution and congestion), and therefore make little net contribution to social welfare.
4. The profusion of goods produced in rich economies complicates life for consumers and introduces large social and private costs associated with uncertainty in decision-making. The net contribution of these goods to social welfare is less than commonly reckoned.

Additional arguments along similar lines could be given, all possessing merit. However, a careful analysis of such arguments, including those above, reveals that, while economic growth itself may not be undesirable, the *wrong kind of growth* is.

These arguments also suggest something more important but more subtle—that economic "growth" *as measured in terms of standard indicators,* like GNP per capita, may represent little, if any, improvement in social welfare and may conceivably be associated with a decline in society's well-being.

Let's first consider the effects of the prevailing *kind* or *direction* of growth. In doing so, we shall concentrate on the *composition of output* that is hidden in a strictly macroeconomic approach in which we proceed as if GNP were a single "good." Many individuals who criticize growth view it as increased production of polluting automobiles, noisy jet planes, sprawling suburban developments of "ticky-tacky," and so on through the conventional list. These individuals would presumably be happy to see increases in the production of noiseless and nonpolluting electric transit; attractive schools, playgrounds, and public parks; and well-designed, racially and socially integrated neighborhoods. The development of such things would also constitute growth, but growth consisting of outputs in proportions different from those already in existence.

Growth, in the sense of more output per person of certain things, is surely desirable. It may, however, be undesirable for a rich economy to continue growing without a major change in its output mix—toward more public goods and less public bads than at present.

This brings us to the question of growth indicators and the measured rate of growth. It may be (and probably is) easier for the United States economy to expand automobile transport services by $1 billion per year than to expand public transport services by the same amount. Concentrating on maximizing the rate of growth in real GNP may result in emphasizing growth in those sectors where growth is easiest, rather than in those sectors where growth has the most social value. This emphasis is increased by the undervaluing of public goods in GNP relative to private output because the public goods are counted basically at resource cost, private goods at resource cost plus residual profit.

Finally, we have the problem of understated social costs. It may well be easier to expand output by a technology that uses resources which are becoming depleted and are associated with public bads such as pollution than by a technology that does not impose these social costs. Because social costs do not appear in the standard indicators, a relatively high rate of growth in social welfare may appear as a low rate of growth in real GNP, and a relatively low rate of growth (or decline) in social welfare as a high rate of growth in real GNP.

A high rate of growth in real per capita GNP, as conventionally measured, may not represent a high rate of growth in social welfare, and may even be associated with its decline.

Therefore, we conclude that growth can indeed be bad, or at minimum, less "good" than first supposed. This is not because growth is bad in itself, but because growth in the wrong direction may be bad, and because our conventional measures of growth may appear more impressive for growth in the wrong direction than in the right direction.

The previous discussion refers essentially to growth in output per capita, taking population growth as given. If we treat population growth itself as a policy variable, then the discussion is considerably broadened. Given the limitations on natural resources and the negative externalities (like pollution) directly associated with population size, the arguments against growth as a means of permitting a larger population become compelling, unless our welfare judgment is based on the philosophical view that the world is better off with 101 people at a certain standard of living than with 100 at the same standard. Because such arguments move rapidly into the metaphysical, economists typically assume their policy goal to be the maximization of the per capita welfare of those people actually in existence. If this goal can be accomplished by allowing the population to increase less rapidly, so much the better.

Recap Concentration on rapid growth in output per capita as a policy goal has recently been widely questioned. The crux of the argument against growth is not that growth *per se* is undesirable, but that output may grow in the wrong proportions. Because of divergences between social benefits and the values used in the national accounts, and in the ability of different sectors of the economy to grow rapidly, the most desirable type growth may not generate the highest rate of growth as conventionally measured in terms of GNP.

Economic Development Policy	The problems associated with the development of nations that are poor

Most poor countries can become rich only by development, not mere growth, because the existing growth rate is close to zero and, without basic changes, the country will simply remain poor. The development problem is essentially that of making the transition between a poor, slow-growing economy and an economy for which a respectable level of income per person is simply a matter of continued growth at a new and higher rate. Historically, economic development was not the product of conscious economic policy. The classic case—European industrialization during the eighteenth and nineteenth centuries—obviously depended on the existence of favorable (or at least nonhostile) policies. But these policies were not consciously devised as part of a grand plan for economic development. Modern economics, which evolved with industrialization, explained what was happening rather than what caused it to happen.

Emergence of Development Policy

Economic development is now a matter of policy, for several reasons:

1. Poor countries can see the results of development (which eighteenth-century Europe could not) and, on the whole, like what they see.
2. Simply waiting for development to occur, as Europe did, is not likely to be fruitful.
3. A repetition of the European experience would simply be too slow for countries that are desperately poor and impatient to achieve respectable living standards.
4. Economists now have sufficient knowledge of how economic systems work to formulate development policies.
5. There are now many examples of economic development resulting from conscious policy efforts.

Development policy, by definition, is total policy. To change a poor, stagnant economy into one growing steadily toward modest affluence will require changes in its macroeconomic structure, its pattern of production and trade, and its pattern of income distribution.

Typical Problems

Let us imagine a poor country that we shall call LDC (for less-developed country). We shall assume it to have a per capita real income equivalent of $100—typical of a poor country—and a near zero growth rate. For simplicity we shall suppose that population is not growing. Most of the work force in such a country will be engaged in agriculture, educational standards will be very low, mortality rates quite high (especially infant mortality), and the income distribution unequal with a very few extremely rich people and a huge mass of terribly poor people. It will export agricultural and mining products, using the proceeds to pay for its imports of machinery and other advanced manufactures.

At the beginning of our story, we shall suppose that LDC is locked into the standard situation of the poor country—incomes are so low that people spend the whole of them on consumption leaving no margin of saving to finance, and no spare productive capacity to produce, investment goods. With virtually no net investment, the capital stock does not grow, embodied technological progress is slow or nonexistent, and there is no economic growth.

Possibilities

A new government takes over, perhaps by revolution, perhaps because of newly achieved independence from a former colonial power. This new government has rapid economic development as its chief goal. What must it do to achieve this goal?

First, it can explore the possibility of achieving increased productivity somewhere in the economy, even without increased investment. Agriculture, the chief industry, may be very inefficient for a variety of reasons. Farms may be peasant-owned and, because of family divisions over the years, the size of holdings may simply be too small in the straightforward sense that each peasant family could efficiently work a farm 50 percent larger than the one it actually owns. Looked at from another direction, each family could fully work its existing farm with two-thirds of the current number of family members employed. Thus, there is *disguised unemployment* equal to one-third of the agricultural work force, and this labor could be transferred to other activities without reducing agricultural output. We shall call this the "Asian case."

This surplus agricultural labor is an important potential resource. Unfortunately, its most obvious use—as an industrial force—requires capital and, therefore, investment.

There may be other structural aspects of agriculture that could be changed. Instead of peasant agriculture, there may be ranch agriculture with a very small group of landowners controlling virtually all the land. Social status, under the old regime, may have depended on the number of acres owned with few incentives for the landowners to maximize output per acre or employee. Breaking up and redistributing the holdings, turning gauchos into farmers (a social change they might well resent) may increase agricultural output from the same amount of land and labor. In this case, the development process would be off to a potentially good start because there would be a new surplus of output (compared with the previous situation) that could form the basis for growth. We shall call this the "Latin American case."

Of course, it may be possible to bring about a purely technological increase in productivity by, say, the use of fertilizers, better seed, or just better farming methods. Because this would give more output with the same resources, there would again be a surplus available. Experience has shown, however, that traditional peasant agriculture is often resistant to technological change of this kind, and such change may take many years.

Investment

Regardless of whatever structural change can be brought about within the agricultural sector, investment is required for development. Even if the country did not seek to develop a major industrial sector or capital-intensive agriculture, investment would be required in roads and railroads (to enable agricultural products to be moved), schools and hospitals, communications networks, and other parts of the basic framework, or the *infrastructure,* of the economy.

The ultimate crux of the development process is the ability to bring about a sharp increase in the level of investment. Let's assume that our LDC fits the "Asian case," and that foreign aid and foreign private investment provide only a small fraction of the investment level required.

Difficult Choices

If income is initially $100 per capita with zero investment, and the country wants to increase the level of investment to 10 percent of GNP, then consumption must fall by 10 percent, at least for the starting-up period. When the population is already at a very low living standard, even a temporary decline in that living standard is not an easy policy to pursue. It may require, quite simply, that a higher proportion of the population will have to die of starvation.

The initial development stage is a problem in intertemporal distribution—people must accept a cut in consumption, even starvation, now in order that other people, later on, can achieve a higher living standard than at present.

Any government that depends on popular support, whether implicitly or by vote, will attempt to minimize the effect on the majority of the current population by getting as much of the required saving as it can from the small group of the rich. Typically, however, even total confiscation of the income of the rich will provide only a fraction of what is required, and that fraction only for a year or two because the rich and their incomes will disappear.

In the end, the necessary increase in saving will involve sacrifices by the poor. Part may be voluntary, if LDC's government can appeal to patriotic motives and the crisis nature of the development program. But some form of an explicit or implicit taxation of peasants is likely. Implicit taxation can be levied by inflation—allowing prices to rise faster than money incomes so real incomes are lowered without any apparent direct taxes, while revenue is obtained from direct expansion of the money supply.

If agricultural output can be increased through better technology, the increase in saving is much easier to obtain. Taxes can then be levied to prevent consumption from rising as fast as output. Thus, a surplus can be obtained without any actual reduction in consumption below its previous levels—only a reduction relative to the level that is now possible.

Once past the initial stages, sustained rapid growth will depend on either a shift in the distribution of income toward those who save a great deal (as in Europe's Industrial Revolution), or sustained taxation, implicit or explicit, to keep consumption sufficiently below output (as in the Soviet Union's development).

The Structure of Investment

Development is not just a macroeconomic problem of ensuring a surplus of output over and above consumption that can be used for investment. This investment must take place in appropriate directions, or the increased output that is the aim of development may not be realized.

A steel mill may add to physical output although it produces steel for which there is no local use and which cannot be sold abroad at any price. Its production may appear as an increase in GNP, but on a false accounting basis. However, the social valuation placed on the steel would be zero.

Alternatively, a steel mill may be a valuable investment as part of an industrial complex that produces steel for something that will ultimately be useful to consumers or for machinery for other industries that, in turn, will produce goods for direct use. Nevertheless, it may be less valuable than an equivalent investment in agriculture or transport that will increase exports and enable the country to import more steel, or steel-based goods, than it could obtain by local production with the same resources.

Surplus Agricultural Labor

In the "Asian case," which we have supposed LDC to fit, the main resource available for development is the disguised unemployment resulting from a surplus of agricultural labor relative to land. This surplus labor is effectively a resource with zero social cost to the economy as a whole because its alternative use (remaining on the land) contributes nothing to output. People will not leave the land to work in industry for zero wages, however, so the private cost of labor to the industrial sector will be higher than the social cost. Therefore, a calculation of the net benefit from industrialization that is based on the actual wages paid may understate the true net social benefit. There could be a case for direct or indirect subsidization of industry, paid for by a tax on agriculture.

To be specific, suppose each farm initially supports three adult workers and produces $300 output per year. Due to the surplus of labor relative to land, the same $300 could be produced with only two people. If the third person moved to industry, the farm could provide an income of $150 for each of the two remaining workers, instead of $100 per person. Thus, a tax on the farm of, say, $50 would leave $250 to be divided among two, or $125 per person—making those left on the farm better off than before, while providing revenues for a subsidy of $50 per worker in industry.

No real economy will conform to analysis as simple as this, but the example given illustrates the type of policy problem that arises.

Industrial Structure

Now let's suppose that LDC has decided to industrialize. What industries should be developed? In what order?

On the face of things, LDC is short of investment funds, but has a large potential labor force from its surplus in agriculture. It would thus seem that the most desirable industries would be labor-intensive, using a high ratio of labor to capital.

We must look more deeply, however. A true industrial sector is a complex network of interrelated industries, not merely a collection of isolated factories. We cannot simply pick the most labor-intensive industries and set them going. The new industries will need, among other inputs, electricity—and electricity generation is one of the most capital-intensive industries. On the other hand, the most labor-intensive industries—the service industries—provide outputs for which there is little demand at low-income levels. People need clothes before they need dry cleaners.

Criteria for Choice

Various industrial "menus" can be considered. For each such menu, total labor and capital requirements can be calculated, together with the output mix. In choosing the "menu," LDC will need to consider the following:

1. The desirability of a high ratio of labor to capital over the industrial sector as a whole. This does not necessarily imply a choice of labor-intensive industries (or processes within a particular industry) uniformly over the whole sector, but may well imply a mix of some capital-intensive and some labor-intensive production.

2. The potentialities for technical progress and economies of scale among the various industries and over the industrial complex as a whole. Such potentialities will generally be higher in the more capital-intensive industries.

3. The potentialities for continued long-run expansion of the industrial sector and growth by the addition of new industries. This consideration may tend to favor the early development of basic industries (electricity, metals, chemicals).

4. The constraint imposed by the balance of payments in relation to the available funds for investment, and the technical necessity of importing machinery from abroad. If foreign currency to buy machinery is small relative to total investment funds, the best value per foreign dollar may be technologically advanced machinery. The best industrialization plan may then be a simultaneous development of a few highly sophisticated plants using imported machines and relatively crude plants using local labor and simple machines. As the sector grows and more local machinery becomes available, the simple plants can be upgraded.

5. The potential demand for output mixes of various kinds. An industrial complex whose outputs are not wanted domestically and cannot be sold elsewhere is useless, however well it fits the other criteria.

Planned or Private Choice?

Finally, do all these decisions need to be planned, or can they be left to the private sector? The fact that LDC is initially stagnating is sufficient evidence that policy of some kind is required. This may take the form of subsidies, tariffs, grants of monopoly power, tax concessions, guaranteed profit levels, and so on.

Once the price system becomes extensively manipulated through such policy, planners must keep their eye on the whole picture. Any imagined choice between socialized industries and private industries operating within such a deliberately manipulated price system will tend to come down to the smallest details. Socialization may result in personal political appointments and bureaucracy, and thus in poor management—but private industry operating under guarantees may also have little incentive for good management. On the other hand, the free entry of private firms (even if many firms are nationalized) will draw attention to certain opportunities that planners may have missed.

Unless the government is dominated by an extreme ideology, LDC may well choose the popular middle path in which key plants are nationalized (but perhaps run under contract by experienced private firms), but in which the entry of small private firms is relatively free.

Recap Economic development policy involves choices about almost every aspect of the economy—distribution of income between persons and investment, major occupational changes for a considerable proportion of the population, and major changes in the industrial structure, the scope of the price system, and the market. Economic development policy is the ultimate in total policy.

Capsule Supplement 24.3   **No Perfect Recipe for Development**

There are currently more than a hundred countries of the world that could be classed as "underdeveloped" by any definition, seventy of these being new countries that emerged from the breaking up of colonial empires after World War II. With such a large sample, one might suppose that we could reach some fairly clear conclusions about which policies work well for development and which do not. Unfortunately we cannot, mainly because so few of these countries have shown real development.

Spectacular cases of development in the last quarter century have been rare, Israel being one of the very few countries that has truly moved from a state definable as "underdeveloped" to "developed." Apart from Israel, Taiwan, China, and North and South Korea, development has been generally disappointing, especially considering the optimistic expectations that were held immediately after World War II. Those few exceptions have little in common—two are Communist countries with almost no private sector, two are strongly private-enterprise oriented, while Israel is nominally socialistic but characterized by a large private sector. Taiwan, Israel, and South Korea have received extensive foreign aid (government and/or private) from the United States, while China received little outside help after its early Soviet aid was cut off.

There have been some spectacular cases of *nondevelopment,* especially Ghana and Indonesia, both of which started independent development with ample resources and great expectations (shared by the rest of the world). Unfortunately, the disastrous periods of these two countries do not provide us with any profound lessons—both dissipated capital and foreign exchange on projects that obviously could not have brought an increase in output.

Generally speaking, the last twenty-five years have seen output rise in the underdeveloped countries, but barely ahead of population growth. Per capita incomes have risen very slowly, much more slowly than those of the developed countries as a group, so the gap between the rich countries and the poor has widened, not narrowed.

There have been some underdeveloped countries that have become very rich, but not by any process that could legitimately be called economic development. At last count, for example, the United Arab Emirates—a tiny new (1971) country in the Persian Gulf—had a per capita income level over twice that of the United States, all from oil. The discovery of new oil reserves may indeed lead to genuine economic development (that is, change in the economy other than the mere appearance of oil derricks), as it has in the case of Libya and Tunisia. Oil may also support development in other countries that perform services for the oil-rich ones, as in Lebanon, which traditionally supplied the Middle East with banking and financial services. Discovery of oil is one way to speed development, but oil can only be discovered if it is already there.

Thus, we are forced to conclude that there is no fully proven recipe for raising a poor country up by its own bootstraps. Foreign aid has been important in some cases, but has been a notable failure in others. There is no marked correlation of development with ideology. Both planned and private enterprise have proved successful in some cases and disastrous in others. Relatively high educational levels (Israel, Korea) seem to have been useful and so, obviously enough, are natural resources—but even natural resource endowments can be wasted.

Exercises

1. Calculate the rate of growth of an economy with a constant propensity to save of 0.20 and a technology that gives $1 per year increase in output for every $2 increase in the capital stock.

2. What will be the rate of growth of this economy if the propensity to save falls to 0.10, with the same technology?

3. Calculate the rate of growth of an economy with a propensity to save of 0.10 and a technology that gives $1 in increased output for $3 increase in capital.

4. Taking the data from Table 24.1, consider those who consume in years 1–5 as the "present generation," those who consume in years 6–10 as the "future generation." Comparing the data in "no capital accumulation" with that in "accumulation over five years," calculate the total consumption of each of the two generations (by adding consumption over the relevant years) in each of the two cases. Does the future generation in the accumulation case gain more consumption than the present generation loses compared with the no-accumulation case?

For Thought and Discussion

1. Do you think the United States should stop growing, or slow its growth rate? Give careful consideration to your answer, and the reasons for it.

2. Which would you expect to result in the greater increase in measured GNP over the next five years: $1 billion spent on machinery for manufacturing cosmetics, or $1 billion spent on new school buildings? Justify your answer.

3. If GNP grows by 5 percent and population also grows by 5 percent, then GNP per person is unchanged so individuals are neither better nor worse off, but there are more of them. Should we regard this as an increase in material social welfare because of the increased number of people, or no change because no individual is better off?

4. Should a poor country make its people even worse off (in terms of current consumption) so future generations can be better off?

5. (This requires some background in microeconomics.) If a natural world resource—oil, for example—were obviously and clearly going to be entirely depleted in fifty years at current rates of use, would you expect the price system to bring about a lower rate of use?

Chapter 25
Inflation

Terms and Concepts

Money illusion
Open inflation
Suppressed inflation
Inflationary gap
Demand-pull inflation
Cost-push inflation
Inflationary spiral
Real balances
Inflationary expectations
Real rate of interest
Money rate of interest
Hyperinflation
Wage-price controls

| **Planning the Impossible** | **How an inflationary situation develops** |

In our previous discussion of the macroeconomic operation of the economy, we assumed that expenditure plans were not limited by the productive capacity of the economy. Any disequilibrium in the system was considered to result from a mismatch between total anticipated income and the total expenditure planned on the basis of that income. However, we also assumed that there was always enough idle capacity for real output to expand to meet changes in the equilibrium level of income. Indeed, except in our discussion of growth, we implicitly restricted ourselves to the study of an *underemployed* economy.

In this chapter, our concern is with a quite different problem—the problem that arises when planned expenditure at current prices *exceeds* the economy's productive capacity (full employment output), also valued at current prices. Consider, for example, the case of an economy that produces only anchovy pizzas, which are currently priced at $10 each. The various sectors may plan to spend $11 billion on these delicacies, while the capacity output of the economy may be only 1 billion pizzas (worth $10 billion at current prices).

Let's focus on a more general example. Assume we have an economy with only a household sector and an investment sector (no government). All income is paid to households which have a constant average propensity to consume (and therefore a constant marginal propensity to consume) of 0.8, giving a multiplier of 5 (= 1/0.2). Suppose planned investment is initially $2 billion, with an equilibrium income level of $10 billion equal to a total expenditure of $2 billion investment plus $8 billion (= 0.8 × $10 billion) consumption. We shall assume that the output of $10 billion at current prices represents the current capacity of the economy, and that we are initially in equilibrium at this level with steady prices.

Unattainable Plans

Now suppose the business sector, motivated by unbridled economic optimism, decides to increase investment by 10 percent to $2.2 billion. Of course, such an increase is viewed in *real terms*—that is, businesses plan to buy 10 percent more capital. Given steady prices, this planned increase in real investment is equivalent to a simple 10 percent increase in dollar expenditure. It's immediately apparent that this new level of planned investment is inconsistent with the current total income of $10 billion because, if investment were $2.2 billion, consumption could then be only $7.8 billion—$0.2 billion less than the planned consumption for $10 billion income. The new equilibrium income, in the absence of any physical constraint on output, would be $11 billion, equal to $2.2 billion investment plus

$8.8 billion (= $0.8 \times \$11$ billion) consumption. But because the economy's capacity output at current prices is only $10 billion, an *unattainable set of plans* exists. Something has to give—specifically, the plans of at least one sector must remain unfulfilled.

Adjustment Processes

In order to predict what might happen, we need to examine the various ways in which the economy might adjust to the new investment plans. If the business sector, having decided to increase investment from $2 billion to $2.2 billion, simply proceeds with its plans, the immediate result will be increased orders for *new plant and equipment* placed with manufacturers. Because industry as a whole is operating at capacity, these increased orders cannot be met without some form of readjustment. One possibility is that manufacturers will place the orders on their books to be filled later—in other words, investment plans will be *registered but not fulfilled.* In this case it's the business sector that will fail to achieve its plans. Actual income will remain at $10 billion, with $0.2 billion in unsatisfied demand for investment goods.

Another possibility is that manufacturers will either find it more profitable to produce capital goods than consumer goods, or simply prefer to honor business orders before consumer orders. In this case increased investment orders for plant and equipment will be met by cutting down on the production of household items. As a result, the output of capital goods will increase to $2.2 billion and investment plans will be fulfilled. However, the output of consumption goods will fall from the $8 billion planned to $7.8 billion.

Note that neither of these cases yields an *equilibrium,* and because plans are not fully achieved, actual withdrawals and injections are equated as a matter of accounting. In the first instance, saving remains at its original level ($2 billion), and investment is equal to it because the planned investment increase of $0.2 billion is not actually carried out. In the second instance, investment increases to $2.2 billion and saving increases to meet it because consumers cannot fully carry out their consumption plans—they are *forced* to save $0.2 billion more than planned simply because there is nothing left for them to spend it on. Equality between actual investment and actual saving is achieved by having actual investment fall short of planned investment in one case, and actual saving exceed planned saving in the other.

Price Increases

But we must consider yet another type of adjustment that may occur. The initial increase in planned investment represents an increase of $0.2 billion in total planned expenditure to $10.2 billion—an increase of 2 percent.

Because the output of real goods is limited to $10 billion at current prices, producers may react to the increased demand *by increasing prices*. If they raise all prices by 2 percent, output once valued at $10 billion will now be valued at $10.2 billion and will thus match the *dollar value* of planned expenditure.

However, this will not bring about an equilibrium. Even assuming the investment sector adheres to its investment plans in *dollar terms* and does not change them to allow for the price increase, consumers' *money incomes* will have risen by 2 percent to $10.2 billion. Because consumers are assumed to spend 80 percent of any change in their incomes, the dollar value of planned consumption will rise by $160 million (80 percent of $0.2 billion). To meet this, prices will rise more, planned consumption will rise again, and so on through a multiplier sequence.

Money Illusion

Provided the investment plans of the business sector are stated in *dollar terms* and are not readjusted with price changes, we shall achieve an "equilibrium" at a dollar output of $11 billion ($2.2 billion investment plus $8.8 billion consumption). In reaching this new equilibrium, real output will not have changed from the original capacity level *but prices will have increased by 10 percent*. At the new income level, *consumers* will achieve their plans (they will be spending 80 percent of their $11 billion incomes). But what about the business sector? If it considers its investment plans to have been achieved, it is most certainly subject to an *illusion*. Even though it originally set out to increase investment by 10 percent in order to attain 10 percent more plant and equipment, it ends up spending 10 percent more to obtain the same plant and equipment as before.

Any decision-maker who formulates plans in dollar terms and is satisfied when those plans are achieved in dollar terms, even though prices may have risen so the plans are not achieved in real terms, is said to be working under a *money illusion*.

If businesses do *not* work under a money illusion, the upward pressure on prices will not stop. Let's suppose that the economy has reached an *illusory equilibrium income* at $11 billion, as in our example. The business sector then realizes that although all dollar values have increased by 10 percent, it is actually buying the same physical quantity of capital as before. To increase its real investment, it further increases its dollar investment by 10 percent to allow for the increase in prices. Planned dollar investment will then rise to $2.42 billion ($2.2 billion plus 10 percent of $2.2 billion), but this will simply further increase prices by 10 percent without any resulting increase in real investment. Unless something happens—such as a redistribution of income that changes the propensity to consume, or a change in the rate of price increase of investment goods compared with that of consumption goods so real investment actually does increase—the process will never end.

Open and Suppressed Inflation

Thus, planned expenditures that exceed capacity output cannot be achieved. Something has to give. Generally speaking, we'll expect price stability to break down and prices to start rising. This situation is known as *open inflation*. However, even if prices do not change (as when the government imposes successful price controls), planned expenditures will still not be achievable and there will be *suppressed inflation*.

From ordinary income determination theory, we can compute what the equilibrium level of income (at constant prices) will be for specific levels of planned government and investment expenditure, given taxes and other structural determinants of the economy. If this equilibrium level of real income exceeds capacity output, we'll have an *inflationary gap* and equilibrium simply cannot be attained. The events that accompany this inflationary gap cannot be analyzed in terms of the standard income model because that model is based on the assumption of sufficient capacity to meet equilibrium expenditure demands.

Inflation (open or suppressed) *commences* with excess demand in the sense that total equilibrium expenditure exceeds capacity output. Once having begun, however, inflation is characterized by a dynamic mechanism that must be analyzed in terms of its own special features.

For simplicity, we assume the existence of a well-defined capacity level of output at which the process of inflation begins. In fact, because some industries may reach capacity while the overall economy still has idle resources, inflation may coexist with unemployment. We've already seen from the Phillips curve in Chapter 22 that in most economies, inflation commences at unemployment rates well above zero. The closer an economy comes to attaining full employment, the more marked will be the upward pressure on prices.

Recap If the several sectors of the economy all plan expenditures that exceed the capacity output of the economy, these plans simply cannot be fulfilled as intended. An adjustment must take place. One possibility is that because not enough goods are available to meet demand, some receive the goods they planned for, while others go without. In a market economy, unsatisfied demand of this kind can be expected to put upward pressure on prices. If the original plans are to buy specific quantities of real goods, the increase in prices will not permit the economy to balance because planned dollar expenditures will keep rising as prices rise. As long as plans to buy real goods exceed the output of real goods the economy can produce, there will be an inflationary gap. We have open inflation if prices actually start rising. Under price controls, prices may not actually change, but the gap remains, and we have suppressed inflation.

Capsule Supplement 25.1   **The Monetarist View of Inflation**

While recognizing the inflationary role of excess demand, monetarists emphasize the effect of the quantity of money and its rate of change on inflation. This effect is generally described as follows: an increase in the quantity of money at a rate more rapid than is justified by the real growth of the economy will lead to money balances in excess of those desired. To run these balances down, individuals and firms will increase their rate of planned expenditure. If the economy was originally operating at capacity, this increase in planned expenditure will represent excess demand and initiate inflationary pressures. Prices will rise and—if nothing else changes—the *real* value of money balances will be reduced by the decline in the purchasing power of the dollar. Once the real value of these balances has fallen to the level appropriate to real capacity income, the inflationary pressures will cease and prices will stay at the new, higher level, provided the quantity of money is not increased further.

Thus, the monetarist scenario does not predict a continuous *inflationary spiral* unless the quantity of money is increased continuously as prices rise. The monetarist cure for inflation is basically to reduce the rate of increase in the money supply as prices rise, and to ultimately maintain this rate of increase at a level equivalent to the growth rate in real output.

Even if the inflation is not initiated by an increase in the quantity of money, but is due, say, to an increase in planned investment arising from business expectations, monetarists would argue that the inflation cannot really get going unless the quantity of money is increased. With funds from saving already at capacity levels, and money balances at desired levels, investment plans can be made effective only by an increase in the quantity of money.

The processes described will work only if individuals are willing to hold lower money balances relative to income, in which case excess demand and inflation can occur even if the quantity of money remains unchanged.

The Inflationary Spiral

Inflation is a process that may continue after its initial cause is removed

Once inflationary pressures have led to open inflation with prices actually rising, a variety of effects come into play that tend to sustain and even aggravate the upward trend in prices.

In the previous section we saw that attempts by decision-makers to achieve impossible levels of expenditures *in real terms* will be sufficient to start prices moving upward. As prices rise, the dollar values of these expenditures will be increased in order to keep pace with rising prices, thereby creating more excess demand and causing further price increases. The impossible cannot be achieved. Unless people can either be deluded into believing that they've succeeded in fulfilling their plans (through money illusion) or come to realize that there is nothing to be gained by further attempts, open inflation will continue indefinitely.

Thus, the excess demand that sets off an inflationary process is not removed by a once-and-for-all price increase. *As long as the excess demand is for real goods and those real goods cannot be produced, the excess demand remains and so does the upward price pressure.*

Even worse, the inflationary process can become self-generating so it continues *even if the original excess demand is removed.* Suppose inflation begins because businesses increase planned investment in response to a report that oil has been discovered on the moon. Prices rise steadily for some time. Then, after further exploration, it becomes certain that the oil does not exist in commercial quantities and the investment planned in response to the moon-oil "boom" disappears. What will happen?

Inflationary Expectations

Planned investment may fail to drop back to its pre-inflationary level (even in real terms) because the *inflation itself* may have provided new investment incentives. As long as prices are rising and are expected to continue rising, a firm can profit simply by buying something at today's prices, holding it, and selling it at tomorrow's prices. Moreover, anything that must be purchased in the reasonably near future will cost less today than it will tomorrow. Firms will thus tend to increase inventories of materials for which they anticipate future needs and hasten investment plans in order to buy or build at today's prices.

Of course, the real value of resulting profits will be reduced by the very inflation that has caused them, and such profits may be small or nonexistent if purchases must be made with funds borrowed at high interest rates. Nevertheless, anyone who has cash available can expect to profit by these transactions as long as selling costs (like overhead expenses for a retail store) are less than the expected increase in prices.

The effect on sellers will be the opposite. Those with things to sell will expect higher prices tomorrow and thus will tend to withhold them from sale today. In short, expectations that prices will continue to rise in the future result in buyers hastening their plans and sellers postponing theirs. These *inflationary expectations,* which are partially self-fulfilling, will thus tend to further increase upward pressure on today's prices.

Upward pressures on prices from (1) unsuccessful attempts to fulfill impossible real expenditure plans, and (2) inflationary expectations reflect excess demand in the economy at existing prices. Inflation stemming from these sources is therefore referred to as *demand-pull inflation.*

Cost-Push Inflation

With all due respect to the preceding example in which excess demand leads to increases in the prices of final goods, the actual inflationary process is far more complex. If the seed of inflation has been planted by an increase in planned expenditure, the initial impact will indeed be exclusively on the prices of final goods, with wages remaining unaffected. As a consequence of rising prices, however, profits will increase. The competition among firms for labor and the negotiation of new collective bargaining agreements in an atmosphere of higher profits and rising prices will put upward pressure on wages. Thus, wages will also rise, but only after a time lag.

With higher wage rates, employers (presumably having become accustomed to higher profits per dollar of sales) will feel their profit margins squeezed and wish to increase prices once again. If they can, they will.

Thus, an original price increase during, say, the first quarter of a year will lead to wage and other cost increases in the second quarter, and thus to further price increases during the second quarter, starting a new cycle of price-cost-price increases. This process is referred to as cost-push inflation.

Long verbal battles have been fought by those who place the emphasis on "demand-pull" as the primary cause of inflation and those who place the emphasis on "cost-push" factors. To the extent that inflation is regarded as harmful, and therefore somehow "antisocial," employers tend to emphasize the cost-push aspect because it tends to put the blame for price increases elsewhere.

The Importance of Industry Structure

Cost-push factors will clearly have their greatest effect in industries where prices are controlled, or where they are set by producers rather than determined in competitive markets. Specifically, then, we will expect to observe them most often in regulated industries, monopolies, and oligopolies. In industries that approximate perfect competition, increased costs will affect supply and ultimately price, but there will be no "cost-pushing" in the direct sense. A rise in farm wages may result in a shift in supply schedules for farm products, but farmers are not in a position to simply set prices 10 percent higher because wages have risen 10 percent.

In the case of nonregulated monopolistic industries, of course, monopolists can *always* raise prices as they see fit. If their costs have increased 10 percent, they can increase prices by 10 percent. The real question is whether it is *in the ultimate* interest of monopolists to automatically pass on increases in cost. If demand conditions are completely unchanged, they will lose sales by increasing prices. In general, the only circumstances in which profit-maximizing monopolists will continue to maximize profits by increasing prices by 10 percent when costs have risen (at all outputs) by 10 percent are when *demand* conditions have changed in such a way that customers are willing to buy the same quantity as before at a 10 percent higher price. *In other words, cost-push factors will tend to operate most smoothly when accompanied by demand-pull pressures.*

The Problem of Causal Identification

It should be emphasized that it is no easy matter to "separate" cost-push and demand-pull effects in empirical studies of a real economy. For example, we may observe prices and wages rising at 5 percent per year. But is the increase in wages "pushing" up costs and prices, or are prices and wages being "pulled" up by the steady 5 percent expansion in money incomes? There is fairly general agreement among economists that:

1. cost-push influences do operate to some extent, and introduce lagged price increases, and
2. cost-push influences cannot result in *continued* price increases without the assistance of continued increases in planned dollar expenditures.

Thus, a sufficient reduction in demand can always be expected to result in the *ultimate* cessation of price increases from cost-push influences. However, because of the dynamic character of the inflationary process, prices cannot be expected to stop rising *immediately* after the excess demand is removed. During the relatively short but definite recession in the United States in 1958, for example, prices continued rising from a process that had commenced earlier. In the inflation of the late 1960s, rapid price increases occurred through 1969 and 1970 although fiscal and monetary policy was anti-inflationary to the point that unemployment became uncomfortably high. Cases like this, in which inflation continues even though unemployment is high, provide clear evidence that the inflationary process itself can continue even when the excess of planned demand over capacity output has been removed.

Recap Demand for real goods in excess of real capacity output puts an upward pressure on prices. This, in turn, may initiate a self-sustaining process that continues even if the original excess demand is removed. From the "demand-pull" side, the process is assisted by factors that tend to increase planned demand as a result of the inflation itself. From the "cost-push" side, rising costs tend to push up prices in subsequent periods, even though excess demand may have fallen. Rising costs and prices lead to a further upward cycle in prices. As a result of this *inflationary spiral,* prices may continue rising for some time even if demand falls below capacity output.

Capsule Supplement 25.2   **Inflation Spectaculars**

In the early fall of 1923, German workers took suitcases to work in order to carry away their daily earnings. Upon being paid at the end of each day, they each actually *ran* to the market to buy as much as they could. Why? Because prices were rising by the hour—doubling every two days or so. By November of that year, it took 10 billion marks to buy what had cost a single mark only sixteen months earlier, and the printing presses couldn't produce bills in denominations of tens and hundreds of billions fast enough to avoid the necessity of carrying huge bags of virtually worthless bills denominated in mere millions. This German bout with hyperinflation is the best known of several spectacular episodes in the history of prices. For example, the then-new Soviet economy had a period of hyperinflation from 1921 to 1924 in which prices rose by a factor of 100 thousand. However, the most spectacular of the European hyperinflations was that of Hungary immediately after World War II, during which prices doubled *twice* a day and rose by a factor of a billion billions in the short space of twelve months.

Anyone who has ever collected postage stamps is aware of the German case from the incredible denominations of the stamps of the time. But the hyperinflation in Germany had a much more important impact on economists than on philatelists. For one thing, it took place in a major industrial country, but perhaps more importantly it was *personally experienced* by leading economists, many of whom were German, and even more of whom had German colleagues. The personal impact of hyperinflation on German professors was disastrous because academic salaries were not adjusted weekly, or even daily, like those of production workers. A senior professor's whole monthly salary wouldn't buy even a loaf of bread at the peak of the inflation, and many had to forage for food in the woods or live off the charity of friends and students who had jobs for which wages were adjusted along with prices. Quite a few economists who had been through, or close to, such experiences later migrated to Britain and the United States. Not unexpectedly, their views on policy were dominated by the horrors of inflation.

It's important to realize that these hyperinflations resulted from very special circumstances. The immediate cause of the German inflation was the attempt of the Allies to extract impossible reparations from Germany after World War I. The Russian hyperinflation grew out of the devastation of the economy after the post-Revolution civil war of 1918–20 and the impact of the free-wheeling New Economic Policy. The post–World War II hyperinflations of Greece, Hungary, and China were all the direct consequence of war-related disruptions.

Hyperinflations have generally been relatively short lived—only the Russian one lasted as long as two years—and have proved to be easier to bring under ultimate control than most regular inflations. Because hyperinflation wipes out much of the preexisting pattern of wealth ownership, an affected country is generally willing to accept policy measures requiring major changes in wealth distribution—measures that would face enormous resistance if used to dampen inflation of a more moderate kind. In Germany, the old currency was simply cancelled and replaced by a new mark. Limits were placed on the number of old marks (or billions of them) that could be exchanged for new ones, thus reducing the wealth of those who held monetary assets relative to those who owned physical assets. Similar restricted currency exchanges were used in many countries after World War II. If the population believes that such a currency exchange represents a commitment to new economic policies, the new currency can start functioning like money in normal times.

Continuous inflation is not hyperinflation, and there is no reason why it should become so unless there is a major breakdown in the economy. Several Latin American countries and some others, including Israel, have lived with inflation rates of well over 10 percent per year (regarded as a crisis rate in the United States) for twenty-five years or more, with no acceleration into hyperinflation.

Monetary and Interest-Rate Effects	**Inflation has important effects on the demand for money and the rate of interest**

Inflation is sometimes characterized as "too much money chasing too few goods." Because money is a stock, rather than a flow like income or expenditure, this description is essentially incorrect and should be re-phrased: "too much planned expenditure chasing too few goods." Never-theless, the stock of money may play an important role in the inflationary process and thus should not be ignored.

A full discussion of the role of money in the economy is given in the next chapter. At present we need only note that people hold money against future expenditures whose exact nature and timing are uncertain. They hold money for this purpose rather than other assets because it is *liquid*, that is, because it can be immediately exchanged for goods. This is different from corporate stocks that need to be sold, possibly at a temporarily low price. The amount of money people wish to hold depends on its purchasing power. For it is the ultimate control over real goods and services that provides the rationale for holding money in the first place. We shall use the term *real balances* to mean money holdings expressed in terms of the goods and services people actually purchase, and assume that individuals' desired real balances are related to their customary level of expenditure on goods and services.

One of the most obvious effects of open inflation is that the *purchasing power of the dollar* declines steadily as prices rise. If prices are climbing at a rate of, say, 5 percent per year and are expected to continue doing so, a cash balance of $105 will be required next year to buy the same amount of goods and services purchased this year for $100.

From Money into Goods

Now consider the choice available to someone who is keeping a reserve against purchases of goods and services currently worth $100 but whose prices are rising at a 5 percent annual rate. To hold this reserve in cash for one year, our individual will need $105 to allow for the price increase. On the other hand, if he buys goods worth $100 now, he will be able to sell them for $105 next year. He'll thus be better off if, instead of keeping reserves in dollars, he keeps them in the form of real assets whose prices will rise along with the general price level.

Thus, *inflationary expectations* will make people less anxious to hold money and more anxious to hold goods. There will be a consequent tendency for those possessing cash reserves to exchange them for goods, adding to planned expenditure and thus increasing inflationary pressures.

Thus, moderate inflation affects the demand for money in two opposite ways. Rising prices, by reducing the real value of existing dollar holdings, increase the demand for current dollars (nominal balances) as individuals attempt to sustain their desired level of real balances. On the other hand, the lowered desirability of money as an asset (due to expected future price increases) tends to lower the demand for money relative to income. On balance, we normally expect the increased demand to outweigh the decreased demand, so the net effect of inflation will be an increased demand for nominal balances—the actual number of current dollars held.

The Quantity of Money

The inflationary process cannot continue indefinitely unless fed by increases in the money supply. Unless money balances increase, inflation will continue to reduce the *real* value of existing balances until individuals (and firms) decide to increase the number of dollars they hold. This can be done only by reducing expenditures, and reductions in planned expenditures will ultimately remove the inflationary pressure.

Economists differ in their assessment of the *speed* with which this sequence of events will end inflation. Monetarists are more confident than other economists that this process will occur rapidly enough to be useful.

Interest Rates

Just as the value of money depreciates with inflation, so the real cost of borrowing falls. Consider the real cost to the borrower of $100 for one year at 5 percent per annum in two different situations—one in which prices remain stable, the other in which prices (and incomes) rise at the rate of 10 percent per year. In both cases, the borrower receives $100 now and must repay $105 next year. If prices remain stable, the $105 next year represents the same real goods and services as $105 this year, so the borrower clearly gives up something to accept the loan. If prices rise by 10 percent, however, the $105 repaid by the borrower is worth only $95.54 (= $105/1.10, where 1.10 is the index of price change) in terms of current prices. In other words, the borrower is obligated to repay the loan with *fewer* goods and services than were originally purchased from its proceeds. The *real rate of interest* (the excess of repayment over the original loan in terms of real purchasing power) is actually *negative* in this case—a result that is quite possible under actual circumstances.

The more rapidly prices rise, the less is the cost to the borrower of a loan at a given *nominal,* or *money,* rate of interest. If nominal rates do not rise, it becomes increasingly attractive to borrow, buy goods, sell these goods next year at higher prices, then repay loans with dollars of less value than those originally borrowed. Such behavior adds to planned expenditure on goods, and thus increases inflationary pressures.

Lenders, of course, will be increasingly reluctant to lend for precisely the same reasons that make borrowers increasingly anxious to borrow. In certain economies that have adjusted to chronic inflation, loans are extended in real terms—each borrower is obligated to repay whatever current dollars are required to equal the purchasing power of the original principal of the loan (compounded, presumably, by some designated interest rate).

The effect of inflation is to push up the *money* rate of interest. Everything is working in that direction, with borrowers more eager to borrow and lenders more reluctant to lend at the pre-inflationary rate of interest. Its effect on the *real* rate of interest (the money rate less the rate of inflation) is less certain. Historically, the real rate has typically fallen (often to a negative level) under inflationary conditions. This may be ascribed, in part, to a form of ''money illusion''—an interest rate of 8 percent with inflation of 3 percent seems ''high'' relative to a rate of 5 percent with steady prices, although the real rate is 5 percent in both cases.

Recap Money balances are held against possible future exchange for real goods and services. If prices continue to rise, the command of a given dollar balance over future real goods diminishes. Inflation makes it more attractive to hold assets other than money, the prices of which can be expected to keep pace with inflation. Even so, because the money value of transactions is increasing, there will probably be an increase in the demand for money, but less than in proportion to the price increase. The inflationary process would ultimately come to an end if there were no increase in the quantity of money, but this might take considerable time. Another effect of inflation is to make debt attractive because repayment will be in dollars of less purchasing power. This effect tends to put upward pressure on the nominal rate of interest.

Distributional Effects

How inflation affects the distribution of income

In a real economy, inflationary pressures tend to affect certain markets more directly than others. There are also many institutional factors in the economy that make some prices (and wages) more flexible, or more rapidly adjustable, than others. Moreover, many existing long-term contracts call for settlement in terms of current dollars.

Thus, inflation—especially in the transition from a long period of steady prices to one of rising prices—tends to alter the distribution of income among sectors and especially among different socioeconomic groups.

Fixed Incomes

Inflation most obviously, most directly, and most adversely affects *those individuals whose incomes are absolutely fixed in money terms.* These are primarily retired people or elderly survivors (with no services to sell at current prices) living on life-insurance annuities or pensions with no provisions for increase. An eighty-year-old person who retired at sixty-five in 1960 on a pension of $50 per week received in 1975 the equivalent of only $30 per week at 1960 prices.

Of course, not all retirement incomes are affected this way. Some persons may have provided for retirement by buying corporate stocks whose dividends and capital values keep pace (or more than keep pace) with general price increases. Moreover, individuals who receive government transfer incomes (such as Social Security) generally benefit from periodic cost-of-living adjustments.

Wages and Profits

Wages and salaries that are determined or renegotiated only at infrequent intervals will also tend to lag behind price increases, especially during the early stages of an inflationary period. In the midst of chronic inflation, however, wage contracts (even if negotiated only every two or three years) may allow for anticipated price increases. Such contracts may even include provisions (in the form of *escalator clauses*) for wages to be adjusted automatically with changes in the consumer price index. We can expect that occupations with flexible wage arrangements will generally gain relative to those with less flexible arrangements.

The effect of inflation on firms is variable as well. Regulated industries, like public utilities, must usually argue for price increases on the basis of rising costs, and thus tend to find their prices lagging compared to unregulated industries.

Generally speaking, profits will tend to rise relative to other incomes in the early stages of inflation, because the initial impact of excess demand is on the prices of goods rather than on wages and other costs. Conversely, when inflation is stopped or slowed, profits will tend to fall relative to other incomes, especially when delayed wage increases are still occurring.

Other Effects

There is also a distributional effect that arises from the existence of flexibility in the full employment ceiling of the economy. Capacity output can be stretched somewhat, and inflation, at least to the extent that it reflects excess demand, will add an incentive for this. Marginal businesses, and workers who normally have difficulty obtaining jobs, will tend to benefit from this variety of inflation.

Recap The effects of inflation are not uniform over the economy. Those with incomes contractually fixed in money terms (many pensions, for example) will find their real incomes reduced by inflation. Those able to adjust quickly may find their real incomes increased. Generally, profits will rise in real terms, at least initially, while real wages will tend to remain fairly steady on average, rising for some groups and falling for others.

Is Inflation Bad?

Judging the possible demerits of inflation

A recession can be considered as an unambiguously undesirable state of the economy on the basis of the simplest and most widely acceptable welfare criterion—restoring full employment would result in more output of *all* goods and more income for *everyone*. Even though a recession may have distributional effects from which some may gain, it remains true that by moving to full employment and appropriately redistributing output, everyone could be made better off. Even those who may advocate a temporary recession as a way to achieve some long-run economic goal apparently have to state their argument in terms of a "necessary evil," but an evil nonetheless.

Gains from Inflation

Inflation provides an entirely different case. During moderate inflation, we may well have full employment and a thriving economy. Furthermore, adjustments in relative prices can assume the form of one price rising more slowly than another, rather than one price actually falling, and it is widely agreed that the former imposes fewer institutional problems on the economy than the latter.

One cannot argue, as in considering recession, that inflation is bad because everyone could be made better off without it, because it simply is not true. There will, of course, be distributional effects, but income redistribution in and of itself is not necessarily bad—it all depends on whether the new distribution is regarded as better or worse than the old.

Nor can it be argued that people cannot live with steadily rising prices because they've been doing just that for a long while. In the eighty-five years from 1890 to 1975, consumer prices in the United States were higher than the previous year in sixty-six instances. The only times prices declined significantly over this period were during the major depressions of the 1890s and 1930s. The average annual rate of price increase was 2.3 percent, compounded over the whole period. An outline of the price history of the United States is presented in Table 25.1.

Table 25.1
Consumer Prices in the United States,
1850–1977

Decade ending	Average annual rate of price change over decade (percent)
1860	1.1
1870	4.9
1880	− 1.2
1890	− 0.2
1900	0.2
1910	2.0
1920	11.1
1930	− 1.7
1940	− 1.6
1950	7.2
1960	2.3
1970	3.1
1970–77	6.4

Dangers of Inflation

If moderate inflation is bad, it is not so much because of what it is but because of *what it might lead to.* We've already seen that inflationary processes are self-sustaining in the sense that price increases that are expected to continue will generate influences tending to push them further upward, perhaps even more rapidly. Thus, inflation at a rate of, say, 5 percent per year does not merely tend to perpetuate itself, but contains many elements that tend to *accelerate* the rate of price increase.

A steady price increase of 5 percent per year is one thing, but prices that rise 5 percent this year, 8 percent the next, 12 percent the next, and so on, is another. If prices are expected to accelerate, there will be an even greater incentive to spend now, thus increasing prices even more. In principle, sufficient inflationary expectations can cause such price increases to explode into *hyperinflation,* in which case the overall rate of price increase becomes so rapid that no one can adjust to it. Under these circumstances, the operation of the market economy breaks down. Relative prices become meaningless if all prices double in a matter of days (or even hours) so a shirt today costs more than a refrigerator did yesterday.

The redistributive effects of inflation thus result not from price increases proper, but from ongoing *changes in the rate of price increase.* If prices simply increased at 2.5 percent annually and were expected to continue doing so forever, complete adjustment could be made. Contracts could be written with future (and certain) price changes in mind, and the rate of interest could be adjusted to allow for these changes. Private pensions could be arranged to increase at 2.5 percent per annum because the value of assets from which pension incomes are derived would also be increasing at this rate. A shift from steady prices to inflation, or from a 5 percent to a 10 percent price rise, on the other hand, would bring about redistribution until new adjustments could be made.

The real danger of inflation is that the inflationary process is potentially unstable and can accelerate into hyperinflation and the breakdown of the market economy.

The Open Economy

All our discussion so far has been in the context of a closed economy with no foreign trade sector. The general analysis of inflation that we have given is appropriate for economies connected through trade *only if the rate of inflation is uniform throughout the world*.

For an open economy, inflation introduces major problems when the domestic rate of price increase exceeds that in the rest of the world. Such a situation will lead either to a persistent balance-of-payments crisis or to a steady decline in the exchange rate of the country's national currency, depending on whether there are fixed or flexible exchange rates. Countries like Britain, with a high ratio of trade to GNP, will find inflation a problem primarily in *external* economic relationships. Countries like the United States, for whom trade is less important relative to the domestic economy, will consider it primarily an *internal* problem. The external problems created by inflation are discussed in the final chapter.

Recap Unlike a recession, the elimination of inflation would not make everyone better off. During inflation, the economy is at or near capacity and the effects are mainly distributional. Inflation should not be condemned simply because it changes the distribution of income unless it changes distribution in the wrong direction. The case against moderate inflation is mainly that it is potentially capable of accelerating, and that very rapid inflation can cause a breakdown in the market system. There is little or no case against moderate, steady, inflation because the economy can adjust to it. It may, however, pose special problems for economies with important external trade.

Policy Toward Inflation

A discussion of the curbs
for inflation,
their effectiveness and cost

Most economists would rather be called on to treat a recession than to cure an inflation. Boosting the economy out of a recession can make everyone better off, while putting a damper on inflation may make some, if not everyone, at least temporarily worse off. Furthermore, economists are more confident about their ability to move the economy steadily from recession to near full employment than about their ability to move it steadily from rising prices to constant (or slowly rising) prices.

The Basic Problem

Drastic cures for inflation are always possible. Any policy that will bring the economy's predicted real income well below the full employment level for long enough can be guaranteed to stop the inflationary process in a closed economy. In other words, we can always cure inflation by engineering a sufficiently devastating recession. Gentle cures for inflation, unfortunately, are more difficult to devise.

A recession is a *static* situation that can be cured by eliminating its fundamental cause—insufficient planned expenditure. Open inflation, on the other hand, is a *dynamic* process—it is quite possible to eliminate the fundamental cause of inflation (too much planned expenditure) without stopping the upward price spiral. Thus, while we can cure a recession by gently *increasing* the equilibrium income level toward capacity, we cannot necessarily halt an ongoing inflationary process by gently *decreasing* the equilibrium income level (at current prices) toward capacity.

Indeed, curing a recession does not require exceeding the full employment level of output, but curing an inflation may well require reducing output drastically into recession. It is certainly obvious that if trying to *maintain* the economy at full employment carries a high probability of inflation, as implied by the Phillips curve described in Chapter 22, simply bringing equilibrium income back down to the full employment level will not be sufficient to eliminate inflation.

The existence of inflation, it must be stressed, does not automatically call for a cure at any cost. If we accept the general Phillips curve evidence that under the institutional arrangements of most Western economies, anything approaching zero unemployment will be associated with some degree of inflation, the alternative is relatively high unemployment. We have already shown that moderate inflation is not necessarily bad if it can be kept from accelerating, but high unemployment represents a real loss of potential output. Thus, we must discuss the question of curing inflation by examining how it might be done, without committing ourselves to an anti-inflationary policy if we consider its costs to be too high.

One possible approach is to consider the *inflationary gap* (the excess of demand over capacity output) and the *inflationary process* (the built-in price spiral) as separate problems to be countered by separate policies. The inflationary gap can be eliminated by policies designed to lower planned expenditure, such as a reduction in government expenditure, an increase in taxes, and discouragement of investment by monetary or fiscal measures. While the inflationary process is more difficult to control, reducing inflationary expectations is the key.

Controlling Inflation

The most widely advocated policies designed to deal with the inflationary process are *wage-price controls* or milder *wage-price guidelines* (backed by the threat of controls). Such controls or guidelines will generally permit wages to rise only in proportion to productivity increases, and prices not to rise at all except to finish off lagged adjustments to previous cost increases. Modified versions may permit slow price increases at a "normal" rate of 2 percent or so.

Controls or guidelines will initially act simply as restrictions on the market. If consumers believe they will work, inflationary expectations will fade and the inflationary process will eventually die. If the inflationary gap is removed at the same time, there will be no new inflationary pressure and the controls can be removed.

The problems inherent in wage-price controls are microeconomic rather than macroeconomic in nature. If the economy really did produce only one good, as in simple macromodels, and the general price level were simply the price of this good, there would be no major problem controlling this price. Nor would there be a problem controlling wages if there were a single uniform wage and only one kind of labor. But the general price level is an abstraction, an index number, as is the average level of wages.

Controlling prices means controlling hundreds of thousands of prices of different things. Even an attempt at selective price control means controlling thousands of prices. Simple rules of thumb, like permitting all wages to rise by some fixed percentage or freezing all prices, can be used for relatively short periods. But in the long run it becomes evident that there are (1) special reasons why some prices should be permitted to rise more than others (such as increases in the prices of materials from abroad), and (2) clear inequities in restraining wage increases of those whose incomes have lagged behind in the inflationary spiral. Once simple rules of thumb can no longer be applied, the control mechanism must be developed into a bureaucracy capable of handling enormous numbers of individual applications for wage and price increases.

The enormous size and diversity of the U.S. economy make it much more difficult to operate a full-scale price-and-wage-control system than it is in countries like Finland and Sweden where such systems have been relatively successful.

The success of *quantitative* economic policies requires that they be adjustable more or less continuously in response to the latest information about how far away the economy is from achieving some preestablished target. While fiscal and monetary policies for maintaining full employment satisfy this criterion, wage-price controls and guidelines do not. These must be set well in advance and then be adhered to, lest they lose their credibility. This requires a degree of accuracy in economic forecasting that we do not yet possess. We must consequently face our moment of truth:

Economists know how to stop inflation, but not how to stop it smoothly and without danger of pushing the economy into a recession.

Recap Inflation can always be cured by a sufficient reduction in demand relative to capacity output for a sufficiently long time. Historical experience shows that it may take a long, deep recession to counteract all tendencies for prices to rise because of the dynamic character of the inflationary process. It is necessary, but not sufficient, to remove the excess demand. Even though this eliminates the initiating cause, other policies may be required to stop the inflationary spiral once it is started. Economists do not yet know how to cure inflation without moving the economy into recession. Thus, it may be preferable to live with moderate inflation than to pay the costs of its cure.

Capsule Supplement 25.3   **Controls, Guidelines, Jawbones, and Wishbones**

Prices can be kept from rising, in principle, if the government can devise enforceable price and wage controls. So long as there is excess demand, inflation is merely *suppressed* by such policies. However, if excess demand is removed by other policies, such controls can prevent an inflationary spiral from continuing as a result of its own dynamic momentum.

During World War II, most countries (including the United States) had extensive wage and price controls. They existed with high excess demand and only partially suppressed open inflation. Full price-wage controls present major administrative problems in a market economy as complex as that of the United States. There are hundreds of thousands (perhaps millions) of individual prices, and it is simply not possible to watch all of them. Hence, the controls fall mainly on those things easiest to control, such as rents and standardized goods sold on a national basis. In addition, there are strong incentives to shift resources into the production of goods that are not controlled and to shift goods into black markets and other illegal outlets.

Few would advocate *complete* controls, except under major emergency conditions (such as World War II), simply because of the administrative problems. Those who favor some form of control under inflationary conditions, primarily to lessen inflationary expectations and check the inflationary spiral, generally advocate *selective* controls on major cost-of-living items such as rents, utilities, and food; on important industrial inputs such as steel; and on wages. The presumption is that holding down key prices will suppress the spiral. Unless excess demand is kept down, however, the result may be a shift of resources away from the production of important items.

With the "Phase II" controls introduced in 1971, the Nixon administration attempted a somewhat different kind of selective control. Under this system, firms whose sales were above a certain level—sufficient for them to be regarded as major national suppliers—were under true price control, while very small firms remained virtually uncontrolled. The selection in this case was by size of firm rather than by type of output produced, and the system was based on the realistic presumption that the prices set by the corporate giants would establish the general price level for each class of product. Even if the giants were squeezed somewhat and smaller firms were able to obtain higher prices and profits, this would be in the socially desirable direction of reducing the market share of the giants. That these controls were only modestly successful can be attributed to the attempt to keep them as gentle as possible.

Some kind of control over wages is usually considered essential in any policy of the price-control type. Because productivity grows, wages can legitimately be permitted to rise somewhat—the question being a matter of how much. Consider a two-sector economy in which output per man-hour is rising at a rate of 6 percent in one sector and 2 percent in the other. Wages in the two sectors could rise at rates of 6 percent and 2 percent respectively, but then there would be great pressure from unions in the slow sector to achieve the same wage increase as in the other sector. If wages rise at the same rate in both sectors— somewhere between 2 percent and 6 percent—unions in the more productive sector will argue that their wages lag behind productivity growth. There is obviously no simple solution to such problems.

The administrators of wage and price controls must be given *guidelines* about what the maximum average rate of *price change* is to be, what the expected rate of average *productivity change* is, and so on. These are major policy decisions, and should not be set by the controllers of individual price and wage changes. Even without any formal system of controls, the government may announce such guidelines in the hope that firms and labor unions will adhere to them, if only to avoid actual controls. Guidelines without controls were set up in the mid-1960s. While credited with modest success, these guidelines did not stem the growing inflation.

Labor union leaders are not always opposed to such guidelines, at least not in private. In an inflation, such leaders are subject to great pressure from their constituents for wage hikes designed to counteract the effect of possible future price increases, as well as to make up for those that have occurred since the last contract. Moreover, there is considerable competition between different unions to see which one can deliver the best wage package. Guidelines place a universal and visible figure on record as having been established and thus take some of the pressure off union leadership. For similar reasons, firms in imperfectly competitive industries also find well-devised guidelines to be useful, both in wage bargaining and in pricing policy.

The term *jawboning* means the verbal and political intimidation of firms whose prices have exceeded explicit guidelines or implicit notions about appropriate rates of change. The classic case was the Kennedy scolding of U.S. Steel in 1963, after which the firm cut back its announced price increase. In 1970, when Bethlehem Steel (the second largest producer) took the lead in price increases, Nixon lashed out in protest and again the price rise was cut back. Guideline-setting without verbal intimidation is appropriately termed *wishboning*.

By 1971 it was obvious that jawboning could not handle the continuing inflationary spiral generated by the Vietnam war and expansionist monetary policy.

Starting in August of that year, the Nixon administration imposed a complete freeze on prices and wages for ninety days. The freeze was a holding device to prepare for wage-price controls that were announced in November. Both the freeze and the initial controls, it might be noted, were introduced under standby powers Congress had voted to the president much earlier—powers the president said he did not want and would not use.

Exercises

1. If the real rate of interest were 4 percent and not affected by inflation, what would the money rate of interest have to be at an inflation rate of 4 percent to induce people to hold the same proportion of their assets in the form of money as they would with stable prices?

2. In an economy with a multiplier of 2.5 and capacity GNP of $500 million, by how much could the government increase expenditure without causing inflation if the output of the economy were initially $450 million?

3. If productivity were increasing by a uniform 2.5 percent in all industries, to what average rate of increase should wages be held if the rate of inflation were to be held constant at 2 percent?

For Thought and Discussion

1. The economy is at full employment at stable prices with output per person increasing at 2 percent per year. Everyone's wage or salary increases by 10 percent. Twelve months later, everyone complains that he has been ''cheated'' out of most of his increase in income by inflation. Should the government be blamed, and if so, for what?

2. As a policy-maker, if you had to choose between full employment and a 5 percent annual rate of inflation or stable prices and some unemployment, which would you choose? Why?

3. What is the maximum rate of inflation you would consider tolerable?

4. By what percentage (and in what direction) do you think consumer prices will have changed in twenty-five years? In fifty years? Make your best guess.

5. Compare your answers with what happened over the last twenty-five years, and the last fifty years. (Table 25.1 will give you sufficient information for a general comparison.)

Part 7
Money and Banks

This part, consisting of Chapters 26, 27, and 28, explores the economic relationship of money and banks. Chapter 26 is concerned with the contribution money makes to the economy. Chapter 27 discusses the role played by banks in determining the money supply, and Chapter 28 points out the ultimate control now exercised over the money supply through central banking. A discussion of the nature and appropriate function of monetary policy appears in Chapter 31 with other aspects of macroeconomic policy.

Chapter 26
Money

Terms and Concepts

Transactions balance
Precautionary reserve
Liquidity
Real balance
Nominal balance
Opportunity cost
Liquidity preference curve
Velocity of money
Exchange equation
Quantity theory of money
Currency
Demand deposits
Near-money

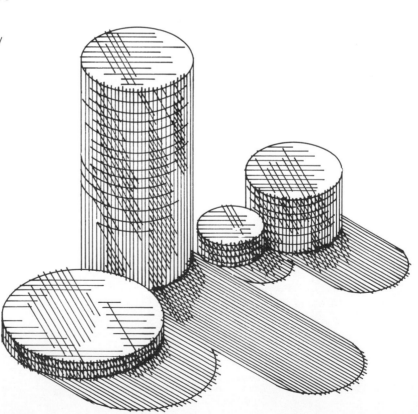

Money and	Why money is discussed
Macroeconomics	in macroeconomics rather than
	in microeconomics, and why it
	is not just another good

Money and Macroeconomics

Why money is discussed in macroeconomics rather than in microeconomics, and why it is not just another good

In macroeconomics, we treat thousands of different goods and services as though they were a single good. Thus, it may seem peculiar that we should focus on one particular thing, money, and give it special treatment. It may also seem strange that money receives so little attention in our study of microeconomics.

The Pervasiveness of Money

Money is studied in macroeconomics simply because it pervades all parts of the economy. A change in the quantity of money, for example, will tend to affect market circumstances in general, rather than the circumstances in any one market to the exclusion of others. Thus, we can say that money influences the quantity and price of our single aggregate good, rather than the relative quantities and prices of the individual components of this aggregate.

Moreover, we choose not to lump money into our aggregate good because the role of money in the economy is fundamentally different from that of, say, pork chops or movies. For one thing, money is not consumed or used *directly* to provide the kind of benefits obtained from food or entertainment—its usefulness derives from the fact that it can be *exchanged* for goods and services. Nor is it *used up* in the process of exchange. A person who receives money in return for goods (or factor services) can, in turn, simply exchange it for other goods and services.

Money exists as a *stock* that circulates from person to person (and firm to firm). At any given point in time, all the money in existence is being *held* by the various members of society (under the mattress, in their pockets, or in bank accounts), even though many of them will immediately pass some of their holdings on to others in exchange for goods and services.

The Social Value of Money

Even though money may not provide benefits comparable to those of ordinary consumption goods, it possesses social value. Indeed, money is productive in the direct sense that, without it, the economy would produce fewer real goods and services.

Consider, for example, the most rudimentary use of money—as a *medium of exchange*. In the absence of something universally acceptable in exchange, we would have multiple barter. A worker in a brewery, for example, might be paid his weekly wage in beer instead of dollars. While he might be persuaded to consume some of this take-home pay directly, he would also need food. To obtain food, he would have to locate individuals willing to accept beer in exchange for bread, salami, radishes, etc. Such a system would obviously require each individual to spend considerable time running about looking for appropriate exchanges. It is the saving of this wasted labor time and effort that makes money productive as a medium of exchange.

But the social value of money is not confined to its usefulness as a medium of exchange. One of money's most important functions derives from its ability to bridge time intervals. Specifically, it functions as a *store of value*, enabling people to make a sale one week followed by a purchase the next week from the proceeds of that sale, those proceeds having been stored in the form of money.

Recap Money is treated in a macroeconomic, rather than a microeconomic, context because its effects are pervasive and influence all other goods rather than just a few. It differs from an ordinary good because its value lies entirely in what it may be exchanged for, not in itself. A system of money has real social value that can be measured in terms of the time and effort otherwise needed to make transactions.

Time, Uncertainty, and Money

How money's usefulness is related to time and uncertainty

In a smoothly operating, instantly adjusting world in which all future events could be predicted with 100 percent certainty, there would be no need for money except as a convenient unit of measurement or *standard of value*. To gain a better understanding of the role of money in a more realistic world of uncertainty, we must consider *why* people want it.

When individuals say that they want "more money," they generally mean that they want *"more income"* with which to buy more goods and services. If they receive more money, they may get rid of it (spend it) quite rapidly, proving that it was not the money itself that was actually desired.

When economists refer to the demand for money, they mean the demand for money to keep as money. If someone receives $100 and keeps it, either under the mattress or in a bank account, that person has demonstrated a demand for more money. But if someone receives $100 and spends it all, that person has demonstrated that the stock of money he was already holding was sufficient for his requirements.

But why would anyone choose to hold money rather than spend it?

Timing Effects

One reason is the *timing of transactions*. A consumer may receive his income at periodic intervals, but wish to consume at a steady rate over time.

For example, he may receive wages of $140 each Friday, but wish to consume at a steady rate over the week. He could, of course, *immediately* convert his wages into stocks of goods and consume these over the week. But for various reasons, it is probably more convenient and economical for him to hold stocks of money rather than goods, and spend these over time. The consumer would thus spend at a rate of $20 per day, running his money balance down from $140 every Friday to zero each Thursday, giving an *average balance* of $70. A balance of this kind is called a *transactions balance*.

Uncertainty

Not only is the timing of transactions likely to be irregular over time, but there may also be *uncertainty* about the *level* of transactions. The consumer may wish to be in a position to meet, say, unforeseeable medical expenses and thus maintain a *precautionary reserve*. Our consumer, for example, may wish to hold an average balance of $100—$70 for transactions purposes and $30 as a precautionary reserve.

Another reason for holding money is that it constitutes an asset, a form of wealth that can be carried forward intact from one period to another. People accumulate assets in order to defer expenditure from the present to the future. They may use part of their income during their working life to purchase assets so they can continue to consume during retirement after income from working has ceased.

But there are many assets available in a market economy that yield a *return* in the form of interest, rent, dividends, or capital gains. Why should anyone hold wealth, or any part of it, in the form of money—which brings no return—as opposed to real estate, stocks, or bonds?

Liquidity

The special property of money, which differentiates it from other forms of wealth, is that it can be *immediately* exchanged for other things. With other forms of wealth, the owner must usually wait until an asset can be sold on the market. This process not only takes time and trouble, but also carries the risk that the asset may have to be sold when its price is temporarily low.

We refer to the immediate exchangeability of money as *liquidity*. Strictly speaking, liquidity differentiates assets that are more or less liquid according to the ease with which they can be exchanged for other things. Corporate stocks, which can generally be sold within a few hours for a small commission, are more liquid than real estate. Because a dollar bill can always be converted directly and immediately into a dollar's worth of things, money is the *most liquid* of all assets.

Liquidity is valuable only because of uncertainty. The degree of immediacy in exchange is unimportant if it is known sufficiently far in advance that an asset is to be exchanged for other things.

Liquidity is important also in transactions balances because of the uncertain *timing* of expenditures relative to receipts. A person may be paid on the first day of the month, but make expenditures in an irregular pattern over the month. If he knew *exactly* when each expenditure was to be made, he could lend at some interest rate under a loan agreement that would bring repayment exactly when needed. While this may seem farfetched for an individual because of the problems involved in making such small loan transactions, large businesses, which also hold money, often make just such loans for periods as short as a day or two.

People hold cash or bank balances against those payments they know they must make, but aren't sure exactly when they'll have to make them. An element of uncertainty even exists with regard to the level of payments on any given day. Will it rain, forcing an individual to take a taxi rather than walk? Will a business opportunity suddenly arise that will be lost unless some payment can be made immediately? These are the kinds of uncertainties that lead individuals and firms to hold a portion of their wealth in the form of money.

Recap What we must explain about money is why it should ever be kept, rather than immediately exchanged for goods. One reason is time—money is kept for exchange at a later date. Another is uncertainty—money is kept because future transactions are not known with certainty. Although other things could be used, money is the most universally and immediately exchangeable commodity when required, that is, it is the most liquid of assets.

Capsule Supplement 26.1   **Yap Stones and Cowrie Shells**

Many people have heard of the great stone disks on the Pacific island of Yap whose ownership changes hands in exchange for goods. These disks are too large to move and some lie buried at the bottom of the sea. Other people have probably heard how members of certain East African tribal societies must "buy" their future brides with cattle, or how cowrie shells were once traded for goods in West Africa. All three things, the stones of Yap, the cattle of East Africa, and the cowries of West Africa have been used as examples of "primitive" monies.

Only the West African cowrie shell, however, should truly be regarded as money. While the others certainly qualify as *assets* or *wealth,* they cannot be categorized as money. The native culture in East Africa functioned without money, in fact. Cattle represented wealth and status only—cattle could not be exchanged for agricultural produce, but only for wives who were not actually "bought" with money but were part of a status exchange. In Yap there was money—not the stone disks that have captured the imagination of so many writers—but mother-of-pearl and the Tridacna shell. The Yap stones are best seen as similar to heirloom jewels or valuable art objects: exchanged only on rare occasions and for very special reasons.

The cowrie shells of West Africa were used as a medium of exchange in both internal and international transactions, and our relatively detailed historical knowledge of them is due to their wide use in exchange with European traders. Indeed, they could be directly equated with European currencies by using an appropriate exchange rate. Dalzel, in his 1793 *History of Dahomey,* quotes a rate of 1 tockey (a string of forty shells) as equivalent to 1-1/5 English pence. The cowries were available in various denominations (5 tockeys = 1 galhina, 5 galhinas = 1 ackey, and so on), each consisting of a specific number of basic shells. We can even trace the exchange rate between the cowries and other currencies and follow its change, just as for other rates of exchange between currencies. In 1883 the rate was 500 cowries per French franc (in the Lobi tribal area). It fell to 800 per French franc during World War I, then rose after the war to only 120 to the franc by the late 1920s. During the world currency crisis of 1932, the use of the cowrie was temporarily revived in northern Nigeria, where it had almost died out.

In simpler societies, the primary functions served by money are its role as a medium of exchange and a store of value. For them liquidity, which is so important in our complex world, is not as important for two reasons: barter is usually possible, and the call for sudden and unanticipated payments is less likely in a society characterized by relatively close personal contacts and comparatively little market activity. In the Yap example, however, where there are two forms of assets, the Tridacna shells and the great stones, we could regard the shells as money precisely because they are more "liquid" than the stones, although the stones certainly function as a store of value and, to some extent, a medium of exchange.

The Demand for Money

What determines the level of money balances an individual will hold

By the demand for money we mean the demand for *money balances* to hold, not the demand for income to spend. Since money is held because it *might* have to be spent, the ultimate reference for money is the *quantity of goods and services over which it has potential command.* Individuals are thereby interested in their *real balances,* that is, in their actual command over goods and services, rather than simply in the number of dollars or *nominal balances* they hold.

The level of the nominal balance constituting a given real balance (or, alternatively, the level of the real balance constituting a given nominal balance) varies over time with changes in the general price level. For example, about $400 was necessary in 1975 to buy the same general collection of goods and services that could be purchased with $100 in 1935.

The demand for money balances represents a desire for ultimate command over real goods and services. Thus it should be measured in dollars of constant purchasing power.

Income

In the last section, we emphasized the importance of holding money balances in order to carry out *transactions* whose timing, and even size, were subject to uncertainty. Now, the level of transactions individuals expect to make is strongly related to their *income*. Clearly, someone with a high income will carry out transactions of a greater total value over a month or a year than will someone with a low income. Thus, we can state the following proposition:

The desired level of transactions balances will depend on income and will rise or fall as income rises or falls.

While this does not necessarily mean that transactions balances will be *proportional* to income, such a proportional relationship is often assumed in simple models.

When an individual's desired money balance is closely proportional to income or expenditure, we can express its magnitude in terms of the *length of time* over which expenditures could be sustained at the current level from the balance alone if the individual's flow of income were to cease. If, for example, an individual's average rate of expenditure were $200 per week and his average money balance were $1,000, we could express his balance as *five weeks of transactions,* or simply *five weeks.*

If all prices were to double, our hypothetical individual would then need to spend $400 per week to obtain the same real goods and services as before, and would require a $2,000 nominal balance. This represents the same *real* balance as before after adjusting for price-level changes. Balances expressed as weeks of real expenditures thus represent real balances and are independent of the price level. We'll further explore this relationship between the level of transactions and real balances in the next section.

The Rate of Interest

Money is held as an asset because of its liquidity, even though a positive return (interest) could be obtained by holding other forms of wealth. The higher the rate of interest, the more is given up by holding, say, $100 in the form of money rather than in the form of a bond—the interest forgone is the *opportunity cost* of holding money. Thus, the higher the rate of interest, the more willing an individual will be to hold assets in a form that brings interest.

The desired level of money balances may be sensitive to the rate of interest, and can be expected to fall when interest rates rise, and rise when interest rates fall.

Despite the logical appeal of this proposition, it seems unlikely that the average person will actually vary his money balance in response to relatively small interest-rate changes. However, almost one-third of all money balances in the United States are held by firms. Because firms possess

Figure 26.1
Liquidity preference curves.

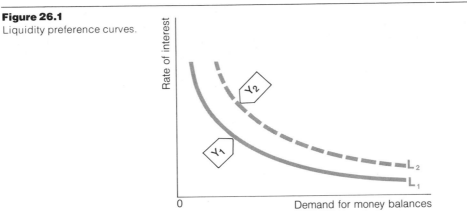

larger average balances, a greater variety of assets, and better information about financial possibilities than most individuals, they are considerably more responsive to such changes.

Economists are primarily interested in the *aggregate* demand for money balances over the economy as a whole, rather than in the demands of specific individuals. Most analyses of the demand for money are thus stated in macroeconomic terms. The general influences on the aggregate demand for money are simply assumed to be the aggregate equivalents of those affecting individual demands. In particular:

The aggregate demand for money balances is assumed to vary directly with aggregate income and inversely with the rate of interest.

Liquidity Preference Curves

The aggregate demand for money is typically depicted by curves that show how the level of desired balances varies with the interest rate. Such curves are called *liquidity preference curves* because variations in desired balances associated with changes in the rate of interest ultimately come from a balancing of the *preference for liquidity* against the *return from interest-bearing assets*.

The traditional liquidity preference diagram is presented in Figure 26.1. Each curve (L_1, L_2, and so on) shows the relationship between the demand for money and the rate of interest *at a given income level*. Each curve slopes downward to the right because the level of desired balances falls as the interest rate rises. Such curves are commonly depicted as more or less vertical above some rate of interest because people (and firms) will presumably desire some minimum level of liquidity even at very high rates of interest.

As income rises from Y_1 to Y_2, we move from one curve, L_1, to another, L_2. The curve corresponding to the higher income level reflects the presumption that a larger money balance is desired at all rates of interest than at the lower income level, and thus lies to the right of the lower income curve.

Empirical Results

Empirical estimates of the demand for money are consistent with the relationships just specified. The authoritative analysis of the monetary sector of the United States economy (the Federal Reserve-MIT macromodel), when simplified to the level of our current analysis, shows that:

1. The demand for the most important form of money, bank deposits, increases in proportion to GNP when the rate of interest is constant.
2. The demand for this type of money decreases when the rate of interest rises—a 10 percent *proportionate* increase in the rate of interest (an increase from 5 to 5.5 percent, for example) causes an approximate 4 percent decline in the level of desired balances.

Recap The demand for money balances represents a demand for ultimate command over real goods and services, and thus will increase if the price level rises. Because the level of transactions is related to income, the demand for money will tend to vary directly with income. Finally, because provision for future payments could be held in the form of interest-bearing assets instead of money, the demand for money will tend to vary inversely with the rate of interest.

| **The Equation of Exchange** | **A brief formal statement of the relationship between money balances, transactions, and the price level** |

In discussing the demand for money, we saw that an individual's desired money balance can be expressed in terms of the number of weeks of transactions it would finance. We also noted that if *real* transactions remain unchanged, a constant balance in terms of weeks of transactions would imply a constant *real balance* even if prices were to change. We'll now examine this relationship in detail, but from a slightly different perspective.

Let T denote the level of *real* transactions (expenditures) per period (a year, say) over the economy as a whole, and M be total *nominal* money balances (measured in ordinary current dollars).

We'll assume that T is measured in *1972 dollars*, the standard measure for real GNP in the United States, and that P is an index of the general price level based on 1972 prices. The aggregate level of *real balances* is then found by dividing nominal balances by the price index, in the same way that real GNP would be found by dividing current-dollar GNP by a price index:

$$\text{real money balances (in 1972 dollars)} = M/P.$$

For example, if current nominal balances are $450 billion and the price index is 1.50 (indicating that it takes $1.50 to buy today what $1.00 bought in 1972), then:

$$\text{current real money balances} = \frac{\$450 \text{ billion}}{1.50} = \$300 \text{ billion}.$$

We can now express these real balances in terms of the number of years of real transactions they would finance:

$$\text{number of years} = \frac{\text{real balances}}{\text{real transactions}}$$
$$= \frac{(M/P)}{T}$$
$$= \frac{M}{PT}.$$

If, in our example, real transactions equal $1,200 billion, then:

$$\text{number of years} = \frac{\$450}{(1.50)(\$1,200)} = \frac{1}{4}.$$

For a typical, real-world economy, this figure will almost always be a fraction less than 1. That is, balances will typically finance transactions for less than a full year.

The Velocity of Money

Rather than working with the number of years of real transactions the balances could finance, economists have chosen to work with the *reciprocal* of this quantity, called the *velocity of money,* and denoted by V. The velocity of money carries a vivid picture of money circulating round and round the economy at greater or less speed. While *some* of the money stock certainly circulates in this way, much does not. For example, a person may receive wages and pay bills in cash, which clearly circulates. But, one may also stash $100 in a cookie jar and wait for a rainy day.

Thus, while we could define velocity as the average number of times a dollar changes hands during a given year, it is more precise to regard V as the number by which we must multiply money balances so they will be exactly sufficient to finance one year's transactions.

However we choose to regard this number, the following relationship holds:

$$V = \text{the velocity of money} = \frac{1}{\begin{array}{c}\text{the number of years}\\ \text{of transactions that}\\ \text{balances will finance}\end{array}}.$$

In terms of M, P, and T, we have

$$V = \frac{PT}{M},$$

and, in our example,

$$V = \frac{(1.50)(\$1,200)}{\$450} = 4.$$

Thus, velocity is defined as the ratio of transactions to money balances, and can be thought of (loosely) as the average number of times a dollar changes hands per year.

The Exchange Equation

If we multiply both sides of the above relationship by M, we obtain the *equation of exchange:*

$$MV = PT.$$

This equation indicates that the number of dollars times the average number of times each is exchanged is equal to the dollar value of transactions made.

Because this equation is derived directly from the definition of V, it necessarily holds for all values of M, P, and T under all circumstances. Such an equation is called a *definitional* or *tautological* equation. It predicts nothing because it is necessarily true under all circumstances.

The level of total transactions in the economy can be taken as proportional to the level of real income. Thus, it is convenient to use income (Y) instead of transactions (T) because we have statistics on income, but not on transactions. The equation then becomes

$$MV = PY,$$

where V is the ratio of income to balances rather than transactions to balances.

Recap The total money stock at any time can be expressed in terms of the number of years of current real transactions it would finance. The inverse of this number is called the velocity of money.

The Quantity Theory

A view of the link between the stock of money and the operation of the economy

The simple quantity theory of money follows directly from the exchange equation when it is assumed that the economy's behavior is such as to *maintain a constant velocity of money,* or at least to restore the velocity to approximately its original level when the adjustment process is completed.

Fact and Theory

Is the velocity of money constant? That is, are money balances maintained in a constant ratio to income? The dispute between those who consider the simple quantity theory useful and those who do not centers primarily around whether or not the particular disputant believes that there is reasonable evidence of constant velocity under the circumstances in which the predictions of the theory are to be used.

Because the demand for money at a given income level depends in part on the rate of interest, the velocity (being the ratio of real income to real balances) also depends on the rate of interest. Consequently, the quantity theory requires that the rate of interest be constant or that the interest effect on velocity be small.

For the moment, let's accept the relationship

$$V = PY/M.$$

It follows that if V is constant, PY/M must remain constant—that is, nominal money balances and the money value of GNP must remain in fixed proportions.

The theory predicts that, if M increases by, say, 10 percent, then the product, PY, will also increase by 10 percent. Significantly, it predicts only what happens to the *product* of P and Y, not what happens to P or Y separately, unless we have more information. In the absence of such information, a 10 percent increase in PY, for example, might reflect a 10 percent increase in P with Y constant, a 10 percent increase in Y with P constant, or a combination of changes in both P and Y.

Full Employment

The clearest prediction of this theory stems from the fact that it is impossible for Y (which represents real GNP) to increase in response to an increase in the quantity of money if the economy is producing at capacity. In this event, any increase in M must result in a proportionately equivalent increase in P.

At full employment, the quantity theory predicts that any increase in the quantity of money will result in a proportional increase in the price level (inflation).

This is the most widely accepted prediction of the quantity theory. Indeed, it has even been observed that under severely inflationary conditions, the velocity of circulation itself tends to rise, thus resulting in a price increase greater than in proportion to the increase in the quantity of money.

Note that the basic theory *does not* predict that a reduction in the quantity of money at full employment will reduce prices. In fact, real output would most likely be reduced in this case.

Below Full Employment

When the economy operates at less than full employment, it is possible for Y to increase. The big question (one of the most important questions in economics) is: Will increasing the quantity of money under these circumstances result in an increase in *real output,* an increase in the *price level,* or (contrary to the assumption of the quantity theory) a reduction in the *velocity of money* so there is little overall effect on output and prices?

The decline in interest in the quantity theory, and therefore in monetary policy, from the 1930s to the 1960s was associated with the belief that this theory contributed little to the analysis or cure of a depressed economy because of the uncertainty of the answer to this question. Although the answer still remains uncertain, economists have become increasingly convinced that there is a possible mechanism by which an increase in the quantity of money can lead to increased expenditure and thus (as we shall see in the next chapter) to increased real output.

Recap The quantity theory goes beyond the simple exchange equation by assuming that the velocity of money will tend to be constant. Given this assumption, the value of total transactions (or current dollar GNP) will vary directly with the quantity of money. At full employment (when real GNP cannot rise), this implies that the price level will rise in proportion to any increase in the money stock. If the economy does not operate at capacity, the prediction is less clear.

Capsule Supplement 26.2 **Evidence on Money and Prices**

Few economists would dispute the existence of a broad relationship between the quantity of money in circulation and the general price level, because there has long been evidence of a link between the two. Before the development of paper money, gold and/or silver formed the basis of the money supply in most countries. Consequently, each new discovery of sources of these precious metals resulted in a period of expansion in the world money supply. Fortunately, we have evidence on the behavior of prices over these periods.

During the fifteenth century, for example, the supply of silver in Europe increased rapidly as a result of the Spanish conquests of Mexico and Peru. Not only did prices rise throughout Europe over this period, but they rose markedly in Castile, the region of Spain that first received the precious metals shipped from the New World. By the middle of the eighteenth century, however, not only had growth in the worldwide stock of precious metals slowed down, but the Industrial Revolution had generated a rapid increase in European real GNP. As output rose and the money supply remained relatively constant, prices fell.

Hence, the effects of the importation of precious metals from the New World and the Industrial Revolution are both consistent with quantity theory predictions. Broadly speaking, so is the relationship between average changes in GNP, the money supply, and the price level in more recent history. The quantity theory relationships, however, do not hold in detail over short periods. From 1955 to 1968, for example, while countries experiencing the greatest rates of increase in the money supply also tended to have the greatest rates of price increase, the correlation was not perfect. Nor did the velocity of money remain constant in any country.

If the quantity of money in a country with relatively constant GNP were to increase tenfold, we would expect the price level to eventually rise in a similar proportion. When we come to smaller movements and shorter time spans, however, the quantity theory is generally a poor predictor because prices will be affected by other, predominately short-term factors. Two such factors are the presence of an inflationary process that continues even after its initiating cause has been removed, and the existence of unemployed capacity that holds back upward pressures on prices.

Simple general relationships, like the quantity equation, may hold on the average and in the long run. But they are of little use in formulating policy concerned with curing short-run economic problems.

What Is Money?   The things that serve as money

Until now our discussion of money has been confined to its *function,* what it does. Having examined the role money plays in the economy, we can now discuss the things that fulfill its requirements.

Because money is held against the likelihood that it may have to be exchanged for real goods and services, it is essential that money be something that preserves this exchange capability intact. It is also crucial that money be freely exchangeable for all goods and services at any time, that is, it must be *universally* acceptable (at least within a given economy) as payment for goods and services. Because money balances are held from one period to another, this universality must *persist over time.* Hence, something that everyone might accept in exchange one month but that would have no general exchange use the next (tickets to the World Series, for example) cannot function as money.

The Importance of Scarcity

It is obvious that something can fill this role of a persistent universally acceptable item of exchange only if

1. it is scarce, and
2. it will remain scarce in the future.

Money must be scarce because no one will voluntarily exchange scarce goods and services for something that is not scarce itself. If the streets of New York were paved with gold, why should Macy's accept gold bricks picked up outside its door in payment for goods produced with scarce resources? Money must also be expected to remain scarce. Otherwise, no one would hold it for fear that it would be useless in future exchanges.

Money is the only thing in the economy that is useful only because it is scarce.

Even though gold and silver possess such qualities as nondeterioration and easy workability, their use as money in the past stemmed primarily from the fact that they were scarce and were expected to remain so.

Modern Forms of Money

In modern economies the two main forms of money are *currency* (paper and coin) and *demand deposits* (checking-account balances in commercial banks).

Currency consists primarily of *bills* (called *bank notes* in most countries outside the United States), which are simply pieces of paper. The government ensures that such currency is kept scarce by directly or indirectly restricting the number of bills issued. Currency is accepted in exchange for the simple reason that recipients know it will, in turn, be accepted by everyone else. This confidence in the currency is partially inspired by laws requiring that legal currency be accepted as payment for any debt. Such laws are by no means essential, however, and generally serve a purpose only at the stage when a country begins using paper money for the first time.

Currency Backing

When bills and bank notes were originally introduced, money was based on *physically scarce* things, like gold and silver. The fact that paper money initially had no constraints on its issue (it could be printed at will) necessitated a long period over which people were gradually accustomed to paper money by being guaranteed its full convertibility into gold and silver, and vice versa. The total value of bills issued during this period was thus constrained by the existing stock of these metals.

After the system of full convertability was curtailed in the United States (in 1933), currency continued to be partially *backed* by gold or silver. Currency backing simply means that the treasury, central bank, or whatever authority issues paper money must hold gold or silver equal in value to a certain proportion of the total currency issued. If a currency is "50 percent gold-backed," the issuing authority must keep gold equal to 50 percent of currency in circulation *even though individuals are not allowed to exchange their bills for gold*.

From a modern perspective, currency backing may be thought of as inherently ridiculous and based on a lack of understanding by the public about the true nature of money. Such backing does, however, possess one aspect of great historical importance: *if a currency must be backed, wholly or partially, by something that is inherently scarce, there is a built-in guarantee that the currency itself will remain scarce*.

Maintained Scarcity

In a modern economic system, currency backing is not only ridiculous, but may result in the currency being kept *too* scarce. For historical reasons, currency-backing laws remain on the books, and may even impose restrictions on monetary management. Nevertheless, the modern situation can best be described as:

The real "backing" of currency is simply the public's confidence that monetary authorities recognize the proper function of money and will act to maintain its scarcity in an appropriate fashion.

For this reason, modern currencies are often called *fiduciary* ("trust") currencies.

Bank Balances

For most purposes in a country like the United States, checking-account deposits fulfill all the major functions of money. Even though they can be converted at any time (at least during banking hours) into currency, such conversion is not generally necessary. Checks are widely accepted in payment of bills, so a bank account and checkbook suffice for most transactions. Of course checks are not *perfect* substitutes for currency because they are inappropriate for many small transactions (which is one reason why currency is still widely used). But not all forms of currency are perfect substitutes. One cannot, at least yet, operate a pinball machine with a $5 bill, nor expect to settle a taxi fare with a $500 bill.

On the whole, individuals (and firms) find it useful to keep some money balances in cash. However, most is kept as demand deposits. In the United States, about three-fourths of the money supply is in demand deposits, the remainder is in currency.

Near-Money

Certain other assets that perform many of the functions of money are referred to collectively as *near-money*. Economists debate rather heatedly over just how ''near'' to money a near-money must be before it can be regarded as money. This is not an empty debate because if controlling the *quantity of money* is an important policy instrument, we must agree on exactly what is to be controlled.

Consider *time deposits*. These are bank deposits that draw interest, cannot be directly transferred by check, and can generally be withdrawn only with prearranged notice. Nevertheless, they bear a relationship to demand deposits not unlike that borne by demand deposits to currency. Because of the rise in interest-rate levels in the United States over the last decade or so, and because of a purely institutional rule that has prohibited banks from paying interest on demand deposits, time deposits have increased enormously relative to demand deposits. In 1950, for example, total time deposits were little more than one-third the level of demand deposits. By the end of 1977, time deposits *exceeded* demand deposits by more than one-half.

Should we count time deposits as part of the total money supply? If we do, why not count short-term government bills, which are virtually as ''near'' to money as time deposits? One possible approach would be to regard various near-monies as ''money,'' but with less *weight* than cash or demand deposits. Because a time deposit of $1.00 is nearly, but not quite, money, we might conclude that its function as money could be performed by, say, a demand deposit of $.95. This is sometimes stated by saying that a time deposit of $1.00 contains $.95 worth of ''liquidity,'' where a $1.00 demand deposit contains $1.00 worth of liquidity. *All* assets under this approach could be assigned a ''liquidity quotient,'' and the total liquidity in the economy could be determined. Unfortunately, it's much easier to enunciate this principle than to actually calculate the appropriate numerical values to be used.

The Quantity of Money

For our simplified models, we shall consider the money supply to consist of those things that comprise what economists commonly refer to as M_1:

1. all cash or currency held by the public, plus
2. all demand deposits in commercial banks.

It should be noted, however, that there are two other definitions of the money supply that have achieved wide use in recent years. These definitions, both of which are more comprehensive and more controversial than M_1, reflect the growing disagreement among economists about whether or not certain near-monies should be regarded as part of the money supply. These definitions are:

$M_2 = M_1$ plus time deposits at commercial banks.

$M_3 = M_2$ plus deposits in savings banks, savings and loan associations, etc.

As stated above, in our discussion of money, we shall refer to the more traditional M_1 concept. The quantity of money so defined can be regulated by controlling those things that constitute it. The supply of currency is controlled directly. The government (or its delegated agent) prints new paper currency or withdraws and burns part of the old whenever it receives currency from the public. The supply of total bank deposits is controlled more indirectly through certain interconnections within the banking system. The relationship between demand deposits and monetary control is discussed in the next two chapters.

Recap Something is money if it functions as money. Its most important property is universal acceptance in exchange, both now and in the future. Because no one will exchange scarce goods for something that is not scarce, money must be scarce and be expected to remain so. Dollar bills are only pieces of paper, but are kept scarce by a monetary authority that limits the number printed. Checking-account deposits also function as money because checks can be used as a means of payment. These deposits are themselves kept scarce through the structure of the banking system. In modern economies, the supply of money conventionally consists of coins, paper money, and checking-account balances.

Capsule Supplement 26.3   **Technological Progress in Money**

As one of the greatest social inventions of all time, money has been the object of innovation ever since it first came into use. The two greatest technological "breakthroughs" were undoubtedly the invention of paper money and the establishment of commercial banking. These both permitted the nominal quantity of money to be varied independently of the physical supply of gold or whatever else might have been previously used. If gold were the only form of money, for example, there could be no *monetary policy* in the real sense because the monetary authority would have no viable policy instruments. Because the usefulness of money depends on its being scarce to *society as a whole* so each *individual* can gain by having more of it, it's not surprising that most innovation in money has been in the same direction—to make money less scarce, or to make scarce money go further.

It has recently been suggested that the combination of the universal credit card and the computer could make money obsolete in its present form. If everyone's financial affairs were monitored by and registered in a computer system to which free access were available, then much of the demand for *transactions balances* might disappear. Every receipt would go instantly into the computer—employers would feed in pay information instead of issuing paychecks. Likewise, each payment would be debited immediately—merchants simply feeding in the amount of each purchase. The computer could be programmed with information about the timing of future receipts, and would clear all payments that could be covered, for example, by next week's wages.

Credit cards already substitute for *cash* in many uses. A traveler need not draw a large quantity of cash to go on a trip, but merely carry a credit card. The traveler must still pay in the end, of course, and must have a *bank balance* sufficient to settle the account when it comes due. Nevertheless, credit cards do permit the substitution of money in the form of bank balances for money as cash, and thus economize on cash.

A rather different problem arises with *automatic credit* at the bank. Many United States banks in recent years, and British banks for a very long time, have permitted a depositor to *overdraw* his bank account to a predetermined limit. If the limit is $100 and this is the transactions balance the individual would normally keep, he may choose to keep his balance at zero and overdraw whenever payments temporarily exceed receipts. Whether this is considered to reduce the quantity of money or not, of course, is ultimately a matter of definition. It can be argued that the individual's bank balance really ought to be measured in relation to −$100 instead of $0, because −$100 is actually his effective base level.

The typical technological developments in money reduce neither the demand for money nor the real money supply. They merely represent ways of using *new things* as money. Because these new things might not yet be counted as part of the money supply, a switch from old forms of money to new forms may initially appear as a reduction in the quantity of money, when *measured in the conventional way*. Major problems in monetary policy are bound to arise if control over the new things is not included in the monetary-authority's powers.

Exercises

1. If, on the average, members of the economy wish to hold money balances equal to two weeks of expenditure and all income is spent, what will be the desired level of money balances when aggregate income is $390 million per year?

2. What will be the desired level of money balances in this economy if nothing changes but the price level, which rises by 10 percent?

3. If the rise in the price level is accompanied by a rise in the rate of interest (no other changes in the economy), would you expect the desired level of money balances to be higher or lower than your answer to question 2? Would it be higher or lower than your answer to question 1?

4. What would the quantity theory predict about the change in the price level if real income rises by 2 percent and the quantity of money rises by 4 percent?

For Thought and Discussion

1. "Money is the root of all evil." What sense of the word "money" do you think is being used in this famous quotation?

2. In the days before paper money, kings occasionally "debased" their country's currency by reducing the proportion of the most valuable metal in the coinage. Would such action damage the monetary system?

3. Immediately after World War II, cigarettes briefly played the role of money in some parts of Europe. Consider the advantages and disadvantages of cigarettes for this purpose.

4. Suppose no one wanted to hold money balances at all, but sought to spend all cash receipts immediately. Could there be a money stock? How would it be held?

5. Suppose all forms of instant communication (telephone, telegraph, radio) disappeared overnight, leaving only the postal service for communication. Would you expect the demand for money balances, income, and interest rates to be unaffected? To change? If so, in what direction?

Chapter 27
Commercial Banks

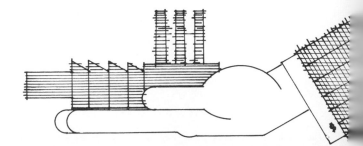

Terms and Concepts

Financial intermediary
The joint probability effect
Balance sheet
Asset structure
Reserve ratio
Bank clearing
Excess reserves
Inside cash
Outside cash
Deposit expansion multiplier

The Economic Function of Banks

How banks increase
the effectiveness of the stock
of cash and the flow
of funds for investment

Commercial banks are *financial intermediaries,* that is, channels through which unspent consumer funds flow to businesses (and governments) that can use these funds. As a by-product of the banks' role in channeling funds, they are important in the overall "creation" of money in the economy.

Let's suppose that an individual wishes to hold a money balance of $100 (for reasons discussed in the previous chapter). This balance, of course, may be held in cash, though at some risk of loss or theft. Consequently, if the individual does not *anticipate* any reason to draw on his money balance in the immediate future, he may seek a convenient and safe place in which to keep it.

One such place is a commercial bank. It will accept his money balance as a deposit in exchange for a believable promise that the individual can claim all or any part of his balance on demand. Presumably, if the safekeeping service is useful to the individual, he will be willing to pay something—however little—for it.

The Joint Probability Effect

Now, let's suppose there are 100 such individuals, each depositing $100 in the same bank. The bank will then have deposits totaling $10,000, all received in the form of cash. If the bank were acting merely as a safe deposit facility, it would lock the cash up in its vaults and stand ready to give any depositor any part of his original deposit on demand. But it is not. The true role of banking comes from the following consideration:

Under normal circumstances, the probability that all depositors will decide to withdraw all their balances at the same time is extremely small.

Suppose our 100 depositors hold their balances primarily for transactions purposes. It is unlikely that all of them will receive incomes and make expenditures at the same time. If $100 represents each individual's *desired* level of money balances, this balance may temporarily run down for some payment, but will ordinarily be built up again.

Each individual's bank balance, therefore, will be expected to fluctuate up and down as deposits and withdrawals are made, with an average over time of $100. At any given time, the bank will receive deposits from those who are building up their balances, and make payments to those who are running them down. Under the circumstances we've outlined, the bank's total withdrawals over a reasonably long period of time will be approximately equal to its total deposits made over the same period of time. On any particular day, however, withdrawals may be greater or less than deposits.

Cash Requirements

If the time patterns of running balances up and running them down differ widely among depositors, then the probability that all depositors will withdraw their balances together is small. There is, of course, the remote possibility that all depositors will wish to withdraw their entire balances, and no one will deposit anything, on a given day. In this case, the cash needed by the bank would exactly equal its total deposits. Banking depends on *probabilities,* however, and we can state the following cash requirement:

A bank needs enough cash on hand to meet the largest excess of withdrawals over deposits that has a reasonable probability of occurring.

Obviously, cash equal to the total balances in depositors' accounts is sufficient to cover all possible eventualities. However, barring special circumstances in which random behavior is eliminated and all depositors act together (such as a run on the bank), a bank can meet its day-to-day cash requirements with much less than its total deposits on account—indeed, with as little as 5 to 10 percent of them.

Let's suppose that our bank with its $10,000 in cash deposits knows from experience that it can meet any anticipated excess of withdrawals over deposits by keeping 25 percent of its total cash deposits on hand. Thus, it needs $2,500 of the cash deposited with it, so it has $7,500 with which to do as it pleases.

Bank Loans

But the bank cannot simply appropriate this $7,500—it is still owed to the depositors. It can, however, *lend* the $7,500 to someone else, thereby balancing its debt or liability to its depositors with a debt owed to the bank (an asset). Of course, the interest derived from such lending activity constitutes the bank's primary source of income.

The Social Usefulness of Banks

Although there may be more intermediate stages, the interest received by the bank comes ultimately from the return on the capital purchased with the loans made. Thus, the cash reserves of the 100 depositors have been channeled, at least in part, into productive use by increasing the available capital stock of the economy. The bank has acted as an intermediary, indeed a creative intermediary, because it has contributed something to the economy that would have been absent had depositors individually lent to firms.

Suppose the bank had not existed, and each depositor had kept $25 in cash under his mattress and lent $75 to a firm to buy machinery. The total loans from the 100 depositors would have been the same as with the bank, but no individual depositor would have been able to immediately obtain $100 in cash—he would have had to first call in his loan to the firm.

The existence of banks enables individuals to keep fully liquid cash balances available to them on demand, while permitting part of aggregate cash balances to be "tied up" in capital production.

This result can be looked at either as increasing the "liquidity" available to individuals, given a fixed level of capital investment, or increasing the productivity of funds yielding a given amount of "liquidity." In any event, the outcome is achieved by a *pooling of probabilities.*

Checks

But even if individuals can withdraw any part of their balances on demand, there are still certain disadvantages of bank balances over cash. Assuming that there is negligible risk of a bank *not* being able to pay a particular individual's withdrawal on demand, most of the disadvantages are institutional in nature. Banks are not open twenty-four hours a day, seven days a week, for example, so balances cannot always be withdrawn exactly when needed. Moreover, the physical location of a bank may prove inconvenient to a depositor at the time he requires cash.

Many of these institutional disadvantages are overcome by the use of *checks.* Instead of trekking to the bank and withdrawing cash to pay a bill, a depositor can simply write a note to the bank instructing it to pay the party concerned out of the depositor's balance. Such a note is a check. Generally speaking, a check is somewhat less acceptable than cash because there is some risk that the payer has insufficient funds in the bank, and thus that the bank will not carry out the instruction on the check. But, a check also has advantages. For instance, it permits financial transactions involving large sums to be settled with a small piece of paper rather than with suitcases full of cash.

Given the advantages and disadvantages of keeping bank balances as compared with cash, most individuals will decide to keep some cash (primarily for small transactions), but maintain the lion's share of their money balances in the form of bank deposits. In the United States, approximately 25 percent of money balances are held in the form of cash (that is, currency), the remainder being held as bank deposits. As would be expected, the cash ratio tends to be higher in countries with less-developed banking systems.

Recap If many individuals deposit their cash balances with a bank, the probability that all depositors will want to draw all their balances out on the same day is extremely small. Therefore, a bank can satisfy all normally expected demands for withdrawals by holding cash balances totaling much less than its total deposits.

The difference between a bank's total deposits and the cash reserves it needs to hold can be lent to the government, businesses, or individuals. Such lending brings interest to the bank, and supplies funds for productive investment.

Capsule Supplement 27.1   **Other Banking Functions**

In the main text, we have concentrated on the role of banks as monetary institutions, a role filled primarily by regular commercial banks with which most checking accounts are held. In doing so, we have greatly simplified the complex functions of banking. Although a bank holding excess reserves will seek to expand its loans, it must find borrowers whose promises to repay are sufficiently believable to qualify as bank assets. Bank loans are extended for many purposes. Even though they have traditionally been extended primarily for business purposes, loans made directly to consumers have been growing. Commercial and industrial loans fell from 41 percent to 33 percent of all loans from 1940 to 1977, while the proportion of loans to individuals rose from 19 percent to 22 percent. Consumer loans are more profitable, commanding a higher rate of interest, but are more risky than commercial loans.

Although commercial banks dominate the monetary side of banking, the other major banking function—channeling funds from individuals and others into business use—is more dispersed. *Savings and loan associations* accept time deposits only and channel funds into mortgage loans for construction. On the other hand, pure *savings banks* allow more flexibility in withdrawal and are more flexible in their use of funds. *Life-insurance companies* also take individual savings (in the form of premiums) and lend these funds. Specialized *investment banks* and other financial corporations channel funds, typically from large-scale lenders, into a variety of uses. Finally, regular *corporations*—not primarily financial in character—have funds from undistributed profits and other sources that they do not plan to use immediately in their own operations, and that can be lent directly or through commercial or investment banks. Even *government agencies* have some funds available.

In 1977, funds made available for investment in the United States exceeded $300 billion. About one-fourth of these funds came from commercial banks and about one-half came from savings institutions (savings and loan associations, insurance companies, savings banks, etc.), the remainder were from nonfinancial corporations and government agencies.

Direct association between commercial banks and industry is generally weaker in the United States than in other countries. In continental Europe and Japan, for example, banks are often major stockholders in regular corporations, and channel funds directly into their associated firms. A recent development in the United States has been the entry of commercial banks into the credit-card business. Since in the long run, credit cards may profoundly affect the level of money balances consumers wish to hold, this would seem to be an appropriate extension of the monetary function of banks.

A Bank's Balance Sheet

The assets and liabilities of a bank

A balance sheet is a table that summarizes what an institution owns or is owed (its *assets*), and what it owes to others (its *liabilities*).

A bank's principal liabilities are its deposits, because each depositor is owed the full balance in the account. To secure initial capital, the bank may have borrowed money or issued stock. Such forms of indebtedness also represent liabilities.

In our previous discussion, we focused on *demand deposits,* so called because they can be withdrawn on demand. Commercial banks also accept *time deposits* that can be withdrawn only after a certain time, or after the depositor has given prior notice. Obviously, a bank doesn't have to keep the same level of cash reserves against time deposits as it does against demand deposits. Also, because time deposits are less convenient to depositors than demand deposits, banks will normally pay interest on them.

Assets

If a bank keeps cash reserves equal to its total deposits, its chief asset will be cash. As we have seen, however, the contribution of the banking system is to channel cash into productive use. Consequently, each bank will extend *loans* equal to a considerable proportion of its deposits. A *loan* is made directly by a bank to an individual or a firm; a loan made to the government involves buying a *bond* or *security*. A bank will normally lend some of its cash reserves to the government, even though the interest rate received is less than that on business or personal loans, because there is generally no risk of default.

But even the degree of "risklessness" of government securities may vary depending on the issuing government body. In general, securities issued by the U.S. Treasury are considered the safest, and therefore carry the lowest rate of interest. Securities (primary bonds) issued by states and municipalities are also generally viewed as quite secure. Occasional crises do occur such as that experienced in late 1975 by New York City, which narrowly escaped default by obtaining "eleventh-hour" federal loan guarantees.

Loans to the government appear on a bank's balance sheet as *government securities*. The process of allocating loans between government and private borrowers, like all banking business, is a matter of balancing a higher return (interest) against a greater risk of default.

Table 27.1 shows an "average" balance sheet for a commercial bank in the United States, that is, the balance sheet that would characterize each of the approximately 15,000 commercial banks in the United States if each were identical in size.

Table 27.1

Average Commercial Bank Balance
Sheet, United States, yearend 1976

Category	Millions	Comment
"Cash"*	$ 13.6	Only $1.2 million actual currency on hand*
Government securities	25.0	
Loans	54.7	Commercial and industrial loans $18.3 million
Physical assets and other	9.8	
Total Assets	$103.1	Must equal total liabilities
Deposits	$ 83.8	$33.7 Demand deposits 50.1 Time deposits
Stockholders' capital and other	19.3	
Total Liabilities	$103.1	Must equal total assets

* Includes reserve deposits with the Federal Reserve System, the nature and function of which are discussed in the next chapter. For the purposes of our present analysis, these can be regarded as equivalent to cash.

Asset Structure

Aside from the distinction between demand and time deposits in the liabilities, the most important feature of a bank's balance sheet is its *asset structure*—the division of total assets among cash, government securities, and ordinary bank loans.

As a business activity, banking consists primarily of organizing and manipulating its asset structure. Cash enables the bank to meet immediate demands for withdrawals, but provides no return. Both government securities and bank loans earn interest, but are not immediately available to meet demands for withdrawals. Government bonds earn less interest than bank loans, but carry little or no risk of default by the borrower. Thus, the bank seeks an asset structure that both provides sufficient cash to meet all withdrawals likely to occur and strikes an appropriate balance between safe but low-earning government securities and more risky but more profitable commercial loans.

In the examples that follow, we shall assume that there are only two assets, cash and loans, ignoring the distinction between different types of loans.

The appropriate division of assets between cash and loans may be determined entirely by the banks, or may be restricted by government (or quasi-government) policy, as is now the case in most countries. To simplify the numerical examples in the remainder of this chapter, we shall assume that banks either desire, or are required, to keep a *reserve ratio* of 20 percent, that is, that banks organize their asset structure so 20 percent of total assets takes the form of cash reserves.

If a bank's total liabilities and total assets remained unchanged, it would have little to do. But continual changes take place—cash flows in and out, deposits rise and fall. It is the reorganization of the asset structure in response to such changes that underlies the monetary role of the banking system in the economy.

Recap A balance sheet is a statement of what an institution owns or is owed (assets) and what it owes to others (liabilities). As a matter of accounting definition, total assets must equal total liabilities. The principal liabilities of a bank are deposits, what the bank owes its depositors. There are two principal assets: cash reserves and loans extended by the bank. The loans are assets because they represent what others owe the bank. Banking as a business activity consists primarily of adjusting the structure of its assets, that is, the ratio of cash reserves to loans.

Capsule Supplement 27.2   **The Development of American Commercial Banking**

There are few economic institutions in the United States whose structures have been more profoundly influenced by historical development than commercial banking. Although commercial banking was well established in Europe during the eighteenth century (though not yet in its modern form), it really didn't develop in the United States until the colonies had achieved independence. As a matter of fact, George Washington maintained his account with the Bank of England throughout the entire American Revolution. Prior to 1838, each new bank required its own private act of incorporation to be passed either by Congress or the appropriate state legislature. Consequently, the number of fully chartered banks remained relatively small although they were supplemented by numerous private banks registered as partnerships.

In 1838, however, New York passed legislation that allowed for "free banking." Under this legislation, any person or group of persons could open a bank if they could satisfy certain requirements, mainly the posting of collateral (government bonds) against all bank notes issued. New York's legislation was soon copied in most other states, and the number of banks rose rapidly over the next half-century—from barely 500 in 1834 to nearly 10,000 in 1895. Although these banks varied enormously in size, asset structure, and quality of management, most were strictly local banks. Poor management, an incautious banking tradition, and localization led to a long history of American bank failures during times of crisis—140 banks failed in 1878 and almost 500 failed in 1893.

Suspicion of the power of bankers resulted in virtual prohibition of the development of branch banking in the United States, and there was no central banking structure through most of the nineteenth century. Local banking is inherently more unstable than branch banking. For instance, the local bank in a corn-growing district will have most of its loans extended to farmers growing corn. Consequently, if the crop fails, so may the bank—just when the local citizens can least afford to lose their deposit balances. A bank with many branches, on the other hand, would presumably have some of its branches in areas where the crop has not failed, and others where most of the borrowers are businesses altogether unrelated to corn production.

Thus, the free banking tradition, together with the opposition to branch banking, has resulted in a unique commercial banking system in the United States consisting of a very large number of banks in a variety of sizes. However, the Federal Reserve System and various banking acts of the twentieth century have imposed more rigorous standards of banking behavior than existed in the nineteenth century.

Check Cashing and Clearing

How checks and payments move within and between banks

Modern commercial banks accept deposits (usually in the form of checks drawn on themselves or other banks), pay on checks issued against these deposits, make loans and receive repayments, and buy and sell government securities. In the remainder of this chapter we examine the effects of each of these activities on both the individual bank and on the banking system as a whole.

First, let's consider what happens when a check is written by an individual depositor. Suppose Claude and Maude both have accounts at First Bank, and Claude pays Maude $100 by drawing a check on his account. Maude may do one of two things: she may *cash* the check, or she may *deposit* the check in her own account. If Maude cashes the check, the bank loses $100 of its cash reserves and, from the bank's point of view, the effect is just the same as if Claude had withdrawn $100 in cash and paid Maude with it.

Balance Sheet Effects

Whether Claude or Maude cashes the check, the effect on the bank's balance sheet is the same. Liabilities (Claude's bank balance) and assets (cash reserves) are simultaneously reduced by $100, as shown on the following balance sheet:

First Bank Balance Sheet

1. Before Check Is Cashed

Assets		Liabilities	
Cash	$ 200	Deposits	$1,000
Loans	800		
	$1,000		$1,000

2. After Check Is Cashed

Cash	$ 100	Deposits	$ 900
Loans	800		
	$ 900		$ 900

Although the bank's assets and liabilities are still in balance, its *asset structure* has changed. Originally, 20 percent of the bank's total assets were in cash. After the check is cashed, this proportion falls to 11.1 percent (1/9). This change may require the bank to make compensating alterations—calling in existing loans, for example—in order to regain the desired asset structure.

On the other hand, if Maude deposits the check, the bank merely makes clerical changes—it reduces Claude's balance by $100, increases Maude's by $100, stamps the check to show the transaction is complete, and returns the canceled check to Claude for his records. There is no change in the bank's overall position. The *total* owed to depositors is unchanged, it just owes $100 less to Claude and $100 more to Maude. Its balance sheet is completely unaffected.

Interbank Transactions

Now, consider the problem of interbank checks. If Claude, with an account at First Bank, writes a check to Maude, with an account at Second Bank, Maude can again do one of two things. She can go to First Bank and withdraw cash directly from Claude's account or, as is usually the case, she can give the check to her own bank with instructions (in the form of a deposit slip) for her bank to collect the cash and deposit it in her account.

Second Bank will wait until the end of the day, collect all the checks deposited in its own customers' accounts that have been drawn against First Bank, then send a messenger to First Bank to collect the corresponding amount of cash. But there will probably also be checks deposited with First Bank that have been drawn against accounts in Second Bank. Thus, rather than have the messenger from Second Bank collect funds from First Bank while his counterpart from First Bank transfers cash in the opposite direction, the banks can agree to simply move the *difference* between the two amounts.

Suppose checks drawn on First Bank and deposited with Second Bank total $983 for the day, and checks drawn on Second Bank and deposited with First Bank total $1,012. Transactions between the two banks can be settled by a *single* transfer of $29 from Second Bank to First Bank, rather than a transfer of $983 in one direction and $1,012 in the other.

Bank Clearing

The process whereby banks periodically compare the amounts owed each other and transfer only the difference is known as *clearing* or *settling*.

With a large number of banks, this clearing is not done on a two-by-two basis, as in the previous example, but is *multilateral*. This results in an even lower volume of actual cash transfers between banks. Under multilateral clearing, each bank pays into, or receives from, a central pool the difference between the total value of its checks deposited in all other banks and the total value of all other banks' checks deposited in its accounts. Its balance sheet is affected only insofar as there is a net loss or gain of cash, the effect being the same as if a depositor in the bank had made a cash withdrawal (or deposit) of that amount.

Recap The bulk of a commercial bank's transactions are carried out by checks that are essentially letters instructing the bank to make certain payments and deduct them from particular accounts. An individual who receives a check normally deposits it, thereby instructing his bank to collect the payment from the bank on which the check is drawn and increase his balance correspondingly. If a check is drawn on one bank and deposited in another, an interbank transaction is involved. Such transactions are carried out by clearing, in which banks balance checks drawn against their accounts against checks from other banks deposited with them. The net difference is the only interbank movement of cash.

Loan Transactions   Bank loans and their consequences

Let's now consider what happens when a bank makes a loan. We shall focus our attention on First Bank, whose liabilities (all deposits) are now assumed to be $1,000,000 and whose assets are assumed to consist initially of $220,000 in cash and $780,000 in loans.

Suppose First Bank agrees to lend $20,000 to Frank Furter, a restaurant owner who happens to be one of its depositors. Once the appropriate documents have been signed, the bank need only make a clerical entry showing a $20,000 increase in Frank's balance. The same result could be obtained simply by issuing Frank a check, which he would presumably deposit in his account. As a result of this transaction, the bank's liabilities increase by $20,000 (more deposits) while its assets also increase by $20,000 (the loan). Its balance sheet is affected as follows:

First Bank Balance Sheet

1. Before Loan to Frank Furter

Assets		Liabilities	
Cash	$ 220,000	Deposits	$1,000,000
Loans	$ 780,000		
	$1,000,000		$1,000,000

2. Immediately after Loan

Cash	$ 220,000	Deposits	$1,020,000
Loans	$ 800,000		
	$1,020,000		$1,020,000

Initial Effects

What effect has this loan had on the bank's overall position? We note the following:

1. Its liabilities and assets have both risen by the amount of the loan. In particular, the bank has increased its total deposits at will by creating an equal amount of assets in the form of loans.
2. Its asset structure has changed. Specifically, the ratio of cash reserves to total assets has fallen from 22 percent to 21.5 percent.

   Thus, although the bank can increase deposits at will by extending additional loans, each new loan reduces the reserve ratio of cash to total assets (which is the same here as the ratio of cash to total deposits). Also the bank increases the risk that it will not have enough cash to meet potential withdrawals. But this is only part of the story.

Subsequent Effects

The overall reduction in the bank's reserve ratio will generally be greater than that associated with the initial effect. After a bank makes a loan, it will usually lose some cash from the borrower's use of the funds. Frank has presumably obtained his loan for some purpose—perhaps to buy a new mustard dispenser for his restaurant. Having obtained the loan, he will proceed to write checks for those items he wishes to buy.

   Some of these checks will probably end up being deposited in other accounts with First Bank, some will be cashed outright, and some will be deposited in other banks. First Bank will lose cash to the extent that checks written by Frank are not redeposited within the bank. If only $5,000 of the checks are paid to other First Bank depositors who choose not to cash them, then First Bank will

1. lose $15,000 cash, and
2. experience a $15,000 reduction in liabilities because Mr. Furter's balance has decreased by $20,000 while other deposits have increased by only $5,000.

The final situation will then be:

First Bank Balance Sheet

3. Final Situation

Assets		Liabilities	
Cash	$ 205,000	Deposits	$1,005,000
Loans	$ 800,000		
	$1,005,000		$1,005,000

The reserve ratio at First Bank has now fallen to 20.4 percent from the 22 percent ratio that existed before the loan was made. Note that if none of the loan had been redeposited in the bank, deposits would have fallen to $1,000,000, cash to $200,000, and the reserve ratio to 20 percent. Under these circumstances, the bank would have no further excess reserves to lend because any further loans would reduce the reserve ratio to a level below 20 percent.

Loans and the Reserve Ratio

We can assume that the banking community considers a reserve ratio of 20 percent or more to be safe, so First Bank is not worried about the consequences of having made the loan to Frank Furter.

Indeed, the loan was presumably made for the very reason that the original reserve ratio (22 percent) was higher than necessary. First Bank merely set out to adjust its asset structure in a way that would increase the ratio of interest-bearing loans to non-interest-bearing cash. This is equivalent to saying that it initially had *excess cash.*

By making loans, a bank can reduce the reserve ratio and increase its return from interest-bearing assets.

The process also works in reverse. If a bank finds that its reserve ratio is too low, it can always raise it by calling in loans. Banks normally extend a proportion of their loans in an open-ended form, requiring borrowers to repay on demand or short notice, for precisely this reason. If Frank Furter's loan were called in, for example, his balance (and thus total deposits) would fall by $20,000, and total assets would fall by the same amount. This alone would raise the reserve ratio (because deposits would fall) but there may also be some inflow of cash as Frank deposits checks or cash to build up his balance again.

When First Bank originally made its loan, and Frank used it to buy equipment, the eventual results were not confined to First Bank alone. We supposed that $15,000 of the $20,000 was either cashed or deposited in other banks. Suppose, in particular, that $4,000 was drawn in cash while $11,000 was deposited in the only other bank—Second Bank. Second Bank thus undergoes the following changes:

1. Total deposits increase by $11,000.
2. To clear these checks, $11,000 flows in from First Bank, thus increasing cash and total assets by $11,000.

If Second Bank initially had cash equal to 20 percent of its deposits, these changes will increase its reserve ratio. Indeed, this ratio would be maintained as long as the bank's cash inflow were equal to 20 percent of its increased deposits—and, of course, the actual inflow in this case is equal to 100 percent of the increase in deposits.

Thus, Second Bank now has a higher reserve ratio (that is, more excess cash) than desired, and will attempt to adjust its own asset structure by extending more loans to its depositors.

We can conclude from this that a change in the volume of lending by one bank will generally affect the lending activity of other banks. Consequently, we need to investigate the relationship between cash movements and loan transactions within a system of more than one bank.

Recap When a bank makes a loan to one of its depositors, it increases the depositor's balance by the amount of the loan. This increases the bank's liabilities (deposits) and assets (loans) by an equal amount. It also changes the asset structure, lowering the reserve ratio. The available reserves place an ultimate limit on the size of loans that can be made. Once a loan has been made, the borrower will write checks, only some of which will be deposited in the lending bank. There will thus be some cash outflow to other banks.

Interbank Cash Flows

What happens when cash flows from one bank to another

Consider a *banking system* consisting, for simplicity, of only two banks— First Bank and Second Bank. As before, we'll assume that the only liabilities are deposits, that the only assets are cash and loans, and that both banks aim to maintain a reserve ratio of 20 percent. For any total level of

assets, we can then calculate each bank's *desired* asset structure as consisting of 20 percent cash and 80 percent loans.

Initial Equilibrium

We shall assume both banks are the same size with initial asset structures at
desired levels and the following balance sheets:

First Bank Balance Sheet/Stage 1*
(Thousands of dollars)

Assets			**Liabilities**	
	Actual	Desired structure relative to actual cash		
Cash	$ 200	($200)	Deposits	$1,000
Loans	800	(800)		
	$1,000	($1,000)		$1,000

* Second Bank Balance Sheet is identical.

The Transfer Process

Let's first consider what happens when a depositor withdraws $10,000 in
cash from First Bank and deposits it in Second Bank.

First Bank simultaneously loses $10,000 in cash and $10,000 in deposits.
Its assets (cash) and liabilities (deposits) change together, so its balance
sheet remains in balance. Its balance sheet will now be as shown, with its
desired asset structure (division of total assets between cash and loans)
indicated along with its actual structure.

First Bank Balance Sheet/Stage 2
(Thousands of dollars)

Assets			**Liabilities**	
	Actual	Desired structure relative to actual cash		
Cash	$190	($190)	Deposits	$990
Loans	800	(760)		
	$990	($950)		$990

In order to obtain its desired asset structure, First Bank wants $760,000
in loans instead of the $800,000 it now has. So it will demand repayment of

$40,000 in loans (note that this is *four times* the value of the cash lost because the desired asset structure is 1/5 cash and 4/5 loans). After repayment (which we can assume involves no cash transfer initially), deposits and loans will both have decreased by $40,000, giving a new balance sheet:

First Bank Balance Sheet/Stage 3
(Thousands of dollars)

Assets			**Liabilities**	
	Actual	Desired structure relative to actual cash		
Cash	$190	($190)	Deposits	$950
Loans	760	(760)		
	$950	($950)		$950

Now let's look at Second Bank. The first impact of the transfer will be for both its cash and deposits to increase by $10,000 making its new balance sheet:

Second Bank Balance Sheet/Stage 2
(Thousands of dollars)

Assets			**Liabilities**	
	Actual	Desired structure relative to actual cash		
Cash	$ 210	($210)	Deposits	$1,010
Loans	800	(840)		
	$1,010	($1,050)		$1,010

Second Bank's asset structure is now out of equilibrium because it has additional cash with no change in its other balance sheet items. We can look at this disequilibrium in either of two ways. One is to note that for deposits of $1,010,000, the bank needs cash reserves of only $202,000. Because the bank's cash is $210,000, we can consider it to be holding $8,000 (= $210,000 − $202,000) in *excess reserves*.

The other way to look at the situation is to note that because it now has $210,000 in cash, the bank's desired asset structure would call for $840,000 in loans—$40,000 more than it actually has.

In the circumstances of our example, Second Bank's reaction to the inflow of cash will be to try to lend someone $40,000. Hypothetically, it could make such a loan to the person whose loan has just been called in by First Bank.

After making the loan, Second Bank will have its asset structure in the desired form, and its balance sheet will be:

Second Bank Balance Sheet/Stage 3
(Thousands of dollars)

Assets			**Liabilities**	
	Actual	Desired structure relative to actual cash		
Cash	$ 210	($210)	Deposits	$1,050
Loans	840	(840)		
	$1,050	($1,050)		$1,050

Final Equilibrium

We now consolidate the Stage 3 balance sheets of the two banks.

Consolidated Balance Sheet/Stage 3
(Thousands of dollars)

Assets (Actual)		**Liabilities**	
Cash	$ 400	Deposits	$2,000
Loans	1,600		
	$2,000		$2,000

The entries in this balance sheet are identical to what they would have been had we presented a consolidated balance sheet at the beginning of our example (in Stage 1). Although the movement of cash from one bank to another has caused one bank's loans to decrease by an amount equal to a multiple of the cash reduction, it has caused an increase in the other bank's loans equal to the same multiple of the cash flow.

Thus, a movement of cash entirely within the banking system (*inside cash*) changes the relative positions of individual banks, but not the overall status of the banking system as long as reserve ratios remain the same in all banks. In particular, total deposits over the economy as a whole (the most important component of the overall *quantity of money*) are unaffected.

Of course, further adjustments may take place after Stage 3 of our example. The recipient of the new loan from Second Bank may make payments that end up in First Bank. Subsequent adjustments will tend to bring the two banks' balance sheets somewhat closer together, but not back to the original situation. In any event, the consolidated balance sheet will remain unaffected.

Recap If cash withdrawn from one bank is deposited in another so it remains within the banking system, the first bank finds its ratio of cash reserves to total assets is too low, while the second finds its ratio too high. Suppose all banks want their asset structure to consist of $1 cash for every $4 in loans. A bank that loses $10,000 in cash will then reduce its loans by $40,000, and the bank that receives the $10,000 will increase its loans by $40,000. As long as the cash remains within the system (inside cash), its movement from bank to bank will not affect the total level of loans and deposits in the banking system as a whole.

The Deposit Expansion Multiplier

What happens when cash flows into the banking system from outside

We shall now examine what happens to the banking system when there is an increase in *outside cash,* that is, cash that comes from outside the banking system.

Outside cash is any cash not originally held by a bank. It could be newly minted coins or freshly printed paper money, cash or its equivalent from outside the economy altogether (gold from overseas payments, for example), or even cash that households have previously kept hidden under floorboards and mattresses.

Let's suppose the government pays for $10,000 worth of services purchased from the private sector with newly printed money. The recipient will deposit it in, say, Second Bank. If we suppose that both First and Second Banks are initially as in Stage 1 of the previous section, Second Bank's balance sheet will now be the same as it was after the cash transfer from First Bank:

Second Bank Balance Sheet/Stage 2
(Thousands of dollars)

Assets		Desired structure relative to actual cash	**Liabilities**	
	Actual			
Cash	$ 210	($210)	Deposits	$1,010
Loans	800	(840)		
	$1,010	($1,050)		$1,010

The bank will expand loans by $40,000, as in the previous section, to bring the level up to the desired $840,000. If it does this, its deposits will also increase by $40,000, making its Stage 3 balance sheet:

Second Bank Balance Sheet/Stage 3
(Thousands of dollars)

Assets			**Liabilities**	
	Actual	Desired structure relative to actual cash		
Cash	$ 210	($210)	Deposits	$1,050
Loans	840	(840)		
	$1,050	($1,050)		$1,050

Final Equilibrium

In this case, there has been no loss of cash from First Bank, whose balance sheet remains unchanged. We can set up the consolidated balance sheet for Stage 3 by adding the unchanged items in First Bank's balance sheet to those in Second Bank's Stage 3 balance sheet (the original consolidated balance sheet in Stage 1 is shown for comparison):

Consolidated Balance Sheet
(Thousands of dollars)

Stage 1

Assets (Actual)		**Liabilities**	
Cash	$ 400	Deposits	$2,000
Loans	$1,600		
	$2,000		$2,000

Stage 3

Assets		**Liabilities**	
Cash	$ 410	Deposits	$2,050
Loans	1,640		
	$2,050		$2,050

If we compare Stage 1 with Stage 3, we see that the entry of $10,000 of outside cash into the banking system has:

1. increased cash in the system by $10,000;
2. increased loans in the system by $40,000; and
3. increased deposits in the system by $50,000.

The increase in deposits is a *multiple* (here it is 5) of the increase in cash.
Entry of outside cash into the banking system will result in total deposits within the system being expanded by a multiple of the increase in cash.

The Value of the Multiplier

It is not difficult to see what this multiple will be. If all banks keep a reserve ratio (ratio of cash to total assets) of r percent, then an increase of $1 in total assets will require an increase of r in cash. Thus, an increase of $1 in cash can support an increase of $1/r$ in total assets. Because total liabilities equal total assets, and we assume deposits to be the only liability, deposits will then rise by $1/r$ for every dollar of outside cash coming in.

If the desired reserve ratio is r *percent, deposits in the banking system as a whole will increase by a multiple of new cash from outside, which is equal to* $1/r$. *If the reserve ratio changes, so will the multiplier.*

The reverse will be true if cash *leaves* the banking system. If the government withdraws cash and burns it, for example, banks will have to reduce loans, and deposits will fall. The process is simply the reverse of that previously described.

If the banking system loses cash to the outside, deposits will fall by a multiple of the loss, the value of the multiplier being $1/r$.

Interbank Adjustments

In discussing this multiplier process, we conveniently stopped when Second Bank had made new loans and reached its desired asset structure (Stage 3). Of course, there will be further transactions as the proceeds of these loans are spent. However, these will involve interbank transfers only, and, as we have seen, the consolidated balance sheet for the banking system will be unaffected. Thus, the full effect on the banking system as a whole is shown by Stage 3, further adjustments affecting only relative situations of the banks within the system.

Note that deposits in the banking system increase by a multiple of the amount of outside cash entering the system. Because bank deposits are an important form of money, banks can be said to be *creating money* by this process of multiplied expansion. In other words, $10,000 of outside cash has entered the system but $50,000 of deposits result. The banking system has "created" $40,000—not the whole $50,000, because the cash could have been used as money in any case.

As long as reserve ratios remain constant, we cannot consider an individual bank to be "creating" money. In focusing on the operation of an individual bank, we cannot distinguish between inside cash flows (in which the extra deposits created by one bank are balanced by deposit reductions in other banks) and outside cash flows (where the extra deposits are not balanced off). To the individual bank, an inflow of cash looks the same whether it comes from another bank or from outside the system.

On the other hand, the banking *system* can be said to "create" money in the sense that it multiplies outside cash and thus generates deposits (which are part of the total money supply) in excess of the cash it receives. Even the banking system cannot create money from nothing, however, and the expansion in bank deposits requires either a change in the reserve ratio or a change in the system's cash.

The Multiplier Sequence

The multiplied effect of outside cash may be better understood if viewed as a sequence. Rather than focus on the final equilibrium position, let's concentrate on excess reserves and trace the flow of successive loans through the system.

Suppose $10,000 in outside cash is deposited with First Bank. This bank now has an additional $10,000 in deposits against which it requires only an additional $2,000 in cash to satisfy a reserve ratio of 20 percent. Thus, it has $8,000 in excess reserves. It can make a *cash* loan of $8,000 that, after having been made, may be deposited either in First Bank or some other bank. Whichever bank receives the deposit has an increase of $8,000 in both cash and deposits. Because this bank needs to hold only $1,600 in additional cash (20 percent of $8,000), it has excess reserves of $6,400 with which it can make a cash loan. This will increase some bank's deposits and cash by $6,400, giving it excess reserves of $5,120—$6,400 less 20 percent of $6,400, or 80 percent of $6,400—and permit yet a further loan equal to this amount.

Each successive excess of reserves and its corresponding loan will be equal to 80 percent of the previous loan. The successive loans will generate deposits of an equal amount, the deposits being successively: $10,000; $8,000; $6,400; $5,120; $4,096; . . . This is a geometric series, the sum of which approaches $50,000 if we take a sufficient number of successive rounds of loans.

In general, if the ratio of cash to total assets is r percent, the excess reserves associated with a cash deposit of $1 will be $$(1 - r)$. For outside cash of $1, the first loan will be $$(1 - r)$. The next will be $$(1 - r)$ times this amount, written as $$(1 - r)^2$, and so on. Thus, the total loans (hence deposits) derived from the initial dollar will be given by the sum of the series:

$$1 + (1 - r) + (1 - r)^2 + (1 - r)^3 + \ . \ . \ .$$

From elementary algebra, this is the sum to infinity of a geometric series with common ratio $(1 - r)$. This sum is given by

$$1/[1 - (1 - r)] = 1/r,$$

which is the same as the multiplier given in the preceding section.

Recap If cash deposited in a bank does not come from another bank but from outside the banking system (outside cash), the bank will find its reserve ratio too high and will expand loans. For a reserve ratio (of cash to total assets) of 20 percent, the bank will expand loans by $400 for every $100 of additional cash. Its deposits will rise by $500—$400 against new loans, $100 against the additional cash. Because there is no loss of cash by other banks, there will be a net increase of deposits in the banking system. For a reserve ratio of r percent, deposits in the banking system will rise by $1/r$ for every dollar of outside cash that enters the system. Although these deposits may not all remain with the bank originally receiving the cash, the total within the system will not be changed by subsequent interbank cash flows.

Exercises

1. The appropriate reserve ratio for a hypothetical economy is 10 percent. Draw up the balance sheet for a commercial bank in such an economy that is in equilibrium with loans totaling $74.7 million.

2. Suppose another economy requires a 25 percent reserve ratio. Due to some institutional change in the economy, it is now considered safe for banks to hold only 20 percent of their assets in cash. If the cash in the banking system remained unchanged at $1 billion, by how much will deposits have changed when the new equilibrium is reached?

3. An economy has two kinds of commercial banks. Country banks are small with few depositors and find a cash ratio of 25 percent necessary. City banks with many depositors find a 20 percent cash ratio perfectly adequate. If a depositor withdraws $1,000 from a country bank and deposits it in a city bank, what will happen to:
   a. total country bank deposits?
   b. total city bank deposits?
   c. total deposits in the banking system?

For Thought and Discussion

1. Banks are commonly regarded as sources of great power within the capitalist system. With what aspects of their banking functions is this power especially associated?

2. The Soviet Union has a banking system. Should this surprise you?

3. The United States is unique in having very large numbers of commercial banks (and some are enormous) rather than a small number of very large banks with branches spread throughout the country. What arguments can you think of both for and against the American system?

4. Suppose all bank accounts and all credit-card accounts were linked to a central computer so all checks and credit charges were instantaneously debited to the drawer and credited to the recipient. In what way would the desired asset structure of banks under this system be different from what it is at present?

Chapter 28
Central Banks and the Money Supply

Terms and Concepts

Central bank
Reserve deposits
Lender of last resort
Reserve ratio
Open market operation

Federal Reserve System
Board of Governors
Federal Open Market Committee
Discounting
Discount rate

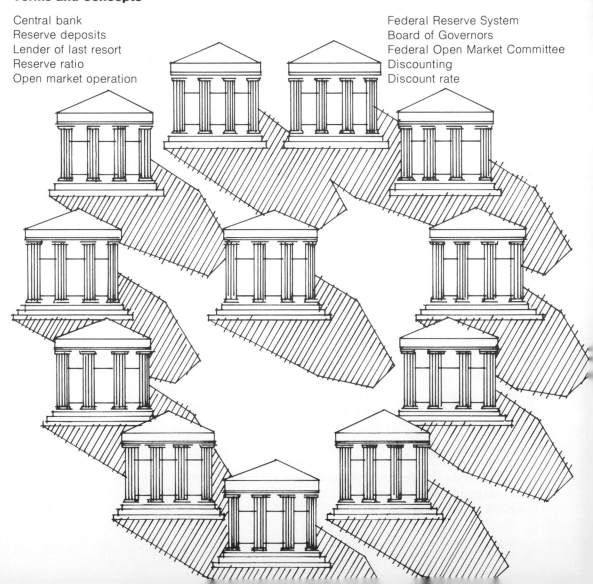

The Money Supply with no Central Bank

How the money supply is determined under a system of commercial banks

It's quite possible for an economy to have a banking system comprised of independent banks (perhaps with some centralized check-clearing arrangement) with no formal controls of any kind other than those designed to minimize simple fraud and embezzlement. Indeed, the banking system in the United States was essentially like this throughout the nineteenth century.

Before we consider the nature of *central banks* and the type of control such banks typically exercise over the banking system in general and the money supply in particular, we should consider how the money supply is determined in an unregulated banking system. This is simply a matter of putting together what we already know from the last two chapters.

The Quantity of Money

In an economy with commercial banks, those items that serve as money are:

1. cash, consisting of coins and paper currency, and
2. bank deposits, consisting of checking-account balances.

It's important not to misconstrue the role of cash in the money supply. Total cash, other than what the government or issuing authority keeps in its vaults, is distributed between two sectors:

1. *the public,* as cash in pocketbooks, cookie jars, and vending machines.
2. *the banks,* as cash held in reserve against demands by depositors.

Only cash in the hands of the public constitutes part of the money supply. The reason for this is simple. A given individual's total money balance consists of his own cash plus his bank balance. While a cash reserve is kept by the bank to back up his account balance, it is the *deposit,* not the cash behind it, that counts as money to the individual.

Bank Cash

Although the cash reserves of banks are not part of the money supply, they *determine* the level of deposits and hence the level of an important part of the money supply. As we showed in the last chapter, the total deposits a bank can safely sustain depend directly on the cash reserves it possesses. If all banks maintain a 20 percent ratio of cash to deposits, then total deposits will be five times the cash reserves of the banking system. This ratio is often maintained by varying loans, as described in the last chapter.

Now, $1 in cash and $1 in deposits are such extremely close substitutes to the public that we regard them as equivalent in determining total money balances. Alternatively, with a 20 percent reserve ratio, $1 in cash held in bank reserves rather than in the hands of the public will back up *$5 in deposits*—equivalent to $5 cash in the hands of the public.

Cash in bank reserves is thus more "high powered" than cash in the hands of the public because $1 in bank cash contributes more than $1 to the money supply. Although bank cash is not itself part of the money supply, it creates deposits that are.

The Money Supply

The supply of money consists of cash in the hands of the public plus bank deposits, and the level of bank deposits is determined by the quantity of cash held by the banking system. Therefore, the total quantity of money in an economy with an uncontrolled banking system depends ultimately on the quantity of cash available, given the structure and financial habits of the economy. The exact relationship between the quantity of cash and the quantity of money depends on two main factors:

1. the ratio that the public wishes to maintain between its own cash and its own deposits. Cash can only remain as reserves in the banking system to the extent that the public's demand for cash is satisfied. The public can always demand that banks supply it with cash or, for that matter, that banks accept surplus cash for deposit.

2. the ratio between cash reserves and deposits that banks find it prudent to maintain. It is this ratio that determines how many dollars of deposits the banking system will maintain for each dollar of cash reserves.

Usually the ratio in which the public holds its own cash to its own deposits will be about the same as the cash ratio in the banking system. The greater the proportion of his money balance the average individual wants to hold as cash, the greater the proportion of cash the average bank needs to hold against withdrawals.

An Example

Given these two ratios, we can determine the exact relationship between the quantity of money and the total quantity of cash. Suppose, for simplicity, that (1) the public wants to hold $20 in cash for every $100 it holds in bank deposits, and (2) banks wish to hold $20 in cash reserves for every $100 in deposits.

The $100 in deposits requires total cash of $40: $20 held by the public and $20 by the banking system. Or we can say that $40 in total cash will be divided equally between the public and the banks, and will generate $100 in total deposits. The quantity of money associated with $40 total cash will be

$120—the $100 in deposits, and the $20 in cash held by the public. In this example, the quantity of money will be three times the quantity of total cash, and an increase or decrease in cash will cause a threefold increase or decrease in the quantity of money.

Control of the Cash Supply

Because the quantity of money is determined by the quantity of cash, even in an uncontrolled banking system, the quantity of money can be controlled if the quantity of cash can be regulated.

In reality, this control is less certain than suggested by simple examples. The public may vary the ratio of its own cash to deposits, causing the quantity of money to vary unpredictably even though total cash remains constant. With no controls, the cash reserve ratios of banks are freely determined by their own view of the balance of risk (too little cash) against profitability (a high ratio of loans to cash), and thus may vary. If the reserve ratio falls or business conditions worsen, the public may try to increase its *own* cash holdings as a safety measure, further decreasing bank cash and thereby causing a contraction in deposits, and thus in the money supply.

Even when varying the quantity of cash results in a proportionate variation in the total money supply, it may not be possible to vary the quantity of cash as needed. An extreme example is when the currency is either gold or paper currency with 100 percent gold backing. In this case, the quantity of cash, and thus the quantity of money, is determined by the quantity of gold—over which policy authorities presumably have little direct control.

In the days of the full gold standard (prior to the twentieth century), a country's gold stock, and thus its quantity of money, depended on the inflow and outflow of gold resulting from international transactions. The quantity of money was thus tied directly to the country's balance of payments and was determined automatically rather than as a matter of policy. With fiduciary paper currency, in which the amount of currency can be varied freely (at least within limits), the currency-issuing authority possesses the ultimate control over the quantity of money.

In modern economic systems, ultimate control over the quantity of money has passed largely to institutions known as *central banks,* the functions of which are carried out in the United States by the Federal Reserve System.

Recap With a simple system of commercial banks, bank reserves consist entirely of cash (currency). The stock of currency is divided between the public and the banking system in a proportion determined primarily by the public's division of its money balances between currency and deposits. The amount of currency held by banks determines the level of total deposits, once the safe ratio of cash to other assets is established. Thus, the overall supply of currency determines the level of bank deposits, and, as a consequence, the total quantity of money.

Banker's Banks

**How banks can obtain
some of the conveniences
they supply**

In the simple banking system analyzed in the previous chapter, the cash reserves of each bank fulfilled two main roles—reserves against the cash withdrawals of depositors, and reserves from which to pay *other banks* when check clearing called for a net transfer.

On the average, a bank's net receipts of cash from other banks on some days and its net payments to other banks on others will tend to even out over time. Because it's inconvenient to cart cash into the bank one day, only to cart it out again the next, the bank-clearing process is obviously greatly simplified if all of this back-and-forth movement of cash can be avoided.

Central Banks

The solution to this problem is to grant banks the ability to operate with checks instead of cash. If one bank owed $1,000 to another, it could simply pay this amount by check rather than by a cumbersome transfer of cash. To do this, of course, it would require a bank account.

For a bank to secure the full advantages provided by a bank account, we need a "banker's bank," or *central bank*. The depositors in a central bank are other individual commercial banks. Almost every country in the world has a bank that functions in this way—the Bank of England, the Bank of France, the Bank of Italy, the Bank of India, and so on. The United States does not have a true central bank of this kind, although many central bank functions are carried out by the *Federal Reserve System*, which we shall discuss later in this chapter. Because the ultimate functioning of the Federal Reserve System is similar to that of a central bank, we shall first consider the working of a system with a true central bank, then discuss the special features of the American arrangement.

In such a system, if First Bank owes Second Bank $1,000 as the result of the current clearing, it can pay Second Bank by drawing a check (or its equivalent) against its account with the central bank. Second Bank, like an ordinary depositor, can then decide whether to "cash" the check or merely deposit it in its central bank account.

A central bank thus gives banks the same basic advantages that an ordinary bank gives its depositors. Just as an individual's bank deposit is as good as cash most of the time, even though he still needs to keep some cash in his pocket, so a commercial bank's deposit with the central bank is as good as cash most of the time, even though it still needs to keep some cash in its vault.

The Importance of Safety

It is essential that the central bank, if it is to fulfill the role of a banker's bank, be extremely *safe*. Commercial banks must feel absolutely certain that the deposits they hold at the central bank (*reserve deposits*) can be converted into cash at any time as they may occasionally require additional cash on short notice to supply withdrawals by their own depositors. Unless this condition is met, commercial banks cannot consider their reserve deposits equivalent to cash in their own vaults.

We might note that the first central bank, the Bank of England, created so much confidence on this score that the phrase "safe as the Bank of England" passed into everyday use as a description of ultimate solidity.

Central Bank Asset Structure

The central bank will obviously be completely safe in the above sense if it holds cash equal to 100 percent of its deposits, which are the reserve deposits of the commercial banks. But it is still safe if it holds something less than 100 percent cash reserves. Just as the probability that all a commercial bank's customers will simultaneously wish to withdraw their deposits in cash is negligible under normal circumstances, so the probability that all commercial banks will simultaneously wish to cash their reserve deposits is negligible.

Thus, the central bank need not hold cash equal to 100 percent of reserves—it can hold less. That part of its total assets not held as cash or its equivalent, however, must be held in minimum-risk form. The commercial loans that collectively constitute a major asset of commercial banks are far too risky for the central bank, which lends primarily to the safest borrower—the government. Typical noncash assets of the central bank are thus loans to the government in the form of bonds (long-term loans) and treasury bills (short-term loans).

Lending Reserves

A central bank can extend its usefulness to its customers (the commercial banks) with little reduction in safety by providing a limited program of loans to the commercial banks themselves. For example, a central bank can lend extra reserves to commercial banks whose reserves temporarily bear too low a ratio to their deposits, just as a commercial bank can lend extra deposits to one of its own customers. Central banks normally do this only on a very restricted, short-run basis, however, and then only after the commercial bank has "explained" (like a commercial bank customer seeking a loan) exactly why it needs the loan and exactly how and when it will be repaid. The particular way in which the central bank makes such loans varies from country to country with the institutional arrangements linking the central bank to its commercial bank depositors. The amounts of these loans (called "discounts and advances" in the United States system) will typically be small relative to government loans and hence to total assets. Because a central bank's loans to commercial banks are made only under stringent conditions (and usually carry a relatively high rate of interest), the central bank is often described as a *lender of last resort.*

Recap Commercial banks can expedite their interbank transactions by holding accounts with a central bank, a special bank that bears the same kind of relationship to commercial banks as these do to their depositors. Deposits with the central bank are considered equivalent to cash reserves by commercial banks. In a highly developed banking system, these reserve deposits become the primary reserves of commercial banks. As for the central bank, it need not hold 100 percent cash against these reserve deposits and thus can make loans, but only those with highest safety—to the government, and sometimes to its commercial bank "customers."

Capsule Supplement 28.1   **The Bank of the United States, 1791–1811, 1816–36**

The United States once had a bank that might have actually become a true central bank. This was the Bank of the United States, which was born in 1791, was allowed to die in 1811, was resurrected as the Second Bank of the United States five years later, then was murdered and buried in 1836.

The formation of the original Bank of the United States was the work of George Washington's secretary of the treasury, Alexander Hamilton, as part of a comprehensive package of economic policies designed to get the new nation off to a successful start. The bank was modeled after the Bank of England to function not only as the government's bank but also as a commercial bank with the right to open branches. It was not a government-owned bank (although the government subscribed to 20 percent of its initial capital). In its key role, it depended on being the government's chosen banking instrument.

Opposition to the Bank arose from several sources. Virginia landowners feared dominance by Northern merchants and financiers, New Yorkers and Bostonians were jealous (the Bank was in Philadelphia), and the Western states disliked the Bank's dampening of the exuberant and incautious lending policies of local banks. Its charter was renewable after twenty years, and opposition grew sufficiently to prevent its renewal. In 1811 the first Bank of the United States disintegrated.

Financial chaos following the War of 1812 was sufficient to provide support for the central bank's revival. Thus, the Second Bank of the United States came into being in 1816. This bank got off to a bad start because of poor management. Although it eventually became a successful operation, it gradually began to generate the same kind of opposition that had arisen against the first bank, being regarded along the Western frontier as an attempt of the wicked East to inhibit the development of the new territories. The election of Andrew Jackson put one of the Bank's leading opponents in the White House and, although Jackson's veto of the 1832 charter renewal still left four more years for another renewal attempt, he decided to "murder" the Bank by withdrawing the government's deposits. Two treasury secretaries had to be appointed before Jackson was able to have his orders carried out, but they eventually were.

The demise of the Bank of the United States did not do what the more naive had expected, destroy the financial power structure. It moved immediately from Philadelphia to Wall Street and continued to thrive. The death of the Bank, however, removed the last chance for the institution of a true central bank. Although the Bank of the United States was not a full central bank in the modern sense, neither was the Bank of England at the time. Both, it can be presumed, would have developed along the same lines. As it happened, the United States was left with a freewheeling and relatively unstable banking system. From 1836 until the creation of the Federal Reserve System in 1913, the government operated without the full control of monetary policy afforded by a central bank.

Central Bank Control over Money

How the central bank becomes the ultimate controller of the money supply

Under a modern system of central banking, the "cash" reserves of commercial banks consist almost entirely of reserve deposits with the central bank. For this reason, we shall no longer use the term *cash* and shall refer simply to *reserves*. The behavior of commercial banks is still governed by their adjustment of asset holdings to maintain the desired structure. In this adjustment, the *reserve ratio* (the ratio of reserves to deposits) is the key.

The total quantity of money is equal to commercial bank deposits plus that part of total currency in the hands (and pockets) of the public. As pointed out earlier in the chapter, currency held in the banking system cannot be counted because it is being held as partial backing for deposits that are already included.

The level of commercial bank deposits is determined by the level of reserve deposits with the central bank (plus bank-held currency, a minor item) and by the reserve ratio. The currency holdings of the public are determined by the public itself as the public is always free to exchange deposits for currency or currency for deposits.

The Money Supply

Thus, the quantity of money is determined by the following four factors:

1. the *quantity of currency,*
2. the *quantity of reserve deposits* with the central bank,
3. the *reserve ratio,* which determines the level of deposits sustainable by the banking system for a given level of reserves and bank-held currency, and
4. the *ratio of currency to deposits* chosen by the public, which determines how much of the currency is held by the public.

Instruments of Regulation

The quantity of money can be varied by varying either of the two quantities (currency or reserves) or the reserve ratio. The other ratio (of publicly held currency to deposits) is not open to policy manipulation because it is entirely determined by the choices of firms and individuals. Because currency plays a minor part in the assets of commercial banks, we can consider that the chief instruments for varying the quantity of money are the *level of reserves* and the *reserve ratio.* The quantity of currency is adjusted primarily to satisfy the demands of the public, not to affect bank deposits.

Without a central bank, the reserve ratio is determined (as outlined in the previous chapter) by balancing the risk of having withdrawals exceed the readily available cash against the profitability of bank loans. Under given circumstances, there will be some ratio that can be considered sufficiently high for safety, yet sufficiently low for profitability.

A central bank, either by virtue of the legal powers given to it or the threat of depriving a commercial bank of its useful services, can prescribe the reserve ratio for commercial banks, and thus vary total deposits by varying this ratio. If the central bank raises the reserve ratio from 20 percent to 25 percent, commercial banks will be able to keep only $400 in deposits for every $100 in reserves, instead of $500 as previously. With unchanged reserves, total deposits would have to fall by 20 percent and commercial banks would have to call in old loans and severely limit new ones.

The reserve ratio can be raised *above* the level considered prudent by the commercial banks, but it cannot easily be reduced below that level. If 20 percent were considered the minimum safe ratio by commercial banks, lowering the legal ratio below this level would have no effect—banks would simply refuse to expand their loans further. If changing the reserve ratio is to be an important instrument, therefore, the "normal" reserve requirement must be set higher than the level banks would choose of their own accord.

Reserve Level Changes

Changing the level of reserves rather than the reserve ratio also requires careful technique. Because reserves are deposits held by commercial banks and are as good as cash, the central bank does not want to make a *free gift* to commercial banks by simply giving them more reserves—although it could do so in principle. Nor does it want to reduce reserves simply by changing the figures on its books (though it could do this in principle). Then reserves would cease to possess their key property—that they are as good as cash in the eyes of commercial banks.

As mentioned in the previous section, the central bank can increase the reserves of commercial banks by extending loans to them, and reduce reserves by calling in such loans. There is, however, another way to influence the level of reserves indirectly: through *open market operations*.

Recap Because deposits with the central bank form the bulk of the reserves commercial banks must hold against ordinary deposits, the level of commercial bank deposits and thus the money supply can be varied by changing the level of these reserves. Alternatively, because the central bank usually has legal or other powers to set the reserve ratio, the money supply can be varied by changing this ratio.

Open Market Operations

An important technique for influencing the money supply

One straightforward way in which a central bank can increase reserve deposits is for it to buy something from the public and pay for the purchase with its own check. In practice, central banks confine such purchases to securities, and then almost entirely to government securities like bonds, although they can and do purchase commercial securities on occasion.

Suppose the Central Bank pays for $1,000 worth of government bonds with its own check for $1,000. These bonds, it should be noted, are not newly issued ones purchased directly from the government. They are ordinary government bonds already held by individuals or firms and purchased in the same way anyone would purchase them, *on the open market*—hence, the name of the operation. Let's suppose that the seller has an account with First Bank, and deposits his check there. First Bank will credit his account with $1,000 and pass the canceled check on to Central Bank for payment. Central Bank completes the check-clearing process by adding $1,000 to First Bank's balance with it.

The Stage 1 *changes* in the balance sheets of First Bank and Central Bank will be as follows:

Balance Sheet Changes/Stage 1

First Bank

Assets	Liabilities
Reserves (+ $1,000 at Central Bank)	Deposits + $1,000

Central Bank

Government securities + $1,000	Reserve deposits + $1,000

Final Equilibrium

First Bank now has $1,000 in additional deposits and $1,000 in additional reserves. Because the reserves are as good as cash for banking purposes, and because they have not been transferred from any other *commercial* bank, they are equivalent to *outside cash*. As shown in the previous chapter, when outside cash enters the banking system, deposits will increase by a multiple of the new cash, the exact multiple being determined by the reserve ratio. For a reserve ratio of 20 percent, the increase of $1,000 in new reserves will ultimately lead to an increase of $5,000 in total deposits within the commercial banking system. The ultimate changes in the consolidated balance sheets of all commercial banks will be:

Balance Sheet Changes/Stage 3

Consolidated Commercial Banks

Assets		Liabilities	
Reserves	+ $1,000	Deposits	+ $5,000
Loans	+ $4,000		
	+ $5,000		+ $5,000

Even though some of the increased deposits in First Bank may have leaked out to other commercial banks, the totals over all commercial banks will not be changed. Central Bank's balance sheet will undergo no changes after Stage 1.

Thus, the central bank can increase the quantity of money by $5 for every $1 in securities it buys on the open market (assuming a 20 percent reserve ratio).

Reserve deposits can be *decreased* in a similar fashion: Central Bank need only *sell* $1,000 in bonds for which it receives a check drawn on some commercial bank. When the check is paid, the commercial bank's reserve deposits at Central Bank will go down by $1,000 while its own deposits will also go down by $1,000. Central Bank reduces both its liabilities (reserve deposits) and assets (government bonds) by $1,000. Eventually, total commercial bank deposits will fall by $5,000, including the initial $1,000 reduction in the bond-buyer's account.

The Rate of Interest

This method of varying reserves and thus the money supply will also have effects on the *rate of interest*. If the central bank buys bonds, it adds to the existing demand for bonds and increases their prices. To see how this affects the rate of interest, suppose we have a bond that initially sold for $100, yields an annual "coupon" of $5, and is redeemed at face value after one year. The buyer will receive a total of $105 for his initial $100—a 5 percent return. Now, suppose the central bank had initially entered the bond market, causing the price of the bond to rise to $101. The buyer will still receive $105 after one year, but on an outlay of $101—slightly less than a 4 percent return.

Varying the quantity of money by buying or selling bonds in the open market will thus tend to have the following effects on interest rates:

1. *An increase in the quantity of money will be associated with a fall in interest rates.*
2. *A reduction in the quantity of money will be associated with a rise in interest rates.*

Automatic Influences

In addition to the various discretionary means of varying the quantity of money, there are automatic means (unless specific countermeasures are taken) that also operate through the central bank.

The most important of these are international transactions. Let's suppose that all international payments are made in gold and that anyone receiving gold must turn it over to the central bank. If an exporter sells abroad and receives $10,000 in gold, he takes the gold to his own bank, which credits him with $10,000. The commercial bank then sends the gold to the central bank and receives a $10,000 addition to its reserve deposits. From then on, the process is standard—commercial banks' deposits can increase by $50,000 because the $10,000 in gold becomes converted into a reserve deposit. Because each $1 of gold results in $5 of deposits, gold constitutes "high-powered" money. Losing gold by making payments abroad will have a similar effect, reducing the quantity of money.

One of the features of modern central banking that is very important in some countries (less so in the United States) is that the discretionary control over the quantity of money by reserve variation can be used to *offset* changes in the quantity of money that would otherwise result from the pattern of international payments.

Recap One of the most important techniques of influencing the money supply (especially in the United States) is open market operations. If the central bank buys government securities from the public, it issues its own check. That check is deposited with a commercial bank, and ultimately becomes added to that bank's reserve deposits with the central bank. The additional reserves permit expansion of commercial bank deposits, so the supply of money is increased by a multiple of the original open market transaction. The money supply can be reduced in a corresponding way by the sale of securities by the central bank.

The Federal Reserve System

How the Federal Reserve System functions as a central bank in the United States

The functions of a central bank in the United States are performed primarily by the Federal Reserve System (the "Fed"), although the Treasury Department also performs certain minor functions performed elsewhere by central banks (keeping nominal ownership of gold reserves, for example).

The Basic Structure of the Fed

Just as the organization of the commercial banking system in the United States is eccentric by world standards (thousands of individual banks, some quite small, rather than a few huge banks with branches all over the country), so the central bank is different in structure from that of most other countries. An American central bank, if set up along the lines of most other central banks, would be a single bank called the "Bank of the United States," would be either a public or quasi-public corporation, and would be backed by legislation that gave it wide discretionary powers over *all* commercial banks. Its policy would be set by its chairman or president, who would be expected to resign if he had major policy differences with the government.

The Federal Reserve System, in fact, is a group of twelve regional banks (see Figure 28.1), each owned cooperatively by its "member" banks. Even though less than 40 percent of all commercial banks in the United States

Figure 28.1
The Federal Reserve System showing boundaries of the Federal Reserve districts and their branch territories.

January 1977

Drawn by R.W. Galvin, Cart.

LEGEND

━━ Boundaries of Federal Reserve Districts

— Boundaries of Federal Reserve Branch Territories

⭐ Board of Governors of the Federal Reserve System

⊙ Federal Reserve Bank Cities

• Federal Reserve Branch Cities

Source: *Federal Reserve Bulletin.*

actually belonged to the Federal Reserve System in 1977, member bank assets represented almost 75 percent of all commercial bank assets.

When founded in 1913, the Federal Reserve System was not a full central bank. Among other things, the Fed was not originally established to control the volume of deposits in the banking system. The structure of the system was tightened in 1935, however, and its powers as a true central bank were expanded.

Although the decentralized structure of the Fed still formally exists, it now operates in practice like a single bank with regional branches. Ultimate control is exercised by the Board of Governors of the Federal Reserve System, referred to either as the "Board of Governors" or the "Federal Reserve Board"—the latter being the official name prior to the 1935 reorganization. The seven governors are appointed by the president to very long terms (fourteen years), with one governor replaced every two years. The president also designates one governor as chairman (for a four-year term). Nevertheless, the governors have traditionally assumed their responsibility to be to Congress rather than to the executive branch.

The Federal Reserve System's primary powers are over its member banks. However, because they account for more than 75 percent of the commercial banking in the United States, we can analyze the system as though it covered all commercial banks.

The Balance Sheet of the Fed

Let's first look at the balance sheet of the Federal Reserve System, shown in Table 28.1. In light of our previous discussion of central banks, some items are immediately recognizable. "Deposits" are the reserve deposits of member banks and thus the reserves on which the quantity of money—through public deposits in commercial banks—is based. On the asset side, "U.S. government securities" are the holdings of bonds and other government securities we expect the central bank's portfolio to contain. "Discounts and advances" are the loans to commercial banks that constitute extra reserves—note how small this item is in the United States.

The item "Gold certificates" on the asset side can be regarded as equivalent to "gold reserves." The Federal Reserve System does not hold gold, but hands it over to the Treasury in return for gold certificates. While the Treasury may physically keep the gold in Fort Knox, much is held in Federal Reserve Bank vaults—even though the Fed is not the nominal owner.

This leaves the item "Federal Reserve notes" on the liabilities side. The Fed is the nation's currency-issuing authority, as well as its central bank. Indeed, the notation "Federal Reserve Note" appears on all but some old paper currency. This notation is, however, subordinate to "The United States of America," and the bills carry the signatures of the U.S. treasurer

Table 28.1
Federal Reserve System Outline
Balance Sheet, December 31, 1977
(Billions of dollars)

Assets		Liabilities	
Gold certificates	11.7	Federal Reserve notes	93.2
U.S. government securities	102.8	Deposits	35.6
Discounts and advances	.3	Other items	9.0
Other items	23.0		
Total	137.8	Total	137.8

Source: *Federal Reserve Bulletin*, February, 1978.

and secretary of the treasury, not of Federal Reserve officials—emphasizing that the currency is ultimately "backed" by the country, not the bank.

Currency

Why does paper currency appear as a "liability"? The reason for this and the place of currency in the balance sheet is best appreciated historically. The first bank notes were privately issued pieces of paper that could be converted, on demand, into gold or whatever happened to constitute legal money. Thus, every note that a commercial bank issued was a potential demand for gold (assuming this was the ultimate legal money). The bank took on the *liability* to redeem its notes in gold, so every note issued appeared as a liability of the bank in exactly the same way (and for the same reason) that deposits constitute a liability.

Federal Reserve notes can no longer be redeemed for gold or anything except other Federal Reserve notes. Nevertheless, the accounting tradition has been preserved.

The Powers of the Fed

Putting aside the currency issue, which is dealt with differently in most other countries, the Fed has the same general powers as any central bank over the money supply. It can do the following:

1. vary reserve deposits by *open market operations*.
2. vary reserve deposits by extending loans to commercial banks, that is, by engaging in *discount operations*.

3. vary the *reserve ratio* within prescribed limits that, under present law, are 10 percent and 22 percent for the most important class of commercial banks.

While the favored method of the Federal Reserve System has always been open market operations, the central banks of other countries exhibit a variety of individual favorites among these three main control methods.

Successful open market operations require a well-developed and smoothly operating market in government securities that the monetary authority can enter and leave without causing major disruptions. Such a market exists in the United States, but not in many smaller countries. The Fed must also operate as an ordinary trader, which it cannot do if it buys and sells directly. Consequently, it keeps its open market trading a secret, buying and selling through numerous regular brokers who mix "Fed" business with regular transactions. Because open market operations typically account for between 5 and 10 percent of all transactions in government securities, such delicate handling is mandatory.

Decisions about open market operations are made on a day-to-day basis by the *Federal Open Market Committee.* This committee consists of the seven members of the Board of Governors plus five of the presidents of the twelve regional Federal Reserve Banks.

Open market operations, as already pointed out, tend to simultaneously affect the *quantity of money* and the *rate of interest.* At different times, due either to different circumstances or to different approaches to the use of monetary policy, the emphasis may be on varying the quantity of money *or* varying the rate of interest, but the two are nonetheless closely linked.

Sometimes open market operations are used on a short-term basis to assist government loan programs. A large issue of new government bonds will tend to depress the securities market (raise the rate of interest). The Federal Reserve System can "even out" potential fluctuations by open market buying during the issue period, followed by slowly selling over succeeding weeks or months.

Discounting

It should be apparent from its balance sheet that while discounting is used as an instrument by the Federal Reserve System, the level of loans is far too low for them to have a major influence on reserves or the money supply.

Strictly speaking, the Fed distinguishes between *advances,* which are direct loans of extra reserves, and *discounts,* which are, in effect, purchases of securities already held by commercial banks at a cost (or discount) to the commercial banks. Although the most important part of "discounts and advances" is actually *advances,* the process has come to be called *discounting.*

Like any central bank, the Federal Reserve System has two main ways of operating its "discount window": it can vary the *discount rate* (the rate of interest it charges) widely and offer relatively unlimited discounts or advances to any commercial bank willing to pay the going price, or it can vary the discount rate comparatively little and *ration* advances with greater or less stringency, as appropriate.

Because the discount rate of any central bank is regarded as an important indicator of interest rates generally, any decision to vary this rate must take into account the effects on the overall interest-rate structure of the economy. Consequently, such variations are made cautiously.

The Federal Reserve System has not traditionally made great use of its authority to change the reserve ratio—unlike the Bank of England, which uses such authority as a primary instrument of policy. Changing the reserve ratio is an instrument of great power, especially for *reducing* the quantity of money. But it is rather extreme in operation—best used in crisis situations such as Britain experiences at frequent intervals. Reserve ratio changes have very direct effects on the volume of commercial loans, and hence the quantity of money, but only indirect effects on interest rates.

The Fed's Relation to the Government

The Federal Reserve System is the *monetary authority* of the United States. It can fully control the *quantity of money* and exert great influence on the *interest-rate structure,* the two basic instruments of *monetary policy.*

Although it is nominally part of the "government" in the broad sense, the Federal Reserve System is not under the immediate control of the administration, and not always amenable to administration policy suggestions. In principle, the Federal Reserve System can be legislated out of existence in case of irreconcilable disagreement, but only under major crisis conditions. There are two main reasons why the Fed may refuse to carry out monetary policy in the manner desired by the administration.

1. The Fed's governors and executives may simply disagree with the government's assessment of the economic situation, the general methods to be used to cope with the situation, or the nature and role of monetary policy in the overall policy mix.

2. The Fed may have *technical* disagreements with the government on how to best use the instruments at its disposal. Because it is closely associated with the banking community, the Federal Reserve System is reluctant to use certain policies (such as reserve ratio changes) whose effects are potentially disruptive. After all, the Fed is charged with maintaining the smooth and efficient operation of the banking system as well as with conducting broad monetary policy.

Recap Central banking functions in the United States are carried out by the Federal Reserve System. The Fed is composed of twelve bankers' banks, "owned" cooperatively by commercial banks, but under ultimate government control. The Federal Reserve System also controls the supply of currency. It regulates the supply of money primarily by open market operations, resorting to reserve ratio changes only on rare occasions. Although under ultimate government control, the Federal Reserve System has considerable independence. Consequently, its monetary policy may not always be well coordinated with the macroeconomic policies of the administration.

Capsule Supplement 28.2   **The Control of Currency in the United States**

Discussions of central banking and the money supply emphasize the level of reserve deposits at the central bank and the resulting level of regular deposits at commercial banks. But currency is still an important part of the money supply. In the United States, the Federal Reserve System has control over paper currency, the most important part of the total. One of its tasks is to provide a supply of currency that is responsive to public need. As has been pointed out in the main text, although the total quantity of money can be determined by the monetary authority, the proportion of this held as currency is determined by the public. This proportion varies seasonally, being especially high at Christmas.

How does the Fed keep the supply of currency at the appropriate level? When an individual wants additional currency, he cashes a check drawn on a commercial bank, which pays him from the relatively small stock of currency it keeps on hand. At times of increased demand for currency, commercial bank withdrawals in cash will exceed cash deposits, and its small currency stock will soon be depleted. The commercial bank will thus seek to hold more currency, the public demand being translated into a demand by the commercial banks. The commercial bank can obtain currency on demand from the Fed—in effect, by "cashing" a check drawn on its reserve deposits. By law, the Federal Reserve System can only issue notes if their value is covered by government securities, gold, and certain other types of collateral. When the notes are issued, the counterbalancing assets are not eligible for other use.

When the commercial bank pays out the currency to the public, its reserves fall by the full amount of the currency transactions even if it obtains new currency from the Fed because the value of the new currency will be deducted from its reserve deposits at the Fed. Consequently, it must find increased reserves.

With a general increase in the demand for currency, the Fed must be prepared to increase bank reserves. It will do this by engaging in open market operations and buying government securities from the public. These activities also help to restore its portfolio of securities, depleted by the collateral it had to put aside against newly issued currency.

If the demand for currency falls (as it does after Christmas), the process works in reverse. Commercial banks find their currency stock building up, so they deposit it at the Fed and increase their reserves. The Fed can then "unissue" the currency and take its collateral off the shelf. Open market operations (selling securities this time) will bring reserves down again. Thus, the volume of currency in circulation can be varied, keeping the total stock of money at any desired level.

Exercises

1. Suppose the public wishes to hold 20 percent of its total money balances as cash and the remainder in the form of bank deposits, and that banks wish to hold cash reserves equal to 10 percent of deposits. What total amount of cash will be required for use both by the banks and the public for a total money supply of $100 million? (Assume there is no central bank.)

2. An economy has a central bank that requires each commercial bank to hold 25 percent reserve deposits against its total checking-account deposits. Reserve deposits of all commercial banks total $10 billion. What will the public's total deposits with the commercial banks be if the banks have no excess reserves?

3. By how much will public deposits with commercial banks rise if the central bank changes its rules to require only 20 percent as the reserve ratio, assuming the other data to be the same as in question 2?

For Thought and Discussion

1. In the nineteenth and early twentieth centuries, there was much support for the central bank being independent of the current administration. What arguments could be (or have been) used in favor of such independence? What are the arguments against independence?

2. In some countries, the same bank that acts as the central bank is (or has been) also engaged in commercial banking operations. Would you expect such an arrangement to interfere with either central banking operations or the commercial banking system as a whole? How?

3. If banks were used to make only cash deposits and cash withdrawals so there were no checks used, but loans (in cash) could be made by banks, would there be any role for a central bank?

4. Would a socialist society need banks?

5. A recent study shows that there is a high degree of correlation between the degree of development of a nation's banking system and the degree of its overall economic development. Does this surprise you? What would explain the relationship?

Part 8
Macroeconomic Policy

This part, consisting of Chapters 29 through 32, is concerned with consolidating the material in Parts 5 (Macroeconomics), 6 (Applications of Macroeconomic Analysis), and 7 (Money and Banks) into a unified presentation of macroeconomic policy in which monetary and fiscal policy are considered as means for attaining essentially similar ends. Chapter 29 discusses the general aims of macroeconomic policy in relation to the means of carrying out that policy. Chapters 30 and 31 present the details of fiscal and monetary policy, respectively, and Chapter 32 deals with the practical problems of policy and of choosing the mixture of monetary and fiscal means to implement it.

Chapter 29
Aims and Instruments of Macroeconomic Policy

Terms and Concepts

Structural unemployment
Frictional unemployment
General unemployment
Modified Phillips curve
Policy possibility curve
Fiscal policy
Monetary policy
Direct and indirect policy

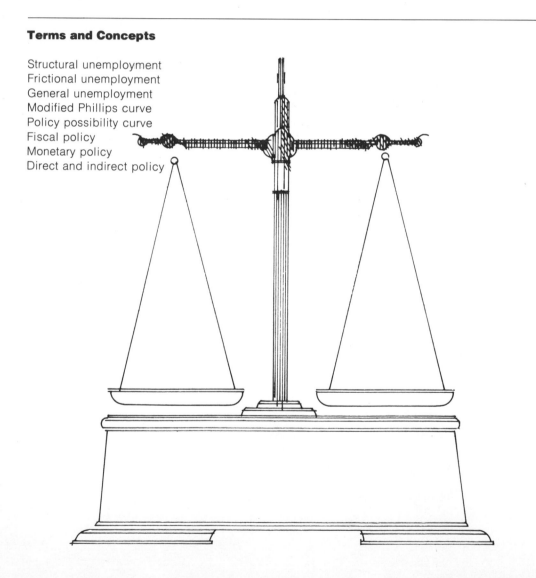

General Objectives

What distinguishes macroeconomic policy objectives from other objectives of economic policy

Macroeconomic policy is concerned with such things as the level of aggregate output and employment, the rate of economic growth, and the general level of prices. Of course, because anything that affects the economy as a whole will necessarily affect its parts, the macroeconomist must also consider the potential effects of macro policy on economic efficiency, income distribution, and the balance of payments, even though they may not be the main concerns of that policy.

The ideal macroeconomic policy is generally considered to be one that achieves the following primary objectives:

1. A level of aggregate real output that is always close to capacity.
2. A stable price level, or one that rises only slowly.
3. A steady growth of capacity—and of real output because it should be kept near capacity—at a rate appropriate for the economy. (The appropriate rate of growth could very well be zero.)

We can summarize the primary objectives as full employment with appropriate growth and price stability.

Because such policy should also ensure that allocative, distributional, and international policy goals are not disturbed, we can add the following secondary objectives:

4. The preservation of economic efficiency and the optimal output mix.
5. The preservation of a desirable or acceptable income distribution.
6. The preservation of balance in international payments.

A Choice Cannot Be Avoided

These objectives are not independent of each other, and those problems of macroeconomic policy that are not merely technical come mainly from their interdependence. Not only are they interdependent, they are, to some extent, competitive. In particular, full employment and price stability are competing objectives insofar as inflationary influences exist at less than full employment and increase as the economy approaches capacity. Alternatively, growth and full employment do not generally conflict because full employment and rapid growth are both promoted by a high level of investment. However, rapid growth and price stability do usually conflict.

Thus, it is probable that the policy-maker will have to make *choices* about the emphasis given to different objectives. Consider, for example, the choice between a combination of relatively high unemployment with zero inflation and a combination of low unemployment with some inflation. Each combination affects different groups in different ways, and each choice will be objected to by those representing the groups that the choice adversely affects. In most countries, the alternative ultimately chosen can generally be predicted from a knowledge of the political party in power.

All economists would agree that each primary objective, considered in isolation, is desirable. When it is a matter of choice among combinations, none of which provide for the attainment of all objectives, the task of professional economists becomes difficult. They must define the available options as clearly as possible and analyze how each sector of the economy will be affected by each alternative.

Recap Macroeconomic policy is the branch of economic policy whose primary focus is on the economy's performance as measured by such macroeconomic variables as the level of output, the rate of growth, and the price level. The macroeconomic policy-maker must also remember distributional and microeconomic objectives, although they are secondary. The primary aim of macroeconomic policy is usually the composite objective of full employment and growth without inflation. The real choice, however, is between more or less employment plus growth, coupled with more or less inflation.

Capsule Supplement 29.1   **Balance of Payments Problems: A Preview**

In Chapter 35 we shall take up the policy problems posed by the existence of economic relationships with other countries and the implications of these problems on the internal operations of the domestic economy. Because we should be aware of these problems, even at this stage, our present purpose is to briefly preview them.

A nation's balance of payments reflects the net effect of all payments made by residents to foreigners and of all receipts by residents from abroad. The most important of these are payments for goods imported and receipts for goods exported. A country can finance an excess of payments abroad over receipts from abroad only by lowering its existing stock of foreign currencies or gold. Obviously, such an excess (known as a *balance of payments deficit*) cannot be sustained indefinitely and must therefore be watched by policy-makers.

Generally speaking, expansionary policies at home will increase imports (because people will buy more imported goods as well as more domestic goods when their incomes rise) and reduce exports (because there is more domestic demand for the goods produced at home). Such policies will thus run the danger of increasing a balance of payments deficit, if one exists, or creating one if it does not. On the contrary, contractionary policy will tend to reduce a balance of payments deficit. The balance of payments situation, therefore, might be an important constraint on policy-makers. If the country is in recession and has a balance of payments deficit, a policy of internal expansion may not be feasible unless appropriate measures are taken to reduce the balance of payments deficit by means that do not simply counteract the initial expansionary effects themselves. One such policy is *currency devaluation,* changing the rate at which the domestic currency is exchanged for foreign currency.

Until we take up the international aspects of policy in Part 9, we shall assume that the balance of payments and other international problems do not constrain policy-makers in their choice among the instruments available for achieving domestic economic goals.

What Is "Full Employment"?

A discussion of the full employment concept

As was indicated in Chapter 22, the capacity output of the economy is not really a clearly defined level but a zone within which output can be contracted a little without laying off workers or expanded a little with the existing labor force.

In analyzing the operation of the economy, we have used the terms *capacity, potential,* and *full employment* interchangeably because we have been interested primarily in characterizing a *level of output.* When we discuss "full employment" as an objective of policy, we must be careful to distinguish between the two uses of the term. It may describe either:

1. the *capacity output* of the economy, or
2. some "ideal" degree to which the *labor force* is actually employed.

In practice, these two may not be the same. "Capacity output," as a working concept in policy decisions, will usually occur at a level at which not all workers are employed. In a dynamic market economy it is inevitable that there will be *some* unemployment not only at "capacity" but even in the zone beyond the nominal capacity level within which we would consider the economy to be "stretched."

One of the most important reasons for the existence of some unemployment, even though the economy may be considered to be operating at or beyond capacity, is hidden by the aggregation that underlies the macroeconomic approach.

Structural Unemployment

Although we may treat it as such in simple models, the labor force is not homogeneous. It consists of a variety of workers who possess a broad range of educational backgrounds and skills. It's quite possible to have a situation in which 1,000 electrical engineers cannot find work in their own field, while the building industry is short 1,000 plumbers. The 1,000 electrical engineers will become unemployment statistics, even though there are 1,000 unfilled vacancies elsewhere—and even if there are 10,000 unfilled vacancies elsewhere.

As the economy changes, labor force requirements in different geographical areas and industries change. People may lose their jobs in one location while there are unfilled vacancies (in their own skills) elsewhere. They may migrate to where the jobs are, but will appear on the unemployment rolls in the transition period. The type of unemployment in which people with certain skills or in certain geographical areas are unemployed even though there are unfilled vacancies elsewhere or in other occupations is commonly referred to as *structural unemployment*. The specific case of workers who have been "structurally displaced" but who are in the process of moving between jobs is known as *frictional unemployment*.

Some structural unemployment is inevitable in a dynamic economy like that of the United States, where the costs of flexibility in labor use fall primarily on labor. Its effects on the individual can be alleviated by unemployment benefits (shifting some of the costs to society) or separation pay (shifting some of the costs to firms). But structural unemployment can only be reduced by programs that help "fit" the unemployed to the unfilled vacancies, like training and retraining, subsidizing interregional migration, and eliminating trade-union entry barriers.

General Unemployment

Our primary interest here is with *general unemployment,* that is, unemployment related to below-capacity operation of the economy. This brings us back to the problem we faced at the beginning of the chapter—defining "full employment."

One proposed definition is that full employment exists when the number of unfilled vacancies in the economy is equal to the number of persons unemployed. Despite its surface plausibility, this is just as arbitrary a definition as any other. The practical problem is that information on unfilled vacancies is quite poor compared with information on unemployment. Ultimately, we can probably do no better than to consider full employment as the unemployment rate that from past experience appears to be consistent with the level of frictional unemployment that is simply unavoidable, even at "full capacity." Most economists put this "full employment" rate at around 4 percent for the United States.

General unemployment implies that there are unemployed workers who have skills that would be in demand if the economy were operating at capacity. Thus, in the most straightforward sense, general unemployment implies the existence of unused resources and suggests that the economy is not on its production possibility frontier. Therefore, unemployment is unambiguously *bad* in the sense that there would be more output, and hence more goods for everyone if the economy were to move to full employment.

The same argument, of course, could be used with reference to unused capital equipment or unused land. It's the *social* consequences of the unemployment of people that leads to our emphasis on this aspect of general underutilization. If jobs are available, even those whose incomes derive from property can sell their personal services if their property incomes fail. The sale of personal services is thus the ultimate source of income of everyone and the *only* substantial source of income of all but a very few.

Distributional Effects

Moderate unemployment of the kind associated with recessions in the United States since 1944 (5 to 9 percent) distributes much of the burden of a fairly small change in the economy onto a small group, the unemployed. In real economic disasters, like the depression of the thirties, property owners are severely affected and distribution shifts away from property owners and the unemployed to those fortunate enough to remain employed. Indeed, while total wages in the United States fell by 42 percent from 1929 to 1933, other incomes fell by almost 70 percent.

Unemployment hits the economically weakest workers the hardest because the first to become unemployed are usually the unskilled (who are the poorest), the young (who may be denied work experience that would bring them lifetime benefits), and the old (who find it hardest to obtain new jobs even if unemployment eases). Relatively well-off skilled workers between twenty-five and forty-five are more likely to retain their jobs. Thus, unemployment causes many social inequities.

To revert to the question we have sought to answer in this section, we can state:

"Full employment" as a macroeconomic objective does not necessarily (or usually) mean zero unemployment, rather it is the level of unemployment that is structurally associated with capacity output.

Recap For a variety of reasons, the economy may be considered to be fully employed even though unemployment is not zero. Because labor is not homogeneous, one sector of the economy may be at capacity with unfilled vacancies for one type of labor, while labor of another kind remains unemployed. For the United States, "full employment" is conventionally taken to correspond to 4 percent unemployment.

Growth as an Objective

The place of the growth rate among macroeconomic objectives

Growth normally plays a minor role among the primary objectives of macroeconomic policy in the United States, being dominated by the goals of full employment and minimal inflation. The reasons are straightforward enough: the United States is already one of the richest countries in the world, and its economy, as presently structured, typically exhibits a growth in capacity output of more than 4 percent in an average year of full employment, a rate some ecologists would consider too high already. Real output fails to grow in step with capacity only when the full employment objective is not achieved, and capacity output generally fails to show growth only under conditions of deep recession.

Thus, in the United States, growth is essentially subordinate to full employment. If full employment is attained, the resulting growth rate is usually considered acceptable. For many other countries, however, growth is a very important objective. Britain, for example, which has grown slowly in recent years, possesses an outdated industrial structure, which could be revamped more rapidly if the rate of growth were greater. Then there are the poorer countries for which growth is necessary to attain an acceptable living standard, not just a second (or third) car in every garage.

Possible Conflicts

There is no conflict between full employment and rapid growth in the poorer countries because full employment is a prerequisite for rapid growth just as in the United States. The emphasis on growth as such, however, may influence the choice of policy instruments with which to achieve full employment, increased investment being more desirable than increased consumption.

More importantly, for a country whose major objective is growth, any balancing of full employment against inflation becomes a balancing of full employment *plus growth* against inflation. The case against accepting inflation is necessarily weakened, and a country seeking rapid growth is more likely to accept policies that carry a high risk of inflation than is a country for which growth is a subordinate objective.

Putting potential conflicts between the objectives of growth and minimal inflation aside, the major conflicts between rapid growth and other objectives are outside the general sphere of macro policy. For example, a high rate of growth is likely to be in conflict with distributional objectives because an increased level of saving (necessary for increased growth) can be more easily obtained by making the income distribution more unequal— especially by increasing the share of profits in national income. Other arguments against high rates of growth were discussed in Chapter 24.

Some types of investment, such as housing, may have a high social priority but lead to little growth in future GNP. A policy concerned primarily with high growth will shift investment away from projects of this kind into such others as industrial plant and equipment.

In our further discussions of macroeconomic policy, we shall take an "American" approach, treating growth as subordinate to full employment.

Recap The rate of growth will be higher when the economy operates near capacity than when it is in recession. For a country like the United States, the growth objective therefore tends to be linked with, but is subordinate to, the full employment objective.

Full Employment Without Inflation?

The policy choice between different combinations of employment and inflation

The ultimate question in macroeconomic policy is whether it is really possible to achieve what can legitimately be called "full employment" in an economy with a large private sector without having inflation.

Output does not consist of a single good, but is an aggregate of many individual goods, each of which is produced in its own industry with different input requirements and capacity levels. Even with unemployment of, say, 5 or 6 percent, some industries may already be operating at plant capacity. Furthermore, because labor is not homogeneous, specific types of skilled labor may be in short supply even though unemployment exists for workers in other occupations.

Thus, excess demand will be apparent in some markets *before* true full employment is reached. This excess demand will generate an upward movement in certain prices and will tend to increase planned investment in those industries already operating at capacity. Hence, a self-generating inflationary process may be in operation before full employment is reached.

The Problem Zone

There is, therefore, a zone close to the full employment level in which further reduction in unemployment is coupled with an increasing probability of inflation or with an increasing rate of existing inflation. Many economists argue that true full employment without inflation is simply impossible, that the choice is between different levels of unemployment associated with different rates of inflation. Thus, we can choose a little less unemployment if and only if we are willing to accept a little more inflation. The level of unemployment at which there is *no* real likelihood of inflation is thus higher than would generally be accepted as "full employment," at least in those economies for which empirical investigation of this relationship has been carried out. For the United States it seems to be around 7 to 8 percent.

The quantitative evidence of the relationship between unemployment and inflationary influences is based on the *Phillips curve* (discussed in Chapter 22), which relates rates of unemployment and rates of wage change for historically observed data.

The same name has been given to related, but different, curves drawn to show the relationship between the rate of unemployment and the rate of price increase. Such a *modified Phillips curve* is presented in Figure 29.1, which illustrates the historical relationship between unemployment and the rate of price increase in the United States for the period 1956 to 1977, with a free-hand curve drawn to approximate the best fit for the pre-1970 period. The curve has the general shape of the original Phillips curve.

Taken at face value, the data shown in the figure suggest that the rate of inflation increases rapidly as unemployment declines. More sophisticated investigations of this relationship exist than can be summarized in a simple diagram. For a zero rate of price increase, the evidence is unreliable because of the relative lack of historical instances, but extrapolation shows associated unemployment rates of 7 percent or higher.

Historical data can only show that the economy *has not succeeded* in combining low unemployment with zero inflation, not that it *cannot* do so. Unfortunately, economists have offered no evidence that they know how to break with this historical precedent.

Policy Possibilities

If we accept a Phillips-type curve as firm evidence about possibilities, we can regard it as a *policy possibility curve.* Economic policy, or at least economic policy as currently known, can then potentially achieve a point on the curve of Figure 29.1, for example, but not a point to the left of it. The policy-makers must then *choose* the most acceptable combination possible—some will choose less unemployment with more inflation, others more unemployment with less inflation. Note that in some years (the period from 1973 to 1977, for example) the economy does not even come close to attaining its previous "Phillips" combinations.

Whether or not a particular quantitative relationship is accepted, there is little doubt that low unemployment carries with it a high probability of, or even certainty of, inflation. The most desirable policy objective would be to *shift* the Phillips curve so a lower level of unemployment is consistent with a given rate of inflation. This, unfortunately, is something economists have not yet discovered how to do. In principle it ought to be possible, but we do not yet have a sufficiently clear analysis of the detailed behavior of the economy in the zone near true full employment.

Full employment with zero inflation, ideal policy objective that it is, is not yet a feasible target. There is simply a choice between being nearer to full employment with higher inflation or inflationary pressure, or being further from full employment with less inflationary pressure. The ultimate policy-maker has to decide where in the range (from 4 percent unemploy-

Figure 29.1

The relationship between the level of inflation and the level of unemployment in the United States, 1954–77.

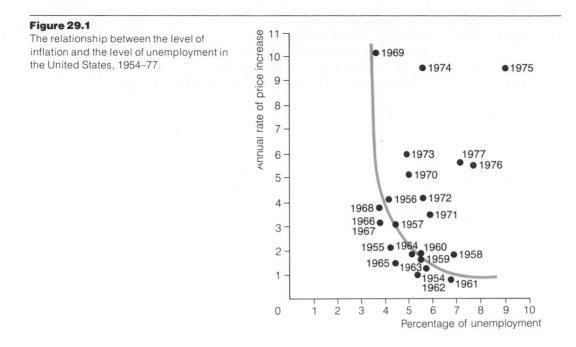

ment, which is effectively zero, to, say, 8 percent) the economy is to operate, balancing the consequences of *some* unemployment against the consequences of *some* inflation.

Recap Although full employment without inflation would be a desirable objective, we do not know how to bring it about. The real choice is between higher unemployment and less inflation, or lower unemployment and more inflation, the attainable combinations being given by a policy possibility curve. A main aim of policy research is to learn how to shift this curve to give more desirable combinations.

The Instruments of Macroeconomic Policy

A brief description of the instruments available for carrying out macroeconomic policy

Macroeconomic policy involves the manipulation of the relationships between capacity output and planned expenditure or, equivalently, between capacity output, planned withdrawals, and planned injections. It attempts to achieve a level of actual real output as close to the capacity level as policy-makers consider desirable, given their view of the trade-off between unemployment and the risk of inflation. It also involves corrective measures, based on the same kind of manipulations, when output strays from its desired level or unacceptable inflation becomes apparent.

Two major sets of instruments for affecting policy are available to the government:

1. Its power to tax and its control of an important slice of the total expenditure of the economy. All policy instruments that are related to the government's control of revenue and expenditure, and appear typically (but not invariably) in the government *budget,* are known collectively as *fiscal policy.* This term is derived from an old word (''fisc'') meaning purse.

2. Its power, exercised directly or indirectly, over the quantity of money and certain other financial assets such as government securities. The instruments related to the government's power as the ultimate monetary authority are known collectively as *monetary policy.*

Figure 29.2 illustrates the relationship of these policies.

It should be made clear at the outset that monetary and fiscal policies represent not two different policies with two different objectives but *two different sets of instruments* for carrying out macroeconomic policy in general. They represent alternative means, not different ends. In principle, macroeconomic policy can be carried out by a broad spectrum of fiscal-monetary combinations that vary from primary emphasis on fiscal methods at one end to primary emphasis on monetary methods at the other. In a recession, for example, the government might lower interest rates (generally regarded as an act of monetary policy), increase the budget deficit (fiscal policy), or lower interest rates *and* run a deficit (a mixture of monetary and fiscal policy). Because typical fiscal and monetary policies affect the economy somewhat differently (even when aimed at the same primary target), the results will vary with the particular mix of monetary and fiscal policies chosen. Theoretically, it is possible to choose an *optimal mix* of monetary and fiscal policies for each set of circumstances.

Direct and Indirect Policies

From an analytical point of view, we can divide the instruments of macroeconomic policy somewhat differently.

1. *Direct injection-withdrawal techniques.* If the government increases its own expenditures, it makes a *direct* injection into the income-consumption loop. Similarly, if it increases total tax revenues, it makes a *direct* withdrawal.

2. *Indirect injection-withdrawal techniques.* If the government manipulates the tax structure to encourage investment (by reducing taxes for firms that invest, for example), it is *inducing* an injection in the form of increased investment expenditure rather than making it directly. Similarly, if it redistributes income (say by increasing tax rates on high incomes and reducing

Figure 29.2
How different types of policy operate on different flows within the economy.

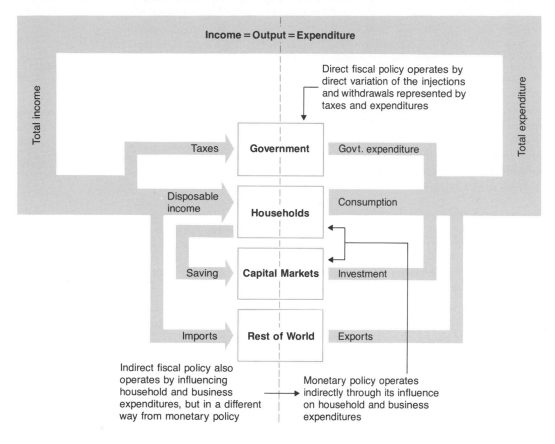

Income = Output = Expenditure

Total income

Direct fiscal policy operates by direct variation of the injections and withdrawals represented by taxes and expenditures

Taxes **Government** Govt. expenditure

Disposable income **Households** Consumption

Saving **Capital Markets** Investment

Imports **Rest of World** Exports

Total expenditure

Indirect fiscal policy also operates by influencing household and business expenditures, but in a different way from monetary policy

Monetary policy operates indirectly through its influence on household and business expenditures

them on low incomes) so as to increase the economy's overall propensity to consume, it is inducing a reduction in withdrawals (less saving). All monetary techniques operate indirectly, either by changing interest rates and thereby inducing changes in investment expenditure, or by changing money balances and inducing changes in consumption expenditures. Indirect techniques rely on inducing firms or consumers to spend or save more. Consequently, these results are less certain and less controllable—especially the size of their effects—than direct techniques.

This classification cuts across the traditional division between fiscal and monetary policy. Although monetary policy is *indirect,* fiscal policy may be *direct or indirect.* From a structural point of view, indirect fiscal policies have more in common with monetary policy than with direct fiscal policy.

Recap The main instruments of macroeconomic policy are those that result from the government's use of its budget (fiscal policy) and from its use of monetary powers (monetary policy). These are different sets of instruments, not different policies. We can also separate direct techniques (direct withdrawals and injections by the government) from indirect techniques (inducements for firms or households to vary their withdrawals and injections).

Capsule Supplement 29.2 **The American Budget Process**

Each January, the president of the United States presents to the Congress his budget for the fiscal year commencing the following July. Due to the complexities of the congressional system, however, this budget represents little more than fiscal fantasizing by the administration. Many months will pass before the fiscal realities of the budget year (which may have already started by then) are settled. How envious economic policy-makers in the United States must be of the British Chancellor of the Exchequer who presents his budget at 4:00 P.M. on the Budget Day, has key legislation passed by both houses of Parliament during the evening, and declares new taxes and other policies effective as of the opening of the next day's business.

The budgeting process in the United States is the most protracted of any major country. Formulating each annual budget begins many months prior to January with preliminary estimates by the smaller governmental units that are approved, disapproved, or modified at successive stages of assembly by larger units. The recommendations of larger units are then compiled by the Budget Bureau into final form, which involves presidential decision. The overall fiscal impact is not considered until the final stages—usually the weekend before presentation to Congress.

Although it may seem unbelievable, Congress never considers the administration's fiscal policy as a whole nor does it vote on the budget as a whole. The budget presented to Congress is immediately split up into individual parts—appropriations for the various agencies and departments, and proposed methods of raising revenue, each of which is the subject of detailed hearings and debates before both the House and Senate. Decisions on each piece of the budget are made independently and with no reference to the budget as a whole by various congressional committees. Defense appropriations are scrutinized by the Armed Services Committee of both chambers, and education appropriations by the Education and Labor Committee of the House and the Labor and Public Welfare Committee of the Senate. But at no time is there any formal consideration of whether the country would be better off by a transfer of resources from defense to education or vice versa.

Alternative means of achieving the same goals will also be separated instead of considered together. Support of some industry by tax advantages would go to Ways and Means (House) and Finance (Senate), the same support by special loan programs would go to Banking and Currency, while support by direct subsidy would go to Interstate and Foreign Commerce (House) and Commerce (Senate).

The net result is that Congress has enormous control over the details of the budget, but no real control over its fiscal impact. The administration may find its broad fiscal plan destroyed by the combined result of the many changes in appropriations and revenue provisions made by the many different committees and voted on piecemeal in both chambers. We might characterize fiscal policy in the United States as being the outcome of a random process that may bear little relationship to the formal budget. Not only does the budget implementation process take six months longer than in most European countries, but the outcome is uncertain. Thus, the initial budget loses one of its most important potential strengths as a policy instrument—its believability as a statement about what will actually occur within the economy.

Exercises

1. There are only two kinds of labor in the economy, plumbers and carpenters, and it is impossible to move from one category to another without several years of retraining. Suppose there are 1,000 unemployed carpenters and 1,000 unemployed plumbers, and each increase of $1 million in GNP causes an increase of 75 in the demand for carpenters and 25 in the demand for plumbers. By how much must GNP be increased to remove all unemployment?

2. If GNP were increased to the level required for question 1, would you anticipate inflationary pressure and, if so, from what source?

3. Take the data in question 1 and assume that "full employment" means that the number of unfilled vacancies (without reference to type of labor) must be as great as the number unemployed (again without reference to type of labor). What increase in GNP will be needed to bring the economy to this level?

4. Will there be inflationary pressure under the conditions in question 3?

For Thought and Discussion

1. If the attainable possibilities for the economy were truly represented by the curve in Figure 29.1, what point on the curve would you aim for?

2. If there are many vacancies for unskilled labor but unemployed electrical engineers, should the engineers be induced (by withholding unemployment benefits, for example) to take the unskilled jobs? Why or why not?

3. Is it dishonest to refer to 4 percent unemployment as "full employment"?

4. The government increases its expenditures by $1 million, paying for this by printing new currency. Is this fiscal policy, monetary policy, or both?

5. A government that spends $1 million clearly spends it on something in particular. If it expands the money supply, it does not directly control where the increased private expenditure goes. Does this mean that monetary policy causes less "interference" in the economy than fiscal policy?

Chapter 30
Fiscal Policy

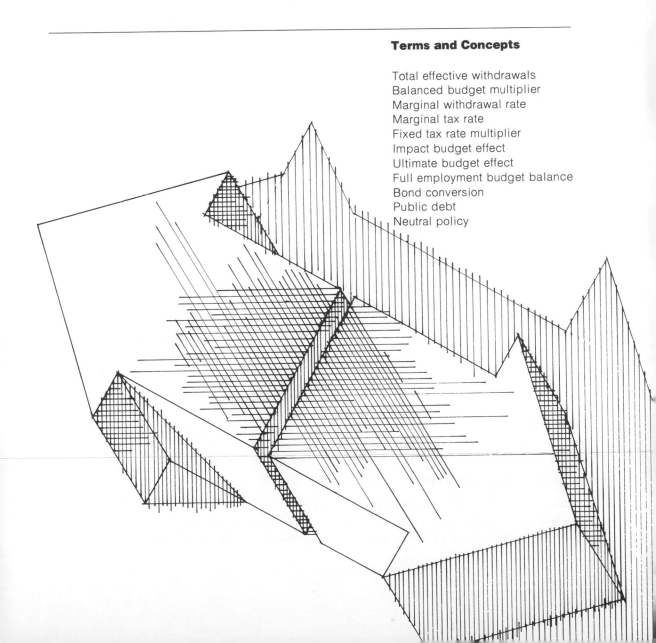

| **Direct** | **The basic principles** |
| **Fiscal Policy** | **of direct fiscal policy** |

The effects of direct fiscal policy—changes in taxes and government expenditures—can be determined by applying the income-expenditure analysis described in Chapters 21 and 22.

Government expenditure represents an *injection* into the income-consumption loop, while taxation represents a *withdrawal* from it. If the policy objective is a desired level of real output, and planned injections and withdrawals from other sectors of the economy are known, the government can determine the level of injections and withdrawals it must make itself in order to attain the objective.

Effects of Taxes on Saving

It is safe to assume that government expenditures will not affect other injections in the economy; however, we cannot assume that taxes will not affect other withdrawals. On the contrary, increased taxes will normally *lower* other withdrawals because they will lead to lower saving from any given level of income. Households base their consumption and saving decisions on their *disposable* income (income after taxes), so higher taxes lead to lower disposable incomes and to lower saving, as well as lower consumption expenditures. Thus, because of the offsetting effect of the change in saving, the change in *total effective withdrawals* will be *less* than the initial tax change alone, as Figure 30.1 shows.

Let's take a simple example. Suppose households consume 80 percent of their disposable income, thus saving 20 percent. Now consider the effect of a $100 million tax increase. Because disposable incomes will fall by $100 million, saving will decline by the amount *that would have been saved* out of $100 million if left in the hands of the households—that is, by $20 million. Total withdrawals will increase by only $80 million, the $100 million increase in taxes *less* the $20 million reduction in saving.

Similarly, if taxes were *cut* by $100 million, disposable incomes would increase by that amount. But consumers would save $20 million out of their increased disposable incomes so total withdrawals would be *reduced* by $80 million ($100 million less $20 million), not the full $100 million represented by the tax cut.

The Net Policy Effect

Although government expenditures *may* sometimes affect other injections such as investment, there is nothing direct or essential about such effects, nor will they necessarily be in any one particular direction even if they

Figure 30.1

The effects of a tax change on the economy.

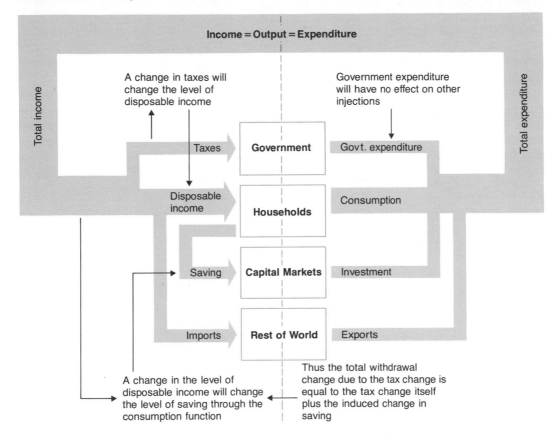

occur. We can therefore assume that government expenditures are generally independent of, and thus have no effect on, other injections.

The *net* effect on the economy of a simultaneous change in both government expenditure and taxes will correspond to the combined effects of the *government expenditure* itself and the *total withdrawals* associated with the tax change. Note that the effect on the government's budget is the combined effect of the change in expenditure and the *actual change in taxes,* not the total withdrawals resulting from the tax change.

For the example already given, with a propensity to consume of 80 percent, an increase of $100 million in *both* government expenditures and taxes would leave the budget balanced (assuming that it was balanced originally). Injections would increase by $100 million (government expenditures) while total withdrawals would increase by only $80 million (the tax less the change in saving). For the economy as a whole, injections would exceed withdrawals, and there would be *upward pressure* on the economy even though the government budget would remain in balance.

Because most economies formulate taxes as *rates relative to income* rather than as lump sums, we shall defer a detailed discussion of tax effects to the next section and concentrate on expenditure effects only, assuming tax revenues to be fixed.

An Example

The general principles of operating direct fiscal policy through expenditures can be illustrated using the simplest Keynesian model. Suppose the consumption function is such that households spend 80 percent of their disposable (after-tax) income at all income levels. The average and marginal propensities to consume are thus equal to 0.8.

Assume also that government tax revenue is fixed at $100 billion. At each level of total income (= total output), we can compute total withdrawals. These will be $100 billion (the tax) *plus* 20 percent of income less tax (household saving). Table 30.1 shows withdrawals for various levels of total output.

For the economy represented by the data in Table 30.1, the equilibrium level of output will be the level at which total injections and total withdrawals are equal. To determine this level of output, find the total withdrawal figure in column 5 that corresponds to total planned injections. Then locate the associated output level in column 1. Or, working in reverse, once we find the desired output level, the corresponding level of total withdrawals given in column 5 is the amount of total injections needed. To achieve a desired output level of $600 billion, for example, we would need total injections of $200 billion.

Direct fiscal policy in this simple model consists of the following steps:

1. Choosing the desired output level.
2. Determining the planned injections from sources other than the government, basically private investment.
3. Fixing the level of government expenditure so total injections (government expenditure plus investment) are at the level appropriate to the target output.

Suppose the target output level, chosen after considering the various policy options among different employment levels and different inflation risks, is $900 billion. To sustain output at this level, total injections of $260 billion are needed. If planned private investment is $200 billion, govern-

Table 30.1
Relationship of Withdrawals to Output
with Fixed Tax Revenue of $100 billion.
(Billions of dollars)
(APC = MPC = 0.8)

(1) Total output = Total (national) income	(2) Disposable income (1) − tax	(3) Household saving 20% of (2)	(4) Household consumption	(5) Total withdrawals (3) + tax
400	300	60	240	160
500	400	80	320	180
600	500	100	400	200
700	600	120	480	220
800	700	140	560	240
900	800	160	640	260

ment expenditure must be $60 billion. If planned private investment is only $150 billion, government expenditure must be increased to $110 billion. Note that the government will run a budget surplus ($40 billion) in the first case and a budget deficit ($10 billion) in the second because revenue is assumed to remain fixed at $100 billion.

General Rules

It is not difficult to formulate general rules that relate budget surpluses and deficits to the expansion and contraction of the economy. Changing a budget that is initially in balance in an economy that is initially in equilibrium has these effects:

1. *A change to a budget deficit is always expansionary if expenditures and taxes both increase.* Because the increase in total withdrawals associated with an increase in taxes is always less than the increase in taxes, and because a deficit requires that the increase in expenditures exceed the increase in taxes, the resulting increase in total injections will necessarily exceed the increase in total withdrawals, and upward pressure will result.

2. *A change to a budget deficit is generally expansionary if expenditures and taxes both decrease; but may be mildly contractionary if the deficit is sufficiently small.* If the deficit is achieved by reducing taxes by only slightly more than expenditures, the reduction in total injections may exceed the reduction in total withdrawals because the reduction in withdrawals (by virtue of the effect on saving) is necessarily less than the reduction in taxes alone. In this case, the resulting deficit will be mildly contractionary. If the deficit is sufficiently large, however, the reduction in total withdrawals will

exceed the reduction in expenditures, and the effect will be expansionary.

3. *A change to a budget surplus is always contractionary if expenditures and taxes both decrease.* Because the reduction in total withdrawals associated with a reduction in taxes is always less than the reduction in taxes, and because a surplus requires that the reduction in expenditures exceed the reduction in taxes, the resulting reduction in total injections will necessarily exceed the reduction in total withdrawals, and downward pressure will result.

4. *A change to a budget surplus is generally contractionary if expenditures and taxes both increase, but may be mildly expansionary if the surplus is sufficiently small.* If the surplus is achieved by increasing taxes by only slightly more than expenditures, the increase in total injections may exceed the increase in total withdrawals as the increase in withdrawals (by virtue of the effect on saving) is necessarily less than the increase in taxes alone. In this case, the resulting surplus will be mildly expansionary. If the surplus is sufficiently large, however, the increase in total withdrawals will exceed the increase in expenditures, and the effect will be contractionary.

5. *A balanced budget change is mildly expansionary if expenditures and taxes both increase, and mildly contractionary if they both decrease.* If expenditures and taxes increase by the same amount (maintaining budget balance), total withdrawals rise by less than the increase in taxes. Because there is an excess of total injections over total withdrawals, the effect is expansionary. The equivalent argument, in the reverse direction, holds for a uniform reduction in expenditures and taxes.

The Balanced Budget Multiplier

We can work out the exact effect of a balanced budget change quite easily. If taxes and injections both rise by $1 million, the excess of injections over withdrawals is equal to the amount that would be saved from a $1 million increase in income. This excess is wiped out when income does, in fact, increase by $1 million, and thus the new equilibrium income is $1 million higher than before.

If the budget is kept in balance, GNP will rise or fall by the same amount that government expenditures and taxes (which are equal) rise or fall. Because this relationship holds for all values of the marginal propensity to consume, we can conclude that the value of the balanced budget multiplier is unity.

Recap Direct fiscal policy is fundamentally based on the fact that government expenditures are injections and taxes are withdrawals. On the withdrawal side, however, we must note that a change in taxes will affect disposable income and thus the level of saving. Because of this effect on saving, the change in total withdrawals that results from a change in taxes is necessarily less than the change in actual tax revenues. A budget deficit (excess of expenditure over tax revenue) is generally expansionary, while a budget surplus is generally contractionary.

Fixed Tax Rates

The analysis of fiscal policy when tax revenues vary directly with income

Most real economies levy taxes at fixed rates on the level of sales or income. Consequently, tax revenues automatically increase when the economy expands and decrease when it contracts. When a government announces plans to increase expenditures without increasing taxes, it usually means that it does not plan to increase tax *rates*. An increase in expenditure with no increase in *total* taxes would imply a reduction in tax rates that would surely be announced by any red-blooded politician as a *cut* in taxes.

To discuss fiscal policy in a reasonably realistic setting, we need to examine the effects of varying government expenditure when tax rates, rather than tax revenues, remain fixed. We shall confine our discussion to income taxes and assume a constant marginal tax rate, that is, a rate such that the proportion of each additional dollar of income paid in taxes remains the same at all income levels.

The general effect of levying taxes at a constant marginal rate is not difficult to assess. Any increase in injections that causes incomes to rise will automatically cause an increase in withdrawals (in the form of income taxes), so the increase in injections less withdrawals will be less than if total tax revenues were fixed. Thus, having taxes fixed as rates rather than as totals necessarily reduces the expansionary power of a dollar of expenditure. The contractionary power of a dollar cut in expenditure will be reduced in a similar way as withdrawals will fall with income.

A Numerical Example

Suppose the marginal propensity to consume out of disposable income is 0.8, and that the marginal tax rate is 0.25. Out of an increase of $100 in income, $25 will go to additional income-tax payments, so disposable income will rise by only $75. Consumption expenditure will rise by 80 percent of the rise in disposable income, that is, by $60 (= 0.8 × $75) in this case. The remainder of disposable income ($15) will be saved.

Thus, a $100 increase in total income generates a $60 increase in consumption expenditure. Stated differently, a $100 increase in total income generates a $40 increase in total withdrawals—$15 in saving and $25 in taxes.

In terms of income-expenditure analysis, the result is exactly the same *as if* the marginal propensity to consume were only 0.6 instead of 0.8, or the marginal propensity to save were 0.4 instead of 0.2. The multiplier is 2.5 (= 1/(1 − 0.6) instead of 5, as it would be with the same consumption function and fixed tax revenue.

It is convenient to think in terms of the *marginal withdrawal rate* (*MWR*), which specifies the increase in total withdrawals associated with an increase in national (not disposable) income. This clearly depends on both the *marginal tax rate* (*MTR*) and the *marginal propensity to save* (*MPS*).

Algebraic Relationships

We can calculate the relationships as follows:

1. Each additional dollar of *national* income increases
   a. taxes by an amount equal to $$MTR$,
   b. disposable income by the remainder, $(1 - MTR)$.
2. Each additional dollar of *disposable* income increases saving by an amount equal to $$MPS$.
3. An increase in disposable income of $(1 - MTR)$ will thus increase saving by an amount equal to $$MPS \times \$(1 - MTR)$.
4. The increase in total withdrawals is equal to the increase in taxes *plus* the increase in saving.

Because the increase in total withdrawals per additional dollar of income is *MWR,* we have

$$MWR = \underset{\substack{\text{(increase} \\ \text{in taxes)}}}{MTR} + \underset{\substack{\text{(increase in} \\ \text{saving)}}}{MPS \times (1 - MTR)}.$$

Because *MTR* lies between 0 and 1, $(1 - MTR)$ is positive. Thus the term $MPS \times (1 - MTR)$ is positive. It follows that *MWR* is greater than *MTR.*
   This relationship can be rearranged to give

$$MWR = MPS + MTR \times (1 - MPS).$$

Because *MPS* is less than unity, the term $MTR \times (1 - MPS)$ is positive. Thus, *MWR* is necessarily greater then *MPS,* so *MWR* is greater than *both* *MTR* and *MPS.*
   For the numerical example given, we have $MTR = 0.25$, $(1 - MTR) = 0.75$, $MPS = 0.2$, and $MPS \times (1 - MTR) = 0.2 \times 0.75 = 0.15$. Thus,

$$MWR = 0.25 \text{ (increase in taxes)} + 0.15 \text{ (increase in saving)} = 0.4.$$

Note that a fixed tax revenue would be equivalent to having a zero marginal tax rate. Given $MTR = 0$, the equations above would give $MWR = MPS$, and the only withdrawal affected by income would be the level of saving.

The Multiplier with Fixed Tax Rates

Because each dollar of increased income generates $$MWR$ in increased withdrawals, we need $$MWR$ in increased injections to produce $1 in increased income. The *fixed tax rate multiplier* is the ratio of the increased income to the injection needed to generate it, and is $1/MWR$, or 2.5 (= 1/0.4) in the numerical example given previously.

The multiplier associated with a fixed tax rate has a *smaller* value than the simple multiplier associated with a fixed level of tax revenue. The fixed tax revenue multiplier is equal to $1/MPS$ because saving is the only withdrawal that changes with income. The fixed tax rate multiplier is equal to $1/MWR$, MWR being greater than MPS. Note that, in the numerical example above, the multiplier is *halved* compared with its value for fixed revenue, even though the marginal tax rate is only 0.25.

The increase in *tax revenue* is MTR times the increase in national income. Each dollar increase in government expenditure generates an increase in national income given by the multiplier, that is, by $\$1/MWR$. Thus, the increase in tax revenue that results from a $\$1$ increase in government expenditure is $MTR \times (\$1/MWR) = \$MTR/MWR$. Because MWR is always greater than MTR, the last amount is necessarily *less* than $\$1$. In our numerical example, it's $\$0.25/0.4$ or 62.5 cents.

Therefore, as might be expected, the increase in tax revenue is always less than the increase in expenditure if expenditure increases while tax rates are kept constant. If the government's budget were initially balanced, it would have a deficit after the expenditure increase.

If government expenditure is *reduced* with a fixed tax rate, this same analysis holds, but in reverse. Because disposable income will be reduced by less than national income, the downward multiplier will be reduced the same way as the upward multiplier. Tax revenues will fall, but by less than the reduction in expenditure. If the budget were initially balanced, it would move into a surplus.

Note that the multiplier with a constant tax rate applies to changes in *investment* or any *other injection*, as well as to changes in government expenditure.

Recap In modern economies, taxes are set in terms of tax rates—as percentages of incomes or sales. This necessitates a modification of such basic income-expenditure relationships as the multiplier. An increase in injections that causes a rise in incomes will increase taxes, and thus withdrawals. Multiplier effects, given taxes that vary with income level, will be less than would be predicted from the consumption function alone. They will depend on both the marginal propensity to consume and the marginal tax rate.

Capsule Supplement 30.1   **Taxes**

In laying the foundations of fiscal policy, we have not discussed taxes much, except to state that they can reasonably be assumed to vary directly with income. This does not mean that our analysis is necessarily confined to income taxes *per se* because there are many other types of taxes (sales taxes, for example) for which total payments rise and fall with income.

Not all taxes depend on income, at least in the short run. Property and estate taxes, for example, depend on the stock of wealth rather than on the current level of income—although a prolonged recession may reduce wealth as well as income and eventually lead to a reduction in receipts from these taxes. Taxes based on wealth accounted for approximately 15 percent of total federal, state, and local tax receipts in 1977. They were especially important in state and local government for which they represented more than 40 percent of tax receipts.

In the United States and other federal systems, fiscal policy is the responsibility of the federal government, rather than local and state governments, so we are primarily interested in federal taxes. At the federal level, income-type taxes account for between 85 and 90 percent of U.S. tax revenue. Consequently, the model of fiscal policy based on income-type taxes is a reasonable representation of reality. These income-related taxes are of three main types: the individual income tax, the corporate income tax, and Social Security contributions. Although called "contributions" and having some relationship to potential future benefits, Social Security contributions have the same fiscal effects as income taxes and should be treated as such.

Sales and excise taxes are related to *expenditure* rather than income. Their totals move up and down with income because expenditure moves up and down with income, but their detailed effects are somewhat different from the effects of a true income tax. An income tax must be paid regardless of how the income is used, but a sales tax can be avoided simply by not spending income. In other words, income taxes fall on both consumption and saving, while sales taxes fall only on consumption. Thus, although an increase in income taxes will lead to total withdrawals that are *less* than the tax because saving is reduced, sales taxes may lead to withdrawals *greater* than the tax because saving may increase (although this is only a possibility). The differences in effects between these different types of taxes can be neglected in discussing broad principles of policy, but they must be taken into account in actual policy decisions.

Different taxes will affect the distribution of income in different ways, and equivalent fiscal effects can be associated with widely different distributional effects. This is another example of the important proposition that economic policy is many-sided and policy-makers must consider their package of policies as a whole at some stage.

Taxes may be levied on the basis of almost any criterion, provided it is objectively measurable. It must also satisfy the old canon of taxation (constitutionally established in the United States) that equal taxes should be paid by those in "equal" situations. Nevertheless, income taxes predominate in the United States. After World War I they became the most important source of federal revenue, and in recent years they have become an important source of state and local revenue, growing rapidly in their relative importance.

Not all countries rely so heavily on income taxes. This stems from a variety of reasons, many of which are related to problems of collection. An important source of revenue in Europe, for example, is the *value added* tax. This is similar to a sales tax but, unlike an ordinary sales tax, is paid on raw materials and intermediate goods, as well as on final products. Manufacturers pay a sales tax on everything they buy and collect it on everything they sell. They pay the government the excess of their collections over their payments, which is equivalent to paying the tax on the difference between the value of what they sell and the value of the materials they have used—equivalent to a tax on the value added in production, hence the name. Such a tax is easily collected and has many desirable properties as a local or regional tax. Indeed, it may well turn up in the United States. A similar type of tax, called a *turnover tax*, is used in the Soviet Union.

Measuring the Budget Effect	Introducing the concept of the full employment budget

Measuring the Budget Effect

Introducing the concept of the full employment budget

The government *budget* (and as far as fiscal policy is concerned, we can confine ourselves to the budget of the central government) is a statement of the planned expenditures and anticipated receipts of the government for some future financial period—usually a twelve-month period commencing soon after the budget is made public. If the twelve-month period does not coincide with the regular calendar year, it is called a *fiscal year*. In the United States, the fiscal year runs from July 1 to June 30. The year starting on July 1, 1979 and ending June 30, 1980 is known as Fiscal 1980.

Budgets originated to keep governments honest, rather than to show the macroeconomic impact of their operations. The actual budgets of most central governments must be manipulated somewhat to bring them into a form that shows what economists want to know. We shall not worry about these detailed problems, but concern ourselves with the budget of a central government in the context of a simple macromodel.

Impact and Ultimate Effects

There are two different effects of fiscal policy, both of which need to be considered in preparing the budget:

1. The *impact effect* of the budget. Will the budget, when it first becomes operative, exert upward or downward pressure on the economy? We were looking at the impact effect earlier in the chapter when we discussed the general effects of budget surpluses and deficits.

2. The *ultimate effect* of the budget. If tax rates and government expenditures remain fixed, will the economy reach balance at full employment or below it, or will the budget run the economy into inflation?

The impact effect of the budget depends on the relationship between expenditures and total withdrawals *when the budget is introduced*. The ultimate effect depends on the relationship between expenditures and total withdrawals *after income has been changed by the budgeting policy*. Because tax revenues change with income, the two effects will differ.

An Example

Consider a situation in which tax rates are fixed at 25 percent of income, full employment income is $100 billion, and government expenditure of $20 billion will exactly bring about full employment equilibrium, given the consumption function and private investment plans.

At full employment, therefore, the appropriate fiscal policy would require government expenditure to be $20 billion, taxes would be $25 billion (25 percent of $100 billion), and the government would have a *surplus* of $5 billion.

Now, for whatever reason, suppose the economy is neither in equilibrium nor at full employment, and national income is only $80 billion. If the government budgeted expenditures of $20 billion, its immediate tax receipts would be only $20 billion (25 percent of $80 billion) and its budget would be in balance. If the economy were even more depressed, with an income of only $60 billion, the budget would be initially in *deficit* (by $5 billion) with expenditures of $20 billion, because taxes would be only $15 billion (25 percent of $60 billion).

We have three different budget results—a surplus, a balance, and a deficit—all associated with the *same expenditure* and the *same rate of tax,* each depending on the level of national income at the time of the budget. If sustained, each budget will bring the economy to full employment equilibrium from its existing level, and yield an ultimate budget surplus of $5 billion.

Let's look at this from another point of view. The economy is depressed with an income of only $60 billion instead of the $100 billion corresponding to full employment. Because we want an expansionary impact effect, a budget deficit would seem appropriate. As far as the impact effect itself is concerned, the larger the deficit, the greater the expansionary effect—but this gives us no guide to where the economy will finally settle. Will a deficit of $1 billion move us to full employment? $5 billion? $10 billion? All will move the economy upward, but to what level?

The Full Employment Budget Balance

The easiest way to find the answer is not to consider the deficit or surplus associated with each possible expenditure level under current circumstances, but to determine what the planned expenditure level would imply at full employment. We do this by calculating the *full employment surplus or deficit,* that is, the relationship between the planned expenditure level and the total tax revenue that would be obtained at full employment.

Whatever the present level of income, we know that a government expenditure of $20 billion will be sufficient to bring the economy to full employment under the assumed saving behavior and tax structure. Suppose the current level of income is only $60 billion. Tax revenues at this income level will be $15 billion, so if expenditures are raised to $20 billion to move the economy to full employment, there will be a current *deficit* of $5 billion. Nevertheless, if the expenditures are sustained and the economy reaches full employment, tax revenues will then be $25 billion, giving a surplus of $5 billion. In this case, $20 billion in expenditures would give a *current budget deficit* of $5 billion, but would ultimately lead to a *full employment surplus* of $5 billion because of the increased revenue at full employment.

If the economy started from an income level of only $40 billion, the current tax revenue would be only $10 billion. The government expenditure necessary to attain full employment would still be $20 billion and the tax revenues at full employment would still be $25 billion, as before. In this case, the expenditure needed to reach full employment would represent a current deficit of $10 billion, but would still ultimately lead to a full employment surplus of $5 billion. No matter what the initial position, the expenditure needed to attain full employment would always be $20 billion. This would always lead to a full employment surplus of $5 billion—the actual or current budget deficit or surplus depending on the initial level of income and the tax revenue at that level.

The ultimate effect of the budget can be found by calculating the full employment surplus or deficit. Given fixed tax rates, the full employment surplus or deficit for a given level of planned expenditure is the same, whatever the starting point.

The full employment surplus or deficit need not be that required to achieve a full employment equilibrium. We might, for example, wish to boost the economy rapidly from an income level of $60 billion by initially running a deficit of $15 billion, thus increasing the impact effect. If sustained to full employment, this budget would clearly be inflationary. By computing the surplus associated with full employment equilibrium, we would know this to be true and thus would plan to cut back on expenditure as the economy approaches full employment.

Note that the full employment budget idea does not presume that there should be a balanced budget at full employment. Whether there will be a full employment surplus, deficit, or balance depends entirely on planned private injections and withdrawals, and the relationship of these to what is required to sustain the target output.

Recap Because tax revenues vary with income, a budget containing a specific level of expenditures and fixed tax rates will show a balance that depends on the current level of national income. If the economy is depressed, tax revenues will be less and the budget will exhibit a greater deficit or a smaller surplus than the same expenditures and tax rates would yield at high employment levels. To compare budgets introduced in different states of the economy, it is useful to calculate the full employment budget balance—the surplus or deficit that the same expenditure and tax rates would give at full employment.

Financing Deficits

How governments can spend more than they receive in tax revenue

Direct fiscal policy implies flexible use of the budget. Sometimes the budget may show an actual surplus and sometimes an actual deficit. We now examine how a government can finance a deficit—when its expenditure is in excess of its revenue—and how it must handle a surplus.

The government obtains resources for its own use by both coercion and exchange. Because tax revenues represent the government's use of coercion, everything over and above these revenues must be obtained by exchange. Consequently, if expenditures exceed tax revenues, the government must cover the difference by exchange, that is, it must sell something to the public that has been produced without using resources from the public, and that the public is willing to buy.

There are two things the government can sell to the public that satisfy these requirements under all normal circumstances—*money* and *government bonds*. A government can finance a deficit with either one, or with a combination of them.

Financing with New Money

The government can "sell" money in the simple sense that it, or its agent, has control of the money supply and thus can increase the quantity of money. It can, for example, simply print new dollar bills and make payments with them, although there are more roundabout and subtle ways of increasing the money supply through the banking system. In any case, newly created money is just as good as existing money, and the government can use it (perhaps by a very circuitous route) to pay for the goods and services it buys from the private sector. Because expenditures paid for with new money do not require revenues, a deficit can be financed this way.

Of course, the public must be willing to *hold* the increased stock of money. If the stock is larger than the public wishes, people will attempt to reduce their balances by increasing expenditure. This introduces a new element into the situation. Financing a deficit by monetary expansion necessarily introduces an element of *monetary policy*. Such deficit financing is, in fact, a combination of fiscal *and* monetary policy. Thus, deficit financing is more expansionary than would be predicted from treating it as fiscal policy alone.

On the other hand, *some* proportion of a deficit *ought* to be financed by monetary expansion because an increased quantity of money will be required if output is rising—assuming there was monetary equilibrium at the original output level. Under the simplest "quantity theory" circumstances, a 10 percent increase in real output would require a 10 percent increase in the quantity of money if prices were to remain stable, interest rates constant, and the velocity of money circulation undisturbed.

Financing with Bonds

The government can also sell *bonds*—promises to pay annual interest of a certain amount and to repay the nominal value at some stated time in the future. Like money, bonds can be printed at will and sold to the public.

Although an individual or corporation can sell its "promises to pay" only to the extent that buyers consider them believable (and often only if they can exhibit sufficient real assets to cover repayment if necessary), the government is relatively unlimited in its ability to sell such promises. The government has the ultimate coercive power to levy taxes with which it can pay the interest on its bonds. Even a government can stretch the believability of its promises to the breaking point, of course, but we shall assume that ours is well within this limit.

Selling bonds to cover a deficit commits the government to pay interest on these bonds until redeemed. Generally speaking, this represents a commitment to pay interest indefinitely into the future. Although individual bonds are indeed redeemed when they come due, repayment is usually made by selling new bonds (a process called *conversion*)—often to the very same persons whose existing bonds have reached maturity. The *public debt* (the total face value of all bonds held by the public) rarely declines. Just as the expansion of incomes resulting from a deficit creates the demand for *some* new money, so the existence of a steady deficit implies the demand for new government bonds.

Suppose a deficit of $10 billion is necessary to maintain the economy at full employment equilibrium. Assume the economy is kept in equilibrium by a $10 billion excess of government injections over government withdrawals. Then *private* withdrawals must exceed private injections by $10 billion as total injections and withdrawals are necessarily equal at equilibrium. In a simple model, private withdrawals are *saving;* private injections are *investment*. Thus, the deficit implies that funds borrowed for private investment are less (by $10 billion) than total funds available for lending (saving). By selling bonds, the government can borrow precisely the amount it needs from the surplus saving that private investment is not using. If it borrows less, there will be surplus funds for lending, and interest rates will fall.

It is only when the economy reaches balance, when total planned withdrawals equal total planned injections, that the deficit is necessarily equal to the excess of saving over investment. During the process of adjustment, this will not be true.

Neutral Policies

Even if fiscal policy involves a budget deficit, we can consider it as being *neutral* with respect to monetary factors if:

1. the amount of financing by new money is just sufficient to maintain the desired ratio of money balances to income at the new level, and
2. the amount of financing by borrowing is just sufficient to fill the gap that would otherwise exist between saving available for lending and the borrowing for private investment.

Under these circumstances, the quantity of money will be maintained in its existing ratio to income, and interest rates will remain unchanged.

Surpluses

A government surplus presents the same types of problems as a deficit—some of the government revenue must remain unspent by the government or anyone else. The government has the same options (but in reverse) as when it runs a deficit. Instead of selling new money, it can dispose of old money, using the surplus to reduce the money stock. The economy must be induced to get along with a smaller stock of money—by lower real incomes, lower prices, or higher interest rates. All of these side effects are usually desirable in the anti-inflation context of a budget surplus. A surplus can also be used to retire a portion of the public debt. Bonds reaching maturity can be paid off with the surplus, rather than by issuing replacement bonds.

Recap If a government plans to spend more than it receives in revenue, it must somehow finance the gap (the budget deficit). It can do this by selling something to the public that is produced without any outlays—either newly created money or government bonds. An increase in either the quantity of money or government borrowing has some aspects of monetary policy. However, if the economy is expanded through a government deficit, it will normally require additions to the money stock. Moreover, if a deficit is required to balance injections against withdrawals, there is generally a demand for additional government securities. Thus, a deficit can potentially be financed without upsetting the demand-supply relationships for money and securities. In this case fiscal policy is said to be neutral with respect to monetary factors.

Capsule Supplement 30.2   **Supporting the Public Debt**

Can a government go bankrupt paying the interest on its public debt? The answer to this question is no, if the public debt is held *internally* (by residents of the country), because interest on the public debt is simply a *transfer*. The public debt (and the interest accruing from it) is owed by the government (the citizens it represents) to the public (those same citizens).

Suppose everyone in a nation of 100 million had the same income and held the same number of government bonds. A $10 billion increase in the public debt at an interest rate of 5 percent would then require the sale of $100 in bonds to every individual with a commitment to pay each $5 annually in interest. But this interest would be paid by increasing taxes. Since everyone has the same income, the taxes would amount to $5 per person. Thus, everyone would receive $5 more in interest and pay $5 more in taxes—leaving him exactly where he started.

Public debt interest has an effect on the economy only because those who *receive* the interest and those whose taxes *pay* the interest are not exactly the same people. There is a net transfer from those who pay high taxes and have no bonds to those who hold bonds and pay no taxes. This transfer obviously results in a redistribution of income. Accentuating this redistribution is the fact that government bond interest is often given *preferred* tax treatment (not federal bond interest in the United States, however). In any event, interest on the public debt is always a major nuisance to governments that inherit it. Given the political facts of life, especially that tax increases are unpopular, rising interest on debt tends to reduce the government's potential level of discretionary expenditure.

Public debt held *externally* (bonds purchased by foreigners) does not lead to a simple redistribution effect. The interest on such debt must ultimately be paid by transferring goods from the bond-selling country to the foreigners, implying a real reduction in the goods available domestically.

Macroeconomic Tax Policy

Notes on the use of tax changes rather than expenditure changes

The government may choose to pursue a fiscal policy through tax changes rather than through expenditure changes. Cutting taxes, like increasing expenditures, is expansionary; increasing taxes, like cutting expenditures, is contractionary.

In any realistic situation, the government is constrained to manipulate tax *rates* rather than total tax revenues. It can, of course, manipulate the tax rate to bring in a certain total revenue at some specified income level—but if it miscalculates the income level, its revenues will differ from those planned.

The Effect on the Multiplier

As we showed earlier in the chapter, the tax rate influences the overall multiplier effect of changes in government expenditure and investment. Lowering the tax rate increases the ratio of disposable income to total income. Because the propensity to consume is related to disposable income, this leads to a higher level of consumption expenditure associated with a given level of national income. Reducing the tax rate thus increases the effective multiplier, while increasing the tax rate reduces the effective multiplier.

In the numerical example given earlier, a tax rate of 25 percent and a propensity to consume of 0.8 gave a multiplier of 2.5. A tax rate of 16.6 percent (1/6) would give a multiplier of 3; a tax rate of zero, a multiplier of 5 (the simple multiplier). Increasing the tax rate from 25 percent to 37.5 percent would lower the multiplier to 2, and a tax rate of 75 percent would give a multiplier of only 1.25. Different propensities to consume would give different multiplier values, but the effect of tax rate changes would be in the same direction.

Cutting tax rates to expand the economy from some given level will result in a greater *full employment* budget deficit than achieving the same result by increased expenditure because the taxes on the increased income are lower.

Tax versus Expenditure Changes

The expansionary effects of a tax cut are subject to more uncertainty than expansion by direct expenditure. It may happen that households do *not* increase consumption when their disposable income is increased by a tax cut. The immediate impact of increased expenditure is a direct increase in income of at least the amount of the expenditure even if the multiplier effect turns out to be very weak. A tax cut may conceivably fail to yield any expansion at all.

There is an asymmetry in the practical application of expenditure changes and tax changes. Because increased expenditure represents a frontal attack on insufficient planned total expenditure, while tax cuts represent only an *inducement* for private spending increases, expenditure changes may be preferred for expansionary policy. On the other hand, when contraction is needed, it may be politically or socially difficult for the government to make large cuts in expenditure, and tax increases may represent the more expedient option.

Other Considerations

The choice between expenditure changes and tax changes is not a matter of macroeconomic policy alone. Expansion by increasing government expenditure will increase the ratio of government goods and services to those produced in the private sector. Expansion by cutting taxes will increase the ratio of private goods and services to those produced by the government. The choice between the two will be heavily influenced by the policy-maker's judgment about the optimum ratio of goods supplied through the government to those supplied through the market—a judgment with strong political and even ideological content.

As in the case of expenditure, the *type* of tax change as well as the aggregate effect is important. With a progressive income-tax system, an *across-the-board* income-tax change (such as a 10 percent surcharge or a 10 percent refund on all taxes) will change the disposable incomes of the rich relatively more than those of the poor. Because the propensity to consume generally declines with income, across-the-board tax changes will tend to be less efficient in generating changes in expenditures than tax changes having more effect on low-income groups. The evidence on this last point is unclear, however, and across-the-board changes can be made, after all, without restructuring the entire system of taxation.

Indirect Fiscal Policy

Tax changes may be designed to influence *investment* rather than consumption. At certain times, the United States has used special depreciation allowances giving tax advantages to firms choosing to invest during some particular period. Whether this should be regarded as *fiscal* policy is another matter—it is more strictly a manipulation of prices because the budgetary effects are relatively small. In any case, it is certainly an *indirect* policy rather than a direct one, and carries the usual uncertainty about effects. By how much will investment increase if we allow firms to depreciate investments at double the normal rate? In cases like this, our estimates will usually be much closer to pure guesswork than they are in assessing the direct effects of an increase in government expenditures.

Recap Governments can pursue fiscal policy objectives by varying taxes (meaning tax rates) rather than government expenditures. Reducing tax rates will be expansionary; increasing them will be contractionary. There is more uncertainty about the effect of tax cuts than there is about the effect of changes in government expenditures. Special types of tax change can be used for indirect fiscal policy—encouraging private investment by special tax concessions, for example.

Capsule Supplement 30.3   **Tax Expenditures**

In 1974, the United States government supported religious and charitable institutions to the extent of about $4.5 billion. It did not do this directly—indeed the Constitution would have prohibited government donations to churches in any case—but indirectly in the form of forgone income taxes on gifts made by private individuals. If provision for the deduction of charitable donations from income before computing tax had not existed, the government would have had $4.5 billion more in revenue in 1974, which it could have spent as it chose. We refer to the $4.5 billion as a *tax expenditure* because it is a tax concession that has the same effect on the budget as an additional $4.5 billion in expenditure. Tax expenditures have many political attractions because *direct* government payments are not involved. A minor amendment to a tax bill may provide farmers or oil firms or home owners with an indirect subsidy that would be politically unacceptable if it were shown as a direct subsidy. Because tax rates are less than 100 percent, taxpayers must always pay *some* of the costs of whatever is allowed as a deduction, and this is generally regarded as desirable.

There are, however, strong arguments against the use of tax expenditures. Could the government have made better use of $4.5 billion by directly supporting education, hospitals, and similar causes instead of by subsidizing gifts of individuals and firms? The answer is unclear, but it is certainly a possibility. The distributional effects are surely counter to usual social aims—home owners are preferred to tenants, the poor man's real sacrifice of $100 to a favorite charity goes with little or no subsidy, while the rich man's may carry an additional $223 gift from the government. Such projected tax expenditures as allowing the deduction of college fees would give a government subsidy of as much as 70 percent on the college education of the very rich, but only a few percent to the poor.

The strongest arguments against tax expenditures relate to the very features that make them politically attractive—their lack of visibility. If it would not be politically possible to spend $1 million on something by direct expenditure, it is difficult to argue that it would be socially desirable to achieve the same objective by tax expenditure, especially because the government can assure exactly where the expenditure goes in the direct case, but has no real control in the tax expenditure case. Although tax expenditures will be less than the total costs of any project financed this way (since there must always be some cost to the taxpayer), the government loses control over the *amount* as well as the direction of the expenditure. It may be socially desirable to have an expenditure of $100 million in a certain direction that would cost the government, say, $50 million in lost tax. Actual expenditure may turn out to be $200 million, which is more than optimal, while the government loses $100 million in taxes. For $100 million in *direct* expenditure, instead of $100 million in *tax* expenditure, the government could have obtained *exactly* what it wanted.

Then there are the inevitable institutional effects. Taxpayers are prone to devise schemes that fulfill the *letter* of the tax law in such a way as to maximize their private benefits, perhaps failing to achieve desired social objectives altogether. In addition, such expenditures are most beneficial to taxpayers in the highest tax brackets and thus represent a significant loss of tax revenue. The United States government already pays, in tax expenditure, 70 percent (the highest tax rate) of much of the expenditure through foundations, over which it has no control at all.

Total tax expenditures in the United States were estimated at $72 billion in 1974—an amount more than one-fourth as great as actual federal expenditures made directly. The largest tax expenditures were those made to promote sav-

ing by corporations (the special treatment of capital gains) and home ownership (the special treatment of owner-occupiers compared with tenants).
More specific items were tax expenditures to help the oil industry (depletion
allowances), to promote business operation in less-developed countries, to
promote Western Hemisphere trade, and to promote education and charitable
institutions.

Exercises

An economy has a constant tax rate equal to 10 percent of income. The full
employment income level is $400 million. To sustain this level, the govern-
ment must add $50 million in expenditures to investment and other injec-
tions. The following exercises both refer to this economy.

1. Calculate each of the following:
   a. The full employment budget balance (the surplus or deficit for the
      budget that will just sustain full employment).
   b. The actual surplus or deficit at an income level of $300 million for a
      budget that has the full employment balance shown in question a.
2. The economy is depressed at an income level of $250 million. The gov-
   ernment boosts the economy with a budget having an initial deficit of $20
   million.
   a. What is the full employment balance for this budget?
   b. Will such a budget bring about sustained full employment?

For Thought and Discussion

1. Government expenditures accounted for less than 5 percent of GNP in
   the nineteenth century compared with approximately 20 percent in more
   recent times. What would this imply about the effectiveness of fiscal
   policy in the nineteenth century?
2. Examine the most recent federal budget you can locate. Compare the
   probable impact and ultimate effects of this budget.
3. It was once often said, and sometimes still is, that because households
   must make their expenditure fit their revenue, the government should
   also. Do households ever spend more than their income? Is there any
   validity in this analogy?

Chapter 31
Monetary Policy

What Can Monetary Policy Do?

The potential scope of monetary policy

The most obvious thing that the monetary authority can do is change the number of dollars available in the economy. However, changing the quantity of money is not an objective of policy; it is only an instrument. Hence, the ultimate effects of monetary policy depend on the *results* of changes in the money stock.

Because money must end up being held as money balances by firms and individuals, the results of changes in the quantity of money can be expressed simply and clearly as *whatever changes in the economy are necessary to induce firms and households to hold the new level of money balances*.

The Demand for Money

As we saw in Chapter 26, the demand for money, by which we mean the demand for nominal balances in simple current dollars, depends on:

1. *the ratio individuals collectively wish to maintain between their "real" balances (in constant dollars) and their "real" incomes or expenditures*. This can be expressed as the number of weeks of real expenditure their balances could finance. Its inverse is the velocity of circulation.

2. *the level of real income*. In conjunction with the ratio between desired real balances and real income, the level of real income will determine the desired level of *real* balances.

3. *the price level*. This converts the demand for real balances, in terms of constant dollars relative to some base year, into the demand in terms of current dollars. That is, it converts the demand for *real balances* into the demand for *nominal balances*.

4. *the rate of interest*. Because, to some extent, money and interest-bearing assets are substitutes, the money balances individuals wish to maintain will be inversely related to the rate of interest. For example, increased interest rates will induce people to shift some of their checking-account deposits into savings bonds. This lowers the ratio of money balances (but not necessarily total assets) to income. Monetarists, unlike Keynesians, would predict monetary effects even under circumstances that leave the rate of interest unchanged.

Fundamental Monetary Power

The government's power to change the quantity of money is power to change the *nominal quantity* (the actual number of current dollars) only. It is possible that under some circumstances, an increase of 5 percent in the nominal quantity may result in a 5 percent price increase. In this case, the *real* quantity (or level of *real balances*) remains unchanged.

Hence, an increased number of dollars may be absorbed by the public if there is any one of the following:

1. An increase in the ratio of desired balances to incomes (or, equivalently, a fall in the velocity of circulation).
2. A fall in the interest rate.
3. An increase in the price level.
4. An increase in real income.
5. Any combination of the above effects.
6. A mixture in which some changes occur in the "wrong" direction but whose overall net effect is in the "right" direction, such as a rise in interest rates whose effect is more than outweighed by that of a rise in the price level.

Cause and Effect

To list conditions under which an increase in the quantity of money would be absorbed in the private sector does not prove, of course, that any of these conditions will be *caused* by an increase in money.

As an analogy, consider a market for apples that is initially in equilibrium. Now, suppose the government decides to put a large stock of apples on the market. We know from ordinary supply and demand analysis that people will generally be willing to consume more apples only if (1) their incomes rise, (2) the price of apples falls, or (3) the price of other fruit rises. Will the increase in the supply of apples *cause* any of these changes to occur?

We can answer this question by considering the *mechanism* of the apple market. There is a well-established mechanism whereby an increase in the supply of apples will lead to market behavior that will cause the price of apples to fall. On the other hand, there is no mechanism by which an increase in the supply of apples will cause, say, major increases in incomes.

Thus, although increased incomes would certainly permit absorption of an increase in the apple supply, we would never assert that an increase in the apple supply would *cause* the requisite increases in incomes.

The Mechanism

But money should not be confused with apples—it exerts a more persuasive influence on the overall economy than any ordinary good—and there are mechanisms by which a change in the quantity of money, through *real balance effects* (see Chapter 26), will affect expenditure and thus income. While economists agree on the list of changes among which the potential effects of monetary policy will be found, there is disagreement on *which* of these changes will actually take place as a direct result of monetary policy.

Keynesians emphasize the effect of monetary policy on the interest rate and the sensitivity of investment to this rate. The demand for money is

Figure 31.1
The ingredients of Keynesian monetary policy.

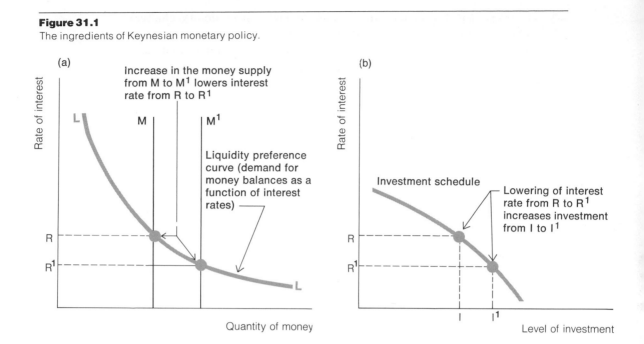

considered primarily in terms of *liquidity preference,* that is, as a choice between liquid but non-interest-bearing money and interest-bearing assets. The demand for money declines as the interest rate increases, so an increase in the quantity of money will lower interest rates, as shown in Figure 31.1(a). The fall in interest rates, in turn, will increase the level of investment, as shown in Figure 31.1(b). The increased investment increases total injections and thus exerts an expansionary effect on the economy.

The *modern (or "new") monetarists* emphasize the direct relationship between the quantity of money and the level of expenditure and income. While not ruling out a subsidiary mechanism of the Keynesian type, their major argument is that an increase in money balances raises the ratio of balances to expenditure above the desired level. As a result, expenditure (including consumption) increases, causing economic expansion. The process of expansion visualized is simply that people find their money balances higher than desired and attempt to run them down by spending more. The consumption function shifts (temporarily), planned consumption rises, and the economy receives an upward boost.

The Direction Is Clear

The predicted *direction* of the ultimate effect is the same in both cases leading us to conclude that an increase in the money supply is expansionary. However, the Keynesian mechanism depends on monetary changes being able to induce changes in the rate of interest and on investment being sensitive to the rate of interest—both in doubt. Consequently, monetary policy plays a minor role in the Keynesian approach.

The modern monetarists, while pointing to the mechanism through which their scenario could come about, emphasize this less than they do the *historical evidence* that there has always been a close association between the quantity of money and the level of money income. The classic study of this association is *A Monetary History of the United States, 1867–1960,* by Milton Friedman and Anna Schwartz, in which the authors contend that the quantity of money *dominates* all other factors, including fiscal policy measures, in determining the level of income.

Recap Monetary policy operates by changing the quantity of money. Its effects will be the changes in the economy needed to induce the public to hold the resulting stock of money. Such changes may occur in the velocity of circulation, the rate of interest, the level of real income, or the price level. "Keynesian" monetary policy emphasizes interest-rate effects on investment. "Monetarist" monetary policy emphasizes the relationship between money balances and income. Both views predict income effects in the same direction.

Capsule Supplement 31.1   **The Political Economy
of Monetary Policy**

In an important survey of post–World War II economic policy in Western Europe and the United States, E. S. Kirschen and associates noted that monetary policy has generally been favored by governments on the political right and avoided by governments on the political left. This observation comes as little surprise, because advocacy of monetary policy has long been associated with political conservatism, and advocacy of Keynesian fiscal policy with political-left liberalism.

There are two major reasons for the political associations of monetary policy. One is simply a matter of history and personnel selection—the banking profession has long been linked in the public mind with conservatism in the primitive sense of caution and suspicion of change. The other, and the more important, is the indirect nature of monetary policy and the implied delegation of power to the banking community.

The prime mechanism of monetary expansion in a modern economy is the expansion of bank loans. If the government decides to use expansionary monetary policy through the banking system, it can control the potential level of new loans but it cannot control, in detail, the direction of these loans. Decisions about which businesses and persons receive the new loans are left to the bankers themselves, a fact that gives these bankers considerable power with respect to the types of economic activity promoted.

Alternatively, if the government chooses to expand the economy through fiscal policy, it can decide in detail where to "aim" its increased expenditures. Political conservatives, who generally favor minimal direct government intervention, prefer monetary policy specifically because the government does not make the final allocative decision. Those farther to the left favor fiscal policy specifically because allocative decisions are not delegated to bankers.

This difference in attitude derives largely from consideration of the distributional effects of the alternative approaches. Although many will benefit from an economic expansion, whether brought about by monetary or fiscal policy, the immediate effects of monetary policy are likely to be most beneficial to the business sector and to the rich. Banks rarely expand their loans by extending credit to the poor. They do so by making additional loans to businesses and low-risk (that is, well-off) personal customers. The expansion of business may increase employment and thus the incomes of the poor, but this is a secondary, rather than a direct, effect. Alternatively, fiscal policy can have virtually any distributional effect the government chooses. The increased expenditure could conceivably be directed to the rich, but it is *possible* to aim fiscal policy directly at the poor.

The politics of the situation is thus built into the structure of the monetary sector, and is likely to persist. In principle, the monetary authorities could specify the purpose for which new loans are to be made—a practice common outside the United States, but rare within it. Even though this would give some control over final allocation, it would still provide weaker regulation than is possible through fiscal policy.

Quantity versus Interest Rates

Whether we should focus on the quantity of money or the rate of interest in assessing monetary policy

The indicator that has traditionally been the quantitative index of monetary policy is the *rate of interest*. Monetary policy is considered "tight" if interest rates are kept higher than normal, and "easy" if interest rates are kept low.

Interest-Oriented Policy

If monetary policy is used exclusively to influence the rate of interest, the effect of such policy on the quantity of money is considered superfluous. The central bank, if it wishes to lower interest rates, orders the quantity to be increased until interest rates have dropped to the required level, then orders the quantity to be held there. It might not even take note of what the new quantity is, except as part of its back-room statistical bookkeeping.

In the United States, the Federal Reserve System's direct actions have traditionally been measured by their effect on interest rates. The Federal Open Market Committee determines the desirable range within which to maintain interest rates, then instructs its executives to buy and sell government securities (*via open market operations*) to keep interest rates within this range. Only when the change in the money supply is markedly out of line is the interest-rate objective modified. In some cases, especially when smoothing the market for issues of new government securities, the money supply has been treated entirely as a secondary matter. Thus, the Federal Reserve System (along with other central banks, such as the Bank of England) has generally regarded change in the quantity of money as a side effect rather than a principal policy variable. The recent emphasis on viewing the *quantity of money* rather than the rate of interest as the principal policy variable for monetary policy has mainly been due to the influence of the modern monetarists.

The Relationship Between Interest Rates and Quantity

Because the quantity of money does affect interest rates, at least in the short run, the monetary authority, by itself, cannot achieve a target rate of interest *and* a target quantity of money simultaneously, unless, of course, they happen to coincide.

To monetary authorities whose professional lives have been spent following interest rates, it involves a considerable change in viewpoint to treat interest rates as a secondary matter. Yet, if these authorities agree that the quantity of money is important, as they now do, and also that the interest rate is important, they must make some kind of choice about which they wish to influence most.

Monetarists argue that interest-rate effects, in any case, will be short term. Increasing the quantity of money, according to their analysis, may temporarily lower interest rates, but the ensuing expansion of the economy will ultimately result in income and price effects that offset this decline.

Quantity-Oriented Policy

Emphasis on the *quantity of money* introduces an important technical problem. If the quantity of money is a critical measure of economic policy, we need to define "money" clearly. For the purposes of our basic analysis, we have assumed that money consists of currency in the hands of the public and checking-account deposits in commercial banks. But there are other assets, such as time deposits in commercial banks and perhaps savings-account deposits, that serve many of the same functions as checking-account deposits. Are these part of the money supply? This question is an important one because these other things may change at different rates than checking-account deposits, giving different rates of change for the money supply depending on which definition is used. Many current policy disputes are based on just such matters of definition.

If monetary policy is being used to achieve macroeconomic objectives, there is at least no conflict in *direction* between quantity objectives and interest-rate objectives. When the economy is depressed, an increase in the quantity of money will be expansionary both through direct effects and through reduced interest rates. Similarly, in an inflation, a reduction in the money supply (or, in a growing economy, a reduction in its rate of expansion) will have a dampening influence regardless of its specific effects.

Lags in Monetary Policy

There is, however, the problem of *lags*. If the quantity of money directly affects income six months in the future, while the interest rate operating through investment indirectly affects income twelve months in the future, there may be a conflict. For example, if a slowdown is expected in six months that will be gone in twelve, monetary policy may produce direct effects at the appropriate time. However, the policy may produce unwanted indirect effects later on, as the investment induced by events of the previous year boosts an already fully employed economy.

Conflicts between quantity and interest-rate objectives may also arise when monetary policy is used for achieving non-macroeconomic objectives. One of the more ignoble, but traditional, roles of the monetary authority is to hold down interest rates during periods of heavy government borrowing. If quantity effects are significant, inflation may well be an undesired consequence of what is normally regarded as a simple piece of good government business. Monetarists have frequently attacked such use of monetary policy for just this reason.

Recap Monetary policy can be assessed by looking at either the quantity of money or the rate of interest. Until quite recently, attention was focused on the rate of interest rather than on the quantity of money. The Federal Reserve System and other central banks varied the money supply to achieve a target interest rate, barely taking into account the actual level of the money supply. Because the quantity of money affects the rate of interest, the monetary authority cannot attain arbitrarily chosen targets for both the quantity and the interest rate. Recent emphasis on the quantity of money has introduced technical problems of defining and measuring it.

The Price Level

The price effects of monetary policy

If we reduce the Keynesian and monetarist views of the economy to their simplest terms, we can state them as follows:

1. The Keynesian model ignores price changes and predicts the level of *real output* as that for which injections and withdrawals are equal, provided the economy is below full employment.
2. The monetarist model assumes that there is an underlying constancy between the quantity of money (in current dollars) and the level of income or output (also in current dollars), so we can predict the *money value of output* from the quantity of nominal money.

The money value of output, of course, is equal to real output multiplied by the relevant price index. In principle, Keynesian and monetarist predictions are not in conflict because they can be made equivalent by an appropriate adjustment of the price level.

It would be very neat if we could use the Keynesian model to predict the level of real output, the monetarist model to predict the value of output, then calculate the change in the price level by comparing the two. However, we know that changing the quantity of money influences the level of real output as well as the value of output, and we have ample evidence that changes in real output when the economy is close to full employment have effects on the price level. Figure 31.2 illustrates the two views and their relationship.

Unknown Division of Effects

There is nothing in the monetarist analysis itself that predicts how much of any change in the value of output will be due to a change in real output, and how much will be due to a change in the price level. There is nothing in the Keynesian analysis itself that predicts what, if any, price effects will result from changes in real output—the constant price level that is usually specified in the simple Keynesian model is only an *assumption*.

The division of the effects of changes in the quantity of money between price and real output changes is one of the great unknowns of economics. We can merely state that a consensus among economists would probably be reached on the following:

1. At well below full employment (depression or deep recession conditions), price effects are likely to be small. Expansionary policies, whether monetary or fiscal, will tend to raise real output rather than prices.
2. At or above full employment, expansionary influences of any kind can *only* result in price increases.
3. When the economy is near, but not yet at, full employment, some price increases will inevitably result from further expansion.
4. Under inflationary conditions, when prices have been rising for some time, further increases in prices will likely result from cost-push and other dynamic influences. Deflationary monetary policy (especially a

Figure 31.2
Two views of the relationship between the level of GNP in real terms and in its
dollar value.

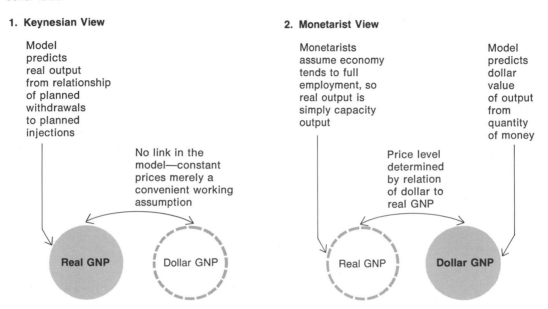

1. **Keynesian View**

Model
predicts
real output
from relationship
of planned
withdrawals
to planned
injections

No link in the
model—constant
prices merely a
convenient working
assumption

Real GNP   Dollar GNP

2. **Monetarist View**

Monetarists
assume economy
tends to full
employment, so
real output is
simply capacity
output

Model
predicts
dollar
value
of output
from
quantity
of money

Price level
determined
by relation
of dollar to
real GNP

Real GNP   Dollar GNP

reduction in the money supply) may thus reduce real output and induce
a recession, while prices continue to rise.

Recap Monetary policy may be able to affect the level of money income without
influencing interest rates. But monetary policy cannot differentiate between affecting real income and affecting the price level. Which of these occurs will depend on the state of the economy.

Techniques of Monetary Policy

**Some institutional details about
the use of monetary policy**

It is important to realize that each economy possesses its own unique
banking institutions and its own unique relationships among the government, the treasury, and the banking system. Over the years, certain techniques for carrying out monetary policy under various circumstances have
been developed in each system.

Monetary authorities traditionally are technically conservative—they do not experiment with new policy techniques unless forced to do so. Because the acceptability of money depends on confidence, and because money is still regarded by the general public as somewhat mysterious, there is merit in the argument that sudden changes in policy technique may have unexpected and possibly undesirable effects.

Emergency Techniques

Unusual techniques have been used in unusual circumstances. There are several cases (including that of Germany) in which a "new" money unit has been introduced. Of itself, this means nothing because it doesn't matter what the nominal money unit is actually called. But if such a move heralds a fundamentally new monetary *policy,* it can have profound effects on expectations and thus on behavior. Hyperinflation can only be cured when the public believes a completely new approach is being taken. Consequently, "new" money is an important psychological weapon.

New money also permits direct manipulation of money balances. This can be done by issuing, for example, a new "heavy dollar" stated to be worth ten old dollars. All prices and wages are then recalculated in the new units. But cash and bank balances are allowed to be converted into new dollars only at the rate of, say, twenty old to one new. In effect, this *halves* everyone's nominal balances and thus the quantity of money.

This example has been given merely to demonstrate that monetary policy is not *necessarily* confined to the use of a few well known techniques. We shall now consider the more traditional operation of monetary policy.

The Role of Banks

Increasing the quantity of money in most economies is carried out *through the banking system.* In the United States, for example, the most common way to increase the quantity of money is through open market operations by the Federal Reserve System (outlined in Chapter 28). The immediate impact of expansionary open market operations will be to increase commercial-bank reserve deposits with the Fed. The increased reserves will result in a multiplied increase in private deposits in commercial banks, and thus in private money balances.

Increased reserves result in increased private deposits through the expansion of bank loans. Bank loans are made primarily to businesses. The expansion of such loans may thus present problems if the economy is depressed.

It is likely that the number of business loans considered "safe" from the banker's point of view will be small if the economy is depressed. Bankers may choose to keep a higher ratio of reserves to deposits than necessary rather than make loans with undue risk, and the expansion of the money supply predicted from the simple analysis may not take place. Long-standing doubts that monetary policy, as traditionally used, can really be effective under depressed conditions are obviously not eliminated by this consideration.

On the other hand, the same mechanism tends to make monetary policy especially effective under inflationary conditions. Because of the incentive to invest during an inflationary period that is expected to continue, it is highly desirable to dampen business expenditure. Contracting or slowing down growth in the money supply through a reduction in business loans will obviously achieve this end.

Reserve Ratios

The other basic technique for controlling the money supply—changing the required ratio of reserves to deposits—works through the nonfinancial sector in basically the same way as open market operations. If the reserve ratio is reduced in order to increase the money supply, the money supply will increase only if business loans can actually be expanded.

Thus, there are major doubts about the effectiveness of monetary policy under depressed conditions. Commercial banks *can be forced* to reduce loans and thus deposits when the monetary authority wants to contract the money supply simply because there is a legal limit on the ratio of deposits to reserves. But banks *cannot be forced* to expand loans and deposits under depressed conditions. The central bank can expand the reserve deposits of the commercial banks, but cannot prevent the commercial banks from keeping these as "excess reserves" and allowing the effective reserve ratio to rise. Under stable business conditions, it is the *profitability* of loans that induces commercial banks to expand them as far as permissible. But depressed business conditions may reduce such profitability (after allowing for risk) to zero. Under these circumstances, the central bank may find itself unable to increase the quantity of money.

Indeed, the central bank may even lose some of its control over the money supply under boom conditions. Although it may reduce ordinary deposits, ingenious "near-monies" that cannot be controlled easily by the central bank may be created.

Thus, the techniques of monetary policy are not always as certain in their operation as they may seem from simple models.

Recap In most countries, monetary authorities tend to rely on traditionally defined techniques even though other techniques are potentially available. In the United States, monetary policy is carried out primarily through the use of open market operations by the Federal Reserve System. Reliance on bank credit expansion to increase the quantity of money can present problems under depressed economic conditions because banks may not increase loans even though they have been given enough reserves to do so.

Automatic Monetary Policy	**Whether we should increase the quantity of money at a fixed rate**

One view of monetary policy, associated particularly with Milton Friedman, though not accepted in its entirety by all monetarists, is that it should be essentially *automatic* rather than discretionary.

The basic idea is a simple one. Each economy has a fairly steady growth rate of real output at full employment (around 4 percent in the United States). Starting from a position of price stability and full employment, the monetary authority "automatically" increases the quantity of money at a steady amount per year, whatever the growth rate of real output is.

Seasonal Effects

Detailed implementation of such a policy is not as automatic as it may sound. For one thing, the volume of transactions does not increase steadily over the course of a year, but is subject to *seasonal* variations. Consequently, the money supply must be adjusted to this seasonal cycle, while increasing at the appropriate rate on average. In addition, the appropriate balance between the components of the money supply—currency and deposits particularly—must be maintained. This balance varies somewhat, with its own seasonal pattern. Currency holdings rise temporarily near Christmas, for example, because of the seasonal increase in shopping activity.

Automatic Policy

The automatic growth rule is advocated not as just a useful rule-of-thumb way to maintain an appropriate money supply as a background for other activities, but as the *mainstay of macroeconomic policy*. In particular, fiscal policy is supposed to remain *neutral* in the sense that it should not be manipulated to adjust to short-term fluctuations in activity.

If everything works smoothly and ideally, real output in the economy grows at its steady 4 percent, the money supply increases in step, the ratio of money balances to incomes remains unchanged, and there are no net influences that change either real output or the price level. A modified version would have the money supply grow at, say, 5 percent to allow for a small rate of price increase (1 percent). This rate is generally considered helpful in maintaining flexibility in relative prices.

Random Influences

Any real economy is subject to a variety of random influences that tend to divert it from a smoothly charted course. Just how well an automatic policy can deal with these influences determines its usefulness.

A simplified version of the operation of the Friedman policy is:

Suppose some random influence has pushed the economy below its full employment level, real output has fallen, and there is unemployment. The quantity of money will then be high relative to the lowered level of activity. The public will regard its money balances as exceeding current needs and will try to run them down somewhat by increasing expenditure. In the aggregate, the balances cannot be run down (they are fixed by the money supply), but the attempts to change them will increase expenditure and exert an expansionary influence on the economy. This expansion may initially cause prices as well as real output to increase. At the same time, unemployment is exerting downward pressure on wages. Rising prices and falling wages will make expansion of (real) output profitable. As a subsidiary effect, the excess of the money supply over requirements at the depressed level of output will lower interest rates and thus encourage investment. All the influences are in the same direction—toward the ultimate expansion of *real output*.

Now, suppose we are at full employment, and prices start to rise. Money incomes will increase along with the price level, but money balances will not, except insofar as real output is growing too. Money balances will become low relative to income levels, and expenditures will be reduced in an attempt to build balances back up. The rate of interest will rise, discouraging investment. The influences are again all in the same direction, dampening the inflationary pressures.

Devotees of Friedman thus predict self-generated readjustments of the economy to any divergences from steady growth with full employment and price stability.

Lags and Adjustment Speeds

No claim is made, however, for *instantaneous* readjustment. Hence, the economy, if pushed downward, will go through a period of unemployment and recession (perhaps mild) before recovery. If pushed upward, it will go through a readjustment phase with some inflation and possibly even a recession before settling down.

As is so often the case with macroeconomic policy, it's the problems of *lags* and *speeds of adjustment* that are crucial in determining policy choices. Unfortunately, our information about adjustment speeds is very poor. Would we accept the Friedman policy if readjustment to a downward push meant unemployment of 8 percent for two years?

There is really nothing in automatic monetary policy to suggest that we might not supplement it by other policies to increase the speed of adjustment, even though many of its advocates believe that we need not do so. Nevertheless, even if the extreme monetarist view that the quantity of money is virtually the *only* thing that matters is not widely accepted, the quantity of money will never again be ignored as it was for over a generation.

Perhaps the most important impact of the Friedman policy is that it forces us to ask: Why should the money supply *not* grow in step with the growth of real output? We may not believe that the adjustment processes will be rapid or certain enough to accept automatic growth of the money supply as *all* we need for macroeconomic policy, but it does seem reasonable that the policy-maker should provide a case for diverging from the principle of automatic growth. At least an automatic growth rate (like a full employment budget in fiscal policy) provides an *origin* from which divergences can be measured.

Recap Because the desired ratio of the money stock to total income is relatively constant, the money stock should grow in step with the economy. Some monetarists have argued that the monetary authority should increase the money supply at a steady rate. This rate should be chosen with reference to the growth rate of the economy, and no attempt should be made to vary the supply in response to short-term economic fluctuations. While this view is not generally accepted, it provides a criterion against which monetary policy can be measured.

Capsule Supplement 31.2   **Monetary Policy in the United States**

Because Keynesian fiscal policy did not exist prior to 1940, monetary policy was considered the primary way to solve the problems associated with economic fluctuations prior to World War II. A crucial argument of the new monetarists (Friedman and his associates) has been that this early monetary policy was simply *bad* monetary policy—an important point because the new monetarists can hardly afford to rest their case for monetary policy on the miserable performance of the U.S. economy in the 1920s and 1930s.

We can measure actual monetary policy over this period using the yardstick proposed by the new monetarists—a steady 4 percent annual growth in the money supply. One glance at the figures shows that the money supply has not grown at a constant rate since 1920. Annual rates of change (based on a six-month average) varied from increases of as much as 34 percent (during World War II) to decreases of as much as 20 percent (in 1921).

Not only did the rate of change in the money supply vary greatly from one period to another, but, in many critical instances, it varied in precisely *the wrong direction.* This is most apparent during periods of recession. The first of these, for the time span we're considering, occurred during 1921, at which time (as indicated) the money supply declined rapidly. During the 1924 recession, the rate of increase of money fell sharply to nearly zero, but did not turn negative as it had in 1921. In the next recession (1927), the rate of increase again fell sharply, and temporarily turned negative. During the booms between these periods of recession, the rate of increase was high—typically more than 10 percent.

During the boom of 1929, however, monetary policy finally seemed to be on the right track: the quantity of money was kept fairly steady and was not increased rapidly to put upward pressure on the situation. From then on, however, monetary policy proved a disaster. As the economy started downhill into the Great Depression, the money supply was reduced, accentuating the general contraction. Indeed, the quantity of money declined consistently from 1930 right through to the depth of the Depression in mid-1933. This decline became almost precipitous as the economy moved toward bottom—the money stock fell at an annual rate of between 10 and 20 percent for one year—from August, 1931 to August, 1932. After a brief leveling off, the rate of decline again rose to more than 10 percent for the final months of the great downward slide.

There was another recession in 1938. Again the money supply was reduced, but the rate of decline was considerably less than in the earlier recession periods. World War II was a special case. The money supply increased rapidly throughout the war as a conscious part of the total policy required to support the huge wartime expenditure.

Since World War II, wild fluctuations in the rate of change of the money supply have not reappeared. There have been periods of modest reductions in the quantity of money (the largest being a 3 percent decline at annual rates for a few months during 1960) and periods of relatively rapid expansion (though always less than 10 percent prior to 1971). In 1971, with the economy in recession (but also in inflation), the annually based rate of expansion reached 22 percent for a brief period. Overall, however, the post–World War II picture has been one of modest fluctuations in the rate change in the money supply.

Would expansionary (or at least, non-contractionary) monetary policy have prevented the Great Depression? We cannot be sure, but we can be confident that the actual monetary policy of the time only made things worse. The Depression was long enough and deep enough for monetary policy to have had important effects even if we do not accept the new monetarists' optimism about the rapidity with which the economy can respond to monetary factors.

Exercises

1. If real GNP is expanding at a steady annual rate of 3.5 percent and the nominal quantity of money (actual dollars) is increasing at a steady annual rate of 2.5 percent, is monetary policy expansionary, contractionary, or neutral?

2. Under the conditions of question 1, will the rate of interest be rising, falling, or constant? (Assume no changes in the economy other than the steady growth of real output and the money supply.)

3. Under the conditions of question 2, would the monetarist scenario predict rising, falling, or steady prices?

4. At what rate will the money (current dollar) GNP be increasing under the monetarist scenario?

For Thought and Discussion

1. If the monetary authority considered its function to be the maintenance of a constant rate of interest, what would happen to the money supply during an upswing in the economy? During a downswing?

2. If the economy were in a depression and banks refused to increase loans because of doubts about the solvency of potential borrowers, what policies could be devised to expand the money supply?

3. If your bank balance were magically increased overnight, would you be more likely to run out and spend the increase in a period of inflation or a period of depression?

4. It is often claimed that monetary policy preserves greater freedom of individual choice than fiscal policy because the effects of monetary policy are more evenly dispersed through the economy. From your knowledge of the mechanism of monetary expansion, would you agree with this assessment?

5. Suppose we knew for certain that monetary restriction in a period of inflation would lead to high unemployment this year with little effect on price changes, but by next year unemployment would be down and prices would have stopped rising. Would you adopt the policy under these circumstances?

Chapter 32
Practical Problems of Policy

Terms and Concepts

Predictive accuracy
Policy safety
Destabilizers
Expectations
Automatic stabilizers
Discretionary policy
Restorative policy
Anti-recession policy
Anti-inflation policy
Linkage effects
Wage-price controls

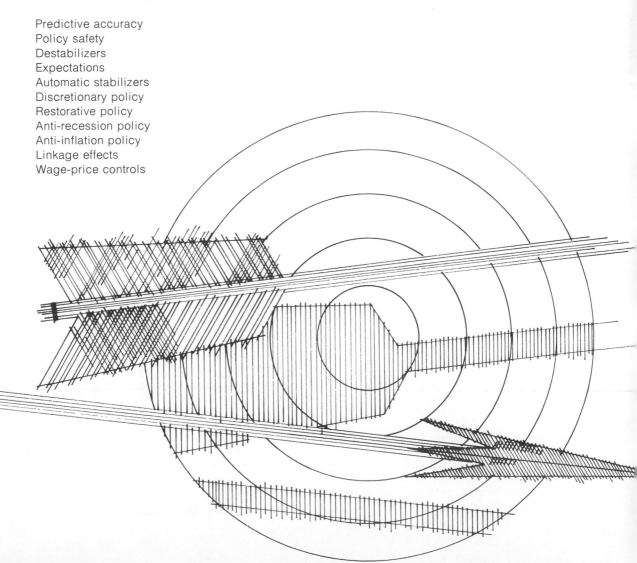

Some Basic Choices

**The basic decisions
facing the policy-maker**

We assume the aim of macroeconomic policy to be full employment without inflation, if attainable. If it is not attainable, we normally assume the aim to be some mixture of relatively high but not full employment and relatively low but not zero rate of price increase.

Given these aims and our knowledge of the various policy instruments available, the practical problems of macroeconomic policy boil down to the following:

1. *What* is required? Does the economy need boosting, dampening, or to be left in peace?
2. *Which* of the various policy instruments available is the best to use?
3. *How much* application of the appropriate policy instruments is called for? If interest rates are to be raised, should they go up by 0.5 percent, 1 percent, or 2 percent?
4. *When* should the policy be applied? For example, is it already too late if the economy's divergence from its desired state has already become clear and obvious?

The Importance of Quantities

Prior to the development of Keynesian analysis, formal thinking about economic policy was largely confined to the "what" and "which" problems. The economic models used were qualitative rather than quantitative—they predicted the *direction* in which a certain policy would move the economy, but not the relationship between the amount of policy and the amount of result. Policy economists had "seat-of-the-pants" views about "how much" and "when," but little hard knowledge.

Early Keynesian economists, with a model no more sophisticated than that set out in Chapter 22, introduced quantitative ("how much") economic policy. At first it seemed very simple—the multiplier is, say, 5, so the exact increase in government or induced expenditure needed to boost the economy by $100 is $20. For many reasons, however, this was not so simple in practice. Specifying the consumption function (and hence the multiplier) proved to be more difficult than in the basic model, and it became evident that more complex models were needed.

Dynamic Problems

Along with the development of such models came increased attention to the dynamic aspects of both the economy and economic policy. This introduced the "when" problem and, as the analysis developed, it became clear that "how much" and "when" could not be separated. The simple multiplier became a dynamic sequence that related current actions to results in the current quarter, the next quarter, the quarter after that, and so on. Because current actions will still have effects next year and the year after, it follows that *last year's* actions still influence the economy at present and will continue to do so.

These *lags* in relationships between actions and consequences mean that the economy can never be viewed as "starting from scratch." We must be able to predict the continuing consequences of former policies before we can predict the results of present policies. While investment may currently be low, last year's tax changes may be in the process of generating a large increase. To build policy on the basis of actual current investment levels may lead to an undesired effect—inflation rather than full employment.

Economic policy must be aimed at a *moving target,* not a stationary one. Current actions will have their main impact later—perhaps in six months, perhaps longer. Thus, such actions must be designed to meet the conditions prevailing then rather than those prevailing now.

The Importance of Prediction

Attempting to hit an economic target "on the nose" is like trying to shoot down one missile with another. It involves an exact *prediction* of the paths of both the target and the interceptor. However, the Newtonian mechanics that determines missile paths is subject to more clearly established laws than those of economic behavior. Therefore, the missile problem is ultimately much simpler than the economic one.

In any event, economic policy does possess one advantage over missile interception. The latter is completely worthless (and may be disastrous) if the target is missed by even a small distance. But in economic policy a direct hit is usually unnecessary. Even missing by a considerable amount may still be better than nothing—providing the direction in which the economy is moved is appropriate. In any event, it always remains true that *accurate policy requires accurate prediction.*

Unfortunately, accuracy in prediction is something economists have not yet been able to produce with sufficient *reliability* to serve as a firm foundation for policies designed to hit exact targets. The complex macromodels used to simulate the operation of the economy are relatively new. Moreover, they often give predictions that, although reasonably consistent in a broad context, are sufficiently different to hinder attempts at exact targeting.

Safety

Given the uncertainty about the accuracy of predictions, *safety* becomes an important consideration in policy choice. A policy that will solve everything if it is on target, but will have undesired effects if off target, may be inferior to a policy that will have less undesirable off-target effects but is less efficient on target. The policy-maker's model may show that with the economy in recession, a $100 million increase in government expenditure will give ''full employment'' and an acceptable 2 percent price increase, but that $110 million will start an inflationary process that will be hard to stop. But what if the predictions were slightly wrong and only $90 million were needed? In this event, an increased expenditure of $100 million may lead to inflation. Thus, something less than a $100 million increase in expenditure may be chosen as safe, rather than the predicted $100 million.

Safety is normally increased by

1. making small policy moves rather than large jumps to avoid the danger of *overshooting* a target; and
2. ''building into'' the economy as much automatic self-regulation as possible, so it will tend toward the desired state even in the absence of conscious policy.

Safety, derived from either of these methods, will usually be achieved at the expense of speed—and long-lasting unemployment (or inflation) is made only slightly less unpalatable by the knowledge that cautious policy or built-in self-regulation will cure it *eventually*.

The relative degrees of safety, speed, and accuracy differ among specific policy instruments and between monetary policy and fiscal policy in general. Indeed, the difference in outlook between those who favor monetary policy and those who favor fiscal policy strongly reflects questions of safety, speed, and accuracy. Fiscal policy (if it can be implemented rapidly and flexibly) is potentially fast and accurate, but only to the extent that good prediction is possible. Monetary policy, being more diffuse, is generally slower in its ultimate effect on GNP (not all monetarists would agree with this assessment) and relies heavily on fundamental stability in market behavior.

Recap Macroeconomic policy requires decisions of four kinds: what the economy requires, which policy instruments to use, how much application of these instruments is needed, and when the policy should be put into effect. Economists are much clearer about the ''what'' and the ''which'' than about the ''how much'' and ''when.'' Because of lags in the economy, accurate policy requires accurate prediction, a difficult matter. In its absence, considerations of policy ''safety'' may be relevant.

Capsule Supplement 32.1   **Can Economists Forecast?**

Because of the lags built into the operation of the economic system, good policy depends on good forecasting. All policy measures take some time to become effective after they are actually put into force. Also, some types of fiscal

Forecaster	Deviation of forecast current dollar GNP from actual GNP (billions of dollars)	Number of percentage points deviation of forecast percentage change from actual percentage change in:	
		Real GNP	Prices
1. Large macromodels			
Council of Economic Advisers	+ 8 (+13)	+1.6 (+1.6)	−0.9 (−0.2)
Wharton model	+ 3 (−6)	+0.6 (+0.3)	−0.4 (−1.1)
IBM model	+ 3 (+7)	+1.5 (+1.2)	−1.5 (−0.8)
Michigan model	+13 (−9)	+2.1 (+0.2)	−1.0 (−1.0)
GE model	+13 (−4)	+3.4 (−0.5)	−1.4 (0)
2. Monetarist models			
Federal Reserve Bank of St. Louis	− 4	+0.3	−1.0
Harris Trust (Chicago)	−11 (−2)	+0.3 (+0.9)	−1.2 (−1.2)
First National City Bank (N.Y.)	−13	n.a.	n.a.

policy require considerable lead time to pass through the various legislative stages. For good policy, therefore, we need to predict what is going to happen during at least the next year and prepare the appropriate measures before the events they are intended to influence occur.

How well can we do this forecasting? Despite the growing sophistication of large computerized forecasting models, the answer is: not yet well enough for our policy needs. Let's focus on a specific example. Forecasting was fairly successful in 1968 and 1969 when the economy was continuing along a fairly direct path. The crucial year was 1970, in which the economy changed direction somewhat. To have predicted 1970 correctly would have been an indication that our forecasting and policy analysis was in very good shape.

At the end of 1969, numerous economic forecasts for the United States were made by all kinds of economists using all kinds of techniques. The accompanying table presents a selection of these forecasts showing how close they came to actual events. As a follow-up, the relationship of forecast to actual data for the next year, 1971, is given in parentheses.

Everybody underforecast the extent of inflation that would continue in the economy through 1970—an important failure. The Keynesian models overforecast real growth and thus actual GNP, while the monetarist models underforecast actual GNP. The Wharton model, probably the closest in spirit to the basic Keynesian model, seems to have performed best overall in 1970; it was the only model to be within a fraction of a percentage point in forecasting the rates of change of both real GNP and prices.

If we look at the figures in parentheses showing deviations of forecasts from actual data in 1971, our faith in forecasts is not strengthened. The best forecast was the GE model, which was very close on both real GNP growth and the rate of inflation. But this same model had the worst forecast performance in the previous year. (The Harris Trust model was close on dollar GNP, but only because the large errors in real GNP and prices offset each other.) The Wharton model, which did well in 1970, performed only moderately well in 1971, although it still came out best on average over the two years.

Note that the Council of Economic Advisers model, which is the official government forecast and is based on the most updated figures, did not shine in either year and was furthest out in its 1971 forecast for total GNP. Most economists laughed when the Council's 1971 forecast was issued because there is always a "seat-of-the-pants" feeling about these things. As a matter of fact, the National Association of Business Economists forecast for 1971, based on a poll of members, was no worse than most other forecasts. Back to the drawing board?

| **Automatic Stabilizing Influences** | **How built-in policies can provide stability** |

Many monetarists believe that the economy is inherently stable and that, if the quantity of money is adjusted steadily to the growth of real output, there is little need for specific adjustment policies except to deal with influences originating outside the economic system proper, such as wars and crop failures. These individuals argue that the historical ups and downs of the economy have been due to unstable monetary policy. For example, instead of maintaining an automatic growth in the money supply in the 1930s, the quantity of money was reduced. This belief is based on the historical relationship between the quantity of money and the level of GNP some six months later, and on a very broad and undetailed description of the way in which changes in real balances affect spending.

Destabilizers

Keynesians and others accept the idea that a steady, or steadily increasing, money supply will generate many stabilizing influences, but these will neither be as certain nor as rapid as the monetarists believe, and more note should be taken of known destabilizing influences.

Among the chief destabilizing influences are the following:

1. The multiplier effect, where an initial decline (or increase) in expenditure somewhere in the economy will decrease (or increase) other incomes and thus other expenditures.
2. The accelerator effect, where a fall in output will lead to a decline in investment, lowering expenditure, and thus lowering output further, with an equivalent upward push on output if output increases.

3. Expectation effects, where the expectation of bad (or good) times ahead will tend to lower (or raise) investment plans and thus help cause the expectations to come true.
4. The inflationary process, which will sustain inflation even though its initiating causes have been removed.

Stabilizers

Even without modern economic policies specifically designed for the purpose, there are some structural, behavioral, and institutional relationships in the economy that are more stabilizing (or less destabilizing) than they might appear at first sight.

A downward movement starts with, say, a drop in planned investment. If planned saving remains at the previous level, equilibrium cannot be sustained and the economy will begin to move downward. In the simple macromodel, planned saving comes only from households and thus falls only when incomes fall. But, in the United States and most industrial economies, much of the saving is business saving in the form of depreciation reserves and undistributed corporate profits. To some extent, investment and business saving are linked, and business saving can usually be expected to fall if investment falls—though not necessarily to the same extent. Thus, it is the decline in investment *less* the decline in business saving that must be matched by a decline in *household* saving through a fall in income.

As incomes start to fall, households tend to adhere to high consumption levels dominated by permanent income effects. In the short run, household saving declines rapidly with income in the next period reaching equilibrium at a level not too far below the original level. If incomes remain lowered, however, households gradually adjust to their new permanent income. This adjustment involves an increase in the propensity to save and further downward pressure on incomes. Thus, while permanent income effects will not ultimately prevent income reductions, they will slow the downward pressures for a time.

For a while, too, the downward pressure of accelerator effects will be comparatively small. Investment plans must be made ahead, and will probably be carried out if businesses believe that any recession that may have commenced is only a temporary one. Indeed, a slackening in the economy may ease supply conditions in capital-producing industries and encourage some investment plans to be speeded up. Thus, the economy will not necessarily start on a precipitous downward path when investment and incomes fall initially.

Expectations

Much depends on expectations. The more optimistic are those making expenditure plans concerning the short-lived nature of the recession, the stronger are the influences tending to reduce the potential decline in income. It might even be argued that the greatest stabilizing factor in the United States since World War II has been the *expectation* that the government would simply not permit a recession to become a depression.

Policy Stabilizers

There are, however, more concrete policy measures that act as potential stabilizers. One of these is the *progressive income tax*. Because the *rate* of tax is lower on low incomes than on high incomes, a fall of, say, 5 percent in pretax incomes will result in a less than 5 percent decline in disposable incomes. Because consumption plans are based on disposable income, the downward influence from falling consumption will be lessened by the progressiveness of the income tax. Progressive taxation was not specifically introduced for this purpose—it was originally instituted for income redistribution—but the stabilizing influence has become an important side effect as the ratio of income-tax collections to total incomes has grown.

A second stabilizer built into the system is the *automatic growth of government transfer payments* as the economy declines. As incomes fall and unemployment rises, both unemployment benefits and welfare payments will increase. This tends to mitigate the decline in personal income and thus the decline in planned consumption expenditure.

None of these stabilizing influences individually, nor all of them together, can *prevent* a decline in activity under continuous downward pressure. Expectational influences (continuing with investment plans, temporarily sustaining high consumption levels) may indeed prevent short-run downward pressure from causing a real downslide. The more the economy actually moves downward, however, the more these influences fade out. Tax and transfer payment influences, on the other hand, become stronger the greater the decline, but never strong enough to restore the economy to its original full employment level. Unemployment benefits are less than wages, so a rise in unemployment always reduces incomes.

Automatic Stabilization Is Incomplete

Considered as part of a self-regulating system, "automatic stabilizers" work in the right direction but either fade rapidly or are designed so they cannot fully restore the economy. To maintain incomes at full employment levels, unemployment benefits, for example, would theoretically have to be set at a level *higher* than wages to make up for the loss of earnings among those still employed. Obviously, paying individuals who give up no leisure *more* than those who give up forty hours a week would have major distributional, efficiency, and social effects that would be generally unacceptable.

The verdict on both automatic monetary policy and automatic stabilizers is that they will *assist* in stabilizing the economy but will either fail to bring it back to the desired state, or will not do so quickly enough to avoid the need to use other policies.

Recap The economy has both stabilizing and destabilizing influences built into it. Monetarists, unlike Keynesians, are inclined to consider the overall result to be stable. However, the effects of the multiplier and the accelerator, as well as expectations and the inflationary spiral, are generally considered to be destabilizing. Policy can be designed to have built-in stabilizing influences. Among such built-in stabilizers in most advanced economies are the progressive income tax and the commitment to unemployment benefits and other forms of income support.

Discretionary Policy

Why discretionary policy is necessary, and what types of policy instruments are available for restoring the economy

The ideal economic policy would maintain the economy in its desired state, reacting immediately and appropriately to every minor tendency to deviate from this state. Perfect maintenance would require perfect prediction because each deviating tendency would have to be caught before it would actually take effect. Automatic policies of the kind discussed in the previous section can never ensure such maintenance because they rely on restorative influences that appear only after actual deviations occur.

Given the present "state of the art" in economics, problems of prediction seem to rule out maintenance policy as a practical goal, except perhaps in certain periods when few unusual influences occur. A modified form of this type of policy (called *fine tuning*) was attempted in the United States during 1964–68 but did not succeed in catching the birth stages of the 1967–71 inflation.

Restoring the Economy

Restorative policies, designed to bring the economy back to the desired state after deviation has already become apparent, remain the chief tools of macroeconomic policy-makers. Because these do not depend on complete accuracy in prediction and complete quantification of effects, economists are more confident about restoring the economy to high employment with low inflation than about keeping it right on the line. The primary restorative problems are thus those of increasing economic activity when output is below capacity and reducing inflation when the rate of price increases is considered too high.

Anti-Recession Policy

When moving the economy out of a *recession*, economists are quite confident, in principle. If a recession exists, it is because equilibrium output is below the full employment level. This situation, in turn, exists because planned private expenditure, plus the current level of government expenditure, is insufficient to sustain full employment. Thus, without disturbing planned private expenditure, the government need merely increase its own expenditure sufficiently to fill the gap or induce a rise in planned private expenditure.

Increased government expenditure is an old prescription, the application of which is subject to two practical problems. One is that government expenditure must be increased in a way that does not reduce private planned expenditure to the same extent; the other is that the sheer size of the required increase in government expenditure may not be feasible.

The size problem cannot be ignored in a depression or major recession. Actual United States GNP in 1933 was $56 billion, full employment GNP was at least $100 billion. To have filled the gap by government expenditure *alone* would have required that it increase expenditure approximately six-fold, from $8 billion to $48 billion. In the 1956 recession, about $43 billion would have been required to achieve full employment—less than 50 percent more than the then-current government expenditure, but still a substantial increase.

But these estimates ignore the multiplier effect. If the government increases its expenditure *without increasing its revenue*, GNP will rise by an amount equal to the increase in expenditure times the multiplier. Early estimates of the marginal propensity to consume put the multiplier close to 4, suggesting that government expenditure needed to be increased only by about one-fourth of the gap between actual and full employment GNP. This would have implied a 150 percent increase in expenditure in 1933 and a 12 percent increase in 1958.

The possibility of the government spending its way out of a recession in a fairly straightforward way would thus generally appear to be an economically feasible fiscal policy. Whether such spending is *politically* feasible is another matter—especially if the requisite increase in expenditure requires both a substantial government deficit and rapid implementation. An alternative to increased government spending is for the government to induce private expenditure to rise by the necessary amount.

Indirect Policies

Even though induced changes in private expenditure can be initiated by fiscal policies (tax cuts, for example), such inducement is generally considered to be the special preserve of monetary policy. Monetary policy is used primarily to influence interest rates or the quantity of money; the "classical" approach to anti-recession policy was based on the presumption that lowering the interest rate sufficiently would greatly increase investment, and possibly consumption, because of lowered saving.

It is now doubted whether the rate of interest can be pushed below a certain minimum level by ordinary monetary policy. Thus, the scope for interest-rate reduction depends very much on this rate's initial level. If the interest rate is initially high, it can be pushed down, but if it is initially low, it may be difficult or impossible to move it down further. In any case, most modern investment theory and empirical investigation suggest that investment is relatively insensitive to the rate of interest, or far less sensitive than visualized in classical analysis.

No method of encouraging private investment seems likely to be capable, by itself, of generating the massive increases necessary to move the economy out of major stagnation. Allowing a very generous short-term multiplier of 3, it would have required a doubling of investment in 1933 to reach full employment when interest rates were already low, business profits nonexistent, and such things as tax concessions irrelevant.

Using monetary theory to increase the quantity of money, rather than attempting to further reduce interest rates, is what modern monetarists prescribe. In this view, as the quantity of money is increased, the ratio of money balances to current expenditure becomes higher than desired, and firms and individuals react by increasing their expenditure. In terms of the Keynesian model, the effect is to increase both investment (through balances held by firms) and the marginal propensity to consume. Because the multiplier rises with the marginal propensity to consume, the mechanism—if it works as suggested—would be more powerful than that operating through interest rates alone.

Under conditions of depression or major recession, however, there is no guarantee that this mechanism will actually work. Although the monetary authorities can always increase commercial bank reserves ("high-powered money"), an increase in checking-account deposits (which form the actual balances of firms and households) requires commercial banks to increase loans—which they may be unwilling to do under unfavorable business conditions. Thus, monetary policy may not be able to increase the quantity of money as required.

Anti-Inflation Policy

In dealing with *inflation,* the principles are similar but the directions are reversed. Fiscal policy necessitates a reduction in government expenditure, or an increase in taxes, or both. Because many government expenditures represent fixed commitments, the requisite reduction in planned total expenditure will almost certainly require increased taxes.

Monetary policy will be operated with emphasis on either raising interest rates or reducing the quantity of money—there is no conflict because both are associated with a "tight" monetary policy. Increased interest rates will deter investment, while a lower quantity of money will reduce planned expenditure as attempts are made to run up individual balances.

The relative efficiencies of monetary and fiscal policies tend to be reversed as compared with anti-recession policy. Even though tax increases are politically unpopular and require considerable time to become operative (in the United States at least), the quantity of money can be reduced rapidly by raising reserve requirements and forcing commercial banks to call in loans. Banks cannot be forced to *increase* loans, but they can be forced to *reduce* them.

For reasons discussed in greater detail in Chapter 25, curing inflation by fiscal and monetary policy alone may be almost impossible without *some* overshoot into recession. This is because of the built-in dynamic of the inflationary process, operating through cost-push and inflationary expectations. Wage-price controls (discussed in the last section of this chapter) may be able to prevent such an overshoot.

Recap Due to imperfect prediction and the fact that automatic stabilizers are only partially effective, most policy consists of restoring the economy to some desired state from which it has already diverged. The policy prescriptions for restoring high employment after a recession are well codified, such restoration being achievable with a sufficient increase in government expenditure. However, the required magnitude of such an increase may be very large under severely depressed conditions such as those that existed in the 1930s. Policies operating on the money supply or rate of interest are also possible, but have less certain effects. Eliminating inflation without bringing on a marked recession is a more difficult policy objective for which monetary policy may be more useful than fiscal policy.

Does the Type of Expenditure Matter?

The effects of different kinds of government expenditure

Government expenditure decisions influence the *output mix* of the economy and the distribution of *incomes and goods* within the economy—matters of the highest policy importance. Our concern here, however, is simply whether the type of expenditure affects the *macroeconomic* consequences of fiscal policy. In other words, we want to know whether an additional $1 million of government expenditure on congressional salaries has the same effect on national income as an additional $1 million spent on interstate highway construction.

Usefulness Not Critical

From the point of view of income generation, it doesn't really matter whether the *immediate* result of the expenditure is to create something "useful" or not. If the government were to spend $100 million to give jobs to the unemployed by hiring workers to dig holes and then fill them in, there would be no difference in the impact on incomes than if the workers were used to rebuild slums, paint subways, clean streets, or implement rural electrification projects. As a matter of fact, it would make no real difference if the jobless were simply given incomes and not required to work at all.

Of course, given that there are many useful things that can be done in any real economy, it would be a waste not to use resources efficiently. Spending $100 million on slum remodeling rather than digging and filling holes would have the same general income-increasing effect *and* would increase social welfare by the results of the project. The hole-digging example is nonetheless important. It illustrates the fact that lack of imagination about what to do in society is no excuse for failing to boost a flagging economy. The holes may have no use in themselves, but the income generated will induce increases in the output of real goods and services.

Type-of-Expenditure Effects

From a pure income-generating point of view, the important considerations for government expenditure are:

1. Who receives the initial (first-round) income from the expenditure?
2. Does the expenditure affect expenditure plans in *other* sectors?

The marginal propensity to consume is not uniform over society. It is generally expected to be lower among the rich than among the poor. Thus, expenditure that initially increases the incomes of the rich will have a lower multiplier effect than expenditure that initially increases the incomes of the poor. In many cases, simple redistribution from the rich to the poor may increase society's overall propensity to consume sufficiently to increase the equilibrium level of income noticeably without increasing total government expenditure.

When the government's objective is to slow down the economy, rather than speed it up, things work in reverse. It will be more effective to cut expenditure that generates incomes for the poor than expenditure that generates income for the rich, and the economy will be dampened by redistribution from the poor to the rich. Such considerations add to the problems of controlling inflation—the appropriate macro policies conflict with distributive objectives, whereas the two are in harmony when the economy is being boosted.

Linkages

Another consideration of expenditure policy important from the income-generating point of view is the effect on expenditure in other sectors. Increasing government expenditure by building public housing, for example, may *reduce* planned construction investment in the private sector. On the other hand, increased expenditure on the space program (which would never be undertaken in the private sector) may *encourage* additional private investment in aerospace, electronics, and other related industries, adding to the income-generating results of government policy.

Unfortunately, from a moral and political point of view, war (or the threat of war) provides just about the ideal form of government expenditure for expanding the economy. The basic expenditure is on something the private sector will not supply by itself, and the effect of the expenditure is to stimulate private investment in many related fields.

Although there are those who maintain that capitalism needs war or the threat of war to prevent collapse from lack of income-generating expenditure, there are other forms of government expenditure that would be equally effective—massive development of urban transport, for example—but only if carried out on a sufficiently large scale (like defense and space) to generate additional, related private investment.

Recap The income-generating effect of government expenditure does not depend on the ultimate "usefulness" of the expenditure. However, the effect does depend on who initially receives the expenditure and whether the expenditure affects other injections. The income-generating effects can be expected to be greatest for expenditures whose initial effect is to increase incomes of the poor and on goods not normally provided in the private sector. Some types of expenditure may even have linkage effects that increase private investment.

Fiscal, Monetary, or a Mixture?

How the policy-maker should decide between various combinations of monetary and fiscal policy

Because both fiscal and monetary policy can be used to achieve macroeconomic policy objectives, the two sets of policy instruments are often treated as rivals—fiscal *versus* monetary policy.

Although, in principle, both types of policy can be used to achieve similar objectives, they are not direct substitutes for each other. Each has its own special effects and is therefore generally more effective under special circumstances.

The Public-Private Mix

To take the broadest difference first, fiscal policy has a significant impact on the relationship of the public to the private sector. Fiscal policy is both easier to employ and more effective when government expenditure is high relative to expenditure in the private sector. If the government increases its spending to boost the economy, it becomes committed to certain types of expenditure. When dampening, rather than boosting, is required, the government is more likely to raise taxes than to cut back on its recently developed commitments. The use of fiscal policy thus *tends* to enlarge the government sector relative to the private sector. Monetary policy, on the other hand, works entirely through the private sector, and is compatible with a small government sector.

Those who believe, either for ideological reasons or on the basis of efficiency and social-welfare considerations, that the economy should consist predominantly of the private sector will tend to favor monetary over fiscal policy.

Microeconomic Effects

The effects of monetary policy are diffused, but not any more evenly over the economy than are the effects of fiscal policy. Contractionary monetary policy will increase interest rates, and thus discourage borrowing and investment. The activity most prominently discouraged under these circumstances is *new construction.* The need for housing is not a short-term cyclical need, but a long-term one—and a marriage or baby boom may be having its peak effects just when monetary policy is cutting new construction down to almost zero. Alternatively, expansionary monetary policy in a recession may make low-interest loans for housing more readily available, even though there may be no buyers and thus no expenditure generated.

In short, while such potential effects of monetary policy on the output mix can be predicted, they cannot be easily manipulated. Fiscal policy, with which it is possible to vary expenditures and taxes in a highly selective fashion, can achieve both a desired output mix and broad macroeconomic objectives at the same time.

It is possible, in principle, to have *selective* monetary policy. Commercial banks can be instructed to lend for some purposes and not for others, a common practice in many planned economies and some others closer to the American pattern. Most advocates of monetary policy, however, consider the lack of explicit selection a virtue—interest rates change and act as prices on the basis of which priorities are established by private firms and households.

Policy Interdependence

Fiscal and monetary policy are not truly independent. How one works will depend on the prevailing character of the other. "Pure" monetary policy is generally visualized as operating in a context in which fiscal policy is *neutral,* in the sense of having a strictly *balanced budget.* Similarly, "pure" fiscal policy assumes neutral monetary policy in the sense that *interest rates* are kept constant.

Neutral policy, however, is still policy. Suppose the economy is depressed, but possesses an equilibrium money supply. If income is expanded by fiscal policy with no action by the monetary authority, the existing money supply will then be inappropriate for the higher incomes at the old interest rates. We will expect interest rates to rise. Neutral monetary policy, in this case, will require increasing the quantity of money more or less in proportion to the increase in income. This turns out to be a very positive policy. If the appropriate increase in money supply were not made, interest rates would rise, reducing investment and diminishing the effectiveness of the fiscal policy.

Because monetary and fiscal policy can have similar broad effects but differ in their detailed impact, the "best" policy is inevitably a *mixture* of fiscal and monetary policy, the mix being varied according to requirements. During the 1930s, attempts at expansionary fiscal policy were swamped by an inappropriate monetary policy. If both fiscal and monetary policy had been expansionary, the outcome would have been much different.

Fiscal policy would seem to have some advantage in anti-recession action; monetary policy, in combatting inflation. In either case, however, reinforcement by the other policy cannot hurt and will generally help.

Institutional Factors

Institutional factors may be important in choosing the policy mix. Because the budgetary process in the United States involves passage of complex legislation through Congress, *rapid* changes in fiscal policy are difficult to achieve unless a crisis situation exists. In principle, presidents could be voted discretionary fiscal powers, such as the power to vary tax rates within specified limits, but Congress is reluctant to lose control of such matters.

Even under less complex political arrangements than those of the United States, the instruments of monetary policy can be manipulated more rapidly than those of fiscal policy. However, this does not mean that the *effects* are always immediately apparent.

Empirical Evidence

Some evidence about lags between policy implementation and effects can be derived from computer simulation with the more elaborate macromodels. Simulation based on the Federal Reserve–MIT Model (Table 32.1) shows the time patterns for three types of policy. Hence, while monetary policy can perhaps be initiated more rapidly, it appears to work more slowly than fiscal policy.

Recap Fiscal and monetary policy can achieve similar broad objectives, but with different side effects. Fiscal policy generally alters the relationship between government output and private output. Monetary policy affects the private sector, but not uniformly. For example, interest-rate changes affect construction more than other industries. There are also institutional and political factors, as well as the speed of both implementation and response, that affect the policy choice. Some mixture of fiscal and monetary policy is generally appropriate.

Table 32.1
Simulation Based on the
Federal Reserve–MIT Model

Policy	Proportion of ultimate effect on GNP obtained within		
	6 months	1 year	2 years
Fiscal I (tax cut)	45%	90%	almost complete
Fiscal II (expenditure increase)	63%	106%	112%
Monetary	8%	17%	80%

(Fiscal II shows figures over 100 percent because there is an overshoot. The effect on GNP declines after two years, and the ultimate effect (100%) is less than the medium-term effects.)

Wage-Price Controls

The appropriate use of wage-price controls

Apart from safety, health, and, more recently, antipollution regulations, the only direct controls that have been extensively used in the United States are those on prices and wages during periods of inflation. Such controls were used during World War II; modified controls appeared during the Korean conflict (1950–53); and wage-price controls appeared again during the 1971–72 inflationary period.

The case for such controls was presented in Chapter 25. It is based on the distinction between the initiating cause of an inflation (excess of planned demand over available supply) and the self-perpetuating inflationary dynamic (inflationary spiral) whereby the inflation, once started, leads to increasing prices that create the need for wage increases that, in turn, lead to higher costs and higher prices. Removing the initiating cause is a matter for fiscal and/or monetary policy, but the spiral may continue even after the initiating cause is removed. Wage and price controls provide a policy that addresses the dynamic process itself. Thus, wage-price policy is not a *substitute* for fiscal and monetary policy but a *supplement* to it. It can dampen the inflationary spiral once the causes of inflationary excess demand are removed, but will ultimately break down into widespread avoidance and black market activity if excess demand is not otherwise removed.

The use of wage and price controls during such periods as World War II, when excess demand was inevitable and sustained, was simply an attempt to moderate the effects of an inflation whose causes could not be reversed. The wage and price controls instituted in 1971 provide a better example of the use of such policies as an option, rather than a political necessity. When the controls were imposed (in August, 1971), the U.S. economy was in a period characterized by simultaneous inflation and recession. Such a combination clearly implies that there is no problem of excess demand (because the economy is operating at less than full capacity), and thus that the inflation must be due to the continuation of an inflationary spiral started during an earlier period. Such a situation provides the ideal circumstances under which to use wage-price policies—to act on the mechanism of the spiral itself. Thus, the 1971 price controls were an appropriate use of such policies although it might be argued that they should have been introduced much earlier than they were.

The chief problems of wage-price policies and other direct controls are administrative. It's one thing to discuss appropriate changes in general price levels and average wages in simple macromodels and quite another to reach appropriate decisions about tens of thousands of pay scales and hundreds of thousands of commodity prices. For these purely administrative reasons, wage and price controls are most practical when they can be imposed for relatively short periods (say, two years or less), enabling use of simple rules-of-thumb like allowing all wages and/or prices to change in the same proportion. For longer periods, such simple rules are bound to introduce major distortions and inequities.

The 1971 Nixon controls made an attempt at administrative simplicity by concentrating on controlling prices set by firms with large market shares and controlling wages negotiated in major collective bargaining contracts. They were designed to be short-period controls to dampen the inflationary spiral with minimum administrative complexity.

Recap Wage-price controls are appropriate supplements to fiscal and monetary policy in some circumstances, especially during inflation. Although fiscal and monetary policy can deal with the initiating cause of inflation, the self-sustained inflationary spiral may continue even after the initial inflationary cause is removed. Wage and price controls act directly on the dynamics of this spiral.

Exercises

1. List as many differences as you can between the side effects of:
    a. a 10 percent increase in income taxes across the board, and
    b. an increase in interest rates designed to achieve the same level of aggregate demand as the tax increase.
2. Compare the consequences of:
    a. undershooting, and
    b. overshooting on a policy designed to achieve exact full employment.
3. List the problems likely to arise if wage-price controls are kept in force permanently.

For Thought and Discussion

1. How would your choice between monetary and fiscal policy be influenced by your view of whether the economy needs more or fewer public goods?

2. One type of automatic policy that has been suggested is that the government act as "employer of last resort," guaranteeing employment to all at a wage equal to the lowest wage paid in the private sector. Would such a policy maintain the economy at capacity output?

3. Would the effects be different if the government offered to employ everyone at the wage last received in the private sector?

4. Your policy aim is to boost the overall economy, but especially to encourage the construction of suburban homes for owner occupancy. Given the alternatives of either a constant money supply with a budget deficit financed by selling bonds, or expansion of the money supply with no change in the budget, which would be most likely to achieve your objectives?

5. If the aim were to increase the supply of urban rental housing for the poor, would you give the same answer as in question 4?

Part 9
International Economics

This part, consisting of Chapters 33 through 35, is concerned with the effects of economic relationships among different countries. Chapter 33 considers the reasons why countries trade with each other, and the effects of such trade on their domestic economies. Chapter 34 is concerned with the ways in which payments are made between different countries, and with the balance of payments, foreign-currency relationships, and international monetary relationships. Chapter 35, which should be read even by those not especially concerned with international economic affairs, discusses the effects of international relationships on the general problems of economic policy.

Chapter 33
International
Trade

Terms and Concepts

Free trade
Capital-intensive industry
Labor-intensive industry
Trading possibility frontier
Exchange rate
Comparative advantage
Terms of trade
Gains from trade
Tariffs
Infant-industry argument
Senile-industry argument

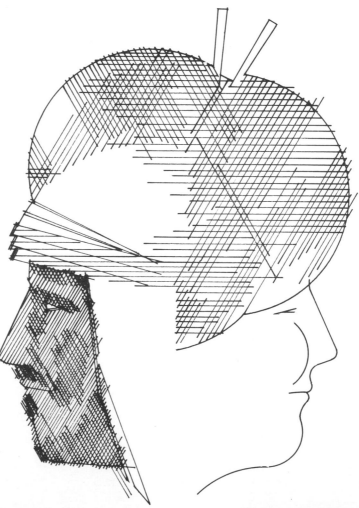

Why Trade?

**The reasons why countries choose
to trade with one another**

Countries engage in trade for the same reason that individuals within a given economy engage in exchange—mutual gain. Indeed, *free trade,* in which there are no government restrictions or taxes imposed on the trading parties, is simply exchange among *individuals* in two different countries. The two countries themselves "trade" only in the sense that the international transactions of individuals in each country are normally aggregated for record-keeping purposes.

Individual exchanges can be presumed to improve the position of all traders involved. Consequently, if no one is made worse off, free trade can be presumed to improve the welfare of both countries. We'll examine the gains from free trade in more detail later.

Trading as a Country

It is possible, of course, for a country to trade *as a country.* Its government would determine how much of its various commodities should be traded and on what terms they should be exchanged for those of other countries, instead of leaving trading decisions to individuals. Such a government could carry out its trading policies either by *direct controls,* through a state trading agency charged with handling all international transactions, or by *indirect controls,* which merely influence the terms on which private individuals may trade. Soviet-type economies typically carry out their trade policies through direct state trading. Economies like those of Western Europe and the United States influence trade by indirect methods, of which the best known is the imposition of special taxes called *tariffs.*

The relationship between two trading countries, each with complete centralized control of trade, is analogous to that between two individuals attempting to strike a bargain. If neither country is being coercive, we can presume that both governments believe their respective countries are better off by the agreed trading conditions. Otherwise, at least one country would refuse to trade. Coercion, of course, has been known to exist. One of the oldest uses of military conquest, or the threat of it, was to force the weaker country to trade under unfavorable conditions. Colonies or client countries have also been "exploited" in the sense that unfavorable trading conditions have been imposed on them.

Although the existence of trade without coercion allows both countries to gain *when compared to the absence of trade,* this does not mean that every trading arrangement is equally satisfactory to both trading parties. Much of the theory of international trade is concerned with assessing the effects on the countries involved of such different trading arrangements as free trade, trade under various tariff structures, and centralized trade control.

Recap Trade between countries takes place for the same reason as trade between individuals within a country: both sides can gain from it. Trade between individuals (or individual firms) in different countries without government intervention is known as free trade. If governments intervene in international trade, they typically do so by imposing taxes, called tariffs, on traded goods.

The Expansion of Economic Possibilities

How trade can expand economic possibilities

Generally speaking, trade enables a trading country to attain consumption points lying outside its production possibility frontier. We shall illustrate this with an example of two countries, each capable of producing two goods, applesauce and dental floss. One of the countries, Capitalia, is well provided with machinery so it can use production methods with high ratios of capital to labor. The other country, Ruralia, has no capital and must use techniques that require labor only.

The outputs per man-day of these two goods in each country are:

| | Output Per Man-day | |
	Dental floss (meters)	Applesauce (liters)
Capitalia	4	10
Ruralia	1	5

Note that because capital is available in Capitalia, the output per man-day is *greater for both goods* than in Ruralia. On the other hand, the use of capital makes more difference in dental-floss production than in applesauce production. We can thus refer to dental-floss production as being more *capital-intensive,* because a man-day of labor in Capitalia can produce four times as much dental floss as in Ruralia, but only twice as much applesauce.

Ruralia has no capital at all, while Capitalia is assumed to have as much as it will ever need. Thus, the production possibilities in *both* countries are determined by *the availability of labor*. If Capitalia has a population of 1 million households and Ruralia 2 million, with one worker per household, we can easily calculate the production possibilities of the two countries in isolation.

Production Possibilities

Capitalia, with 1 million man-days of labor available, could produce 4 million meters of dental floss if all labor were used to produce dental floss,

Figure 33.1

Production possibility frontiers for two countries with different resource endowments.

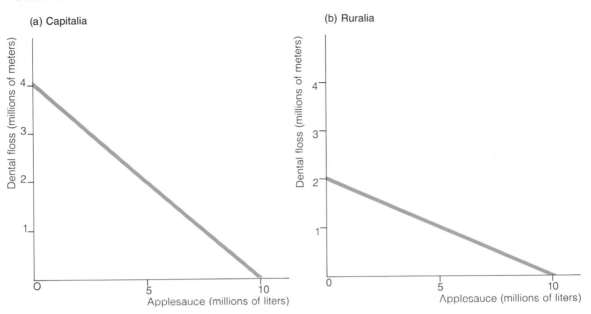

(a) Capitalia

(b) Ruralia

or 10 million liters of applesauce if all labor were used to produce applesauce. Various allocations of labor between dental-floss and applesauce production will give points on the straight-line production possibility frontier shown in Figure 33.1(a). This frontier has a constant marginal rate of transformation of 2.5 liters of applesauce per meter of dental floss because a worker who moves from applesauce to dental-floss production will increase dental-floss output by 4 meters per day, but reduce applesauce output by 10 liters per day.

Ruralia, with 2 million man-days of labor available, could produce 2 million meters of dental floss if all labor went into the dental-floss industry, or, like Capitalia, 10 million liters of applesauce if all labor were to be concentrated in applesauce production. The resulting production possibility frontier is the straight line shown in Figure 33.1(b). The marginal rate of transformation in Ruralia is 5 liters of applesauce per meter of dental floss because one man-day gives 1 meter of dental floss or 5 liters of applesauce.

If both countries had the same standard of applesauce consumption at 3 liters per household per day, then Capitalia, in isolation, would produce and consume 3 million liters of applesauce (requiring 300 thousand workers), and be able to produce 2.8 million meters of dental floss with the 700 thousand remaining workers. Ruralia, for the same applesauce consumption level, would produce and consume 6 million liters of applesauce (remember, it has double Capitalia's population) using 1.2 million workers, with 800 thousand workers still available to produce 800 thousand meters of dental floss.

At the specified applesauce consumption level, Capitalia can provide 2.8 meters of dental floss per household; Ruralia, only 0.4. Capitalia is a richer country than Ruralia because it has more resources—ample capital as well as labor.

Trading Possibilities

Now let's consider the possibilities of trade between the two countries. In Capitalia, 1 meter of dental floss can be exchanged for 2.5 liters of applesauce, while in Ruralia it can be exchanged for 5 liters of applesauce. Suppose we pick an exchange rate between 2.5 and 5—say 4. At this rate, someone in Capitalia could exchange a meter of dental floss for 4 liters of applesauce—obtaining more applesauce than at Capitalia's isolated exchange rate. A person in Ruralia, on the other hand, could exchange 4 liters of applesauce to obtain a meter of dental floss—obtaining a meter of dental floss for less applesauce than at Ruralia's isolated exchange rate.

Thus, if trade were freely permitted, individuals in both countries would do better by international exchange at some rate like 4 liters of applesauce per meter of dental floss than they could by exchange within their own country in isolation. *Both* sides can gain only if the international exchange rate lies *between the rates in isolation*. A Ruralian would be happy to exchange 2 liters of applesauce for a meter of dental floss, but a Capitalian would be unwilling to exchange a meter of dental floss for only 2 liters of applesauce internationally when he could get 2.5 liters internally.

Traders in both countries gain from exchange at an appropriate rate only when trade takes place *in one particular direction*. In our example, Capitalians will trade dental floss for Ruralian applesauce; they will never trade their applesauce for Ruralian dental floss. Trade in the reverse direction would mean that Capitalians would give up 4 liters of applesauce for 1 meter of Ruralian dental floss when they only need to give up 2.5 liters at their isolated internal rate. And the Ruralians would give up 1 meter of dental floss for only 4 liters of applesauce instead of the 5 liters they could obtain at the internal rate. Both sides will thus *lose* from trade in the wrong direction.

Economic Possibilities

We are now ready to consider the effect of trade at the rate of 4 liters of applesauce per meter of dental floss on the economic possibilities in both countries.

Suppose Capitalia produces no applesauce, but manufactures dental floss

Figure 33.2

How trade can expand the economic possibilities for both countries beyond what each could produce in isolation.

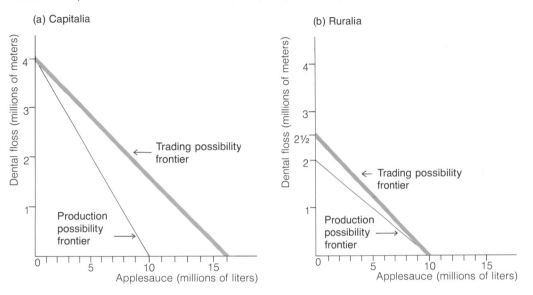

exclusively with the objective of exchanging some dental floss for applesauce. If Capitalia exchanges none, it will have 4 million meters of dental floss. If it exchanges all of its dental floss for applesauce, it will receive 16 million liters compared with the 10 million liters it could produce in isolation. By retaining some dental floss and trading the rest, it can attain combinations of these two goods represented by the *trading possibility frontier* in Figure 33.2(a).

Similarly, Ruralia, by producing only applesauce, and trading some for dental floss, can attain product combinations represented by points on the line joining 10 liters of applesauce (its maximum production) and 2.5 million meters of dental floss (the amount it could obtain by exchanging its complete applesauce production), shown in Figure 33.2(b).

For both countries, the trading possibility frontier lies beyond the production possibility frontier, except at one point. *The economic possibilities of the two countries, now represented by trading possibilities rather than production possibilities, are greater with trade than in isolation.*

Recap If two countries differ in their production possibilities, they can both gain from trade in the direct sense that the trading possibility frontier of both countries lies farther out than the production possibility frontier.

The Principle of Comparative Advantage

What determines which goods a country exports and which it imports

In the previous analysis, we showed that, for two countries *with different internal rates of transformation between two goods,* individual traders in both countries will gain from trade and the two countries themselves will gain in the sense of expanding economic possibilities, if

1. the international exchange rate between the two goods (which is equivalent to the *terms of trade* between the countries in this example) lies between the two internal transformation rates; and
2. trade takes place in one particular direction—Capitalia producing dental floss and exchanging it for Ruralian applesauce.

Direction and Advantage

We shall concentrate here on the *direction* of trade. Why do both countries gain if Capitalia exchanges its dental floss for Ruralian applesauce, while both countries lose if Capitalia exchanges its applesauce for Ruralian dental floss? The reason is that Capitalia's production possibilities are such that it must sacrifice less applesauce to produce a given quantity of dental floss (10 liters to get 4 meters) than Ruralia must (20 liters to get 4 meters). In other words, Capitalia can produce *relatively* more dental floss than applesauce with one man-day of labor than Ruralia can. To summarize, Capitalia has a *comparative advantage* in the production of dental floss.

Ruralia, on the other hand, can produce relatively more applesauce than dental floss with one man-day of labor than Capitalia can. That is, it must sacrifice less dental floss to produce a given quantity of applesauce (2 meters to get 10 liters) than Capitalia must (4 meters to get 10 liters). Ruralia thus has a comparative advantage in the production of applesauce. The direction of trade in which gains are made is thus related to comparative advantage in the following way:

When a country has a comparative advantage in the production of a good, it normally gains from trade if it exports that good.

Efficiency and Comparative Advantage

Comparative advantage and the consequent gains from trade depend only on the *relative* productivity of the industries in each country. Capitalia gains by importing Ruralian applesauce even though its own applesauce industry may be considered more "efficient" than Ruralia's because one man-day of Capitalian labor produces twice as much applesauce as one man-day of Ruralian labor (10 liters compared with 5). The gains occur because Capitalian dental-floss production is *even more* ''efficient'' in this sense than its applesauce production relative to Ruralia.

By using one man-day to produce 4 meters of dental floss, then trading this dental floss to Ruralia for 16 liters of applesauce (assuming an exchange rate of 4 liters of applesauce per meter of dental floss), Capitalian labor can *indirectly* ''produce'' 16 liters of applesauce—60 percent more than by direct internal production. Similarly, one man-day of Ruralian labor used to produce 5 liters of applesauce that is exchanged for 1.25 meters of dental floss has indirectly ''produced'' 1.25 meters of dental floss—25 percent more than by direct internal production.

A country may be the world's ''most efficient'' producer of some product, yet still gain by importing this product rather than producing it if it is even more efficient producing other products.

Sources of Comparative Advantage

There are many reasons why a country may have a comparative advantage in one product rather than in another. Differences in natural resources can be important—tropical countries have an extreme comparative advantage in producing tropical agricultural products, for example. Differences in skills or technology are also an important determinant of comparative advantage. In our example, Capitalia's comparative advantage in dental floss results because

1. dental-floss production is more capital-intensive than applesauce production; and
2. Capitalia has more capital than Ruralia.

There is a general presumption that a country will tend to export goods that use intensively those production factors with which it is best endowed. The United States tends to export technologically advanced (capital-intensive) manufactured goods because it has a high ratio of capital to labor; Australia exports the (land-intensive) products of ranching because it has a high ratio of land to labor. But even countries that possess similar factor endowments may exchange different models of automobiles or different types of machine tools. Consequently, the factor endowment rule should be viewed only as a broad guide to expectations.

Of course, the real world consists not of two countries trading in two goods, but of dozens of countries trading in thousands of goods. From the viewpoint of any one country, however, we can regard the ''rest of the world'' as an approximation to a single country. Our country will tend to export goods in which it has a comparative advantage relative to the average over the rest of the world, and import those for which it has an equivalent kind of comparative disadvantage.

Figure 33.3

At an exchange ratio of three liters of applesauce per meter of dental floss, both countries gain, but the gain is relatively greater for Ruralia.

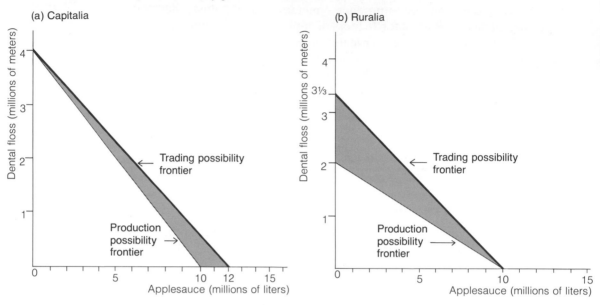

Recap The difference between the production possibility frontiers of two countries can be expressed as the difference in internal rates of transformation between different goods in the two countries. Of two countries with different rates of transformation between, say, dental floss and applesauce, the country that can produce the highest ratio of dental floss to applesauce from given resources is said to have a comparative advantage in dental-floss production. The other country then must have a comparative advantage in applesauce production. Both countries gain from trade only when each exports the good in which it has a comparative advantage.

The Terms and Volume of Trade

What determines the volume of trade and the price relationship between traded goods

We have already seen that traders *in both countries* will be willing to exchange dental floss and applesauce only at exchange rates lying between the isolated transformation rates in the two countries.

For the numerical example given, the transformation rates were 2.5 and 5

Figure 33.4

At an exchange ratio of four liters of applesauce per meter of dental floss, both countries gain, but the gain is relatively greater for Capitalia.

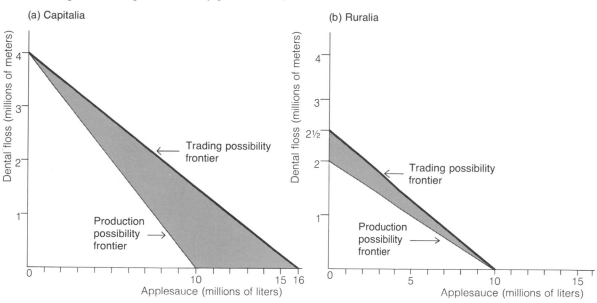

liters of applesauce per meter of dental floss. We arbitrarily chose 4 liters of applesauce per meter of dental floss as a potential exchange rate for international trade. Other exchange rates are possible, as long as they lie between 2.5 and 5.

Trade and the Price Ratio

Figures 33.3 and 33.4 show the relation between the isolated production possibilities and the trading possibilities for Capitalia and Ruralia under each of two exchange rates between dental floss and applesauce—3 liters of applesauce per meter of dental floss in Figure 33.3, and 4 liters of applesauce per meter of dental floss in Figure 33.4. Comparing the diagrams, we can see immediately that:

1. Capitalia's trading possibility frontier lies farther beyond its production possibility frontier at an exchange rate of 4 liters of applesauce per meter of dental floss than at a rate of 3 liters of applesauce per meter of dental floss.
2. The situation is reversed for Ruralia—its expansion of economic possibilities is greater at an exchange rate of 3 liters of applesauce per meter of dental floss than at 4 liters of applesauce per meter of dental floss.

Capitalia has a comparative advantage in dental-floss production, so it exports dental floss. Its gain from trade is greater when the price of dental floss in terms of applesauce (its import) is greater—at 4 liters of applesauce per meter of dental floss. Ruralia, on the other hand, exports applesauce and its gain from trade is greater when the price of applesauce in terms of dental floss (its import) is greater—at ⅓ meter of dental floss per liter of applesauce.

The Terms of Trade

The price of a country's exports in terms of its imports is called the *terms of trade* for that country. A higher price of exports in terms of imports is referred to as *more favorable terms of trade* relative to a lower price of exports in terms of imports. In our example, each country exports one good and imports one good so the terms of trade are directly related to the exchange rate between applesauce and dental floss. The price of dental floss in terms of applesauce (so many liters of applesauce per meter of dental floss) represents Capitalia's terms of trade; its inverse (so many meters of dental floss per liter of applesauce) represents Ruralia's terms of trade.

Because the terms of trade of the two countries are reciprocally related, more favorable terms of trade for one country imply less favorable terms of trade for the other.

In general, we can conclude that:

For two trading countries, the more favorable the terms of trade to one, the greater the gain in economic possibilities to that country and the less the gain to the other. In the absence of coercion, however, the terms of trade will not be such that either country loses from trade.

Gains Depend on Volume

The *actual* gains from trade depend on both the economic possibilities opened up and consumer interest in those possibilities. To take up our example again, if Ruralians had no interest in dental floss and wanted only applesauce (either because of poor dental hygiene or poverty), there would be no advantage derived from trade because there would be no Ruralian who would wish to exchange applesauce for dental floss. Expanded economic possibilities would thus lead to no actual gain.

The more interested the Ruralians are in dental floss and the Capitalians in applesauce, the greater will be the volume of exchange and, because each exchange involves a gain, the greater will be the total gain. In other words, actual gains from trade depend on two things—the *terms of trade* and the *volume of trade*. However, these two factors are not totally independent.

A country may succeed in having such favorable terms of trade that its exports are too expensive for anyone in the rest of the world to buy. Thus, the country would have highly favorable terms of trade, but zero volume, and would derive no gain at all from the existence of trade. The country would be better off with "worse" terms of trade that would increase its volume of trade and thus its gains from trade.

Recap For both countries to gain from trade, the price ratio of the traded goods must lie between certain limits that depend on the internal production conditions in the two countries. The ratio of the price of a country's export good to the price of its import good is called the terms of trade. A country's gains from trade depend on both the terms of trade and the volume of trade. For a given volume, a country will gain more the higher the price of its export is relative to the price of its import, that is, the more favorable its terms of trade.

The Effects of Tariffs

How one country may sometimes gain at the expense of others by imposing tariffs

In our simple two-country, two-good example, we have shown that in the absence of coercion, three things occur:

1. Trade will take place in a particular direction, with each country exporting the good in which it has a comparative advantage—Capitalia will export dental floss and Ruralia will export applesauce, never the reverse.
2. The terms of trade will lie between the domestic transformation ratios between dental floss and applesauce in the two countries.
3. The exact terms of trade (the exchange rate between dental floss and applesauce) will determine the relative gains from trade for the two countries.

The terms of trade are not arbitrary, but depend on the combined effects of:

1. the production possibilities in the two countries;
2. consumer preferences in the two countries;
3. internal market structures (perfect competition versus imperfect competition) in the two countries; and
4. the trading arrangements.

If there is free trade with perfect competition in both countries and no transport costs, then there is, in effect, a single worldwide market for each good. A Ruralian can exchange applesauce for dental floss in the Capitalian market as easily as in the Ruralian market because it costs nothing to transfer goods from one market to another. Likewise, a Capitalian can buy applesauce in the Ruralian market as easily as in the Capitalian market. It is obvious that, in equilibrium, the price of applesauce relative to the price of dental floss will be the same in both countries, otherwise everyone would shift to the market with the more favorable terms.

If both countries used the same money (say gold bars), the actual money prices of both goods would be the same in both countries. Even if the monies differed, the *relative* prices of the goods would remain the same in both countries. We shall take up the discussion of different monies in the next chapter.

Demand Conditions

With the equivalent of a single world market for each good, the exchange rate between applesauce and dental floss will be determined by the world demand relative to the world supply of the two goods. It is not possible to illustrate the equilibrium determination with simple demand and supply curves because the problem is one of general equilibrium—any change in the price of dental floss relative to applesauce will affect the terms of trade and thus the incomes of citizens in the two countries. It is easy to see, however, that the greater the extent to which consumers are interested in dental floss relative to applesauce over the world as a whole, the higher will be the price of dental floss relative to applesauce and the more favorable the terms of trade will be to Capitalia.

Tariffs and the Terms of Trade

If the government of either country abandons a free-trade policy, it may attempt to improve its terms of trade by imposing a tax or *tariff* on imports. Suppose Ruralia imposes such a tariff on dental floss (its import). The price of dental floss relative to applesauce will then be higher for Ruralian citizens than it will be in the Capitalian market, because the Ruralians must pay the price including the tariff. The tariff will thus cause Ruralia's demand for dental floss from Capitalia to fall. But, in the two-country world, Ruralia's demand for dental floss represents an important share of total demand, so the fall in Ruralia's demand will tend to cause the price of dental floss to fall relative to the price of applesauce, and thus for Ruralia's terms of trade to improve.

Tariffs and the Volume of Trade

It might seem from the preceding argument that a country gains by imposing a tariff, and the higher the tariff the better. But the mechanism by which Ruralia improves its terms of trade involves lowering its own demand for dental floss. By doing so, Ruralia reduces its volume of trade. By making the tariff high enough, dental floss may indeed become so expensive to Ruralians that they may not buy any, in which case the favorable terms of trade are worthless and lead to no gain.

Thus, the use of tariffs to improve the terms of trade also lowers the volume of trade. Improving the terms of trade tends to increase the gains from trade, while lowering the volume tends to reduce these gains. It can be shown that there is an "optimum" tariff that maximizes the gain from trade. At this tariff level the improved terms of trade are not yet offset by too great a fall in volume.

The use of tariffs to manipulate the terms of trade requires that the tariff-imposing country's share of world trade be sufficient for its demand to affect total world demand. *Such manipulation can be successful only if a country is either a major consumer or a major producer of the traded good.*

The Worldwide Effect

Although a tariff can improve one country's terms of trade, it necessarily worsens the terms of trade of other countries. Because a tariff restricts the volume of trade, the loss to trading partners from the combination of worsened terms of trade and lowered volume is greater than the gain derived by the tariff-imposing country from better terms of trade in spite of lowered volume.

Furthermore, if one country improves its terms of trade by the use of tariffs, its trading partners may *retaliate* by imposing their own tariffs. Retaliation can improve the terms of trade of the partners from what they were before retaliation, but it does so by further reducing the volume of trade. Thus, a "tariff war" may lead to *all* countries being made worse off than under free trade.

Recap The terms and volume of trade are related, just as prices and quantities are in an ordinary market. If a country is sufficiently important in trade to influence demand or supply conditions, it can improve its terms of trade by imposing a tariff. Imposing a tariff, however, will reduce the volume of trade. A country gains from a tariff only to the extent that the gain from better terms of trade is not outweighed by the loss from lower volume. If one country imposes tariffs, others may retaliate. The final result may be to make all countries worse off than under free trade.

Capsule Supplement 33.1   **The Common Market**

Although it would be extremely difficult if not impossible to arrange universal free trade, it is possible for a group of countries to institute free trade among themselves with a common tariff against the outside world. Such a group of countries is said to constitute a *customs union*. The world's most extensive customs union is the group of Western European nations known formally as the *European Economic Community* (EEC), and informally as the *Common Market*. The Common Market was a joint outgrowth of the United States' most successful foreign-aid effort, the post–World War II European Recovery Program (more commonly called the Marshall Plan after the then secretary of state) and the resolution of many war-weary Europeans that Europe would not again become a collection of small rival countries. Experiments, started in 1952 with the European Coal and Steel Community, proved so successful that plans were drawn up to extend the concept of a unified market to cover all goods. The Netherlands, Belgium, and Luxembourg had already formed a true customs union (Benelux) in 1948, which promised to be a success.

In 1958, the European Economic Community was formed by France, Italy, West Germany, and the three Benelux countries. The treaty of incorporation called for all internal tariffs between member countries to be abolished in stages over a ten-year period, and for the diverse external tariffs of the members to be unified into a common tariff. After a decade of intense step-by-step negotiations, internal trade restrictions were abolished and external tariffs were unified.

The success of the Common Market countries was spectacular during the 1960s, especially compared with the stagnating economy of Britain and the decelerating economy of the United States. It remains uncertain whether this success actually derived from the Common Market arrangements or simply resulted from complete postwar economic recovery. It's certainly true that Japan, whose economy was also smashed by war, showed spectacular growth during the same period without the help of any favorable trading arrangements. In any case, no one has ever suggested that the Common Market arrangement has *hurt* its members.

The year 1971 marked a major new step in the history of the organization—its decision to admit Britain to membership. While Britain had initially been offered charter membership, it had declined at that stage. France later vetoed British attempts to join in 1963 and 1968. The decision to admit Britain opened the door for Norway, Denmark, and Ireland, all of whom had previously wanted to join but had such strong trading relationships with Britain that they could not afford to do so if Britain remained outside the organization. Norway eventually decided not to join after all, and the newly enlarged Common Market came into being at the beginning of 1973 with a total membership of nine countries, and with plans to achieve true economic integration by 1980.

The enlarged Common Market commands all the important natural resources of Western Europe (except for some in Spain), has a population larger than that of either the United States or the Soviet Union, and possesses tremendous resources of capital and technology. *Size* had always been a key factor in the decision to form the group, and one of the strongest original motives had been to create a market for the output of the community's industries comparable in size to that of the United States, enabling economies of massive scale to be fully exploited. This goal was achieved, as was the beginning of another—to form a group with *political,* as well as economic, power comparable to that of the superpowers.

The success of the European Common Market has inspired various attempts to achieve similar results elsewhere. Groups of countries in Latin America, the Caribbean, and Africa have attempted to create various forms of expanded markets. In no case, however, have the countries been willing to go as far as the European nations in abolishing trade restrictions among members and in imposing a common external tariff. Consequently, no success as spectacular as that of the Common Market has emerged.

Internal Effects	Why trade brings
of International	**internal changes**
Trade	**to the economy**

If a country opens its doors to trade, the internal structure of the economy will inevitably be affected. The gains from trade occur *only* because the country switches from producing all of its own requirements to producing more of its export goods and less of its import goods.

Broadly speaking, America has a comparative advantage in producing complex capital goods (like aircraft and machinery) and a comparative *disadvantage* in producing certain types of goods associated with the early stages of industrialization, like cotton textiles. The expected result of America freeing its trade is that it will export more airplanes and import more textiles. Increased trade will thus cause the internal structure to shift to more aircraft production and less textile production.

An increase in aircraft production might present certain problems, such as a shortage of appropriate skills and equipment, but these will generally be temporary and self-correcting. The decline of the textile industry will also produce problems, and these will be more difficult for policy-makers to ignore.

If textile workers could simply move into the expanding aircraft industry, obviously there would be no difficulty. But it's unlikely that textile workers will be trained in skills appropriate to the aircraft industry—and it will generally be true that those industries that expand through trade will differ greatly from those that contract.

Thus, the effect of trade will be to distribute income away from workers with certain skills, and away from firms in the declining industries. If textile workers (and machines) are truly useless elsewhere in the economy, then part of the argument in favor of trade disappears, as this argument depends on the *import-competing industry being a user of resources that could be employed elsewhere.*

Immobile Resources

The lack of alternatives, if true, applies only to those resources *already* in the textile industry. Sheltering the textile industry *permanently* from foreign competition would result in new workers being trained and worn-out textile machinery being replaced. Because the economy gains from trade, it faces the certain loss of potential gains by protecting those industries that would be hard hit. On the other hand, if it permits trade, it must face the temporary income-distribution problem that will arise.

The most rational policy would be one that removes the tariff on textiles, then temporarily uses some of the gains from trade (perhaps through a temporary sales tax on *all* textiles, local or imported) to pay for the unavoidable dislocation in the domestic textile industry. Hence, the domestic industry could be subsidized, but only insofar as it produces as efficiently as possible with existing *nonmovable* resources.

But rational economic policy is difficult to formulate in the face of strong political pressures. In the circumstances outlined, the textile-workers' unions and the textile-industry owners would both exert political pressure for permanent protection of "their" industry. It would be (and is) argued, for example, that the textile industry is "essential" for national defense. After all, who else would make military uniforms in case of war?

Other Internal Effects

Restructuring the economy as a result of trade is made more difficult if there are strong *regional* factors involved. In most countries, the textile industry is located in certain geographical areas where it is the dominant industry. Restructuring may thus have profound effects on interregional income distribution, giving rise to further political pressure. Such regional domination also increases the likelihood of difficulty in shifting labor to alternative industries.

One of the major social problems in a market economy is that the *costs* of shifting jobs to improve resource allocation are largely borne by individual workers, though the *gains* accrue to society as a whole.

Not all firms in a complex economy must either export goods or be put out of business by imports. Many domestic markets can be shared with imports, with only the inefficient, high-cost firms going out of business. *Foreign competition, in this case, has much the same effect as increased numbers of domestic firms in the industry.* It reduces monopoly power if there is a single domestic firm, or loosens up the oligopoly situation if there are few domestic firms.

Recap Gains from trade occur only when resources are reallocated within each country. Thus, trade necessarily affects the internal structure of the economy—the more trade, the greater the internal effects. If some of the internal changes bring undesired effects, policies are available to remedy them without restricting trade.

Capsule Supplement 33.2 **The General Agreement on Tariffs and Trade (GATT)**

Once tariff barriers have been erected by at least one country, each remaining country can improve its *relative* position by imposing its own tariffs. Because each additional tariff reduces the *volume* of trade, however, it's quite conceivable that *all* countries may actually make themselves worse off than they would be without tariffs. Nevertheless, it still won't be to the advantage of a single country to abolish its own tariff barriers as long as those of other countries remain.

For this reason, existing tariff barriers must be reduced by all countries simultaneously in a mutually cooperative effort. The General Agreement on Tariffs and Trade (called GATT) was drawn up in 1947 for this purpose. Specifically, GATT was designed to dismantle the high tariff barriers that had grown up in the years prior to World War II.

GATT is a central negotiating society. Each "round" of tariff negotiations (which may last several years) is carried out through a large number of bilateral agreements that automatically become multilateral. Suppose, for example, the United States is interested in selling machinery to France, and France in selling textiles to the United States. These countries will bargain, and eventually reach an agreement that France will cut its machinery tariff by so much if America cuts its textile tariff by a certain amount.

Such cuts then apply to *all* textiles (not only French) imported into the United States, and *all* machinery imported into France, because of the *most-favored-nation* clause in the GATT agreement. This clause stipulates that no member of GATT may be treated worse than the "most favored nation"—in effect, that no member country's imports can be charged a higher tariff than those of any other member country, unless special exceptions have been made. Although it has been a lengthy process, GATT has greatly reduced world tariff barriers since the agreement first went into operation. The most recent examples of GATT negotiations have been the sixth or "Kennedy Round," which commenced with the passage of the U.S. Trade Expansion Act in 1962 and concluded in 1967, and the seventh or "Geneva Round," which commenced in 1973 with the purpose of not only addressing tariffs and such nontariff barriers as import quotas and licensing requirements, but also establishing rules of conduct for exporters of important foodstuffs and raw materials.

A more sweeping approach to the removal of trade barriers was to have been the purpose of the International Trade Organization (ITO), initiated after World War II. The United States Senate failed to ratify the agreement setting up this organization, which then died. This failure to support the ITO is evidence that the United States occupies an unusual place in world trade—its own trade represents a large and crucially important slice of total world trade, but the *internal* impact of this trade is far less in the United States than in any other major trading nation.

Trade Policy

Some of the arguments for and against trade restrictions

We have already shown that:

1. Each country gains from trade, unless the trading conditions have been imposed by coercion.

2. Within certain bounds, a particular country may gain by imposing tariffs.
3. Any gain obtained by one country from the imposition of tariffs is more than offset by losses to its trading partners. Free trade is therefore optimal *for the world as a whole.*
4. The expansion or contraction of trade *necessarily* requires a reallocation of resources within each country, with consequent short-run adjustment problems.

Infant Industries

Trade policy is generally discussed in terms of these four propositions. However, there are other considerations that may be used to justify certain trade policies. The most widely known of these is the *infant-industry argument.*

Consider the automobile industry in which there are indivisibilities leading to *increasing returns to scale,* as discussed in Chapter 7. If Venezuela imports automobiles from a well-established manufacturer in Japan whose operations are quite large, the import price will be low, reflecting the ability of the Japanese manufacturer to take advantage of large-scale economies.

A Venezuelan manufacturer, starting out on a small scale, would have high costs and thus would be unable to effectively compete with Japanese imports. However, if this manufacturer were protected from import competition in the initial or "infant" stage of development, he could increase his scale of operations until it was large enough (assuming the country's total market to be of adequate size) to achieve large-scale economies and thus the ability to compete with imports.

This is the essence of the infant-industry argument. It calls for *temporary* tariff protection for a growing industry in which economies of scale (or economies resulting from operating experience) exist. The tariff is imposed during the industry's "infancy," then removed when it has "grown up."

Infant-industry tariffs were imposed early in this century by the then-developing countries, such as Australia and Canada, and have been imposed by subsequent generations of less-developed countries seeking industrial expansion. Few infants have grown up to the point of having tariffs removed, however, because the more advanced industries always seem to keep one step ahead. However, Japan, most of whose modern industry was developed behind tariff and other trade barriers, is clearly competitive in international markets—though tariffs still remain.

Industrialization as a Goal

A modified version of the infant-industry argument, favored by the less-developed countries, is that industrialization is a necessary component of the lengthy process of development. According to this argument, a tariff should be imposed even if the internal market is not likely to be large enough to generate scale economies for many years. The case depends on a presumption that a steel industry, for example, is inherently necessary for long-run development and should be encouraged even if protection is needed for a hundred years.

Occasionally the infant-industry argument appears in the United States. The proposal of providing government support for building the prototype SST was essentially of this kind, although direct subsidy rather than tariff protection was the recommended mechanism.

Senile Industries

Most arguments for tariff protection in the United States come from the opposite end—for protecting a *senile* industry rather than an infant one. Continuous pressures have been exerted over many years for the protection of industries, such as clothing and textiles, in which the United States does not possess a comparative advantage.

As pointed out in the previous section, real problems arise from the decline of domestic industries as a result of increased imports. One of the few things economists agree on virtually unanimously, however, is that tariff protection is *not* the best policy for solving these problems.

World Considerations

Optimal world trade, and especially the expansion of trade by the poorer countries, requires that the richer countries allow certain industries, which are associated with the early stages of development, to decline. These include textiles, iron and steel, and (by now) perhaps even automobiles.

This does not mean that the costs of restructuring the economy should necessarily fall completely on those in the declining industries. There are ways, other than protection, of shifting the burden. Assuming that it's the textile industry that is declining under import competition, economists would consider any of the following policies to be superior to tariff protection:

1. Paying part or even most of the retraining costs for textile workers from general tax revenues.
2. Paying retraining costs partly from a tax on those export industries that will gain from increased trade.
3. Paying retraining costs partly from a sales tax on *all* textiles, whether domestic or imported, because it is textile users who would otherwise lose from the tariff.

Unfortunately, a tariff, even if economically less than optimal, is often politically more attractive than these other schemes, both because it is traditional and because its costs are widely dispersed.

Recap Although free trade is optimal for the world as a whole under static conditions, individual countries may decide to restrict trade. One reason for doing so is the gain derived from improving the terms of trade, discussed in the previous section. Another is the infant-industry argument—that, due to increasing returns to scale, some industries can grow, and thus achieve sufficiently low costs to compete internationally only with protection. The senile-industry argument, that a declining industry should be protected to prevent its total disappearance, is common in the United States.

Capsule Supplement 33.3   **Other Trade Restrictions**

Because they are the most frequently used, tariffs are the form of trade restriction with which trade theory is primarily concerned. There are, however, many other ways of restricting trade. Indeed, due to the negotiations carried out through GATT, the scope for imposing tariffs has diminished over the past thirty years, and the use of other restrictions has grown—even though these have also been subject to negotiation.

Most important among the alternatives to tariffs are quotas. Whereas a tariff is a tax imposed on imports, which places no restriction on the level of imports other than to make them more expensive and thus less attractive to residents, quotas represent a quantitative limit on the allowable level of imports.

Quotas pose a major question of allocation that does not arise in the case of tariffs, specifically: Who is to receive the right to profit from the imports on which quotas are imposed? Suppose imported oil costs $12.50 per barrel, while domestic oil costs $13.00. The domestic price is presumably high enough to cover the costs of domestic production (otherwise there would be none). Consequently, importers will make an additional profit of 50 cents on every barrel imported. There will be no shortage of potential importers. (In United States' practice, the total quota is generally divided among domestic producers approximately in proportion to their domestic output.) This allocation problem—with its associated danger of corruption of public officials—does not occur with tariffs. Under tariff restrictions, everyone who can successfully sell the import at its tariff-increased price is free to do so.

Quotas need not always be applied at the point of import. Many countries, including Canada, require that television stations broadcast a certain proportion of locally produced material or lose their licenses. Although U.S.-produced program material can be *imported* without restriction, it cannot be *sold* without restriction, and the effect is identical to that of an import quota.

Although it may seem paradoxical, a country can sometimes achieve the same result with a tax on *exports* as it would with a tariff on imports. Suppose a country is a major exporter (or the only exporter) of some good. By imposing a tax on the exportation of this good, it raises the price of its exports relative to its imports and improves its terms of trade, just as it could do by means of a tariff. For a small country whose imports are negligible relative to world trade, but whose export of a particular good is significant in world totals, an export tax could improve the terms of trade when a tariff would have no such effect. Thus, we typically find export taxes in small countries with specialized exports.

There are more subtle forms of restriction. Quarantine and health regulations can be used (or misused) to keep out imports of particular goods even when no substantial health hazard is involved. The Aviation Authority, for example, could withhold certificates of airworthiness from imported planes.

Finally, under threat of more drastic action, the importing country can reach an agreement on "voluntary" quotas with the exporting country or the major producers in that country. Japanese manufacturers in several areas (textiles and electronics, for example) have "voluntarily" agreed to restrict exports to the United States under threat of more formal quota imposition.

Exercises

Country A has 1 million inhabitants and produces rice and fish. Its technology is such that it can produce 10 tons of fish and 5 tons of rice per person. Country B has a population of 10 million, and produces the same goods with outputs of 16 tons of fish and 7 tons of rice per person.

1. Draw the production possibility curves for each of the two countries.

2. Which country has the comparative advantage in each good?

3. Would an exchange rate of 2.1 tons of fish per ton of rice enable both countries to gain from trade?

4. Which country might gain by imposing a tariff on the import of rice?

For Thought and Discussion

1. Two countries, East and West, have formerly had closed economies. Now both countries trade. As a result of this trade, there is a total gain of $100 million for both countries together. West's gain is $3 million, East's is $97 million. Is East exploiting West? Should West refuse to continue trading?

2. American shipping lines use American-built ships, the construction of which is very heavily subsidized. They also use American crews, and receive a very large subsidy on operations for so doing. What kind of arguments might be used to support this policy?

3. A country's practice of selling an export good abroad at a much lower price than it is sold domestically is known as "dumping." International trade agreements permit tariffs to be imposed against dumped goods. If

dumping occurs, does the importing country gain by imposing such a tariff?

4. For which goods do you think the United States possesses a comparative advantage with Western Europe? What are the main items of trade between the United States and Europe?

5. If the United States is worried about the depletion of its oil reserves, is the appropriate policy to restrict imports so oil industry development remains profitable in the United States, or to permit unrestricted imports?

Chapter 34
International Payments

Terms and Concepts

Trading deficit and surplus
Gold standard
Balance of payments accounts
Gold-exchange standard
Foreign-exchange reserves
International liquidity
Special drawing rights
Key or reserve currency
Exchange rate
Flexible exchange rate
Fixed exchange rate
Capital flow
Direct investment
Portfolio investment
Balance of payments surplus and deficit
Unilateral transfer
Financing transaction
Current account balance

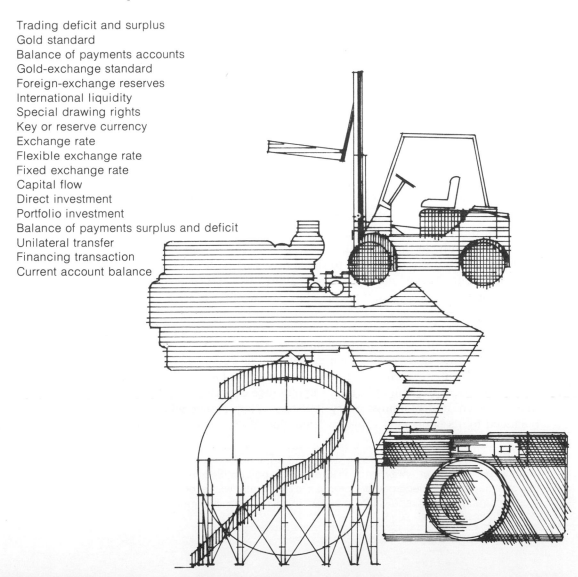

Paying for Imports The simple case of direct exchange

The simple two-good, two-country model used in the last chapter to illustrate the principles of international trade is characterized by *direct exchange* of goods. Ruralia, which has a comparative advantage in applesauce, exchanges this directly with Capitalia for dental floss, in which Capitalia has a comparative advantage. Because there are only two goods, every economic unit, whether an individual consumer or a government, either wants dental floss in exchange for applesauce, or applesauce in exchange for dental floss. Each country, therefore, uses its exports to pay directly for its imports.

Now, suppose dental-floss production in Capitalia slows down or even grinds to a halt. This country will be able to continue importing applesauce at the previously established level *only if it has stocks of dental floss from which to draw*. Of course, such stocks cannot be expected to last indefinitely.

Loans

Now, suppose the dental-floss exporters in Capitalia either have no stocks or wish to deplete them. It may still be possible to maintain the level of imports by *deferring payment*. Applesauce exporters in Ruralia may agree to send applesauce *now* in return for a promise of dental floss *later*. But to do this, they will presumably want more dental floss per liter of applesauce than they would have been willing to accept for immediate payment. If such an agreement were made, the value of dental floss exported *this year* may be less than the value of applesauce imported this year—and a true *trading deficit* will result. In this case, the deficit is financed by the willingness of applesauce exporters in Ruralia to defer receiving payment (dental floss) until next year. Acceptance of deferred payment is equivalent to extending a loan for the period of deferment. Here we would say that Capitalia's trading deficit was *financed* by a loan from her trading partner (Ruralia) or, in usual terminology, a *capital inflow* from Ruralia. A capital inflow is simply a receipt of loans from foreigners.

In the absence of a specific loan agreement, however, direct exchange will automatically result in an equality between the value of exports and the value of imports. So long as Ruralia's applesauce exporters insist on immediate payment in dental floss, every 100 liters of applesauce will be exactly balanced by its equivalent value in dental floss.

Recap Even in a simple two-country, two-good world, imports need not be paid for by exports from current production. Stocks of export goods may be run down, or imports may be obtained against a promise to repay later with export goods. Unless deferred payment (equivalent to a loan) is agreeable to the importer, exports must balance imports.

Universal Money

How universal money permits imports and exports to differ in the short run but links them in the long run

If we have more than two goods and/or more than two countries, the process of direct exchange becomes rather complex. For example, if there are only two countries, but peat moss is produced and traded along with dental floss and applesauce, some applesauce exporters may not want dental floss, but prefer peat moss, while dental-floss exporters may want applesauce. We then face the same problems that arise with barter arrangements within a single country. These problems are obviously increased if a third country is involved.

The Gold Standard

The simplest method of solving the exchange problem when many goods and countries are involved is with some *universally accepted* medium of exchange, or *universal money*. Like a national money, a universal money must be scarce and be expected to remain scarce. Moreover, individuals *in all countries* must have confidence in such money.

We shall thus assume, in our initial analysis of the balance of payments, that there is a universal money (say, gold) that is acceptable as payment for internal and international transactions. Any exporter in any country will accept gold in exchange for his goods. He can then use the gold to buy goods in his own country, to buy goods from abroad, or (if he is a manufacturer) to pay for the resources he has used in production. An importer, therefore, will pay in gold that he has received from his own customers.

The Balance of Payments

Once the direct exchange process is replaced by payments in universal money, the *direct link* between the value of imports and the value of exports is broken. Thus, *with universal money, the value of a country's exports need not equal the value of its imports*.

Capitalia may export dental floss worth 100 million gold dollars, and import applesauce worth 120 million gold dollars. Its exporters will receive 100 million gold dollars for their sales. They will either spend that money in Capitalia or use it to buy imported applesauce. Capitalia's importers, on the other hand, will pay 120 million gold dollars either taken out of its economy or obtained from its exporters. In any event, even if all the gold received from exports was used directly to buy imports, there would still be 20 million gold dollars that would have to be taken out of Capitalia's economy.

An excess of imports over exports for Capitalia is financed by moving gold out of Capitalia. Had exports exceeded imports, the movement would have been in the opposite direction, with Capitalia gaining gold. We can tabulate Capitalia's trade and payments in a set of *balance of payments accounts,* as shown in Table 34.1.

Sign Conventions

Certain important economic conventions are used in the balance of payments accounts that, when followed, make these accounts fairly simple to understand. These conventions all derive from the same basic principle: *The value of anything sold abroad appears as a positive entry, the value of anything purchased abroad as a negative entry.*

From this principle we can see that the gold transaction, although it represents a *loss* of gold, nevertheless appears as a *positive* entry because the gold, in effect, is "sold" to pay for part of the exports. Note that the net balance for all transactions is necessarily zero. A balance of payments *surplus* or *deficit* refers to the balance over *part* of the accounts, not over *all* the accounts.

For our example, we would say that the Capitalian balance of payments shows a *deficit* because the net movement of universal money (gold) is out of Capitalia. If exports had been 120 and imports 100, all the signs in Table 34.1 would be reversed, and Capitalia would show a *surplus.*

The surplus or deficit in the balance of payments is measured differently in more complex cases, but in a simple example like this, it is shown by the balance on goods and services. We would write the "balance" for Table 34.1 as *−20 million gold dollars* showing that there is a deficit of 20 million gold dollars.

In this simple case, Capitalia can run a deficit only by "exporting" gold. Because gold is the universal money, Capitalia is reducing its total money supply—that is, if the deficit is maintained, Capitalians must be willing to reduce their money balances.

Counterpart Transactions

Let's look now at the balance of payments accounts for Capitalia's trading partner, which we shall henceforth refer to as ROW (rest of the world). Capitalia's exports, of course, are ROW's imports, and Capitalia's imports are ROW's exports. The loss of gold from Capitalia is a gain of gold for ROW. ROW's accounts are shown in Table 34.2—the reverse of Capitalia's.

ROW's balance is +20, a *surplus.* In general, because exports from one country are imports into others, and gold sales by one country are purchases by others, *a deficit in one country implies, as a necessary counterpart, a surplus in the rest of the world. Conversely, a surplus in one country corresponds to a deficit in the rest of the world.*

Because ROW gains gold in the example in Tables 34.1 and 34.2, its money balances increase just as Capitalia's fall.

Table 34.1
Balance of Payments Accounts,
Capitalia
(Millions of gold dollars)

Exports of goods and services	+ 100
Imports of goods and services	− 120
Balance on goods and services	− 20
Net gold sales abroad	+ 20
Net balance on total transactions	0

Table 34.2
Balance of Payments Accounts,
ROW counterpart to Table 34.1
(Millions of gold dollars)

Exports of goods and services	+ 120
Imports of goods and services	− 100
Balance on goods and services	+ 20
Net gold sales abroad	− 20
Net balance on total transactions	0

The Link Between Exports and Imports

It might seem that, unlike the direct exchange case, there is nothing to link the value of total exports to the value of total imports, and no reason why countries should not run huge deficits or huge surpluses on an arbitrary basis. However, there are relationships linking imports and exports through individuals' budget constraints.

Let's suppose that Capitalia produces 200 million gold dollars' worth of output, all dental floss. If trading arrangements are represented by Table 34.1, with dental floss as the only export and applesauce as the only import, then Capitalians spend 100 million gold dollars on dental floss (200 million output less 100 million exported) and 120 million gold dollars on applesauce (all imported). This is a total expenditure of 220 million with current income of only 200 million gold dollars. Because expenditure exceeds income, Capitalians are required to reduce their money balances.

Thus, the value of exports and the value of imports are linked through the income-expenditure relationship. If Capitalians wished to keep their money balances at existing levels, their expenditure would necessarily have to equal their income. They would buy, say, 20 million gold dollars less worth of dental floss (leaving 20 million more for exports) or 20 million gold dollars less worth of applesauce (reducing imports by 20 million). Either reduction would bring the balance of payments into equilibrium.

An opposite situation prevails for Capitalia's trading partner, ROW. In the aggregate, ROW *increases* its money balances (with 20 million gold dollars from Capitalia) and spends less than its income. If the citizens of ROW were not willing to spend less than their incomes in the aggregate and accumulate money balances, ROW would not have a balance of payments surplus.

The link between the value of exports and the value of imports is clearly more indirect than in barter exchange, where every import is paid for immediately by an export of equivalent value. In large and complex economies there are many steps, involving many lags, between the relationship of individual expenditures and incomes and the relationship between exports and imports. Yet the export-import relationship is ultimately linked to the expenditure-income relationship and is not just arbitrary.

Monetary Effects

There is another, even more indirect, link. If Capitalia has a balance of payments deficit, it loses gold and thus part of its *money supply*. In the long run, we can expect this to influence the *price level* in Capitalia. From the quantity theory of money, a fall in the quantity of money will tend to lower the price level of Capitalian goods. This will make Capitalia's exports cheaper relative to goods in ROW, tending to increase these exports. It will also make Capitalia's home products cheaper than imports from ROW, tending to reduce imports. Thus the ultimate price-level effects will tend to decrease the balance of payments deficit. This result is reinforced by the fact that ROW's money supply will be rising simultaneously, which will tend to increase the price level there.

The classical (pre-twentieth-century) economists believed that this mechanism was sufficient to preserve a balance of payments equilibrium, on average, over the long run.

The classical gold flow mechanism is no longer relevant because countries now use national rather than universal money and attempt to isolate their respective money supplies from balance of payments changes. Even if the full gold standard were in operation, most economists would now criticize the mechanism as too slow and too disruptive in terms of the unemployment and inflation generated during the period of adjustment.

Recap If there were a universally accepted medium of exchange (such as gold), payments could be made in this medium rather than directly with goods. Then, the value of exports would not need to equal the value of imports; any difference would be balanced by a net gold flow. Total payments, including gold flows, would necessarily equal total receipts. We speak of a surplus or deficit in the balance of payments when we compare specific transactions, not overall payments. In a simple case with only goods and gold, a country will have a deficit if imports exceed exports, that is, if the net gold flow is out of the country. Because a country cannot lose gold indefinitely, exports and imports are ultimately linked.

Special International Money	**Money used universally in international trade, but not in domestic trade**

In the previous section, we discussed the balance of payments with true universal money that could be used both internally and internationally. Historically, the only money that ever approached this degree of universality was gold. Therefore, we normally refer to the universal money system as the *full gold standard*. A full gold standard is consistent with the existence of paper money and other nongold currency, provided there is unrestricted conversion, at will, between gold and these other currencies.

The Gold-Exchange Standard

One modification of a universal money system is special international money universally acceptable for international transactions, even though its use may be restricted internally within each country. Gold, again, has been the primary medium of this kind, and the corresponding system is generally referred to as the *gold-exchange standard*.

Under a gold-exchange standard, *foreigners* can demand, and receive, gold in payment for their exports, but citizens in each country can neither hold gold nor demand it in payment. A typical arrangement would be, say, a United States exporter selling goods to Britain and receiving payment in gold. He could use this gold to buy goods from other foreign countries. But if he wanted to spend his export proceeds within the United States, he would have to hand his gold over to the United States treasury (through the banking system) in exchange for an equivalent value in dollars. Where did the British importer obtain the gold to make the initial payment? It came from official sources (the Bank of England) in Britain, in exchange for pounds.

In this system, only official bodies (which we can consider to be governments) hold international money (gold), and the international money moves only to handle international transactions. The government sells gold in exchange for domestic money only to those making international transactions, and requires that those residents who receive gold from international transactions exchange it for domestic money.

Table 34.3
Balance of Payments Accounts,
Capitalia (gold-exchange standard)

Balance on goods and services	−20
Net transactions in official gold reserves	+20

Balance of Payments Accounts

Balance of payments transactions do not really look any different in this system than on the full gold standard. Any surplus or deficit is balanced by gold movements, but such movements are no longer from private money balances in one country to those in another. Gold now moves from official government holdings in one country to those in another. In the conventional balance of payments format, we would put the information of Table 34.1 in the form of Table 34.3.

Under a gold-exchange standard, the international money (gold) is held by the government, so its quantity is known. During periods in which something like a full gold standard was in operation, gold holdings were dispersed among private individuals and no one knew this quantity. Thus, when gold is used only for official transactions, it is usual to keep track of it, and view the balancing of international transactions in terms of increasing or reducing the gold stock.

Note again the sign convention. A *decrease* in gold reserves appears as a *positive* entry on the balance of payments accounts because it involves a *sale* of something to foreigners, in accord with the fundamental sign convention. An *increase* in gold represents a purchase of gold from foreigners, and appears as a *negative* sign.

Under the gold-exchange standard, the effect of a surplus or deficit is felt on official gold holdings rather than on the total money supply, as in the full gold standard case. This makes the government very *conscious* of the existence of a deficit as it sees its gold stock being depleted.

Balance of Payments Crises

If all countries have gold stocks that are large compared to the value of their trade, and if incomes equal expenditures on the average over a long period, we would not expect balance of payments *crises* to appear.

When reserves are small *relative to potential fluctuations in the balance of payments position,* the balance of payments becomes an important indicator to be watched. A country that has gold reserves of $50 million and exhibits a deficit of $20 million per year will run down its reserves to zero in two-and-a-half years. Whether or not this country has a balance of payments *crisis* when the deficit first appears depends on the probability that a surplus will appear before its reserves are entirely depleted.

Optimum Reserves

Official foreign-exchange reserves have somewhat the same relationship to a country that money balances have to an individual. Their function is to smooth out fluctuations in receipts relative to payments. If the reserves are too small relative to the level of transactions, they can be wiped out by a series of deficits. On the other hand, building up huge reserves by a series of surpluses means that expenditure is less than income, and the country's citizens are obtaining less real goods and services than they could have.

If a country actually runs out of reserves, then something must give. Importers who have promised to pay gold to foreigners will find that the government has no gold to sell them. So they must either cancel all import transactions, ask foreigners to wait for payment (equivalent to borrowing from them), or induce foreigners to accept the money of the importing country instead of international money.

The International Monetary Fund

One economic policy aim is to increase *international liquidity* by expanding the level of reserves relative to the level of trade. The major institution that has evolved over the years to assist in easing the problems of international liquidity is the *International Monetary Fund* (IMF).

The IMF began as a reserve-pooling system. It initially created no new international money, but was designed to make existing international money go further. Each member country has a *quota* with the IMF. This quota is calculated on the basis of a complex formula that allows for the country's size, wealth, and importance in trade (the United States possesses the largest quota). Each member must pay one-fourth of its quota to the fund in gold, the remainder in its own currency. Thus, the fund has a pool of international reserves that consist of gold plus an assortment of national currencies. (Each country, of course, can still maintain its own private reserves, which remain completely outside the IMF.)

Member countries can draw on this pool, but in a restricted way. There is an unrestricted right to obtain any foreign currency in exchange for ones' own currency, up to the level of the gold subscription (one-fourth of the quota), which is usually called the *gold tranche*. But the foreign currency must be exchanged back for the national currency within five years. Foreign-currency borrowing for more than this gold tranche requires special permission, usually granted only if the IMF has been satisfied with the country's economic policies. If the IMF is not satisfied, it can insist on changes.

For obvious enough reasons, many of the national currencies held by the fund are of no interest to anyone and have never been borrowed. The effective size of the fund's pool is thus its holding of currencies in demand—dollars, pounds, marks, yen, francs, and a few others, plus its gold. Because at least one country must have a surplus if another country has a deficit, only some of the members will need to draw on the pooled reserves at any time, so a greater volume of trade can be sustained than if each country had to rely exclusively on private reserves.

A New International Money

In the late 1960s, it became clear that simple reserve pooling did not go far enough and that the IMF should move toward becoming a true international central bank with powers to "create" money. This had been one of the primary aims of the original founders of the fund who observed that the value of world trade was doubling every decade, but world reserves were increasing by only 20 percent per decade. Initially, this aim was not acceptable to the United States. It later changed its views, however, when confronted with a balance of payments crisis of its own.

In 1970, the IMF cautiously began the process of creating an international bank money in the form of *special drawing rights* (SDR's). These are book entries against each country's account, in amounts proportional to its quota, which can be transferred to other countries. If Gabon has no dollars with which to settle its balance with the United States, it can pay with part of its SDR's. In effect, it writes a check on the IMF against its own account, just as a commercial bank in the United States can settle with another commercial bank by a check against its reserve account at the Fed. Because all member countries must accept SDR's in payments, they are as good as gold or any foreign currency.

The IMF can expand the volume of SDR's at any time, simply by agreeing that every country's account will be increased by a certain proportion of its quota. Thus, it can create *new international money*. Note that this creation is more direct than it is in domestic banking systems when new money must normally be "sold" (usually for government bonds, as in open market operations) rather than "given" to all depositors in proportion to their bank balances.

Recap International payments can be carried on with any medium of exchange that is universally acceptable in trade, even though not necessarily acceptable within each country. A country's ability to sustain a balance of payments deficit for any length of time then depends on its reserves of this international money rather than on its total money supply. Smooth trade requires adequate reserves and the available world reserves of gold, the traditional international money, have been too low to perform this reserve function adequately. The International Monetary

Fund (IMF), initially established to permit world gold reserves to be used more efficiently, ultimately moved to create a new international money, special drawing rights (SDR's).

Foreign-Exchange Holdings	Why the residents of one country are often willing to hold the domestic money of another

In discussing the gold-exchange standard, we have assumed that any excess of imports over exports must be balanced by selling gold. This is certainly true if every seller insists on being paid immediately *in his own currency*.

Money of Other Countries

But consider the case of a New Zealand meat exporter selling meat in Britain prior to World War II. At this time, New Zealand sold most of its exports to Britain, and also *bought* most of its imports from Britain. Thus, if the New Zealand exporter accepted payment in *sterling* (British pounds), he could use it to buy British imports himself or easily find (or have his banker find) a New Zealand importer who could use it for the same purpose. Even if he did not spend the sterling immediately, he would be confident that he could buy something with it later. Under these circumstances, the New Zealand resident would be willing to keep the sterling in his bank account—that is, he would be willing to *hold* sterling. In fact, prior to World War II, British pounds were so widely useful that residents of many countries were quite content to keep balances in sterling rather than convert them into gold.

Gold reserves, on the gold-exchange standard, are held because they can be used to settle *any* international transactions when exports and imports are out of balance. Widely acceptable foreign currencies can be used to perform the same function. Even a foreign currency that is *not* widely acceptable can still be useful—it can always be used to settle a deficit with a particular country.

Requirements of a Reserve Currency

In general, the greater the number of countries that a particular currency can be used to settle with, the more useful it is. Nicaraguan cordobas may be useful to Panama or even the United States, but it is unlikely that they will be acceptable to Japan because Japan has little occasion to settle with

Nicaragua. On the other hand, United States dollars, British pounds, and French francs are likely to be accepted by Japan, because Japan has important trading relationships with those countries. The currencies of major trading nations with which most other countries have international transactions are thus the most desirable to hold.

Although most countries hold reserves of several major foreign currencies, sometimes one or two currencies are so useful, so widely held, and so universally accepted by other countries that they become *reserve currencies* or *key currencies*. The British pound served as a reserve currency between the two world wars. Some countries (mainly but not exclusively in the British Commonwealth) had so great a share of their trade with Britain that they held all their reserves in sterling. If they occasionally needed another currency or gold, they obtained it by exchanging sterling.

After World War II, the United States dollar became the primary reserve currency, although the British pound continued to perform some key currency functions. By the late 1960s, however, U.S. dominance in world trade had begun to disappear. Countries often found it more desirable to hold stocks of German marks, French francs, or Japanese yen than of U.S. dollars. None of these became a true key currency because there were simply not *enough* marks, francs, or yen to perform the function, but the dollar had ceased to be the most desirable currency to hold.

Advantages and Disadvantages

Because foreign-exchange holdings perform some of the functions that would otherwise have to be performed by gold or special international money, they add to the world total of international liquidity. A country's international monetary reserves consist of its gold, its rights with the IMF, and its foreign-exchange holdings.

Foreign-exchange holdings, even of "solid" currencies, are never as useful as true international money. Indeed, they are used expressly because there is a *shortage* of international money relative to total international transactions. As substitutes, they are not as good as gold or IMF drawing rights to the countries that hold them. Moreover, they represent a potential headache to the country whose money is being used because at the first sign that this money may cease to be useful, its holders will attempt to exchange it for gold or some different currency. This exchange may precipitate a crisis, as happened with the dollar in 1971. Any country whose money is used extensively as a reserve currency must ensure that its value as money is preserved internationally as well as domestically. As long as this international confidence is maintained, the country obtains a benefit because it can pay for imports with its own money (which costs nothing). Also, it may not have to accept this money back for many years—thereby obtaining low cost "international loans." The cost to the country is the constraint placed on its domestic economic policies; for example, Britain had to endure recession several times to preserve the key currency status of the pound.

Recap The domestic currency of a country may be used as an international money, especially if there are inadequate world reserves of true international monies. Countries may be willing to accept, say, United States dollars or Swiss francs in payment because they feel certain they will be able to use these dollars or francs to buy goods from most other countries, not just from the United States or Switzerland. If Brazil holds reserves of dollars, we refer to these as foreign-exchange holdings. Countries will not hold reserves of foreign currencies they do not believe to have near-universal acceptability. Thus, foreign-exchange holdings consist of currencies of stable countries that are important in world trade—such as those of the United States, Germany, and Japan. Although useful, foreign-exchange holdings are not a perfect substitute for true international currency.

Foreign-Exchange Markets

How international payments can be handled entirely with domestic monies

Let's now turn to the opposite of a universal money system and consider the case in which every country has its own money, completely acceptable internally, but completely unacceptable elsewhere. In the absence of universal money, every seller will demand payment in his *own* currency.

Exchange Markets

Suppose an American importer wants to buy goods in Britain worth £1,000. The British seller will accept only pounds, so the American importer must find pounds somewhere. Let's suppose that, at the same time, a British importer wants to buy goods in America that sell for $2,000, which he must pay for in dollars. The British importer must find dollars somewhere.

If these were the only transactions taking place between Britain and America at this time, the obvious way for the British and American importers to find their dollars and pounds, respectively, would be from each other. Both could carry out their transactions *if the American importer was willing to exchange $2,000 for £1,000 with the British importer, and vice versa.* Because dollars and pounds are different monies, we can regard such transactions as setting an *exchange rate* between pounds and dollars (in this case, 1 pound = 2 dollars). In effect, the Americans are *selling* dollars and *buying* pounds, while the British are selling pounds and buying dollars.

In the absence of any interest in each other's currency other than to buy goods, the demand by Americans for pounds will be equal to the total value of American imports from Britain *valued in pounds*. Likewise, the demand by the British for dollars will be equal to the value of American exports to Britain *valued in dollars*. If the pounds to be paid for the American imports come only from the British importers who need dollars, the *exchange rate* will be given by the following relationship:

$$\text{Exchange rate (number of dollars per pound)} = \frac{\text{Value of American exports in dollars}}{\text{Value of American imports in pounds}}.$$

If Britain and America were the only countries engaged in foreign trade, with American exports of $200 million per year and British exports (= American imports) at £100 million per year, the exchange rate would be $2 per pound.

Now, at this exchange rate, suppose a change in British tastes causes an increase in the amount of U.S. goods the British desire to purchase. Figure 34.1 illustrates the effect of this change. The downward-sloping demand curve for pounds, $D_£$, reflects the fact that British exports (priced in pounds) become more attractive to Americans as the dollar price of pounds falls. Likewise, the upward-sloping supply curve of pounds, $S_£$, reflects the fact that as the dollar price of pounds rises, a given number of pounds buys more dollars, American exports (priced in dollars) become more attractive to the British, and the quantity of dollars demanded (and hence the quantity of pounds supplied) increases.

Given an initial exchange equilibrium of $2 per pound, an increase in the demand for American exports by the British shifts the supply curve of pounds from $S_£$ to $S_£'$. If we assume that the exchange rate is fully flexible (like the price of a consumer good in a typical competitive market), a new exchange rate will be established at $1.5 per pound. At this new "price" for pounds, £120 million (representing the new equilibrium value of American imports in pounds) will be exchanged for $180 million (representing the new equilibrium value of American exports in dollars).

A system in which only national monies are used, and in which the *foreign* currency necessary for international transactions is obtained by exchange on a free market, is a *flexible exchange rate system*.

Fixed and Flexible Rates

Under the simple conditions of our example, there are *no balance of payments surpluses or deficits* with flexible exchange rates. Changes in the volume of exports relative to imports result in changes in the exchange rate—but the value of exports (in dollars) is always equal to the value of imports (in dollars).

With universal money, of course, there is no real distinction between dollars and pounds (except that gold may be made into coins of different

Figure 34.1

The effect on the equilibrium exchange rate between dollars and pounds arising from a change in the British demand for American goods.

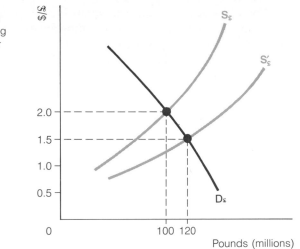

design) and no question of a flexible exchange rate. With the gold-exchange standard, we implicitly assumed that individuals would receive some *fixed* amount of their national money in exchange for their gold. If Americans exchange gold and dollars at a fixed rate with the U.S. Treasury and the British exchange gold and pounds at a fixed rate with the Bank of England, the rate of exchange between pounds and dollars is indirectly fixed. For gold at, say, $40 per ounce in the United States and £20 per ounce in Britain, the rate of exchange would be $2 per pound ($40 divided by £20). Under a gold-exchange standard, therefore, we normally have *fixed exchange rates.*

Under fixed exchange rates, changes in exports relative to imports lead to variations in balance of payments deficits or surpluses and to inflows or outflows of international money. Under flexible exchange rates, such changes lead to variations in the rate of exchange.

Exchange Market Problems

In a developed system of foreign-exchange markets, exchange rates will not fluctuate wildly from hour to hour to equate the demand and supply for a particular currency. There will be both *speculation* and *arbitrage over time* so specialized currency traders will buy up, say, pounds if the price for pounds is less than it is expected to be in the future, or sell them if the price is currently high. *Forward-exchange markets* are developed in which traders can contract to receive foreign currency at a certain date in the future at a price that is clearly stated now.

When all works smoothly, exchange rates will tend to fluctuate only moderately around those rates that will equate *average* demand and supply over a period. Speculation, under some circumstances, can be *destabilizing* and accentuate fluctuations, but speculation is less dangerous for fully flexible exchange rates than for basically fixed exchange rates that are only changed from time to time.

Recap International payments can be made even if there is no international money, not even a domestic money used as such. If Britain and America trade, American producers want payment in dollars, the British in pounds. American goods will be sold in Britain for pounds, but American suppliers can obtain dollars by selling these pounds in exchange. There will be buyers because British exports are being sold for dollars, and their suppliers want to buy pounds in exchange for dollars. Thus, international payments can be handled by foreign-exchange markets in which pounds and dollars are exchanged. If the demand for American goods falls in Britain, American suppliers will have fewer pounds to offer in exchange for dollars. Unless there is an equivalent change in the demand for British goods in America, the rate of exchange between pounds and dollars—the number of dollars that can be bought for one pound—will change. If such changes are not inhibited by any government, exchange rates are said to be flexible. If exchange rates are kept at a specific level, they are said to be fixed, and flows of gold or other international money will occur.

Other Balance of Payments Items

Why there are international payments in addition to those arising from exports and imports

The relationships among countries are much more complex than those implied in our simple examples. Transactions other than imports, exports, and movements of gold and foreign exchange are involved.

Resources, as well as final goods, can move from country to country. When *labor* migrates, its residence and the place in which its income is counted moves with it. But *capital* can move from one country to another without its owners changing residence.

Capital Flows

Capital, the most internationally mobile resource, appears two different ways in the balance of payments: one way when the *capital* itself moves, another when the *income from its services* is paid across international borders.

Consider an American mining company that decides to commence operation in Bolivia. We shall assume that this company is owned in America, and uses its own financial resources to buy equipment worth $10 million in America, which it ships to Bolivia. As the equipment enters Bolivia, it becomes an import. Bolivia's trade balance is changed by −$10 million. Does Bolivia, therefore, lose $10 million in exchange reserves? No, because the import does not have to be paid for. It is, in effect, *lent* to Bolivia by the American corporation. This loan appears in the balance of payments accounts as a *private capital movement*. Under the circumstances given, this type of capital movement is known as *direct investment*. It appears as a capital movement of −$10 million in the United States (an *outflow* of funds) and +$10 million in Bolivia (an *inflow* of funds). The corporation need not have bought the equipment in America. Suppose it was purchased in Germany. It still appears as an import in Bolivia, and the funds corresponding to it still appear as a capital inflow.

Capital flows may take a simpler form. Americans may simply buy $10 million worth of stock in a *Bolivian* corporation—this is called a *portfolio investment*. The funds used to buy the stock will still appear as a capital inflow into Bolivia.

In the balance of payments accounts, a capital outflow appears with a negative sign because the payment is flowing *out* of the country. It is sometimes useful to think of a capital outflow as equivalent to buying stock abroad (literally true for portfolio investment). The country *imports* foreign securities, so the transaction has the same sign as an import. For a country receiving a capital *inflow*, the reasoning is reversed, and the transaction has a positive sign.

Property Income

Stocks and capital equipment owned in one country but used to produce in another will generate flows of *interest* and *dividends* to their owners. In our mining case, dividends will flow *out* of Bolivia and *into* America.

Again, confusion is easily avoided by concentrating on the direction of the implied sales transaction. Bolivia is *buying* capital services from America, so, to it, the transaction is equivalent to an *import*.

Transfers

Not all transactions between countries involve exchange. There are, for example, a wide variety of *unilateral transfers*. Like internal transfers, these are flows that do not represent payments for goods and services. Among the major transfer items that flow between countries are *private remittances*—especially gifts by immigrants to relatives in their country of origin—and *government transfers* (such as foreign aid) that do not constitute direct payment for goods or services.

Table 34.4
United States Balance of Payments
Accounts, 1975
(Millions of dollars)

Basic Transactions	
1. Exports of goods and services	+ 148,410
2. Imports of goods and services	− 132,151
3. Balance on goods and services (1 + 2)	+ 16,259
4. Unilateral transfers	− 4,610
5. Current account balance (3 + 4)	+ 11,649
6. Net capital movements	− 21,271
7. Surplus (+) or deficit (−) in balance of payments (5 + 6)	− 9,622
Financing Transactions	
8. U.S. reserves accepted and retained by foreigners	+ 5,020
9. Errors and omissions	+ 4,602
10. Net total over all transactions (7 + 8 + 9)	000

Current and Capital Items

It is usual to separate *current* items in the balance of payments from *capital* items. Current items include all exports and imports of goods and services (including interest and dividends, which are considered payments for capital services) plus unilateral transfers. Capital items are transactions in actual or implied securities, loans, and promises. The sale of a bond abroad constitutes a *capital* item, the receipt of interest on it a *current* item. Just as goods and services flow in both directions, so does capital. We usually note only *net* capital movements, the difference between the capital flows in the two directions. The net flow will have a minus sign if outflows exceed inflows, a plus sign in the reverse case.

An Example: The U.S. Accounts

Table 34.4 shows a simplified version of the United States balance of payments accounts for 1975. The first six entries in the table show the items that contribute to the surplus or deficit (7). The *financing transactions* for the surplus or deficit are shown in 8 and 9, giving the net total over all transactions in 10.

The year 1975 was chosen for illustration because it is the only recent year in which the United States sold more goods and services abroad ($148,410 million) than it purchased from abroad ($132,151 million), giving a favorable balance on goods and services of $16,259 million. Unilateral transfers totaled $4,610 million ($2,893 million was foreign aid; the remainder, private remittances and other payments abroad). When the balance on goods and services is added to unilateral transfers, we obtain the *current account balance*—the balance on all items that are not capital flows or reserve transactions. This balance was a surplus of $11,649 million.

Despite this surplus on current account, however, the United States suffered an overall balance of payments deficit in 1975 of $9,622 million. This deficit, numbered 7, reflects the significant net outflow of capital ($21,271 million) as indicated in item 6.

In examining the balance of payments accounts, it is not really the officially defined surplus or deficit, or the change in reserves, or any other single figure that is important. Rather it is the *pattern* of the various transactions and how this pattern has changed from year to year (or quarter to quarter in real policy-making) that must be used to decide whether a policy change is called for.

Recap Goods are not the only items that move between countries. Among other items are interest and dividend payments for capital used in one country but owned in another, transfers such as foreign aid, and international capital flows in the form of loans and stock purchases. Although a country's exports may exceed its imports, it may have a net outpayment in these other items sufficient to cause a balance of payments deficit.

Capsule Supplement 34.1 | **Exporting Jobs or Exploiting Foreigners?**

A labor union in the United States goes on strike against the large corporation that employs its members, protesting the corporation's opening a new foreign subsidiary in Central America. Meanwhile, in the country where the new plant is located, local citizens riot in the streets to protest American imperialism and exploitation. This exact coincidence of events has probably never occurred, but the two points of view are expressed quite often.

Does the exportation of capital imply a loss of jobs at home? Does the importation of that capital into another country imply exploitation of that country's labor? We need to examine the apparent contradiction between the viewpoint of local workers, who feel that *they* lose by the export of capital, and that of foreigners who act as if *they* lose by having the capital there.

Most economists would agree that the demand for labor in an economy will be greater, and the wages higher, the more capital there is relative to the available labor supply. Consequently, the local labor union would appear to be acting wisely in opposing the export of capital. Although the income from the exported capital still accrues to the home country, it accrues exclusively to those who own capital. If the capital remained at home, the income from it would still accrue to those same "capitalists," but the greater abundance of capital would tend to increase wages, thus giving labor some gain.

On the basis of this same argument, the foreign workers should welcome the capital, which will raise the ratio of capital to labor in their country and thus raise their wages, even though they may still remain well below those of the home country. In the extreme case, however, labor may be so abundant relative to capital that the wage is unaffected by the opening of one new plant. But even in this case, the plant will provide wages to those employed in it, individuals who would presumably have lacked employment otherwise.

The gains to capital-poor countries from importing foreign capital are real enough, but there are problems as well. To have substantial sectors of the economy owned by foreigners—and typically they will be among the most important sectors—poses a very real threat of political pressure from sources outside the country itself. Even a wealthy and stable country like Canada worries about the fact that much of its industry is owned by the United States. Although a country and its workers may gain economically from imported capital, this gain may be (or may appear to be) small compared with the profits generated by the foreign capital and sent back home. Thus, it is not difficult to feel exploited under these circumstances.

Increasingly, small countries are attempting to find formulas through which they can obtain foreign capital—which they need—with the minimum of these traditional disadvantages. One of these formulas is the restriction of business operations to joint corporations in which there are domestic stockholders as well as foreigners. This formula may make it worthwhile for the foreign corporation to *give* some capital to local individuals in order to promote a joint venture. Alternatively, plants built with loans from foreign corporations may nominally be nationalized and then leased back to the lenders for operation at a small charge.

Exercises

The balance of payments accounts of a hypothetical country in 1979, other than capital flows, in millions of dollars, are: foreign aid to other countries, 840; imports, 1,100; loss of gold reserves, 160; exports, 2,720. All transactions are settled in gold.

1. Attach the appropriate signs to these transactions.
2. Draw up the balance of payments accounts, leaving space in the appropriate place for the capital flows.
3. Did the country have a surplus or a deficit on its balance of payments?
4. What must have been the value and direction of net capital flows?

For Thought and Discussion

1. Decide whether each of the following items would appear as a positive or a negative entry, or no entry, in the United States balance of payments accounts:
   a. Purchase of a TWA airline ticket by a Californian for a trip from New York to Paris.
   b. Purchase of the same ticket from Lufthansa.
   c. Sale of a U.S. government bond to a French citizen.
   d. Proceeds of the Israel bond drive in Madison Square Garden.
   e. Rent of a house in the Bahamas by a New Yorker.
   f. Sale of a new Boeing 747 to KLM airlines.
   g. A birthday gift of $50 from a resident of Los Angeles to a relative in Mexico City.

2. If exchange rates were flexible, what would you expect to happen to the rate of exchange between pounds and dollars if domestic prices were rising annually at 10 percent in Britain and 5 percent in the United States?

3. Suppose a certain state in the United States became independent overnight. What would be the main positive and negative items in the balance of payments with the rest of the United States for the state you have chosen?

4. What factors would you consider in deciding whether to hold the currency of some specific country in your own country's foreign-exchange reserves?

5. At various times, it has been suggested that any shortage of international money could easily be cured by increasing the price of gold in terms of all currencies. How would this expand the supply of international money?

Chapter 35
Economic Policy in an Open Economy

Terms and Concepts

Currency depreciation
Currency appreciation
Import-saving goods
Multilateral aid

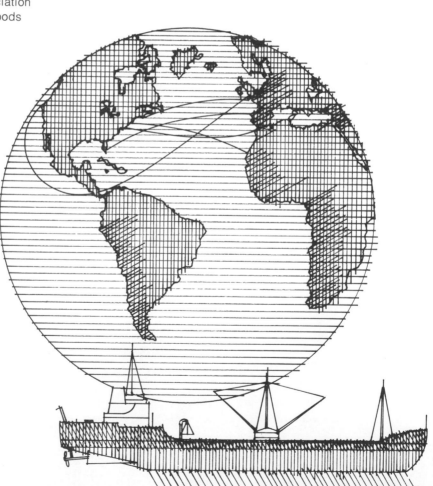

Openness as a Constraint on Domestic Policy

How the balance of payments is affected by domestic activity and policy

The gains from expanding economic possibilities through trade carry with them some loss of autonomy in domestic policy in the trading countries. The balance of payments and/or the exchange rate become policy indicators to be watched along with the unemployment rate, price levels, and other internal indicators.

The existing international monetary framework is based on *managed flexible exchange rates,* rather than on *fully flexible exchange rates.* To the extent that exchange rates are not totally flexible, short-run international effects appear as changes in balance of payments surpluses or deficits. We shall assume the existence of this general framework in the following discussion.

The internal operation of the economy and the balance of payments have a two-way relationship. The internal state of the economy affects balance of payments items, and the balance of payments affects the internal state of the economy.

Domestic Activity and the Balance of Payments

Goods are imported into a country both for final consumption and as inputs into production activities. In both cases, imports can be expected to rise and fall with the level of economic activity. When income rises, consumption rises, including the consumption of imported goods. When output rises, the demand for inputs increases, including imported inputs.

As the internal level of activity rises, the effect on exports, if anything, will be to reduce them because fewer unused resources will be available and internal consumption of export goods will increase. A reduction in the internal level of activity can be expected to increase or maintain a constant level of exports. Thus, even if there are no internal or external price changes, and no change in exchange rates, we would normally expect:

An increase in the level of domestic activity will tend to increase imports and perhaps decrease exports, worsening the balance of payments position of the country. A decline in domestic activity will have opposite effects, improving the country's balance of payments position.

Inflation

The same type of effects will occur if the economy is at capacity and attempts to spend at a higher rate lead to inflation. If the country's general price level rises relative to price levels in the rest of the world and exchange rates remain fixed, there will be adverse effects on the balance of payments.

The increased price of domestic products relative to imports will increase the demand for imports, while the increased price of exports will (except in unusual cases of inelastic demand) reduce export sales.

An increase in a country's general price level relative to changes in prices elsewhere, with fixed exchange rates, will worsen the balance of payments position. Holding back inflation domestically when inflation occurs elsewhere will improve the balance of payments.

Interest Rates

Even changes in the interest rate, an important instrument of domestic policy, will have balance of payments repercussions. If the interest rate rises relative to interest rates in other countries, it will be more profitable to lend in this country than elsewhere. Funds that might have moved abroad at a lower domestic interest rate will stay at home, while foreign funds will be attracted. This will reduce the net capital outflow and increase the net capital inflow. Less capital outflow and more capital inflow both represent *improvements* in the balance of payments because an increase in capital inflow has the same effect as more exports. A fall in the interest rate, of course, will have an opposite effect and cause the balance of payments to deteriorate.

An increase in domestic interest rates relative to those abroad will tend to improve the balance of payments position, while a decrease in the domestic interest rate will tend to worsen the balance of payments.

General Repercussions

Thus, policies designed to achieve essentially domestic objectives, such as full employment, will have repercussions on the balance of payments. Moreover, policy options in an open economy are constrained by potential balance of payments effects. How restrictive such constraints are in practice depends on both the internal structure and the international role of the country concerned. These determine the magnitude of the effects of domestic policy on the balance of payments, and the importance of balance of payments objectives in overall policy.

For the United States, imports of goods and services represent only about 5 percent of GNP. For Britain, the proportion is almost 20 percent, and for Canada it is more than 20 percent. Thus, the repercussions of domestic income policy on the balance of payments can be expected to be noticeably greater *relative to GNP* in countries like Britain and Canada than in the United States.

The repercussions of *interest-rate* policy will be greater on those countries that have major international capital markets than on those that do not. A difference in interest rates between the United States and Britain may set up large capital flows, for example, while a difference in interest rates between the United States and Indonesia will probably have little effect on these countries' respective capital markets.

Recap Domestic activity and domestic policy have important effects on the balance of payments. If activity increases, imports will rise and the home country's balance of payments will "worsen." Inflation will worsen the balance of payments because imports become cheaper at home. Policies that reduce interest rates at home will worsen the balance of payments because capital will flow out for a higher return abroad. The importance of these effects will depend on the extent of trade relative to total GNP.

Capsule Supplement 35.1   **What's Wrong with a Deficit?**

In balance of payments discussions, payments deficits that grow larger are said to "worsen," while those that diminish are said to "improve." This is the jargon of those specialized policy-makers who must watch the level of a country's international reserves, and for whom deficits represent a threat to those reserves. The purpose of this discussion is to associate the balance of payments with overall material welfare rather than the level of reserves.

The economic welfare of a country depends on the quantities of goods and services available for its use. Exports represent domestic production not available to domestic consumers, while imports represent goods available for domestic consumption even though not produced at home.

Thus, a balance of payments deficit represents a situation in which the country's available goods is greater than its own production—the country is better off in a straightforward welfare sense with a deficit than with payments in balance. It is analogous to the situation in which a person is able to spend more than he receives in income, and thus is clearly better off than if he could spend only his income.

There is, of course, a hidden snag. A deficit runs down foreign-exchange reserves and cannot be sustained once these fall to zero and all forms of borrowing are exhausted. A deficit thus implies living beyond the country's means, something that can be done for short periods only. Consequently, a deficit cannot be used to promote a permanent increase in welfare.

Just as there is a welfare *gain* derived from running a deficit, there is a corresponding welfare *loss* associated with curing a deficit. Any policy designed to eradicate a balance of payments deficit must necessarily hurt. Exchange rate depreciation will increase the price of import goods so consumers will be able to afford less, while anti-deficit macroeconomic policy will be contractionist and thus reduce incomes.

The greater availability of goods with a payments deficit than with a payments balance can be useful in anti-inflationary policy. The excess of planned expenditure over capacity production can spill over into the market for imported goods, removing part of the upward pressure on internal prices. If the economy is depressed, however, the demand for imports constitutes a leakage from the domestic income flow, and is thus undesirable.

A flow of foreign aid into a country enables it to achieve the same expenditure level as if it had a deficit equal to the amount of the aid. This is the aim of foreign aid—to raise the expenditure level in the recipient country. Building up exchange reserves means running a surplus, a welfare loss. Poor countries cannot afford the luxury of maintaining expenditures below the level of production, even for a few years. Consequently, they operate with very low levels of reserves.

International Transmission of Activity

How changes in activity
in one country can be transmitted
to others through
the balance of payments

In the last section we outlined the ways in which the domestic level of activity would affect the balance of payments situation. Here we shall look at influences in the reverse direction, and then at the joint effects.

Confining ourselves to the trade balance, we can note that exports represent *domestic income generated by foreign expenditure*. Imports represent the reverse: domestic expenditure that does not generate domestic income. Imports, in effect, represent a leakage or *withdrawal* from the circular flow of income in the domestic economy. Every dollar spent on imports is a dollar that does not generate domestic income. Exports are an *injection*, like investment or government expenditure, because they generate income even though they do not correspond to domestic expenditure.

Balance of Payments Effects

If exports and imports are equal, the domestic expenditure that leaks abroad is exactly balanced by foreign expenditure creating domestic income. There is no net effect. But, if exports *fall* (due to changing demand conditions abroad, for example), the leakage through imports is not balanced by foreign expenditure. Withdrawals from the income flow will exceed injections into it (in the absence of counteracting policy) and the *equilibrium income level* will fall.

The effect will be subject to the multiplier. This is seen easily by noting that a sudden fall in export sales will reduce income in export industries. Domestic expenditure by those providing resource services to these industries will fall, and so on, in a downward multiplier sequence. A sudden *increase* in exports, of course, will have the opposite effect. Domestic income will rise, again to a multiplied extent.

Figure 35.1
The mechanism for international transmission of changes in the level of economic activity.

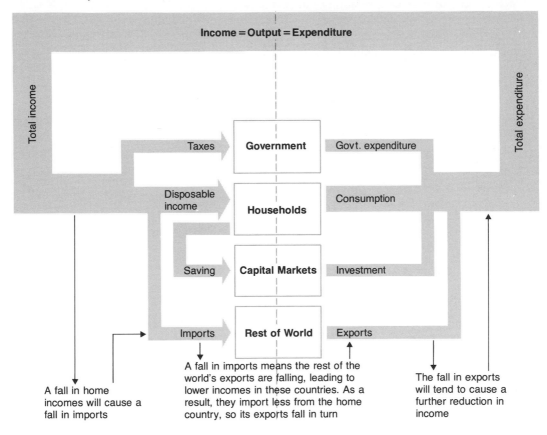

Income = Output = Expenditure

Total income

Total expenditure

Taxes → **Government** → Govt. expenditure

Disposable income → **Households** → Consumption

Saving → **Capital Markets** → Investment

Imports → **Rest of World** → Exports

A fall in home incomes will cause a fall in imports

A fall in imports means the rest of the world's exports are falling, leading to lower incomes in these countries. As a result, they import less from the home country, so its exports fall in turn

The fall in exports will tend to cause a further reduction in income

Although we have concentrated on exports, similar effects occur (but in the reverse directions) if there is a sudden shift from domestic products to imports or vice versa. In general:

An adverse change in the balance of payments (greater deficit or smaller surplus) will exert a downward influence on the level of domestic activity; a favorable change will exert an upward influence.

Two-Way Effects

Let's combine these effects with those of the domestic level of activity on the balance of payments discussed in the previous section. The joint effects are illustrated in Figure 35.1. For simplicity, consider a world consisting of two countries "America" and "Europe," both initially in domestic full employment equilibrium and balance of payments equilibrium. What happens when domestic investment in America falls suddenly, and the government does not take counteracting policy measures?

The first effect, of course, will be a reduced level of activity in America—a recession. The resulting lower incomes will reduce America's imports, and America's balance of payments will move to a surplus.

But America's imports are Europe's exports. The fall in American imports, therefore, will exert a downward pressure on Europe's economy. It, too, will move into a recession—relatively minor, perhaps, compared with America's—and the European balance of payments will move into deficit.

These initial effects will lead to secondary effects. The surplus in America's balance of payments will dampen the internal recession somewhat, while the corresponding European deficit will heighten the recession there. The overall effect will be a recession in America, less severe than would have been the case if America had been a closed economy, coupled with a recession in Europe, where there would have been none under closed economy conditions.

Similar international effects would occur as a result of *inflation* in America, rather than recession. America's demand for imports would rise and its balance of payments would move into deficit, putting upward pressure on Europe's fully employed economy, and generating inflation there as well.

The level of economic activity is transmitted internationally through trade. A domestic recession in one country will tend to spread, causing recession in other countries. Domestic inflation will be spread internationally in the same way.

Asymmetry of Effects

These effects are not symmetrical. Because United States' trade is small relative to its own GNP, but large relative to world trade, the U.S. level of activity has more effect on other countries than these countries' levels of activity have on the United States. An extreme example is Canada. Trade with the United States is large relative to Canada's GNP, while trade with Canada is small relative to U.S. GNP. A severe recession in the United States will inevitably put very strong downward pressures on Canada's economy, but a Canadian recession will have only minor repercussions in the United States.

There is another point we should note. Just as a recession (or inflation) becomes transmitted internationally, so some of the effects are diminished in the initiating country, and *policy measures* become dissipated internationally. Expansionary measures in one country will increase domestic income, part of which will be used to buy imports and thus increase incomes elsewhere. Thus, domestic injections must be *higher* for a given increase in domestic GNP than would be the case in a closed economy. On the other hand, in an open economy, other countries' incomes are boosted.

Recap The balance of payments can influence the level of domestic activity because imports act as a withdrawal and exports, an injection. Increased exports, improving the balance, will boost the economy, while a worsening of the balance of payments position will depress the economy. Because the level of economic activity affects the balance of payments and the balance of payments affects the level of economic activity, there is some international transmission of domestic changes in economic activity. Economic decline in one country will cut its imports. These are the exports of some other country, which will thus also suffer a decline in activity. The strength of the effects will depend on the relative importance of trade in the various countries.

Macroeconomic Policy in an Open Economy

How macroeconomic policy can be influenced by balance of payments considerations

The general problems of attaining, or maintaining, full employment in the face of inadequate investment or other private-sector expenditures are heightened in an open economy by the effects already outlined. Much depends on the sensitivity of the balance of payments to the domestic income level, and on the initial state of the balance of payments and the quantity of foreign-exchange reserves held by the economy.

Problem Combinations

Perhaps the worst situation in which a country can find itself is a deep recession with a large balance of payments deficit and very low international reserves. Ordinary anti-recession macro policy cannot be used because it will worsen the balance of payments deficit and run down remaining reserves. The deficit could be cured by further reduction in income levels, but this will make the recession even worse. This would be a case for permitting *currency depreciation* (lowering the price of the country's currency relative to that of other countries, a process that would be automatic under fully flexible exchange rates). This could generally be expected to correct the deficit if carried out to the appropriate degree. Removing the deficit would itself have an expansionary effect on the economy. Because further expansion by, say, fiscal policy would have adverse effects on the balance of payments once more, the depreciation would have to be large enough to give balanced international payments at *full employment,* not merely at the initial depressed level.

Recession under conditions of a balance of payments surplus poses few policy problems. Any expansionary policy will both reduce unemployment and bring payments closer to balance. Inflation and deficit are also a non-conflicting combination. Restrictive policy, whether carried out by fiscal or monetary methods, will move both the domestic activity level and the balance of payments in the directions desired.

The combination of inflation with a surplus poses more problems for the rest of the world than for the country concerned. Restrictive policy will dampen the inflation but increase the surplus. Surplus countries rarely feel constrained to correct their balance of payments situation because they are accumulating assets (foreign currencies) that have potential future value. But every surplus has corresponding deficits elsewhere, so anti-inflation policy at home will increase *other countries'* deficits. There will be strong pressure from trading partners for the country to permit *currency appreciation* (increase in value relative to others) rather than carry out restrictive fiscal or monetary policy.

International Interdependence

Due to the international transmission of activity levels, it is to the advantage of each country to have every *other* country maintain a high level of employment, stable prices, and balance of payments equilibrium. Anti-recession policy will be easier for each country if other countries pursue corresponding policies, especially when linkages are close.

Furthermore, it is difficult for linked countries to use radically different means for attaining similar policy objectives. Suppose America and Europe both have inflation. Europe proposes to use monetary policy as the cure, increasing interest rates sharply. America, because it does not want to dampen investment in housing, keeps interest rates low but raises taxes. In the absence of direct controls, there will be a massive flow of capital from America to Europe. This will partly maintain the high expenditure level in Europe, which its policy is designed to cut, and reduce the funds for the housing development America is trying to sustain.

Recap Because the balance of payments is affected by the level of activity, macroeconomic policy must take into account the balance of payments effects. This may or may not present major problems. If the economy is depressed and in deficit, boosting it will improve the activity level but worsen the balance of payments. However, if the economy is depressed but in surplus, expansionary policy will reduce both the unemployment and the surplus. Similarly, inflation with a deficit is not a major policy conflict, but inflation with a surplus is.

Capsule Supplement 35.2   **Can We Divide Policy Responsibility?**

All of our economic analysis tells us that economic policy is a highly connected set of decisions, that domestic policy will affect international economic relationships, and that international events will affect domestic policy. Direct logic thus leads to the conclusion that there should be some stage at which economic policy is considered as a whole, when all the repercussions of each piece of proposed policy on areas other than its chief target are examined, and the policy package is judged by its total effect on the economy.

There can be no doubt that, given policy-makers with no human failings, perfect data, and sound economic analysis, the only truly optimal policy package is one that has been considered as a whole and with respect to its total impact. But policy-makers are imperfect, and they are especially imperfect in their ability to absorb the enormous quantity of data involved in total policy decisions. Because of this, it has often been argued that a system in which policy decisions are divided—one policy-maker concentrating on the balance of payments and another on internal full employment, for example—might be suboptimal in principle, but safer in practice and more reliable on average in an imperfect world.

The extreme case is the "Chicago" or "New Laissez-Faire" approach that asserts that the only reliable policy-makers are consumers making consumption decisions and businesses making production decisions, and that there should be an absolute minimum of government policy superimposed on these decision-makers. However, microeconomic analysis shows that the laissez-faire market system deviates greatly from optimality. We are interested here in a much less drastic division of policy responsibility in which the government has extensive policy concerns, but divides responsibility among different branches of government, each branch controlling some instrument of policy and being charged with overseeing some specific policy objective.

The division of responsibility between fiscal and monetary policy has sometimes been considered as the most obvious point at which to make a major allocation of responsibility. In the United States as in most countries, monetary policy is under the control of a semiautonomous Federal Reserve System or central bank, while fiscal policy is under the control of the government proper. Because the two sets of policy instruments are already in two different hands, why not formalize the division by telling the central bank that it should operate monetary policy to keep international payments in balance (for example) without worrying about full employment, while instructing the treasury or budget bureau to operate fiscal policy to preserve full employment without worrying about the balance of payments? Each policy controller would then have a simple, clear objective.

In simple models of the economy, this division of responsibility can work in the sense that, if full employment and the payments balance are the only two goals of policy, both could be achieved under a divided responsibility system—although not necessarily as rapidly as under central policy control. The chief problem is that of allocating the objectives: Should the monetary authority look after the balance of payments and the fiscal authority after full employment, or should the monetary authority look after full employment while the fiscal authority looks after the balance of payments?

The attractive simplicity of this scheme, unfortunately, begins to vanish as we add more objectives and more instruments of policy to the system. For each policy objective, we need a policy instrument that is not required for other objectives. Unfortunately, such objectives as a more equitable income distribution and price stability cannot easily be associated with a unique instrument of policy. Nevertheless, the policy division problem is one that is likely to attract considerable future attention.

Preserving Domestic Policy Autonomy

How to achieve maximum freedom in domestic policy without shutting out the rest of the world

Due to the effects of domestic policy on the balance of payments, and vice versa, policy-makers in an open economy cannot ignore the balance of payments in pursuing domestic policy goals. In particular, full employment policy can be severely constrained by balance of payments considerations.

How can a country protect its autonomy in exercising domestic policy options, yet preserve its potential gains from trade? It can always abandon international trade and shut itself behind a wall of prohibitive tariffs. This would result in more than just a loss of the gains from trade, however, for *some* trade is essential to every economy. In particular, there are some goods that cannot be produced domestically because natural resources or specialized capital or skills are simply not available. Thus, we shall not consider complete economic autonomy as desirable or possible.

The Importance of Reserves

The larger a country's exchange reserves, relative to the size of its balance of payments items, the less *critical* a period of deficit is to it and the more freedom it has in domestic policy.

It is precisely this freedom to exercise domestic policy that is the greatest benefit to a country possessing large international reserves. This consideration was important in setting up the international monetary institutions after World War II within which internal payments still operate to a certain degree. The primary aim of the *International Monetary Fund* (IMF) is to provide more *international liquidity,* that is, to increase the exchange reserves to member countries so countries are not forced to undertake undesirable domestic policies merely to rectify *temporary* balance of payments deficits.

Policy Combinations

Another way to minimize the potential constraints on domestic policy imposed by balance of payments considerations is the use of an appropriate *policy mix,* as discussed in Chapter 32. As we have already seen, restrictive macro policy will rectify a balance of payments deficit, but depress the domestic economy. A combination of internal macro policy and exchange rate changes, however, can simultaneously affect the domestic economy and the balance of payments.

If there are two separate goals to be considered, such as domestic full employment and balance of payments equilibrium, we cannot generally attain both with a single policy measure. An appropriate mixture is thus called for. In some cases, a fiscal-monetary mix may be better than either fiscal or monetary policy alone. Both will affect the level of domestic activity and the balance of payments, but in different proportions. The appropriate proportion may be attained by combination.

One of the strongest arguments in favor of fully flexible exchange rates is that they would provide more autonomy for domestic policy than fixed, or even managed flexible exchange rates. A continuous decline in the exchange rate, however, would still pose major problems. Moreover, autonomy would never be complete, because varying exchange rates would affect the relative prices of domestic and imported goods.

Recap A country will be less constrained by balance of payments considerations in domestic policy if it has large reserves, allowing it to run a deficit if necessary. In the absence of large reserves, domestic targets may be achieved without a balance of payments crisis if a suitable mix of policies is chosen. Flexible exchange rates permit more autonomy in domestic policy than fixed rates do.

Growth and Development in an Open Economy

The special balance of payments problems of developing countries

In a closed economy, growth is determined by the rate of technological change and the rate of capital accumulation, as discussed in Chapter 24. Because technological change itself depends critically on the installation of new types of capital, the major determinant of growth is the rate of capital accumulation, and thus the rate of saving.

In an open economy, and most poorer countries are open economies, additional constraints on the rate of growth and development become apparent. At the same time, there are significant benefits from being open.

Consider a less-developed country, which we shall call LDC, with little industry and a plan for economic development through a sharp increase in its rate of capital accumulation, especially in manufacturing. We shall assume that its trade is initially in balance and that its main exports are agricultural and mineral products.

To increase the rate of capital accumulation from its internal resources, it will need to increase its rate of saving. For a poor country, where average consumption levels are far below what a rich country would consider its poverty level, increasing saving—which means reducing consumption—is no easy task. Nonetheless, we shall assume that it has been achieved. However, this is only the first of LDC's problems.

Capital Equipment

Because LDC has little or no industry, the actual equipment it needs to increase its capital stock cannot be produced domestically, but must be imported. Assuming that trade was balanced before the development plan commenced, an increase in the rate of capital accumulation and thus of importation of capital equipment can be achieved only by one or more of the following:

1. An increase in exports sufficient to pay for the capital.
2. A balance of payments deficit that implies a depletion of gold, foreign currency, and/or other international reserves.
3. Offsetting inflows of foreign funds, such as gifts (foreign aid) or loans from foreign governments or private investors.

The second of these, using up reserves, is possible only in the short run and then only under special circumstances. Certain less-developed countries (Ghana and Malaysia, for example) began their independent existence with large international reserves accumulated in the past that could be used for development purposes. Most poor countries have not been so fortunate, however.

Straightforward foreign aid, if it carries no explicit or implicit commitment to repay, involves no necessity to increase exports. In effect, the new capital equipment is a direct *gift* representing a transfer from one country to another.

The Need to Increase Exports

The other cases all require an increase in exports, either in the present or in the future, as a precondition for development. If the imported capital must be financed directly by exports, the need for an immediate increase in exports is clear. If the capital is financed by any form of foreign loan, there is a commitment to *future* increases in exports although no immediate increases will be required. This is because a loan implies the future payment of both principal and interest—which will only be acceptable if paid in international currency or the currency of the lending country. To obtain the necessary foreign currency in the future, increased exports will be required.

The Double Constraint

The developing country will be constrained in two ways because of its need for capital equipment from abroad. The immediate constraint will be on the amount of foreign financing available, both in aid and loans. This constraint may turn out to be more important than the internal saving constraint. LDC may save $100 million annually, permitting $100 million investment if all equipment could be produced domestically. But it may only be able to finance $50 million of imports annually. Thus the attainable rate of capital accumulation will be less than the saving rate, unless something in excess of $50 million in internal saving can be used to produce simple capital goods (roads built by hand, for example) that do not require imports.

Even if loans can be obtained to cover the total capital LDC is able to finance from saving, there is a second constraint. Because of the commitment to increase future exports, the capital obtained must be used, in part at least, to develop *export* industries rather than those producing domestic goods. We can modify this somewhat—if the capital is used to produce *import-saving* goods, this is just as good as using it to produce exports. Specifically, $10 million of domestic production, which replaces $10 million of former imports, is just as good for the balance of payments as $10 million additional exports. In either case, the structure of the developing economy is constrained by the need to develop ways to make interest payments and loan repayments in the future.

Does this mean that trade is *harmful* to the developing countries? Not at all, since the whole problem arose because the equipment needed for development was assumed to be only available abroad. Without trade, the country could not develop. In reality, the options are not as clear cut. LDC may be able to produce equipment domestically, but only by using far more resources than required to produce exports and use these to pay for the equipment purchased abroad.

Recap A developing country must accumulate capital. If it has insufficient industry to manufacture capital equipment domestically, such equipment will have to be imported. Growth may be constrained as much or more by the need for exports to pay for imported equipment as by the level of saving. Aid or credit from abroad will reduce or eliminate this constraint, but loans from abroad require a future increase in exports to finance repayment.

International Distributional Policy

A note on the international distribution of income

If we look at the world as a whole, the distribution of income is unequal to a degree that would precipitate an instant revolution if it occurred within any one country. Even the guaranteed minimum real income in the United States (represented by welfare support) is far above the real income level of almost everyone in the world who does not live in North America, Europe, or Japan. This is true even after all justifiable adjustments to the standard statistics (real GNP per capita) have been made.

Prior to World War II, there was almost no thought given to the question of international income distribution, but there has been considerable thought (and some action) applied since.

Distribution of Resources, Not Incomes

Given the fantastic inequality of income distribution, and the fact that the primary political unit is the country rather than the world, international distributional policy is mainly confined to questions of distributing the *means for increasing incomes* in poor countries, and not for redistributing *income itself,* at least not directly. Any redistribution can occur only by inducing the rich countries to help the poor on a voluntary basis. Thus redistribution will generally be quite limited and heavily dependent on arguments stressing some kind of self-interest to the rich countries.

Countries obtain some goods by producing them directly, others by producing exports and exchanging them for imported goods. The relative importance of domestic production versus trade varies greatly from one country to another. If we measure it by the ratio of total imports to GNP, it is as high as 72 percent for Trinidad and Tobago (West Indies) and 82 percent for Luxembourg, and as low as 5 percent for the United States and 1 percent for the Soviet Union.

Terms of Trade

For countries in which trade is important—which includes many of the less-developed countries—real income is determined, to a major extent, by the productivity of the export industries and the *terms of trade* or ratio of imported goods obtained per unit quantity of exports.

Less-developed countries typically export farm products, raw materials, or simple manufactures, and import more sophisticated industrial products. The distribution of income between the richer and the poorer countries is thus influenced by the terms of trade (relative prices) of technically advanced manufactures compared with raw materials and simple manufactures. Insofar as these terms of trade have been influenced by policy decisions, they have usually been influenced to the disadvantage of the poorer countries.

One set of proposals for bringing about a redistribution toward the poorer countries has been of the "trade, not aid" kind. Here the rich countries give especially favorable treatment to imports from the poorer countries—or to imports that typically come from the poorer countries. Such proposals still result in an uneven redistribution, however, because they *redistribute* most to those countries that *trade* most. However, these proposals provide an important auxiliary argument against rich countries' tendencies (such as those of the United States) to raise tariffs against simple manufactures, like textiles, that are produced mainly by poorer countries.

Foreign Aid

Most attempts to improve world distribution have attacked the problem differently by concentrating on raising the level of technology and the stock of capital in the poorer countries. Typical foreign-aid programs—such as those of the United States, Britain, France, Germany, Japan, Belgium, Italy, the Netherlands, Canada, Australia, and the U.S.S.R.—involve direct gifts or loans at favorable rates for capital projects, coupled with technical assistance.

National foreign-aid programs are not based on any concerted policy as far as world distribution is concerned. A high proportion of foreign aid goes to former colonies or near-colonies, or to countries in which the donors have a strategic or political interest. The failure of foreign aid to achieve certain political goals ("buy friends") has indeed led to its failure to grow with the world economy.

United States' "gift" aid (as opposed to loans) rose from $2 billion in 1960 to a little over $3 billion in 1975, but fell, relative to GNP during this period, from two-fifths of a cent per dollar of GNP to less than one-fifth of a cent per dollar. At its peak, three years after World War II, it was two cents per dollar of GNP. The course of development loans on subsidized terms has been similar. Although the United States still gives the largest total amount of foreign aid of any country, it is now well down the list in terms of aid given per dollar of GNP.

Multilateral Programs

To avoid the client relationships inherent in direct aid from a particular rich country to a particular poor one, there has been steady pressure on the rich countries to distribute aid on a *multilateral* basis. Multilateral aid implies that the rich countries put money for aid according to some criterion, such as per capita income, into an international "pot," and that this money be distributed to poor countries on the basis of need. The aid available to a particular poor country is then determined by an international agency rather than by a particular country, and the source of the aid cannot be specifically identified with any particular donor. The multilateral idea has steadily gained support, but is not yet operative.

A restricted multilateral scheme, involving loans rather than gift aid, has operated through the International Bank for Reconstruction and Development (IBRD) since World War II. The IBRD obtains funds by selling its bonds, which are jointly guaranteed by its member countries (most countries belong, as they do to the IMF). It lends these funds for specific development projects in less-developed countries. The function of the IBRD is to obtain funds on terms more favorable than the poor countries could obtain by borrowing directly.

Recap The inequality of incomes among countries is much greater than that within most countries. Although there are some policies, such as favored tariff treatment for poor countries, that directly raise incomes in poor countries relative to the rich, most international distribution policy is based on supplying the resources for growth in the poor countries. Foreign aid is a gift from rich countries to poor countries. Loans at subsidized rates also contain a gift component. Such aid, typically granted in the form of capital equipment, represents a very small proportion of the GNP of the donor countries.

Exercises

1. In 1972, one Norwegian krone could be exchanged for 15 cents. It had been 14 cents in 1971. Did the krone depreciate or appreciate relative to the dollar?

2. The dollar purchased ten Argentine pesos in 1972, compared with twenty-five in 1971. Over the same period, the value of the Chilean escudo changed from 14 cents (1971) to 27 cents (1972). Did the peso depreciate or appreciate relative to the escudo?

3. A country borrows $1 billion in capital from abroad, and the increased income generated by the consequent development will result in a $5 million annual increase in imports. If the country must repay 5 percent interest annually to be paid in foreign currency, by how much must the annual exports of the country increase if the balance of payments is not to be worsened by the loan?

For Thought and Discussion

1. The Canadian economy, due to its close links with that of the United States, moves much as the United States moves. Should the Canadian government have the right to consult and be consulted by U.S. policymakers?

2. Although the United States has had a balance of payments deficit for many years, the balance of payments is rarely mentioned in policy discussions. The British balance of payments, on the other hand, has been a topic of concern even to the man in the street. What accounts for the difference?

3. Given a fixed total of potential U.S. foreign aid, would you allocate it to:
   a. the very poorest countries,
   b. those poor countries most friendly to the United States,
   c. those countries most likely to develop rapidly from the aid, or
   d. domestic projects such as clearing slums?

4. Why do countries with balance of payments surpluses usually take less corrective action than those with deficits?

5. If a country's money supply were based ultimately on its gold stock, what would be the effect of a payments deficit in terms of the monetarist scenario?

Glossary:
Standard Economic Terms

AC Standard abbreviation for average cost. For a definition, *see* **Cost.**

Accelerator The hypothesis that the rate of investment is proportional to the rate of change of output or income. Also refers to the numerical value of the ratio.

Aggregation Replacement of a large number of variables by a single variable. Aggregation may involve simple procedures like addition of dollar values or more complex procedures like construction of index numbers.

Antitrust In the policy context of the United States, refers to all policies concerned with imperfect competition of all kinds.

APC Standard abbreviation for the average propensity to consume. *See* **Consumption function.**

AR Standard abbreviation for average revenue. *See* **Revenue.**

Arbitrage Trading on price differentials for the same good in different markets.

Asset Anything expected to possess value in the future.

Asset structure The relative holdings of assets of different kinds.

Automatic monetary policy Monetary policy based on a constant rate of change in the supply of money, without adjustment to short-term economic conditions.

Automatic stabilizers Structural features of economic institutions (the progressive income tax, unemployment pay) that tend to dampen movements of the economy away from equilibrium.

Average product *See* **Productivity.**

Average revenue *See* **Revenue.**

Balance of payments A summary of a country's international payments and receipts (usually presented as a *balance of payments table*) or, more specifically, the difference between receipts from abroad and payments abroad after omitting transactions in gold, foreign currencies, and certain other financial assets. An excess of receipts over payments is a balance of payments *surplus;* an excess of payments over receipts, a balance of payments *deficit.*

Balanced budget The government's budget is balanced if revenues equal expenditures; otherwise, it has a *surplus* (if revenues exceed expenditures) or a *deficit* (if expenditures exceed revenues).

Bargaining Any process in which the buyer and seller reach mutual agreement on terms specific to their individual transaction as compared with the standard market transaction in which the price is determined by the market.

Barrier to entry Any financial, legal, or institutional factors making it difficult or impossible for new firms to enter an industry.

Benefit The numerical value of the gain to a person or society from an action or policy. A loss will appear as a *negative benefit.* A gain that accrues only to the person or group taking the action is a *private benefit.* The total gain to society is the *social benefit.*

Budget Refers either to the maximum expenditure consumers can allocate among the various purchases they wish to make, or to the summary of anticipated revenues and planned expenditures of a government.

Buffer stock Any stock or inventory of a good held with the object of smoothing price fluctuations by selling from stock when prices are unusually high and adding to it when prices are low.

Capital A collective term for the assortment of machines, buildings, and other durable goods that have been manufactured and contribute to production. May also refer to the total current dollar value of these, or to financial resources used to buy them. Capital as an input refers properly to the use of the services of capital. The stock of capital is increased or maintained, in face of inevitable wearing out, by investment.

Capital flow In international transactions, refers to payments associated with investment and other items of a capital nature.

Capital-intensive One production process is said to be capital-intensive relative to another if it uses a higher proportion of capital relative to other inputs.

Cartel A formal and enforceable agreement among producers on prices or other matters affecting potential competition. Illegal within the United States, but United States' firms may sometimes belong to international cartels (air transport, for example).

Central bank A bank that holds the reserves of other banks and possesses ultimate control over the whole banking system, making it the institution responsible for monetary policy.

Characteristic (sometimes attribute) Any property of a good that is relevant to consumers' views of how the good relates to their interests.

Club good A good whose benefits can be shared by more than one person without loss to any, but from whose enjoyment it is possible to exclude others (like a golf course). Compare with **Public good.**

Collusion An informal agreement among firms about matters affecting potential competition. Differs from a cartel in lack of formal sanctions. Compare with **Cartel.**

Comparative advantage The idea that exchange (especially in international trade) is most efficient if each trader offers the particular good in which he has some advantage in production relative to the good he receives in exchange.

Comparative statics The most basic technique of economic analysis at the elementary level, a comparison of two equilibrium positions without concern for the actual dynamic path from one to the other.

Complement Two goods are complements if an increase in the quantity demanded of one is associated with increased demand for the other. (More automobiles will be associated with increased demand for gasoline.)

Conglomerate A large corporation whose size is derived from a variety of activities in many fields, rather than from dominance in a single industry.

Constant returns to scale *See* **Scale.**

Consumer In economics, refers to the individual acting on his own behalf and covers such activities as decisions concerning supply of labor as well as purchase of goods for consumption.

Consumer surplus If a consumer would have been willing to pay $100 for a Super Bowl ticket, but is able to buy at a market price of $25, the $75 difference is his consumer surplus on that transaction.

Consumption In macroeconomics, one of the three broad categories into which aggregate expenditure is divided (the others are investment and government expenditure). Consumption, in this context, refers to all expenditure made outside government that is not for purposes of production.

Consumption function A stable relationship between aggregate consumption and aggregate income, possibly with lag effects. The *average propensity to consume* at a given income level is the ratio of consumption to income. The *marginal propensity to consume* at a given income level is the increase in consumption that will result from an additional dollar of income.

Cost In economic analysis, cost does not necessarily refer to simple dollar outlay but refers to what must be given up in order to attain a stated objective. This concept (*opportunity cost*) covers not only direct payments but such things as the value of opportunities forgone by an owner as a result of devoting his time to his business. *Average cost of production* is total cost of producing a given quantity (cost taken as above), divided by the quantity. *Marginal cost* is the increase in total cost that would result from the production of an additional unit. *Fixed costs* are costs that do not change with the level of output; *variable costs* are costs that do change.

Cost-push inflation An inflationary process in which the main force is the effect of higher wages on costs, leading to higher prices, then to higher wages, and so on.

Demand Either the quantity buyers plan to buy under given circumstances at a specific price, or the list of quantities buyers would plan to buy at each price under given circumstances. The latter is more properly the *demand schedule,* and its graphic depiction is the *demand curve.*

Demand-pull inflation An inflationary process in which the main force is the expansion of incomes, leading to increased demands, higher prices (if output is at capacity), higher wages, and a further increase in incomes leading to another round of the process.

Derived demand Occurs when a good is not demanded for itself, but because it is required to obtain a good that is demanded. The demand for inputs in production is derived from the demand for the goods produced.

Devaluation A change in a country's exchange rate that makes the home currency worth less in terms of foreign currencies.

Differential rent That part of pure rent arising from locational or other differences, as between two plots of land equal in space.

Differentiated products Goods that are identical or very similar in many characteristics, but different in some (like different models of compact cars).

Direct policy Policy carried out by direct manipulation of major components of the economy, for example, government expenditure. *See* **Indirect policy.**

Discount operation In the United States banking system, a method by which commercial banks can increase reserves similar to an individual obtaining a bank loan.

Discretionary policy Policy options on which the policy-maker has not been committed in advance by legislation or other arrangements.

Disequilibrium *See* **Equilibrium.**

Disguised unemployment A situation, often associated with peasant economies, in which the number of people nominally employed is greater than the number that can actually be used.

Disposable income The part of household income that the household may use in any way it wishes. It is normally considered to be total income less income taxes and similar compulsory outlays.

Distributed lag A relationship between two variables in which the values of the causal variable at several points in the past still affect the current value of the affected variable.

Distribution In economics, the whole pattern of how society's output (or benefits) is divided among its members.

Distributional policy That aspect of total policy concerned with how the benefits of an action (or its costs) are distributed over society.

Distributional poverty Poverty entirely due to uneven distribution of benefits over society, as opposed to *general poverty* in which society's outputs are too low to abolish poverty everywhere.

Duopoly *See* **Oligopoly.**

Dynamic profits Short-term profits arising from disequilibrium in the economy, and usually arising from actions that move the economy toward equilibrium.

Dynamics Analysis of the path by which the economy moves from one state to another, as compared with *comparative statics* in which only equilibrium states are compared. *See* **Comparative statics.**

Economic weights Weights designed to represent relative economic values.

Economies of scale *See* **Scale.**

Efficiency Obtaining the maximum output with a given input, or using the minimum input to attain a given output. A process is *technically inefficient* if it uses more of some input, and no less of another, for a given output level, inputs being measured in physical terms. A process is *economically inefficient* if it uses total inputs that have a social value higher than those required for some other way of producing the same output. Technical inefficiency implies economic inefficiency, but economic efficiency does not necessarily imply technical efficiency. An efficient process is one that is not inefficient.

Efficient allocation of resources An allocation of total resources among all possible uses such that there is no rearrangement that will permit the production of more of anything without reducing output of something else.

Elasticity A term widely used in economics to denote the ratio of the percentage change in one variable to the percentage change in another. Being a ratio of proportions, it is a pure number and is independent of units of measurement. *Elasticity of demand* (*supply*) refers to the ratio of the percentage change in quantity demanded (supplied) to the percentage change in price. *Income elasticity* refers to the ratio of the percentage change in quantity demanded (or personal services supplied) to the percentage change in income. A relationship may have *unit elasticity* (numerical value of the ratio equal to unity), be relatively *inelastic* (elasticity less than unity) or relatively *elastic* (elasticity greater than unity).

Engel curve A curve showing the relationship between dollar expenditure on a good and the level of income, the price of the good being constant.

Entrepreneur Used in economics to describe the role of the person or institution who locates market opportunities and production possibilities, and organizes exchange or production to take profitable advantage of these opportunities.

Equilibrium Any situation in balance in the sense that it would tend to persist unless disturbed by a change from outside. As used in both micro- and macroeconomics, equilibrium implies that all decision-makers are doing what they would plan to do under the circumstances given. A market is in equilibrium at a given price (the *equilibrium price*) if the quantity suppliers plan to sell at that price equals the quantity buyers plan to buy. That quantity is the *equilibrium quantity*. In macroeconomics, the economy is in equilibrium at a given level of aggregate income if planned expenditure at that income level is equal to planned output, and thus to anticipated income. *Disequilibrium* means any nonequilibrium state.

Excess demand (supply) If a market is not in equilibrium, the quantity demanded will not equal the quantity supplied at the going price. The difference is *excess demand* (if quantity demanded exceeds quantity supplied) or *excess supply* (in the reverse case).

Excess reserves In the banking system, a situation in which commercial banks have more reserves with the central bank than they require as backing for their current level of loans.

Exchange rate In general, the rate at which any commodity exchanges for another in a transaction. Most often used with reference to the rate of exchange of foreign currency for domestic currency (so many pesos to the dollar).

Externality Any effect of an action that influences persons (or firms) other than those directly involved in the action. If the action is one of consumption, we have a *consumption externality;* if one of production, a *production externality*. Externalities may be ''good'' if the indirect effects are regarded as benefits, or ''bad'' if they are regarded negatively. A snowmobile rider passing through a village generates consumption externalities (noise), in this case normally considered ''bad.'' The existence of one large store in a particular location may increase potential customers for nearby specialty stores—a production externality.

Factor Often used in a technical sense in economics to mean an economic resource, especially in reference to broadly defined categories of resources like ''labor,'' ''capital,'' ''land.'' *Factor markets* are the markets for these basic resources, and *factor prices* consist of wages, rents, interest, and other resource prices.

Financial intermediary An institution, like a bank or insurance company, that receives funds from households and firms and disburses them to firms that require funds for investment.

Firm The standard term in economics for any privately owned or publicly owned business enterprise, covering both the single proprietorship and the giant corporation. A firm is regarded as a single decision-making unit in production.

Fiscal policy Macroeconomic policy carried out primarily by varying government expenditures and/or revenues. Compare with **Monetary policy.**

Fixed exchange rates An international monetary system in which each country fixes the rate of exchange between its currency and others, and takes appropriate action to maintain that rate of exchange.

Flexible exchange rates An international monetary system in which each country's currency is sold in terms of other currencies at a rate determined continuously by the interaction of demand for and supply of the currency.

Full employment Normally refers to some conventionally accepted level of unemployment that is believed to reflect good performance for the economy. It does not normally refer to true zero unemployment.

Full employment budget balance The surplus or deficit the current budget would exhibit if the economy were to achieve full employment with an unchanged tax structure.

General equilibrium The concept of the economy as a connected system, in which the events in any one market or sector depend on events in all other markets or sectors, so true equilibrium in one market is reached only when there is equilibrium in all.

GNP The standard abbreviation for gross national product.

Gold-exchange standard An international monetary system of fixed exchange rates in which net international payments are made in gold, but domestic transactions are not.

Gold standard A domestic and international monetary system in which gold is used as money both domestically and internationally, perhaps supplemented by other forms of money that are freely exchangeable with gold at fixed rates.

Gross investment *See* **Investment.**

Gross national product *See* **National income.**

Human capital By analogy with physical capital, the concept that the knowledge, skill, and even physical strength of humans can be increased by investment in training, education, and special care, so the result of this investment is economically similar to the result of investing in physical capital because it can result in increased production.

Hyperinflation A rate of inflation so high that people are unwilling to hold money for even a few days because of the rapidity with which its exchange value in terms of goods is declining.

Imperfect competition Any competitive structure in which either the buyer or seller can influence the price of the transaction by his own actions, as opposed to *perfect competition* in which each individual buyer and seller makes transactions that are so small a part of the total that they cannot affect the price.

Income Generally used in consumer theory to mean the budget allocated for consumption expenditure rather than income proper.

Income-consumption curve The curve showing how the consumer's chosen collection of goods changes with income, the prices of the goods remaining constant. Compare with **Engel curve.**

Income-consumption loop In macroeconomic theory, the flow from income to consumption expenditure, which then generates further income.

Income effect In the theory of consumer behavior, refers to the fact that a change in the price of a good with money income constant has two effects, one of which is similar to the effect of a change in income with prices constant.

Index number One form of aggregation in which the movement of a large number of different but related variables are summarized by movements of a single number, as when the movements of the large number of prices of items purchased by consumers are summarized by the movement of the consumer price index.

Indirect input If oil is not used directly in the production of textiles, but electricity is used directly and electricity uses oil, then oil is an indirect input into textiles.

Indirect policy Policy carried out by measures designed to induce others to change important components of the economy, as a change in interest rates to induce a change in investment.

Industry Strictly speaking, all firms producing identical products. Also used, however, to cover all firms producing closely similar products.

Infant industry A term used in international trade and development theory to refer to the early stages of an industry that is expected to produce at lower unit cost after being permitted to grow by virtue of tariff protection.

Inferior good *See* **Normal good.**

Inflation A situation in which the rate of increase in prices generally is greater than considered "normal."

Inflationary gap The excess of planned expenditure at existing prices over capacity output at those prices, typically leading to upward pressure on prices.

Inflationary spiral. A self-sustaining dynamic process by which prices continue to rise even though the initiating cause of the inflation may have disappeared.

Infrastructure Social capital in the form of transport, communication, education, and administrative arrangements that are taken for granted in developed countries, but are often lacking in less-developed societies.

Injection In macroeconomics, refers to expenditure (such as government expenditure or business investment) that is not a direct function of income, and is thus "injected" into the income-consumption loop.

International liquidity Refers to the worldwide availability of things acceptable in international monetary transactions.

Investment The act of producing or buying new items of capital, or the financial transactions associated with this act. Over the economy as a whole, the total dollar value of all investment is *gross investment. Net investment* is gross investment less the value of things used to replace worn-out capital, and represents the value of the increase in the capital stock.

Isoquant The list of all input combinations with which a given level of output of some good can be produced, or the curve drawn to depict those combinations.

Joint products Products are joint if the technology requires that one cannot be produced without the other, even though it may be possible to vary the proportions within limits.

Key currency The currency of one country widely held in foreign countries and used to settle international transactions even among countries for which it is not the domestic currency.

Labor-intensive One production process is labor-intensive relative to another if it uses a higher proportion of labor relative to other inputs.

Liquidity An asset's property of being easily and immediately exchangeable for other things at a predictable rate of exchange. Money is regarded as having the maximum possible liquidity.

Long run Does not refer to any calendar time, but to a period sufficient for all dynamic effects to work through to full equilibrium.

Lump-sum tax A tax fixed in amount regardless of any variable, such as income or spending, controlled by the taxpayer.

Macromodel A simplified representation of the economy designed to show the relationship between the important aggregates in the economy.

Marginal A term widely used in economics when referring to small changes from a given position.

Marginal cost *See* **Cost.**

Marginal cost pricing In publicly controlled monopolies, the setting of price equal to marginal cost. This is not profit-maximizing but is socially optimal in appropriate circumstances.

Marginal product *See* **Productivity.**

Marginal propensity to consume *See* **Consumption function.**

Marginal revenue *See* **Revenue.**

Marginal revenue product (of an input) The increase in revenue obtained from the sale of the increased production resulting from the use of one more unit of that input. Under perfect competition, it is identical with *value of marginal product*.

Market Refers to individual markets or to the general institutional structure where goods may be exchanged without coercion, as in the phrase "through the market."

MC Standard abbreviation for marginal cost. *See* **Cost.**

Monetary policy Macroeconomic policy carried out through the banking system rather than through variation in the government budget. Compare with **Fiscal policy.**

Money illusion Reaction to the nominal dollar value of wages or other prices without taking into account changes in the general price level.

Monopolistic competition A market structure of many firms selling similar but not identical products, in which the rivalries of oligopoly are absent.

Monopoly A market structure with only one firm selling the product and no other firms selling closely related products. If, as is often the case with public utilities, the technology is such that the existence of more than one supplier would lead to obvious wasteful duplication of capacity, the structure is a *natural monopoly*.

Monopoly profit The difference between actual profit and the profit of an equivalent perfectly competitive industry, appropriate to all types of imperfect competition, not only pure monopoly.

MPC The standard abbreviation for marginal propensity to consume.

MR The standard abbreviation for marginal revenue.

Multiplier In Keynesian analysis, the increase in total income taken as a ratio of the increase in injections that caused it.

National income Specifically, the sum of all incomes generated in the economy. More generally, refers to all the aggregate concepts that appear in the *national income accounts* of the country. The most commonly used of these is *gross national product,* the total value of all final goods produced in the economy without allowance for capital depreciation. *Net national product* is equal to gross national product less capital depreciation allowances. Net national product and national income are closely related but not identical.

Natural monopoly *See* **Monopoly.**

Near-money Anything that is almost, but not quite, as liquid as what is regarded as money. In the United States, checking-account balances are regarded as money, savings-account balances as near-money.

Negative income tax A policy measure for income redistribution in which those with incomes below some base level receive a payment (negative tax) related to the amount of the deficiency, but less than 100 percent of it.

Net national product *See* **National income.**

NNP Standard abbreviation for net national product.

Nominal quantity of money *See* **Real balances.**

Nonprice competition Competition by product variation, advertising, special services, or any means other than changes in the nominal price.

Normal good A good whose quantity purchased rises with income, as contrasted with an *inferior good,* whose quantity purchased declines with rising income, price being kept constant.

Oligopoly A market structure with a relatively small number of dominant firms, so the actions of any one of these firms have a major impact on each of the others. The primary characteristic of an oligopoly situation is the existence of close rivalries and the necessity for each firm to consider potential reactions of its rivals in formulating its own policy. The most extreme form of rivalry appears in *duopoly,* in which there are only two dominant firms.

Open market operation Action by a central bank in selling securities to, or buying them from, the public through the regular (''open'') market. Such action can be used to influence both interest rates and the overall level of bank balances.

Opportunity cost *See* **Cost.**

Pareto criterion Based on this criterion, a policy is desirable if it makes someone better off and no one worse off, undesirable if it makes someone worse off and no one better off. No judgment is made concerning a policy that makes someone better off and someone else worse off.

Perfect competition A market structure in which the number of traders is so large and the market share of any one so small that no individual trader's action will have a perceptible effect on the market as a whole. Under perfect competition, all traders accept the market price as something over which they have no control. Compare with **Imperfect competition.**

Phillips curve A curve expressing the empirically determined relationship between the level of unemployment and the rate of change of wages for a particular economy. Also used for the relationship between the level of unemployment and the rate of associated inflation; strictly, the *modified Phillips curve*.

Preferences Consumers are presumed to have consistent preferences in that they know which of two collections of goods they prefer: the first to the second, the second to the first, or no preference. If they have no preference, they are said to be indifferent between the collections. Consumers are presumed to act in accordance with their preferences, and those preferences are the basis on which economic judgments must be made.

Price discrimination The charging of different prices for the same product to different buyers or groups of buyers.

Price leadership A market situation in which the price set by a prominent firm (the price leader) is normally followed by other firms in the group, achieving the effects of *collusion* without any direct consultation among the firms. Compare with **Collusion.**

Private benefit *See* **Benefit.**

Production Covers any activity in which the output differs in form, place, or time from any of the inputs, and includes transportation and commerce as well as manufacturing and agriculture.

Production possibility frontier The outer limit of all the possible collections of things the economy can produce with its existing resources and technology.

Production process A specific recipe indicating the quantities of all inputs required to produce a given amount of some good.

Productivity The ratio of output to a specific input (often labor) or an aggregate of inputs. The *marginal product* of an input is the addition to total output resulting from the use of an additional unit of the input. The *average product* of an input is its productivity.

Profit For a firm, the excess of revenues over all costs of production and sale, including those implicit costs (value of owner's time, use of entrepreneur's own capital) that do not appear as direct dollar outlays. The return to capital is regarded as interest rather than pure profit, the owner(s) of the firm receiving a mixture of interest on capital and pure profit.

Progressive tax A tax is said to be *proportional* if the tax represents the same proportion of income at all income levels, *progressive* if it represents a higher proportion of income at higher levels of income, and *regressive* if it represents a higher proportion of income at lower levels of income.

Proportional tax *See* **Progressive tax.**

Public bad *See* **Public good.**

Public good A good whose benefits can be shared by many without loss to any individual, and from whose benefits it is not easy to exclude people. (Compare with **Club good.**) A *public bad* is something regarded negatively that is necessarily shared by many and from which it is not easy for people to exclude themselves—polluted air is a typical example.

Quantity theory of money The hypothesis that, when the economy is at capacity, the price level will vary in direct ratio to the quantity of money.

Real Modifier frequently used in economics to mean that the variable so qualified has been adjusted for changes in the general price level.

Real balances Money balances converted to dollars of constant purchasing power. In the aggregate, these are equivalent to the nominal quantity of money.

Real gross national product Gross national product expressed in terms of dollars of constant purchasing power.

Real wage Wages expressed in terms of dollars of constant purchasing power.

Regressive tax *See* **Progressive tax.**

Rent As a formal term in economics, it refers to the payment for the use of land as space and location only, not to any part of total payment for the use of buildings or improvements. It is also used in a technical sense for payments for the use of any resource that, like pure land, is fixed in total quantity.

Reserve ratio In banking, the ratio of reserves held in the central bank to total assets of the commercial bank. A required minimum reserve ratio is usually determined by the central bank.

Revaluation Strictly speaking, means any change in the rate of exchange of the country's currency for foreign currencies. In the absence of a better word, it is frequently used to mean only an exchange rate revision that increases the value of the domestic currency in terms of foreign currency, *devaluation* being used for change in the reverse direction.

Revenue Receipts of the firm arising from the sale of its output. *Average revenue* is the total revenue received from the sale of a given quantity of output divided by the quantity. For any market in which a uniform price is charged, average revenue is necessarily equal to price. *Marginal revenue* is the increase in total revenue resulting from the sale of an additional unit of output.

Scale, returns to Refers to the extent to which output increases when all inputs are increased in the same proportion. If, for example, all inputs are increased by 50 percent and output also rises by 50 percent, we have *constant returns to scale.* If output rises by more than 50 percent, we have *increasing returns to scale,* and if by less than 50 percent, *decreasing returns to scale.* Increasing returns to scale are sometimes referred to as *economies of scale,* even though this term covers some effects (such as quantity discounts on the purchase of inputs) that are not true increasing returns to scale.

Scarcity Something is scarce in the economic sense if social welfare could be increased by having more of it. Desert land is not scarce in North Africa, but labor is scarce in most economies most of the time.

Second-best problem If the truly best policy solution is unattainable for institutional or other reasons, the next-best policy may be quite different.

Selling cost Advertising or other costs associated with increasing the sale of a product at a given price.

Shadow price An ''ideal'' price that represents the true social value of an additional unit of a good or resource, and that may or may not be well approximated by an actual market price.

Short run A period insufficient to make all adjustments decision-makers would wish to make under the circumstances.

Social cost *See* **Social welfare.**

Social welfare A conceptual indicator that is considered to be improved by a ''good'' policy and made worse by a ''bad'' policy. A policy considered desirable based on the *Pareto criterion* would be presumed to increase social welfare. Social welfare, unlike individual preferences, involves personal judgments in cases in which the Pareto criterion cannot be applied, and thus cannot be free of value judgments.

Speculation Market transactions made with a view to future purchase or sale at different prices, when those prices are uncertain.

Statics *See* **Comparative statics.**

Structural unemployment A situation in which there would be little or no unemployment if all workers could perform all jobs, but in which there is, in fact, an excess supply of some kinds of labor at existing wages together with excess demand for other kinds.

Substitution Refers to the basic idea that the same objective can be achieved in different ways. There is *input substitution* when a change of process results in the use of more of one input and less of another in order to produce the same output. In consumption, a change in the relative prices of goods will lead to a change in the collection purchased. Part of the total effect will be the *substitution effect,* in which some of the good that has become cheaper will be substituted for some of the more expensive good.

Supply The quantity potential sellers would be willing to sell at a given price, or the whole schedule of quantities that would be offered at different prices. The *supply schedule* and *supply curve* are the supply analogs of the equivalent concepts for *demand.* Compare with **Demand.**

Tariff In general, a scale of charges; specifically in international trade, a tax that must be paid on imported goods.

Technical efficiency *See* **Efficiency.**

Technological progress The addition of new processes to the technology that results in increased productivity. If the new processes require new machines and can only be used as the new machines are installed, the technological progress is said to be embodied.

Technology The collection of all known ways of doing things. The collection of all known ways of making things is the *production technology;* the collection of all known characteristics of consumer goods is the *consumption technology.*

Terms of trade The rate of exchange between goods, especially the rate of exchange of exports for imports in international trade.

Trade balance The difference between the total value of goods exported and the total value of goods imported. It is one of the key items in the *balance of payments.*

Transactions balance Money, as currency or bank balances, held to bridge the time gap between receipt of income and anticipated expenditure.

Transfer payment An income receipt, like Social Security or unemployment pay, that is not a payment for rendering current productive services. Such income must be derived by transfer through the tax system from incomes originating in the supply of current services.

Transformation curve Essentially the same as *production possibility curve. See* **Production possibility frontier.**

Unilateral transfer In the balance of payments accounts, a receipt from or payment to another country or individual that is not in payment for goods or services and implies no repayment. Foreign aid (if not in the form of a loan) and immigrant remittances to former homelands are important types of such transfer.

Unit elasticity *See* **Elasticity.**

User charge Charge for a public facility based on the use made by the payer, as opposed to annual tax assessments or other charges not related to use.

Utility A term often used in economics for whatever a consumer has increased by a movement to a new situation considered preferable to the former situation. Equivalent, in most contexts, to *personal benefit* or personal welfare.

Value of marginal product The marginal product of an input in some specific use times the price of the product produced. Under perfect competition it is equal to the *marginal revenue product. See* **Marginal revenue product.**

Variable proportions Refers to the existence of alternative processes in production that permit the use of inputs in different proportions, or the production of joint products in different proportions.

Velocity of money The ratio of the overall level of transactions to total money balances.

Wage-price controls A policy, normally associated with attempts to control inflation, that places specified limits on the rate at which wages and prices can be increased in the private sector.

Welfare economics The branch of economics concerned with the criteria for making normative judgments about the operation of the economy, and with prescriptions based on these criteria.

Withdrawal A technical term in macroeconomic analysis for that part of income not directly spent within the economy by the income recipient, such as saving, taxes, and expenditure abroad.

Index

Printed in U.S.A.

F